NEW YORK STATE

2nd Edition

Where to Stay and Eat
for All Budgets

Must-See Sights
and Local Secrets

Ratings You Can Trust

Fodor's Travel Publications   New York, Toronto, London, Sydney, Auckland
www.fodors.com

FODOR'S NEW YORK STATE

Editor: Debbie Harmsen

Editorial Contributors: Salwa Jabado, Molly Moker, Jess Moss, Mark Sullivan, Caroline Trefler

Writers: Vanessa Ahern, Bethany Beckerlegge, John Blodgett, Gary Catt, Jennifer Edwards, Shannon Kelly, Kate King, Amanda Theunissen, William Travis

Production Editors: Evangelos Vasilakis, Carrie Parker

Maps & Illustrations: David Lindroth, *cartographer*; Bob Blake, Rebecca Baer, *map editors;* William Wu, *information graphics*

Design: Fabrizio La Rocca, *creative director*; Guido Caroti, Siobhan O'Hare, *art directors*; Tina Malaney, Chie Ushio, Ann McBride, Jessica Walsh, *designers*; Melanie Marin, *senior picture editor*; Moon Sun Kim, *cover designer*

Cover Photo: Mohonk Preserve: Peter Guttman

Production Manager: Angela L. McLean

COPYRIGHT

Copyright © 2009 by Fodor's Travel, a division of Random House, Inc.

Fodor's is a registered trademark of Random House, Inc.

All rights reserved. Published in the United States by Fodor's Travel, a division of Random House, Inc., and simultaneously in Canada by Random House of Canada, Limited, Toronto. Distributed by Random House, Inc., New York.

No maps, illustrations, or other portions of this book may be reproduced in any form without written permission from the publisher.

2nd Edition

ISBN 978-1-4000-0897-1

ISSN 1554-5873

SPECIAL SALES

This book is available at special discounts for bulk purchases for sales promotions or premiums. Special editions, including personalized covers, excerpts of existing books, and corporate imprints, can be created in large quantities for special needs. For more information, write to Special Markets/Premium Sales, 1745 Broadway, MD 6-2, New York, New York 10019, or e-mail specialmarkets@randomhouse.com.

AN IMPORTANT TIP & AN INVITATION

Although all prices, opening times, and other details in this book are based on information supplied to us at press time, changes occur all the time in the travel world, and Fodor's cannot accept responsibility for facts that become outdated or for inadvertent errors or omissions. So **always confirm information when it matters**, especially if you're making a detour to visit a specific place. Your experiences—positive and negative—matter to us. If we have missed or misstated something, **please write to us.** We follow up on all suggestions. Contact the New York State editor at editors@fodors.com or c/o Fodor's at 1745 Broadway, New York, NY 10019.

PRINTED IN THE UNITED STATES OF AMERICA

10 9 8 7 6 5 4 3 2 1

Be a Fodor's Correspondent

Your opinion matters. It matters to us. It matters to your fellow Fodor's travelers, too. And we'd like to hear it. In fact, we need to hear it.

When you share your experiences and opinions, you become an active member of the Fodor's community. That means we'll not only use your feedback to make our books better, but we'll publish your names and comments whenever possible. Throughout our guides, look for "Word of Mouth," excerpts of your unvarnished feedback.

Here's how you can help improve Fodor's for all of us.

Tell us when we're right. We rely on local writers to give you an insider's perspective. But our writers and staff editors—who are the best in the business—depend on you. Your positive feedback is a vote to renew our recommendations for the next edition.

Tell us when we're wrong. We're proud that we update most of our guides every year. But we're not perfect. Things change. Hotels cut services. Museums change hours. Charming cafés lose charm. If our writer didn't quite capture the essence of a place, tell us how you'd do it differently. If any of our descriptions are inaccurate or inadequate, we'll incorporate your changes in the next edition and will correct factual errors at fodors.com immediately.

Tell us what to include. You probably have had fantastic travel experiences that aren't yet in Fodor's. Why not share them with a community of like-minded travelers? Maybe you chanced upon a beach or bistro or B&B that you don't want to keep to yourself. Tell us why we should include it. And share your discoveries and experiences with everyone directly at fodors.com. Your input may lead us to add a new listing or highlight a place we cover with a "Highly Recommended" star or with our highest rating, "Fodor's Choice."

Give us your opinion instantly at our feedback center at www.fodors.com/feedback. You may also e-mail editors@fodors.com with the subject line "New York State Editor." Or send your nominations, comments, and complaints by mail to New York State Editor, Fodor's, 1745 Broadway, New York, NY 10019.

You and travelers like you are the heart of the Fodor's community. Make our community richer by sharing your experiences. Be a Fodor's correspondent.

Happy traveling!

Tim Jarrell, Publisher

CONTENTS

MAPS

ABOUT THIS BOOK

Our Ratings

Sometimes you find terrific travel experiences and sometimes they just find you. But usually the burden is on you to select the right combination of experiences. That's where our ratings come in.

As travelers we've all discovered a place so wonderful that its worthiness is obvious. And sometimes that place is so experiential that superlatives don't do it justice: you just have to be there to know. These sights, properties, and experiences get our highest rating, **Fodor's Choice**, indicated by orange stars throughout this book.

Black stars highlight sights and properties we deem **Highly Recommended**, places that our writers, editors, and readers praise again and again for consistency and excellence.

By default, there's another category: any place we include in this book is by definition worth your time, unless we say otherwise. And we will.

Disagree with any of our choices? Care to nominate a place or suggest that we rate one more highly? Visit our feedback center at www.fodors.com/feedback.

Budget Well

Hotel and restaurant price categories from ¢ to $$$$ are defined in the opening pages of each chapter. For attractions, we always give standard adult admission fees; reductions are usually available for children, students, and senior citizens. Want to pay with plastic? **AE, D, DC, MC, V** following restaurant and hotel listings indicate whether American Express, Discover, Diners Club, MasterCard, and Visa are accepted.

Restaurants

Unless we state otherwise, restaurants are open for lunch and dinner daily. We mention dress only when there's a specific requirement and reservations only when they're essential or not accepted—it's always best to book ahead.

Hotels

Hotels have private bath, phone, TV, and air-conditioning and operate on the European Plan (aka EP, meaning without meals), unless we specify that they use the Continental Plan (CP, with a Continental breakfast), Breakfast Plan (BP, with a full breakfast), or Modified American Plan (MAP, with breakfast and dinner), or are all-inclusive (including all meals and most activities).

We always list facilities but not whether you'll be charged an extra fee to use them, so always ask.

Many Listings
- ★ Fodor's Choice
- ★ Highly recommended
- ⊠ Physical address
- ✧ Directions
- ⌖ Mailing address
- ☏ Telephone
- 🖷 Fax
- ⊕ On the Web
- ✉ E-mail
- 🎫 Admission fee
- ☉ Open/closed times
- Ⓜ Metro stations
- ▭ Credit cards

Hotels & Restaurants
- 🏨 Hotel
- ⇌ Number of rooms
- ⚬ Facilities
- ❍ Meal plans
- ✕ Restaurant
- ⚲ Reservations
- ↘ Smoking
- ᛤᛪ BYOB

Outdoors
- ⚐ Golf
- ⚠ Camping

Other
- ☾ Family-friendly
- ⇨ See also
- ⊠ Branch address
- ☞ Take note

Experience New York

WORD OF MOUTH

"New York State is one of our most beautiful states in that almost every inch of it is gorgeous. You almost cannot go wrong."

—Cabovacation

". . . just about anywhere you drive in New York state will be scenic. It really is a very pretty state."

—CAPH52

WHAT'S NEW IN NEW YORK

Mets and Yankees Get New Homes
It's hard to imagine, but it's true. The scent of beer, hot dogs, and Cracker Jacks wafts no more through New York City's two historic baseball stadiums. On November 8, 2008, "The House That Ruth Built" officially closed. Since 1923, it's come to be associated with not only the Yankees but the legacy of baseball itself. The 2009 season opened in New Yankee Stadium, adjacent to the old Yankee Stadium. Not to be outdone by its crosstown rival, Shea Stadium also saw its last baseball game in the 2008 season. The longtime home of the New York Mets has been demolished to make way for Citi Field, which opened at the beginning of the 2009 season.

Politics, For Better or For Worse
New York politics took some hard knocks in 2008. After a stunning victory in 2006, Eliot Spitzer swept into the governor's office, putting the state leadership back in Democratic hands. But in 2008 Spitzer was forced to resign due to his involvement in a prostitution ring. David Patterson, the lieutenant governor, took over the reigns. One of his first directives was to recognize same-sex marriages in New York. Later in the year, former first lady Hilary Rodham Clinton resigned her seat in the Senate to take the position of secretary of state under President Barack Obama. Caroline Kennedy had a brief flirtation with the vacant Senate post, but personal reasons prompted her to withdraw her name from consideration, and Lieutenant Governor Patterson appointed a pro-gun Democrat from upstate, Kirsten Gillibrand.

A New Cork in Wine Country
The Finger Lakes region is second only to Napa in its wine production, with some 100 wineries producing some of the finest wines in the country. One of the region's highlights is its ice wine, a sweet dessert wine made from frozen grapes. New York ice wines have received international acclaim, rivaling Germany and Canada, who have produced some of the best ice wines in the world. Thus, in February 2009, the 1st annual New York Ice Wine festival kicked off with great success, filled with tastings, seminars, live entertainment, and meals prepared by chefs from around the world. Oenophiles should mark their 2010 calendars for this monthlong event.

Woodstock Revisited
If you thought Woodstock was a memory, think again. The historic festival lives on at the Catskill area's Bethel Woods Center for the Arts. A new museum and performance space at the center opened in 2008. It is dedicated to preserving the legacy of the Woodstock Festival and its era. Interactive exhibits, displays, and artifacts are showcased throughout the museum and galleries.

The *Intrepid* Sets Sail Once Again
After being closed two years for renovations, New York's City's beloved *Intrepid* Sea-Air-Space Museum opened its doors on November 2008. Alongside its many permanent exhibits, such as the USS *Growler* submarine, lunar modules, and A-12 Blackbird spy plane, the museum also showcases a British Airways Concorde.

History on the Hudson
Currently closed for extensive renovations, one of the most beautiful historic estates on the Hudson, the 23-room Montgomery Place, plans to reopen in late 2009. The house, in Annandale-on-Hudson, is an exceptional example of

early 19th-century architecture, complete with an inspired interior. The grounds are equally inspiring, with 434 lush acres of orchards, flower gardens, and ancient trees. Sweeping views of the Hudson River and Catskill Mountains highlight this dramatic country home. Though you can't go inside the house, you can still visit the grounds on a self-guided or audio tour.

It's All about Buffalo

Buffalo always seems to fall under the glitzy radar of New York City. Not so in 2008. Suddenly, it seemed as if New Yorkers were discovering a long-lost historic city. The National Trust for Historic Preservation named Buffalo one of its 2009 Dozen Distinctive Destinations, and the *New York Times* listed it as one of its "44 Places to Go in 2009." And why not? Its historic downtown is rich with mansions and some of the world's first skyscrapers, including the art-deco styling of Buffalo City Hall, the Liberty Building, with its two small replicas of the Statue of Liberty, and the terra-cotta tiled Guaranty Building, the tallest building constructed in the 1890s. Frank Lloyd Wright also put his stamp on the city with such structures as the Prairie-style Darwin D. Martin house. The innovative cultural scene rocks with cutting-edge art, music festivals, and theater. Add to that stylish hotels and restaurants, and it's no wonder Buffalo has become a must-see destination.

What New York Urbanites Are Talking about

The most recent season of *Top Chef* was filmed in Manhattan, and the city's foodie population watched closely for sightings of the NYC's culinary stars. New Yorkers are enjoying comparing the (fake) luxurious lifestyles of the cast of *Gossip Girl* with the (slightly less fake) luxurious lifestyles

of the cast of *The City*. Some of them are sad to lose Conan to Los Angeles—Jimmy Fallon is hardly a replacement—but Jon Stewart and Stephen Colbert keep the comedy quotient high.

While the market for buyers in Manhattan is dropping in volume, if not in price, rents are dropping across the board. Many landlords are giving incentives like the first month's rent free to entice tenants. Some renters are even bold enough to renegotiate the terms of their current leases; a few hundred dollars off the cost of living making having roommates as a grown-up that much more bearable.

It's getting harder for locals (and visitors) to partake of their typical vices in the city. Those in New York City also are faced (literally) with calorie counts on the posted menus of fast-food restaurants, so the health benefits—or lack thereof—of burgers and sodas will be front and center whether or not Paterson's proposal passes.

Don't cry for them, Argentina—Broadway has seen quite a few shows drop the curtain for good, including *Gypsy, Spamalot, Spring Awakening, Hairspray, Young Frankenstein,* and *Grease.* Now's the time to catch a performance while you still can.

Hotels are slashing their rates so much here that even New Yorkers are taking the opportunity to sample luxurious digs for the weekend. Don't be surprised if the couple across the hall from you has traveled up north . . . from Greenwich Village. Visitors should eye hotel openings for deals, as opening offers are quite good.

WHAT'S WHERE

The following numbers correspond to chapter numbers.

2 Western New York and Niagara Falls. In summer, more than 750,000 gallons a second rush over Niagara Falls—truly a stunning sight. In Buffalo, a lively waterfront area impresses with a collection of architectural landmarks.

3 The Finger Lakes. Taste your way through 80-plus vineyards and wineries. This region's dramatic landscape has deep gorges and rushing waterfalls contrasted with wide fertile valleys. Dotting the landscape are dairy farms and small villages.

4 The Adirondacks and the Thousand Islands. This outdoor wonderland is filled with thousands of miles of rivers, brooks, and streams, and more than a million acres of forest. The area's hub is Lake Placid, site of the 1932 and 1980 Winter Olympics.

5 Central New York and the Capital Region. The region's crown jewels are the National Baseball Hall of Fame in Cooperstown, the resort town of Saratoga Springs, and the capital, where the Empire State Plaza, with its impressive château architecture and the Romanesque Million Dollar Staircase, is a good introduction to the city.

6 The Catskills. Climbing as high as 4,200 feet, these bluish mountains contain dense forests, rock-walled gorges, and large lakes, and are veined with hiking and skiing trails. One-traffic-light hamlets are the norm and small villages include the arts colony of Woodstock.

7 The Hudson Valley. The untamed beauty here inspired early American painters and seduced the Vanderbilts, Rockefellers, and Astors to build extravagant mansions along the river. Harborside villages hold intimate cafés, small museums, art galleries, antiques shops, and quirky boutiques.

8 New York City. Museums of all kinds, Broadway shows, experiential theater, stylish boutiques, mammoth department stores, comedy clubs, standing-room-only jazz clubs, temples of haute cuisine, and more all thrive in the city that never sleeps.

9 Long Island. Once you pass the suburban sprawl, you come upon the rural areas where farms and vineyards, historic houses, and magnificent mansions of the rich and famous stretch out on this nearly 120-mi-long island east of Manhattan. And don't forget all the beaches and the fabled Hamptons.

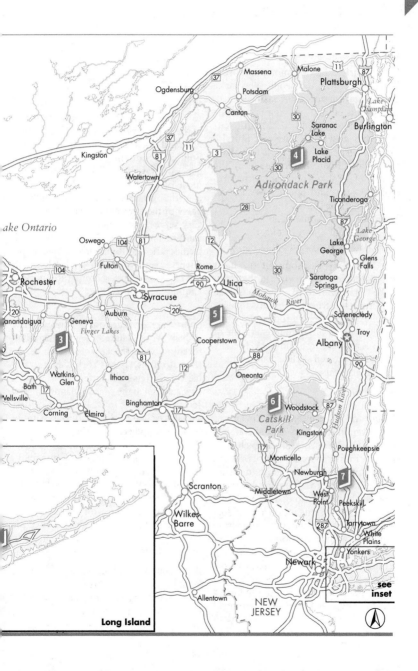

Massena
Malone
Ogdensburg
Potsdam
Plattsburgh
Canton
Lake
Champlain
37
87
11
30
Saranac
Lake
Burlington
Kingston
37
11
3
4
Lake
Placid
Watertown
81
30
Adirondack Park
Ticonderoga
28
87
Lake Ontario
Lake
George
Oswego
104
81
12
Lake
George
Glens
Falls
104
Fulton
Rome
Rochester
90
Utica
30
Saratoga
Springs
Mohawk
River
Syracuse
Schenectady
20
Auburn
20
5
Canandaigua
Geneva
Finger Lakes
Troy
3
Cooperstown
Albany
81
88
90
Watkins
Glen
12
Ithaca
Oneonta
Bath
17
Binghamton
6
Woodstock
Wellsville
Corning
Elmira
17
Catskill
Park
Kingston
Hudson River
Poughkeepsie
17
Monticello
Scranton
Newburgh
7
Middletown
West
Point
Peekskill
Wilkes-
Barre
287
Tarrytown
White
Plains
Yonkers
Newark
see
inset
Allentown
NEW
JERSEY
Long Island

NEW YORK TODAY

The People
With its early influx of immigrants from all over the world, the people who make up the Empire State are not easily defined. Most of this cultural melting pot—some 90%—is clustered in the major cities, mostly New York City and Buffalo. African-Americans and people of Italian, Irish, and German descent make up the majority of the state's population; the largest Dominican- and Jamaican-American population in the United States also make New York their home. The New York City borough of Queens holds the state's largest Asian-American population.

New York City has some of the most focused and energetic people in the country. You may need to live here to get the full picture, but trust us, the city also has its mellow side. Drive around the state, and within short order, the frenetic life of the city is replaced by a laid-back, friendly vibe and the storied skyline transforms to pastoral landscapes.

The Economy
No question that New York City is the banking and finance center in the United States, even in this topsy-turvy economy, and with the New York Stock Exchange, one of the most important in the world. It's also a major communication and media stronghold, with most of major American TV networks broadcasting from Midtown Manhattan. Publishing is also a big industry in the city. Across the state, agriculture dominates, with dairy, apples, cherries, cabbage, maple syrup, and cheese among the top products. New York also produces an astonishing amount of grapes, and with grapes come wine. From the Finger Lakes to Long Island, vineyards are prevalent throughout, second to California in

wine produced. Tourism, education, and electronics round out the industries here.

Politics
When it comes to politics, New York leans to the left, with Democratic strongholds in the major cities of New York City, Buffalo, and Rochester. In the rural areas, the political pendulum swings to the right, generally favoring Republicans; in fact, most of upstate New York is Republican, though Albany shifts to match the party of the current governor. New York City serves as a major spot for political fund-raising, and has also hosted both Democratic and Republican conventions. Diverse New York City is also home to the oldest and largest Young Republican Club in the country.

Sports
Sports are a year-round extravaganza in New York. There's plenty of football to enjoy, with three professional teams (Buffalo Bills, New York Giants, and New York Jets—the latter two sharing a new stadium in the Meadowlands, in New Jersey, beginning in 2010). And professional baseball is always an obsession in New York, where both the Yankees and the Mets consistently add top-name players to their rosters (each team now plays in its own recently built state-of-the-art stadium as of 2009). Fans should visit the National Baseball Hall of Fame in Cooperstown. There you'll find in-depth exhibits of famous players and have the opportunity to relive classic moments in baseball history.

Basketball is popular, too, with the New York Knicks and New York Liberty hooping it up. Each year the state races for the Stanley Cup with three competitive hockey teams: the New York Rangers, the New York Islanders, and the Buffalo Sabres. And don't forget soccer, which is represented by the New York Red Bulls. Add to that to a plethora of minor league teams in all sports, and you'll never be without a game to watch.

The Arts
It's impossible to be culturally bereft in New York. Major cultural institutions hold sway in New York City, including such landmarks as the Metropolitan Museum of Art, the Museum of Modern Art, the Solomon R. Guggenheim Museum, and the Museum of Natural History. Elsewhere in the state are such unique showcases as the Adirondack Museum, overlooking Blue Mountain Lake in the Adirondacks; the Corning Museum of Glass, with its dazzling collection of historic and modern glass sculptures; and the Strong Museum in Rochester, an imaginative interactive children's museum with more than 20,000 dolls, dollhouses, and toys.

The state also nurtures a vibrant performing arts scene, filled with opera, dance, and classical music concerts and festivals. New York City venues are landmarks in their own right, and to see a concert at Carnegie Hall or the Metropolitan Opera House is an experience onto itself. Throughout the summer, festivals fill the state's calendar, from the Glimmerglass Opera in Cooperstown to the Lake George Jazz Festival.

The Media
New York City is the media capital of the country, with dozens of media companies—from print to TV to online—headquartered in Manhattan. Even conservative Fox News is based here. While L.A. still has the major studios,

New York has its share of TV tapings (*The Marth Stewart Show*, *The Late Show with David Letterman*, and *Saturday Night Live*, for example) and movies filmed at sites throughout town.

The Outdoors
New York is about much more than the cities that inhabit it; in fact, the state is filled with acres and acres of wilderness, from mountains and valleys to rivers and lakes. And New Yorkers across the state emerge from their urban playground in droves to take part in the abundance of outdoor offerings. New York is home to many state parks that offer plenty of hiking, skiing, swimming, biking, camping—you name it—opportunities. From the spectacular peaks and crystal clear lakes of the Adirondacks and the rushing waterfalls of Watkins Glenn State Park to the streams and trails of the Catskills and white-sand beaches of Jones Beach State Park, outdoors enthusiasts have plenty of spaces to indulge their activities. Add to that long scenic drives in the lush, rolling countryside of the Hudson Valley or the Finger Lakes region, dotted with hamlets and wineries, and any urban stresses you have will melt away.

QUINTESSENTIAL NEW YORK

If the name "New York" brings to mind images of skyscrapers, Broadway, subways, and round-the-clock activity, what you're really thinking about is New York City. But there's much more to New York than the fabulous city at the mouth of the Hudson River.

Arts and Culture

New York State just may lead the country when it comes to arts and culture. New York City stands tall with its outstanding museums, performing arts venues, and a melting pot of cultures. But having such a great city on the state's pedestal is infectious, and the rest of the state rises to the challenge: outside the city are countless eclectic and fascinating museums, exciting festivals and performances, and cultural experiences unlike those in any other state. From museums on baseball, glass, and contemporary art, to Broadway plays, opera performances, and chamber music festivals, it's all here, there, and everywhere around the state.

Parks and Nature

From Niagara Falls in the northwest corner of the state to the tip of the South Fork of Long Island lies a rich, diverse body of parks and unspoiled wilderness. In the north and central sections, breathtaking trails weave their way through mountains, forests, spectacular cliff-side views, and equally spectacular water spectacles. Toward the south are more mountains and rivers leading to Long Island, where you can soak up the sun on the many ocean beaches that span its shores. You won't need to look far to find a bounty of outdoor experiences here. Your only challenge is finding the time to do it all.

Food and Wine

One of the first things you'll discover as you drive around the state is the variety of cuisine. And it's not just in New York City, either. From the Hudson Valley to the towns of central New York, restaurants creating different takes from local specialties abound. Chefs from all around the state pick through the variety of homegrown ingredients at markets in nearly every town. New York City is no different. Three times a week, growers bring their finest to the famous Union Square market. And that's just the food. New York State also produces some of the best wines in the country. The Finger Lakes region has its pinot noirs, chardonnays, and cabernets, and the North Fork of Long Island yields pinot gris, viogniers, and malbecs, among others. For your next New York meal, savor the whole experience.

History

New York's heritage goes back to the 17th century, when traders brought their wares up and down the Hudson River from the port of New York City. With such a natural harbor and waterway, it didn't take long for a flood of immigrants to move into this natural trading and transportation mecca, and the spread of the state's diverse culture began. From Revolutionary War sites and history museums to Gilded Age mansions and stately monuments, the state is a living embodiment of American history. Nowhere is this evolution of people and culture displayed more poignantly than at the Ellis Island Immigration Museum, an experience not to be missed.

WHEN TO GO

The best time to visit depends on which area of the state you plan to go and what you wish to do. While some museums and historic sites in the Catskills, Adirondacks, and Hudson Valley may close in winter, for instance, you can still find a bounty of places to visit, sights to see, and cold-weather sports to enjoy. In general, summer is the high season throughout much of the state. And while New York City can get very hot and humid in summer, particularly in July and August, that's also one of the best times to visit the city. It's the least crowded, but hosts plenty of street fairs, outdoor concerts, and other activities. Winter is also a popular time to visit the Big Apple, especially during the December holiday season, when store windows are decked out with festive and imaginative holiday displays. For the rest of the state, the weather can be pleasantly warm in summer. Ocean breezes help to cool Long Island's shores; New York's waterways attract people with boats, swimsuits, fishing poles, and sunscreen; and the Catskills, Adirondacks, and Shawangunks offer invigorating hikes and cool refuges. Fall months can be glorious throughout the state. Beginning in late September, the Adirondacks shimmer with spectacular fall foliage, and soon after most of the countryside in the rest of the state follows suit. Peak foliage times usually result in full hotels and B&Bs, so reserve early if you'll be traveling during this time. Vineyards celebrate harvests and new issues in fall, making this a great time to visit wineries in the Hudson Valley, along Lake Erie, on Long Island, and in the Finger Lakes region.

Climate
The weather varies widely throughout the state. It could be sunny in New York City and snowing in the Hudson Valley, for instance. Away from coastal areas, there's plenty of snow in New York, with a statewide seasonal average of 40 inches. More than half the state receives over 70 inches of snow per year. In summer, temperatures range from 70°F to 85°F in the higher elevations of the Adirondacks and Catskills. The summer air can be much more humid in the lower Hudson Valley and the New York City area than the rest of the state. What follows are average daily maximum and minimum temperatures for three major cities in the state.

Forecasts Weather Channel (⊕ *www.weather.com*).

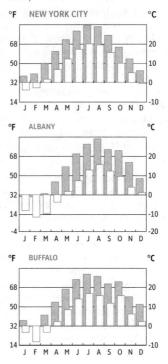

NEW YORK STATE'S TOP ATTRACTIONS

Niagara Falls

Nothing compares to the rush you'll feel standing near the three cascades that make up this natural wonder on both sides of the U.S. and Canadian border. The malls, amusement parks, hotels, tacky souvenir shops, and flashy wax museums that surround the falls today attest to the region's maturation into a major tourist attraction. But despite the hordes of visitors jostling unceremoniously for the best photograph, the astounding beauty of the falls remains undiminished.

Times Square and Broadway

Times Square is the most frenetic part of New York City: a dizzying mix of flashing lights, honking horns, and shoulder-to-shoulder crowds that many New Yorkers studiously avoid. But if you like sensory overload, then the chaotic mix of huge billboards displaying underwear ads, flashing digital displays, on-location television broadcasts, and outré street performers will give you your fix. The Great White Way, otherwise known as Broadway, slashes through Times Square, and is where theater-lovers head to see the razzle-dazzle of the stage.

National Baseball Hall of Fame and Museum

If you're a baseball fan, a pilgrimage to Central New York's Cooperstown should be on top on your list. Besides seeing the actual ball Babe Ruth hit for his 500th home run to Shoeless Joe Jackson's shoes, you'll find out everything you've ever wanted to know about the national pastime's great legends. Plaques bearing pictures and biographies, multimedia displays, and exhibits geared toward children endlessly fascinate. Come during mid- to late-July for the annual induction ceremony.

Catskill Park

Intrepid souls have long flocked to the Catskills. Dreamers, visionaries, artists, writers, poets, and musicians find a corner to call their own in the many hamlets surrounding this park. With 700,000 acres that include ponds, lakes, mountains, campgrounds, and hiking trails, the park still has plenty of room for hikers and other outdoors enthusiasts, not to mention bears, rattlesnakes, and other creatures.

Hudson River Valley's Historic Estates

The Hudson River valley teems with American historical sites, in and around the many towns that make up this scenic region. Crowning a hill overlooking the Hudson River, the Rockefeller's Kykuit mansion houses a mean collection of art and antiques. Take your time walking through the Italian gardens and absorb the opulence and grandeur of the Vanderbilt Mansion National Historic Site farther north in Hyde Park. While in town, pay homage to the country's 32nd president with a tour of FDR's Hyde Park Hudson River estate, which includes a birthplace and burial site, a museum, and a presidential library.

Metropolitan Museum of Art

The largest art museum in North America, the Met in Manhattan pulls in art lovers of all stripes. Treasures from all over the world and every era of human creativity comprise its expansive collection. It's easy to get dizzy circling all the Dutch master canvases, bronze Rodins, and ancient Greek artifacts. If you need a breather, retire to the rooftop café overlooking Central Park.

NEW YORK'S TOP EXPERIENCES

Taste Your Way through the Finger Lakes Wineries

More than 100 wineries dot this region, producing fine pinot noirs, chardonnays, and cabernet francs. The best way to enjoy them is to sample several in a leisurely day trip. You can follow one of the four wine trails, named for the four largest lakes, or explore off the trails. Nearly all the wineries have tasting rooms and gift shops, and many have restaurants, cafés, or picnic grounds with panoramic lake views.

Stroll across the Brooklyn Bridge

"A drive-through cathedral" is how the critic James Wolcott described one of New York's noblest and most recognized landmarks. Spanning the East River, the bridge connects Manhattan island to the borough of Brooklyn. An hour's stroll on the pedestrian walkway (which you share with bicyclists and rollerbladers) is an essential New York experience. Traffic is beneath you, and the views of the New York City skyline are some of the best anywhere.

Explore the Hudson Valley's Towns

You'll find hamlets aplenty along the Hudson River, including Tarrytown, Cold Spring, Beacon, Poughkeepsie, and Saugerties, to name just a few. Each one breathes with its own personality. A driving tour with multiple stops is the best way to explore the region. Stop for a meal, browse the shops of main streets, and enjoy the quaint, historic surroundings.

Hit the Slopes

With several ski resorts and hundreds of trails, the Catskill Mountains draw loads of skiers and snowboarders. About three hours' drive from New York City, the slopes here have vertical drops of 1,100 to 1,600 feet. Facilities offer lessons for all levels of experience. And you can't beat the scenery. If you want to ski like an Olympian, travel farther north to Lake Placid, about a 2½-hour drive northwest of Albany. From this Adirondacks hub you can head to Whiteface or Gore Mountain.

Take a Hike

Scenic trails abound in the North Country, with many trailheads accessible along the routes that traverse the region. Some of the best areas for hiking are in the High Peaks region, near Lake Placid, Keene, and Newcomb. This area is known for its rugged hiking, but you'll find plenty of less strenuous hikes that provide spectacular views and backwoods experiences, whether for half-day or full-day outings. Farther south, the Catskills have more than 200 mi of marked trails.

Get Sprayed on a Niagara Falls Boat Tour

"Explore the roar" on the *Maid of the Mist* boat tour. Of the many ways to experience the falls, this one is one of the wettest. But it's worth it for the close-up views of three of the falls during a spectacular 30-minute ride. Don't worry: waterproof clothing is provided.

Shop and Dine in the Hamptons

On summer weekends, many New Yorkers escape the city and land here to get away from it all, or at least get away from some of it. The Hamptons teem with top restaurants and upscale shops, but the pace is far more relaxed than that of its urban counterpart. Southampton is the center of it all, and its sophisticated-yet-laid-back vibe along the beach is best experienced during a weekday trip.

IF YOU LIKE

Museums

New York City anchors the state with its plethora of world-class museums, but outside the city lies an interesting and eclectic mix of institutions worth a stop on your travels throughout the state.

■ **Corning Museum of Glass, Corning.** Uncover the history of glassmaking while perusing the museum's enormous collection. You can watch a glassblowing demo and even make your own glass souvenir. Walk-in workshops are offered daily.

■ **Munson-Williams-Proctor Arts Institute, Utica.** Come for the Hudson River School paintings, the highlight of this institute, which triples as an art school and a performing arts center. Throughout its eclectic spaces you'll also find a rich sampling of Victorian-era furnishings, Asian prints, and 19th- and 20th-century European paintings.

■ **Museum of Modern Art, New York City.** Japanese architect Yoshio Taniguchi's spacious, soaring-ceilinged galleries suffused with natural light elicit praise, plus there are such masterpieces as Monet's *Water Lilies* and van Gogh's *Starry Night*.

■ **National Baseball Hall of Fame and Museum, Cooperstown.** Baseball, baseball, and more baseball. Everything you could ever know about the game's great legends are on display here.

■ **Strong Museum, Rochester.** Kids love the interactive exhibits, antique-doll collection, and other attractions at the country's second-largest children's museum.

Parks and Nature

Whether you want to sun on the beach or hike and bike in the woods, outdoors enthusiasts will find plenty of spaces to do it.

■ **Jones Beach State Park, Wantagh.** Crowds flock to this 6½-mi stretch of white sand, one of Long Island's most popular beaches, to soak up some sun and cool off in the Atlantic. Big-name musicians play throughout the summer at its amphitheater.

■ **Kaaterskill Falls, Haines Falls.** You might recognize the 260-foot cascade from paintings, because Kaaterskill Falls was a popular subject for Hudson River School artists. A hike of just under a mile brings you to the base of the two-tiered falls.

■ **Minnewaska State Park Preserve, New Paltz.** Bike the historic carriageways or hike past gushing streams and waterfalls at this crown jewel of a park in the Shawangunks. Or just take a walk around the lake, find an open spot with a view, and stop for a picnic.

■ **Niagara Falls.** Nothing, and we're serious about this, compares with the rush of experiencing the three cascades that make up this natural wonder. Whether via a boat tour or from one of the spectacular vantage points, hearing the thunder and observing the sheer volume of three waterfalls here is a one-of-a-kind experience.

■ **Watkins Glen State Park, Watkins Glen.** Glen Creek drops about 500 feet in a span of 2 mi at this stunning park with 19 waterfalls. A 1½-mi gorge trail runs parallel to the creek, and 300-foot-high cliffs border the water.

Family Fun

New York State is crammed with attractions appealing to all sorts of families. Parks, beaches, museums, and historical sites top the list, but there are plenty of unique sites with magic all their own.

- **American Museum of Natural History, New York City.** The hands-down favorite for both visiting and local kids, this museum's many exhibits could entertain most children for a week. The dinosaurs are worth the trip, as is the live Butterfly Conservatory that runs from October to May each year. There are also an IMAX theater, ancient culture displays, and wildlife dioramas with taxidermied creatures that hit the right mix of fascinating and creepy.

- **Lake George.** Family spots don't get much more fun-filled than Lake George. Outdoor activities abound, from Great Escape & Splashwater Kingdom Fun Park and Water Slide World, both filled with wave pools and slides, to Lake George Beach for swimming and volleyball. Indoor activities keep rainy days magical with the House of Frankenstein Wax Museum and the Fort William Henry Museum. Myriad shops, restaurants, and assorted amusements enhance the experience.

- **Saratoga Springs.** Families find much to do at this resort town near Albany. The Children's Museum and Saratoga Spa State Park—with its seasonal skating rink, walking trails, and swimming pool—top the list. Families can indulge their equestrian interests at the National Museum of Racing Hall of Fame, where you can tour the training track.

Food

The Culinary Institute of America, based in the Hudson Valley, is the country's premier culinary college. Between the CIA graduates and New York City's many talented chefs (some of whom are one in the same) the state brims with a palate-pleasing cornucopia of flavors. The following are just the first course.

- **Craft, New York City.** Crafting your ideal meal here is like picking and choosing from a gourmand's well-stocked kitchen—one overseen by the gifted Tom Colicchio, who is also chef at the renowned Gramercy Tavern.

- **DePuy Canal House, High Falls.** Chef-owner John Novi, called "the father of new American cooking" by *Time* in 1984, is still turning out innovative seasonal fare in his cozy, antiques-filled 1797 stone tavern.

- **La Parmigiana, Southampton.** With its warm atmosphere and generous plates of everyone's favorite Italian dishes, this casual spot is a hit.

- **Quarter Moon Café, Delhi.** You might not expect to find innovative cuisine and cool decor in an intimate eatery in a small northern Catskills village, but here it is. The kitchen serves creative fusions of international flavors in eclectic surroundings.

HISTORY YOU CAN SEE

The Hudson River opens its mighty waters to not only New York City but into the heart of the Empire State. New Yorkers are fiercely proud of it all, from the tumbling waterfalls of Niagara to the tall buildings of New York City. Here's a quick look how this state moved from a trading center to a gateway to America.

New Amsterdam and a Revolutionary Victory

About 32 years after Christopher Columbus reached land in the western hemisphere, Giovanni da Verrazano slipped into what was to become New York Harbor. He and the droves of Europeans and others who followed were relative latecomers. People had roamed the woodlands, shorelines, and glens in this area for thousands of years. At the time of European exploration, the Algonquins lived in much of the Hudson Valley, on Manhattan, and on Long Island, whereas the Iroquois ruled the west. Thanks to Henry Hudson's travels and claims in the early 1600s, the Dutch occupied the area and called it New Amsterdam.

In 1626, just a little more than 100 years after Verrazano spotted New York, Peter Minuit, the first Dutch governor of the colony, purchased the island of Manhattan from the Algonquins for $24 worth of tools and trinkets. By 1664, the British acquired the land. They changed the name to New York and transformed it into a major trading port.

The area existed as a British colony until July 9, 1776, when the state declared its independence and became one of the original 13 colonies of the newly christened United States. But the British didn't walk away without a fight. After independence was declared, the first major battle of the American Revolutionary War was fought here. But the British victory was short-lived, and in 1783, General George Washington bade farewell to his officers, following the British evacuation, at Fraunces Tavern.

WHAT TO SEE:
Tour the **Museum of the City of New York** and **Fraunces Tavern**.

Opening up the Empire State

With Manhattan anchoring a natural harbor at the mouth of the Hudson River, it didn't take long for traders to move upstream and discover a trading and transportation gold mine. Wares moved up and down the river, and towns and cities sprang up on its shores. Henry Hudson discovered the area that was to become Albany in 1609. The Dutch moved in shortly thereafter, and established it as a hub for the beaver-fur trade. Albany was chosen as the state's capital in 1797, after the Battle of Saratoga (a turning point in the American Revolution) was fought and won here.

The area's importance, however, really rose with the completion of the Erie Canal in 1825, which linked the Atlantic Ocean with the Great Lakes and opened up new trade and transportation routes. With access to the rich sources of timber and iron ore from the nearby Adirondack Mountains, the region led the Industrial Revolution with the rise of factories and steel. Prosperity continued for the rest of the 19th century along the waterways, as millions of immigrants from Europe and other parts of the world poured into the country at the end of the 19th century and beginning of the 20th century.

1

WHAT TO SEE:
See the exhibits at the **New York State Museum.** The battlefield at **Saratoga National Historical Park** and the **Erie Canal Museum,** in Syracuse, add details to the story.

The Gateway to America

With the waterways of New York State providing new agricultural and industrial opportunities along with New York City's rise as a major commercial port of trade, immigrants thronged to New York. To accommodate this massive influx, New York opened Ellis Island as its main immigration facility. Between 1892 and 1924, some 12 million men and women came through this facility. Some stayed in the city, but many others traveled up the Hudson and through the Erie Canal, settling in towns and cities along the way.

These new citizens brought their cultures and traditions, and the diversity of the state increased significantly, especially in New York City, where this melting pot of cultures flourished like never before. New York's status as gateway to America was solidified in 1886, when France presented the country with the Statue of Liberty, which was placed in the center of New York Harbor. In 1900, New York City unified its five boroughs, becoming the largest city in the country and the most culturally diverse. By the time Ellis Island closed in 1954, the facility had processed the ancestors of 40% of Americans living today.

WHAT TO SEE:
A visit to **Ellis Island** and the **Statue of Liberty** is a moving experience.

A Land of Wealth

The industrial age brought not only prosperity to the state but also enormous wealth to many individuals. Those riches were spread out around the state in the form of mansions, museums, and monuments. The railroad magnates, finance barons, and steel tycoons were not shy in spending and erecting sumptuous estates for their leisure—and, little did they know, for the enjoyment of generations to come. The Hudson Valley, with its rolling hills and lush greenery, became the site of country homes for the Vanderbilts and the Rockefellers. In Buffalo, the wealthy elite built a row of mansions that rivaled those on New York City's Fifth Avenue.

These wealthy individuals also were quite philanthropic; most donated moneys to build museums in the state, ensuring that New York would remain one of the world's key cultural centers.

WHAT TO SEE:
Stroll along **Delmore Avenue** in downtown Buffalo, or visit the **Vanderbilt Mansion National Historic Site** in Hyde Park.

GREAT ITINERARIES

IN AND AROUND THE BIG APPLE

Days 1–3: New York City

For a small bite of the Big Apple, begin your first day at the Empire State Building, taking in the panoramic view of the city. Next head up to the Metropolitan Museum of Art. You could easily spend a whole day here, but you'll exhaust yourself if you do. Luckily, just behind the museum lies beautiful Central Park, where you can relax on a bench, rent a rowboat, or explore a meadow and watch the world go by. Exit the park's south end at 5th Avenue and work your way downtown, browsing the department stores and shops that abound. If you're there at dusk, walk instead south on 7th Avenue toward the bright lights of Times Square.

On Day 2 seek out some history via a ferry trip to the Statue of Liberty and Ellis Island. You can beat the crowds with any early start. Allow yourself about six hours if you plan to do a thorough visit with guided tours. If not, you can be back in Manhattan by lunchtime. After lunch, stroll through the Wall Street area, home of the colonial-era Fraunces Tavern, mid-19th-century Trinity Church, and St. Paul's Chapel, Manhattan's oldest surviving church building. Also here is the World Trade Center site, complete with time line and memorial. Just north are the neo-Gothic Woolworth Building (don't miss the splendid gilded lobby) and City Hall. Hop on the N or R Train to 8th Street, where you can stroll around Washington Square Park and Greenwich Village.

On your last day in town, do what many New Yorkers do on their days off—wander. Make your way to Chinatown for a dim sum breakfast or tapioca-filled soft drink. From here head north to SoHo and NoLita for galleries, chic boutiques, and restaurants. If you haven't eaten by now, hit a café a few blocks north in the happening East Village, home to yet more shops and vintage stores. From Union Square, walk up Broadway to the fashionable Flatiron District with its inimitable Flatiron Building. Take a break in Madison Square and soak up the surrounding skyline. Have dinner in one of the neighborhood's noted restaurants.

Days 4–6: The Hudson Valley

On Day 4, head up to Tarrytown to tour Kykuit or one of the other magnificent homes in the area. Or drive farther north and spend the day at Beacon, for its blend of cool art, old buildings, funky shops, and laid-back restaurants. Alternatively, Cold Spring is a nice day trip if you're traveling by train; if the shops and eateries don't interest you, take a hike—in Hudson Highlands State Park, that is.

On Day 5, head to Hyde Park and tour Franklin D. Roosevelt's home and/or the Vanderbilt Mansion. If you're here on a Friday or Saturday, have dinner at one of the Culinary Institute of America restaurants. If you're staying in Millbrook, check out a winery and one of the gardens.

On Day 6, visit Staatsburg, Annandale-on-Hudson, Tivoli, or Hudson. The stately beaux arts mansion at the Staatsburg State Historic Site; Bard's Frank

Gehry–designed performing-arts center; the stunning gardens and classical revival–style mansion of Montgomery Place; and Frederic Church's Moorish-style home, Olana, are all highlights. Leave some time for strolling and shopping in any of the villages.

Days 7–8: The Catskills

Focus on either the northern or southern Catskills. Woodstock, which has a smattering of shops and restaurants, makes a good base in the northern Catskills. From here you can easily go hiking, canoeing, kayaking, tubing, or fishing, or go to see Kaaterskill Falls. The ski resorts are accessible from here as well: the Hunter Mountain ski area, for example, is 19 mi to the north and the Belleayre Mountain ski area is about 30 mi to the west. Or make quick jaunts into small villages in the area: Mount Tremper (which also makes a good base) and Phoenicia or, closer to Belleayre, Fleischmanns, Margaretville, and Arkville. Be sure to devote a few hours to exploring Woodstock.

In the southern Catskills the area around Monticello has a few good lodging choices, including a magnificent inn in Forestburgh and a golf-focused resort in Kiamesha Lake. If you head west, you can see the site of the famed 1969 Woodstock music festival on the outskirts of Bethel. The area is known for golf and fishing, so you may want to spend time on either or both of these activities.

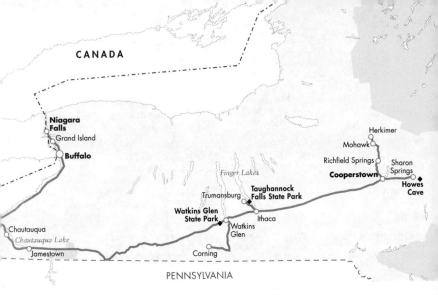

BUFFALO AND UPSTATE

Days 1–3: Niagara Falls

Start in Niagara Falls, and spend two days taking in the sights, crossing to the Canadian side if you wish. On the afternoon of Day 2, head north of the falls to see the Castellani Art Museum or one of the state parks. On Day 3, head south to Buffalo, via Grand Island. If you have kids in tow, consider a visit to the Buffalo Zoological Gardens or the Buffalo Museum of Science. Otherwise, see the Albright-Knox Art Gallery or the Buffalo and Erie County Botanical Gardens. Frank Lloyd Wright lovers should head straight for the Darwin D. Martin Complex (just be sure to have made a tour reservation). In summer you might opt to center your trip on Chautauqua. Make quick trips around Chautauqua Lake and into Jamestown if you have time. Otherwise, take advantage of the Chautauqua Institution's rich cultural offerings.

Days 4–6: The Finger Lakes

Spend Day 4 in Ithaca, a perfect gateway into the region. On the morning of Day 5 take a quick trip to Taughannock Falls State Park in Trumansburg, where the falls are higher than Niagara Falls. In the afternoon, travel to Watkins Glen State Park. Walk the awesome gorge trail (note that the gorge trail is closed in winter) and check out a winery or two. On the morning of Day 6, swing down to Corning to see the Corning Museum of Glass, which is a must-see. Return to Ithaca for dinner and a good night's sleep.

Days 7–9: Cooperstown

Cooperstown deserves two full days, which will give you the chance to see the main sights and to walk about a bit. Classical music fans shouldn't miss the Glimmerglass Opera (July and August). Spend both nights in Cooperstown (many lodgings have a two-night minimum in season). On Day 9, head either north or east. If you're traveling with children, stop at the Petrified Creatures Museum in Richfield Springs on your way north before continuing on to Herkimer to dig for "diamonds" (really quartz crystals) or to take an Erie Canal cruise. Without kids, head straight to Herkimer for the cruise. Boats leave from the Gems Along the Mohawk retail complex, which has a restaurant. If you choose to head east instead, you can do some underground exploring in Howes Cave. A third option is to head northeast to Sharon Springs for lunch.

GATEWAY TO THE NEW WORLD

A quintessential part of a visit to New York, a trip to the Statue of Liberty and Ellis Island takes up the better part of a day. It involves a ferry ride, long lines, security checks, and ultimately, the rare opportunity to stand within the single most powerful symbol of American ideals, not to mention one of the world's great monumental sculptures. It's worth the effort. It's no overstatement to say that these two sights have played defining roles in American culture.

THE STATUE OF LIBERTY

Impressive from the shore, the Statue of Liberty is majestic in person and up close. For millions of immigrants, the first glimpse of America was the Statue of Liberty. You get a taste of the thrill they must have experienced as you approach Liberty Island on the ferry from Battery Park and witness the statue grow from a vaguely defined figure on the horizon into a towering, stately colossus.

What's Here

The statue itself stands atop an 89-foot pedestal designed by American Richard Morris Hunt, with Emma Lazarus's sonnet "The New Colossus" ("Give me your tired, your poor, your huddled masses yearning to breathe free . . ."). This massive pedestal section is now the only area to which visitors have access, and only with timed tickets and after an extensive security check.

Inside the pedestal is an informative and entertaining museum. Highlights include the torch's original glass flame that was replaced because of water damage (the current flame is 24-karat gold and lit at night by floodlights), full-scale copper replicas of Lady Liberty's face and one of her feet, Bartholdi's alternative designs for the statue, and a model of Eiffel's intricate framework.

The observatory platform is a great place for a photo op; you're 16 stories high with all of Lower Manhattan spread out in front of you. You'll then descend to the promenade at the bottom of the base, where you're still four stories high. Be aware that to reach the platform you'll need to walk up 26 steps from the elevator drop-off point.

Liberty Island has a pleasant outdoor café for refueling as well as a large cafeteria. The gift shop sells trinkets little better than those available from street vendors.

Know Before You Go

You're allowed access to the museum only as part of one of the free tours of the promenade (which surrounds the base of the pedestal) or the observatory (at the pedestal's top). The tours are limited to 3,000 participants a day. To guarantee a spot on one of the tours, you must order tickets ahead of time—they can be reserved up to one year in advance, by phone or over the Internet. There are a limited amount of same-day standby tickets available at the Castle Clinton and Liberty State Park ticket offices.

Once you reach the island, there are no tickets available. And without a ticket, there is absolutely no admittance into the museum or observatory. You can get a good look at the statue's inner structure on the observatory tour through glass viewing windows that look straight into the statue. Be sure to try the view from several different viewing spots to get the whole interior. There has been no access to the torch since 1916, however the park service now offers limited access by lottery to the statue's crown.

Liberty Highlights

■ The surreal chance to stand next to, and be dwarfed by, the original glass torch and the copper cast of Lady Liberty's foot.

■ The vistas of New York from the observatory platform.

■ The rare opportunity to look up the skirt of a national monument.

Statue Basics

☎ 212/363–3200,
212/269–5755 ferry
information; 877/523–
9849 ticket reservations
⊕ www.statuecruises.com
✉ Free; ferry $12
round-trip
⊙ Daily 9 AM–5 PM;
extended hours in
summer.

Liberty helicopters

VIEWS OF THE CROWN
Some unique ways to see
Lady Liberty:

**Rise in the Ritz-Carlton
New York Battery Park:**
A swank cocktail lounge 14
stories high with straight
sight lines to the statue.
Liberty Helicopter: Sightseeing tours that fly over the
crown and torch.
Kayak: Free kayak tours of
the harbor depart from the
NYC Downtown Boathouse.

FAST FACT: To move
the Statue of Liberty from
its initial home on a Paris
rooftop to its final home
in the New York Harbor,
the statue was broken
down into 350 individual
pieces and packed in
214 crates. It took four
months to reassemble it.

FAST FACT: The
face of Lady Liberty
is actually a likeness
of sculptor Frederic-
Auguste Bartholdi's
mother—quite a tribute.

FAST FACT: *Liberty Enlightening
the World,* as the statue is officially
named, was presented to the United
States in 1886 as a gift from France
to celebrate the centennial of the
United States, a symbol of unity
and friendship between the two
countries. The 152-foot-tall figure
was sculpted by Frederic-Auguste
Bartholdi and erected around an
iron skeleton engineered by Gustav
Eiffel (the same Eiffel who would
later create the Eiffel Tower).

Foundation of
the pedestal to
torch: 305'6"

Heel to top
head: 111'6"

ELLIS ISLAND

Chances are you'll be with a crowd of international tourists as you disembark at Ellis Island. Close your eyes for a moment and imagine the jostling crowd 100 times larger. Now picture that your journey has lasted weeks at sea and that your daypack contains all your worldly possessions, including all your money. You're hungry, tired, jobless, and homeless. This scenario just begins to set the stage for the story of the millions of poor immigrants who passed through Ellis Island at the turn of the 20th century. Between 1892 and 1924, approximately 12 million men, women, and children first set foot on U.S. soil at the Ellis Island federal immigration facility. By the time the facility closed in 1954, it had processed ancestors of more than 40% of Americans living today.

What's Here

The island's main building, now a national monument, reopened in 1990 as the Ellis Island Immigration Museum, containing more than 30 galleries of artifacts, photographs, and taped oral histories. The centerpiece of the museum is the white-tile Registry Room (also known as the Great Hall). It feels dignified and cavernous today, but photographs show that it took on a multitude of configurations through the years, always packed with humanity undergoing one form of screening or another. While you're there, take a look out the Registry Room's tall, arched windows and try to imagine what passed through immigrants' minds as they viewed lower Manhattan's skyline to one side and the Statue of Liberty to the other.

Along with the Registry Room, the museum's features include the ground-level Railroad Ticket Office, which has several interactive exhibits and a three-dimensional graphic representation of American immigration patterns; the American Family Immigration Center, where for a fee you can search Ellis Island's records for your own ancestors; and, outside, the American Immigrant Wall of Honor, where the names of more than 600,000 immigrant Americans are inscribed along a promenade facing the Manhattan skyline.

The gift shop has a selection of international dolls, candies, and crafts. You can also personalize a number of registry items here as well.

Making the Most of Your Visit

Because there's so much to take in, it's a good idea to make use of the museum's interpretive tools. Check at the visitor desk for free film tickets, ranger tour times, and special programs.

Consider starting your visit with a viewing of the free film *Island of Hope, Island of Tears*. A park ranger starts off with a short introduction, then the 25-minute film takes you through an immigrant's journey from the troubled conditions of European life (especially true for ethnic and religious minorities), to their nervous arrival at Ellis Island, and their introduction into American cities. The film is a primer into all the exhibits and will deeply enhance your experience.

The audio tour ($6) is also worthwhile: it takes you through the exhibits, providing thorough, engaging commentary interspersed with recordings of immigrants themselves recalling their experiences.

Ellis Island Highlights

■ Surveying the Great Hall.

■ The moving film *Island of Hope, Island of Tears*.

■ Listening to the voices of actual immigrants who risked their lives to come to America.

■ Reading the names on the American Immigrant Wall of Honor.

■ Researching your own family's history.

Ellis Island Basics

- ☎ 212/363–3200 Ellis Island; 212/561–4500 Wall of Honor information
- ⊕ www.ellisisland.org
- 🎫 Free; ferry $12 round-trip
- ⊙ Daily 9–5; extended hours in summer.

IMMIGRANT HISTORY TIMELINE

Starting in the 1880s, troubled conditions throughout Europe persuaded both the poor and the persecuted to leave their family and homes to embark on what were often gruesome journeys to come to the golden shores of America.

1880s 5.7 million immigrants arrive in U.S.

1892 Federal immigration station opens on Ellis Island in January.

1901–1910 8.8 million immigrants arrive in U.S.; 6 million processed at Ellis Island.

1907 Highest number of immigrants (860,000) arrives in one year, including a record 11,747 on April 17.

1910 75% of the residents of New York, Chicago, Detroit, Cleveland, and Boston are now immigrants or children of immigrants.

1920s Federal laws set immigration quotas based on national origin.

1954 Ellis Island immigration station is closed.

Ellis Island: New arrivals line up to have their papers examined. ca. 1880 – 1910.

FAST FACT: Some immigrants who passed through Ellis Island later became household names. A few include Charles Atlas (1903, Italy); Irving Berlin (1893, Russia); Frank Capra (1903, Italy); Bob Hope (1908, England); Knute Rockne (1893, Norway); and Baron Von Trapp and his family (1938, Germany).

FAST FACT: In 1897, a fire destroyed the original pine immigration structure on Ellis Island, including all immigration records dating back to 1855.

FAST FACT: Only third-class, or "steerage," passengers were sent to Ellis Island. Affluent first- and second-class passengers, who were less likely to be ill or become wards of the state, were processed on board and allowed to disembark in Manhattan.

Four immigrants and their belongings, on a dock, look out over the water; view from behind.

PLANNING

Admission

There's no admission fee for either sight, but the ferry ride, run by Statue Cruises, costs $12 ($20 with an audio tour). Ferries leaving from **Battery Park** every half hour take you to both islands. (Note that large packages and oversize bags and backpacks aren't permitted on board.) Reserve tickets in advance online—you'll still have to wait in line, both to pick up the tickets and to board the ferry, but you'll be able to pick up a Monument Pass allowing you access to the pedestal of the statue, the museum, and the statue's interior structure. There is no fee for the Monument Pass and you cannot enter inside the statue without it.

Where to Catch the Ferry

Broadway and Battery Pl., Lower Manhattan Ⓜ Subway: 4, 5 to Bowling Green.

When in New Jersey

Directly on the other side of the Hudson River from Battery Park, Liberty State Park is an impressive stretch of green with ample parking and quick ferries to the monuments. Lines are almost never an issue here, something that can't be said about the New York side.

Planning Tips

Buy tickets in advance. This is the only way to assure that you'll have tickets to actually enter the Statue of Liberty museum and observatory platform.

Be prepared for intense security. At the ferry security check, you will need to remove your coat; at the statue, you will need to remove your coat as well as your belt, watch, and any metal accessories. At this writing, no strollers, large umbrellas, or backpacks are allowed in the statue.

Check ferry schedules in advance. Before you go, check www.statuecruises.com.

Keep in mind that even though the last entry time for the monument is at 4:30 PM, **the last ferry to the Statue of Liberty and Ellis Island is at 3:30 PM.** You need to arrive by at least 3 PM (to allow for security checks and lines) if you want to make the last ferry of the day.

Niagara Falls and Western New York

WITH TORONTO

WORD OF MOUTH

"Niagara is worth any miniscule time you have. It IS better from the Canada side, but whatever you can get in is great. Do NOT miss going on *Maid of the Mist* tour."

—Surfergirl

"My husband was a bit skeptical [about the Chautauqua Institution], thinking this might be too much culture for him, but as we drove home, we were already talking about bringing our friends back for a visit."

—LindainOhio

Updated by
Shannon M.
Kelly

As any local will tell you, this is western New York, not "upstate," which suggests a closeness to New York City—and this pastoral parcel of the state couldn't be farther away from that metropolitan morass. Here, oranges and yellows wash over wooded valleys in autumn, snow blankets farm fields in winter, tulips bloom beside the mighty Niagara in spring, and the blue of Lake Erie sparkles brilliantly in summer. The region's bastions of arts and culture—even Buffalo, the state's second-largest city—retain a small-town feel.

By far, Niagara Falls, anchoring the northwest corner of the state and forming the border with Ontario, Canada, is this region's famous tourist attraction. Nearly everyone who sees the falls is struck by the wonder of it. Though not among the world's highest waterfalls, Niagara Falls is, for sheer volume of water, unsurpassed, at more than 750,000 gallons per second in summer. The falls spurred the invention of alternating electric current, and they run one of the largest hydroelectric developments in the world. And it really is all that water, fueled by four of the Great Lakes—Superior, Michigan, Huron, and Erie—as they flow into the fifth, Ontario, that ranks Niagara as one of the planet's natural wonders.

Buffalo is known as the blizzard capital of the United States. In the late 19th and early 20th centuries the city was a boomtown, rich in electricity and steel—well-kept baronial homes along Delaware Avenue are proof of this legacy. Today the city has a more varied economic palette (manufacturing, technology, service industries) and is home to vibrant neighborhoods, fiercely loyal sports fans (go Bills!), and a thriving university, as well as attractions such as a collection of Frank Lloyd Wright homes and the impressive Albright-Knox art museum—worthy of the state's second-largest city.

Down in Chautauqua and Cattaraugus counties, where New York State hugs Lake Erie and borders Pennsylvania, lie slow-paced towns in a region of hills and farms, fledgling vineyards and wineries, fish-filled lakes, and the huge and wild Allegany State Park. For most visitors, however, the main reason to visit is the Chautauqua Institution, with its impressive roster of lectures, courses, and performances spanning arts, education, religion, and recreation during a nine-week summer season. Nine U.S. presidents, from Ulysses S. Grant to Gerald Ford, have delivered addresses here, as have Leo Tolstoy, William Jennings Bryan, Amelia Earhart, and, in more recent years, Jesse Jackson, Ted Koppel, and Al Gore.

TOP REASONS TO GO

Seeing Niagara Falls. An awesome display of natural power that should not be missed, the falls is worth a stop even for a half hour. But if you have time, see it from the Canadian side for superior views.

Falls tours. While you're next to the waterworks, make time for at least one tour—Maid of the Mist, Cave of the Winds, or the White Water Walk—and maybe also a cable car over the whirlpool, a fast-paced boat ride with Whirlpool Jet Boat Tours, or a helicopter ride over the thundering waters.

Buffalo. The state's second-largest city, dating from 1804, has historic buildings, a handful of Frank Lloyd Wright structures, some worthwhile art museums, and the region's top restaurants, music, and theater.

The Chautauqua Institution. This summer-long program of lectures, workshops, and performances has been the number one attraction in southwestern New York since Victorian times.

Allegany State Park. An amazing 65,000-acre expanse of woodsy trails, hilltop views, lakes, and campsites makes for the nature-lover's ultimate playground.

ORIENTATION AND PLANNING

GETTING ORIENTED

Anchored by the tenacious city of Buffalo and the inescapable Niagara Falls, western New York is wedged between Lake Erie to the west, Lake Ontario to the north, Rochester and the Finger Lakes to the east, and the Pennsylvania border to the south. In the northwest corner is the Niagara River, which connects lakes Erie and Ontario and is shared by the United States and Canada.

From Interstate 90 (New York State Thruway), the main entryway to the region, expressway spur Interstate 190 at Buffalo leads across Grand Island to the Robert Moses Parkway into Niagara Falls. The parkway continues north to Lewiston and then Youngstown, where the Niagara River empties into Lake Ontario. The scenic Great Lakes Seaway Trail traces the region's perimeter in the north and west, along lakes Ontario and Erie.

In this chapter, we've started with Niagara Falls, undoubtedly the top attraction in western New York. Seeing the falls from the Canadian side is much recommended, and from there, it's an easy jaunt to pretty Niagara-on-the-Lake and the surrounding wine country. Worthwhile Canadian overnights are Stratford for its prestigious summer theater festival, and Toronto, Canada's metropolitan nerve center. Just 20 minutes from Niagara Falls, Buffalo is an idea hub for day trips to the Erie Canal town of Lockport, or to East Aurora, Darien Lakes theme park, or Letchworth State Park (⇨ *Finger Lakes, Chapter 3*). Buffalo is also the starting point for many a trip south along the Seaway Trail to Dunkirk, Fredonia, Westfield, Chautauqua, and Jamestown. East along

BORDER CROSSINGS

As of June 2009, in order to reenter the United States from Canada by land, citizens and legal residents of the United States ages 19 and older need a passport or a state-issued "enhanced" driver's license that some states, such as New York, are currently offering. By air, a passport is required. Naturalized U.S. residents should also carry their naturalization certificate, and permanent residents should also carry their green card. Children 18 and younger need only a birth certificate. Go to the

Department of Homeland Security Web site (⊕ *www.dhs.gov/travel*) and click on Travel Security for up-to-the-minute information.

■ TIP→Avoid crossing at high-traffic times, especially Friday night and Sunday night. The Rainbow Bridge, connecting Niagara Falls, New York, to Niagara Falls, Ontario, is almost always more congested than Buffalo's Peace Bridge or the Lewiston-Queenston Bridge.

Interstate 86 are Salamanca and Olean, bordering giant Allegany State Park, and Ellicottville, a short drive north of Salamanca, is a popular ski and foodie destination for Buffalonians.

PLANNING

WHEN TO GO

Outside the Holiday Valley ski area, high season runs from Memorial Day through Labor Day, when most cultural activities take place and the Niagara Falls boat rides are operating. In the Chautauqua–Allegany region, some restaurants and B&Bs close between September or October and May. Summer temperatures range from 75°F to 85°F, with occasional light rainfall. The area near Niagara Falls is always misty, a natural refresher in the summertime. Throughout the region, very hot, humid days are infrequent. Winter temperatures create ice-covered tree branches and rocks that sparkle, and the railings and bridges turn almost crystalline.

GETTING HERE AND AROUND
AIR TRAVEL

Buffalo handles most flights to western New York, with nonstop flights to 18 cities on 10 airlines. **Buffalo Niagara International Airport** (BUF ⊠ *4200 Genesee St., Cheektowaga* ☎ *716/630–6000* ⊕ *www. buffaloairport.com*) is about 15 mi east of downtown, off Interstate 90. The **Buffalo Airport taxi service** (☎ *716/633–8294 or 800/5514369* ⊕ *www.buffaloairporttaxi.com*) is the only official taxi service at the airport; it runs 24 hours to most destinations in western New York. Fares from the airport to downtown are metered, but run about $32.

You could fly into Toronto (100 mi north of Buffalo) if you plan to see some of Canada. Jamestown has a small airport, **Chautauqua County Jamestown Airport (JHW** ⊠ *3163 Airport Dr., Jamestown* ☎ *716/484–0204*) with flights to/from Cleveland, Ohio. Some towns in the Chautauqua–Allegany region are closer to the airport in Erie, Pennsylvania,

Erie International Airport (ERI ✉*4411 W. 12th St.* ☎*814/833–4258* ⊕ *www.erieairport.org)*, than to Buffalo's airport.

Toronto has two airports. Most flights arrive at **Lester B. Pearson International Airport (YYZ** ✉*3111 Convair Dr., Mississauga, ON* ☎*416/776–3000* ⊕*www.gtaa.com*), 32 km (20 mi) northwest of downtown. Taxis to downtown Toronto from Pearson cost C$45 or more; rates are fixed based on destination. (Check fixed-rate maps at ⊕*www.gtaa.com*.) **Toronto Airport Express** (☎*905/564–3232* ⊕*www.torontoairportexpress. com*) offers 24-hour coach service daily to several major downtown hotels and the Toronto Coach Terminal (Bay and Dundas streets). It costs C$18.50 one way, C$29.95 round-trip.

Toronto's City Centre Airport (YTZ ✉*Ferry terminal at Bathurst St. and the lakefront* ☎*416/863–2000* ⊕*www.torontoport.com/Airport.asp*), in the Toronto Islands, is a five-minute ferry ride from downtown. It is served by **Porter Airlines** (☎*416/619–8622 or 888/619–8622* ⊕*www.flyporter. com*), which has flights from a handful of cities in Canada and from Newark. Porter Airlines runs a free shuttle between Union Station and the ferry terminal. (Call Porter with any questions, rather than the airport.)

BUS TRAVEL

Greyhound (☎*800/231–2222* ⊕*www.greyhound.com*) has a line running from Toronto to New York City, with a stop in Buffalo. **Megabus** (☎ *877/462–6342* ⊕*www.megabus.com*), a discount line, operates the Toronto–New York City route, with a stop in both downtown Buffalo and at the Buffalo Niagara International Airport. **Short Line Coach USA** (☎*800/631–8405* ⊕*www.coachusa.com/shortline*) travels between New York City and nearly all towns and cities in the region. **Adirondack, Pine Hill, and New York Trailways** (☎*800/858–8555 or 800/225–6815* ⊕*www.trailwaysny.com*) links most of the towns and cities in the region with New York City and much of the rest of New York and neighboring states.

CAR TRAVEL

Driving is generally the easiest way to get around, with a few exceptions. Toronto has excellent public transportation, and a car isn't necessary to get around downtown. Chautauqua is largely a no-car zone, but there are parking lots near the main gates. In Niagara Falls most major sights are clustered in a walkable area around the falls, and you should not have any trouble parking in Niagara Falls or Buffalo. But asides from these exceptions, towns and cities aren't easily traversed by public transportation.

Access to western New York from the east and south is primarily via Interstate 90, the New York State Thruway. Getting to Niagara Falls, Ontario, from Niagara Falls, New York, is a 10-minute drive when borders are clear. Some neighborhoods in downtown Buffalo (Elmwood, Allentown) are easy to explore on foot; traveling from neighborhood to neighborhood is best by car, however. Transport between Buffalo and Toronto by bus and train is frequent and convenient; getting around Toronto by subway and streetcar is preferred. Note, however, that border wait times on a bus or train are much longer than if you're traveling by car, since every passenger must be processed.

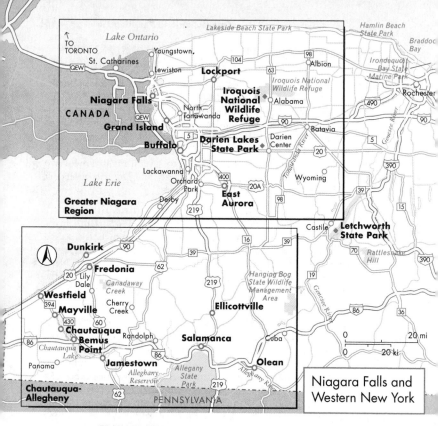

Niagara Falls and
Western New York

TRAIN TRAVEL

Amtrak (☎ *800/872–7245* ⊕ *www.amtrak.com*) connects Buffalo and
Niagara Falls with Toronto, the Finger Lakes, Rochester, central New
York, Albany, the Hudson Valley, and New York City, as well as Cleve-
land, Ohio. In Albany you can switch to Adirondacks-bound trains.

RESTAURANTS

Fast-food chains are well represented in Niagara, and apart from a few
good Italian and hotel-restaurant options, it's best to make the trip to
Lewiston (7 mi north), Buffalo, or Niagara-on-the-Lake (in Canada)
for an above-average meal.

Buffalo has given the world two classics: Buffalo chicken wings and beef
on weck. You'll come across both throughout the region. The former is
served mild, medium, or hot, alongside blue-cheese dressing and celery.
The latter consists of roast beef, carved on the spot, and heaped on a
fresh, flaky kimmelweck roll that has been sprinkled with coarse salt.

In the Chautauqua–Allegany region, finding anything other than American or (often Americanized) Continental cuisine is rare. A few restaurants stand out for their excellent use of abundant farm-fresh local
produce, especially around Chautauqua.

2

Casual dress is usually acceptable and reservations usually aren't necessary at any but the priciest restaurants. Outside Buffalo, restaurants may close by 9 PM for dinner, and in smaller towns, many restaurants are closed Sunday evenings and Monday. In the Chautauqua area, some restaurants open only in the summer season.

HOTELS

In Niagara Falls, lodgings consist mainly of chain hotels, with a few exceptions, such as the historic Red Coach Inn and the glitzy Seneca Niagara Casino Hotel. Niagara Falls, Ontario, tends to have higher-quality options. Buffalo has its fair share of major chains, plus a handful of independent, historic hotels and B&Bs. In the Chautauqua–Allegany region, you can get VIP attention as you chat with a B&B owner over a homemade country breakfast at one of the many historic inns. Most towns have a couple of chain options as well. During the Chautauqua Institution season, reservations in that area should be made as far in advance as possible.

Most of the area's hotels are moderately priced. High-season rates apply from Memorial Day through Labor Day everywhere except at the Holiday Valley and Peek'n Peak ski resorts.

The **Inns of Chautauqua County** (⊕ *www.bbonline.com/ny/chautauquainns*) has information about nine lodgings in the area. The **Western New York Bed & Breakfast Association** (⊕ *www.bbwny.com*) represents more than a dozen member B&Bs in the region.

WHAT IT COSTS IN U.S. AND CANADIAN DOLLARS					
	¢	$	$$	$$$	$$$$
RESTAURANTS	under $10	$10–$17	$18–$24	$25–$35	over $35
	under C$8	C$8–C$12	C$13–C$20	C$21–C$30	over C$30
HOTELS	under $100	$101–$150	$151–$200	$201–$300	over $300
	under C$75	C$75–C$125	C$126–C$175	C$175–C$250	over C$250

Restaurant prices are for a main course at dinner (or at the most expensive meal served). Hotel prices are for two people in a standard double room in high season, excluding tax.

VISITOR INFORMATION

New York State Tourism (☎ *800/225–5697* ⊕ *www.iloveny.com*) maintains a comprehensive list of local tourism boards. **Ontario Travel** (☎ *800/668–2746* ⊕ *www.ontariotravel.net*).

NIAGARA FALLS

20 mi north of Buffalo, 80 mi south of Toronto, 90 mi west of Rochester.

Niagara Falls has inspired artists for centuries. English painter William H. Bartlett, who visited here in the mid-1830s, noted that "you may dream of Niagara, but words will never describe it to you." Although cynics have called it everything from "water on the rocks" to "the second major disappointment of American married life" (Oscar Wilde)—most visitors are truly impressed. Missionary and explorer Louis Hennepin, whose books were widely read across Europe, described the falls in 1678 as "an incredible Cataract or Waterfall which has no equal." Nearly two centuries later, Charles Dickens declared, "I seemed to be lifted from the earth and to be looking into Heaven." Henry James recorded in 1883 how one stands there "gazing your fill at the most beautiful object in the world." The thundering cascades were dramatically immortalized by Hollywood in 1953, when Marilyn Monroe starred as a steamy siren, luring her jealous husband down to the crashing waters in the film *Niagara*. The film single-handedly spurred the modern-day popularity of the falls as a vacation destination.

> ## NIAGARA FALLS IN ONE DAY
>
> If you have only a day in Niagara Falls, go on a *Maid of the Mist*, Cave of the Winds, or White Water Walk tour for a close look at the falls. (Bring a change of clothes.) You can picnic at Whirlpool State Park to see the whirlpool. It's worth it to cross the Rainbow Bridge to the Canadian side, where you have much better views of the cascades. From there, you can do the Whirlpool Aero Car, a cable-car ride over the whirlpool. Dinner with a view of the falls, and seeing them lighted up at night, is a nice way to end the day.

The falls prompted the invention of alternating electric current, and they drive one of the world's largest hydroelectric developments. As with many other geographic features, Niagara's origins are glacial. Thousands of years ago the glaciers receded, diverting the waters of Lake Erie northward into Lake Ontario. (Before that, they had drained south; such are the fickle ways of nature.) There has been considerable erosion since, more than 7 mi in all, as the soft shale and sandstone of the escarpment have been washed away. Wisely, there have been major water diversions for a generating station (1954) and other developments (1954–63) that have spread the flow more evenly over the entire crest line of Horseshoe Falls. The erosion is now down to as little as 1 foot every decade. At this rate it will be some 130,000 years before the majestic cascade is reduced to an impressive rapids somewhere near present-day Buffalo, 20 mi to the south.

The malls, amusement parks, hotels, tacky souvenir shops, and flashy wax museums that surround the falls today (mainly on the Canadian side) attest to the region's maturation into a major tourist attraction. But despite the hordes of visitors jostling unceremoniously for the best photographic vantage point, the astounding beauty of the falls remains undiminished, and unending.

VISITOR INFORMATION

Niagara Tourism & Convention Corp. (⊠ *345 3rd St., Suite 605, Niagara Falls* ☎ *716/282–8992 or 800/338–7890* ⊕ *www.niagara-usa.com*).

NIAGARA FALLS, NEW YORK

There are actually two cities called Niagara Falls—one on the U.S. side and the other immediately across the Niagara River in Canada. You can walk from one to the other across the Rainbow Bridge (bring your passport!). The view from Goat Island on the American side is a must, and the Cave of the Winds tour is excellent. Though the city of Niagara Falls is developing slowly, there's little for tourists outside the Niagara Falls State Park boundaries and the city noticeably struggles with deterioration.

WHAT TO SEE

 Aquarium of Niagara. Dive into Niagara's other water wonder. This is a close encounter with more than 1,500 aquatic animals, including sharks, piranhas, sea lions, octopus, and moray eels. The aquarium has sea-lion demonstrations and penguin feedings daily, and an outdoor harbor-seal exhibit. ⊠*701 Whirlpool St.* ☎*716/285–3575 or 800/500–4609* ⊕*www.aquariumofniagara.org* ☜*$9.50* ⊙*Late May–early Sept., daily 9–7; early Sept.–late May, daily 9–5.*

 Castellani Art Museum. The collection at this museum, in a gray marble–faced building on the Niagara University campus (just north of the city), encompasses more than 5,000 works—paintings, drawings, photographs, prints, and sculptures—with an emphasis on modern and contemporary art. Charles Burchfield, Alexander Calder, Salvador Dalí, Willem de Kooning, April Gornick, Keith Haring, David Hockney, Marsden Hartley, Amedeo Modigliani, and Cindy Sherman are among those represented here. An Underground Railroad interpretive center includes historic photos, video, and artifacts; Niagara Falls was one of the last stops on the "railroad" for slaves escaping to Canada. ⊠*Niagara University, Rte. 104 W* ☎*716/286–8200* ⊕*www.niagara. edu/cam/* ☜*Free* ⊙*Tues.–Sat. 11–5, Sun. 1–5.*

Earl W. Brydges Artpark State Park. The 150-acre park, on a bluff overlooking Niagara Gorge, is dedicated to the performing and visual arts (⇨*Nightlife and the Arts, below*), but also has historic sights, such as an American Indian burial mound dating from AD 140. You can fish, hike, and picnic in the park. Summer brings a slew of family-oriented events and activities. ⊠*450 S. 4th St., Lewiston* ☎*716/754–4375* ⊕*nysparks. state.ny.us* ☜*Parking $6 (June–Aug. during scheduled events; free otherwise)* ⊙*Daily dawn–dusk.*

 Goat Island is a wonderful spot for a quiet walk and a close-up view of the rapids. Pedestrian bridges give you access to Luna Island and the Three Sisters Islands. The Cave of the Winds tour leaves from Goat Island.

There are two main automobile entrances to the park, both off Robert Moses Parkway. The south entrance takes you over a bridge to Goat Island; the north entrance puts you near the visitor center. ⊠*Off Robert Moses Pkwy.* ✑ *Box 773, 14302* ☎*716/278–1796* ⊕*nysparks.state. ny.us* ☜*Parking $10.*

 Historic Lewiston. During the War of 1812, the Americans made a failed attempt to invade Canada from Lewiston, in the Battle of Queenston.

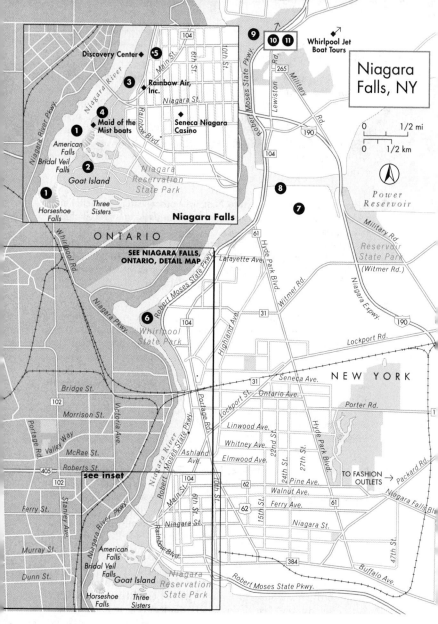

Niagara Falls, NY

Niagara Falls

0   1/2 mi
0   1/2 km

Power Reservoir

Discovery Center ◆ **⑤**

③ ◆ Rainbow Air, Inc.

Niagara St.

④

◆ Maid of the Mist boats

Seneca Niagara Casino

①

American Falls

Bridal Veil Falls

②

Goat Island

①

Horseshoe Falls

Three Sisters

Niagara Falls

⑨

⑩ ⑪ Whirlpool Jet Boat Tours

Niagara River Pkwy.

Niagara River

Rainbow Blvd.

Main St.

6th St.

10th St.

Robert Moses State Pkwy.

Lewiston Rd.

Military Rd.

265

190

104

Niagara Reservation State Park

⑧

⑦

ONTARIO

SEE NIAGARA FALLS, ONTARIO, DETAIL MAP

Reservoir State Park (Witmer Rd.)

Military Rd.

Lafayette Ave.

Hyde Park Blvd.

Witmer Rd.

Niagara Expwy.

61

31

Whirlpool Rd.

Niagara Pkwy.

Niagara River

Robert Moses State Pkwy.

⑥

Whirlpool State Park

104

Highland Ave.

Lockport Rd.

190

Bridge St.

102

Morrison St.

Victoria Ave.

Portage Rd.

Valley Way

McRae St.

Roberts St.

405

102

see inset

Ferry St.

Stanley Ave.

Murray St.

Dunn St.

American Falls

Bridal Veil Falls

Goat Island

Horseshoe Falls

Three Sisters

Niagara Reservation State Park

Main St.

6th St.

10th St.

Rainbow Blvd.

Niagara St.

104

NEW YORK

Seneca Ave.

Ontario Ave.

31

Lockport St.

Linwood Ave.

Whitney Ave.

Elmwood Ave.

Ashland Ave.

Portage Rd.

15th St.

22nd St.

24th St.

27th St.

Hyde Park Blvd.

Porter Rd.

1

TO FASHION OUTLETS

Packard Rd.

Niagara Falls Bl.

62

Pine Ave.

Walnut Ave.

Ferry Ave.

Niagara St.

61

62

384

Robert Moses State Pkwy.

Buffalo Ave.

47th St.

The town has further historic significance as the last stateside stop on the Underground Railroad and as the birthplace of Niagara Falls; today's Niagara Gorge is the result of the falls' movement south to their current location. This community of 2,700 is a clean, quiet, small-town contrast with Niagara Falls, which is about a 10-minute drive south. Center Street, lined with restaurants, shops, a pub, and a café, leads down to the waterfront, where the Barton Hill Hotel and Whirlpool Jet Boat launch are located. Lewiston has a virtually nonstop festival calendar in summer, with waterfront concerts almost daily. The **Historical Association of Lewiston, Inc.** (✉*469 Plain St., Lewiston* ☎*716/754–4214* ⊕*www.historiclewiston.org*) has information about events and attractions. ✉*Center St. between N. 9th St. and the waterfront.*

> **CANADIAN OR AMERICAN SIDE?**
>
> Overall, Canada has the superior views and a more-developed waterfront, with better (and more-expensive) restaurants, attractions, and hotels. In contrast, the American waterfront is lined with state parks, ideal for hiking and picnicking—an altogether different experience. From the American side, views are generally of the river rapids, gorge, and whirlpool, rather than the falls. If you only have time for a drive-by, or don't want to deal with the border crossing, you can get your Niagara Falls fix stateside. But if you have even a few hours to spare, it's worth it to experience the Canadian side, too.

❶ Niagara Falls. North American Indians called it Onguiaahram, or Thundering Waters. For hundreds of years, visitors to Niagara Falls have marveled at the sheer immensity of the surging walls of water. Its awe-inspiring views today are enhanced by misty early mornings, sun-streaked rainbows, and grand after-dark illumination with spotlights that penetrate the night sky.

FodorsChoice ★

Part of the longest unfortified border in the world, Niagara Falls is actually three cataracts: the American Falls and Bridal Veil Falls, in New York, and the Horseshoe Falls, in Ontario. American Falls is the highest (70–110 feet tall), but not by much, and it's about half as wide as the Canadian cascade (950 feet long). Bridal Veil is the smallest of the three. Several small islands dot the river here. Goat Island, part of Niagara Falls State Park, separates Horseshoe Falls from the U.S. falls and offers spectacular vantage points of both sides. Little Luna Island sits between the two U.S. cascades, between Goat Island and the mainland.

❸ Niagara Falls State Park. This park hugs the Niagara River bordering the Horseshoe and American and Bridal Veil falls. It includes several islands: Goat Island—with several attractions—Luna Island, and Three Sisters Islands. Established in 1885 to protect the public's access to the land surrounding the falls, this is the oldest state park in the country. It was designed by noted landscape architect Frederick Law Olmsted, who also designed New York City's Central Park.

FodorsChoice ★

NIAGARA FALLS TOURS—AMERICAN SIDE

Cave of the Winds. In this walking tour, an elevator takes you down 175 feet into the gorge, where you follow walkways to an observation deck less than 20 feet from the thundering waters of Bridal Veil falls—you will get drenched (it's called Hurricane Deck for a reason). Souvenir ponchos and sandals are provided. ⊠ *Departures from Goat Island, next to American Falls, Niagara Falls State Park* ☎ *716/278–1730* ⊕ *www.niagarafallsstatepark.com* ✉ *$11* ⏲ *May–Oct., daily from 9 AM; closing times vary.*

☾ ★ *Maid of the Mist.* View the three falls from up close during a spectacular 30-minute ride on the world-famous boat tour, in operation since 1846, when it was conducted with wooden-hulled, coal-fired steamboats. Today double-deck steel ships tow passengers on 30-minute journeys to the foot of the falls, where the spray is so heavy that ponchos must be distributed. The *Maid of the Mist* tour originating from the Canadian side of the falls (⇨ *Niagara Falls, Ontario*) is almost exactly the same. ⊠ *Departures from dock next to Prospect Point Observation Tower, Niagara Falls State Park* ⏦ *151 Buffalo Ave.,*

14403 ☎ *716/284–8897* ⊕ *www.maidofthemist.com* ✉ *$13.50* ⏲ *Departures every 15 mins daily Apr.–late Oct.*

Rainbow Air, Inc. Helicopter Tours. For rare aerial views of the falls and some impressive vacation photos, take a day- or nighttime helicopter ride. The 10-minute tours are on a first-come, first-served basis. ⊠ *454 Main St.* ☎ *716/284–2800* ⊕ *www.rainbowairinc.com* ✉ *$90* ⏲ *May–Oct., daily 9 AM–dusk; Apr. and Nov., weekends 9 AM–dusk.*

Whirlpool Jet Boat Tours. Veer around and hurdle white-water rapids on a one-hour thrill ride that follows Niagara canyons up to the wall of rolling waters, just below the falls. Children must be at least six years old for the open-boat Wet Jet Tour and four years old for the Jet Dome Tour, in a (dry!) covered boat. Tours departs from Lewiston, New York, a 15-minute drive north of Niagara Falls and from Niagara-on-the-Lake, Ontario. Reserve ahead; check the Web site for discounts. ⊠ *115 S. Water St., Lewiston* ☎ *905/468–4800 or 888/438–4444* ⊕ *www.whirlpooljet.com* ✉ *$57* ⏲ *Daily late Apr.–Oct.*

The **Niagara Scenic Trolley** (✉ *$2*) travels a 3-mi route through the park, picking up and dropping off passengers at six locations. The **Niagara USA Discovery Pass** (✉ *$33*) includes Niagara Scenic Trolley tickets and admission to the Aquarium of Niagara, *Maid of the Mist,* Cave of the Winds, the Prospect Point Observation Tower, and the Niagara Gorge Discovery Center. It's available from the Prospect Park Visitor Center.

■**TIP**➔Hours of operation for all park attractions change according to weather and season. It's best to call ahead to make sure your timing is right.(⇨ *For the* **Cave of the Winds** *and* **Maid of the Mist** *tours, see Niagara Falls Tours box.*)

4 The **Prospect Park Visitor Center** (☎716/278–1796 ☒*Free* ⊙*Hrs vary; call ahead*) is surrounded by gardens and has tourist information, exhibits, and a snack bar. The visitor center's Adventure Theater shows the "thrill film" *Niagara: Legends of Adventure* (☒ *$11*), *on a 45-foot-tall screen*. The 282-foot-tall **Prospect Point Observation Tower** (☎716/278–1796 ☒*$1; free with Maid of the Mist ticket* ⊙*Hrs vary; call ahead*) offers dramatic views of all three falls from an observation deck high above the gushing waters. When the *Maid of the Mist* is in operation, you can take a glass elevator to boat launch at the base of the tower. The **Niagara Gorge Discovery Center** (☎716/278–1070 ☒*$3*) explains, through interactive exhibits and a multiple-screen movie, the natural history of the falls and the Niagara Gorge and their formation.

8 **Niagara Power Project Visitors Center.** Niagara Falls generates power at one of the largest hydroelectric plants in the world (the largest in New York State). The visitor center, 4½ mi north of the falls, has more than 50 hands-on exhibits, including an operating model-size generator, and educational displays on energy efficiency and hydroelectric power generation. Atop the Robert Moses Power Plant, the visitor center has sweeping views of the Niagara Gorge. ✉*5777 Lewiston Rd. (Rte. 104), Lewiston* ☎716/286–6661 or 866/697–2386 ⊕*www.nypa.gov* ☒*Donations accepted* ⊙*Daily 9–5.*

10 **Old Fort Niagara.** The earliest part of the fort was built as a French castle in 1726, and the complex later played a critical role in the French and Indian War (1754–63). You can watch colorful displays of cannon and musket firings, historical reenactments, 18th-century military demonstrations, and take part in archaeological programs. The fort is inside Fort Niagara State Park (⇨*Sports and the Outdoors*), 15 mi north of Niagara Falls. ✉ *Rte. 18F, off Robert Moses Pkwy., Youngstown* ☎716/745–7611 ⊕*www.oldfortniagara.org* ☒ *$10* ⊙*Sept.–June, daily 9–5; July and Aug., daily 9–7.*

6 **Whirlpool State Park.** From this park 2 mi north of Niagara Falls you get great views of the giant whirlpool that occurs in this part of the Niagara River. A sharp turn in the river is responsible for the swirling waters. Steps and trails lead down 300 feet into the gorge, where you may fish. It's a nice place for a picnic while watching the cable car from the Canadian side glide hundreds of feet above the whirlpool. ✉*Off Robert Moses Pkwy.* ☎716/284–4691 ⊕*nysparks.state.ny.us* ☒*Free* ⊙*Daily dawn–dusk.*

SPORTS AND THE OUTDOORS

PARKS AND NATURAL AREAS The 202-acre **Earl W. Brydges Artpark State Park** (⇨ *What to See, above*) is primarily visited for its performing- and visual-arts facilities, but you may also fish, hike, picnic, and cross-country ski here. Summer brings a slew of family-oriented events and activities.

Fort Niagara State Park is at the edge of the Niagara River where it empties into Lake Ontario, 15 mi north of Niagara Falls. Facilities include picnic tables, swimming pools, hiking trails, fishing access, a boat-launch site, and playgrounds. In winter you may cross-country ski or sled here. The grounds surround the Old Fort Niagara complex

(⇨ *What to See, above*). ✉ *1 Main-tenance Ave., off Rte. 18F and Robert Moses Pkwy., Youngstown* ☎*716/745–7273* ⊕*nysparks.state. ny.us* ✉ *$6 per car mid-June–early Sept.* ⊙*Daily dawn–dusk.*

Hiking trails along the Niagara Gorge wind through **Whirlpool State Park** (⇨ *What to See, above*); some lead down 300 feet into the gorge, where you may fish.

NIAGARA REGION DRIVING TOURS

Greater Niagara Travel (⊕*www. greaterniagara.com*) has a number of interesting **driving tours** on its Web site, including a tour of Underground Railroad sites, an Erie Canal Tour, a War of 1812 tour, and an architectural tour of Buffalo.

SHOPPING

Kate Spade, Coach, Banana Republic, Brooks Brothers, J. Crew, Michael Kors, Saks Fifth Avenue, Nike, and Ann Taylor are just a handful of the more than 150 stores at the **Fashion Outlets** (✉*1900 Military Rd.* ☎*716/297–0933*), which draws as many Canadian as American shoppers for the substantial deals.

NIGHTLIFE AND THE ARTS

★ **Artpark State Park** (✉*450 S. 4th St., Lewiston* ☎*716/754–4375 or 800/659–7275* ⊕*www.artpark.net*), Niagara's premier performing-arts center, hosts reasonably priced, world-class musical theater, dance performances, and classical, big-band, pop, and jazz concerts. Performances are held in the 2,400-seat Mainstage Theater or the outdoor amphitheater, which will be completely renovated for the 2010 season. Free Tuesday- and Wednesday-evening concerts, from June through August, draw big crowds, and this is the summer home of the Buffalo Philharmonic Orchestra.

The 82,000-square-foot **Seneca Niagara Casino** (✉*310 4th St.* ☎*716/299–1100 or 877/873–6322* ⊕*www.snfgc.com*) complex, which includes a hotel and performance venues, is owned by the Seneca Nation. The 24-hour casino is in a giant airplane-hangar-style space with a large stained-glass mural at one end, and has more than 3,200 slot machines and 100 table games, including baccarat, craps, roulette, and several styles of poker. Unlike Canadian casinos across the river, free alcohol is served on the gaming floor, and smoking is allowed (though the smoke is not cloying, it's noticeable). Big acts like Michael Bolton perform at the events center; smaller performers occasionally take the stage at the 443-seat Bear's Den.

WHERE TO EAT

The best stateside restaurants in the area tend to be in Lewiston, about 10 mi north of Niagara Falls, New York. If you're seeking a five-star dining experience, it's worth the 30-minute drive (if border crossings are clear) to Niagara-on-the-Lake.

$ ✕**Brickyard Pub & B.B.Q.** The polished-wood dining room and bar, decorated with vintage signs, are separated, which helps with noise control during Buffalo Bills games at this Southern-inspired neighborhood joint. Slip into a booth and order a rack of baby back ribs, a chicken-and-

SOUTHERN

rib platter with homemade corn bread, fried Cajun-spice catfish, or a po'boy sandwich, and choose from a long list of bourbons and beers. Locals say that everything, from the stew to the fish fry to the barbecue, is top-notch. ⊠ *432 Center St.,Lewiston* ☎716/754–7227 ☐*AE, D, MC, V.*

$ ✕**Buzzy's.** Many say the Buffalo-style wings at Buzzy's are better than
PIZZA   those at Buffalo's Anchor Bar. An institution since 1953, this no-frills place with bland decor and windows facing Route 62 serves build-your-own pizzas, eight specialty pies, calzones, and a dozen or so subs and hoagies. The wings and chicken fingers—fresh, not frozen—come with blue-cheese dip and a choice of 10 sauces, including one called Suicide, which the menu warns is "very hot—no refunds or exchanges." ⊠*7617 Niagara Falls Blvd./Rte. 62* ☎716/283–5333 ☐*AE, D, MC, V.*

$$ ✕**Carmelo's Ristorante.** On Lewiston's historic main street (Center Street),
ITALIAN   Carmelo's has a classy small dining room with an oiled wooden bar,
★   dark-wood beamed ceiling, partial stone walls, and white tablecloths. Fresh and often local ingredients are used in pastas, like homemade ricotta gnocchi with rapini and sweet sausage or slow-cooked veal, pork, and pancetta Bolognese, and in entrées, such as peppercorn-encrusted ahi tuna with a ginger-soy glaze. ⊠*425 Center St., Lewiston* ☎716/754–2311 ⚭*Reservations essential* ☐*AE, D, DC, MC, V* ⊘*No lunch.*

$$ ✕**Clarkson House.** This local institution occupies an antiques-filled 19th-
AMERICAN   century building. Cloth-covered tables contrast with hardwood floors and old wood beams. The menu blends contemporary, American, and Continental dishes; steaks—New York strip and Kobe flatiron among them—are a specialty. You have a large choice of starters, such as shrimp cocktail, baked Brie, crab cakes, and teriyaki tenderloin skewers. Reservations are essential on weekends. ⊠*810 Center St., Lewiston* ☎716/754–4544 ☐*AE, MC, V* ⊘*Closed Mon. No lunch weekends.*

$ ✕**Como Restaurant.** Since 1927, the Antonacci family has been serv-
ITALIAN   ing traditional dishes from the south of Italy like veal à la Francesca, chicken cacciatore, and veal Parmesan. The interior is an explosion of floral wallpaper, pastoral-scene murals, glitzy chandeliers, and faux grapevines. ⊠*2220 Pine Ave./U.S. 62A* ☎716/285–9341 ☐*AE, D, MC, V.*

$$ ✕**Top of the Falls.** Just feet from the brink of Niagara Falls, this spot with
AMERICAN   panoramic views lives up to its name. The scenery is awesome, as is the
★   thick New York strip steak. The signature Buffalo chicken wrap (crispy chicken fingers, hot sauce, lettuce, and blue cheese in a flour tortilla) is a good choice for lunch. ⊠*Niagara Falls State Park, Goat Island, off Robert Moses Pkwy.* ✉*Box 773, 14302* ☎716/278–0348 ☐*AE, D, MC, V* ⊘*Closed Oct.–early May.*

WHERE TO STAY

$$$–$$$$ ▦**Barton Hill Hotel & Spa.** New-built but mimicking Federal-era design, this stone hotel faces the Niagara River. Many rooms have four-poster beds; all have detailed moldings, heavy draperies, reproduction Greek Revival armchairs, and more-contemporary luxuries such as electric fireplaces, flat-screen TVs, and some whirlpool baths. Ground-floor rooms have hardwood flooring. The hotel has a full spa and salon

with multiple massage and beauty treatments. The Whirlpool Jet Boat tours leave from right across the street. **Pros:** Lewiston's top hotel; lovely rooms and common areas; views of Niagara River from some rooms. **Cons:** pricey; no tubs in some rooms; electric, not gas, fireplaces. ⊠*100 Center St.,Lewiston* ☎*716/754–9070 or 800/718–1812* ⊕*www.bartonhillhotel.com* 🛏*68 rooms, 10 suites* ♿*In-room: DVD (some), refrigerator (some), Wi-Fi. In-hotel: restaurant, room service, bar, gym, spa, water sports, laundry service, Internet terminal, Wi-Fi, parking (free), no-smoking rooms* ▤*AE, D, DC, MC, V* ℗*CP.*

¢–$$ ⊞**Comfort Inn The Pointe.** At the entrance to Niagara Falls State Park, this is the closest hotel to the falls in the United States. Some rooms overlook the Niagara River on its breathtaking tumble; others have views of the Canadian skyline, the state park, or the city. The rooms are standard, but with such scenery about 500 feet away you won't spend much time in them. **Pros:** walking distance to *Maid of the Mist,* Rainbow Bridge, Cave of the Winds, and other attractions; nice views from some rooms. **Cons:** cookie-cutter decor; somewhat dated. ⊠*1 Prospect Pointe* ☎*716/284–6835 or 800/284–6835* ⊕*www.comfortinnthepointe.com* 🛏*117 rooms, 1 suite* ♿*In-room: Wi-Fi. In-hotel: gym, Wi-Fi, parking (free), laundry service, no-smoking rooms* ▤*AE, D, DC, MC, V* ℗*CP.*

$$ ⊞**Crowne Plaza Niagara Falls.** The classiest of Niagara Falls chain hotels since a $25 million renovation in 2006, this six-story hotel is across the street from the Seneca Niagara Casino. Rooms have two queen beds or one king, with fluffy white duvets and blackout blinds. Suites are twice the size of rooms. The grand ground floor, with Egyptian limestone flooring, has lounge areas with plush couches, a Starbucks, and a spacious, polished bar and grill with flat-screen TVs. Parking isn't free, but it's not bad at $3 per day. **Pros:** right across the street from the Seneca Niagara Casino; updated rooms. **Cons:** some rooms quite a walk to the elevator; no tubs in most rooms. ⊠*300 3rd St.* ☎*716/285–3361* ⊕*www.crowneplaza.com/niagarafalls* 🛏*367 rooms, 24 suites* ♿*In-room: refrigerator (some), Wi-Fi. In-hotel: restaurant, room service, pool, gym, laundry facilities, laundry service, Internet terminal, parking (paid), no-smoking rooms* ▤*AE, D, DC, MC, V.*

$ ⊞**Rainbow House Bed & Breakfast.** Antiques, quilts, hand-painted furniture, and stenciled walls give this turn-of-the-20th-century Victorian B&B its folksy charm. Honeymooners love this spot; a wedding chapel on the premises lets them have the ceremony, reception, and honeymoon all in one place. The Honeymoon Suite has an antique fireplace and a porch with a swing. Note that there are cats on the premises. **Pros:** friendly owner; 10-minute walk to falls and five-minute walk to casino; homemade cinnamon rolls get rave reviews. **Cons:** only one room (Garden Room) has a bathtub; wall-to-wall carpeting detracts from historic look; bathrooms could use upgrading. ⊠*423 Rainbow Blvd.* ☎*716/282–1135 or 800/724–3536* ⊕*www.rainbowhousebb. com* 🛏*3 rooms, 1 suite* ♿*In-room: no TV, no phone, refrigerator (some). In-hotel: no kids under 9, parking (free), no-smoking rooms* ▤*MC, V* ℗*BP.*

DAREDEVILS & HONEYMOONERS

Over the years, the glory of Niagara Falls has brought out professional daredevils, as well as the self-destructive amateurs. In 1859, the French tightrope walker Blondin successfully crossed Niagara Gorge, from the American to the Canadian side, on a 3-inch-thick rope. On his shoulders was his reluctant, terrified manager; on both shores stood some 100,000 spectators. "Thank God it is over," exclaimed the future King Edward VII of England, after the completion of the walk. "Please never attempt it again."

But others did. From the early 18th century, dozens went over in boats, rubber balls, and those famous barrels. Not a single one survived—until schoolteacher Annie Taylor in 1901. Emerging from her barrel, she asked, "Did I go over the falls yet?"

The stunts were finally outlawed in 1912, but nothing stops the determined: in 1985 two stuntmen survived a plunge, and two years later, canoe expert Nolan Whitesell (with a legal permit) mastered the rapids below the falls.

Besides daredevils, the other thing that springs to mind at the mention of Niagara are honeymoons. The first high-profile honeymooners arrived in 1801: Aaron Burr's daughter Theodosia and her husband. Shortly after, in 1804, Jerome Bonaparte (brother of Napoléon) and his bride, the daughter of a prosperous Baltimore merchant, followed suit. By the mid-1800s honeymoons at Niagara had become quite the rage and were a definite status symbol for young couples. Though Niagara Falls doesn't hold the cachet it once did, it remains a quintessential honeymoon spot. Today more than 50,000 couples honeymoon here every year, many of them staying in opulent suites in one of the casino hotels.

$$$ ⌂ **Red Coach Inn.** Established in 1923 and modeled after an old English ★ inn, the Tudor-style building has spectacular views of Niagara Falls' upper rapids from street-facing suites. The size of apartments, suites have full kitchens and living rooms, one or two bedrooms, and some have a second bathroom. Rooms and suites are furnished with antiques, gas fireplaces (some), and four-poster beds with toile duvets. Champagne and cheese is served upon arrival. The dark-wood restaurant ($$), with three meals daily, has snug seating, plush chairs, a stone fireplace, and a patio. Rib-sticking dinners might include sirloin with garlic-herb butter or an 8-ounce lobster tail. **Pros:** walking distance to Goat Island and Rainbow Bridge; extra-large suites. **Cons:** rooms in back face parking lot; not many king-size beds. ⊠ *2 Buffalo Ave.* ☎ *716/282–1459 or 800/282–1459* ⊕ *www.redcoach.com* ⦿ *16 rooms, 15 suites* ⌂ *In-room: kitchen (some), refrigerator, Wi-Fi. In-hotel: restaurant, room service, bar, parking (free), no-smoking rooms* ⊟ *AE, D, DC, MC, V* ⏀ *CP.*

$ ⌂ **Seneca Niagara Hotel.** This 26-story glass hotel, opened in 2006 as ★ part of the Seneca Niagara Casino complex (⇨ *Nightlife, above*), is a beacon of rainbow-LED-light glam in downtown Niagara Falls. Rooms are spacious and contemporary in design, in caramel tones, with floor-to-ceiling windows (some with views of the river and the skyline of Niagara Falls, Ontario), big flat-screen TVs, and large bathrooms with oversize showers. Suites have stand-alone Jacuzzis at the foot of the bed. The hotel has four restaurants (Asian, Italian, steak, and Southern), a 24-hour café, and the requisite buffet, here the size of a basketball court. **Pros:** toniest hotel in town; full-size spa and salon; multiple on-site restaurants. **Cons:** no in-room Wi-Fi, casino atmosphere can be overwhelming. ⊠ *310 4th St.* ☎ *877/873–6322 or 716/299–1100* ⊕ *www.senecaniagaracasino.com* ⬫ *486 rooms, 108 suites* ⬧ *In-room: safe, DVD (some), Internet. In-hotel: 6 restaurants, room service, bar, pool, gym, spa, Internet terminal, Wi-Fi, parking (free), no-smoking rooms* ▤ *AE, D, DC, MC, V.*

NIAGARA FALLS, ONTARIO

130 km (81 mi) south of Toronto via the QEW (Queen Elizabeth Way).

After enjoying the falls from the U.S. side, you may want to walk or drive across Rainbow Bridge to the Canadian side, where you can get a far view of the U.S. falls and a close-up of the Horseshoe Falls. You may park your car for the day in any of several lots on the Canadian side and hop onto a People Mover bus, which runs continuously to all the sights along the river. The amusement parks and tacky souvenir shops that surround the falls attest to the area's history as a major tourist attraction. Most of the gaudiness on the Canadian side is contained on Clifton Hill, which has more wax museums than one usually sees in a lifetime.

VISITOR INFORMATION

Niagara Falls Tourism (⊠ *5515 Stanley Ave., Niagara Falls, ON* ☎ *905/356–6061 or 800/563–2557* ⊕ *www.niagarafallstourism.com*) can help plan your trip. Phone lines are open from 8 to 6 daily.

WHAT TO SEE

❹ Clifton Hill. This is the most crassly commercial district of Niagara Falls, lined with haunted houses, wax museums, and fast-food chains that include a House of Frankenstein Burger King. Attractions are typically open late (11 PM), with admission ranging from C$7 to C$13. They include the 175-foot-tall **SkyWheel**, whose enclosed compartments are heated and air-conditioned; the **Guinness World Records Museum;** the **Ripley's Believe It or Not! Museum;** and the **Hershey Store,** marked by a six-story-high chocolate bar at the base of Clifton Hill. The strip is undergoing a C$100-million construction project aimed at creating a more modern, streamlined amusement center, with roller coasters and two water parks; the estimated completion date is 2015. ⊕ *www.cliftonhill.com.*

❷ Marineland. The daily marine shows at this theme park star killer whales, dolphins, harbor seals, and sea lions. Aquarium exhibits include a beluga whale habitat with underwater viewing areas and kids can also pet and feed deer. Among the many rides is Dragon Mountain, the world's largest steel roller coaster. Marineland is in the midst of constructing a C$160 million aquarium complex that will include an exotic-marine-species reef

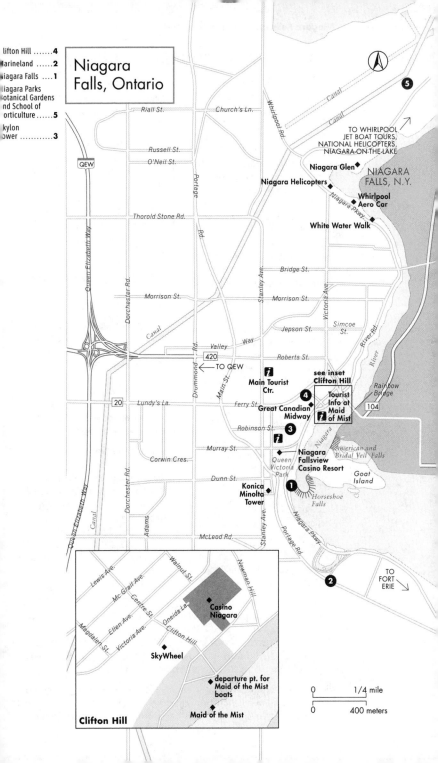

Niagara Falls, Ontario

QEW

Riall St.
Church's Ln.

Russell St.
O'Neil St.

Portage Rd.

Whirlpool Rd.

Canal
Canal

TO WHIRLPOOL
JET BOAT TOURS,
NATIONAL HELICOPTERS,
NIAGARA-ON-THE-LAKE

Niagara Glen◆
Niagara Helicopters◆

NIAGARA
FALLS, N.Y.

Whirlpool
Aero Car◆

White Water Walk◆

Niagara Pkwy.

Thorold Stone Rd.

Bridge St.

Stanley Ave.

Dorchester Rd.

Morrison St.
Morrison St.

Simcoe
St.

Jepson St.

Victoria Ave.

River Rd.

Canal

Valley Way

420

TO QEW

Roberts St.

see inset
Clifton Hill

Rainbow
Bridge

🛈
Main Tourist
Ctr.

20

Lundy's La.

Main St.

Ferry St.
🛈
Great Canadian
Midway

4

Tourist
Info at
🛈 Maid
of Mist

104

Robinson St.
3
🛈

Drummond Rd.

Murray St.

Corwin Cres.

Queen
Victoria
Park

Niagara
Fallsview
Casino Resort

American and
Bridal Veil Falls

Goat
Island

Niagara

Dunn St.

Konica
Minolta◆
Tower

1

Horseshoe
Falls

Dorchester Rd.

Stanley Ave.

Adams

McLeod Rd.

Portage Rd.

2

TO
FORT
ERIE

Queen Elizabeth Way

Canal

Clifton Hill inset:

Lewis Ave.
McGrail Ave.
Centre St.
Walnut St.
Newman Hill

Magdalen St.
Ellen Ave.
Victoria Ave.
Oneida La.
Clifton Hill

Casino
Niagara◆

SkyWheel◆

departure pt. for
Maid of the Mist◆
boats

Maid of the Mist◆

Clifton Hill

0 _____ 1/4 mile
0 _____ 400 meters

NIAGARA FALLS TOURS—CANADIAN SIDE

Journey Behind the Falls. An elevator takes you to an observation deck that provides a fish's-eye view of the Canadian Horseshoe Falls and the Niagara River. From there a walk through tunnels cut into the rock takes you behind waterfalls where the roar is thunderous, and you can glimpse the back side of the crashing water through two portals. ✉ *Tours begin at Table Rock Center, 6650 Niagara Pkwy.* ☎ *905/371–0254 or 877/642–7275* ⊕ *www.niagaraparks.com* 🎫 *Dec.–mid-Apr. C$9, mid-Apr.–Nov. C$12* ⊙ *From 9 AM year-round; closing times vary.*

★ *Maid of the Mist.* This tour is almost the same as the one that leaves from the U.S. side of the falls ⇨ *Falls Tours in Niagara Falls Tours—American Side box earlier.* ✉ *Departures from the foot of Clifton Hill, 5920 River Rd.* ☎ *905/358–0311* ⊕ *www.maidofthemist.com* 🎫 *C$14.50* ⊙ *Departures every 15 mins May–late Oct.*

National Helicopters. These 20-minute tours with a bit of narration fly over the falls and wine country. ✉ *Niagara Stone Rd., Niagara-on-the-Lake* ☎ *905/641–2222 or 800/491–3117* ⊕ *www.nationalhelicopters.com* 🎫 *C$139.*

Niagara Helicopters. A nine-minute flight passes over the giant whirlpool, up the Niagara Gorge, and past the American Falls and the Horseshoe Falls. ✉ *3731 Victoria Ave.* ☎ *905/357–5672 or 800/281–8034* ⊕ *www.niagarahelicopters.com* 🎫 *C$115.*

★ **Whirlpool Aero Car.** In operation since 1916, this antique cable car crosses the Whirlpool Basin in the Niagara Gorge. This trip is not for the fainthearted, but there's no better way to get an aerial view of the gorge, the whirlpool, the rapids, and the hydroelectric plants. ✉ *3850 Niagara Pkwy., 4½ km (3 mi) north of falls* ☎ *905/371–0254 or 877/642–7275* ⊕ *www.niagaraparks.com* 🎫 *C$11* ⊙ *Mid-Mar.–mid-Nov., daily. Hrs vary.*

Whirlpool Jet Boat Tours. ⇨ *Falls Tours in Niagara Falls, New York, above.* The tour, which departs from Niagara-on-the-Lake, is also available from Lewiston, New York. ✉ *61 Melville St., Niagara-on-the-Lake* ☎ *905/468–4800 or 888/438–4444* ⊕ *www.whirlpooljet.com* 🎫 *C$57* ⊙ *Late Apr.–Oct., daily.*

White Water Walk. Descend by elevator to the bottom of the Niagara Gorge and walk beside the Niagara River. The gorge is rimmed by sheer cliffs as it enters the giant whirlpool area. ✉ *4330 Niagara Pkwy., 3 km (2 mi) north of falls* ☎ *905/371–0254 or 877/642–7275* ⊕ *www.niagaraparks.com* 🎫 *C$8.50* ⊙ *Mid.-Mar.–Nov. daily, weather permitting.*

and interactive dolphin area. The park is 6 km (4 mi) south of downtown Niagara Falls. ✉ *7657 Portage Rd.,off Niagara Pkwy. or QEW (McLeod Rd. exit)* ☎ *905/356–9565* ⊕ *www.marinelandcanada.com* 🎫 *C$39.95* ⊙ *Mid-May–June and mid-Sept.–mid-Oct., daily 10–dusk; July–mid-Sept., daily 9–dusk; ticket booth closes at 5.*

❶ **Niagara Falls.** From Canada, the mighty Horseshoe, American, and Bridal Veil falls are all in full view from the developed waterfront. Tourist buses run up and down the Niagara Parkway, stopping at vantage points and

Fodor'sChoice

★

to experience one of the many tours that get you even closer to the falls. From sky-high viewpoints like the 775-foot-tall Skylon Tower, some with restaurants, you can see the entire Niagara Gorge. ⇨*For more information, see Niagara Falls, New York, above.*

❺ **Niagara Parks Botanical Gardens and** ☺ **School of Horticulture.** Since 1936, this institution has been graduating professional gardeners; it has 100 acres of immaculately maintained gardens. Within the Botanical Gardens is the **Niagara Parks Butterfly Conservatory,** housing one of North America's largest collections of free-flying butterflies—at least 2,000 butterflies from 50 species around the world are protected in a climate-controlled, rain forest–like conservatory. ✉*2405 Niagara Pkwy.* ☎*905/356–8119 or 877/642–7275* ⊕*www.niagaraparks.com* ✉*Gardens free, Butterfly Conservatory C$11* ⊘*Daily 9–5; later closing times May–Nov.; call or check Web site for details.*

❸ **Skylon Tower.** The best view of the great Niagara Gorge and the entire ☺ city is from this tower, 775 feet above the falls. The indoor-outdoor ★ observation deck has visibility up to 128 km (80 mi) on a clear day. The revolving dining room is another reason to visit. The lower level has a gaming arcade and a 3-D theater. ✉*5200 Robinson St.* ☎*905/356–2651 or 800/814–9577* ⊕*www.skylon.com* ✉*C$12.95* ⊘*Mid-June–early Sept., daily 8 AM–midnight; early Sept.–mid June, daily 11–9.*

NIGHTLIFE AND THE ARTS

The casinos are entirely nonsmoking and are open 24 hours.

Niagara Fallsview Casino Resort (✉*6380 Fallsview Blvd.* ☎*888/325–5788* ⊕*www.fallsviewcasinoresort.com*), Canada's largest privately funded commercial development, crowns the city's skyline, overlooking the Niagara Parks with picture-perfect views of both falls. Within the 30-story complex is Canada's only casino wedding chapel, a glitzy theater, spa, shops, and, for the gaming enthusiasts, 150 gaming tables, 3,000 slot machines, and plenty of restaurants. The Las Vegas–style Avalon Ballroom showcases a wide array of talents, from Reba MacIntyre to Brian Wilson to Jay Leno.

WHERE TO EAT

Dining in Niagara Falls is expensive. Even a meal at a fast-food joint will cost you a few bucks more than it would a few miles up the road. And while many of the priciest restaurants have fab views of the falls, their food pales in comparison to what you'd find in Niagara-on-the-

---

SUMMER FIREWORKS AND WINTER LIGHTS

Adding to the ambience of nightly illumination are **Fireworks Over the Falls** displays every Friday and Sunday evening at 10 PM from late May to early September. If you don't have a falls-view hotel room, try the patio of the Falls-view Casino Resort.

From November to early January, the **Winter Festival of Lights** (☎*905/374–1616 or 800/563–2557* ⊕*www.wfol.com*) illuminates the entire Niagara Parkway running from the Whirlpool Bridge to the Dufferin Islands with more than 1 million lights.

Lake. Still, it can be worth it for the romance of a meal with a view.

$$$$\
CONTINENTAL

✕ **17 Noir.** On the second floor above the Fallsview Casino, 17 Noir has the best food with a view in town. Start out with fresh oysters or aged prosciutto and Parmesan, then move on to Australian or American Kobe beef with sautéed wild mushrooms and spring vegetables, seared organic salmon with artichokes in lobster ravioli, or lemon-herb-crusted Alberta lamb with Yukon potato–parsnip mash and a rapini-and-rosemary reduction. The space is dramatically modern, with a profusion of red, black, and gold; views of the falls are from window-side table or one of two patios. ⊠ *Fallsview Casino Resort, 6455 Fallsview Blvd.* ☎ *905/358–3255, 888/325–5788 reservations* ⌖ *Reservations essential* ▤ *AE, MC, V* ⊘ *No lunch.*

$$$\
AMERICAN

✕ **Elements on the Falls.** Run by Niagara Parks, Elements serves standard American-Canadian fare, but it's the setting that's extraordinary—you sit perched at the edge of Horseshoe Falls, behind tall windows or on the terrace. The dining room, completely overhauled in 2008, is contemporary and whimsical, with swooping, wavelike ceilings and pillars that look like birch bark. The kitchen serves familiar food, such as slow-roasted prime rib, and familiar-with-a-flourish, such as a Caesar salad with lemon-pepper-garlic grilled shrimp. Window seats can't be reserved. ⊠ *Table Rock Center, 6650 Niagara Pkwy., just above Journey Behind the Falls* ☎ *905/354–3631* ⊕ *www.niagaraparks.com* ⌖ *Reservations essential* ▤ *AE, MC, V.*

WHERE TO STAY

One reason to spend the night here is to admire the falls illumination, which takes place every night of the year. Even the most contemptuous observer will be mesmerized as the falls change from red to purple to blue to green to white, and finally all the colors of the rainbow in harmony.

If you prefer a B&B, consider one of the many excellent choices 20 km (12 mi) north in Niagara-on-the-Lake and make the falls a day trip.

$$–$$$

⌂ **Country Inn & Suites.** If you're on a budget but not willing to stay at a dingy motor lodge, this seven-story hotel that opened in 2007 is probably your best choice. Guests commend the friendly staff and the cleanliness of the rooms, which are decorated in the generic, contemporary style of a chain hotel but have the advantage of being fairly new. Some rooms have Jacuzzi tubs (right in the room, not in the bathroom). **Pros:** low-cost parking ($6 per day); within walking distance of Clifton Hill and falls. **Cons:** few rooms have views; melee of Clifton Hill right outside. ⊠ *5525 Victoria Ave.,* ☎ *905/374–6040 or 888/201–1746* ⊕ *www.countryinns.com/niagarafallson* ⇆ *49 rooms, 59 suites* ⌂ *In-room: refrigerator (some), Internet. In-hotel: pool, gym, laundry* *facilities, Internet terminal, parking (paid), no-smoking rooms* ▭AE, D, MC, V ❚◎❚CP.

$$$–$$$$ 🏨 **Niagara Fallsview Casino Resort.** The C$1-billion price tag of this casino-resort means there are touches of luxury everywhere: natural light streams through glass domes and floor-to-ceiling windows, chandeliers hang in grand hallways, and frescoes lend an aristocratic feel. All bright and colorful rooms in this 35-story hotel tower overlook the Canadian or American Falls. The hotel is in a casino-entertainment complex (⇨ *Nightlife and the Arts, above*). The romantic 17 Noir (⇨ *above*) is one of Niagara Falls' best restaurants, the ground-floor Galleria mall has a number of other options. The spa, renovated in 2008, has a full range of massages and facials, as well as wraps and Vichy treatments. **Pros:** first-class accommodation and entertainment; the most glamorous address in Niagara Falls. **Cons:** overwhelming popularity means rooms fill up fast. ✉*6380 Fallsview Blvd.* ☎*905/358–3255 or 888/946–3255* ⊕*www.fallsviewcasinoresort.com* ➬*289 rooms, 85 suites* ⚥*In-room: safe, kitchen (some), refrigerator (some), Internet. In-hotel: 4 restaurants, room service, pool, gym, spa, laundry service, Internet terminal, parking (paid), no-smoking rooms* ▭*AE, MC, V.*

$$$ 🏨 **Sheraton Fallsview Hotel and Conference Centre.** Most of the oversize
★ guest rooms and suites in this upscale high-rise hotel have breathtaking views of the falls, and even basic family suites have wide floor-to-ceiling window bays that overlook the cascades. Loft Suites are spacious, and the Whirlpool Rooms have open whirlpool baths that look out to the bedroom and the falls beyond. A Cut Above Steakhouse has a weekend dinner buffet and à la carte entrées. **Pros:** family rooms available; stellar views; convenient to Fallsview Casino. **Cons:** busy; impersonal service; daily charge for Internet. ✉*6755 Fallsview Blvd.* ☎*905/374–1077 or 800/618–9059* ⊕*www.fallsview.com* ➬*366 rooms, 36 suites* ⚥*In-room: safe (some), refrigerator, Internet, Wi-Fi. In-hotel: 2 restaurants, bar, pool, gym, parking (paid), no-smoking rooms* ▭*AE, D, DC, MC, V.*

BUFFALO AND GREATER NIAGARA

North of the falls on the U.S. side along the Niagara River is an area rich in orchards and vineyards. To the south, about a 20-minute drive away, is Buffalo, situated on Lake Erie. Nestled between lakes Erie and Ontario lie acres of rolling farmland, part of the Great Lakes Plain, which stretches north from the Appalachian Plateau. Once you're on the Canadian side of the falls—an essential jaunt for anyone who wants to get the full experience—pretty Niagara-on-the-Lake is just a 10-minute drive away. Another hour and change north through the vineyard-rich region wedged between Lake Ontario and the Niagara Escarpment brings you to Toronto, Canada's largest city and cultural center, worthy of at least an overnight.

GRAND ISLAND

12 mi south of Niagara Falls, NY.

The low and flat Grand Island is the largest of the islands dotting the Niagara River between Buffalo and Niagara Falls. (In fact, it's larger than Manhattan.) Two spectacular high-arching bridges ($1 toll) link it to the mainland. Once farmland, much of the island is now residential, and many of its inhabitants commute to Buffalo. **Beaver Island State Park** (⊠*2136 West Oakfield Rd., Exit 18B off I–290* ☎*716/773–3271* ⊕*nysparks.state.ny.us/parks* ✉*$7 per car* ☉*Daily dawn–dusk*), at the southern tip of the island, is a flat, grassy, sparsely treed expanse crossed with biking and walking-running paths (including a long boardwalk along the Niagara River), plus a sandy beach for swimming, a golf course, and driving range. ☺ **Martin's Fantasy Island** (⊠*2400 Grand Island Blvd.* ☎*716/773–7591* ⊕*www.martinsfantasyisland. com* ✉*$24* ☉*May–Sept., daily 11:30–8:30*) has more then 100 rides, including a wooden roller coaster, a 140-foot-tall swing ride, and a petting zoo, and a water-park area with a wave pool, swirling slides and chutes, and a log-flume ride.

CRUISE **Grand Lady Cruises** (⊠ *Holiday Inn Grand Island, 100 Whitehaven Rd.* ☎*716/774–8594 or 888/824–5239* ⊕*www.grandlady.com* ✉*$22–$55* ☉*Mar.–Oct.; call for schedule*) offers two- and three-hour cruises on the upper Niagara River above the falls. Lunch, dinner, and themed cruises also are available, beginning in May, as are charters.

WHERE TO STAY

$ ⊡ **Holiday Inn Grand Island Resort.** The large, six-story riverfront hotel is adjacent to a golf course and a marina. All rooms have balconies or patios, which are larger in the east-facing river-view rooms. All rooms will be completely renovated, with new furnishings and flat-screen TVs, by the end of 2009. The hotel has a pubby lounge, an arcade room, massage treatments, and a larger-than-average fitness room. Grand Lady cruises leave from the hotel's back door. **Pros:** best option on Grand Island; many rooms have nice views; large, attractive pools and dining room, both with floor-to-ceiling river views. **Cons:** unattractive exterior; no breakfast included. ⊠*100 Whitehaven Rd., east side, at the river* ☎*716/773–1111 or 800/465–4329* ⊕*www.myholidayinn.com* ✒*255 rooms, 8 suites* ♿*In-room: refrigerator (some), Wi-Fi. In-hotel: restaurant, room service, bar, pool, gym, water sports, laundry facilities, laundry service, Internet terminal, Wi-Fi, parking (free), some pets allowed, no-smoking rooms* ▤*AE, D, DC, MC, V.*

BUFFALO

21 mi southeast of Niagara Falls, NY.

Snow, the Buffalo Bills, and the gateway to Niagara Falls are just some of the things that come to mind when most people think of Buffalo. While it is true that the city is hit by at least one to four memorable snowstorms a year, Buffalo doesn't actually receive a great deal of snow compared to many other cities in New York. Buffalo is indeed a great sports town with tough professional teams, but it is also the home of Buffalo wings, beef on weck (thin-sliced roast beef and fresh horseradish on a hard roll crusted with salt and caraway seeds), and sponge candy (a confection of chocolate-covered caramelized sugar with a slight molasses flavor that is at first crisp, then melts in your mouth). The city also boasts world-class architecture, a leading cancer-research institute, and one of the four research universities of the State University of New York.

The city's growth began in the early 1800s, when ships from the Great Lakes transported millions of bushels of grain from Midwest farms to Buffalo. The Erie Canal, completed in 1825, connected Buffalo to Albany (and Lake Erie to the Hudson River), allowing the grain to be distributed along the East Coast, and Buffalo became known as the "Queen City on the Lake." Railroad tracks laid alongside the Erie Canal continued the great migration of products. Laborers were needed to handle the boats, grain, and, later, the steel mills. Thousands of immigrants came to fill those jobs, bringing rich ethnic diversity to the city.

At the turn of the 20th century, Buffalo had a booming economy, and majestic mansions sprang up along Delaware Avenue, known as Millionaires' Row. Ornate structures erected during these boom years included some of the world's first skyscrapers, such as the 13-story steel-and–terra-cotta 1896 Guaranty Building (28 Church Street), designed by Louis H. Sullivan.

Today, Buffalo has a rich cultural scene that includes contemporary art at the Albright-Knox Gallery and free summer Shakespeare performances in Delaware Park—one of several Buffalo parks designed by noted landscape architect Frederick Law Olmsted. The city's six institutions of higher learning infuse youth into neighborhoods like Elmwood, whose eponymous main avenue is known for its boutiques, used-book stores, hip bars, and eateries; historic, bohemian Allentown district; and Chippewa Street (or the Chippewa District), known for its nightclubs and jazz bars. Far from mere university crawls, these neighborhoods are frequented by Buffalonians of all ages.

Though it is the state's second-largest city, Buffalo is definitely "small town" when compared to its glamorous downstate big sister. Still, the city has a distinct style, a product of its rich ethnic, cultural, and architectural history. Friendliness and affordability are also selling points. Distances aren't great, and it's easy to get around.

VISITOR INFORMATION

Buffalo Niagara Convention & Visitors Bureau (✉ *617 Main St., Suite 200, Buffalo* ☎ *800/283-3256* ⊕ *www.visitbuffaloniagara.com*).

WHAT TO SEE

❶ Albright-Knox Art Gallery. Twentieth-century art is well represented here.
★ The gallery's collections are especially rich in postwar American and European art, including Jackson Pollock, Jasper Johns, and Andy Warhol. Works by Pablo Picasso, Vincent van Gogh, Claude Monet, Henri Matisse, and Pierre-Auguste Renoir are here as well. On Sunday afternoons in July and August, free jazz performances are held on the massive front steps. The museum's restaurant, Muse, serves dinner and a highly acclaimed brunch. ✉ *1285 Elmwood Ave.* ☎ *716/882-8700* ⊕ *www.albrightknox.org* ▭ *Museum $10, parking $5* ⊙ *Wed. and weekends 10–5, Thurs. and Fri. 10–10.*

⓬ Buffalo and Erie County Botanical Gardens. Even in the middle of winter you can soak in the sights and scents of the tropics under the domes of this Victorian glass conservatory. The greenhouses shelter cacti, fruit trees, palms, and orchids. The American Ivy Association certified the claim of the largest ivy collection of any botanical garden in the world. Formal gardens and a park with a golf course (the park is popular with runners) surround the conservatory. Guided tours are given by reservation. ✉ *2655 S. Park Ave.* ☎ *716/827–1584* ⊕ *www.buffalogardens. com* ▭ *$4* ⊙ *Tues., Wed., and Fri.–Sun. 10–5, Thurs.10–7.*

❽ Buffalo and Erie County Naval and Military Park. A guided-missile cruiser,
ᘓ destroyer, and a World War II submarine are on display at this 6-acre waterfront site, the largest inland naval park in the nation. ✉ *1 Naval Park Cove* ☎ *716/847–1773* ⊕ *www.buffalonavalpark.org* ▭ *$8* ⊙ *Apr.–Oct., daily 10–5; Nov., weekends 10–4.*

❼ Buffalo City Hall & Observation Tower. This broad-shouldered art-deco architectural masterpiece rises from the heart of downtown. An elevator to the 25th floor, then three flights of (unmarked) stairs take you to an observation deck; though you can't go outside, it has spectacular views of the city and the Lake Erie waterfront. ✉ *65 Niagara Sq.* ☎ *716/851–5891* ▭ *Free* ⊙ *Weekdays 8–4.*

❺ Buffalo Museum of Science. Exhibits cover everything from anthropology
ᘓ to zoology. One exhibit uses the stories of three mummies to explore what daily life was like for ordinary citizens in ancient Egypt. ✉ *1020 Humboldt Pkwy., at Rte. 33 and MLK Park* ☎ *716/896–5200* ⊕ *www. sciencebuff.org* ▭ *$7* ⊙ *Mid-June–Aug., Mon.–Sat. 10–5; Sept.–mid-June, Wed.–Sat. 10–5, Sun. noon–5.*

❹ Buffalo Zoological Gardens. Endangered Amur (Siberian) tigers, Asian ele-
ᘓ phants, and Indian rhinos are among the nearly 1,000 wild and exotic animals found in this natural setting in Delaware Park. The grounds include an interactive, mock, field-research station, and a rain-forest exhibit opened in 2008. At this writing the zoo has secured funding to open an on-site children's zoo, which will feature farm animals historically found in the Erie Canal area. ✉ *300 Parkside Ave.* ☎ *716/837–*

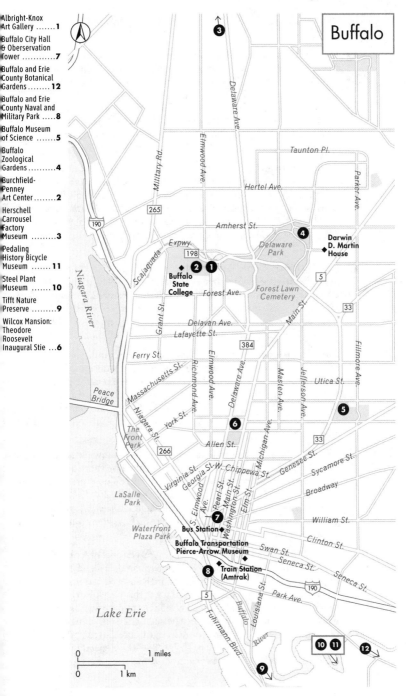

Buffalo

3900 ⊕*www.buffalozoo.org* ▣*Zoo $9.50, parking $3.25* ☉*July and Aug., daily 10–5; Sept.–June, daily 10–4.*

❷ **Burchfield-Penney Art Center.** This premier showcase for western New York artists reopened in a new, $33 million, 84,000-square-foot space in November 2008. The museum spotlights the works of watercolorist Charles Burchfield (1893–1967) and handcrafted objects from the Roycroft Arts and Crafts community. It is New York State's first LEED-certified art museum. ⊠*Buffalo State College, Rockwell Hall, 1300 Elmwood Ave.* ☎*716/878–6011* ⊕*www.burchfield-penney.org* ▣*$7* ☉*Tues., Wed., Fri., Sat. 10–5, Thurs. 10–9, Sun. 1–5.*

❸ **Herschell Carrousel Factory Museum.** The old factory contains two oper-
☾ ating carousels—one from 1916 and a smaller "kiddie carousel" from the 1940s—as well as a menagerie of hand-carved carousel animals, some quite elaborate. ⊠*180 Thompson St., North Tonawanda* ☎*716/693–1885* ⊕*www.carrouselmuseum.org* ▣*$5* ☉*Apr.–early June and Sept.–Dec., Wed.–Sun. noon–4; early June–Aug., Mon.–Sat. 10–4, Sun. noon–4.*

⓫ **Pedaling History Bicycle Museum.** More than 400 rare and unique bicycles
☾ and related antiques and memorabilia are on display at one of the larg-
★ est bicycle museums in the world. Orchard Park is 12 mi south of Buffalo. ⊠*3943 N. Buffalo Rd., Orchard Park* ☎*716/662–3853* ⊕*www. pedalinghistory.com* ▣*$7.50* ☉*Apr.–mid-Jan., Mon.–Sat. 11–5, Sun. 1:30–5; mid-Jan.–Mar., Fri., Sat., and Mon. 11–5, Sun. 1:30–5.*

⓪ **Steel Plant Museum.** Photos, exhibits, and memorabilia pay tribute to
☾ western New York's steel workers and what was once the largest steel plant in the world, Bethlehem Steel. The museum is in the Lackawanna Public Library, 6 mi south of Buffalo. ⊠*Lackawanna Public Library, 560 Ridge Rd., Lackawanna* ☎*716/823–0630* ⊕*steelpltmuseum.org* ▣*Free* ☉*Mon. and Wed. 1–9, Tues. and Thurs.–Sat. 9–5 (closed Sat. July–early Sept.).*

❾ **Tifft Nature Preserve.** Five miles of nature trails, boardwalks, and a cattail marsh make this wildlife refuge near the Lake Erie shore an ideal place for hiking, bird-watching, and picnics. The 264-acre preserve is part of the Buffalo Museum of Science (⇨*above*). ⊠*1200 Fuhrmann Blvd.* ☎*716/825–6397 or 716/896–5200* ⊕*www.sciencebuff.org* ▣*$2 suggested donation* ☉*Grounds daily dawn–dusk. Visitor center Wed.–Sat. 10–4, Sun. noon–4.*

❻ **Wilcox Mansion: Theodore Roosevelt Inaugural National Historical Site.** After President William McKinley was assassinated at the Pan-American Exposition in Buffalo in 1901, Theodore Roosevelt was inaugurated as the nation's 26th president in the library of this Greek Revival mansion. You can take guided tours and view exhibits and gardens. Architectural walking tours are also available. The site underwent a major yearlong renovation in 2008 to rebuild the carriage house and to update and add exhibits. ⊠*641 Delaware Ave.* ☎*716/884–0095* ⊕*www.nps.gov/thri* ▣*$8* ☉*Weekdays 9–5, weekends noon–5.*

SPORTS AND THE OUTDOORS

The National Football League's **Buffalo Bills** (⊠*Ralph Wilson Stadium, 1 Bills Dr., Orchard Park* ☎*716/648–1800 or 877/228–4257* ⊕*www. buffalobills.com*) has a strong following. The **Buffalo Sabres** (⊠*HSBC Arena, 1 Seymour H. Knox III Plaza* ☎*716/855–4444 Ext. 82 or 888/223–6000* ⊕*www.sabres.com*) is a National Hockey League team. The **Buffalo Bisons** (⊠*Dunn Tire Park, 275 Washington St.* ☎*716/843– 4373* ⊕*www.bisons.com*), a triple-A affiliate of the Cleveland Indians, plays minor-league baseball.

SHOPPING

Elmwood Avenue, from approximately Bryant Street to Auburn Avenue, is a walkable strip with a handful of boutiques selling shoes, clothing, chocolate, gifts, and pet supplies. It also has a food co-op, cafés (locals get their daily fix at Spot Coffee), and restaurants.

NIGHTLIFE AND THE ARTS

Check out the free *ArtVoice* weekly paper for current events.

NIGHTLIFE **Elmwood Avenue** near the state college, **Allen Street,** and **Chippewa Street,** downtown, are dotted with bars and nightclubs. The **Lafayette Tap Room** (⊠*391 Washington St.* ☎*716/854–2466* ⊕*www.lafayettetaproombbq. com*), a blues bar, has a few seating areas, a couple of bars, and two stages where national and local acts perform. Jazz, blues, country, and reggae musicians perform at grungy **Nietzsche's** (⊠*248 Allen St.* ☎*716/886–8539* ⊕*www.nietzsches.com*) in Allentown. There's a show most nights.

For martini swilling, head to a classy restaurant bar. **Stillwater** (⊠*481 Delaware Ave.* ☎*716/886–2220*) is a favorite for its unique decor: an indoor courtyard with a starlit ceiling above, and a giant movie screen showing arty images. Known as something of a pickup spot, **Mother's** (⊠ *511 Rhode Island St.* ☎*716/882–3509*) has an eclectic clientele that ranges from suited lawyers to baseball-capped B-boys. Its low-beamed ceilings and stone walls give it a wine-cellar feel. The patio is open seasonally.

THE ARTS The theater district is at the north end of Main Street, between Chip-
★ pewa and Tupper streets.

The 18,690-seat **HSBC Arena** (⊠*1 Seymour Knox III Plaza* ☎*716/855– 4100* ⊕*www.hsbcarena.com*) presents family shows and concerts with big-name musicians. It's also a major sports venue. **Shea's Performing Arts Center** (⊠*646 Main St.* ☎*716/847–1410* ⊕*www.sheas.org*) pres-ents concerts, opera, dance, and touring theater performances in an old movie palace reminiscent of a European opera house. The **University at Buffalo Center for the Arts** (⊠*North Campus, 103 Center for the Arts* ☎*716/645–2787* ⊕*www.ubcfa.org*) encompasses four theaters, the largest of which is the 1,744-seat main stage. Operas, concerts, dance performances, theatrical productions, and musicals are among the events that take place here. The **Buffalo Philharmonic Orchestra** (⊠*71 Symphony Cir.* ☎*716/885–5000 or 800/699–3168* ⊕*www.bpo.org*) plays a variety of classical and pop concerts throughout the year at

CLOSE UP

Wright Sites

The Buffalo area is home to several buildings by renowned architect Frank Lloyd Wright (1867–1959).

The Darwin D. Martin House, part of the **Darwin D. Martin House Complex** in Buffalo's Parkside East Historic District, is considered one of the finest examples of a Wright prairie-style structure. The estate was commissioned in 1902 by Darwin Martin, a wealthy Buffalo businessman who would become one of Wright's most loyal patrons. The first Wright house on the property was the **George Barton House** (at 118 Summit Avenue), built in 1903 for Martin's sister and brother-in-law. The final touches were applied to Martin's own house in 1907. The estate also includes the **Gardener's Cottage** (285 Woodward Avenue). At this writing, the complex is undergoing a multiyear restoration. Restored in the first phases of the work were the pergola, conservatory, and carriage house. The final phase is a restoration of the house interiors, which will likely continue through 2010. The site remains open for tours during restoration. ✉125 Jewett Pkwy. ☎716/856–3858 ⊕darwinmartinhouse.org ☒Tours $15, free 2nd and 4th Thurs. each month ☉Tours by appointment.

Around the same time, Wright also designed the **Walter V. Davidson House** (57 Tillinghast Place) and the **William R. Heath House** (72 Soldier's Place), both of which are private residences.

The Martins liked their Buffalo home so much that they also commissioned Wright to design their summer estate. The centerpiece of the 8½-acre **Graycliff** estate is the two-story main house, built circa 1926. Its cantilevered balconies take advantage of its position atop a 70-foot-cliff overlooking Lake Erie. The estate is undergoing an extensive multiphase, multiyear restoration. At this writing, all exteriors have been completed and interiors are in progress. The property is about 18 mi south of Buffalo. ✉6472 Old Lake Shore Rd., Derby ☎716/947–9217 ⊕graycliff.bfn.org ☒Tours $15 ☉Tours Apr.–Nov. and Christmas season by appointment.

In 1928 Darwin Martin commissioned a family mausoleum—a project he dropped after his fortunes were pummeled by the following year's stock-market crash. In 2004, Buffalo's Forest Lawn cemetery (near Delavan Avenue) built the concrete-and-granite **Blue Sky Mausoleum** from plans owned by the Frank Lloyd Wright Foundation. ✉ Forest Lawn Cemetery, 1411 Delaware Ave. ☎716/885–1600 ⊕www.forest-lawn.com ☒Free ☉Apr.–Oct., daily 8–7; gates close earlier during daylight savings months (times vary).

At this writing, the **Buffalo Transportation/Pierce-Arrow Museum** is building a winged gas station from unfinished Wright plans (it hopes to finish in fall of 2010). A former Wright apprentice is involved with the project, which, once built, won't actually function as a station but will rather complement the museum's collection of cars and automobile memorabilia and artifacts. ✉263 Michigan Ave. ☎716/853–0084 ⊕www.pierce-arrow.com ☒$7 ☉Mar.–Dec., Sat. noon–5; and by appointment.

Klienhans Music Hall, which was designed by architects Eliel and Eero Saarinen and is renowned for its excellent acoustics. Bring a picnic basket and a blanket and enjoy free full-length plays with **Shakespeare in the Park** (⊠ *Delaware Park, behind Rose Gardens* ⌂ *Box 716, 14205* ☎ *716/856–4533* ⊕ *www.shakespeareindelawarepark.org*) most nights from late June through August.

Tralf Music Hall (⊠ *622 Main St.* ☎ *716/852–2860* ⊕ *www.tralfmusichall.com*) hosts first-class jazz, blues, rhythm and blues, rock, and alternative acts. The box office opens two hours prior to shows.

FESTIVALS
AND FAIRS
Allentown Arts Festival (⌂ *Box 1566, Ellicott Station, 14205* ☎ *716/881–4269* ⊕ *www.allentownartfestival.com*), a nationally acclaimed fine-arts–and–crafts show, brings nearly 500 exhibitors, food vendors, live music, and outstanding people-watching to the Allentown district for two days in mid-June. Nautical displays and a midway with rides and games are set up along the Eric Canal for eight days in late July during **Canal Fest of the Tonawandas** (⌂ *Box 1243, North Tonawanda, 14120* ☎ *716/692–3292* ⊕ *www.canalfest.org*).

WHERE TO EAT

$ ✕ **Anchor Bar & Restaurant.** Anchor claims to have originated Buffalo
AMERICAN wings. Some people dispute that, but many come to sample the ground-
★ breaking invention in bar food. Try them hot for the full experience. A buffalo's head hanging on the wall is about all the atmosphere you need. ⊠ *1047 Main St.* ☎ *716/886–8920* ▤ *AE, D, DC, MC, V.*

$$$$ ✕ **Buffalo Chophouse.** Meat lovers splurge on what some rate the best
STEAK steaks in western New York. Expensive but not stuffy, the two-level wood-paneled dining room with red-satin banquettes and warm lighting buzzes with conversation and Sinatra. Start your meal with fresh raw oysters or tuna tartare, and move on to the main event: succulent rib eye, filet mignon, prime rib, and chateaubriand. Non-beef entrées include free-range chicken breast in a lemon-thyme sauce, grilled salmon, and steamed king crab legs. ⊠ *282 Franklin St.* ☎ *716/842–6900* ♠ *Reservations essential* ▤ *AE, D, DC, MC, V* ⊙ *No lunch.*

$$ ✕ **Coles.** Since 1934, this pubby place has served up its specialty sand-
AMERICAN wiches, among them a stack of ham, turkey, and Swiss with onions and Russian dressing on marble rye. Also on the menu: pot roast on a roll with caramelized onions and cheddar; sesame-encrusted yellowfin tuna salad; and, for dinner, lobster ravioli in a crab-vodka sauce and barbecue ribs. It's a huge space, with two dining rooms—one a true pub with wooden booths, checkerboard floors, and '50s-era sports pennants, and the other a sunroom with a fireplace at one end. Sidewalk seating is available in summer. The gigantic, multipage beer menu, with rare brews from around the world, is sure to impress. ⊠ *1104 Elmwood Ave.* ☎ *716/886–1449* ▤ *AE, D, DC, MC, V.*

$$$ ✕ **Hutch's.** The menu and 20 or so nightly specials, handwritten on
CONTINENTAL a card and delivered to your table, consists of an equal number of
★ small and large plates: grilled prawns with linguine, fresh zucchini, and Parmesan; pan-seared beef tenderloin au poivre with a brandy-cream sauce; tomato-mozzarella-prosciutto salad; smoked salmon with capers and horseradish. The wine list is long, with many good options.

The small, two-room dining space hums with conversation; it's traditional, with exposed-brick-and-cream walls with black trim, but livened up by colorful art and unobtrusively defiant leopard-print carpeting. Some tables are in the attached, brick-walled bar. ⊠ *1375 Delaware Ave.* ☎*716/885–0074* ⌖*Reservations essential* ▤*AE, D, DC, MC, V* ⊘*No lunch.*

$ ✕**The Left Bank.** This urban bistro occupies a dark, brick-walled space
CONTINENTAL   humming with conversation and music from the bar. You feel just as at home ordering drinks and one of the many tapas-size dishes as full meals. Small plates might include fried oysters with tomato, corn, and jalapeño salsa or Gorgonzola fondue for two, scooped up with portobello mushroom "fries" and asparagus spears. Pasta-heavy entrées include the homemade ravioli of the day, seafood linguine, and pork tenderloin with Grand Marnier–cranberry sauce. Some complain of slow service—order a martini and settle in. Brunch is served on Sunday. ⊠ *511 Rhode Island St.* ☎*716/882–3509* ▤*AE, D, DC, MC, V* ⊘*No lunch Mon.–Sat.*

$$$ ✕**Rue Franklin.** A tried-and-true spot for an excellent meal, Rue Franklin
CONTINENTAL   has a changing menu with French and contemporary Continental fare, such as braised short ribs in a red-wine sauce or skate in a soy–beurre blanc sauce. French doors open onto a beautiful landscaped courtyard for summer dining. The hushed interior of this sophisticated restaurant, with soft colors and swagged windows, is just as pretty. ⊠*341 Franklin St.* ☎*716/852–4416* ⌖*Reservations essential* ▤*AE, DC, MC, V* ⊘*Closed Sun. and Mon. No lunch.*

WHERE TO STAY

$–$$ 🏨**Beau Fleuve.** Each of the rooms at this circa-1881 bed-and-breakfast
★   in the historic Linwood district is furnished to celebrate one of the various nationalities of the people who settled Buffalo. You may choose the French, the Irish, or the German room, among others. Rooms have antiques, down comforters, and William Morris wallpaper. A candlelit breakfast awaits you in the morning. **Pros:** impeccable decor; location in quiet, residential area; lounge with drinks and snacks available 24 hours. **Cons:** most bathrooms lack tubs; some bathrooms don't connect directly to bedroom. ⊠*242 Linwood Ave., at Bryant St.* ☎*716/882–6116 or 800/278–0245* ⊕*www.beaufleuve.com* ⇆*4 rooms, 1 suite* ⌂*In-room: no TV (some), DVD (some), Wi-Fi. In-hotel: parking (free), no-smoking rooms* ▤ *AE, D, MC, V* ⊙*BP.*

$$ 🏨**Hampton Inn & Suites Buffalo Downtown.** Stay at this five-story hotel in a 1920 building just off Chippewa Street for spacious, updated rooms and suites with views up busy Delaware Avenue. Rooms have traditional decor with fluffy white duvets; some have whirlpool tubs (some in the bedroom rather than the bathroom) or gas fireplaces. **Pros:** downtown core location; popular martini bar (the Chocolate Bar) on ground level; nice pool with decorative floor-to-ceiling windows, beveled ceilings, and statues. **Cons:** standard, unexciting breakfast; parking lot not secured; in-room hot tubs a bit large for space. ⊠*220 Delaware Ave.* ☎ *716/855–2223 or 800/444–2326* ⊕*www.hamptoninnbuffalo.com* ⇆*108 rooms, 29 suites* ⌂ *In-room: kitchen (some), Internet, Wi-Fi. In-hotel: 2 restaurants, room service, pool, gym, laundry facilities, laundry*

2

service, Internet terminal, parking (free), no-smoking rooms ⊟*AE, D, DC, MC, V* ⦿ *CP.*

$ 🏨**Holiday Inn–Downtown.** The eight-story chain property is in the historic Allentown neighborhood, across from the Wilcox Mansion, and near the downtown business district. Rooms have large windows, desks, and contemporary furnishings. **Pros:** central but quiet downtown location; good restaurant. **Cons:** thin walls; no breakfast included. ✉*620 Delaware Ave.* ☎*716/886–2121 or 800/465–4329* ⊕*www.hibuffalodowntown.com* 🛏*168 rooms* ♿*In room: refrigerator (some), Internet, Wi-Fi. In-hotel: restaurant, bar, room service, pool, gym, laundry facilities, laundry service, Internet terminal, Wi-Fi, no-smoking rooms* ⊟*AE, D, DC, MC, V.*

$–$$ 🏨**Hyatt Regency Buffalo.** Fronted by a fountain and incorporating some of the original 1923 facade, this contemporary theater-district hotel connected to the convention center has an '80s-chic glass atrium with a café and great views of surrounding historic buildings. Rooms were upgraded in 2008 and 2009, and are contemporary, with earth tones and warm woods and ergonomic desk chairs. Suites have whirlpool tubs and CD players. Until the new gym opens in late 2009, guests can use the health club across the street. E.B. Green's restaurant (named after the architect of the building) earns high marks for its steaks, in particular. **Pros:** convenient for convention-goers; friendly staff; comfortable beds. **Cons:** fee for Wi-Fi and parking; no pool. ✉*2 Fountain Plaza* ☎*716/856–1234* ⊕*www.buffalo.hyatt.com* 🛏*380 rooms, 16 suites* ♿*In-room: refrigerator (some), Internet. In-hotel: 2 restaurants, room service, laundry service, Internet terminal, parking (paid), no-smoking rooms* ⊟*AE, D, DC, MC, V.*

$$–$$$ 🏨**Mansion on Delaware Ave.** Built in the 1860s in the Second Empire
Fodor'sChoice style, this beautiful mansion was thoroughly renovated for the hotel's
★ opening in 2001. The decor is classy yet up-the-minute: hand-carved original walnut pocket doors paired with midcentury-modern sofas and contemporary paintings by local artists. Beds are dressed in down duvets and Frette linens. Some rooms have fireplaces and whirlpool tubs. Complimentary cocktails are served in the evening. **Pros:** offers the amenities (e.g., 24-hour butler service, free car service to downtown) of a much larger property; large buffet breakfast with unusual options. **Cons:** only one room with king-size bed; no views to speak of; frequent wedding parties. ✉*414 Delaware Ave.* ☎*716/886–3300 or 800/448–8355* ⊕*www.themansionondelaware.com* 🛏*25 rooms, 3 suites* ♿*In-room: DVD, refrigerator (some), Internet, Wi-Fi. In-hotel: room service, bar, gym, laundry service, Internet terminal, Wi-Fi, parking (free), no-smoking rooms* ⊟*AE, D, DC, MC, V* ⦿*CP.*

LOCKPORT

16 mi east of Niagara Falls.

The city of Lockport has five sets of operating locks along the Erie Canal. The busy lock system still operates in much the same manner as it did nearly a century ago. The historic district downtown surrounds the canal and locks, which you may see in action. Locks 34 and 35 can

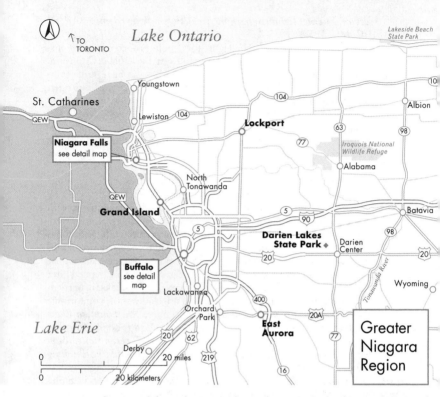

be viewed from the Big Bridge and Pine Street Bridge. Museums and historic sites trace the heritage of the canal and lock system and the town that grew up around them.

CANAL TOUR

The narrated two-hour **Lockport Locks & Erie Canal Cruises** travel the canal, viewing historic buildings and passing through five locks. ⊠ *210 Market St.* ☎ *716/433–6155 or 800/378–0352* ⊕ *www.lockportlocks.com* 🎟 *$14.50* 🕐 *Early May–mid-Oct., daily; call for schedule.*

Gain admission to eight of the town's sites and gain access to a hop-on, hop-off narrated **trolley tour** (July and August only) with the **Tour Lockport pass** (☎ *716/439–0431* 🎟 *$24*), available from the Erie Canal Discovery Center and other sights.

DARIEN LAKES STATE PARK

25 mi east of Buffalo, 30 mi southeast of Lockport.

The centerpiece of this 1,850-acre park is 12-acre Harlow Lake, which has a sandy beach. Hiking, bridle, and cross-country skiing trails vein the grounds, which are hilly and wooded and include a 158-site campground (open daily from June through September and on weekends the rest of the year) with showers and a comfort station. Fishing, picnicking, snowmobiling, and ice-skating are among the other activities you might pursue here. Some hunting is allowed in season. ⊠ *10289 Harlow Rd., Darien Center* ☎ *585/547–9242 or 585/547–9481* ⊕ *nysparks.state. ny.us* 🅿 *Parking $6* ⊙ *Daily dawn–dusk.*

🔆 **Darien Lake Theme Park Resort.** The Ride of Steel will have your heart racing faster than the 70 mph this roller coaster reaches. It's one of six coasters at this theme park, which has more than 100 rides in all. The Viper coaster turns you upside down five times. The water park has the Big Kahuna—a more than 700-foot-long, twisting tube ride—the Grizzly Run rapids, a log flume, a wave pool, and various twisted chutes and slides. The complex includes a 20,000-seat concert amphitheater, eateries, a hotel, and a mammoth campground with 1,200 sites. ⊠ *9993 Allegheny Rd., off Rte. 77, Darien Center* ☎ *585/599–4641* ⊕ *www. godarienlake.com* 🅿 *Day pass $34 ($20 before Memorial Day and after Labor Day), parking $7* ⊙ *Early May–mid-Oct.; call for schedule.*

EAST AURORA

20 mi southwest of Darien Lakes, 20 mi southeast of Buffalo.

East Aurora has earned the nickname Toy Town, U.S.A. because of the many toy companies that have been based in this tiny town over the years. It remains the headquarters of Fisher-Price, which is connected to a unique toy museum. East Aurora is also the locale of two National Historic Landmarks—the honeymoon cottage of President Millard Fillmore and his wife, Abigail, and the Roycroft Campus, an Arts and Crafts movement community founded in 1895 by writer, publisher, and craftsman Elbert Hubbard. Visit the Roycroft Inn to see the murals painted by Barbizon artist Alex Fournier and for the original examples of Roycroft Mission-style furniture.

WHAT TO SEE

Elbert Hubbard-Roycroft Museum. A 1910 Craftsman bungalow contains furniture, glass pieces, books, and other items related to the Roycroft movement and its founder, Elbert Hubbard (1856–1915). A writer and frequent lecturer, Hubbard died along with his wife aboard the *Lusitania.* ⊠ *363 Oakwood Ave.* ☎ *716/652–4735* 🅿 *$5* ⊙ *June–Oct., Wed. and weekends 1–4; tours by appointment.*

Millard Fillmore House Museum. In 1826, when Millard Fillmore was just a young lawyer, he built this simple house. The man who was to become the 13th U.S. president lived here for only four years. A National Historic Landmark, the house has been restored and refurnished to reflect life in the early 19th century. ⊠ *24 Shearer Ave.* ☎ *716/652–8875* 🅿 *$5* ⊙ *June–mid-Oct., Wed. and weekends 1–4 (last tour at 3:30); mid-Oct.–May, by appointment.*

Roycroft Campus. A center for New York's Arts and Crafts movement at the turn of the 20th century, this 9-building community (it originally held 14 buildings) was once home to as many as 500 craftsmen, aka Roycrofters. The community was founded in 1895 by Elbert Hubbard, who had met William Morris during his travels in England. Existing campus buildings include the Roycroft Inn, the 1902 blacksmith shop and the furniture-making and bookbinding building (both now housing artisan and antiques shops); and the old chapel, now the town hall. ⊠*Main and Grove Sts.* ☎*716/652–3333 or 888/769–2738* ⊕*www. ralaweb.com* ⊠*Free* ⊗*Daily 10–5.*

⟳ **Toy Town Museum.** Rare and one-of-a-kind toys are on display at this museum, which also houses a collection of Fisher-Price toys from 1931 to the present; a huge fully furnished dollhouse; circa-1970 puppets from the locally syndicated *Commander Tom Show*; and changing exhibits. The Fisher-Price toy store is next door. ⊠*636 Girard Ave.* ☎*716/687–5151* ⊕*www.toytownusa.com* ⊠*Free* ⊗*Mon. and Tues. noon–5, Wed.–Sat. 10–5, Sun. noon–4.*

SHOPPING

Several artisan shops, including Roycroft Antiques, the Copper Shop, and Roycroft Potters, occupy space in the **Roycroft Campus** (⊠*31 and 37 S. Grove St.* ☎*No phone*) buildings. Buy art, jewelry, Arts and Crafts furniture, and home accessories. Everything you'd expect to find in an old-fashioned five-and-dime—and some you wouldn't—is for sale at **Vidler's 5 and 10 Cent Store** (⊠*676–694 Main St.* ☎*716/652–0481 or 877/843–5377*). Its 15,000 square feet houses Elvis lunchboxes, giant Pez dispensers, John Deere collectibles, scented candles, moisturizers, kitchen supplies, cards, fabrics, and toys. The Vidler family opened the place in 1930 and still owns it.

NIGHTLIFE AND THE ARTS

FESTIVALS AND FAIRS
Held at the Roycroft Campus, the **Roycroft Festival** (⊠*Roycrofters at Large Association, 21 S. Grove St.* ☎*716/655–7252* ⊕*www.ralaweb. com*) encompasses an antiques show, juried art show, and crafts and art sale with live entertainment twice a year. The two-day festivals are held in late June and early December.Notable and historic toys from various periods and manufacturers are on display during three-day **ToyFest** (⊠*636 Girard Ave.* ☎*716/687–5151* ⊕*www.toytownusa. com*), which also brings a parade, an antique-car show, rides, and other entertainment to the Toy Town Museum. The event is usually held in late August.

WHERE TO EAT AND STAY

$$
AMERICAN
✕**Roycroft Inn Restaurant.** Several cozy rooms with fireplaces and wood beams and pillars are furnished with Arts and Crafts pieces and embellished with arched stained-glass windows. An enclosed sunroom with wicker chairs looks out onto the viney covered patio, open in warm weather. The fare is American: duck confit with apricot chutney, smoked mozzarella ravioli in a garlic–white wine sauce, oven-roasted salmon in a puff pastry with wild mushrooms, leeks, and roasted-red-pepper sour cream. Breakfast is served daily (brunch on Sunday). ⊠*40 S. Grove St.* ☎*716/652–5552* ⊟*AE, D, DC, MC, V.*

$
ECLECTIC
★
✕**Tantalus.** The name is a nod to the son of Zeus in Greek mythology, but the tome of a menu in this semicasual, rustic-industrial space—with huge windows, cement floors, and Mexican-style woven rugs hung from

2

exposed piping—hails from seemingly every part of the old and new worlds: a Cuban sandwich on homemade rustic bread; a "filled burger," stuffed with feta, kalamata olives, and sun-dried tomatoes; house-made ricotta ravioli with prosciutto in Gorgonzola-arugula sauce; plus 20 pizzas, a page of salads, and entrées of duck, fish, pork, and beef. Thursday is Mexican day. The wine and beer lists are equally lengthy and varied. ⊠ *634 Main St.* ☎*716/652–0341* ⊟*AE, D, MC, V.*

$–$$ **Roycroft Inn.** Original and reproduction Roycroft Arts and Crafts fur-
★ nishings fill the rooms at this lovely three-story inn on the old Roycroft Campus. Most accommodations here are three-, four-, or five-room suites. Some have two twin beds or a queen-size bed and a pullout queen sleeper. Bursts of bright color—in a throw rug or pillow or a bedcovering, for example—play off the straight lines of the Mission furniture and the neutral walls. **Pros:** good on-site restaurant (⇨*above*). **Cons:** thin mattresses; no views; breakfast not included in rate. ⊠*40 S. Grove St.* ☎*716/652–5552 or 877/652–5552* ⊕*www.roycroftinn.com* ⇨*5 rooms, 23 suites* ⸂*In-room: Internet, Wi-Fi. In-hotel: restaurant, room service, bar, Internet terminal, parking (free), no-smoking rooms* ⊟*AE, D, DC, MC, V.*

SIDE TRIPS IN CANADA

NIAGARA-ON-THE LAKE

15 km (9 mi) north of Niagara Falls.

One of the country's prettiest and best-preserved Victorian towns, B&B-filled Niagara-on-the-Lake borders Lake Ontario at the mouth of the Niagara River, directly across the water from Old Fort Niagara. It's the launch point for wine tours in the region, and since 1962 has been considered the southern outpost of fine summer theater in Ontario because of its acclaimed Shaw Festival.

GETTING AROUND

Niagara-on-the-Lake can easily be explored on foot. Parking downtown is metered and limited. Walking east along central **Queen Street,** you get a glimpse of the town's architectural history. At No. 209 is the handsome **Charles Inn,** built in about 1832 for a member of Parliament. At No. 5 is the **Niagara Apothecary** (☎*905/468–3845* ⊕*www.niagaraapothecary. ca*), restored to look like the 1866 pharmacy it once was, glass-fronted walnut cabinets display vintage remedies such as Merrill's System Tonic, which "Purifies the Blood and Builds up the System." *L0S 1J0*

TOURS Horse-drawn, narrated carriage tours with **Sentineal Carriages** (☎*905/468–4943* ⊕*www.sentinealcarriages.ca*), which pick up from the intersection of King and Queen streets, are a popular way to see town. The **Whirlpool Jet Boat Tours** (⇨*Niagara Falls*) leave from the end of Melville Street, near the Harbour House hotel.

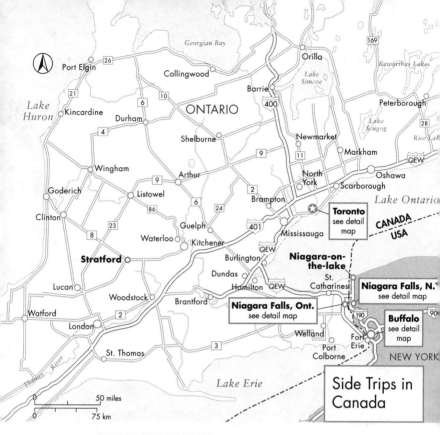

Side Trips in
Canada

VISITOR INFORMATION

The Niagara Peninsula is home to about 60 wineries that stretch 30 mi north of Niagara-on-the-Lake. Wine festivals are frequent between spring and fall. For a map of the entire wine route, pick up the free **Official Guide to the Wineries of Ontario,** updated yearly, at the tourism board (☎800/263–2988 ⊕*www.tourismniagara.com*) or at various attractions in town. You also can download or order it from the **Wine Council of Ontario** (☎905/684–8070 ⊕*www.winesofontario.org*).

NIGHTLIFE AND THE ARTS

Fodor'sChoice
★

The **Shaw Festival** (☎905/468–2172 or 800/511–7429 ⊕*www.shawfest. com*) is the only theater festival in the world specializing in the plays of George Bernard Shaw and his contemporaries. The season runs from April through December. All shows are staged in one of three town-center theaters.

WHERE TO EAT

A number of wineries have restaurants. Especially in summer, make reservations whenever possible. Many restaurants serve dinner only until 9 PM.

$$$$
FRENCH

✕**Hillebrand Vineyard Café.** After a complimentary winery tour and tasting, you can settle down to a superb meal. Culinary masterpieces may include Ontario lamb loin with ravioli and turnip-and-potato gratin or halibut with white beans, chorizo, and wild prawns; the menu changes every six weeks. The tossed salad is a beautiful composition of organic greens, sun-dried blueberries, and roasted crisp garlic. The pastry chef's desserts are incredible too: a bittersweet chocolate cup is filled with vanilla ice cream and topped with candied hazelnuts. ⊠ *1249 Niagara Stone Rd., at Hwy. 55* ☎ *905/468–7123 or 800/582–8412* ⊕ *www.hillebrand.com* ⊟ *AE, D, MC, V.*

$$$$
CONTINENTAL
✕**Peller Estates Winery Restaurant.** Frequently cited as the best restaurant in town—an impressive feat considering the competition—Peller manages refinement without arrogance. The colonial revival dining room is anchored by a huge fireplace at one end and has large windows overlooking the estate vineyards. The ever-changing menu has included succulently tender diver scallops with pancetta in a tomato-and-tarragon sauce and cabernet-braised rib eye with lobster knuckles and tomato risotto. Tasting menus are available. Desserts, like a sea-salt brownie with a crème fraîche ice-cream sandwich, offer a lighthearted twist. ⊠ *290 John St. E* ☎ *905/468–4678* ⩲ *Reservations essential* ⊟ *AE, D, DC, MC, V.*

WHERE TO STAY

Luxury hotels in historic buildings are a dime a dozen here, and nearly all are fabulous, but the Niagara wine region also has over 100 B&Bs whose service and quality can rival some of the priciest hotels. **Niagara-on-the-Lake Historic Bed & Breakfasts** (⊕ *www.historicbb.com*) maintains an online list of historic B&Bs, all built before 1850 and all walkable to Queen Street. The **Niagara-on-the-Lake Bed & Breakfast Association** (☎ *905/468–0123* ⊕ *niagarabedandbreakfasts.com*) has a comprehensive listing.

$$$$
★
▨**Harbour House.** A classy nautical theme pervades this luxurious boutique hotel one block from the Niagara River. The building's 1880s maritime, cedar-shingled look is topped off with a gambrel roof. Spacious rooms have cozy touches like gas fireplaces, feather-top beds, and Frette robes, as well as DVD and CD players. You can sample local preserves and homemade pastries at breakfast and attend wine-and-cheese tastings in the afternoon. **Pros:** staff caters to every need; afternoon wine tastings are a wonderful opportunity to meet new people. **Con:** no restaurant; gym and spa facilities off-site. ⊠ *85 Melville St.* ☎ *905/468–4683 or 866/277–6677* ⊕ *www.harbourhousehotel.ca* ⤍ *29 rooms, 2 suites* ⋔ *In-room: Internet, Wi-Fi. In-hotel: Internet terminal, parking (free), some pets allowed, no-smoking rooms* ⊟ *AE, MC, V* ⎮◎⎮*BP.*

$$$–$$$$ 🖼 **Shaw Club Hotel & Spa.** For a rare contemporary experience in Niagara-on-the-Lake, stay at this boutique hotel with sleek, gorgeous rooms, oversize artwork, and some in-room fireplaces. Techno perks include iPod docks, 42-inch plasma TVs in bedrooms and smaller TVs in bathrooms, surround sound, and complimentary cappuccinos. Zee's restaurant, serving a Continental menu, is popular in particular for its wraparound patio dining. Annex rooms and standard rooms are traditional rather than modern; the former have Jacuzzi tubs. **Pros:** dreamy beds; good restaurant; Shaw Festival Theatre across street. **Cons:** standard and annex rooms don't have the same modern decor and amenities. ⊠*92 Picton St.* ☎*905/468–5711 or 800/511–7070* ⊕*www.shawclub.com* ↘*30 rooms, 1 suite* ⚙*In-room: refrigerator, DVD, Internet, Wi-Fi (some). In-hotel: gym, spa, Internet terminal, Wi-Fi, parking (free), some pets allowed, no-smoking rooms* ☐*AE, D, DC, MC, V.*

TORONTO

130 KM (82 mi) from Niagara Falls via QEW.

"Toronto is like New York, as run by the Swiss," actor Peter Ustinov is rumored to have said. Indeed, this is a big, beautiful, and efficient city, one that has emerged from relative obscurity over the past half century to become the center of culture, commerce, and communications in Canada. With its colorful ethnic mix, rich history, and breathtaking architecture, Toronto is nonstop adventure for the willing tourist, from the top of the CN Tower to as far as the eye can see.

GETTING AROUND

Traffic is dense and parking expensive within the city core. If you have a car with you, leave it at your hotel when exploring the city. ■**TIP➔ In the city, take taxis or use the excellent Toronto transit system (TTC). A single ride costs C$2.75 and one-day passes are C$9.** For more information, go to the Toronto Transit Commission's Web site at ⊕*www.ttc.ca.*

VISITOR INFORMATION

Tourism Toronto (☎*416/203–2600 or 800/499–2514* ⊕*www.torontotourism. com*).

WHAT TO SEE

★ **Art Gallery of Ontario.** The AGO's collection ranges from AD 100 to
❷ the present, with works by Rembrandt, Hogarth, Rothko, Oldenburg, and more. Such northern lights as Emily Carr and David Milne are on display in the Canadian Wing. A C$254 million, four-year expansion, designed by Toronto native son Frank Gehry, was completed in late 2008. ⊠*317 Dundas St. W, Chinatown* ☎*416/979–6648* ⊕*www. ago.net* ☑*C$18; free Wed. after 6 PM* ☉*Wed.–Fri. 10–8:30, Tues. and weekends 10–5:30* Ⓜ*St. Patrick.*

❹ **CN Tower.** The tallest freestanding tower in the world, at 1,815 feet
☾ and 5 inches high, was built in 1976 as a telecommunications tower.
Fodor's Choice Glass-front elevators zoom up the exterior to the four observation
★ decks, including the **Glass Floor Level,** 1,122 feet above the ground.

The excellent **360 Revolving Restaurant** is at 1,150 feet. All levels provide spectacular panoramic views of Toronto, Lake Ontario, and the Toronto Islands. ☒*301 Front St. W, Harbourfront* ☎*416/868–6937, 416/362–5411 restaurant* ⊕*www.cntower.ca* ⚑*From C$22* ⊘*Sun.– Thurs. 9* AM*–10* PM*, Fri. and Sat. 9* AM*–10:30* PM Ⓜ*Union.*

❸ Fort York. The founding of Toronto occurred in 1793 when the British built this fort to protect the entrance to the harbor. Twenty years later the fort was the scene of the bloody Battle of York. The Americans won this battle—their first major victory in the War of 1812—and razed the provincial buildings during a six-day occupation. Exhibits include restored barracks, kitchens, and gunpowder magazines, plus changing museum displays. ☒*100 Garrison Rd., Harbourfront* ☎*416/392– 6907* ⊕*www.toronto.ca/culture/fort_york.htm* ⚑*C$6* ⊘*May–Aug., daily 10–5; Sept.–Apr., weekdays 10–4, weekends 10–5* Ⓜ*Bathurst, then streetcar 511 south.*

❻ Historic Distillery District. North America's best-preserved collection of Victorian industrial architecture is in this historic enclave in downtown Toronto. Formerly the Gooderham & Worts Distillery (founded in 1832), the Distillery has been developed as a center for arts, culture, and entertainment. This 13-acre cobblestone site includes a picturesque pedestrian-only village that houses more than 100 tenants—including galleries, artist studios and workshops, boutiques, a brewpub, restaurants, and bars. Outdoor events are frequent in summer. ☒*55 Mill St., Old Town* ☎*416/364–1177* ⊕*www.thedistillerydistrict.com* ⚑*Parking C$5* ⊘*Mon.–Wed. 11–7, Thurs. and Fri. 11–9, Sat. 10–9, Sun. 11–6; tenant hrs vary* Ⓜ*King, then streetcar 504 east.*

❺ Hockey Hall of Fame and Museum. Even if you're not a hockey fan, it's worth a trip here to see this shrine to Canada's favorite sport. Exhibits include the original 1893 Stanley Cup, as well as displays of goalie masks, skate and stick collections, and a replica of the Montréal Canadiens' locker room. ☒*30 Yonge St., Financial District* ☎*416/360–7765* ⊕*www.hhof.com* ⚑*C$13* ⊘*Sept.–June, weekdays 10–5, Sat. 9:30–6, Sun. 10:30–5; July and Aug., Mon.–Sat. 9:30–6, Sun. 10–6* Ⓜ*Union.*

❶ Royal Ontario Museum. Canada's largest museum, the ROM has more than 6 million items among its science, art, and archaeology exhibits. The Chinese Sculpture Gallery displays 25 stone Buddhist sculptures dating from the 2nd through 16th century. The ultramodern Michael Lee-Chin Crystal gallery—a series of interlocking prismatic cubes spilling out onto Bloor Street—opened in 2008. ☒*100 Queen's Park, Yorkville* ☎*416/586–5549* ⊕*www.rom.on.ca* ⚑*C$22* ⊘*Sat.–Thurs. 10–5:30, Fri. 10–9:30* Ⓜ*Museum.*

SPORTS AND THE OUTDOORS

Toronto has many professional sports teams, including Major League Baseball's **Toronto Blue Jays** (☎*416/341–1234* ⊕*www.bluejays.com*); the NBA's **Toronto Raptors** (☎*416/815–5600* ⊕*www.raptors.com*); and the NHL's **Toronto Maple Leafs** (☎*416/870–8000* ⊕*www.mapleleafs.com*), whose games always attract rabid, sell-out crowds.

SHOPPING

The block-long **Eaton Centre** (✉220 Yonge St., Dundas Square Area ☎416/598–8560 Ⓜ Dundas, Queen) shopping complex houses restaurants and more than 200 stores. If it's funky or fun, it's found on **Queen Street West.** The best boutiques are concentrated from University Avenue to Spadina Avenue, with fashionable stores as far west as Bathurst Street and beyond. The **Yorkville** neighborhood, near Bay and Bloor, is *the* place to find names like Prada, Cartier, Hermès, and Canada's high-style department store, Holt Renfrew.

NIGHTLIFE AND THE ARTS

The city's impressive artistic and after-dark options range from Toronto Symphony Orchestra performances and Broadway-caliber musicals to touring bands at grungy rock venues and stand-up at Second City. The best sources for information are the free weekly newspapers *NOW* (⊕ *www.nowtoronto.com*) and *Eye Weekly* (⊕ *www.eyeweekly. com*), and daily papers the *Toronto Star* (⊕ *www.thestar.com*) and *The Globe and Mail* (⊕ *www.theglobeandmail.com*).

Nightlife centers around Queen Street West, the Annex (Bloor Street, between Spadina and Bathurst), and Little Italy (College Street, between Bathurst and Ossington) for bars and small music venues, and around Adelaide Street, from University Avenue to Peter Street, for clubs. The area around Church and Wellesley streets, northeast of the downtown core, is the so-called "gaybourhood."

TORONTO INTERNATIONAL FILM FESTIVAL

For 10 days each September, downtown is dominated by the **Toronto International Film Festival** (☎416/967–7371 or 416/968–3456 ⊕ www.tiffg.ca), which hosts red-carpet world premiers as well as less-hooplahed premiers of independent and foreign films. Tickets can be purchased online beginning in July. You can also buy tickets at TIFF booths set up around the city during the festival, or on a "rush" basis the day of the screening.

WHERE TO EAT

$$$$
CANADIAN
✗**Canoe.** Look through huge windows on the 54th floor of the Toronto Dominion Bank Tower and enjoy the breathtaking view of the Toronto Islands and the lake while you dine. Classics include foie gras and truffles. A seven-course tasting menu takes you from coast to coast with dishes like roast hind of Yukon caribou with zucchini corn-bread cobbler and partridge-berry juice. ∎TIP➔ **Canoe's restaurant and lounge is a great place to sample Niagara wines.** ✉*Toronto-Dominion Center, 66 Wellington St. W, 54th fl., Financial District* ☎416/364–0054 △*Reservations essential* ▤*AE, DC, MC, V* ⊙*Closed weekends* Ⓜ*King.*

$$
★
CANADIAN
✗**Jamie Kennedy Wine Bar.** This sleek, spare wine bar and dining room is amazingly popular, due in part to the charm of owner-chef Kennedy, who has been at the forefront of the Canadian food movement for more than 20 years. Sit on comfy bar stools and watch as Kennedy sautés, grills, seasons, and cooks. From the daily-changing list of 21 items, favorites are an oval scoop of pâté with the chef's own pickled veggies, and tempting artisanal cheeses. ✉*9 Church St., Old Town* ☎416/362–1957 △*Reservations essential* ▤*AE, DC, MC, V* Ⓜ*Union.*

2

$$$$ ✕**Lai Wah Heen.** In an elegant room with a sculpted ceiling, etched-
CHINESE glass turntables, and silver serving dishes, the service is formal; here
mahogany-color Peking duck is wheeled in on a trolley and presented
with panache. Excellent choices from the 100-dish inventory include
wok-fried shredded beef and vegetables in a crisp potato nest. At lunch,
dim sum is divine. ⊠*Metropolitan Hotel, 108 Chestnut St., 2nd fl.,
Chinatown* ☎*416/977–9899* ⌦*Reservations essential* ▤*AE, DC,
MC, V* Ⓜ*St. Patrick.*

$$$ ✕**Sotto Sotto.** A coal cellar in a turn-of-the-20th-century home was dug
ITALIAN out, its stone walls and floor polished, and a restaurant created. The
menu of more than 20 pasta dishes gives a tantalizing tug at the taste
buds. Gnocchi is made daily. Cornish hen is marinated, pressed, and
grilled to a juicy brown, and the swordfish and fresh fish of the day are
beautifully done on the grill. ⊠*116A Avenue Rd., Yorkville* ☎*416/962–
0011* ▤*AE, DC, MC, V* ☉*No lunch Sun. and Mon.* Ⓜ*Bay.*

WHERE TO STAY

$$$ ▦**Gladstone Hotel.** Artist-designed guest rooms place an emphasis on
everything that is one-of-a-kind—even the soaps are handmade and
locally produced. The hand-operated 1904 elevator is one of three
still working in Toronto. In the Racine Room, maroon-velvet furnishings complement a stack of several vintage steamer trunks hiding the
TV and DVD player. The two-story Rock Star suite contains a wraparound view of the city and a turret bedroom. **Pros:** friendly, bohemian
ambience; truly unique property and experience. **Cons:** downtrodden
neighborhood; many blocks from downtown core. ⊠*1214 Queen St.
W., Queen West* ☎*416/531–4635* ⊕*www.gladstonehotel.com* ⌘*34
rooms, 3 suites* ⌂*In-room: kitchen (some), DVD, Wi-Fi. In-hotel: restaurant, bars, Wi-Fi, no-smoking rooms* ▤*AE, MC, V* Ⓜ*Osgoode,
then streetcar west.*

$$$$ ▦**The Hazelton Hotel.** The full celebrity treatment begins from the
moment you step into the discreet reception area. Stunning guest rooms
feature sumptuous furnishings, 9-foot ceilings, floor-to-ceiling windows,
individual doorbells, and (soundproof) French doors opening out onto
balconies. No expense is spared in the marble bathrooms, with their
fog-free LCD TVs built into the mirror, three showerheads, plunge
tubs, and heated floors. Celebrity-chef Mark McEwan runs the hugely
popular lobby restaurant One. **Pros:** Toronto's hottest address; well-
equipped gym and spa; great in-room amenities. **Cons:** can be hard
to get a room. ⊠*118 Yorkville Ave., Yorkville* ☎*416/963–6300 or
866/473–6301* ⊕*www.thehazeltonhotel.com* ⌘*77 rooms* ⌂*In-room:
safe, refrigerator, DVD, Internet (some), Wi-Fi (some). In-hotel: restaurant, room service, pool, gym, spa, laundry service, parking (paid),
no-smoking rooms* ▤*AE, D, DC, MC, V* Ⓜ*Bay.*

$$ ▦**The Suites at 1 King West.** This all-suites hotel, the tallest residential
building in Canada, rises 51 stories above the city's downtown business
and shopping core. Each suite has a washer-dryer unit and equipped
kitchen. A 24-hour concierge, a connection to the PATH, and com-
plimentary limousine service within the downtown area are bonuses.
Many rooms face the atrium, but for a little more you can request a
suite facing south on an upper floor for a magnificent view of the lake

and Toronto Islands. **Pros:** great views from upper floors; central locale. **Cons:** slightly inexperienced front desk staff; slow elevators. ⊠*1 King St. W, Financial District* ☎*416/548–8100 or 866/470–5464* ⊕*www. onekingwest.com* ⚏*570 condominiums* ⌂*In-room: safe, kitchen, refrigerator, DVD, Internet. In-hotel: restaurant, gym, parking (paid), no-smoking rooms* ☰*AE, DC, MC, V* Ⓜ*King.*

OFF THE BEATEN PATH

In July 1953, Alec Guinness, one of the world's greatest actors, joined with Tyrone Guthrie, probably the world's greatest Shakespearean director, beneath a hot, stuffy tent in a quiet town about a 90-minute drive west of Toronto. This was the birth of the **Stratford Festival,** which now runs from April to early November and is one of the most successful and admired festivals of its kind.

The early years brought giants of world theater to the tiny town: Christopher Plummer, Jason Robards Jr., and Maggie Smith. Stratford's offerings are still among the best of their kind in the world, with at least a handful of productions every year that put most other summer-arts festivals to shame. Today Stratford is a city of 32,000 that welcomes over 500,000 visitors annually for the Stratford Festival alone.

Stratford Festival performances—now a mix of Shakespeare, works by other dramatists, and popular musicals—take place in four theaters, with 15 different productions mounted during the season. The festival also offers numerous non-play concerts, workshops, tours, and lectures. ⊠*55 Queen St., Stratford* ☎*519/273–1600 or 800/567–1600* ⊕*www. stratfordfestival.ca.*

CHAUTAUQUA-ALLEGHENY

The Chautauqua–Allegheny area covers the southwestern part of the state, bordered by Pennsylvania on the south, Lake Erie on the west, and the Buffalo and Finger Lakes regions on the north and east, respectively. The region includes the Chautauqua Institution—one of the nation's most respected educational and cultural institutions—ski resorts, an active and industrious Amish community, the beautiful Allegany State Park, and the expansive Allegany Indian Reservation, which includes the city of Salamanca.

Chautauqua County takes its name from its largest lake, which is 22 mi long. French explorers landed on the Lake Erie shores of the Chautauqua area in 1679. Their quest was for a southward passage to the Ohio and Mississippi rivers, and the route connecting Lake Erie with Chautauqua Lake, known as the Portage Trail, offered an answer. Indeed, the dispute between France and England over possession of this trail led to the French and Indian War.

GETTING HERE AND AROUND

Fredonia, Dunkirk, Westfield, Mayville, Chautauqua, Bemus Point, and Jamestown are all within Chautauqua County, which is bordered to the west by Lake Erie. Cattaraugus County encompasses the Allegany State Park area, incorporating Salamanca, Ellicottville, and Olean. The

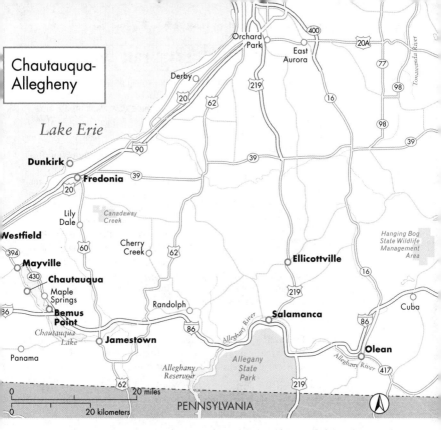

Chautauqua-Allegheny

Lake Erie

Dunkirk

Fredonia

Lily Dale

Canadaway Creek

Westfield

Mayville

Chautauqua

Maple Springs

Bemus Point

Chautauqua Lake

Panama

Jamestown

Cherry Creek

Randolph

Alleghany Reservoir

Allegany State Park

Ellicottville

Hanging Bog State Wildlife Management Area

Salamanca

Allegany River

Cuba

Olean

Allegheny River

Orchard Park

East Aurora

Derby

0   20 miles

0   20 kilometers

PENNSYLVANIA

Interstate90 New York State Thruway runs along Lake Erie from Buffalo to Pennsylvania; I–86 runs east–west and is the main route from Jamestown to Olean. Most other roads in the region are small country routes or small-town main streets. A car is a necessity.

VISITOR INFORMATION

Cattaraugus County Tourism (☞ *Ellicottville, Olean, Salamanca* ☎ *800/331–0543* ⊕ *www.enchantedmountains.info*). **Chautauqua County Visitors Bureau** (☞ *Bemus Point, Chautauqua, Dunkirk, Fredonia, Jamestown, Westfield* ⊠ *Chautauqua Institution Welcome Center, Rte. 394, Chautauqua* ☎ *800/242–4569* ⊕ *www.tourchautauqua.com*).

FREDONIA AND DUNKIRK

50 mi southwest of Buffalo.

Dunkirk, one of the few harbors along the east coast of Lake Erie, was named after Dunkerque in northern France, and in 1851 became the terminus of the longest railroad in the world. Dunkirk's historic lighthouse was built in 1875 and is still operating. The town has a tiny boardwalk with a few craft and gift shops fronting the marina, next to the Clarion Hotel, but not much else.

THE CHAUTAUQUA–LAKE ERIE WINE TRAIL

Chautauqua County is the country's largest grape-growing area outside of California and is the Concord grape capital of America. Sweet grapes thrive here, so traditionally the area has been a supplier for juices and jams (Welch's was based here until 1982). But in the 1960s, locals started experimenting with wines. Johnson Estate Winery, the first estate winery in New York, opened in 1961; today there are 21 wineries along the trail.

Cold winters make wine-quality grape-growing a challenge. Many wines are made from native labruscas (try a Concord wine for

something unique) or French hybrids (Vidal ice wines are a good buy). But these days, wineries are also cultivating hardier European vinifera varieties, like Riesling.

The 50-mi **Chautauqua Wine Trail** (⊕ *www.chautauquawinetrail.org*) roughly follows Route 20, from about 6 mi northeast of Fredonia to North East, Pennsylvania. Wineries generally feel more homegrown that those in Niagara-on-the-Lake or the Finger Lakes, which can be a refreshing change of pace. Tastings begin as early as 11 AM and cost no more than $5.

About 4 mi inland across Interstate 90 is the pretty village of Fredonia. It's home to Fredonia State University (better known as SUNY Fredonia), a provider of several cultural opportunities.

Fredonia and Dunkirk lie in a grape- and wine-producing area. The Chautauqua–Lake Erie Wine Trail (⇨ *box, above*) begins just north of Fredonia along Route 20.

WHAT TO SEE

Dunkirk Lighthouse and Veterans Park Museum. A beacon in the dark since 1826, this lighthouse still operates every night, using a Fresnel lens dating from an 1875 update, when the brick surround was built. (The 1826 structure is still intact inside.) On the first floor of the keeper's house are nautical history exhibits and rooms showing how the keeper and his family would have lived; the second floor is the veterans museum. Coast Guard boats on display include a 45-foot buoy tender. You can take a guided tour up to the tower. ⊠*1 Lighthouse Point, left on Point Dr. N off Rte. 5, Dunkirk* ☎*716/366–5050* ⊕*www.dunkirklighthouse.com* ☜*$6 grounds, museum, and tour; $1 grounds only* ⊙ *May, June, Sept., and Oct., Mon., Tues., and Thurs.–Sat. 10–2 (last tour at 1); July and Aug., Mon., Tues., and Thurs.–Sat. 10–4 (last tour at 2:30).*

OFF THE
BEATEN
PATH

Lily Dale Assembly. This religious colony of Victorian houses 8 mi south of Fredonia was founded on the shores of Lake Cassadaga in 1879, during a period of increased interest in Spiritualism, which believes that the spirits of the dead live on and that some people can communicate with them. Today the world's largest spiritualist community has a summer season with workshops, medium readings, a research library, lectures, and a variety of recreational activities, including fishing, swimming, and picnicking. Lily Dale has lodging, restaurants, and its own volunteer fire department. You can go for the day or stay overnight, but call ahead for readings with the most popular mediums. ⊠*5 Melrose Park, west of Rte. 60, Lily Dale* ☎*716/595–8721* ⊕*www.lilydaleassembly.com* ▣*Day pass $10 ($5 after 6 PM)* ⊙*Late June–last Sat. in Aug.*

SPORTS AND THE OUTDOORS

☽ **Lake Erie State Park.** On a bluff overlooking Lake Erie, this park has spectacular scenery. You may swim, hike, bike, fish, and picnic here in warm-weather months. The trails are used for cross-country skiing and snowmobiling in winter. A campground (open late April to late October) includes 102 campsites and 10 cabins. The park is off Route 5 about 9 mi south of Dunkirk. ⊠*5905 Lake Rd., Brocton* ☎*716/792–9214, 800/456–2267 camping reservations* ⊕*nysparks. state.ny.us/parks* ▣*$7 late Apr.–late Oct., free late Oct.–late Apr.* ⊙*Daily 8 AM–10 PM.*

NIGHTLIFE AND THE ARTS

FESTIVALS AND FAIRS Get a rundown of all the festivals year-round at ⊕*www.festivalsfredonia. com.*

America's Grape Country Wine Festival. Making its debut in August 2008, this annual two-day festival in Dunkirk celebrates New York State wines. Other attractions are a farmers' market, music, and homemade foods and crafts. Events take place at the county fairgrounds. *Exit 59 on I-90.* ☎*800/965–4834* ⊕*www.agcwinefestival.com.*

☽ **Chautauqua County Fair.** A large part of this seven-day fair, held at the end of July, centers on animals: livestock exhibits, horse shows, goat-milking contests. Other attractions include demolition derbies, tractor pulls, line dancing, magic shows, and carnival rides. ⊠*Chautauqua County Fairgrounds, 1089 Central Ave., Dunkirk* ☎*716/366–4752* ⊕*www.chautauquacountyfair.org.*

Red, White & Blues Festival. One of Fredonia's most popular annual events, this festival, held the first weekend after Labor Day, brings blues music to various indoor and outdoor venues around town, accompanied by local wines (and a few brews) and plenty of food. ☎*888/373–3664* ⊕*www.festivalsfredonia.com.*

WHERE TO EAT

Fredonia also has an outpost of the popular and casual **Ellicottville Brewing Company** (⇨*Ellicottville*), at 34 West Main Street, with much the same ambience and menu.

$$ ✕**The Brick Room.** Entrées, such as grilled shrimp over a fried grits cake
CONTINENTAL with Tasso ham (spicy smoked ham), French green beans, and cherry
★ tomatoes in a beurre blanc sauce, are inventive and expertly prepared. The menu is seasonal, but starters have included fried green tomatoes with chipotle aioli. Congenial but classy, the compact, Napa-esque dining room—gleaming light-wood floors and tables, exposed-redbrick walls, and French doors that open to the street—buzzes with conversation. ⊠*49 W. Main St., Fredonia* ☎*716/672–5547* ▤*AE, D, DC, MC, V* ⊙*Closed Tues.*

$
AMERICAN
✕**Demetri's on the Lake.** The deck overlooking Lake Erie and much-loved Greek-American comfort food are the reasons to eat at this diner that serves three meals daily. (The scruffy dining room lacks atmosphere—it's best to go when the weather is cooperating so you can dine alfresco.) Lamb, chicken souvlaki, prime rib, steak, and seafood entrées go well with the extensive wine list. ✉*6 Lake Shore Dr. W, Dunkirk* ☎*716/366–4187* ▤*AE, D, MC, V.*

WHERE TO STAY

Area hotels fill up quickly and far in advance during university-related events at SUNY Fredonia, such as commencement, in May, and parents' weekend, in late September.

$–$$
🏨**Clarion Hotel Dunkirk.** The brick four-story chain hotel overlooks Lake Erie's Chadwick Bay. Rooms are standard, with contemporary furniture; some have in-room whirlpool tubs. In the Windjammer's restaurant, a boat wheel, a fish tank, and huge windows overlooking the marina create a nautical theme. Menu options include Delmonico steak, salmon, and chicken Alfredo. **Pros:** rooms in back have view of marina and Lake Erie; nice restaurant. **Cons:** indoor pool in a windowless room under harsh fluorescent lights; room furnishings a bit outdated (though they are gradually being renovated). ✉*30 Lake Shore Dr. E, Dunkirk* ☎*716/366–8350* ⊕*www.clariondunkirk.com* ⤳*127 rooms* &*In-room: refrigerator (some), Internet, Wi-Fi. In-hotel: restaurant, room service, bar, pools, gym, laundry facilities, laundry service, Wi-Fi, parking (free), no-smoking rooms* ▤*AE, D, DC, MC, V.*

¢–$
🏨**White Inn.** Victorian frills and florals are in full effect at this handsome inn, originally the White family residence. Some of the building dates from 1868; it became an inn in 1919. Victorian antiques and reproduction pieces furnish the rooms, which have wall-to-wall carpeting and (very) floral wall coverings and may have white-wicker furniture or carved-wood four-poster beds. The restaurant serves mostly Continental fare that includes entrées such as pecan-encrusted chicken and prime rib (Friday and Saturday only). **Pros:** on Fredonia's main strip within walking distance of shops and restaurants; big breakfasts. **Cons:** furnishings need updating; no views; poor soundproofing. ✉*52 E. Main St., Fredonia* ☎*716/672–2103 or 888/373–3664* ⊕*www.whiteinn.com* ⤳*12 rooms, 11 suites* &*In-room: refrigerator (some), Internet, Wi-Fi. In-hotel: restaurant, laundry service, Wi-Fi, parking (free), some pets allowed, no-smoking rooms* ▤*AE, D, DC, MC, V* ⦿*BP.*

WESTFIELD

15 mi southwest of Fredonia.

As the home of a Welch's plant, Westfield calls itself the grape-juice capital of the world. Several wineries are nearby, off U.S. 20. Antiques stores and craft shops cluster around the village square, and scattered throughout Westfield are Federal-style mansions. At nearby Cassadaga Lake is the Lily Dale Assembly, a spiritualist center begun in 1879 that still attracts mediums and the psychically curious.

2

WHAT TO SEE

McClurg Mansion. The handsome 14-room Federal-style mansion on the Westfield village green was built in 1820. The Chautauqua County Historical Society runs the house, which is on the National Register of Historic Places and is decorated in high Victorian style. Displays include Civil War documents and American Indian and military artifacts. ⊠*15 E. Main St.* ☎*716/326–2977* ⊕*www.mcclurgmuseum.org* ⊠*$5* ⊘*Tues.–Sat. 10–4.*

SHOPPING

More than 40 vendors participate in the **Cross Roads Farm & Craft Market** (⊠*Country Rte. 21/Sherman Westfield Rd., Sherman, 5 mi south of Westfield, just south of Hardscrabble Rd.* ☎*716/326–6278 or 877/512–7307* ⊕*www.thecrossroadsmarket.com* ⊘*May–Dec., Sat. 9–5*). The mix includes handcrafted furniture, jams, cheeses, Western wear, hand-knit sweaters, wooden toys, and candles.The owners of **Landmark Acres Antiques** (⊠*232 W. Main St.* ☎*716/326–4185* ⊕*www.landmarkacres. com* ⊘*Thurs.–Mon. 1–5*) have been stocking their shop with a well-edited collection of 18th- and 19th-century antiques since 1975.**Vinewood Acres Sugar Shack** (⊠*7904 Rte. 5* ☎*716/326–3351* ⊕*www. sugarshack1.com* ⊘*Thurs.–Mon. 1–5*) sells 29 fruit syrups, from maple to quince, and 15 fruit butters, all homemade from the farm's own produce. Customers are offered tastings of the syrups, poured over ice cream. The Sunday pancake breakfast (March–December) is popular.

WHERE TO EAT

$ ✕**Sapore Restaurant, Coffee & Wine Bar.** With its Italian–Latin Amer-
ECLECTIC ican fusion menu focusing on simple dishes made with local, fresh, and organic ingredients, and an Old-World-meets-urban-café decor—exposed-brick walls, local art, a gleaming cappuccino machine on the bar—this place is quite the cosmopolitan departure in this pocket of the state. The San Francisco–trained chef might whip up seared scallops over ginger-marinated cabbage or pappardelle topped with tomatoes and cracked-pepper mascarpone. Sapore is open all day as a café, and also serves breakfast. ⊠*7 E. Main St.* ☎*716/326–7707* ⚑*Reservations not accepted* ▤*AE, D, DC, MC, V* ⊘*Closed Sun. and Mon. in Nov.–Apr.*

$$$ ✕**William Seward Inn.** At this historic B&B (⇨*below*) you can eat in
CONTINENTAL one of the two tiny floral dining rooms, one with a fireplace, seating 16 each, or on the petite front patio. The chef, formerly of the Peek'n Peak Resort, is praised in particular for his seared Chilean sea bass with a citrus beurre blanc and for Stilton-encrusted beef tenderloin in merlot sauce. These favorites are always on the menu; other entrées, salads, and appetizers—such as the watermelon gazpacho—change seasonally. ⊠*6645 S. Portage Rd., 3 mi east of Westfield town center* ☎*716/326–4151 or 800/338–4151* ⚑*Reservations essential* ▤*AE, D, MC, V* ⊘*Closed Mon. and Tues. No lunch.*

$$ ✕**ZeBro's Harbor House.** Locals admit that only the fish fry is stellar at
SEAFOOD this casual local joint, but the view of sparkling Lake Erie from the outdoor patio, just 100 feet from the rocky waterfront, is what keeps them coming back, particularly around sunset. Plus, it's the only place

in town open on Monday. The menu is largely seafood, and portions are huge. The concrete patio with metal tables, and the dark, carpeted dining room are nothing to gawk at; keep your gaze fixed lakeward. Dinner is only served until 8 PM Sunday. Reserve for a sunset-hour table. ⊠ *8254 1st St., at the end of N. Portage Rd.* ☎*716/326–2017* ⊟*AE, D, MC, V.*

WHERE TO STAY

$–$$ 🏨**Candlelight Lodge.** Built in 1851, this Italianate brick Victorian mansion, listed on the National Register of Historic Places, has inlaid flooring, leaded- and stained-glass transoms, paneled pocket doors, and ornate fireplaces. The owners are antiques dealers (⇨ *Landmark Acres Antiques, Shopping*), and rooms are crammed with Civil War–to Victorian-era pieces. The four-suite Captain Storm House, an 1892 Queen Anne revival next door, follows much the same style. Stores and restaurants are within walking distance; the Chautauqua Institute is a 20-minute drive. **Pros:** lovely building; amazing antiques; large suites. **Cons:** no breakfast on-site; some bathrooms need updating; owners live off-site. ⊠*143 E. Main St./U.S. 20* ☎*716/326–2830* ⊕*www. landmarkacres.com* ⇖*6 rooms, 7 suites* ♨*In-room: no phone, no TV (some), kitchen (some), refrigerator, Wi-Fi. In-hotel: Wi-Fi, parking (free), no kids under 12, no-smoking rooms* ⊟*D, MC, V.*

$$–$$$
Fodor'sChoice
★

🏨**William Seward Inn.** This lovely 1837 Greek Revival inn sits on a secluded, grassy property between Westfield and Chautauqua. Rooms are traditionally furnished with period antiques and reproductions: some are dressed in flirty florals and ruffles, others have a more tailored look, with handsome four-poster beds; a few have balconies and fireplaces. The modern-built Carriage House rooms are the largest, with double whirlpool baths. Big, gourmet breakfasts, which could include amaretto-soaked French toast or four-cheese-and-tarragon omelet, are served in the cozy dining room (⇨ *Where to Eat*). **Pros:** new owners (2008) renovating all rooms in detailed period style; congenial rather than stuffy; care taken in details. **Cons:** bathrooms in historic part of inn are small and quirky; some rooms have only full-size bed. ⊠*6645 S. Portage Rd., 3 mi east of Westfield town center* ☎*716/326–4151* ⊕*www.williamsewardinn.com* ⇖*12 rooms* ♨*In-room: DVD (some), Internet, Wi-Fi. In-hotel: restaurant, room service, spa, bicycles, laundry service, Wi-Fi, parking (free), some pets allowed, no-smoking rooms* ⊟*AE, D, MC, V* ⊚*BP.*

CHAUTAUQUA AND MAYVILLE

10 mi southeast of Westfield.

The 856-acre village of Chautauqua, bordering Chautauqua Lake, is something of a Mayberry, with Victorian homes lining its narrow, hodgepodge streets. It's overtaken entirely by the Chautauqua Institution in the summer months, attracting as many as 180,000 visitors each season. Few cars are allowed inside the town gates (which serve as ticket collection booths for the institution); parking lots are at the gates. From late June through August, the institution fee is levied on anyone passing through the gates, even if you're overnighting on the grounds. Entry is free off-season.

Immediately outside the Chautauqua gates, you're in Mayville, though its center lies a few miles northwest. The small town of around 1,700 residents contains a number of restaurants and reasonably priced hotels in close proximity to the institution.

WHAT TO SEE

★ **The Chautauqua Institution.** It all began in 1874, when John Heyl Vincent, a Methodist minister, and Lewis Miller, an industrialist, set up a training center for Sunday-school teachers here. The Chautauqua Institution rapidly grew into a summer-long cultural encampment. More than 2,000 events take place here in summer, including lectures, art exhibitions, outdoor symphonies, theater, dance performances, opera, and open-enrollment classes.

> ### AMISH COUNTRY
>
> Chautauqua and Cattaraugus counties have three Amish communities, most in Chautauqua County. From their workshops and farms dotting the countryside they sell handmade furniture, quilts, rugs, jams, maple syrup, produce, and much more. The **Chautauqua County Visitors Bureau** (☎ 866/908–4569 ⊕ www. tourchautauqua.com) has downloadable maps with shops marked. Click on "Shopping" on the site.

The village has small winding streets lined with gas lights and beautiful Victorian houses, which are often outfitted in bright colors, turrets, multiple gables, and gingerbread trim. The **Miller Bell Tower** is the most recognizable landmark on the lakeshore and has become the symbol of the institution; tunes are played three or four times a day, and the Miller Bell is rung manually 15 minutes before amphitheater lectures and evening programs.

Seats for the Chautauqua Symphony Orchestra and other large events held at the 6,500-seat **Chautauqua Amphitheater** are on a first-come, first-served basis. Musicians as diverse as Peter, Paul, and Mary; 10,000 Maniacs; Glenn Miller; and Natalie Cole have performed in the theater, which has a roof and houses an enormous pipe organ. **Norton Memorial Hall,** a 1,365-seat art-deco building, is where the Chautauqua Opera Company presents four English-language operas each season.

The institution's recreational activities complement its cultural opportunities. You may fish, swim, play tennis, golf, or rent sailboats, motorboats, or canoes from the concessions on the lake. The village, a National Historic District, also includes B&Bs, hotels, inns, guesthouses, apartments, and condominiums, as well as several restaurants and eateries. You may use a car when dropping off and picking up your luggage, but otherwise car usage is extremely limited here. Lots near the entrance gates offer daily and long-term paid parking. A free shuttle bus and tram travel through the campus during the season. Narrated bus tours of the grounds are available. ⊠ *1 Ames Ave.* ☎ *716/357–6250, 716/357–6200, or 800/836–2787* ⊕ *www.ciweb.org* ✉ *Day/evening pass (7 AM–midnight) $53; discounts for partial-day passes and late-season visits* ☉ *Late June–Aug.*

SPORTS AND THE OUTDOORS

BOAT TOURS The **Chautauqua Belle** steamship makes trips around Chautauqua Lake, departing from Mayville and Chautauqua. ☎716/269–2355 ⊕*www.chautauquabelle.com* ☒*$15* ⊙*Memorial Day–Labor Day*. The yacht-like **Summer Wind** has sightseeing, breakfast, brunch, lunch, dinner, and entertainment cruises, departing from Lucille Ball Memorial Park. ☎716/763–7447 or 716/665–2628 ⊕*www.thesummerwind. com* ☒*$16–$80* ⊙*Mid-May–mid-Oct.; check Web site for current schedule.*

GOLF The best golf course in the area is 25 mi southwest of Chautauqua at the **Peek'n Peak Resort** (☒*1405 Old Rd., Clymer* ☎716/355–4141 ⊕*www.pknpk.com*). The 18-hole, par-72 upper course regularly hosts PGA tournaments. The 18-hole lower course is fun, too, but lacks the impressive views. On-site are a driving range, putting practice area, and pro shop. In winter, the resort opens its 27 downhill runs (ranging from beginner to black-diamond) to skiers and snowboarders. It also has snow tubing and cross-country and snowmobiling trails.

The Donald Ross–designed, 18-hole course at the **Chautauqua Golf Club** (☒*4731 W. Lake Rd., Chautauqua* ☎716/357–6211 ⊕*golf.ciweb.org*) has been a fixture in Chautauqua since 1924; a second 18-hole course was opened in 1994. Both courses are par-72. A practice facility has a driving range and putting greens.

NIGHTLIFE AND THE ARTS

FESTIVALS
AND FAIRS
Craft Festivals at the Chautauqua Institution. Two annual shows are held in early July and again in mid-August, during the Chautauqua Institution season. More than 60 artists and craftspeople participate, displaying their paintings, jewelry, pottery, carvings, and other works. ⊕*Chautauqua Craft Alliance, Box 89, Mayville 14757* ☎716/753–0240 ⊕*www. chautauquacraftalliance.org.*

WHERE TO EAT

Despite the cultural offerings of the Chautauqua Institution, quality culinary options in the immediate area are few. Locals frequently stray to Bemus Point, Jamestown, and Westfield for fine dining.Reservations are necessary in summer.

$$
ITALIAN
✗**Olive's.** In the Chautauqua Suites hotel, this restaurant puts a twist on traditional in northern Italian dishes such as seared salmon in a pinot grigio–butter sauce and slow-roasted pork served in the style of osso buco with an herb-reduction-and-mascarpone polenta. Lunches consist of pasta, paninis, and pizzas—the Calvatore is topped with cremini and portobello mushrooms, truffle oil, and fontina. Chef Andrew Culver has worked at Washington, D.C.'s Mandarin Oriental, and at the White House. Some pastries—such as a lemon butter-cream tart—are imports from the owners' Bonjour Cafe & Patisserie, on Mayville's main street. ☒*Chautauqua Suites, 215 W. Lake Rd., Mayville* ☎716/753–2331 🖶*AE, D, DC, MC, V.*

$$
AMERICAN
✗**Webb's Captain's Table Restaurant.** The restaurant, which serves American fare with an emphasis on seafood, has a deck overlooking the lake. Dishes include broiled au gratin sea scallops, blackened wild Atlantic

salmon, prime rib, veal cordon bleu, and vegetable lasagna. Some local wines and brews (12–18 on tap), as well as picks from around the world, accompany meals. ⊠*115 W. Lake Rd./Rte. 394, Mayville* ☎*716/753–3960* ⊟*AE, D, MC, V* ☽*Daily 11:30* AM*–11:30* PM.

WHERE TO STAY

The Chautauqua Institution publishes an extensive list of on-campus accommodations, including apartments, houses, condominiums, hotels, inns, and rooms in denominational houses operated by various religious groups. The list is available on the institution Web site, or you may request a copy by telephone. Some condos are available on a weekly basis, although most apartments are available only during the nine-week season. Many people who attend the summer program return year after year, so places tend to book up early. Mayville, Bemus Point, and Jamestown are all close enough to be viable options if you're attending the institution.

$$$$ ⊡ **Athenaeum Hotel.** One of few options within the Chautauqua Institution gates, this Victorian hotel faces Chautauqua Lake and is steps from the amphitheater. Opened in 1881, the Athenaeum frequently hosted Thomas Edison and was one of the first electrified hotels in the country. These days, however, modern advances (like central air-conditioning) are lacking, furnishings are threadbare, and the building is in dire need of restoration. It's pricey for the quality of rooms, though three meals a day are included. We've included the hotel in this book not because we strongly recommend it but because it is one of only two hotels on the grounds of the institute, and for some, location trumps quality and cost. Dinner (for those not staying at the hotel) is a five-course prix-fixe affair. **Pros:** fantastic location if attending the Chautauqua Institution; friendly staff; good food. **Cons:** deteriorated; expensive; parking lot is a golf-cart ride or five-minute walk away. ⊠*26 S. Lake Dr., Chautauqua* ☎*800/821–1881 or 716/357–4444* ⊕*www.ciweb.org/athenaeum-home* ⇶*155 rooms* &*In-room: refrigerator (some). In-hotel: restaurant, room service, laundry service, Wi-Fi, parking (paid), no-smoking rooms* ⊟*AE, D, MC, V* ☽*Closed early Sept.–mid-June* ⦿|*FAP.*

$–$$ ⊡ **Peek'n Peak Resort & Spa.** A quiet retreat for golf lovers or skiers, Peek'n Peak also has a nice spa. Lodging options range from inn rooms with two queen beds to detached, multistory Clubhomes with five bedrooms, five bathrooms, full kitchens, and two-car garages. With the exception of units in the Inn at the Peak, which are dated (but share a building with the dining room, pub, spa, and pool), lodgings are updated, clean, and spacious, with large windows and some fairways and slopes views. **Pros:** good group and off-season rates; friendly staff; beautiful surroundings. **Cons:** isolated; rooms in main inn inferior. ⊠*1405 Old Rd., Clymer, 25 mi southwest of Mayville* ☎*716/355–4141* ☎*716/355–4141* ⊕*www.pknpk.com* ⇶*107 inn rooms, 12 suites, 12 Fairways suites, 84 condos, 50 town homes, 13 detached houses* &*In-room: DVD (some), kitchen (some), refrigerator (some), Wi-Fi. In-hotel: 2 restaurants, bar, golf courses, tennis court, pool, gym, spa, children's programs (ages 4–12), laundry facilities, parking (free), no-smoking rooms* ⊟*AE, D, MC, V.*

$$–$$$ 📺**The Spencer Hotel & Spa.** Rooms at this Victorian hotel are individually decorated and named for great authors. The decor varies considerably from room to room. The Agatha Christie room is decked out with fern-print wallpaper that has a sort of psychedelic effect; the Isabel Allende room has cactus murals on the walls and a desert-hue theme. Some rooms are small and cramped, whereas others are quite capacious. Many have hand-painted murals or faux finishes on the walls or ceilings. Gardens surround the inn, which stays open all year. During the Chautauqua Institution season, the minimum required stay is a week. **Pros:** central air; massage treatments. **Cons:** small, unimpressive breakfast; weak Wi-Fi signal; limited parking near hotel (most parking in a lot several blocks away). ✉*25 Palestine Ave., Chautauqua* ☎*716/357-3785 or 800/398-1306* ⊕*www.thespencer.com* ➴*19 rooms, 4 suites* ⌂*In-room: DVD (some), kitchen (some), Internet, Wi-Fi. In-hotel: bicycles, Internet terminal, Wi-Fi, parking (free), some pets allowed, no-smoking rooms* ▤*MC, V* ⏹*CP.*

$–$$ 📺**Webb's Lake Resort.** The family-owned and -run complex across the street from Chautauqua Lake includes a two-story motel, Webb's Captain's Table restaurant (⇨*Where to Eat*), a candy store dating from 1947, and an 18-hole miniature-golf course. Rooms have traditional-contemporary furnishings; a couple have fireplaces. Furnishings are outdated and bathrooms smaller in the older portion of the hotel. All rooms facing the road have whirlpool tubs and balconies. **Pros:** all rooms to be renovated by 2011; nice restaurant. **Cons:** obstructed view of lake; on busy road; some ongoing renovations until 2011. ✉*115 W. Lake Rd./Rte. 394, Mayville* ☎*716/753-2161* ⊕*www.webbsworld. com* ➴*50 rooms, 1 suite* ⌂*In-room: refrigerator (some), Internet, Wi-Fi. In-hotel: restaurant, bar, pool, gym, water sports, laundry facilities, Internet terminal, parking (free), some pets allowed, no-smoking rooms* ▤*AE, D, MC, V.*

BEMUS POINT

9 mi southeast of Chautauqua.

Bemus Point is the largest community on the north shore of Chautauqua Lake. Its main attractions are its waterfront and its handful of good restaurants. In summer the population swells with vacationers who come from all over New York and Canada to enjoy the lake and the Chautauqua Institution, which is on the opposite shore.

SPORTS AND THE OUTDOORS
Long Point State Park. This busy, 320-acre park on Chautauqua Lake has a swimming beach, changing rooms, a modern boat-launch facility, a marina, and a playground. You may hike, bike, snowmobile, and cross-country ski here, or simply have a picnic. Muskellunge are a draw for fishing enthusiasts, but the lake also has bass, pike, and other fish. In winter you may ice fish. ✉*4459 Rte. 430* ☎*716/386-2722* ⊕*nysparks. state.ny.us/parks* 🅿*Parking $5 May–Sept.* ☉*Daily dawn–dusk.*

WHERE TO EAT

¢ ╳ **Bemus Point Inn.** The tablecloths are
AMERICAN plastic, the floors are linoleum, and everyone seems to know everyone else at this no-frills greasy spoon, famed locally for its huge cinnamon rolls. The all-American menu includes sandwiches (e.g., grilled cheese and bacon) served with chips and a pickle, breakfast all day, and homemade pies. It closes at 2 PM. ✉ *4958 Main St.* ☎ *716/386–2221* ▭ *No credit cards* ⊘ *No dinner.*

$$ ╳ **Italian Fisherman.** Eat indoors or
SEAFOOD outside on the multilevel covered deck overlooking Chautauqua Lake. (Heat torches warm deck diners up on cool days.) The eatery is known for seafood and Italian dishes—cioppino, large sautéed shrimp with spicy tomato sauce over pasta, grilled catch of the day. The drinks list is extensive, and the place often hosts live music and other entertainment. ✉ *61 Lakeside Dr.* ☎ *716/386–7000* ▭ *AE, D, MC, V* ⊘ *Closed late Sept.–Apr. No lunch in Sept.*

> **CONCERTS BY THE LAKE**
>
> Every Saturday and Sunday in summer visiting artists—ranging from classical to jazz to rock to bluegrass—and/or the Bemus Bay Pops Orchestra perform on a floating (anchored) stage beside the Italian Fisherman restaurant. On summer weeknights, there are outdoor movies, dance performances, and other shows. Boaters sidle right up to the stage to watch and listen. The best thing? It's always free.

JAMESTOWN

11 mi southeast of Bemus Point.

Jamestown, founded in 1811, is at the eastern end of Chautauqua Lake. One of its claims to fame is that it was the childhood home of Lucille Ball. It was here that Ball first performed her wacky comedy acts, which are now commemorated every year during the Lucille Ball Hometown Celebration. Another well-known Jamestown native was Roger Tory Peterson, who wrote and illustrated the *Peterson Field Guides,* which document the flora and fauna of various U.S. regions.

Lucille Ball's grave is in Jamestown, in the Lake View Cemetery, just down the street from the Comfort Inn and Hampton Inn. Her birthplace is at 69 Stewart Avenue, and her childhood home is at 59 Lucy Lane, in Celoron, 3 mi west of Jamestown.

WHAT TO SEE

Fenton History Center. Reuben Fenton, governor of New York from 1865 to 1869, had this brick Italianate mansion built in 1863. It contains Victorian period rooms (some quite ornate) and exhibits showcasing the history of Chautauqua Lake, the life and career of Lucille Ball, and Jamestown's Swedish and Italian communities. Also of interest are the archival and genealogical library and the Civil War exhibits. ✉ *67 Washington St.* ☎ *716/664–6256* ⊕ *www.fentonhistorycenter. org* ▭ *$5* ⊘ *Early Jan.–Thanksgiving, Mon.–Sat. 10–4; Thanksgiving–early Jan., Mon.–Sat. 10–4, Sun. 1–4*

Lucille Ball–Desi Arnaz Center. Ball's turquoise-and-silver-sequin cowgirl costume from a 1976 "Donny and Marie" episode, video interviews with childhood friends, and original *Here's Lucy* scripts are a few of the items on display in the Lucy-Desi Museum, which follows the lives and careers of the two comedy stars. The adjoining Desilu Playhouse centers solely on the *I Love Lucy* show, with a replica of the couple's TV apartment, a 1953 Emmy, and an interactive display where you can try your hand at the Vitameatavegamin commercial. ■ TIP→Two annual festivals—Lucy-Desi Days, over Memorial Day weekend, and Lucille Ball's Birthday Celebration, in early August—celebrate the two stars. ⊠ *10 W. 3rd St.* ☎ *716/484–0800* ⊕ *www.lucy-desi.com* 🖾 *$15* ☉ *Mon.–Sat. 10–5:30, Sun. 1–5.*

Roger Tory Peterson Institute of Natural History. Named for Jamestown native and noted naturalist Roger Tory Peterson (1908–96), who wrote the seminal *Field Guide to the Birds* in 1934 (which spawned today's best-selling Peterson Field Guides series), this 27-acre center seeks to educate children about nature. You may hike the wooded trails, or explore one of the natural-history exhibits. The gallery shows a selection of works by Peterson and others. ⊠ *311 Curtis St.* ☎ *716/665–2473 or 800/758–6841* ⊕ *www.rtpi.org* 🖾 *$5* ☉ *Center Tues.–Sat. 10–4, Sun. 1–5; grounds daily dawn–dusk.*

OFF THE BEATEN PATH

Panama Rocks. The rock outcropping here, 14 mi west of downtown Jamestown, spans 25 acres. The park has caves, 60-foot-high cliffs, and crevices said to have been used by American Indians for shelter and as places to keep meat cool in summer. Outlaws are also said to have used the rocks as hiding places. As you hike along the 1-mi self-guided trail here, you may find rare mosses, wildflowers, ferns, and oddly shaped tree roots. ⊠ *11 Rock Hill Rd., Panama* ☎ *716/782–2845* ⊕ *www. panamarocks.com* 🖾 *$6* ☉ *May–mid-Oct., daily 10–5.*

WHERE TO EAT

$$$
ECLECTIC
★

✕**MacDuff's.** An intimate and elegant dining experience awaits you at this eight-table restaurant in an 1873 town house with red-clothed tables, upholstered Queen Anne chairs, and brass chandeliers and sconces. The menu leans French in preparation, but Continental in substance: the twin tenderloin fillets with port, Stilton cheese, and green-peppercorn sauce is the signature dish, or you might try veal scaloppine in a blackberry cream sauce. Desserts include lavender crème brûlée and homemade orange ice cream served in a bittersweet chocolate shell. The extensive wine and liquor selection includes 40 single-malt Scotches. ⊠ *317 Pine St.* ☎ *716/664–9414* ▤ *AE, MC, V* ☉ *Closed Sun. No lunch.*

$$
CONTINENTAL

✕**Scallion Bistro.** A 5-mi drive west of town (and easily accessible from Chautauqua) on a block-long cobblestone street ending at the lake, Scallion Bistro is a favorite of locals in the know. Try citrus-glazed salmon over fruit salsa, topped with horseradish butter and fried parsnips; or pan-seared chicken breast wrapped with Italian ham, over lobster succotash. There's a Tuscan feel, with faux-finish walls and hanging colored-glass lamps and an "arcaded" wall separating the dining room from bar. It's nice enough for a romantic dinner, but low-key enough to foster boisterous conversation and to have a (low- to-no-volume) flat-screen TV in the bar. ⊠ *60 Chautauqua Ave., Lakewood* ☎*716/763–0051* ⚛*Reservations essential* ▤*AE, D, MC, V* ⊙*Closed Sun. and Mon. No lunch*.

¢   ✕**Timothy's.** In addition to great coffee, this low-key java joint decorated
AMERICAN   in bright, primary colors serves breakfast sandwiches, bakery items, and desserts. Lunches are panini and salads, including some vegetarian options. It's open 8 AM–6 PM weekdays and 9 AM–3 PM Saturday. ⊠*106 E. 3rd St.* ☎*716/484–8904* ▤*No credit cards* ⊙*No dinner. Closed Sun*.

WHERE TO STAY

$$ ▦**Hampton Inn & Suites.** A step up from the Comfort Inn across the street, this fairly new hotel (built in 2006), has a large breakfast and lobby area and updated rooms in neutrals with cherrywood headboards, the Hampton's signature striped wallpaper, and large bathrooms with granite countertops, slate floors, and some Jacuzzi tubs. Some have views of trees and a cemetery. The hotel is entirely no-smoking. **Pros:** right off thruway and Lucille Ball's grave site; the nicest chain option in town. **Cons:** tiny pool looking directly onto parking lot; some rooms have views of McDonald's and a gas station; no Wi-Fi. ⊠*4 W. Oak Hill Rd.* ☎*716/484–7829* ⊕*www.hamptoninn.com* ⇋*71 rooms, 28 suites* ⚘*In-room: refrigerator, Internet. In-hotel: pool, gym, laundry facilities, laundry service, Internet terminal, Wi-Fi, no-smoking rooms* ▤*AE, D, DC, MC, V* ⦿*CP*.

$ ▦**Radisson Hotel Jamestown.** This eight-story chain hotel is in Jamestown's business district. Rooms have luxurious mattresses, large windows, cushy leather desk chairs, granite-countertop bathrooms, and traditional furnishings in muted color schemes. The hotel was completely renovated in 2008. **Pros:** walking distance to Lucy-Desi Museum and historic downtown; great views of city and hills beyond on upper floors. **Cons:** immediate area dead on weekends. ⊠*150 W. 4th St.* ☎*716/664–3400 or 800/528–8791* ⇋*143 rooms, 3 suites* ⊕*www. radisson.com* ⚘*In-room: refrigerators (some), Wi-Fi. In-hotel: 2 restaurants, room service, bar, pool, gym, laundry facilities, laundry service, Wi-Fi, parking (free), no-smoking rooms* ▤*AE, D, DC, MC, V*.

ELLICOTTVILLE

35 mi northeast of Jamestown.

Holiday Valley, a popular regional ski resort, is Ellicott's main draw. This is where Buffalo and Rochester area residents go to get in some weekend skiing. But the small village also has a cute main street with some good restaurants, an old-fashioned candy shop, and clothing boutiques.

WHAT TO SEE

☾   **Griffis Sculpture Park.** More than 200 sculptures by prominent local,
★   national, and international artists are displayed in a variety of natural settings at this 400-acre park. Kids enjoy touching and climbing on the pieces, which actually is allowed here. About 10 mi of hiking trails vein

the park, which is 7 mi north of Ellicottville. Ask for directions at your hotel or bring a map of the area, as it's a bit off the beaten path. ⊠*6902 Mill Valley Rd., East Otto* ☎*716/667–2808* ⊕*www.griffispark.org* ⊠*$5* ☉*May–Oct., daily dawn–dusk.*

Nannen Arboretum. Begun in 1977 as an adjunct to the Cornell Cooperative Extension facility, the arboretum occupies 8 acres with more than 400 unusual trees and shrubs. The herb garden has 300-plus species, and there's a popular Japanese meditation garden. The entrance is marked by a little shack on the far side of the Cooperative Extension Center parking lot. ⊠*28 Parkside Dr.* ☎*716/699–2377 or 716/945–5200* ⊠*Free* ☉*Daily dawn–dusk.*

SPORTS AND THE OUTDOORS

SKI AREA The **Holiday Valley Resort** (⊠*Rte. 219* ☎*716/699–2345* ⊕*www.holidayvalley.com*) has a 750-foot vertical drop, 56 trails, 95% snow-making coverage, a snowboarding area, three base lodges, 13 lifts, and a skiing and snowboarding school. For night skiing, 37 trails are lighted. Trails in the golf-course area may be used by cross-country skiers and snowshoers. Full-day lift tickets are $57. The resort includes ski-out-your-back-door accommodations (⇨*Where to Stay, below*). In summer the 18-hole golf course, golf school, tennis courts, three pools, and mountain-biking trails are the main attractions.

WHERE TO EAT

$$ ✕**Dina's.** This relaxed space has a rustic elegance exemplified by a long
AMERICAN polished-wood bar, pressed-tin ceiling, unfinished-wood columns and
★ bare beams, antler chandeliers, banquette seating, and an exposed-brick wall with artfully peeling cream-color paint. Hearty fare like dry-rub ribs with a side of mac-and-cheese are joined on the menu by pasta and pizzas, including one with red-pepper pesto, prosciutto, cappicola, fresh mozzarella, goat cheese, and basil. Locals frequently stop in just for the cakes, pies, and oversize cookies, which you can savor with a cappuccino. Breakfast is served daily. ⊠*15 Washington St.* ☎*716/699–5330* ⊟*AE, D, MC, V.*

$ ✕**Ellicottville Brewing Company.** The trendy, rough-hewn microbrewery
AMERICAN restaurant draws a young crowd. The shepherd's pie is popular, and the menu also includes English-style fish-and-chips and assorted grilled steaks. You may eat outside in the German beer garden, which has a brick patio and vines climbing the walls. Tours of the brewery are available. This is the original; there's a Fredonia offshoot as well. ⊠*28A Monroe St.* ☎*716/699–2537* ⊟*AE, MC, V* ☉*Closed Mon. in May, June, and Sept.–Nov.*

WHERE TO STAY

The ski season is the peak season here.

$$–$$$ 🏨**Inn at Holiday Valley.** The inn is at the base of the Holiday Valley ski resort's (⇨*Sports and the Outdoors, above*) Sunrise Quad ski lift. In winter a free shuttle brings guests to the main chalet. All rooms have patios or balconies, most with mountain views; suites have cathedral ceilings, fireplaces, wet bars, and jetted tubs. The decor is traditional but streamlined. Other pluses: an outdoor hot tub, flat-screen TVs in all

rooms, and facilities for hiking, biking, cross-country skiing and snow-shoeing in addition to the downhill trails. In late 2009, the resort will open another lodging option, the 79-condo-unit Tamarack Hotel. **Pros:** suites very large; ski lifts and golf course right outside your door. **Cons:** indoor pool small; room decor somewhat outdated. ⊠*681 Rte. 219 S* ☎*716/699–2345 or 800/323–0020* ⊕*www.holidayvalley.com* ➪*95 rooms, 7 suites* ⚭*In-room: refrigerator (some), Internet. In-hotel: res-taurant, bar, golf course, pool, gym, spa, bicycles, laundry facilities, parking (free), no-smoking rooms* ⊟*AE, D, DC, MC, V* ⽥*CP.*

$–$$ 🏨 **Jefferson Inn of Ellicottville.** White rockers sit on a wraparound porch of this Victorian house just off Ellicottville's main strip, within walking distance of shops, restaurants, and bars. The B&B rooms are homey, with simple furnishings; the suite has a sitting area with a fireplace. The efficiencies are suitable for those with children or pets. A three-course breakfast is served at a communal table (not included for efficiency guests). **Pros:** thoughtful extras like sweets, tea and coffee, and cold drinks at all hours; luxurious mattresses; within walking distance of Ellicottville's main drag; outdoor hot tub. **Cons:** king beds are two twins pushed together; some furnishings and accents outdated. ⊠*3 Jefferson St.* ☎*716/699–5869 or 800/577–8451* ⊕*www.thejeffersoninn.com* ➪*4 rooms, 1 suite, 2 efficiencies* ⚭*In-room: kitchen (some), no TV (some), DVD (some), Internet. In-hotel: some pets allowed, no-smoking rooms* ⊟*AE, D, MC, V* ⽥*BP.*

SALAMANCA

12 mi south of Ellicottville.

Salamanca, on the broad Allegheny River, has the distinction of being the only U.S. city on an American Indian reservation (the Allegany Indian Reservation). The region was settled by the Seneca Nation, which leases the land to the government. The small but well-executed Seneca Iroquois National Museum is worth a visit.

WHAT TO SEE

Salamanca Rail Museum. A fully restored 1912 passenger depot offers a fascinating look at the history of the Erie Lackawanna Railroad, whose anticipated arrival led to the creation of the city of Salamanca. Exhib-its include old switches and lanterns, an extensive collection of vin-tage photographs, and a restored red caboose outside. ⊠*170 Main St.* ☎*716/945–3133* ⊠*Donations accepted* ⊗*Apr. and Oct.–Dec., Tues.– Sat. 10–5, Sun. noon–5; May–Sept., Mon.–Sat. 10–5, Sun. noon–5.*

Seneca Iroquois National Museum. The history and current culture of the Seneca Nation and of the Iroquois Confederacy is explored at this museum on the Allegany Indian Reservation. Displays include a par-tially reconstructed longhouse, silver and beadwork, baskets, corn-husk items, sculptures, and paintings. ⊠*794–814 Broad St.* ☎*716/945–1738* ⊕*www.senecamuseum.org* ⊠*$5* ⊗*May–Nov., daily 9–5; Dec., Mar., and Apr., weekdays 9–5; call for hrs in Feb.*

NIGHTLIFE AND THE ARTS

A glitzy lobby with Seneca Nation–inspired hieroglyphs and green-lighted endemic-stone walls marks your entry to the **Seneca Allegany Casino** (⊠*777 Seneca Allegany Blvd., just south of Rte. 86* ☎*888/913-3377* ⊕*www.senecaalleganycasino.com*). The 22,000 square feet of gaming space encompasses around 2,300 machines, 40 table games, a bar and high-rollers' lounge, as well as a separate poker room, which is the only portion still owned by the Seneca Nation. The mega-complex has a hotel (⇨*Seneca Allegany Hotel, Where to Stay*), a salon and spa, and several restaurants, including the requisite buffet. Big-name acts from the Goo Goo Dolls to Brooks & Dunn have played the big stage.

WHERE TO STAY

$–$$ 🏨 **Seneca Allegany Hotel.** Opened in 2008 and due for another expansion of a couple of hundred rooms, this 11-story hotel is in a casino complex with restaurants, bars, a deli and two cafés, plus a spa-salon, large fitness center, and a rooftop pool with a great view toward Allegany State Park. Rooms include corner suites with 46-inch plasma TVs, standard king or queen rooms, and suites. All rooms have Jacuzzi tubs. **Pros:** at least partial forest-and-hills views from all rooms; very nice pool and full-size spa. **Cons:** smoking in casino is noticeable; casino lights and action a bit much for some. ⊠*777 Seneca Allegany Blvd., just south of Rte. 86* ☎*888/913–3377* ⊕*www.senecaalleganycasino. com* ⇦*212 rooms, 12 penthouse suites* ⌂*In-room: Internet. In-hotel: 4 restaurants, room service, bar, pools, gym, spa, no-smoking rooms* ▭*AE, D, DC, MC, V.*

ALLEGANY STATE PARK

★   *Northern park entrance in Salamanca, 65 mi south of Buffalo.*

Allegany State Park's 65,000 acres make this the largest park in the state system. More than 85 mi of trails vein the park, which encompasses forest, meadow, lakes and streams, and hills, and borders Pennsylvania's Allegheny National Forest to the south. Hikes here range from short, easy strolls to an 18-mi trek over rugged terrain. The park has sandy swimming areas, bridle trails, boat launches and rentals, fishing, miniature golf, mountain-bike rentals, tennis courts, and picnic areas. The 90 mi of snowmobiling trails are a big draw in winter. Lodging options (all year-round) include 424 tent and RV sites, 375 rustic winterized cabins with single beds (no bedding), and seven cottages with heat and electricity. The park's Red House Restaurant, at the Tudor administration building in the Red House area, is open seasonally. In general, the Quaker Area (western) portion of the park is more remote than the (eastern) Red House Area. ⊠*Entrances at I–86 Exits 18–21* 🏠 *2373 State Park Rte. 1, Ellicottville 14731* ☎*716/354–9121, 716/354–2182, 800/456–2267 camping reservations* ⊕*nysparks.state.ny.us* 🅿*Parking $7* ⊙*Daily dawn–dusk.*

SPORTS AND THE OUTDOORS

The park has 18 hiking trails that cover more than 50 mi. In winter, six of the trails, covering 25 mi, double as cross-country ski trails, and form the **Art Roscoe Ski Touring Area.** The same six trails are used for mountain biking in warm weather. Quaker Lake, within the park, has a boat launch and swimming beach; you can also swim at Red House Lake.

SNOWMOBILING

Snowmobiling is hugely popular in western New York. Chautauqua County alone has more than 400 mi of groomed trails. Cattaraugus County also has nearly 400 mi of snowmobile trails, not including the 90 mi of trails at Allegany State Park. You may also snowmobile in the Darien Lakes, Fort Niagara, Lake Erie, Letchworth, and Long Point state parks. Pick up trail maps at county tourism offices.

OLEAN

20 mi east of Salamanca.

Olean, founded in 1804, is a community of 16,000 nestled in hills formed by receding glaciers. It's home to St. Bonaventure University, two community colleges, and manufacturers of assorted goods from Cutco knives to Drusser Rand turbines. The old public library, a National Historic Landmark facing the tree-lined town square, has been converted into a restaurant (⇨ *Old Library Restaurant, Where to Eat*). From Olean you may follow a paved path—on foot, skates, or by bicycle—along the Allegheny River.

WHAT TO SEE

★ **Rock City.** Perched at the edge of the Allegany Mountains, Rock City is believed to have the largest exposure of quartz conglomerate in the world. Some of the towering prehistoric rock formations are several stories high. Pathways lead you over top and down through narrow crevices enclosed by huge boulders. Wear athletic footwear. ⊠ *505 Rock City Rd., 5 mi south of Olean on right* ☎ *716/372–7790* ⊕ *www. rockcitypark.com* ☜ *$4.50* ☉ *May–Oct., daily 9–6.*

WHERE TO EAT

$ ✕ **Beef 'N' Barrel.** This casual restaurant with round-back chairs and low-
AMERICAN hung stained-glass lamps is known for its generous portions, in-house bakery, and friendly staff. The menu is beef focused, with a special emphasis on roast-beef sandwiches (including the beloved French dip, with a side of au jus) and platters. Juicy roast beef is carved up and served on hard rolls; accompaniments may include German or American potato salad, baked beans, salad, mashed potatoes, fries, or coleslaw. Burgers, salads, and soups round out the menu. ⊠ *146 N. Union St.* ☎ *716/372–2985* ▤ *AE, D, DC, MC, V* ☉ *Closed Sun.*

$$ ✕ **Old Library Restaurant.** In a National Historic Landmark building,
ECLECTIC what was the town library, built in 1910 with funds from Andrew Carnegie, was converted to a restaurant in 1983. It retains most of its original architecture—parquet flooring, stained-glass windows, inlaid ceilings. Dining is in hushed, bookshelf-lined, front "library" rooms or

a mezzanine overlooking a central atrium. The menu is diverse, with Italian, French, and American dishes. Six-cheese ravioli is served with pesto cream and sautéed spinach; sautéed antelope medallions come with peppercorn sauce; a surf-and-turn combo joins New York strip steak and jumbo scampi. Sunday brunch is served. ⊠ *120 S. Union St.* ☎*716/373–9804* ⊟*AE, D, MC, V* ☉*No lunch.*

WHERE TO STAY

¢ ☐**Old Library Bed & Breakfast.** The 1895 Victorian B&B, facing the tree-lined main square, has original oak, mahogany, and maple woodwork, including parquet floors, and stained-glass windows. Guest rooms, which vary considerably in size, are generally outfitted in a country look, with period antiques and some brass beds; new mattresses were installed in all rooms in 2008. The Old Library restaurant is next door. **Pros:** good restaurant; great price. **Cons:** basement rooms somewhat dreary; could use some room-furnishing upgrades; no tubs (showers only) in some rooms. ⊠ *120 S. Union St.* ☎*716/373–9804 or 877/241–4347* ⊕*www.oldlibraryrestaurant.com* ⇴*7 rooms, 2 suites* ☖*In-room: Wi-Fi. In-hotel: restaurant, room service, no-smoking rooms* ⊟*AE, D, DC, MC, V* ⦿*BP.*

The Finger Lakes

WORD OF MOUTH

"Ithaca and Geneva, although beautiful, are not as quaint as Skaneateles. If you want quaint go with Skaneateles. If you want great access to the wineries Ithaca and Geneva are great locations . . . and Belhurst Castle always pleases."

—annikany

"The views along the Gorge Trail [in Watkins Glen State Park] are absolutely stunning and quite overwhelming. We've hiked in the Grand Canyon and when we first experienced this area last October [we] were amazed at the comparable beauty and intimacy of this area."

—natf

Updated by
Shannon Kelly

The Finger Lakes stretch like narrow north–south slashes across western central New York. Their names evoke the tribes of the Iroquois Confederacy that dominated this area for more than two centuries. From east to west, the lakes are Otisco, Skaneateles, Owasco, Cayuga, Seneca, Keuka, Canandaigua, Honeoye, Canadice, Hemlock, and Conesus.

Iroquois legend has it that the Finger Lakes were formed when the Great Spirit placed his hand in blessing on this favored land, leaving behind an imprint. Geologists offer another explanation: retreating Ice Age glaciers created the lakes about a million years ago. The intense grinding pressure of the ice masses gouged deep holes in the earth, creating the long, narrow lakes that lie side by side, as well as deep gorges with their rushing falls (the Finger Lakes has more than 1,000 waterfalls, many around Ithaca), and the wide fertile valleys that extend south for miles.

Five of the six Iroquois nations inhabited the Finger Lakes Region. After the American Revolution, European-Americans received tracts of land here in lieu of pay for their war service. The region flourished as an agricultural heartland, bolstered by the construction of the Erie Canal, completed in 1825.

In the 19th and early 20th centuries the Finger Lakes became a land of dreamers and doers. Joseph Smith had a vision leading to the founding in 1830 of the Mormon Church at his home in Palmyra, north of Canandaigua. Elizabeth Cady Stanton and Susan B. Anthony worked for women's suffrage here, and Seneca Falls, site of the Women's Rights Convention of 1848, is considered the birthplace of the women's movement. Frederick Douglass proselytized for the abolition of slavery near his home in Rochester and Harriet Tubman, who lived in Auburn, smuggled slaves to Canada along the region's many Underground Railroad stops. George Eastman invented the Kodak camera in Rochester. Mark Twain wrote *The Adventures of Huckleberry Finn* at his summer home in Elmira. Glenn H. Curtiss put Hammondsport on the aviation map by flying his *June Bug* just under a mile in 1908.

This rich history spawned institutions of higher learning and of the arts that continue to thrive: Rochester's world-famous Eastman School of Music, Ithaca's Cornell University, Syracuse University, and the Corning Glass Works (and Steuben Glass) and the Corning Museum of Glass, to name a few.

Much of the Finger Lakes region still shows its rural roots. Dairy farms, small villages, and stunning 19th-century architecture dot the landscape. Today the region thrives on its viticulture. Those deep glacial lakes create a microclimate that moderates temperatures along their

TOP REASONS TO GO

Wineries: Finger Lakes wineries are coming in to their own, and touring vineyards has become quite the industry for this part of the state. Follow the organized wine trails or just pop into a local winery for a tasting.

Gorges and waterfalls: "Ithaca is gorges," proclaim the bumper stickers, and it's true. The south-center Finger Lakes region is littered with canyons and waterfalls. Farther west is the dramatic Letchworth State Park and its 17-mi gorge.

Outdoor adventure: More than 25 state parks, a national wildlife refuge, a national forest, and all those lakes make for excellent hiking,

biking, boating, fishing, or just taking in the scenery.

History lessons: This corner of the country was a hotbed of change, innovation, and progressivism in the 19th century—a place where suffragists rabble-roused, secretaries of state orated, and abolitionists converged. Museums and historic homes pay tribute to these movers and shakers of centuries past.

Food: fresh and local: From roadside farm stands to winery restaurants, the Finger Lakes region seems to be experiencing a culinary renaissance, with chefs drawing from the abundance of this agriculturally rich region.

shores, protecting grapevines from cold winters and hot summers. The region has more than 100 wineries, and touring vineyards is one of the top tourist activities. Meanwhile, B&Bs are sprouting like weeds and restaurants are honing their menus to focus on the region's fresh bounty in produce, dairy, meat, and wine.

ORIENTATION AND PLANNING

GETTING ORIENTED

The major cities in the region are Rochester, in the region's northwest corner, and Syracuse, in the northeast corner. Interstate 90 (the New York State Thruway) links the two cities. The region's western boarder is Interstate 390, which runs north–south through Rochester; Interstate 81, the eastern border, crosses Interstate 90 in Syracuse. Ithaca, at the southernmost tip of Cayuga Lake, is a southern Finger Lakes hub.

The Finger Lakes are strung across the heart of the region, south of Interstate 90. Parallel to Interstate 90, Route 5/U.S. 20 travels (from west to east) through Canandaigua, Geneva, Seneca Falls, Auburn, and Skaneateles. The historic Erie Canal, part of the state park system, meanders its way west to east roughly parallel to Interstate 90. To the north lie the high bluffs and sandy beaches of Lake Ontario; the Chemung and Susquehanna rivers border the region on the south.

The Seaway Trail along Lake Ontario makes for spectacular driving or biking. Other scenic routes wind along and around the lakes, passing through villages and farmland. Many wineries lie along these roads,

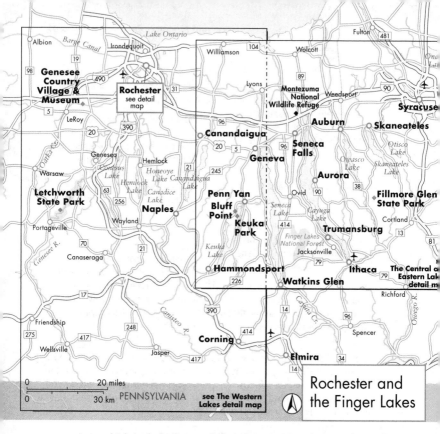

Rochester and
the Finger Lakes

which include Cayuga Lake's Routes 89 and 90, and Routes 14 and 414 on the western shore of Seneca Lake.

The region can be broken down into smaller areas and toured roughly from west to east and centered on the lakes, with Rochester and Syracuse serving as bookends. Another way to explore the region is to treat it as two halves, north and south; make your way across one half and then circle back across the other half.

PLANNING

WHEN TO GO

Lined with beaches, parks, campgrounds, and marinas, the Finger Lakes are most enjoyable in the warm-weather months. Autumn, when the leaves turn and grape-harvesting season is in full swing at the wineries, is actually the most popular time to visit. Still, Labor Day marks the end of the lake season and many lakeside attractions, restaurants, and places to stay are open only in summer and early fall (usually until early October). Most reopen in April or May. Winters are beautiful here: the hills are blanketed with snow and winter-sports enthusiasts will find ample diversions. Driving can be treacherous, however, especially near the lakes, so it's best to stay close to hubs like Syracuse, Rochester, and Ithaca.

GETTING HERE AND AROUND

Rochester and Syracuse are the main hubs for air travel in the Finger Lakes. Fly into these cities if you plan to travel along the Route 5/U.S. 20 road connecting Canandaigua, Geneva, Seneca Falls, Auburn, and Skaneateles. Ithaca and Corning have smaller airports and might be better bases for the southern tier of Hammondsport, Elmira, Watkins Glen, and Trumansburg.

You can also reach Rochester and Syracuse by Amtrak, a route that connects to Toronto and New York City. Other cities and towns in the Finger Lakes cannot be reached by train. Nearly all towns and cities have bus connections.

Once you arrive, driving is really the only way to get around. None of the cities have great public transportation systems. Interstate 90, the New York State Thruway, connects Rochester and Syracuse in about an hour and a half, but most of the historic Finger Lakes towns are along rural roads south of the interstate. Route 5/U.S. 20 is a fairly well-maintained roadway, but the smaller lakeside routes and winding, hilly roads around Ithaca and Watkins Glen can be treacherous in winter. Major routes to the west and east are Interstate 390, connecting Rochester to Corning, and Interstate 81, south of Syracuse to Binghamton (cut west to Ithaca on Route 13 at Cortland).

Wine tours, in limos, vans, or buses, are readily available around the major lakes.

RESTAURANTS

The larger cities offer a full range of dining options, from trendy restaurants to ethnic eateries. Ithaca and Rochester, in particular, are havens for vegetarian and ethnic fare. Some restaurants outside the urban areas are increasingly emphasizing fresh, local, and organic cuisine. Regional wines often show up on menus. (The region's Rieslings, which have garnered high praise, are perfect summer and early-fall sips.) But American restaurants, diners, family-style spots, and pizza parlors are still the norm; steaks, chops, and prime rib are standards, as are Italian-American dishes. ■ TIP → **For the full Finger Lakes experience, be sure to visit pick-your-own orchards, farmers' markets, and wine-tasting rooms.** The Web site of Edible Finger Lakes magazine (⊕ *www.ediblefingerlakes.com*) is a good resource, as are tourism boards and wine-trail organizations.

HOTELS

Lodging options in the cities range from full-service hotels to budget chain properties and individualized B&Bs. Outside the cities you're likely to find lodgings in converted farmhouses and mansions, where two-night-minimum stays are often required on weekends, especially in summer and early fall. The **Finger Lakes Bed & Breakfast Association** (☎ *800/695–5590* ⊕ *www.flbba.org*) has extensive B&B listings.

Many properties outside cities close in mid- to late fall and reopen close to Memorial Day. Book as far in advance as possible, particularly for summer and early fall. Lakeside rentals, from simple cottages to luxury homes, are good options for families and for stays of a week or longer. **Finger Lakes Premier Properties** (☎ *315/536–2201 or 888/414–5253* ✪ *www.fingerlakespremierproperties.com*) has a large selection of vacation rentals. Many tourism offices have information about vacation rentals.

WHAT IT COSTS					
	¢	$	$$	$$$	$$$$
RESTAURANTS	under $10	$10–$17	$18–$24	$25–$35	over $35
HOTELS	under $100	$100–$150	$151–$200	$201–$300	over $300

Restaurant prices are for a main course at dinner (or at the most expensive meal served). Hotel prices are for two people in a standard double room in high season, excluding tax.

VISITOR INFORMATION

Finger Lakes Visitors Connection (✉ *25 Gorham St., Canandaigua* ☎ *585/394–3915 or 877/386–4669* ✪ *www.visitfingerlakes.com*). **Finger Lakes Tourism Alliance** (✉ *309 Lake St., Penn Yan* ☎ *315/536–7488 or 800/530–7488* ✪ *www.fingerlakes.org*).

ROCHESTER

30 mi northwest of Canandaigua, 90 mi west of Syracuse.

First known as the Flour City in the early 1800s, for the mills that were powered by the Genesee River, Rochester became the Flower City when nurseries and seed production replaced the grain industry. Industrialists and entrepreneurs shaped the city at the turn of the 20th century, and photography pioneer George Eastman played a particularly key role. His Eastman Kodak Company is practically synonymous with the city and remains one of its top employers. Xerox and Bausch & Lomb were founded here as well, but today the city is as focused on its world-class educational institutions.

In downtown Rochester you can still see some nice examples of early-20th-century architecture, including the 1930 art-deco Times Square Building, topped with 42-foot aluminum wings pointing skyward. Neighborhoods east and southeast of the downtown core are worth a gander for their large Federal, Greek Revival, and Victorian homes. Corn Hill, Rochester's first residential neighborhood, is just blocks south of downtown. A mile or so to the east is the Park Avenue area of shops and restaurants, interspersed with tree-lined residential streets. To the north, the waterfront Charlotte (say it like a native: Shar-LOT) neighborhood has taverns, restaurants, and a rock-and-roll bar, but Ontario Beach Park is its point of pride.

Rochester is a vibrant city where theater, music, film, and visual arts flourish; almost every night there's a performance of some sort. This, along with the many parks, frequent festivals, professional sports teams, and proximity to the Finger Lakes wine trails make it a city worth visiting.

GETTING OUTDOORS

BIKING

The terrain in the region, although flat in many places, especially along the old railbeds that now serve as multipurpose trails, can be quite hilly. The terrain in the south has more hills, with some steep inclines. Roads are well paved, shoulders are wide, and traffic is relatively light.

The Canal Way Trail System follows the historic Erie Canal waterway. **NYCanal.com** (☎ *585/234–7708* ⊕ *www.nycanal.com*) provides information and maps online. The **Ontario Pathways Rail Trail** (☎ *585/234–7722* ⊕ *www. ontariopathways.org*), a former railway, is now a 23-mi multiuse trail. The **Keuka Outlet Trail** (⊕ *www. keukaoutlettrail.net*) is a 6-mi hiking and biking trail that begins in Penn Yan and snakes between Keuka and Seneca lakes.

The Web site of the Ithaca-based **Finger Lakes Cycling Club** (⊕ *www.flcycling.org*) has information about trails, tours, races, and local bike shops.

FISHING

Because of their unique physical attributes, each of the Finger Lakes is known for different species. Large- and smallmouth bass are found in all the lakes. Brown, lake, and rainbow trout inhabit most, except Conesus and Honeoye. Yellow perch, landlocked salmon, northern pike, pickerel, bullhead, and walleye are common, too. Cayuga Lake, the longest of the lakes, has the greatest fishing diversity. Seneca Lake is especially known for its rainbow and lake trout. Tiger muskie are found in Conesus and Otisco lakes.

The region is also veined with many rivers and streams teeming with trout, bass, pike, bullhead, and walleye. The major tributaries of Canandaigua, Cayuga, Keuka, Owasco, and Seneca lakes often offer up large specimens; most of these waters offer miles of public access. For game fishing, head north to Lake Ontario. Sodus Bay has some of the best fishing year-round, including ice fishing in winter.

All the lakes have municipal and/ or state launches and private marinas. Keuka, Seneca, and Cayuga have the greatest number of public launches. Some lakes, like Conesus and Honeoye, can be crowded in summer; others, such as Hemlock and Canadice lakes, are practically undeveloped. Boat rental is available at marinas. Charter boats are also available; check with the Finger Lakes Tourism Alliance or county tourism offices for details.

Fishing licenses and regulations may be obtained at town clerk's offices, fishing-gear retailers, or by phone from the state. For fish and wildlife information, sporting conditions, licenses, and a list of marinas, contact the **New York State Department of Environmental Conservation** (☎ *866/933–2257 fishing licenses, 845/256–3000 general information* ⊕ *www.dec.ny.gov*).

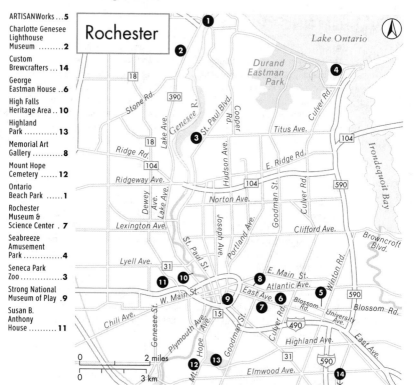

GETTING HERE AND AROUND

Rochester lies north of the Interstate 90 New York State Thruway. Auxiliary highways that lead into the city are Interstate 590, Interstate 490, and Interstate 390. Downtown, Interstate 490 becomes the Inner Loop, a beltway surrounding the city center. Rochester's Amtrak station and main bus terminal are downtown; the airport is southwest of downtown. Megabus drops off passengers at Eastview Mall, southeast of downtown. A car is essential for getting around the city.

Airport Information Rochester International Airport (✉ *1200 Brooks Ave., Rochester* ☎ *585/753-7000* ⊕ *www.monroecounty.gov*).

Bus Information Adirondack, Pine Hill, and New York Trailways (☎ *800/776-7548, 800/225-6815, or 800/858-8555* ⊕ *www.trailwaysny.com*). **Greyhound** (☎ *800/231-2222* ⊕ *www.greyhound.com*). **Megabus** (☎ *877/462-6342* ⊕ *www.megabus.com*).

Train Information Amtrak (☎ *800/872-7245* ⊕ *www.amtrak.com*).

VISITOR INFORMATION

Visit Rochester (✉ *45 East Ave., Suite 400, Rochester* ☎ *585/546-3070 or 800/677-7282* ⊕ *www.visitrochester.com*).

WHAT TO SEE

5 **ARTISANWorks.** Inside this former cannon factory, nearly every inch of the more than 60,000-square-foot bohemian art-gallery-meets-studio-space is chockablock with art, much of it for sale. Some of the 500,000 pieces have a pedigree: Roy Lichtenstein, Andy Warhol, Frank Lloyd Wright, and Gordon Parks, though about 80% of the collection is local. The eclectic space also includes artist studios, a dinner theater, a courtyard, and a two-story firehouse with a real 1958 pumper truck. The rooftop sculpture garden gives you a view of the city skyline. ⊠ *565 Blossom Rd., Suite L* ☎ *585/288–7170* ⊕ *www.artisanworks.net* ⊡ *$12* ⊙ *Fri. and Sat. 11–6, Sun. noon–5.*

2 **Charlotte Genesee Lighthouse Museum.** The lighthouse stands about a mile south of Lake Ontario, giving you an idea of how the landscape has changed since the 40-foot-tall stone structure was erected in 1822. In the 1960s a group of local high school students saved the structure—the second-oldest American lighthouse on Lake Ontario—from rumored demolition. ⊠ *70 Lighthouse St.* ☎ *585/621–6179* ⊕ *www. geneseelighthouse.org* ⊡ *Donations accepted* ⊙ *Early May–late Oct., weekends 1–5.*

14 **Custom BrewCrafters.** If you enjoy a microbrew at a Rochester bar or restaurant, chances are it was brewed here. The 6,000-square-foot brewery makes more than 50 beers (20 kegs at a time), which are served throughout western New York. Tours explain the brewing process, and free samples let you taste brews that have won at the Great American Beer Festival in Denver as well as at other national and local competitions. The 25-mi drive to the brewery from downtown (Route 31 to Route 65 south) takes you from city to country in about 20 minutes. ⊠ *93 Papermill St., Honeoye Falls* ☎ *585/624–4386* ⊕ *www.custombrewcrafters. com* ⊡ *Free* ⊙ *Weekdays noon–8, Sat. 10–6, Sun. noon–6. Brewery tours weekends on drop-in basis, weekdays by appointment.*

6 **George Eastman House.** The sprawling colonial-revival mansion, once the home of Eastman Kodak's founder, has been restored to its early-1900s appearance. The elephant head on the wall in the conservatory is an eye-catcher, and the rest of the house gives a glimpse into the life and times of the man who brought photography to the masses. Much of the second floor is used as gallery space. The grounds include a rock garden with scallop-shaped flower beds, a formal terrace garden with more than 90 types of perennials, a cutting garden, a lily pool, and a grape arbor. The **International Museum of Photography and Film,** connected to the mansion, has changing exhibits about the history of photography and film technology; the permanent collection includes tens of thousands of photos, books, and films as well as photographic equipment. Also here is the **Dryden Theatre,** which shows movies ($7) and hosts film festivals. ⊠*900 East Ave.* ☎*585/271–3361* ⊕*www. eastmanhouse.org* ☒*$10* ⊙*May daily 10–5; June–Apr., Tues., Wed., Fri., Sat. 10–5, Thurs. 10–8, Sun. 1–5. House tours Tues.–Sat. at 10:30 and 2, Sun. at 2. Garden tours May–Sept. Tues.–Sat. at 11:30 and 3, Sun. at 3.*

❿ **High Falls Heritage Area.** Stand on a bridge over the Genesee River, watch and listen to the High Falls cascading 96 feet, and feel the power that drove Rochester's flour mills in the 19th century. The Triphammer Forge, a reconstructed waterwheel, is one of the largest in the state. Frontier Field and Eastman Kodak world headquarters are across the street. The **High Falls entertainment district** has pubs, clubs, and restaurants, as well as frequent events in summer and a laser show every Thursday, Friday, and Saturday night from Memorial Day to Labor Day. The **High Falls Visitor Center** (⊠*60 Brown's Race* ☎*585/325– 2030* ☒*Free* ⊙*Wed.–Fri. 10–5, Sat. noon–6, Sun. 1–5*) has a museum, with interactive exhibits, that give an overview of Rochester history. ⊠*Commercial St. and Browns Race* ⊕*www.centerathighfalls.org.*

⓭ **Highland Park.** Established in 1888, this was Rochester's first public park. Site of the hugely popular **Lilac Festival,** Highland Park has more than 500 varieties of lilacs. Walking paths crisscross the park and lead to a reservoir that provides an unobstructed view for miles to the south. The **Lamberton Conservatory** (⊠*180 Reservoir Ave.* ☎*585/753–7270* ☒*$3* ⊙*Daily 10–4*), built in 1911, houses arid desert species and lush tropical vegetation. It's incredibly popular on snowy winter days. At the corner of Mt. Hope and Reservoir avenues, a block west of the Lamberton Conservatory, is the squat **Warner Castle** (☎*585/473–5130* ⊕*www.rcgc.org* ☒*$1 donation* ⊙*Tues.–Thurs. 9–4*). Headquarters of the Rochester Civic Garden Center, it has art exhibits and educational materials about gardening. ⊠*South and Highland Aves.* ☎*585/256– 4950* ⊕*www.monroecounty.gov* ☒*Free* ⊙*Park daily 6* AM–11 PM.

❽ **Memorial Art Gallery.** More than 5,000 years of art is contained within the 14 exhibit rooms at this museum, opened in 1913. Egyptian coffins, medieval tapestries, impressionist paintings, European masters, and African carvings are on permanent display. The collection of American art is strong and regional artists are represented and compete in juried shows here. ⊠ *University of Rochester, 500 University Ave.* ☎*585/276–8900* ⊕*www.mag.rochester.edu* ☒ *$10* ⊙*Wed.–Sun. 11–5, Thurs. 11–9. Tours Thurs. at 6:30, Fri. at 2, Sun. at 1.*

⓬ **Mount Hope Cemetery.** Formed by a glacier that left undulating terrain upon its retreat, the 196 rolling acres of this cemetery are as much a park as they are the final resting place for more than 370,000 people. Among the more famous laid to rest here are suffragist Susan B. Anthony and anti-slavery leader Frederick Douglass. The cemetery, dedicated in 1838, is one of the nation's oldest. Many headstones retain Victorian symbols such as the anchor, crown, obelisk, or sheaf of wheat. The city owns the cemetery, but a caretakers group called the Friends of Mount Hope Cemetery offers tours. ⊠*1133 Mt. Hope Ave.* ☎*585/428–7999* *cemetery, 585/428–7970 tours* ⊕*www.fomh.org* ✉*Free; Thurs. twilight tours $4* ☉*Daily dawn–dusk. Tour May–Oct., Sat. at 1, Sun. at 2 and 2:30; mid-May–early Aug. Thurs. twilight tours at 7* PM.

❶ **Ontario Beach Park.** The showcase of the Charlotte neighborhood, the restored park recalls its days as the "Coney Island of the North." The 1905 **Dentzel Carousel** ($1) has three rows of animals—pigs, giant rabbits, and giraffes as well as horses—and is one of only about six such Dentzel menagerie carousels still operating in the country. Free concerts are held on Wednesday nights in summer. To get here, take Lake Avenue all the way north until you reach Lake Ontario. ✉*Entrances on Lake and Beach Aves.* ☎*585/256–4950* ⊕*www.monroecounty.gov* ✉*Free* ☉*Daily 7* AM*–11* PM.

NEED A BREAK?

Finish your day at Ontario Beach Park with a true Rochester treat: **Abbott's Frozen Custard** (✉*4791 Lake Ave.* ☎*585/663–8770*). You can spot this Rochester institution, opened in 1926, by the line on a hot afternoon. The custards—thicker and creamier than ice cream due to a slow-churning process—are made fresh daily in old-fashioned flavors ranging from chocolate almond to black cherry to butterscotch.

❼ **Rochester Museum & Science Center.** Everyone in the family can play with hands-on exhibits that focus on science and technology and their impact on our daily lives, as well as some nature and local cultural-heritage exhibits. Highlights include Light Here/Light Now, an optics exhibit; the interactive Expedition Earth, which delves into how the region was formed; a Seneca Indian exhibit; and the **Strasenburgh Planetarium,** which presents astronomy and laser-light shows and large-format films about space and Earth. ✉*657 East Ave.* ☎*585/271–4320* ⊕*www. rmsc.org* ✉*Museum $10, planetarium $10* ☉*Mon.–Sat. 9–5, Sun. noon–5.*

❹ **Seabreeze Amusement Park.** The Jack Rabbit, a wooden roller coaster built in 1920, is the most famous ride at this park on the Lake Ontario shore. Sampling all the water rides, the log flume, the carousel, the bumper cars, and the midway makes for a very full day. ✉*4600 Culver Rd.* ☎*585/323–1900* ⊕*www.seabreeze.com* ✉*$23, $16 after 5* PM ☉*Mid-June–early Sept., Sun.–Thurs. noon–10, Fri. and Sat. noon–11; late May–mid-June, call for days and hrs.*

❸ **Seneca Park Zoo.** Exhibits at this zoo along the Genesee River include Rocky Coasts, providing aboveground and underwater viewing of a polar bear, penguins, and sea lions; A Step Into Africa, a re-creation of Tanzania's Ngorongoro Crater with African elephants and olive baboons; and a cougar exhibit in which you can crawl through a tunnel to see the cats up close. During your day in the wild, you might also spot Bornean orangutans, white rhinos, Arctic wolves, and meerkats, among other beasts. ✉*2222 St. Paul St.* ☎*585/336–7200* ⊕*www. senecaparkzoo.org* ✉*Nov.–Mar. $7, Apr.–Oct. $9* ☉ *Nov.–Mar., daily 10–4; Apr.–Oct., daily 10–5*

9 Strong National Museum of Play. Play is taken seriously at the second-largest children's museum in the country, home to the world's largest collection of toys, dolls, and play-related artifacts and to the **National Toy Hall of Fame.** Within its 282,000-square-foot footprint are interactive exhibits like Reading Adventureland, where you follow a yellow-brick road into a pop-up book of life-size literary creations; Sesame Street (created in collaboration with Sesame Workshop); a pint-size market where kids run the store; and an indoor butterfly garden and aquarium. Also on display are some of dolls and dollhouses of museum founder Margaret Woodbury Strong (1897–1969), who collected some 17,000 dolls throughout her life. ⊠ *1 Manhattan Sq.* ☎ *585/263–2700* ⊕ *www.strongmuseum.org* ⊑ *$10* ⊗ *Mon.–Thurs. 10–5, Fri. and Sat. 10–8, Sun. noon–5.*

11 Susan B. Anthony House. The west-side street where suffragist Susan B. Anthony lived from 1866 until her death in 1906 looks much like it did in her day. The tree out front is bigger, of course, but many of the neighboring houses still look the same. You can tour the three-story redbrick Victorian and picture Anthony working to get women the right to vote. The visitor center next door was the home of a sister. A park one block north has a statue of Anthony and friend Frederick Douglass having tea. ⊠ *17 Madison St.* ☎ *585/235–6124* ⊕ *www.susanbanthonyhouse. org* ⊑ *$6* ⊗ *Tues.–Sun. 11–5.*

SPORTS AND THE OUTDOORS

The Erie Canal has shifted from being a transportation route to a recreation area. You can rent a replica packet boat or join a public tour. Joggers and bicyclists enjoy a paved path alongside the waterway. Golfers can choose from nearly 60 area courses, and gardeners can glean ideas from the nearly two dozen parks, many designed by Frederick Law Olmsted. Birders flock to **Braddock Bay State Park** in Greece to watch for hawks and many other species.

Corn Hill Navigation (☎ *585/262–5661* ⊕ *www.samandmary.org* ⊑ *$13* ⊗ *May–Oct.; schedules vary*) offers cruises on the packet boat *Sam Patch* and the wooden double-decker the *Mary Jemison* along the Erie Canal May through October. The *Sam Patch* passes through a canal lock, leaving from 12 Schoen Place, in Pittsford. The boat was named for a 19th-century Evel Knievel who, after successfully leaping into Niagara Falls and into Rochester's High Falls (with a pet bear), met his maker upon his second plunge into High Falls in 1829. The *Mary Jemison* cruises past historic sights in downtown Rochester as the captain narrates. It leaves from Corn Hill Landing, at Exchange Boulevard and Plymouth Avenue South.

PARTICIPANT SPORTS

GOLF   The **Greystone Golf Club** (⊠ *1400 Atlantic Ave., Walworth* ☎ *800/810–2325* ⊕ *www.234golf.com*), about 15 mi east of Rochester, has a 7,200-yard links-style course that features changes in elevation and undulating greens. The open landing areas belie challenges on the many memorable holes. High-season greens fees for 18 holes (with cart) are $50–$58. The challenging, 18-hole championship course at **Mill Creek Golf Club** (⊠ *128 Cedars Ave., Churchville* ☎*585/889–4110* ⊕*www.millcreekgolf.com*), opened in 2005, spans 7,100 yards. There's also a short course, a pro shop, bar, and restaurant. Greens fees are $44–$64 for 18 holes with a cart. Mill Creek is 18 mi southeast of Rochester, just north of Interstate 90.

SPECTATOR SPORTS

The **Rochester Americans** (⊠ *Blue Cross Arena, 1 War Memorial Sq.* ☎*585/454–5335* ⊕*www.amerks.com*), an American Hockey League team, is affiliated with the National Hockey League's Buffalo Sabres. The team, nicknamed the Amerks, is a perennial contender and has won several Calder Cup championships. The season runs October to April. Ticket prices are $10–$22.

Some of baseball's greats—Stan Musial and Cal Ripken Jr., to name two from different eras—played for the **Rochester Red Wings** (⊠ *Frontier Field, 1 Morrie Silver Way* ☎*585/423–9464* ⊕*www.redwingsbaseball. com*). The Triple-A International League team's downtown stadium is across from the High Falls entertainment district. Tickets are $6.50–$10.50. Soccer may be a foreign sport in much of the rest of the country, but in Rochester it's a fan favorite. The **Rochester Raging Rhinos** (⊠ *460 Oak St.* ☎*585/454–5425* ⊕*www.rhinossoccer.com*) play in the A-League, a step below Major League Soccer, although they've defeated top teams many times. The season runs from May to September. Tickets are $14–$20.

SHOPPING

The village of **Pittsford,** about 6 mi southeast of downtown, is the city's most upscale neighborhood and has some of its best shopping. In **Pittsford Plaza** (⊠ *3349 Monroe Ave., off the Monroe Avenue exit on I–590, Pittsford* ☎*585/424–6220*), you find discount department stores, boutiques, chain stores, a nice wine store (Century Wines), restaurants, and a Wegmans grocery store. Farther east, in the village proper, the two blocks south of the intersection of Main Street and Monroe Avenue are lined with restaurants and shops.

Schoen Place encompasses a row of jewelry and artisan shops across from the Erie Canal. **Northfield Common** (⊠ *50 State St./Rte. 31 at Schoen Pl., just over covered bridge heading out of town on State St., on left, Pittsford* ☎*No phone*), adjacent to Shoen Place, houses a mix of crafters, restaurants, and art galleries.

NIGHTLIFE AND THE ARTS

NIGHTLIFE

The quirky, grungy **Bug Jar** (⊠ *219 Monroe Ave.* ☎*585/454–2966* ⊕*www.bugjar.com*) is a small bar and music venue with mostly alt-rock and punk acts and DJs some nights. National and local acts play at **High Fidelity** (⊠ *170 East Ave.* ☎*585/325–6490* ⊕*www.highfidelityrochester. com*), a fixture of the East End nightlife scene. The music ranges from DJ spins to rock to jazz, and you're as likely to discover a new favorite as to enjoy familiar sounds. **The Old Toad** (⊠ *277 Alexander St.* ☎ *585/232–2626* ⊕ *www.theoldtoad.com*) is a classic English pub with a long beer list and a British staff.

Nearly all popular music acts that are too big for small-club/bar venues or too small for an arena end up at the 1,300-capacity **Water Street Music Hall** (⊠ *204 N. Water St.* ☎ *585/546–3887* ⊕ *www.waterstreetmusic. com*).

THE ARTS

The performing arts are highly valued in Rochester. Several theaters offer productions many nights of the week. Rock and jazz are favorites in the clubs on Alexander Street and East Avenue in the East End, on Monroe Avenue in the city, and in the St. Paul Quarter downtown.

DANCE   The world-renowned **Garth Fagan Dance** (☎ *585/454–3260* ⊕ *www. garthfagandance.org*), a modern-dance troupe, is based here but spends most of the time touring.

FESTIVALS   **Corn Hill Arts Festival.** The two-day event, held the weekend after the July
AND FAIRS   4th weekend, brings more than 200,000 people to one of Rochester's oldest neighborhoods to browse works by more than 400 artists and crafters and to partake in the food and live entertainment. ⊠ *Exchange Blvd. and Plymouth Ave.* ☎ *585/262–3142* ⊕ *www.cornhill.org.*

Fodor'sChoice   **Lilac Festival.** Held in early or mid-May, this 10-day event heralds the
★   start of Rochester's festival season. If the more than 1,200 lilac bushes (in 500 varieties) won't cooperate (Mother Nature is on her own schedule, after all), you can ogle the tulips, magnolias, or other blooms. When your eyes and nose have had their fill, arts and crafts, garden tours, and live entertainment beckon. ⊠ *Highland Park, South and Highland Aves.* ☎ *585/325–4720* ⊕ *www.lilacfestival.com.*

Park Avenue Summer Arts Fest. Rochesterians cannot get enough of arts and crafts, fried dough, or chatting with their neighbors. The two-day Park Avenue Summer Arts Fest, which falls on the first full weekend in August, is the last big blowout of summer. ⊠ *Park Ave. between Alexander St. and Culver Rd.* ☎ *585/473–4482* ⊕ *www.rochesterevents.com.*

FILM   The 535-seat **Dryden Theatre** (⊠ *George Eastman House, 900 East Ave.* ☎ *585/271–3361* ⊕ *www.dryden.eastmanhouse.org*), on the grounds of the George Eastman House, shows classic, art-house, and foreign films most nights at 8 PM, with matinees on Sunday. It also hosts several film festivals each year. The art-deco **Little Theatre** (⊠ *240 East Ave.* ☎ *585/258–0444* ⊕ *www.thelittle.org*) shows art-house and foreign films on five screens and also hosts movie festivals. The café is a destination in itself, with live jazz and sweets that make you forget about buckets of popcorn.

MUSIC   The **Eastman School of Music** (⊠ *26 Gibbs St.* ☎ *585/274–1100* ⊕ *www. esm.rochester.edu*) hosts frequent visiting and student performers— mostly classical—throughout the school year.

THEATER Touring Broadway shows and occasional musical performances are mounted at the **Auditorium Theatre** (⊠ *885 E. Main St.* ☎ *585/222–5000* ⊕ *www.rbtl.org*).

★ **Geva Theatre Center** (⊠ *75 Woodbury Blvd.* ☎ *585/232–4382* ⊕ *www.gevatheatre.org*), the city's leading professional theater for resident shows and the largest regional theater in the state, presents about seven shows a year on its 552-seat Mainstage space. Its 180-seat Nextstage theater mounts edgier, more experimental productions.

WHERE TO EAT

$ ✕ **Hogans Hideaway.** The clientele—from suit-wearing execs to hoodie-clad students—is as varied as the menu at this pubby restaurant with
AMERICAN wooden booths and brick walls. Specials fill five 4-foot-square blackboards, change daily, and feature many fish dishes, such as basil-pesto-crusted salmon fillet. The regular menu includes sandwiches and soups, which make for a cheap but filling meal. Diners spill onto a patio in summer. ⊠ *197 Park Ave.* ☎ *585/442–4293* ⚖ *Reservations not accepted* ⊟ *AE, D, MC, V* ⊘ *No lunch Sun.*

$ ✕ **Mr. Dominic's.** The family-run Italian restaurant, a staple in Charlotte
ITALIAN since the mid-1970s, draws a loyal clientele from throughout the city. Homemade pastas—gnocchi, lasagna, veal and lobster ravioli, four-cheese manicotti—are a specialty, but then again so are the steaks, chops, and seafood. It's two blocks from Lake Ontario, which makes it especially busy in summer. ⊠ *4699 Lake Ave.* ☎ *585/865–4630* ⊟ *AE, D, MC, V* ⊘ *No lunch Sat.–Mon.*

$$ ✕ **Restaurant 2 Vine.** In a century-old garage, 2 Vine frequently tops the
★ list of Rochestarians' favorite restaurants. A vine-covered arbor leads
CONTINENTAL into a two-room space with booth and table seating, soft lighting, and wood-beamed ceilings. The front room has huge windows and a long polished-wood bar. Mussels are steamed, served in white wine with shallots and black peppercorns, and accompanied by a side of frites; lamb chops are grilled and paired with Swiss chard in a lemon-thyme sauce. Most of the ingredients are local and organic. ⊠ *24 Winthrop St., off East Ave.* ☎ *585/454–6020* ⚖ *Reservations essential* ⊟ *AE, D, DC, MC, V* ⊘ *Closed Sun. No lunch.*

¢ ✕ **Schaller's Drive-In.** Opened in 1956, the family-owned and -operated
AMERICAN restaurant has retained a *Happy Days* feel. Place your order and the cashier yells it out amid the din. Burgers topped with Schaller's secret hot sauce are the most popular choice, followed by a Rochester specialty, white hot dogs, also known as "white hots" (sausage-size, natural-casing dogs made with pork, beef, and veal). The restaurant, west of Ontario Beach Park in the town of Greece, is particularly popular with the beach crowd. Take out on a sunny day or eat in the bright

dining room. ⊠*965 Edgemere Dr., Greece* ☎*585/865–3319* ⊸*Reservations not accepted* ⊟*No credit cards.*

$$ ✕**Tapas 177.** Spanish-style appetizers and entrées draw from Latin and
ECLECTIC European roots, as does the music and decor, at this below-street-level
restaurant. The decor, with candlelight, brick arches, and curtained-off cubbyhole seating is Morocco-meets-Paris, and the menu, which changes weekly, highlights seafood, with options for vegetarians well as carnivores. You might choose from chicken empanadas or Thai-glazed barbecued ribs (on the tapas menu) or wasabi-pea-encrusted tuna or guava-chipotle beef fillet (among the main dishes). A full martini menu includes chocolate, melon, lemon, and orange varieties. The specialty dessert—bananas wrapped in a fried, cinnamon-and-sugar-covered tortilla—is always available. ⊠*177 St. Paul St.* ☎*585/262–2090* ⊟*AE, D, DC, MC, V* ⊘*Closed Sun. No lunch.*

$$ ✕**Tastings.** Going to the grocery store was never like this. Run by Roch-
ECLECTIC ester grocery giant Wegmans, this upscale, brick-walled and polished-
★ wood restaurant is adjacent to the huge, flagship Pittsford store. Chefs use the best of the supermarket's fresh, seasonal ingredients, turning out such contemporary fare as a blackened pork chop in an apple-bacon jus and seared red snapper with a lemon couscous, spinach, and curried cauliflower puree. Sushi is also available, as is a three-course chef's choice sushi menu and reasonably priced four- and five-course tastings menus. The open kitchen lets you watch the preparations; two chef's tables put you in the front row. ⊠*3195 Monroe Ave., Pittsford* ☎*585/381–1881* ⊟*AE, D, MC, V* ⊘*Closed Sun. and Mon.*

WHERE TO STAY

A spate of economical chain hotels can be found near the airport and in Henrietta, a southern suburb with big-box stores and a mall.

$–$$ 📖**Dartmouth House B&B Inn.** On a residential street off boutique- and café-lined Park Avenue, this 1905 Tudor dwelling has been the home of owners Ellie and Bill Klein for 50 years. The decor is a jumble of patterned wallpapers; original features (like some claw-foot tubs); furniture from various periods (Italian and French provincial, early American, contemporary); and quirky touches like vintage dresses hung in closets. Guests have access to a library of classic VHS movies. **Pros:** in a quiet, pretty, and central neighborhood; lavish six-course breakfasts. **Cons:** one room not connected to its bathroom; small room TVs and only one suite has cable. ⊠*215 Dartmouth St.* ☎*585/271–7872 or 800/724–6298* ⊕*www.dartmouthhouse.com* 🛏*3 rooms, 1 suite* △*In-room: Wi-Fi. In-hotel: Internet terminal, parking (free), no kids under 12, no-smoking rooms* ⊟*AE, D, DC, MC, V* ⊘*Closed Jan. and Feb.* ⊺❘*BP.*

$–$$ 📖**Edward Harris House.** This 1896 Georgian home is impeccably furnished and decorated in a mix of Victorian and modern country-cottage style, with lovely moldings and fireplaces, hardwood floors, tasteful floral fabrics and antique and reproduction furniture. The two larger rooms are the most impressive, with more completely executed decor. A room with a twin bed called the Sleeping Porch can be tacked onto the Cottage Suite. Breakfast is served in a pretty dining room or on a side patio in warm weather. **Pros:** great location in one of Rochester's best neighborhoods; beautifully decorated; all rooms have fireplaces. **Cons:** two small resident dogs. ✉*35 Argyle St.* ☎*585/473–9752* ⊕*www. edwardharrishouse.com* ✍*5 rooms* ♿*In-room: DVD, Internet, Wi-Fi. In-hotel: Wi-Fi, parking (free), no kids under 10, no-smoking rooms* ☐*AE, D, MC, V* ⏍*BP.*

$–$$ Ⓗ**Hyatt Regency Rochester.** Rooms at this downtown high-rise hotel either look out onto some of the city's finest examples of 19th-century architecture or face Lake Ontario or the Genesee River. The hotel is within walking distance of the Blue Cross Arena and Geva Theatre Center. Guest rooms and corridors were completely renovated in 2006 and 2007; beds are topped with down duvets and bathrooms are granite. **Pros:** good option in downtown; only hotel downtown with a pool. **Cons:** area does not feel safe at night; fee for Internet and parking. ✉*125 E. Main St.* ☎*585/546–1234* ⊕*www.rochester.hyatt.com* ✍*319 rooms, 17 suites* ♿*In-room: refrigerator (some), Wi-Fi. In-hotel: restaurant, bar, room service, pool, gym, laundry service, Internet terminal, Wi-Fi, parking (paid), no-smoking rooms* ☐*AE, D, MC, V.*

$$–$$$ Ⓗ**The Inn on Broadway.** Our pick for Rochester's top hotel, the Inn on ★ Broadway is in the East End within blocks of the Eastman and Geva theaters, Strong Museum, and various dining and nightlife options. A private club originally occupied the 1929 building, and refinement lingers in the air. Every room is unique, but all have featherbeds (queen or king), down comforters, and thick towels; some have hardwood floors, gas fireplaces, and two-person Jacuzzi tubs. Deluxe rooms have baths with multiple showerheads. A sitting area with a small library is a B&B–style touch. **Pros:** individually decorated rooms; great staff; elegant steak house with amazing wine list. **Cons:** views are nothing special; some occasional city noise. ✉*26 Broadway* ☎*585/232–3595 or 877/612–3595* ⊕*www.innonbroadway.com* ✍*17 rooms, 6 suites* ♿*In-room: kitchen (some), DVD (some), Internet, Wi-Fi. In-hotel: restaurant, bar, Internet terminal, parking (free), no-smoking rooms* ☐*AE, D, DC, MC, V.*

$$–$$$ Ⓗ**Renaissance Del Monte Lodge.** The modern hotel is next to the Erie Canal, 6 mi southeast of downtown Rochester. Rooms have doorbells and traditional furnishings; all rooms received new carpeting and huge flat-screen TVs in 2009. Beds have luxurious sheets, specially washed to preserve softness, and down pillows and comforters. The spa offers massages, facials, body wraps, manicures, and pedicures. The Erie Grill, an intimate candelit restaurant, overlooks the canal, serves a seasonal American menu that emphasizes game meats in cooler weather. **Pros:** top-notch property in a great neighborhood; nice spa. **Cons:** rooms don't overlook canal (some have partial canal views). ✉*41 N. Main St., Pittsford* ☎*585/381–9900 or 866/237–5979* ⊕*www.renaissancehotels. com* ✍*97 rooms, 2 suites* ♿*In-room: refrigerator, Internet, Wi-Fi. In-hotel: restaurant, bar, room service, pool, spa, laundry facilities, laundry service, Internet terminal, parking (free), no-smoking rooms* ☐*AE, D, DC, MC, V.*

$$ Ⓗ**The Strathallan Hotel.** Suites here are either one-bedrooms, with full kitchens and living rooms, or studios, with kitchenettes and living areas separated by shelving units. Every other suite has a balcony, with views toward downtown or the residential neighborhood. The interior was renovated from top to bottom in 2009, and suites are furnished with microfiber sectional sofas, contemporary wood-veneer furniture, and stainless-steel appliances. At the highly regarded Grill at Strathallan, seafood and beef dishes have some Asian influences. **Pros:** walking distance to Rochester Museum and Science Center and George Eastman House; good restaurant. **Cons:** unattractive exterior. ⊠*550 East Ave.* ☎*585/461–5010 or 800/678–7284* ⊕*www.strathallan.com* ⇱*151 suites* ⚲*In-room: safe, kitchen, Internet, Wi-Fi. In-hotel: restaurant, bar, room service, gym, laundry facilities, laundry service, Internet terminal, parking (free), no-smoking rooms* ▤*AE, D, MC, V.*

EN ROUTE

Genesee Country Village & Museum. This 750-acre living-history museum has 68 buildings that were moved from throughout the region to re-create 19th-century life in the Genesee Valley. The complex includes the **John L. Wehle Gallery of Wildlife & Sporting Art.** The 175-acre **Genesee Country Nature Center,** which has exhibits and 5 mi of interpreted hiking trails, is open all year. You may cross-country ski and snowshoe here. Mumford is 20 mi southwest of Rochester. ⊠*1410 Flint Hill Rd., Mumford* ☎*585/538–6822* ⊕*www.gcv.org* ⛁*$14* ⊗*June–Oct. Tues.–Sun. 10–5.*

SIDETRIP: LETCHWORTH STATE PARK

Fodor's Choice
★

54 mi southwest of Rochester.

The Genesee River snakes its way through this 14,350-acre park. The sheer cliff walls of the 17-mi gorge soar nearly 600 feet in some spots, which is why the park is often called the Grand Canyon of the East. The river spills over three large waterfalls—one 107 feet high—and the long and narrow park encompasses awesome rock formations and dense forest. Some 66 mi of trails are used for hiking, biking, horseback riding, snowmobiling, and cross-country skiing. Many activities here center on water; you may go fishing, white-water rafting, or kayaking, or swim in one of two pools. Ice-skating, snow tubing, and horse-drawn sleigh rides round out the winter options. ■TIP→ **The most impressive views of the gorge and the Glen Iris Inn are in the southern part of the park, near the Castile entrance.** Park accommodations include tent and trailer campsites (open mid-May to mid-October) and winterized cabins. The Glen Iris Inn and restaurant was originally the retreat of park founder William Pryor Letchworth. ⊠*Off I–390 Exit 17; Castile entrance off Rte. 19A, Castile* ☎*585/493–3600* ⊕*nysparks.state.ny.us* ⛁*Parking $6 Apr.–Oct., free Nov.–Mar.* ⊗*Daily dawn–dusk.*

WHERE TO EAT AND STAY

$$$
AMERICAN

✕**The Glen Iris.** A wraparound porch overlooks the gorge and a waterfall at this restaurant within Letchworth State Park. American and European fare on the seasonal menu might include entrées such as chicken breast over spinach fettuccine in a garlic-cream sauce, salmon with a barbecue maple glaze cooked on a cedar plank, and slow-roasted prime rib with fresh horseradish. The dining room is in keeping with the Victorian style of inn; large windows take in the park setting. ⊠7 *Letchworth State Park, Castile* ☎585/493–2622 ▤*AE, D, MC, V* ✆*Closed Nov.–late Mar.*

$–$$ ▧**Genesee Country Inn.** This exquisitely restored 1833 mill sits in a rural town en route to Letchworth State Park. Rooms are immaculate and decorated in historic country-cottage style with handcrafted and antique pieces. A bubbling creek with a waterfall runs alongside the inn, in view of the patio and flowering garden. The huge breakfast, with homemade granola and maple syrup tapped on-site is a high point. **Pros:** lovely accommodations; peaceful location. **Cons:** not much to see or do nearby. ⊠*948 George St., Mumford* ☎585/538–2500 ⊕*www. geneseecountryinn.com* ➪*9 rooms, 1 suite* ⚷*In-room: Internet, Wi-Fi. In-hotel: Internet terminal, Wi-Fi, parking (free), no-smoking rooms* ▤*D, MC, V* ⏍*BP.*

¢ ▧**Glen Iris Inn.** Within Letchworth State Park, this country inn overlooks the park's tallest waterfall. Park founder William Pryor Letchworth had used the mansion as a retreat; it became an inn in 1914. Interiors are Victorian in style. Smaller standard rooms have one double or two twin beds, but the suites, with queen beds, are spacious. The Cherry Suite has a whirlpool tub, a private porch, and chevron-patterned hardwood floors. Also available are contemporary lodge rooms and three houses. **Pros:** within the state park; steps from the gorge. **Cons:** only suites have gorge views; limited Wi-Fi. ⊠*7 Letchworth State Park, Castile* ☎585/493–2622 ⊕*www.glenirisinn.com* ➪*12 rooms, 4 suites* ⚷*In-room: no TV, Wi-Fi. In-hotel: restaurant, Wi-Fi, no-smoking rooms* ▤*AE, D, MC, V* ✆*Closed Nov.–Mar.*

WESTERN LAKES

Possibly best known for its sloping vineyards and numerous wineries, the area is rich in history and has scenery that can be enjoyed in any season—whether or not you're interested in wine. **Keuka Lake,** approximately 18 mi long, is Y-shaped, with the villages of Penn Yan and Branchport at its northern end and Hammondsport—the so-called Cradle of Aviation—at its southern end. **Canandaigua Lake,** the westernmost of the major Finger Lakes, includes Squaw Island, one of the few islands in the region. Legend has it that many Seneca women and children escaped slaughter by hiding on the island during the 1779 Clinton-Sullivan campaign to drive the tribe out of west-central New York.

CANANDAIGUA

28 mi southeast of Rochester on Route 5/U.S. 20.

Long a favorite vacation destination for Rochester residents, this small city (population about 11,200) sits at the north end of 16-mi-long Canandaigua Lake. It was here that the 1794 Pickering Treaty was signed, brokering peace between the Iroquois and the U.S. government. Canandaigua's majestic courthouse, which still looms over Main Street, was the site of Susan B. Anthony's trial and conviction—she was found guilty of treason for voting in the 1872 election.

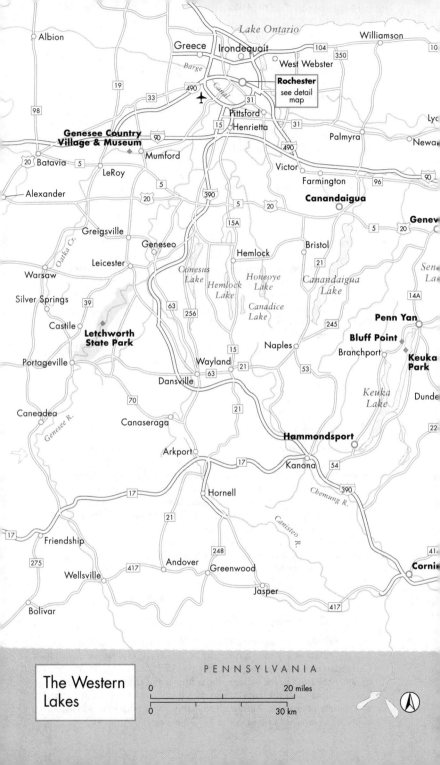

The Western Lakes

The wide main street with granite curbing is lined with stately Victorians in the north end of town. Heading south you pass through a downtown area with shops before you come to the lake. City Pier, which dates from 1847, is home to an eclectic mix of boathouses. Nearby Kershaw Park is a perfect place for a swim or a stroll.

GETTING HERE AND AROUND

Canandaigua is south of Interstate 90 and on Route 5/U.S. 20, at the northern tip of Canandaigua Lake. The closest bus, train, and air links are in Rochester, accessible by car via Interstate 490.

VISITOR INFORMATION

Canandaigua Chamber of Commerce (⊠ *113 S. Main St., Canandaigua* ☎ *585/394–4400* ⊕ *www.canandaiguachamber.com*).

WHAT TO SEE

Granger Homestead and Carriage Museum. The Federal-style house was completed in 1816 by Gideon Granger, postmaster general for presidents Thomas Jefferson and James Madison. It contains what's known as a flying staircase, and its nine rooms have hand-carved woodwork and many of the original furnishings and paintings. Free guided daily tours are available. The carriage house displays 93 horse-drawn vehicles, including an undertaker's hearse. The many annual events include a Civil War encampment in September and a Festival of Trees in November and December. The museum runs 45-minute narrated carriage tours of Canandaigua on Friday and Sunday, June through September. The trips cost $20, and reservations are required. ■ TIP➔ **Weather permitting, sleigh rides are offered on Sunday at 1 PM, January–March.** ⊠ *295 N. Main St.* ☎ *585/394–1472* ⊕ *www.grangerhomestead.org* ☑ *$6* ⊙ *Late May–Oct., Tues. and Wed. 1–5, Thurs. and Fri. 11–5 (June–early Sept., also weekends 1–5).*

New York State Wine & Culinary Center. At this waterfront educational center you can attend a dinner hosted by a local winery, take wine or food workshop, watch guest chefs in action, get expert advice on the various wine trails, or peruse the gift shop for locally made honey, pottery, and other food- and wine-related items. The center has more than 400 classes each year for the general public, including wine basics, various types of wine pairing, and cooking classes that focus on local foods. Most are a few hours in length and you can often arrange same-day signups. Drop-in classes are always available on weekends. A tasting room offers wine and beer flights, and the on-site restaurant serves a seasonal menu highlighting local food and wine. ⊠ *800 S. Main St.* ☎ *585/394–7070* ⊕ *www.nywcc.com* ☑ *Center free; classes $20–$80; wine and beer tasting $2–$7* ⊙ *Late May–mid-Oct., Mon.–Sat. 10–9, Sun. noon–9; mid-Oct.–late May, Tues.–Thurs. 10–6, Fri. and Sat. 10–9, Sun. noon–6.*

Fodor'sChoice
★ **Sonnenberg Mansion and Gardens.** The grounds at this 52-acre estate are a magnificent example of late-Victorian gardening and design. The rose garden overflows with 4,000 bushes; the other themed plantings include Japanese, pansy, blue-and-white, and rock gardens. An early-1900s conservatory houses the orchid collection and other exotic

plants. The stunning 1887 Queen Anne mansion was built as a summer home by a wealthy New York City banker and his wife, who became Canandaigua's biggest benefactress. The library, the couple's favorite room, looks out on the Italian garden. The great hall features a massive leaded-glass window and an 1874 Steinway. Walking tours are offered weekdays at 1 and weekends at 10 and 1 from Memorial Day through September. The **Finger Lakes Wine Center** (☎ *585/394–9016* ◷ *Mid-May–early Oct., daily 11–4:30*), on the Sonnenberg Gardens' grounds in a building near the parking lot, has a tasting room with a rotating selection of wines and sells wines and specialty foods from throughout the Finger Lakes region. ✉ *151 Charlotte St.* ☎ *585/394–4922* ⊕ *www. sonnenberg.org* 💲 *$10* ◷ *Early May–late May and early Sept.–mid-Oct., daily 9:30–4:30; late May–early Sept., daily 9:30–5:30.*

SPORTS AND THE OUTDOORS

☾ **Roseland Waterpark.** The park has several large waterslides, a water flume, a lazy river with huge inner tubes fitting up to five people, a wave pool, and a lake where you can rent canoes and paddleboats. ✉ *250 Eastern Blvd.* ☎ *585/396–2000* ⊕ *www.roselandwaterpark.com* 💲 *$20* ◷ *June–Sept., hrs vary.*

BOAT TOUR   **Canandaigua Lady.** This replica 19th-century paddle wheeler plies Canandaigua Lake for narrated one- to three-hour tours, lunch, dinner, and themed cruises, and custom trips. ✉ *Steamboat Landing, 205 Lakeshore Dr.* ☎ *585/396–7350* ⊕ *www.steamboatlandingonline.com* 💲 *$15–$45* ◷ *May–mid-Oct., Tues.–Sun.; tour times vary.*

Captain Gray's Boat Tours. Local history is shared during one-, two-, and three-hour tours offered by Captain Gray, who has been cruising Canandaigua Lake in steel-enclosed boats for more than a quarter century. ✉ *City pier, S. Main St.* ☎ *585/394–5270 June–Oct., 607/664–7299 Nov.–May* ⊕ *www.captaingrays.com* 💲 *$8.50–$17.50* ◷ *July and Aug., tours daily; June, Sept., and Oct., tours weekends.*

FISHING   Lake trout as well as rainbows and browns can be found in Canandaigua Lake, which is 262 feet deep and hosts the **Canandaigua Lake Trout Derby** (⊕ *www.canandaiguachamber.com*) on the first weekend in June. Captain Bill Reeser runs **Happy Hooker Charters** (✉ *City pier, S. Main St.* ☎ *315/331–1265*). From April through October he takes up to six people out on Canandaigua Lake in his 25-foot boat. You might wind up just as happy as the client who, in 1992, hooked a 22¼-pound lake trout—the biggest on record from the lake. Captain Bill supplies the bait and tackle.

GOLF   The highly regarded **Bristol Harbour Resort Robert Trent Jones Championship Golf Course** (✉ *5410 Seneca Point Rd.* ☎ *585/396–2200 or 800/288–8248* ⊕ *www.bristolharbour.com*), 11 mi south of Canandaigua, is a par-72, 6,200-yard course with a pro shop, a golf school, and spectacular lake views. Greens fees are $54–$79 for 18 holes, including cart.

SKI AREA   With a 1,200-foot vertical drop, the **Bristol Mountain Resort** (✉ *5662 Rte. 64* ☎ *585/374–6000* ⊕ *www.bristolmountain.com*), south of town, has the highest vertical rise on any ski area between the Adirondacks and the Rockies. The area has 33 slopes and trails, almost all with lighting and snowmaking capability. The longest run is 2 mi; about half of the runs are for intermediate skiers, with about 20% for advanced skiers and 30% for beginners. Skiing and snowboarding lessons are available. The Nordic Center, at the summit, has 3 km (2 mi) of trails for snowshoeing and cross-country skiing. The season usually runs from November through first week in April. In fall you can take in the foliage on a chairlift ride; hiking back down is an option.

SHOPPING

South Main Street between Ontario and Saltonstall streets is the heart of the shopping district in downtown Canandaigua. **Nadal Glass** (⊠*20 Phoenix St.* ☎*585/394–7850*), in a former firehouse just off South Main Street, specializes in handblown glass that's also sold in galleries throughout the country.

The Cheshire Union Gift Shop & Antique Center (⊠*4244 Rte. 21 S* ☎*585/394–5530*), 5 mi south of Canandaigua, occupies a 1915 schoolhouse with tin ceilings and black-and-white photos of former students on the walls. A deli and grocery store are downstairs; antiques and a wide selection of gifts fill the former classrooms upstairs.

NIGHTLIFE AND THE ARTS

The state-of-the-art outdoor amphitheater at the **Constellation Brands Marvin Sands Performing Arts Center** (⊠*Finger Lakes Community College, Rte. 364 and Lincoln Hill Rd.* ☎*585/325–7760* ⊕*www.rbtl. org*) is the summer home of the Rochester Philharmonic Orchestra. It also hosts internationally known rock, blues, jazz, and pop musicians, with seating for 15,000 under a band shell and on the grass-covered hillside.

FESTIVALS
AND FAIRS
Historic Downtown Canandaigua Arts Festival. More than 200 arts and crafts vendors line the downtown sidewalks for this annual festival, held on a weekend in mid-July. ⊠*S. Main St.* ☎*585/394–7110* ⊕*www. bardeenenterprises.com.*

Waterfront Art Festival. More than 150 local and national artists display their work on the north shore of Canandaigua Lake as part of this juried show. The event is held the last full weekend in July. ⊠*Kershaw Park, Lakeshore Dr.* ☎*585/383–1472* ⊕*www.waterfrontartfestival.com.*

WHERE TO EAT

$$ ✕**Casa de Pasta.** Tucked away on a side street in downtown Canandaigua, this Italian restaurant offers an intimate setting with burgundy linens and candles on each table. The menu includes shrimp scampi, homemade potato gnocchi, and braciola (thin slices of beef rolled with a filling of prosciutto, sliced egg, Parmesan, and onions). ⊠*125 Bemis St.* ☎*585/394–3710* ▤*MC, V* ⊘*Closed Mon.*

$$ ✕**Doc's Lakeside.** This seafood-and-steaks restaurant next to the New York State Wine and Culinary Center has live Maine lobsters delivered daily. Shrimp and lobster scampi and inventive daily fish specials are the chef's calling card, but the seasonal menu could include sole stuffed with crab or linguine Alfredo topped with shrimp, scallops, and

lobster. Steaks, pork, and poultry are available. The attentive wait-staff is trained in wine pairings. A nautical decor (think lighthouses and life preservers) fits the location, within walking distance to the waterfront. ⊠ *726 S. Main St.* ☎ *585/394–3460* ⊟ *AE, D, MC, V* ⊘ *Closed Mon. Nov.–mid-Mar. No lunch Tues.*

$ ✕ **Eric's Office.** Vintage signs and
AMERICAN photos and tablecloths printed with Victorian-era newsprint add interest to this casual place on the north end of town. The menu is a mix of bar food, salads, wraps, and sandwiches: batter-fried shrimp, a Reuben, a chicken BLT, burgers, chips topped with shredded cheddar and bacon. The dinner menu adds entrées to the mix, such as beef tenderloin dusted with coffee, chocolate, and spices, pan-seared and served with a port wine sauce. Locals warm the stools in the front-room bar. ⊠ *2574 Macedon Rd., at N. Main St.* ☎ *585/394–8787* ⊟ *AE, MC, V* ⊘ *Dining room closed Sun.*

$$ ✕ **Steamboat Landing.** The enviable location overlooking the lake is the
AMERICAN number one attraction at this restaurant with exposed wood beams, two-story windows, and a huge fireplace. You may opt to sit on the outside patio overlooking lake. The menu of steak, pasta, seafood, and poultry includes dishes like grilled salmon with dill sauce, chicken topped with artichoke hearts, and roast prime rib. The lobster bisque is a must. Breakfast is served Sunday; Friday night is a seafood buffet. ⊠ *205 Lakeshore Dr.* ☎ *585/396–7350* ⊟ *AE, D, MC, V* ⊘ *No dinner Sun. Jan.–Mar.*

WHERE TO STAY

$$–$$$ ⊞ **1795 Acorn Inn.** This 18th-century stagecoach inn has elegant, spa-
★ cious guest rooms furnished with a well-assembled blend of antique and contemporary country pieces. All rooms have down comforters and thick robes. In the Hotchkiss Room, which has a fireplace, French doors lead out to a walled terrace. A renovated barn 25 feet from the back door contains the private Barn Suite, with a kitchen and king-size sleigh bed. Grassy grounds, with stone walls, gardens, and a hot tub, surround the inn, which is a 10-minute drive outside the city. **Pros:** contemporary feel; plenty of privacy; peaceful location. **Cons:** no room phones. ⊠ *4508 Rte. 64 S* ☎ *585/229–2834 or 866/665–3747* ⊕ *www.acorninnbb.com* ⇄ *4 rooms, 1 suite* ⌂ *In-room: no phone, DVD, Wi-Fi. In-hotel: Wi-Fi, no kids under 12, no-smoking rooms* ⊟ *AE, D, MC, V* ⊘ *Closed Mon.–Wed. Nov.–Apr.* ⊠*BP*

$–$$ ⊞ **Bed & Breakfast at Oliver Phelps.** The gracious hosts at this B&B win accolades from past guests. In a stately Federal-style home with original olive-green clapboards, rooms are tastefully decorated with a mixture of antique and reproduction furniture and accents, with some gas fireplaces and four-poster, canopy, or ironwork beds. Guests share a hot tub enclosed in a gazebo for all-weather use. **Pros:** near Granger Homestead, walking distance to Sonnenberg Mansion. **Cons:** some rooms have no tub. ⊠*252 N. Main St.* ☎*585/396–1650 or 800/926–1830* ⊕*www.oliverphelps.com* ⮐*5 rooms* ⟡*In-room: no phone, DVD (some), Wi-Fi. In-hotel: bicycles, Wi-Fi, no kids under 12, no-smoking rooms* ⊟*AE, MC, V* ⦿*BP.*

$$–$$$ 🏨 **Bristol Harbour Resort.** All the rooms at this Adirondack lodge–style hotel have gas fireplaces, heated bathroom floors, rustic decor with wood on the walls and wool blankets on the beds, and balconies with spectacular lake views. Guests share an outdoor hot tub. The Lodge Restaurant serves contemporary American and grill fare, from burgers to maple-glazed pork tenderloin. You may cross-country ski or snow-shoe on the grounds in winter (rentals available) or play the 18-hole championship golf course. Ski packages with Bristol Mountain are available. **Pros:** all rooms have lake view; peaceful location. **Cons:** balconies are shared; limited breakfast in off-season. ⊠*5410 Seneca Point Rd.* ☎*585/396–2200 or 800/288–8248* ⊕*www.bristolharbour.com* ⮐*30 rooms, 1 suite* ⟡*In-room: Internet, Wi-Fi. In-hotel: restaurant, golf course, beachfront, water sports, pool, gym, Internet terminal, Wi-Fi, no-smoking rooms* ⊟*AE, MC, V.*

$$–$$$ 🏨 **Inn on the Lake.** The waterfront inn next to the city pier has spacious grounds with a pool, a sand-volleyball court, and a barbecue grill. A large lobby-lounge extends out onto a deck overlooking the lake. Rooms are upgraded every few years and are contemporary in decor; those with lake views have either a patio or balcony. More lake views are found in the elegant, contemporary Max on the Lake restaurant, with a menu of steak, seafood, and pasta. **Pros:** right on the water; good location; lakeside dining and lounging. **Cons:** some rooms overlook parking lot; pricey suites. ⊠*770 S. Main St.* ☎*585/394–7800 or 800/228–2801* ⊕*www.theinnonthelake.com* ⮐*86 rooms, 48 suites* ⟡*In-room: safe, refrigerator (some), Wi-Fi. In-hotel: 2 restaurants, bar, room service, pools, gym, laundry facilities, Internet terminal, Wi-Fi, some pets allowed, no-smoking rooms* ⊟*AE, D, MC, V.*

¢ 🏨 **Miami Motel.** A pink-and-turquoise neon sign on Route 5/U.S. 20 welcomes you to this 1953 motor lodge, transformed into an art-deco-style motel. Each room is individually decorated, with some '50s and '60s lamps and furnishings mixed with more-modern pieces. Rooms have comfortable queen beds with better-than-average linens; some have hot tubs. **Pros:** newly overhauled; low prices; convenient to shopping. **Cons:** unattractive surroundings; outside town. ⊠*4126 Rte. 5/U.S. 20* ☎*585/394–6700* ⊕*www.motelmiami.com* ⮐*28 rooms* ⟡*In-room: no phone, refrigerator, Internet, Wi-Fi. In-hotel: Wi-Fi, some pets allowed, no-smoking rooms* ⊟*AE, D, DC, MC, V* ⦿*CP.*

$$–$$$ 🏨 **Morgan Samuels Inn.** A tree-lined drive leads to this 1810 English-style mansion on 42 country acres. The mansion served as an upstate hideaway for playwright-actor Judson Morgan and was later the home of industrialist and Johnson administration official Howard Samuels. Three rooms have French doors that open onto balconies. The master suite has French inlaid-wood antiques, a king-size bed, a double hot tub, and floor-to-ceiling windows with window seats. Common areas include a wicker-furnished Victorian porch with views of the gardens. **Pros:** countryside location; some fireplaces. **Cons:** far from town

and lake; spotty Wi-Fi. ⊠*2920 Smith Rd.* ☎*585/394–9232* ⊕*www.morgansamuelsinn.com* ⟩*5 rooms, 1 suite* ⚲*In-room: no phone, no TV, Wi-Fi (some). In-hotel: tennis court, Wi-Fi, no kids under 12, no-smoking rooms* ▭*AE, D, MC, V* ⊺*BP.*

PENN YAN

25 mi southeast of Canandaigua.

The small village, which incorporated in 1833 and took its name from its early Pennsylvania and Yankee residents, is at the north end of Keuka Lake. Penn Yan is the seat of Yates County as well as home to Birkett Mills, one of the largest producers of buckwheat in the world. Visitors come here mainly for the wineries, spectacular lake views, summer recreational opportunities, and vibrant fall foliage. A drive down the main street, with its shops, restaurants, and Victorian-style houses, is a drive through small-town America. Members of the Mennonite community mix in with the traffic in their horses and buggies.

GETTING HERE AND AROUND
At the intersection of State Routes 54, 54A, and 14A, this town is equidistant from Rochester, Syracuse, Corning, and Ithaca (about an hour and a half from each) and is accessibly only by car.

VISITOR INFORMATION
Yates County Chamber of Commerce (⊠*2375 Rte. 14A, Penn Yan* ☎*315/536–3111 or 800/868–9283* ⊕*www.yatesny.com*).

WHAT TO SEE
Oliver House Museum. The museum of the Yates County Historical Society is in an 1852 house that was the residence of the Olivers, a well-known local family of physicians. Guided tours lead you through the Victorian rooms and historical exhibits. Revolving exhibits may cover period furniture, costumes and textiles, carpentry and blacksmithing tools, American Indian artifacts, paintings and photographs, and decorative arts. ⊠*200 Main St.* ☎*315/536–7318* ⊕*www.yatespast.org* ⊡*Free* ☉*Tues.–Fri. 9–4.*

SPORTS AND THE OUTDOORS
BOAT TOURS In season, cruises aboard the **Viking Spirit** depart daily at 5 PM from the Viking Resort. A trip around Keuka Lake takes an hour or so, during which you can take in the views of the surrounding shore, hills, and vineyards. ⊠*680 E. Lake Rd./Rte. 54* ☎*315/536–7061* ⊕*www.vikingresort.com* ⊡*$12* ☉*Mid-May–mid-Oct.*

Esperanza Rose. The lunches and dinners aboard this 65-foot vintage yacht are surprisingly good. Sightseeing cruises are also available. ⊠*3537 Rte. 54A, Bluff Point* ☎*315/595–6618* ⊕*www.esperanzaboat.com* ⊡*Sightseeing cruise $19* ☉*Mid-May–late Oct.*

SHOPPING
Penn Yan is home one of the largest buckwheat producers in the country, **Birkett Mills** (⊠*163 Main St.* ☎*315/536–3311*). You can buy its products—kasha, its own buckwheat cookbook, buckwheat pillows—from

its headquarters on Main Street. When the **Windmill Farm & Craft Market** (⊠*3900 Rte. 14A* ☎*315/536–3032*) opened in 1987 as an outlet for local producers and craftspeople, it had fewer than 100 vendors. Today this 29-acre farm and crafts market is host to more than 200 vendors and craftspeople, many of them members of the Mennonite and Amish community. Offerings include farm-fresh produce, quilts, furniture, and sweets. It's open Saturday 8–4:30 from late April through mid-December.

NIGHTLIFE AND THE ARTS

FESTIVALS
AND FAIRS
Yates County Fair. The fair, one of the oldest in the state, is held over five days in early July. Traditional activities include a demolition derby, amusement rides, kids' games, petting farms, 4-H exhibits, and various musical performers. ⊠*Penn Yan Fairgrounds, Old Rte. 14A* ☎*315/536–3111* ⊕*www.yatesny.com.*

WHERE TO EAT

$$
AMERICAN
✕**Esperanza Mansion.** It's worth eating here for the view alone. When the weather cooperates, you can sit on a hillside veranda with the whole of Keuka Lake before you. The formal dining room, decorated in 19th-century splendor, is another option. The two executive chefs create seasonal menus with entrées such as filet mignon with a chanterelle demi-glace, scallops and shrimp tossed with white wine and garlic butter over linguine, and roasted turkey and Brie wrapped in a puff pastry and topped with a cassis sauce. Brunch is served Sunday. ⊠*3456 Rte. 54A, Bluff Point* ☎*866/927–4400* ▤*D, MC, V* ⊘*Closed Jan. and Mon. and Tues. No dinner Sun. Feb.–Apr., Nov., and Dec.*

$
AMERICAN
✕**Essenhaus Restaurant.** With its airy dining space, tall windows, and ceiling fans, this country-style eatery a few miles north of town instantly makes you feel welcome and comfortable. Many of the dishes and baked goods served here—like "church supper ham loaf" (a ham-and-sausage meat loaf) and shoofly pie—are inspired by the area's Mennonite community. Others, like pot roast or beer bratwurst, are pure American and German country cooking. The gift shop carries items crafted by local Mennonites. Breakfast is served Monday to Saturday and brunch on Sunday. ⊠*1300 Rte. 14A* ☎*315/531–8260* ▤*MC, V* ⊘*No dinner Sun.*

WHERE TO STAY

$$–$$$
▥**Esperanza Mansion.** The stately 1838 Greek Revival mansion sits on a hill overlooking Keuka Lake, 16 mi north of Hammondsport. Some guest rooms are in the mansion, but most are in the separate two-story inn building. Rooms may have four-poster and sleigh beds, armoires, and decorative fireplaces. Whitewashed furniture and quilted bedspreads give the inn a more casual cottage feel. Linger over a cocktail on the outdoor terrace and drink in the lake, surrounding hills, and farms. **Pros:** impeccable decor; spectacular views from rooms. **Cons:** expensive rates; locals say restaurant is inconsistent. ⊠*3456 Rte. 54A, Bluff Point* ☎*315/536–4400* ⊕*www.esperanzamansion.com* ⋺*9 mansion rooms, 21 inn rooms* ⚲*In-room: Internet, Wi-Fi. In-hotel: restaurant, bar, Internet terminal, Wi-Fi, no-smoking rooms* ▤*AE, D, MC, V* ⊘*Closed Jan. and Sun.–Tues. Feb.–Apr., Nov., and Dec.* ⦿*CP.*

$–$$　　🕆 **Top O' the Lake Bed & Breakfast.** Classic and clean (rather than frilly) country accents fill the rooms of this 5,000-square-foot mid-1800s Italianate house, which has crown moldings and fluted pillars inside and is surrounded by 8 acres of woods and a huge grassy field. Rooms have hardwood floors and are individually decorated, some with four-poster beds and mahogany furnishings. The wraparound porch with wicker chairs and palms would be at home in Savannah. **Pros:** radiant-heat floors in some rooms; three blocks from both lake and town. **Cons:** only one room with bathtub; owners have pets. ⊠*128 South Ave.* ☎*315/536–8070* ⊕*www.topothelake.com* ⇨*5 rooms* ♨*In-room: no phone, Wi-Fi. In-hotel: no kids under 12, no smoking rooms* ▤*MC, V* ⏀*BP.*

$–$$　　🕆 **Trimmer House Bed & Breakfast.** The Queen Anne Victorian, built in
★　　1891 by a wine merchant, has spacious guest rooms with lovely, traditional furnishings like sleigh beds, Oriental carpets, and claw-foot tubs. The suite has a fireplace and a private veranda. Guests share a formal Victorian library with a fireplace. The breakfast buffet includes pancakes or waffles made with locally produced buckwheat. Next door, the B&B has a 2,000-square-foot, two-bedroom 1904 Arts and Crafts guesthouse with Stickley and Mission-style furniture. **Pros:** walking distance to town; private beachfront; outdoor hot tub. **Cons:** one room has full-size bed. ⊠*145 E. Main St.* ☎*315/536–8304 or 800/968–8735* ⊕*www.trimmerhouse.com* ⇨*4 rooms, 1 suite, 1 2-bedroom house* ♨*In-room: DVD, Internet, Wi-Fi. In-hotel: Internet terminal, Wi-Fi, no-smoking rooms* ▤*AE, MC, V* ⏀*BP.*

EN ROUTE　　Route 54A runs along the west shore of Keuka Lake, between Hammondsport and Penn Yan. Driving north from Hammondsport (and then east from Branchport), you come to **Bluff Point,** which sits on a headland between the two branches of the wishbone-shape lake and offers breathtaking views of the water. At the end of the bluff is pretty Garrett Chapel, built in 1931, which has spectacular grounds (grounds open daily dawn to dusk). From Bluff Point, detour east through the hamlet of Keuka Park (the home of Keuka College) and take a long, leisurely ride along Skyline Drive, which gives you more spectacular views of the lake.

HAMMONDSPORT

22 mi south of Penn Yan.

Hammondsport, a small village nestled between soft hills at the southern end of Keuka Lake, is close to a number of quality wineries and an excellent wine-touring base. Native son Glenn Curtiss made the world's first publicly observed, preannounced flight here—a 5,090-foot trip aboard the *June Bug* in 1908. Hammondsport has interesting stores, including antiques shops and local crafts purveyors, and there are several small restaurants in town and along the lake.

GETTING HERE AND AROUND

A car is essential for getting to Hammondsport, on State Route 54. The small Corning airport is the closest (about 40 mi away) but flights from

Rochester or Syracuse (both about 70 mi away) are generally cheaper and more direct.

VISITOR INFORMATION

Steuben County Conference & Visitors Bureau (⊠ *1 W. Market St., Suite 301, Corning* ☎ *607/936–6544 or 866/946–3386* ⊕ *www.corningfingerlakes.com*).

WHAT TO SEE

★ **Glenn H. Curtiss Museum.** Just outside Hammondsport, this museum honors Curtiss and his early aviation experiments. The Hammondsport native made the first public preannounced flight when he flew his *June Bug* plane more than 5,000 feet outside the village on July 4, 1908. Exhibits include aircraft, engines, a collection of antique motorcycles, and hands-on models for kids. A restoration shop is open to the public and staff is available to answer questions. ⊠ *8419 Rte. 54* ☎ *607/569–2160* ⊕ *www.glennhcurtissmuseum.org* ⌗ *$7.50* ⊗ *May–Oct., Mon.– Sat. 9–5, Sun. 10–5; Nov.–Apr., daily 10–4.*

WINERIES **Bully Hill Vineyards.** The views of Keuka Lake from here are spectacular. The wine is less so, and the tours are touristy, but the tastings are fun. A tour of the vineyard and winery includes the **Greyton H. Taylor Wine Museum** (☎ *607/868–4814* ⊗ *Mid-May–Oct., Mon.–Sat. 9–5, Sun. 11:30–5*), which focuses on 18th-century wine-making equipment. Lunch and dinner are available at the Bully Hill Restaurant. ⊠ *8843 Greyton H. Taylor Memorial Dr., off Rte. 54A* ☎ *607/868–3226* ⊕ *www.bullyhill.com* ⌗ *Tour free, tastings $2 and $5* ⊗ *Mon.–Sat. 9–4, Sun. 11:30–4.*

★ **Dr. Konstantin Frank Vinifera Wine Cellars.** Many consider Dr. Frank's the best wine in the Finger Lakes. The winery, overlooking Keuka Lake, was started in the early 1960s and is run by the grandson of the founder. A Ukrainian immigrant, Dr. Frank was a pioneer in growing classic European grapes in the region. Cabernet francs, Rieslings, pinot noirs, and chardonnays (all European, or vinifera, varietals) are among Dr. Frank's offerings. The Rieslings are excellent, and the pinot noirs are really coming into their own. Also look for *rkatsiteli* (ar-kat-si-*tel*-lee), a spicy wine made from an Eastern European grape. ⊠ *9749 Middle Rd., off Rte. 76* ☎ *607/868–4884* ⊕ *www.drfrankwines.com* ⌗ *Free* ⊗ *Tasting room Mon.–Sat. 9–5, Sun. noon–5.*

Heron Hill Winery. Beautiful Keuka Lake views are one of the draws at this winery built by John and Josephine Ingle in 1977. John Ingle maintains the winery's Ingle Vineyards, which were planted on the western shore of Canandaigua Lake in 1972 and feature chardonnay, cabernet franc, merlot, Riesling, and pinot noir grapes. Heron Hill's winemaker, Thomas Laszlo, oversees the Heron Hill Vineyards, which were planted here in 1968 and include chardonnay and Riesling grapes. The Heron is open from May through October. ⊠ *9301 County Rte. 76* ☎ *607/868–4241 or 800/441–4241* ⊕ *www.heronhill.com* ⌗ *Tastings $2 and $5* ⊗ *Mon.–Sat. 10–5, Sun. noon–5.*

Replica seaplanes constructed at the Glenn H. Curtiss Museum are flown each September at the three-day **Seaplane Homecoming** (⊠*Depot Park, Water St.* ☎*607/569–2160* ⊕*www.seaplanehomecoming.org*).

SHOPPING

The Village Square is where you find most of the shopping in town. The merchandise at the **Cinnamon Stick** (⊠*26 Mechanic St.* ☎*607/569–2278*) includes Christmas ornaments, teddy bears, candles, glassware, jewelry, chimes, and fancy-food items. **Opera House Antiques** (⊠*61–63 Shethar St.* ☎*607/569–3525*) is a multi-dealer shop in a 1901 opera house off the Village Square. Furniture, jewelry, silverware, and linens are among the offerings. From January through March it's just open weekends.

WHERE TO EAT

$$
AMERICAN
✕**Bully Hill Restaurant.** A spectacular view of Keuka Lake awaits you at this breezy patio café, part of the Bully Hill Vineyards. The food is eclectic: Maryland crab cakes, buffalo burgers, or sage-and-prosciutto-stuffed chicken breast with three-cheese fettuccine. Lunch includes sandwiches and salads. Bully Hill wines are available, of course. ⊠*8843 Greyton H. Taylor Memorial Dr.* ☎*607/868–3490* ▤*AE, D, MC, V* ⊘*Closed Dec.–Apr. No dinner Sun.–Fri.*

$
AMERICAN
✕**Lakeside Restaurant.** This casual spot—one of the best choices in the area for lake views—occupies an 1880s cottage on the west side of Keuka Lake. The food is American: prime rib, fried shrimp, bacon-wrapped beef tenderloin, barbecue chicken, a variety of steaks and chops, and a Friday fish fry. Outside, a fire pit and 150 seats overlook the bluff of Keuka Lake. ⊠*13780A W. Lake Rd.* ☎*607/868–3636* ▤*AE, D, MC, V* ⊘*No dinner Sun.–Tues. Nov.–Apr.*

$
CONTINENTAL
✕ **Snug Harbor.** The well-trained waitstaff here is as impressive as the finely presented contemporary American fare. Dishes on the seasonal menu might include calamari with a cilantro and chili sauce, baked Moroccan chicken with almonds and spicy honey, or seafood Thai curry. Vegetarian and vegan dishes are available, and bar food is served all day. Lift your eyes from the plate long enough to take in the view of Keuka Lake from the dining room or the two verandas and dining room. Docking for boats is available. ⊠*9068A Snug Harbor Dr.* ☎*607/868–7684* ▤*AE, D, MC, V.*

WHERE TO STAY

$
▦**Amity Rose Bed & Breakfast.** The smell of freshly baked cookies welcomes you to this turn-of-the-20th-century home. Guest-room furnishings are a blend of Victorian and country-romantic styles. Two rooms have whirlpool tubs, three have electric fireplaces, and one has a private porch. The living room also has a gas fireplace. **Pros:** well maintained; walking distance to lake; near village square. **Cons:** overly frilly country decor; cash only. ⊠*8264 Main St.* ☎*607/569–3402 or 800/982–8818* ⊕*www.amityroseinn.com* ⇨*3 rooms, 1 suite* ⌂ *In-room: no phone, no TV, Wi-Fi. In-hotel: no kids under 12, Wi-Fi, no-smoking rooms* ▤*No credit cards* ⊘*Closed Jan.–Mar; occasionally open off-season (call ahead)* ⦿|*BP.*

$$$ ⛺**Elm Croft Manor Bed & Breakfast.** Stately columns stand guard at the entrance of this 1832 Greek Revival mansion sitting amid gardens and surrounded by vineyards. The elegant interior has a formal look, with period antiques throughout, and individually decorated rooms, some with four-poster beds, richly patterned wallpapers or fabrics, or marble baths. Monogrammed robes and rooms stocked with complimentary beverages and hors d'oeuvres are nice extras. Common areas include a formal parlor and dining room and a screened-in porch with wicker furniture. **Pros:** chef-prepared breakfast; the area's most luxurious inn. **Cons:** not lakeside; expensive for area. ⊠*8361 Pleasant Valley Rd.* ☎*607/569–3071 or 800/506–3071* ⊕*www.elmcroftmanor.com* ⇆*4 rooms* ⌂*In-room: refrigerator, no TV, no phone, Wi-Fi. In-hotel: Internet terminal, Wi-Fi, some pets allowed, no-smoking rooms* ☰*AE, MC, V* ⊘*Closed late Oct.–Apr.* ⏃*BP.*

CENTRAL LAKES

Each stretching nearly 40 mi and creating a virtual microclimate, **Cayuga Lake** and **Seneca Lake** are the two largest Finger Lakes. Hillsides cup lake warmth, extending the growing season, which is why so many grapes are grown on the sloping shores of Seneca and Cayuga. East–west travel has always been stymied by the length of the lakes. To reach a destination 3 mi across a lake you might have to travel north, then south, for two hours. As a result, glorious swaths of countryside are little touched by visual change. You might drive for an hour without seeing another moving vehicle or losing sight of a magnificent lake.

WATKINS GLEN

36 mi south of Geneva.

Watkins Glen State Park, one of the state's premier natural wonders, is one reason to visit this small village (population 2,500). On the south edge of Seneca Lake, this residential community attracts boaters, who sail from Seneca Harbor. This is also wine and car-racing country. U.S. car racing, which had been halted because of World War II, was revived in Watkins Glen in 1948. Until the current speedway opened in 1956, the competing cars would roar through the center of the village. Area wineries range from large-production operations to intimate family-run vineyards. The Rieslings are among Seneca Lake's most celebrated wines.

VISITOR INFORMATION
Schuyler County Chamber of Commerce (⊠*100 N. Franklin St., Watkins Glen* ☎*607/535–4300 or 800/607–4552* ⊕*www.schuylerny.com*).

WHAT TO SEE
Fodor'sChoice
★ **Finger Lakes National Forest.** On a ridge between the southern ends of Cayuga and Seneca lakes, 9 mi north of Watkins Glen, the national forest offers more than 30 mi of easy-to-moderate hiking trails through a variety of terrain. The land was patched together when the federal

government purchased about 100 farms between 1938 and 1941. The forest encompasses 16,032 acres, so you might feel like you have the place to yourself—regardless of whether you're camping, cross-country skiing, fishing, or hunting. The forest's altitude is higher than most surrounding points, so great vistas are yours for the hiking. Trail maps are available at some trailheads and at the visitor center. ⊠ *Visitor Center, 5218 Rte. 414, Hector* ☎*607/546–4470* ⊕*www.fs.fed.us/r9/ gmfl* ⊠*Free* ☉*Forest daily dawn–dusk. Visitor center mid-May–Nov., weekdays 8–4:30, Sat. noon–4:30; Dec.–mid-May, weekdays 8–4:30.*

Watkins Glen International Raceway. "New York's Thunder Road" rumbles from June to September. The season's highlight is the **NASCAR Series,** in mid-August. On a Thunder Road Tour ($25; May–October, most days at noon), you drive the track in your own vehicle behind a pace car. Call for schedules and prices. You can get tickets, souvenirs, and merchandise at The Shop, at 4 North Franklin Street, downtown. ⊠*Track: 2790 County Rte. 16* ☎*607/535–2486 or 866/461–7223 info and tickets, 607/535–2338 (The Shop) for Thunder Road Tour* ⊕*www.theglen.com.*

Fodor'sChoice **Watkins Glen State Park.** The main entrance to this park is in down-
★ town Watkins Glen. Campgrounds are scattered around the beautiful Glen Creek. The waters drop about 500 feet in 2 mi and include 19 waterfalls. The easy 1½-mi **gorge trail** runs parallel to the creek, and 300-foot cliffs border the water. One bridge spans 165 feet over the water. The park also has an Olympic-size pool. "Timespell," a computerized light-and-sound show, explains the geological development of the gorge. It's screened on the sides of the glen. The gorge isn't accessible in winter. ⊠*Franklin St. near Rte. 17/Old Corning Rd.* ☎*607/535–4511* ⊕*nysparks.state.ny.us* ⊠*Parking $7 late May–early Sept., $6 weekends Apr.–late May and early Sept.–Oct.; free at other times* ☉*Daily dawn–dusk. Gorge trail, visitor center, and restrooms closed Nov.–Mar.*

SPORTS AND THE OUTDOORS

Captain Bill's Seneca Lake Cruises. Captain Bill Simiele and his son and daughter run meal cruises (some with music) and hour-long sightseeing cruises from the end of Franklin Street. Cruises range from $11 for sightseeing excursions to $30–$43 for lunch and dinner cruises. ⊠*1 N. Franklin St.* ☎*607/535–4541* ⊕*www.senecaharborstation. com* ☉*Mid-May–mid-Oct.; call for schedules.*

WHERE TO EAT

$$ ✕**Castel Grisch.** Strudel, Swiss fondue, sauerbraten, and schnitzels high-
CONTINENTAL light the largely German and Hungarian menu at this restaurant, part of Castel Grisch winery. In warm weather you can sit on a veranda taking in the vineyards, hills, and the lake in the distance. Steak and duck preparations, as well as American fare (burgers and such), also are available. ⊠*3380 County Rte. 28* ☎*607/535–9614* ☐*D, MC, V* ☉*No dinner Mon.–Wed. or mid-Dec.–Apr.*

$ ✕**Wildflower Cafe.** Burgers made with locally produced beef are piled
ECLECTIC with bacon and blue cheese; vegetarian entrées (like soy-based "ribs"

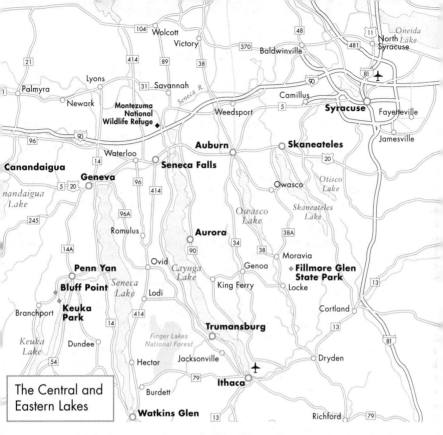

The Central and Eastern Lakes

with barbecue sauce) are plentiful, wines and brews are local, and coffee is fair-trade and organic at this casual restaurant near the entrance of Watkins Glen State Park. Oak, brass, and stained glass accent the interior. Also available: jambalaya, soy-sauce-marinated sirloin over soba noodles, plus soups, salads, and pizzas. ⊠*301 N. Franklin St.* ☎*607/535–9797* ▭*AE, MC, V.*

WHERE TO STAY

$$–$$$ ★ 🖼 **Inn at Glenora Wine Cellars.** Every room has a view of Seneca Lake at this inn 10 mi north of Watkins Glen, built in 1999 to complement the on-site Glenora winery (Seneca Lake's oldest winery, opened in 1977). All rooms are furnished with Mission-style pieces and have either a balcony or patio; Vintners Select rooms have fireplaces. The restaurant, Veraisons, serves three upscale-American meals a day in a cathedral-ceiling dining room with a stone fireplace, a patio, and excellent lake views. **Pros:** all rooms have lake views; nice rooms; well placed for Keuka- and Seneca Lake wine tours. **Cons:** a bit far from Watkins Glen. ⊠*5435 Rte. 14, Dundee* ☎*607/243–9500 or 800/243–5513* ⊕*www. glenora.com* ⟳*30 rooms, 1 cottage* ♿*In-room: refrigerator, DVD (some), Internet, Wi-Fi. In-hotel: restaurant, room service, bar, gym, Internet terminal, Wi-Fi, no-smoking rooms* ▭*AE, D, MC, V.*

$–$$ ⊞ **Seneca Lake Watch Bed and Breakfast.** The Queen Anne Victorian with a watchtower, just north of town and across the street from Seneca Lake, has porches and four out of five rooms with lake views. Accommodations are large and have modern bathrooms; two rooms have private sundecks. The common area has a telephone, fireplace, and piano. Porches wrap around the house, and a lawn gazebo is lighted at night. **Pros:** warm hosts; spacious rooms. **Cons:** decor too frilly for some; no TVs or room phones. ⊠ *104 Seneca St.* ☎ *607/535–4490* ⌨ *5 rooms* ♿ *In-room: no phone, no TV, Wi-Fi. In-hotel: Wi-Fi, no kids under 12, no-smoking rooms* ⊟ *AE, MC, V* ⦿ *BP.*

$$$–$$$$ ⊞ **Watkins Glen Harbour Hotel.** This upscale hotel opened in 2008 in an enviable location at the south end of Seneca Lake adjacent to a marina and waterfront boardwalk. Rooms have a seaside-cottage decor, with white beadboard headboards, hardwood floors, and a blue-and-white color scheme. All rooms have flat-screen TVs and oversize walk-in showers, and suites have wine refrigerators. The Blue Pointe Grille serves American and Continental fare; in summer you can have drinks on the harborside patio. Captain Bill's boat tours and the Seneca Harbor Station restaurant are next door. **Pros:** large rooms; up-to-the-minute amenities; walking distance to everything in town. **Cons:** pricey rates; some shared balconies. ⊠ *16 N. Franklin St.* ☎ *607/535–6116* ⊕ *www.watkinsglenharborhotel.com* ⌨ *98 rooms, 6 suites* ♿ *In-room: refrigerator, Internet, Wi-Fi. In-hotel: restaurant, room service, bar, pool, gym, laundry service, Internet terminal, Wi-Fi, no-smoking rooms* ⊟ *AE, D, MC, V.*

GENEVA

36 mi north of Watkins Glen.

In the Seneca Lake city of Geneva (population 13,000), wonderful examples of Federal, Victorian Gothic, and Jeffersonian architecture, among other styles, document two centuries of history. South Main Street row houses dating from the 1820s line Pulteney Park, designed in 1794 as Geneva's original town square. Emancipation celebrations were held here in the 1800s, with Frederick Douglass and Sojourner Truth delivering orations. A bare-breasted sculpture named *Peace* presides over the park, which is not even a block away from the campuses of Hobart and William Smith colleges. A former Finger Lakes steamship port and manufacturing center, Geneva remains an agricultural hub; Cornell University's Agricultural Experiment Station is based here.

GETTING HERE AND AROUND
Geneva, on Route 5/U.S. 20, is about an hour from Syracuse and Rochester via Interstate 90. It's accessible only by car.

VISITOR INFORMATION
Seneca County Tourism (⊠ *1 DiPronio Dr., Waterloo* ☎ *315/539–1759 or 800/732–1848* ⊕ *www.visitsenecany.net*).

WHAT TO SEE

Prouty-Chew House. The 1829 mansion, run by the Geneva Historical Society, contains period rooms and local history exhibits. It's a good place to orient yourself to Geneva's rich social and cultural history. ⊠ *543 S. Main St.* ☎ *315/789–5151* ⊕ *www.genevahistoricalsociety.com* ✉ *Donations accepted* ⊙ *Sept.–June, Tues.–Fri. 9:30–4:30, Sat. 1:30–4:30; July and Aug., Tues.–Fri. 9:30–4:30, weekends 1:30–4:30.*

WORD OF MOUTH

"Geneva, at the northern tip of Seneca Lake is a beautiful spot, with good access to the northern bits of the finger lakes. The Watkins Glen State Park is worth about 4 hours of sightseeing, in my humble opinion."

—gb944

Fodor'sChoice **Rose Hill Mansion.** Six huge Ionic columns front this restored 1839 Greek
★ Revival mansion overlooking Seneca Lake. The 21 rooms open to the public include servants' quarters, the children's playroom, the kitchen, dining room, and parlors. Some rooms are outfitted with the Empire-style furnishings that were used from 1850 to 1890 by the prosperous farm family that lived here. Guided tours of the house begin with an introductory film and are given on the hour weekdays and on the half hour weekends. The grounds include boxwood gardens. ⊠ *3373 Rte. 96A* ☎ *315/789–3848 May–Oct., 315/789–5151 Nov.–Apr.* ⊕ *www.genevahistoricalsociety. com* ✉ *$7* ⊙ *May–Oct., Tues.–Sat. 10–4, Sun. 1–5.*

WINERIES Other wineries near Geneva that are worth checking out are White Springs Winery, Billsboro Winery, and Ventosa Vineyards. For information, contact the **Seneca Lake Wine Trail** (☎ *877/536–2717* ⊕ *www. senecalakewine.com*).

★ **Fox Run Vineyards.** Some of the region's best wines are produced at this winery, opened in 1990 in a converted Civil War–era dairy barn on the shores of Seneca Lake. All the wines are winners, but the Rieslings, gewürtztraminer, and dry reds are particularly notable. In 2008, Fox Run was the first New York State winery in 22 years to be chosen as one of the top 100 wineries in the world by *Wine and Spirits* magazine. Tours are given every hour on the hour (weather permitting) until 4 PM. A café serves homemade soups, salads, and sandwiches, prepared fresh daily by the CIA-trained chef; all of Fox Run's wines are available by the glass in the café. Note: it has an address in Penn Yan, but is actually closer to Geneva. ⊠ *670 Rte. 14, Penn Yan* ☎ *800/636–9786 or 315/536–4616* ⊕ *www.foxrunvineyards.com* ✉ *Tours free, tastings free–$2* ⊙ *Mon.–Sat. 10–6, Sun. 11–6.*

OFF THE
BEATEN
PATH

Sampson State Park and Military Museum. Swim, fish, boat, and walk for miles at this 1,852-acre park on the shore of Seneca Lake. The museum honors the nation's second-largest naval training station during World War II. The Air Force took over the station during the Korean War, and an Air Force Museum, in the same building, tells that story. A boat launch and 120 berths surround the marina, next to a gravel swimming beach. More than 240 campsites are nestled among wooded areas.

Tennis courts, playgrounds, and a concession stand, open in summer, are also part of the complex. ⊠*6096 Rte. 96A, Romulus, 13 mi southeast of Geneva* ☎*315/585–6392 park, 315/585–6203 Naval Museum, 315/585–5999 Air Force Museum* ⊕*nysparks.state.ny.us* ⊠*Parking $7 late June–early Sept., $6 weekends May–late June and early Sept.– late Oct.; free at other times. Museums free* ☉*Park daily dawn–dusk. Museums Memorial Day–Columbus Day, Wed.–Sun. 9:30–3.*

SPORTS AND THE OUTDOORS

ひ **Seneca Lake State Park.** The longest stretch of accessible public lakeshore in the Finger Lakes extends for 2 mi here at the northern tip of Seneca Lake. A children's splash playground with brightly colored water fountains and benches is a popular draw. A tree-lined walking and biking path along the shore leads from the park to downtown Geneva. Other amenities here include picnic tables, a swimming beach, and a marina. The view south from here is spectacular. ⊠*1 Lakefront Dr. (Rte. 5/U.S. 20), 1 mi east of town* ☎*315/789–2331* ⊕*nysparks.state. ny.us* ⊠*Parking $7 mid-June–early Sept., $6 at other times* ☉*Daily dawn–dusk.*

FESTIVALS
AND FAIRS
The angler who hooks the biggest fish at the **National Lake Trout Derby** (⊠*Lakeshore Park, 35 Lakefront Dr.* ☎*315/781–2195* ⊕*www. laketroutderby.org*) wins a whopping $5,000. A total of about $21,000 is awarded each year at the Memorial Day weekend event.

NIGHTLIFE AND THE ARTS

The 1894 **Smith Opera House** (⊠*82 Seneca St.* ☎*315/781–5483* ⊕*www. thesmith.org*) presents stage productions, concerts, and films. The exterior of the theater, built by Geneva philanthropist William Smith, is Richardson Romanesque. The interior was gutted in 1930 and spruced up into an elegant movie palace with art-deco and baroque details. Along with Radio City Music Hall, it's one of the few remaining atmospheric theaters still in use. Films are frequently shown, and the stage has hosted George M. Cohan, Billy Joel, Bruce Springsteen, and other performers. Tours are given by appointment.

WHERE TO EAT

$$
CONTINENTAL
✕**The Cobblestone Restaurant.** Continental fare is served with contemporary flair at this restaurant in an 1825 Greek Revival farmhouse. Dishes might include veal scaloppine, bourbon-glazed duck, or goat-cheese-and-vegetable lasagna. The breads and pastas, as well as the chocolate soufflé, are made on the premises. Fireplaces add to the elegant but cozy ambience. Balcony and porch dining are seasonal alternatives. ⊠*3610 Pre-Emption Rd.(Rte. 5/U.S. 20)* ☎*315/789–8498* ⊟*AE, D, MC, V* ☉*Closed Mon.*

$
ECLECTIC
★
✕**Ports Cafe.** Overlooking the water about 3 mi south of Geneva, this casual eatery serves eclectic fare. The chef prepares fresh-cut fish and steak specials daily, in addition to a regular menu that moves from Indian to Mexican in dishes like tandoori chicken in an almond-onion curry and house-smoked spareribs with honey corn bread. Finger Lakes wines accompany your meal, and the staff is trained in wine pairing. Nachos, calamari, and other small plates are always available.

Reservations are essential in summer, especially around sunset. ✉*4432 W. Lake Rd./Rte. 14* ☎*315/789–2020* ▤*AE, D, MC, V* ⊙*Closed Sun. and Mon. No lunch.*

WHERE TO STAY

$$–$$$ 🏨**Belhurst Castle.** The 1889 castle, complete with tower, is listed on the National Register of Historic Places. You can stay in the original stone structure, but better rooms are found in the charming Georgian Revival mansion or in the modern Vinifera Inn, which has less personality but king-size beds, gas fireplaces, and two-person showers. The formal restaurant and lounge have lake views. Belhurst has its own winery, and a wine-tasting room and gift shop are on-site. **Pros:** historic buildings; lovely grounds. **Cons:** restaurants disappointing; rooms could use maintenance. ✉*Rte. 14 S* ☎*315/781–0201* ⊕*www.belhurst.com* ⇨*30 rooms, 9 suites, 2 houses* ♿*In-room: refrigerator (some), DVD (some), no TV (some), Internet, Wi-Fi. In-hotel: 2 restaurants, bars, pool, Internet terminal, no-smoking rooms* ▤*MC, V* ⦿*CP.*

$$$–$$$$ 🏨**Geneva on the Lake.** Here's a slice of Europe at the edge of Seneca ★ Lake. Formally manicured grounds and Italian Renaissance architecture call to mind Tuscany. The stunning white manor house, built in 1914, has fireplaces of imported marble and rich upholstery and tapestries. Rooms are furnished with different styles of Stickley furniture. Ten suites have two bedrooms. Studios have living rooms and Murphy beds. Spend a summer afternoon playing lawn games, fishing, or taking a pontoon boat ride on Seneca Lake. **Pros:** lovely formal gardens; pool overlooking the lake; stately historic property. **Cons:** small dining room; long gaps between room renovations. ✉*1001 Lochland Rd./ Rte. 14* ☎*315/789–7190* ⊕*www.genevaonthelake.com* ⇨*23 suites, 6 studios* ♿*In-room: kitchen, DVD, Internet, Wi-Fi. In-hotel: restaurant, room service, pool, gym, water sports, bicycles, laundry service, Wi-Fi, no-smoking rooms* ▤*AE, D, MC, V* ⦿*CP.*

SENECA FALLS

11 mi east of Geneva.

Seneca Falls is a classic. The former mill town has wide streets lined with century-old homes, 19th-century storefronts, and a sprinkling of small parks. Movie director Frank Capra visited Seneca Falls in the 1940s, and some say the Bedford Falls setting of *It's a Wonderful Life* was modeled after the village. (You might notice the similarities between the Bridge Street bridge and the bridge from which George Bailey ponders his fate in the movie.)

The falls that powered many factories here in the 1800s were flooded long ago to create Van Cleef Lake and a canal through the village's midsection. In 1848, the village was the site of the first Women's Rights Convention, during which attendees declared that "all men and women are created equal." The convention was organized by reformer Elizabeth Cady Stanton, who raised seven children here.

GETTING HERE AND AROUND

On Route 5/U.S. 20, Seneca Falls is about an hour from Syracuse and Rochester via Interstate 90. It's accessible only by car.

VISITOR INFORMATION

Seneca County Tourism (⊠ *1 DiPronio Dr., Waterloo* ☎ *315/539–1759 or 800/732–1848* ⊕ *www.visitsenecany.net*).

WHAT TO SEE

Seneca Falls Historical Society Museum. Elaborate woodwork and Victorian furniture decorate the 1855 Queen Anne mansion on Cayuga Street, which is lined with grand homes. A female ghost is said to wander its 23 rooms. ⊠ *55 Cayuga St.* ☎ *315/568–8412* ⊕ *www.sfhistoricalsociety. org* ☑ *$3* ⊙ *Sept.–June, weekdays 9–4; July and Aug., weekdays 9–4, weekends 1–4.*

☾ **Seneca Museum of Waterways and Industry.** Why did reform movements flourish in the Finger Lakes? Many of the answers are at this museum, where narratives of water power, transportation, industry, and cultural history are interwoven to tell the story of 19th-century Seneca Falls. The museum has interactive exhibits for kids, who are urged to ask questions of tour guides. ⊠ *89 Fall St.* ☎ *315/568–1510* ⊕ *www. senecamuseum.com* ☑ *Free* ⊙ *Mid-June–Aug., Tues.–Sat. 10–4, Sun. noon–4; Sept.–mid-June, Tues.–Sat. 10–4.*

★ **Women's Rights National Historical Park.** Elizabeth Cady Stanton, Lucretia Mott, and a handful of other pioneers in the women's rights movement organized the first Women's Rights Convention in the Wesleyan Chapel in Seneca Falls in 1848. Today, the park incorporates the site of the convention (the Wesleyan Chapel Declaration Park), a visitor center, and several off-site historic homes of key convention participants. Exhibits and an orientation film at the **visitor center** explore the development of the women's rights movement in the United States.

The gathering of 300 women and men at the Wesleyan Chapel in 1848 produced the Declaration of Sentiments, the bedrock document of the modern women's rights movement. It proclaimed—audaciously, at the time—"that all men and women are created equal." Today the document's words are etched on a 140-foot-long wall between the national park's visitor center and the adjacent **Wesleyan Chapel Declaration Park** (⊠ *136 Fall St.* ☎ *315/568–0024*), which encompasses a steel structure housing remnants of the chapel. Tours are given daily at 10:30 and 1:30 and more frequently in summer.

The meticulously restored **Elizabeth Cady Stanton House** (⊠ *32 Washington St.* ☎ *315/568–0024* ☑ *Free*) is where one of American feminism's most important leaders shaped social reform as she raised seven children. Stanton's feminist colleague, Susan B. Anthony of Rochester, was a guest in the house. A tour helps you to understand Stanton's charisma and power. The house, a mile east of the Declaration Park and visitor center (across the canal), is open early March through mid-December, with tours daily at 11:15 and 2:15 and more frequently in summer.

The **M'ClintockHouse** (Memorial Day–Labor Day, Thursday–Sunday 1–4) and the **Hunt House** (not open to public) are in the village of Waterloo, 3 mi west of Seneca Falls. Inquire about tours at the park visitor center. ⊠ *Visitor center, 136 Fall St.* ☎ *315/568–0024* ⊕ *www.nps.gov/ wori* ⊠ *Free* ⊙ *Visitor center daily 9–5, grounds daily dawn–dusk.*

SPORTS AND THE OUTDOORS

Cayuga Lake State Park. A swimming beach, bathhouse, boat launch, playground, campground, and trails are the key attractions in this 190-acre park. You can also fish at the park, on the north end of Cayuga Lake and 2 mi from Seneca Falls. ⊠ *2678 Lower Lake Rd.* ☎ *315/568–5163* ⊕ *nysparks.state.ny.us* ⊠ *Parking $7 late June–late Oct.; free at other times* ⊙ *Daily dawn–dusk.*

Cayuga-Seneca Canal. The 12-mi-long Cayuga-Seneca Canal links the northern ends of Seneca and Cayuga lakes and connects to the Erie Canal near the Montezuma National Wildlife Refuge. Locks enclose boats in bathtublike mechanisms that fill with water and float the boat to the next level. (Locks are in service during daylight hours from May to mid-November.) The decorative lamps along the canal near downtown Seneca Falls make this a great place for walkers, night or day. Victorian-style benches provide seating. The **Ludovico Sculpture Trail** stretches along the canal's south bank in Seneca Falls. ⊠ *9 Seneca St.* ☎ *315/568–5797 Seneca Falls Lock, 800/422–6254 NYS Canals* ⊕ *www.nyscanals.gov.*

★ **Montezuma National Wildlife Refuge.** The area between the Finger Lakes and Lake Ontario was a huge wetlands until settlers began draining it more than 200 years ago. Montezuma, a 7,000-acre remnant of the giant swamp, is a major stopover for thousands of migrating birds. The numbers peak in mid-April and early October. More than 320 species of birds have been identified at the federally managed site since its establishment in 1937. Look for eagles that raise their young here. You can take a 3½-mi self-guided car tour of the refuge; start at the visitor center, where you pick up a brochure with information about the wildlife you see on the tour. The visitor center has limited winter access; call for seasonal hours. The refuge entrance is 5 mi east of Seneca Falls, at the north end of Cayuga Lake. ⊠ *3395 Rte. 5/U.S. 20* ☎ *315/568–5987* ⊕ *www.fws.gov/r5mnwr* ⊠ *Free* ⊙ *Refuge daily dawn–dusk; visitor center Apr.–Nov., weekdays 10–3, weekends 10–4.*

SHOPPING

Polo Ralph Lauren, Coach, Calvin Klein, Brooks Brothers, London Fog, J. Crew—you'll recognize most of the names you see at the **Waterloo Premium Outlets** (⊠ *655 Rte. 318, Waterloo* ☎ *315/539–1100*). Laid out in arcs forming a loose circle, the stores have exterior entrances connected by a covered walkway. **Sauder's Store** (⊠ *2168 River Rd.* ☎ *315/568–2673*) is an authentic Mennonite market, with Pennsylvania Dutch meats and cheeses and hundreds of bulk containers brimming with baking supplies, candies, and spices. The eclectic inventory mix includes fresh produce, children's books, simple toys, and wooden sheds. Young people in traditional Mennonite garb staff the store, which John Sauder's family has run for decades. A farmers' market with 15 or so vendors selling fresh flowers, plants, crafts, produce, and other goods is held Friday 9 to 7.

NIGHTLIFE AND THE ARTS

FESTIVALS
AND FAIRS
Empire Farm Days. For three days every August, tens of thousands of farmers and hobby agriculturalists gather in a field filled with vendors promoting everything from giant tractors to alpaca fur. Food booths, operated by community not-for-profit groups, sell sausage sandwiches, ice cream, and other fare. ⊠ *Rodman Lott & Sons Farms, Rte. 414, just south of Seneca Falls* ☎ *585/526–5356* ⊕ *www.empirefarmdays.com.*

WHERE TO EAT

¢   ✕ **Connie's Diner.** The chrome-trimmed diner, run by the Caratozzolo

AMERICAN
family, serves nothing except tasty comfort food. Eggplant Parmesan,
★   linguine with clam sauce, and liver and onions are popular dishes. The lasagna is made from an old family recipe. The homemade pies—especially the coconut cream and raspberry—are glorious. Connie's is 3 mi west of Seneca Falls. ⊠ *205 E. Main St., Waterloo* ☎ *315/539–9556* ⚑ *Reservations not accepted* ▭ *No credit cards* ⊘ *Closed Mon.*

$$$ ✕ **Henry B's.** Seneca Falls' go-to restaurant for a classy dinner, Henry

ITALIAN
B's serves Italian-American fare in a dark-wood, white-tablecloth, low-lighted environment with a full bar up front. The homemade gnocchi with fresh basil pesto is a top seller; other entrées include pan-seared pork chops stuffed with pancetta, Gorgonzola, and spinach and huge servings of pasta loaded with rich ingredients that feed two to three people. ⊠ *84 Fall St.* ☎ *315/568–1600* ▭ *AE, D, MC, V* ⊘ *No lunch.*

$ ✕ **Knapp Winery Restaurant.** Part of a winery 11 mi south of Seneca Falls,

SEAFOOD
this eatery uses fresh produce grown in its own gardens. The food is contemporary, and the menu changes every two months. Try crab cakes with chipotle aioli or salmon over white-truffle risotto, or choose from burgers, wraps, and salads. The covered patio overlooking the flower garden and vineyard is nice in warm weather. The restaurant is open daily till 5 PM. ⊠ *2770 County Rd. 128, Romulus* ☎ *607/869–9271* ▭ *AE, D, MC, V* ⊘ *Closed early Dec.–Mar. No dinner.*

¢   ✕ **ZuZu Cafe.** You get free wireless with the espresso drinks, paninis, and

CAFE
wraps at this cavernous café. The place, filled with leather sofas and two-seater tables, is named after ZuZu, the daughter of the George Bailey character in the 1946 cinema classic *It's a Wonderful Life.* The café is open for breakfast and lunch, but is only open past 5:30 on Friday, when it serves until 8 PM. ⊠ *107 Fall St.* ☎ *315/568–2230* ▭ *AE, MC, V* ⊘ *No dinner Sat.–Thurs.*

TRUMANSBURG

30 mi south of Seneca Falls.

A few miles west of Cayuga Lake, Trumansburg is a self-contained rural outpost but also something of an Ithaca exurb. The village is known for its summer music festival and its tidy Victorian homes, as well as for Taughannock (pronounced Tuh-*gan*-nik) Falls State Park.

3

GETTING HERE AND AROUND

Trumansburg is just over 10 mi northwest of Ithaca along State Routes 96 and 89. You need a car to get around.

VISITOR INFORMATION

Ithaca/Tompkins County Convention & Visitors Bureau (⊠ *904 E. Shore Dr., Ithaca* ☎ *607/272–1313 or 800/284–8422* ⊕ *www.visitithaca.com*).

SPORTS AND THE OUTDOORS

Fodor'sChoice
★
Taughannock Falls State Park. Stunningly steep shale cliffs and rock surround the 215-foot-high Taughannock Falls, which are 30 feet higher than Niagara Falls. A level ¾-mi path takes you from the parking lot to the falls. Autumn is perhaps the most dramatic time of year to see the gorge, but the waterway is breathtaking any time of year. And, unlike many of the rim trails that surround other Finger Lakes gorges, the trail at the glen's bottom here is open all year. Camping and swimming are allowed in season. The park, which straddles Route 89, has playgrounds, a boat launch, and picnic grounds fronting Cayuga Lake. ⊠ *Rte. 89, 8 mi north of Ithaca* ☎ *607/387–6739* ⊕ *nysparks.state. ny.us* ⊠ *Parking $7 Memorial Day–Labor Day and weekends Apr., May, Sept. and Oct.; free at other times* ⊙ *Daily dawn–dusk.*

NIGHTLIFE AND THE ARTS

FESTIVALS
AND FAIRS
Finger Lakes Grassroots Festival. The music ranges from Cajun and zydeco to African and reggae at this four-day festival that raises money to fight AIDS. The event is held in July on the fairgrounds; four-day passes cost $75 to $110. Limited tent and vehicle camping is available on-site. ⊠ *Trumansburg Fairgrounds, Rte. 96* ☎ *607/387–5098* ⊕ *www. grassrootsfest.org.*

WHERE TO EAT AND STAY

$$
AMERICAN
✕ **Hazelnut Kitchen.** A cozy spot with checkered-tile flooring, mismatched silverware, and an open kitchen, this restaurant serves up rustic-elegant meals without pretension. The chefs, Philly transplants, use local locally grown produce, grass-fed beef, and cheeses from local dairies. The menu changes monthly, but past diners have tucked into cheddar-and–Ithaca Nut Brown Ale soup, pâté made in-house on baguette toasts with Dijon mustard, jam, and cornichons and grilled hanger steak with hand-cut fries and malt-vinegar aioli. ⊠ *53 E. Main St.* ☎ *607/387–4433* ▤ *D, DC, MC, V* ⊙ *Closed Tues. and Wed. No lunch.*

$–$$
▥ **Taughannock Farms Inn.** The 1873 Victorian main house sets the tone for this elegant, 12-acre property, which also includes four guesthouses varying in style and number of rooms. You may choose a room with Victorian antiques and no TVs in the original structure; take one of the modern-built but Victorian-style units in the Edgewood house; or opt to stay in a room or suite in one of the guesthouses with country-cottage decor. Taughannock Falls State Park surrounds the 12-acre property and the state park lakeshore is across the street. **Pros:** most rooms have lake views; restaurant has glassed-in porch. **Cons:** no Wi-Fi. ⊠ *2030 Gorge Rd./Rte. 89* ☎ *607/387–7711 or 888/387–7711* ⊕ *www.t-farms. com* ⇆ *20 rooms, 2 suites* ⌂ *In-room: no TV (some), DVD (some), refrigerator (some), Internet. In-hotel: restaurant, bar, no-smoking rooms* ▤ *AE, D, MC, V* ▮◎▮*CP.*

ITHACA

12 mi south of Trumansburg, 55 mi southwest of Syracuse.

Home to both Cornell University and Ithaca College, eclectic Ithaca is the multicultural and intellectual capital of the central Finger Lakes region. The diverse restaurant scene and array of arts venues contribute to Ithaca's urbane air. And the setting, amid steep hills and waterfalls at the southern tip of Cayuga Lake, is spectacularly beautiful.

GETTING HERE AND AROUND

Ithaca is served by one small airport, 5 mi northeast of town. Flying into Syracuse is an option. The nearest interstate highway is Interstate 81 (the route to Syracuse), about 20 mi east of town. Getting to Ithaca by car means at least 20 mi of driving along rural state routes. Greyhound and Trailways serve Ithaca and the city has a bus system, but a car by far is the best way to get around.

Airport Information Ithaca Tompkins Regional Airport (⊠ *72 Brown Rd., Ithaca; north of Rte. 13, 4½ mi northeast of downtown* ☎ *607/257–0456* ⊕ *www. flyithaca.com*).

VISITOR INFORMATION

Ithaca/Tompkins County Convention & Visitors Bureau (⊠ *904 E. Shore Dr., Ithaca* ☎ *607/272–1313 or 800/284–8422* ⊕ *www.visitithaca.com*).

WHAT TO SEE

Cornell Plantations. The 200 acres of plants and trees adjacent to the Cornell University campus are primarily organized in collections—peonies, rock-garden species, rhododendrons, old-time vegetable and flower gardens, conifers, flowering crabapples, wildflowers. There's even a section for poisonous plants. The winter garden includes evergreens, conifers, and assorted plants with interesting cold-weather colors and textures. The complex's arboretum includes an area with sculptures. Walking and bus tours are available; call ahead for seasonal times. Some tours are free and others are $5. ⊠ *1 Plantations Rd., off Rte. 366* ☎ *607/255– 2400* ⊕ *www.plantations.cornell.edu* 🖃 *Free* 🕙 *Daily dawn–dusk.*

Cornell University. With its historic buildings, weave of natural and manmade spaces, Cayuga Lake views, and two spectacular gorges, the campus of this private university is considered one of the most beautiful in the country. Founded in 1865, Cornell is a mixture of modern structures and ivy-covered 19th-century buildings. Wear your walking shoes; there is almost no public parking near the campus center. Free 75-minute tours of the campus leave daily from Day Hall, at Tower Road and East Avenue.

Four miles of trails lead through the 220-acre **Sapsucker Woods Sanctuary,** part of the **Cornell Lab of Ornithology** (⊠ *159 Sapsucker Woods Rd.* ☎ *607/254–2473 or 800/843–2473* ⊕ *www.birds.cornell.edu*). Bird artist Louis Agassiz Fuertes named the woods after two yellowbellied sapsuckers he had spotted in the area. A computer touch screen leads you through interpretive displays. The visitor center is open weekdays 8–5 (until 4 on Friday), Saturday 9:30–4, and Sunday 11–4.

Cornell University's I. M. Pei–designed **Herbert F. Johnson Museum of Art** (⊠ *University Ave.* ☎*607/255–6464* ⊕*www.museum.cornell.edu*) houses more than 30,000 works of art: American and European impressionist paintings, some contemporary pieces, and an extensive collection of Asian art and artifacts. But the most stunning sight here may well be the unforgettable views of Cayuga Lake. The museum is open 10–5 Tuesday through Sunday; entry is free. ⊠ *Cornell Visitor Relations Center: 1 Main Campus Rd.* ☎*607/254–4636* ⊕*www.cornell.edu* ☉*Weekdays 8* AM*–10* PM*, Sat. 8–5. Tours daily at 9, 11, 1, and 3.*

3

☺ **Museum of the Earth.** Experience the natural history of New York State
★ through exhibits called "Beneath an Ancient Sea," "Where Dinosaurs Walked," and "A World Carved by Ice." Whale and mastodon skeletons, along with audiovisual theater presentations, help prepare museumgoers for hands-on labs featuring fossils, dinosaurs, and ice. The on-site Paleontological Research Institution runs the museum. ⊠*1259 Trumansburg Rd./Rte. 96* ☎*607/273–6623* ⊕*www.museumoftheearth. org* ☎*$8* ☉*Late May–early Sept. Mon.–Sat. 10–5, Sun. 11–5; early Sept.–late May, Mon. and Thurs.–Sat. 10–5, Sun. 11–5.*

☺ **Sciencenter.** A tide-pool touch tank and a two-story kinetic ball sculpture are among the 100-plus exhibits at this hands-on museum catering to youngsters. The Sagan Planetwalk, a to-scale solar-system walking tour around the city, honors scientist Carl Sagan, who taught at Cornell University. Outside there's a wooden playground. ⊠*601 1st St.* ☎*607/272–0600* ⊕*www.sciencenter.org* ☎*$7* ☉*Tues.–Sat. 10–5, Sun. noon–5.*

SPORTS AND THE OUTDOORS

Buttermilk Falls State Park. Water cascades over 10 falls through a ¾-mi gorge, dropping close to 500 feet, at this park on Ithaca's south end. A swimming hole sits at the base of the falls, and the park also has playing fields, a campground (open mid-May to mid-October), and hiking trails through woodlands and wetlands. Nearly all the trails are closed in winter. The park is about 3 mi south of the city. ⊠*Rte. 13* ☎*607/273–5761 May–Oct., 607/273–3440 Nov.–Apr., 800/456–2267 camping reservations* ⊕*nysparks.state.ny.us* ☎*Parking $7 Memorial Day–Labor Day and weekends Apr., May, Sept. and Oct.; free at other times* ☉*Daily dawn–dusk.*

Robert H. Treman State Park. A dozen waterfalls, including Lucifer Falls, which has a 115-foot drop, are the highlight here. Nine miles of well-maintained hiking trails lace the park, which also offers swimming, fishing, a campground, and a playground. The trails all close for winter in early November. The park is 5 mi south of the city, near Buttermilk Falls State Park. ⊠*Rte. 327* ☎*607/273–3440* ⊕*nysparks.state.ny.us* ☎*Parking $7 Memorial Day–Labor Day and weekends Apr., May, Sept. and Oct.; free at other times* ☉*Daily 8* AM*–dusk.*

SHOPPING

Ithaca Commons (⊠*State St. between Cayuga and Aurora Sts.*), the historic center of Ithaca, is a pedestrian mall with specialty book and clothing stores as well as dozens of restaurants. Sculptures and gardens give the former motorway some texture and provide an inviting backdrop for festivals and itinerant musicians. The **Downtown Ithaca Business Improvement District** (☎607/277–8679 ⊕*www.downtownithaca.com*) maintains a Web site with a map of the shops and restaurants.

The open-air **Ithaca Farmer's Market** (☎607/273–7109 ⊕*www.ithacamarket.com*) is perhaps Ithaca's hottest ticket on a weekend morning. Artwork, food, plants, and flowers, all local, fill the 80-plus stalls. The market is open seasonally. Weekends (May–October, Saturday 9–3, Sunday 10–3; April, Saturday 9–3; November and December, Sat. 10–3) are at **Steamboat Landing**, off Route 13, a mile north of downtown. A Tuesday market (May–October, 9–2) is held at **Dewitt Park**, at Cayuga and Buffalo streets.

NIGHTLIFE AND THE ARTS

FESTIVALS AND FAIRS
Ithaca Festival. Hundreds of poets, dancers, musicians, and other performers and artists entertain tens of thousands of people at this four-day arts festival in late May or early June, which centers around the Commons and Stewart Park. A parade is part of the festivities. ☎607/273–3646 ⊕*www.ithacafestival.org*.

WHERE TO EAT

$
AMERICAN
✕**The Antlers.** Steak and seafood feature prominently on the menu at this country inn about 5 mi east of downtown. Baby back ribs are simmered in a house barbecue sauce, a buttery London broil is served with baked stuffed shrimp, and haddock is baked and topped with tomatoes, olives, capers, and raisins. Sit in front of the fireplace and sip local wine under the watchful gaze of the deer heads mounted on the walls. ✉*1159 Dryden Rd.* ☎607/273–9725 ▤*AE, D, MC, V* ◔*No lunch*.

$$$
STEAK
✕**John Thomas Steakhouse.** A two-story 1848 farmhouse on the grounds of La Tourelle Country Inn is home to this restaurant that specializes in grilled meats but also serves chicken and fish dishes (and a vegetarian entrée). Filet mignon, prime rib, strip steak, and porterhouse are among the choices. Sides, such as garlicky mashed potatoes, are served family style. In summer you may eat outside on the deck, with views of the lawns, gardens, and La Tourelle. The restaurant is about 3 mi south of downtown, near Buttermilk Falls State Park. ✉*1152 Danby Rd./Rte. 96B* ☎607/273–3464 ▤*AE, D, DC, MC, V* ◔*No lunch*.

$
CONTINENTAL
✕**Just a Taste.** On the Commons, this tapas place is a bistro-style storefront that manages to be romantic despite the fact that you're sitting elbow to elbow with other diners. Menus of small plates might include rare grilled flank steak with homemade kimchi, marinated scallops with walnut-garlic aioli, or spinach salad with pears, goat cheese, and bacon. Small portions mean room for dessert; don't overlook the cornmeal shortbread with a wine-soaked dried-fruit compote and whipped cream. This tiny place gets packed, even on weeknights. ✉*116 N. Aurora St.* ☎607/277–9463 ⌂*Reservations essential* ▤*AE, D, DC, MC, V* ◔*No lunch*.

$
VEGETARIAN
★
✕**Moosewood.** Since its founding in 1973, this downtown restaurant has been at the forefront in the field of creative vegetarian cooking, and its cookbooks are known worldwide. The menu changes daily, and everything is prepared from fresh ingredients. Past menus have

included spinach-and-cheese ravioli in a red-pepper-basil sauce and haddock with lemon, thyme, tomatoes, and topped with dill pesto. A vegan option is always available. The setting is casual: chunky blond-wood tables and booths and lively conversation fill the space. You may also dine outside on a patio. ⊠ *215 N. Cayuga St. (entrance on Seneca St.)* ☎ *607/273–9610* ⊟ *AE, D, MC, V* ⌖ *Reservations not accepted* ⊘ *No lunch Sun.*

$ ✕ **Taste of Thai.** Finding foreign fare in the Finger Lakes can be a chal-
THAI lenge, but not in this university town. Ithaca has several Thai restaurants, and this family-owned and -operated choice is a favorite both for its consistent food and its location on the Commons. The casual but classy place has orange faux-finish walls and is decorated with Buddha statuettes. Ithacans of all ages come for the moderately priced and expertly spiced curry, noodle, and seafood dishes. It's a buzzy, convivial place. ⊠ *216 E. State St.* ☎ *607/256–5487* ⊟ *AE, D, MC, V* ⊘ *No lunch weekdays.*

WHERE TO STAY

■ **TIP →** Ithaca is a university town, so book far in advance during busy events like graduation and orientation at Cornell University and Ithaca College. Rooms also book up during big events at the Watkins Glen speedway.

¢–$ 🏠 **Grayhaven Motel.** The lodging is in a suburban spot 3 mi from downtown. Motel rooms are simple, with no-frills furnishings. Rooms in the separate lodge building have wood-covered walls and vaulted ceilings. A cottage and a carriage house contain several rooms and suites. Picnic tables and Adirondack chairs, sprawled across the lawn, offer a respite after hikes at Buttermilk Falls State Park, 1 mi away. **Pros:** varied room options; economical rates. **Cons:** basic decor. ⊠ *657 Elmira Rd.* ☎ *607/272–6434* ⊕ *www.grayhavenmotel.com* ↘ *17 rooms* ⌂ *In-room: refrigerator, kitchen (some), DVD (some), Wi-Fi (some). In-hotel: gym, some pets allowed, no-smoking rooms* ⊟ *AE, D, MC, V* ⊘ *Closed mid-Nov.–Mar.*

$$ 🏠 **Inn on Columbia.** An 1830s Greek Revival mansion was completely renovated to create the main building of this unconventional B&B. Accommodations are rooms, suites, and cottages, some a block away from the main inn. The design is contemporary, with custom-designed furniture by architect and co-owner Kenn Young. Suites and cottages have gas fireplaces. Kenn's wife Madeline, a chef, prepares breakfast. The owners are fairly hands-off. **Pros:** near Ithaca Commons; more private than most B&Bs. **Cons:** not all guests get full breakfast. ⊠ *228 Columbia St. 14850* ☎ *607/272–0204* ⊕ *www.columbiabb.com* ↘ *4 rooms, 4 suites, 2 cottages* ⌂ *In-room: DVD (some), Internet (some), Wi-Fi (some). In-hotel: kitchen, laundry service (some), Wi-Fi, some pets allowed, no-smoking rooms* ⊟ *No credit cards.* ⦿ *BP, CP.*

$$–$$$ 🏠 **La Tourelle Resort & Spa.** This three-story inn sits on 70 acres on a hill 3 mi from downtown. You can hike into Buttermilk Falls State Park or fish in one of the two on-site ponds. Rooms vary in configuration and style: king rooms (many with fireplaces, hot tubs, and balconies) have swagged windows, light-wood furniture, and an overall feminine feel. A tower room has curved walls and a round bed. The John Thomas

Steakhouse occupies a farmhouse on the grounds; the inn building also has a bistro. **Pros:** on-site spa with full range of treatments; spacious rooms. **Cons:** older rooms need upgrading. ⊠*1150 Danby Rd./Rte. 96B* ☎*607/273–2734 or 800/765–1492* ⊕*www.latourelle.com* ⇆*53 rooms, 1 suite, 1 cottage* ⌂*In-room: safe, refrigerator, DVD, Internet (some), Wi-Fi (some). In-hotel: 2 restaurants, bar, spa, tennis courts, gym, Internet terminal, some pets allowed, no-smoking rooms* ⊟*AE, DC, MC, V* ⓘⓄⒾ*BP.*

$$$–$$$$ 🏨 **Statler Hotel at Cornell University.** Cornell's School of Hotel Administration operates this nine-story hotel, as well as an Italian restaurant and two cafeterias. Guests have access to university recreational facilities, including the pool, golf course, basketball court, and ice-skating rink. Rooms, with contemporary furnishings, have beautiful campus views. Suites are spacious and have one full and one half bath. The hotel and dining facilities are closed during the university's Thanksgiving and Christmas recesses. **Pros:** on campus; nice upper-floor views; eager staff. **Cons:** pricey rates; valet is the only parking option. ⊠*130 Statler Dr.* ☎*607/257–2500 or 800/541–2501* ⊕*www.statlerhotel.cornell. edu* ⇆*138 rooms, 15 suites* ⌂*In-room: refrigerator, Internet, Wi-Fi. In-hotel: restaurant, room service, bar, gym, laundry service, Internet terminal, Wi-Fi, no-smoking rooms* ⊟*AE, D, DC, MC, V.*

$$–$$$ 🏨 **William Henry Miller Inn.** Rooms at this inn, an 1880 Queen Anne
Fodor's Choice downtown, are imaginatively decorated to highlight alcoves, built-in
★ shelves, curved walls, and steeple views of the city center. Furnishings are traditional and pretty: European armoires, cherrywood sleigh beds and four-poster beds, and wood shutters. Breakfast is excellent, with treats like a homemade English muffin topped with scrambled eggs, smoked salmon, and asparagus, plus fresh juice and assorted muffins. A dessert buffet is offered in the evening. **Pros:** every detail attended to—down to the hand-ironed sheets; modern bathrooms; walking distance to Cornell and Ithaca Commons. **Cons:** small TVs. ⊠*303 N. Aurora St.* ☎*607/256–4553 or 877/256–4553* ⊕*www.millerinn.com* ⇆*8 rooms, 1 suite* ⌂*In-room: DVD (some), Internet, Wi-Fi. In-hotel: laundry service, Internet terminal, Wi-Fi, no kids under 12, some pets allowed, no-smoking rooms* ⊟*AE, D, DC, MC, V* ⓘⓄⒾ*BP.*

AURORA

27 mi north of Ithaca.

Stretching nearly a mile along the east shore of Cayuga Lake, Aurora has long been one of the prettiest 19th-century villages in upstate New York. Historically sensitive renovations beginning in 2001 freshened a number of commercial and residential buildings on Main Street, where colonial, Federal, and Victorian structures mix with examples of other architectural styles. A cluster of quality restaurants and one-of-a-kind shops helps make this a worthy destination. Wells College, established in 1868, anchors the south end of town. Built into a hillside overlooking Cayuga Lake, Wells was a women-only institution until trustees decided to admit men in 2005.

GETTING HERE AND AROUND

Aurora is directly north of Ithaca along lakeside State Route 90, but also 20 mi from Seneca Falls and from Auburn. It's accessible only by car.

VISITOR INFORMATION

Cayuga County Office of Tourism (⊠ *131 Genesee St., Auburn* ☎ *315/255–1658 or 800/499–9615* ⊕ *www.tourcayuga.com*).

WHAT TO SEE

MacKenzie-Childs. The design studios and factory of this home-furnishings empire occupy a Victorian farmhouse and other attractive buildings on a bluff overlooking Cayuga Lake. A 15-minute studio-tour video plays continuously in the visitor center, where artisan demos are given Friday and Sunday 11–4. You can tour the "farmhouse," a late-1800s Second Empire–style home that's been renovated and decorated with MacKenzie-Childs products. The extensive, 75-acre grounds include gardens, trails, and a shop devoted to MacKenzie-Childs wares. ⊠ *3260 Rte. 90* ☎ *315/364–7123* ⊕ *www.mackenzie-childs.com* ☒ *Free* ☉ *Visitor center daily 10–5. Farmhouse tours June–Columbus Day, daily at 10, 11, 1, 2, 3, and 4; rest of yr, weekdays at 11, 1, and 2.*

SHOPPING

Bet the Farm (⊠ *318 Main St.* ☎ *315/294–5643*) sells its own wines— made at Damiani Wine Cellars in Hector—as wells as unique dips, sauces, cheeses, chocolates, and more in an adorable shingle-house shop. **Jane Morgan's Little House** (⊠ *347 Main St.* ☎ *315/364–7715*) stocks good-quality women's slacks, sweaters, skirts, dresses, and tasteful accessories. The staff is very helpful. The store is in a two-story brick building in the center of Aurora. Victoria and Richard MacKenzie-Childs, creators of the MacKenzie-Childs brand, sell their Alice-in-Wonderland-esque housewares at **Home Again** (⊠ *1671 Rte. 90* ☎ *315/364–8615*), 4 mi south of Aurora.

WHERE TO EAT

$$$
AMERICAN
✕ **Aurora Inn.** Well appointed but not overdone, the Aurora Inn is the spot for fine dining in town. The food is mostly classic American and the seasonal menu uses many fresh, local ingredients. Dinner could be veal Oscar (with crab cakes and béarnaise sauce), pan-seared scallops, or rack of lamb. The pastry chef whips up decadent desserts. You can eat inside or out: the formal dining room with floor-to-ceiling windows opens out onto a spacious patio overlooking Cayuga Lake. Breakfast is served daily. ⊠ *319 Main St.* ☎ *315/364–8888* ▤ *AE, D, MC, V* ☉ *Closed Nov.–Apr. No lunch or dinner Mon. and Tues. in May, Sept., and Oct.*

¢
AMERICAN
✕ **Dorie's.** The Victorian-style café has about a dozen tables and counter seating inside, as well as a deck overlooking Cayuga Lake. The menu features soups, sandwiches, and salads, plus ice cream, floats, and shakes, and a good-size list of hot-drink concoctions (caffeinated and otherwise). It also has a case of baked goods, a rack of daily newspapers, a small selection of gifts, and a selection of hand-scooped candies sold by the bag. ⊠ *238 Main St.* ☎ *315/364–8818* ▤ *MC, V* ☉ *No dinner.*

The Wine Trails

One of the top reasons to visit the Finger Lakes is the wine. The region has three American Viticultural Areas, a federal designation. The Finger Lakes designation encompasses the four largest lakes. Cayuga and Seneca lakes, considered microclimates, have their own designations. Because of their size and depth, the lakes heat and cool more slowly than the surrounding land, moderating shore temperatures and extending the growing season.

Pinot noir, chardonnay, Riesling, cabernet franc, merlot, and cabernet sauvignon are among the fine wines produced in the region. Before the second half of the 20th century, only American Indian grapes, or *vitis labrusca,* which produce very sweet wines, were grown here. The belief was that the than more-delicate European *vitis vinifera* varietals wouldn't survive the climate. Dr. Konstantin Frank, a Ukrainian immigrant who settled in the area in the 1950s, challenged that belief and successfully started growing vinifera vines.

Today the region is home to more than 100 wineries, including Dr. Konstantin Frank Vinifera Wine Cellars, still considered the best by many. Although native grapes (Concord, Catawba, Niagara, Delaware) are still grown here, winemakers have been experimenting with new varieties, often with the help of Cornell University's College of Agriculture and Life Sciences.

WINE TRAILS
Nearly all the wineries have tasting rooms and gift shops, and many have restaurants, cafés, or picnic grounds with panoramic lake views. The trail associations sponsor events throughout the year. Not all Finger Lakes wineries are associated with the trails; Rochester's *Democrat & Chronicle* newspaper maintains a more comprehensive list and information at ⊕ *www.fingerlakeswine.com.*

The **Canandaigua Wine Trail** (☎ *877/386–4669* ⊕ *www. canandaiguawinetrail.com*) includes just five wineries, in Fairport, Canandaigua, and Naples, and two wine centers in Canandaigua.

The **Cayuga Wine Trail** (☎ *800/684– 5217 or 607/869–4281* ⊕ *www. cayugawinetrail.com*) has 16 wineries stretching from Seneca Falls down to Ithaca, with most concentrated on the western-central lakefront. Montezuma Winery, on the trail, is known for its mead (honey wine).

The **Keuka Lake Wine Trail** (☎ *800/440–4898* ⊕ *www. keukawinetrail.com*) encompasses nine wineries. Recommended: Dr. Konstantin Frank Vinifera Wine Cellars, Heron Hill, and Ravines Cellars in Hammondsport; Hunt Country Vineyards in Branchport; and Rooster Hill in Penn Yan. Wineries are more or less evenly distributed along the outer edges of the lake.

More than 30 wineries make up the **Seneca Lake Wine Trail** (☎ *877/536–2717* ⊕ *www. senecalakewine.com*). Some favorites are Fox Run Vineyards in Penn Yan, Glenora Wine Cellars in Dundee, and Lamoreaux Landing Wine Cellars in Lodi.

⊄ ✕**Fargo Bar & Grill.** A brick building across the street from the Aurora
AMERICAN Inn houses this tavern, a once-crusty bar now outfitted with dark-wood
paneling, rough-hewn beams, and crackling fireplaces. The food is pub
fare with a bit of flair. The most popular item is the burger, topped with
raw or caramelized onions and a choice of cheese, served with hand-cut
fries. Also on the menu are pulled-pork sandwiches, spicy black bean
burgers, and barbecue chicken sandwiches with apple-smoked bacon.
A TV resides over the bar and there's a pool table in back. ⊠*384 Main
St.* ☎*315/364–8006* ⊟*AE, D, DC, MC, V.*

WHERE TO STAY

$$$–$$$$ ⊞**Aurora Inn.** Most guest rooms in this luxurious 1833 Federal-style
brick inn have balconies with lake views; some have fireplaces and
whirlpool tubs. Furnishings are a rich and historically appropriate mix
of antiques and reproductions. Paintings and Oriental rugs outfit the
common rooms downstairs. Modern amenities include flat-screen TVs,
Bose CD players, Frette linens, terry robes, and marble bathrooms. The
restaurant serves elegant American fare. **Pros:** pristine property; every
detail is addressed. **Cons:** expensive rates. ⊠*391 Main St.* ☎*315/364–
8888* ⊕*www.aurora-inn.com* ➪*10 rooms* ⚲*In-room: safe, kitchen
(some), DVD, Internet, Wi-Fi. In-hotel: restaurant, bicycles, water
sports, Wi-Fi, no-smoking rooms* ⊟*AE, D, MC, V* ❍❘*BP* ⊗*Closed
Nov.–Apr.*

$$$–$$$$ ⊞**E. B. Morgan House.** Under the same management as the Aurora
Inn and less than a half mile up the road, the E. B. Morgan House is
equally as impressive and has many of the same luxurious amenities
(terry robes, Frette linens). The lakefront 1858 Italianate mansion is
filled with a mix of tasteful modern, reproduction, and antique pieces.
Three rooms have carved-wood four-poster beds. All rooms have mar-
ble baths. A full breakfast is available at the Aurora Inn May–October;
the on-site Continental breakfast includes a hot entrée and fresh muffins
or scones. **Pros:** gorgeous lakefront property; attention to detail; daily
wine-and-hors d'oeuvres hour. **Cons:** abbreviated breakfast off-season;
expensive. ⊠*431 Main St. 13026* ☎*315/364–8888* ⊕*www.aurora-inn.
com/eb_morgan_house* ➪*7 rooms* ⚲ *In-room: safe, kitchen (some),
DVD, Internet, Wi-Fi. In-hotel: restaurant, bicycles, water sports,
Wi-Fi, no-smoking room* ⊟*AE, D, MC, V* ❍❘*CP.*

CORNING AND ELMIRA

Corning and Elmira anchor the Finger Lakes region in the south, about
10 mi north of the Pennsylvania border. Route 17 links the two, and
both are bisected by the Chemung River.

CORNING

43 mi southwest of Ithaca, 106 mi southeast of Rochester.

One of the world's glass centers, Corning has an appropriate nickname:
Crystal City. The Corning Museum of Glass, housing the world's larg-
est collection of glass art, is one of New York State's major tourist

attractions. The town's restored 19th-century buildings along Market Street, Corning's main commercial strip in the Historic Gaffer District, has interesting storefronts and restaurants and is also worth a visit.

GETTING HERE

Airport Information **Elmira-Corning Regional Airport** (⊠ *276 Sing Sing Rd., Horseheads* ☎ *607/795–0402* ⊕ *www.ecairport.com*).

VISITOR INFORMATION

Finger Lakes Wine Country (⊠ *1 W. Market St., Corning* ☎ *607/936–0706 or 800/813–2958* ⊕ *www.fingerlakeswinecountry.com*).**Steuben County Conference & Visitors Bureau** (⊠ *1 W. Market St., Suite 301, Corning* ☎ *607/936–6544 or 866/946–3386* ⊕ *www.corningfingerlakes.com*).

WHAT TO SEE

☼ **Corning Museum of Glass.** One of the world's premier glass museums, the Corning Museum of Glass displays pieces ranging from contemporary glass sculpture to Frank Lloyd Wright and Louis Comfort Tiffany stained-glass windows to glassware crafted by Egyptians 3,500 years ago. About 10,000 of the more than 45,000 glass objects in the museum's collection are on display at any one time. Interactive exhibits show the history, beauty, and creativity of 35 centuries of glasswork. Glassmaking demonstrations are given throughout the day and a workshop encourages you to make your own glass souvenir ($10–$30); even preschoolers may participate. In the 18,000-square-foot gift shop you can buy works from local or internationally known glass artists, from a $5 glass-bead bracelet to a $17,000 Pepi Hermann cut-crystal platter, as well as utilitarian items, like the namesake CorningWare. Also available is Steuben Glass, founded in Corning; Steuben masterpieces have been presented as gifts to foreign heads of state and are in museums around the world. The museum adjoins a glass studio, which serves as a workshop for professional gaffers and an educational center for glass students. ⊠ *1 Museum Way* ☎ *800/732–6845* ⊕ *www.cmog.org* ⊡ *$12.50, $16.50 combination ticket with Rockwell Museum* ☉ *Late May–early Sept., daily 9–8; early Sept.–late May, daily 9–5.*

FodorsChoice
★

Rockwell Museum of Western Art. The museum has the largest collection of Western American art in the East. Art from the 19th and 20th centuries and American Indian artifacts and works show the people, places, and ideas of the West. Kids get to use special interactive backpacks as they go through the displays. The museum occupies an 1893 building, the old city hall, in the historic Market Street district. A Southwestern restaurant is on the premises. ⊠ *111 Cedar St.* ☎ *607/937–5386* ⊕ *www.rockwellmuseum.org* ⊡ *$6.50, $16.50 combination ticket with Corning Museum of Glass* ☉ *Late May–early Sept., daily 9–8; early Sept.–late May, daily 9–5.*

WHERE TO EAT

$ ✕ **Market Street Brewing Co.** Five beers—two lagers, and a red, pale, and dark ale—are brewed on-site throughout the year. Each season brings one or two specialty brews. The kitchen incorporates Thai, Southwestern, Mexican, Caribbean, and Italian influences, among others, in dishes such as pork osso buco, Jamaican jerk chicken, a salmon fillet glazed

ECLECTIC

with the brewery's D'Artagnan ale, coconut-battered shrimp appetizer. Sandwiches and burgers are also available. Beer suggestions accompany entrée descriptions. ⊠ *63–65 W. Market St.* ☎*607/936–2337* ⊟*AE, MC, V* ⊘*Closed Sun. and Mon. Nov.–Apr.*

$
AMERICAN

✕**Spencer's Restaurant and Mercantile.** This cozy family-oriented roadhouse with country music (live Friday and Saturday nights) is decorated with a rustic, eclectic mix of log-cabin-type paneling, hanging baskets, wooden shutters, and Christmas lights. The large and varied menu includes chicken and biscuits, steak, chops, fish fry, seafood, and American-style pasta dishes. ⊠ *359 E. Market St. Extension* ☎*607/936–9196* ⊟*AE, D, DC, MC, V.*

$$$
STEAK

✕**Tony R's Steak & Seafood.** Upscale dining has arrived in Corning. A historic bank was transformed into a stylish dining room in 2008, preserving the old vault as a private dining room. There's a 300-square-foot glass-enclosed wine locker, huge stone fireplaces, and a wildebeest mounted on one wall. Aged steaks, Alaskan king crab legs, and veal saltimbocca help fill out the long menu. The prices can be hard to swallow, but tapas in the bar are a more affordable option. ⊠ *2–6 E. Market St.* ☎*607/937–9277* ⚘*Reservations essential* ⊟*AE, D, MC, V* ⊘*No lunch weekends.*

WHERE TO STAY

$–$$
⊞**Radisson Hotel Corning.** In downtown Corning, this hotel is steps from Market Street, the Rockwell Museum, and the Corning Museum of Glass. Rooms have such traditional furnishings as dark-wood desks and big leather chairs, many have king-size beds, and some have bathrooms with granite countertops and brushed-steel fixtures. Guests share a 10-person hot tub outside. **Pros:** great location, near top attractions. **Cons:** decor not particularly inspiring; wireless Internet only in main building. ⊠ *125 Denison Pkwy. E* ☎*607/962–5000 or 800/333–3333* ⊕*www.radisson.com/corningny* ⟿*176 rooms, 1 suite* ⚐*In-room: kitchen (some), Internet (some), Wi-Fi (some). In-hotel: restaurant, room service, bar, pool, gym, Internet terminal, laundry facilities, laundry service, some pets allowed, no-smoking rooms* ⊟*AE, D, DC, MC, V.*

$–$$
⊞**Rosewood Inn.** The 1855 home is three blocks from downtown and less than 1 mi from the Corning Museum of Glass. Guest rooms, decked out in Victorian style, have antiques, plush towels, and 300-thread-count sheets. Some have canopy beds. Only the suites, both on the first floor, have kitchenettes. Porch-sitting in summer is replaced by 4 PM tea and cookies by the parlor fireplace in winter. **Pros:** friendly hosts; walking distance to Market Street. **Cons:** decor may be overly ruffled for some. ⊠ *134 E. 1st St.* ☎*607/962–3253* ⊕*www.rosewoodinn.com* ⟿*5 rooms, 2 suites* ⚐*In-room: kitchen (some), no phone (some), no TV (some), Wi-Fi. In-hotel: Wi-Fi, no kids under 12, no-smoking rooms* ⊟*AE, D, DC, MC, V* ⚭*BP.*

ELMIRA

19 mi southeast of Corning via I-86 and Rte. 17.

Settled in 1788, Elmira was the site of one of the battles of the Sullivan-Clinton expedition of 1779, during which a colonial army routed American Indians allied with the British. The city got its industrial start in the 19th century with lumbering and woolen mills. Confederate soldiers were held at a prison camp here during the Civil War; conditions were so bad that thousands of prisoners died.

Elmira's most famous resident, Samuel Clemens (aka Mark Twain), spent more than 20 summers at Quarry Farm, which belonged to his wife's family. He is buried in Elmira's Woodlawn Cemetery. The city has also been known as the "soaring capital of America," since it hosted the first national soaring contest in 1930.

VISITOR INFORMATION
Chemung County Chamber of Commerce (⊠ *400 E. Church St., Elmira* ☎ *607/734–5137* ⊕ *www.chemungchamber.org*).

WHAT TO SEE
Mark Twain's Study. Twain wrote *The Adventures of Huckleberry Finn* and *The Adventures of Tom Sawyer* in this study built for him by his sister-in-law and her husband. The octagonal shape was inspired by a Mississippi riverboat pilothouse. The study was moved to the Elmira College campus in the 1950s and is part of the school's Center for Mark Twain Studies. Cross the street to visit the (free) Mark Twain Exhibit to learn more about Twain's connection to Elmira or to buy books in the gift shop. ⊠ *Elmira College, 1 Park Pl.* ☎ *607/735–1941* ⊕ *www. elmira.edu* ⊡ *Free* ⊙ *May–early Sept., Mon.–Sat. 9–5, Sun. noon–5; early Sept.–mid-Oct., Sat. 9–5, Sun. noon–5; or by appointment.*

ⓒ **National Soaring Museum.** Dozens of sailplanes and gliders, dating from
★ the late 19th to the late 20th century, are on display at this museum, part of Harris Hill Park. Movies and exhibits help explain and explore the heritage of gliding. You can even take a sailplane ride ($70; April–November weather permitting; reservations required). ⊠ *Harris Hill Park, 51 Soaring Hill Dr., off Rte. 17, 10 mi west of downtown Elmira* ☎ *607/734–3128* ⊕ *www.soaringmuseum.org* ⊡ *$6.50* ⊙ *Daily 10–5.*

Woodlawn Cemetery. Mark Twain rests in the Langdon family plot, with his daughter Clara and son-in-law, Ossip Gabrilowitsch, at his feet. A 12-foot-tall monument marks the spot (12 feet, in river terminology, is 2 fathoms, or "mark twain," the derivation of Clemens' pen name). ⊠ *1200 Walnut St.* ☎ *607/732–0151* ⊕ *www.friendsofwoodlawnelmira. org* ⊡ *Free* ⊙ *Daily dawn–dusk.*

WHERE TO EAT
$$ ✕ **Hill Top Inn.** A giant wreath with a shamrock beckons from a hill,
AMERICAN making this family-owned restaurant, in operation since 1933, hard to miss. The menu has mostly seafood, steak, and chops: filet mignon, scallops in cheese-and-cream sauce, and Irish surf and turf (with lamb

chop and langostinos). Open-air dining is an option on the deck and terrace. ⊠*171 Jerusalem Hill Rd.* ☎*607/732–6728 or 888/444–5586* ▤*AE, D, DC, MC, V* ☉*Closed Sun. No lunch.*

\$\$ ✕**Tanino Ristorante.** Worth the 6-mi drive north of town, family-owned
ITALIAN and -operated Tanino's, as it's called, serves more-authentic Italian than is usually found in this area: meals start with bread and olive oil rather than bread and pats of butter, and the wine list is one of the region's lengthiest. Ignore the strip-mall exterior and head into the casual, comfortable dining room with a fireplace. The large menu includes about a dozen choices each of pasta (cheese ravioli, penne alla vodka), seafood, poultry, veal, and beef entrées, plus popular brick-oven pizzas. ⊠*1–3 Ithaca Rd., Horseheads* ☎*607/739–7013* ▤*AE, D, MC, V* ☉*No lunch weekends.*

EASTERN LAKES

Skaneateles Lake and **Owasco Lake** are in the eastern part of the region, near Syracuse. Of the 11 lakes, these two are medium in size. The village of Skaneateles is mentioned simultaneously with the lake of the same name. Skaneateles, lake and village, set the standard for Finger Lakes hospitality; a number of municipalities attempt to emulate its accent on tourism. Owasco Lake isn't as closely identified with Auburn, several miles from the lake's northern end. But it does feed the Owasco Outlet, which powered Auburn's industrial heritage, and the lake continues to be a huge contributor to the Auburn area's quality of life.

AUBURN

27 mi west of Syracuse.

Around 28,000 people live in Auburn, an urban outpost in rural Cayuga County. Despite a somewhat shabby downtown, the city has a number of beautiful and remarkably intact buildings dating from the early 1800s. The Auburn Correctional Facility, built in 1817 and still used as a maximum-security state prison, subcontracted inmate labor to local businesses until the 1890s. Cheap prison labor combined with water power streaming in from Owasco Lake and railway transportation routes in every direction conspired to make Auburn one of upstate New York's most important 19th-century industrial centers.

GETTING HERE AND AROUND
Highway Route 5/U.S. 20 passes through Auburn, which is easily reached via Route 5 from Syracuse. Auburn is not accessible by public transport.

VISITOR INFORMATION
Cayuga County Office of Tourism (⊠*131 Genesee St., Auburn* ☎*315/255–1658 or 800/499–9615* ⊕*www.tourcayuga.com*).

WHAT TO SEE

Cayuga Museum of History and Art. The history and culture of Cayuga County, which stretches from Lake Ontario to outside Ithaca, is carefully curated in exhibits here. Some of the focus is on the Auburn Correctional Facility, which has shaped the area for three centuries and is the oldest continually operating prison in the nation. ⊠ *203 Genesee St.* ☎ *315/253–8051* ⊕ *www.cayuganet.org/cayugamuseum* ☜ *$3 suggested donation* ⊙ *Feb.–Dec., Tues.–Sun. noon–5.*

★ **Fort Hill Cemetery.** Some of Auburn's most famous residents are buried at Fort Hill, an outstanding example of the parklike burial grounds resulting from the rural-cemetery movement of the early 1800s. Rising over a middle-class residential and commercial neighborhood near downtown, Fort Hill is a great place for a quiet walk under giant trees and for views of the city. Among those buried here are William H. Seward, who served in the cabinets of two U.S. presidents; Harriet Tubman, who liberated hundreds of slaves; and Captain Myles Keogh, who fought (and died) alongside General George Custer at Little Big Horn. ⊠ *19 Fort St.* ☎ *315/253–8132* ⊕ *www.cayuganet.org/forthill* ☜ *Free* ⊙ *Daily dawn–dusk.*

Harriet Tubman Home. The property's simple white clapboard house is where, beginning in 1890, Harriet Tubman tended to elderly African-Americans; the adjacent brick house served as her primary residence. Before Emancipation, Tubman led more than 300 slaves to freedom in the North. At the encouragement of William Seward, an abolitionist who served in two presidential cabinets, she settled in Auburn in the late 1850s. Seward and his family lived on the same road, a mile closer to town. The brick house isn't currently open to the public (though it's being restored for future visits), but Tubman's carved wooden bed and her Bible are displayed in the white clapboard building. Tours are given hourly. ⊠ *180 South St.* ☎ *315/252–2081* ☜ *$4.50* ⊙ *Feb.–Oct., Tues.–Fri. 10–4, Sat. 10–3; Nov.–Jan., by appointment.*

★ **Seward House.** William H. Seward (1801–72), a governor of New York, U.S. senator, and secretary of state under Presidents Abraham Lincoln and Andrew Johnson, lived in this distinguished Federal-style home. The Seward family occupied the house (built in 1816–17) until 1951, and virtually every object here—the furnishings, the library, the tableware—was theirs. ⊠ *33 South St.* ☎ *315/252–1283* ⊕ *www.sewardhouse.org* ☜ *$7* ⊙ *July–mid-Oct., Tues.–Sat. 10–4, Sun. 1–4; mid-Oct.–June, Tues.–Sat. 10–4; tours on the half hr.*

Willard Memorial Chapel. Fourteen brilliant stained-glass windows are the centerpiece of the chapel interior, a Louis Comfort Tiffany creation with mosaic-inlay floors and nine leaded-glass chandeliers. It's the only known Tiffany-designed chapel interior still intact. A lunchtime music series is held here in July and August. ⊠ *17 Nelson St.* ☎ *315/252–0339* ⊕ *www.willardchapel.org* ☜ *$3 donation* ⊙ *Sept–June, Tues.–Fri. 10–4; July and Aug. Tues.–Fri. 10–4 and Sun. 1–4.*

SPORTS AND THE OUTDOORS

Emerson Park. The 133-acre park, 3 mi south of downtown Auburn, includes a beach on Owasco Lake, three boat-launch sites, picnic shelters, a playground, and a snack stand open daily in summer. Lifeguards are on duty Memorial Day to Labor Day. ⊠ *E. Lake Rd./Rte. 38A* ☎ *315/253–5611* ⊕ *co.cayuga.ny.us/parks/emerson* ⊠ *Parking $2* ⊙ *Daily dawn–dusk.*

NIGHTLIFE AND THE ARTS

The **Finger Lakes Drive-In** (⊠ *1056 Clark Street Rd. [Rte. 5/U.S. 20])* ☎ *315/252–3969* ⊠ *$5*), open nightly from spring through early fall, is one of the country's few remaining outdoor-movie venues. The place, 3 mi west of Auburn, shows many first-run films and is popular with families. The **Merry-Go-Round Playhouse** (⊠ *Emerson Park, Rte. 38A, 2 mi south of U.S. 20* ☎ *315/255–1785* ⊕ *www.merry-go-round.com*), a professional summer theater, produces up to six classic American musicals from late May to October.

WHERE TO EAT AND STAY

$$ ✕ **Balloons.** Since 1934, Balloons has been a local favorite for its prompt
ITALIAN service, uncomplicated menu, and warm welcome. The concrete wall
★ of the Auburn Correctional Facility is right across the street, but Balloons, with its original art-deco decor, is a transporting experience. Sizzling steaks are the specialty, but you can also go for heaping platters of spaghetti and meatballs, surf and turf, or rattlesnake pasta (chicken and pasta with a spicy chipotle sauce), all accompanied by an iceberg salad topped with the original secret-recipe house dressing. ⊠ *67 Washington St.* ☎ *315/252–9761* ⊟ *AE, MC, V* ⊙ *Closed Sun. and Mon. No lunch.*

$-$$ 🛏 **Springside Inn.** The red clapboard inn, built in 1851, is across the road from Owasco Lake. Guest rooms all have wood floors and Victorian antiques; some have claw-foot tubs. According to local legend, Harriet Tubman hid runaway slaves in the woods behind the inn. Guests may use the inn's dock. The restaurant, open for dinner Thursday through Saturday and brunch on Sunday, serves Continental and American fare. A five-bedroom guesthouse is also available. **Pros:** updated rooms; close to the lake. **Cons:** so-so breakfast. ⊠ *6141 W. Lake Rd./Rte. 38 S* ☎ *315/252–7247* ⊕ *www.springsideinn.com* ⇆ *5 rooms, 2 suites, 1 house* ♿ *In-room: refrigerator (some), kitchen (some), DVD, Internet, Wi-Fi. In-hotel: restaurant, bar, room service, Internet terminal, Wi-Fi, no-smoking rooms* ⊟ *AE, MC, V* ⓘ⍔ *CP.*

$$$-$$$$ 🛏 **10 Fitch.** Guests rave about this early-1900s stucco house in Auburn's historic district. The antiques mixed with funky MacKenzie-Childs furnishings, cushy modern armchairs, and contrasting patterns make a bold statement, but it all comes together beautifully. Romance and privacy is key in the spacious, uniquely decorated rooms. In the English suite, the four-poster canopy bed faces a fireplace and the huge bathroom has 14-foot ceilings, a claw-foot tub, a two-person shower, and a dressing area. A veranda a fire pit is a popular place to wind down. **Pros:** guests get the royal treatment; multiple package options. **Cons:** expensive; books up quickly. ⊠ *10 Fitch Ave.* ☎ *315/255–0934* ⊕ *10fitch.*

com ↪3 *suites* ♿*In-room: no phone, refrigerator (some), DVD, Wi-Fi. In-hotel: Wi-Fi, no kids under 17, no-smoking rooms* ⊟*AE, D, MC, V.* ¶○¶*BP.*

OFF THE BEATEN PATH

The limestone-and-shale **Fillmore Glen State Park** (⊠*1686 Rte. 38, Moravia* ☎*315/497–0130* ⊕*nysparks.state.ny.us* ⊠*Parking $7* ☉*Daily dawn–dusk*), 17 mi south of Auburn, has five waterfalls and a stream-fed, stone-walled swimming pool. Named for the nation's 13th president, the park also has a replica of the cabin where Millard Fillmore was born. (The actual site is 5 mi east.)

SKANEATELES

18 mi southwest of Syracuse.

On a former stagecoach route, Skaneateles—officially pronounced skanny-atlas (though you'll hear skinny-atlas from locals, too)—presides over the northern tip of a stunning, 16-mi-long lake with the same name. The village has dodged the so-called urban renewal that destroyed the face of many Finger Lakes communities. Instead, it has treasured most of its Greek Revival and Victorian homes and neat-as-a-pin look. Some shops and restaurants are decidedly upscale, and this 2,600-person village is the Beverly Hills of the mostly modest region. Nevertheless, tradition hasn't been forsaken, and you can still treat yourself to plain vanilla ice-cream cones. A cozy graciousness born of prim front porches and subdued commercialism pervades, and community bands perform at the Victorian gazebo at lakeside Clift Park.

GETTING HERE AND AROUND

U.S. 20 takes you from Auburn to Skaneateles, which is also a quick drive from Syracuse along Routes 5 and 321. You must have a car in Skaneateles.

VISITOR INFORMATION

Skaneateles Area Chamber of Commerce (⊠*22 Jordan St., Skaneateles* ☎*315/685–0552* ⊕*www.skaneateles.com*).

WHAT TO SEE

Creamery Museum. Lake history and local farming take center stage at this 1899 barn-style building where butter bound for New York City was produced. Exhibits here also feature the prickly, cone-shape teasel—a plant used in mills to "tease" the nap of wool. Skaneateles was a teasel-growing center until the 1950s, when synthetic fabrics replaced much of the demand for wool. ⊠*28 Hannum St.* ☎*315/685–1360* ⊕*www.skaneateleshistoricalsociety.org* ⊠*Free* ☉*May–Sept., Thurs.– Sat. 1–4; Oct.–Apr., Fri. 1–4.*

SPORTS AND THE OUTDOORS

BOAT TOURS Cruise Skaneateles Lake or the Erie Canal with **Mid-Lakes Navigation** (⊠*11 Jordan St.* ☎*315/685–8500* ⊕*www.midlakesnav.com*). Brunch, dinner, and sightseeing cruises on Skaneateles Lake depart from mid-May through September. One tour is on a 1937 mailboat. Erie Canal tours, which include sightseeing tours and two-, three-, and

A HANDLE ON THE LAKES

Iroquois legend holds that the Finger Lakes are hand imprints that were left in the soil after the Great Spirit blessed the land. Of the 11 Finger Lakes, 10 do resemble fingers. (Keuka Lake, which is Y-shaped, is the exception.) Geologists say retreating glaciers carved out these north–south lakes. The six that are more than 10 mi long are the major lakes. Their names (all but one American Indian), lengths, and depths follow, from east to west: Otisco ("Waters Dried Away"): 6 mi long, 66 feet deep. Skaneateles ("Long Lake"): 15 mi long, 350 feet deep. Owasco ("Crossing Place"): 11 mi long, 177 feet deep. Cayuga ("Boat Landing"): 40 mi long, 435 feet deep. Seneca ("Place of the Stone"): 36 mi long, 632 feet deep. Keuka ("Canoe Landing"): 22 mi long, 157 feet deep. Canandaigua ("Chosen Place"): 16 mi long, 262 feet deep. Honeoye ("Finger Lying"): 5 mi long, 30 feet deep. Canadice ("Long Lake"): 3 mi long, 91 feet deep. Hemlock (not named by American Indians): 8 mi long, 98 feet deep. Conesus ("Always Beautiful"): 9 mi long, 59 feet deep.

four-day excursions—depart from Baldwinsville, 25 mi northeast of Skaneateles.

NIGHTLIFE AND THE ARTS

★ Chamber music reigns during the monthlong **Skaneateles Festival** (⊠*97 Genesee St.* ☎*315/685–7418* ⊕*www.skanfest.org*), which starts in early August. Pianist Jon Nakamatsu is among the many other acclaimed musicians who have been featured in the program. Performances, ranging from $12 to $30, are held in First Presbyterian Church and at the Brook Farm estate.

WHERE TO EAT

$ ✕**Doug's Fish Fry.** Go for the fried-fish sandwich and clam chowder,
SEAFOOD stay for the down-home atmosphere at this Skaneateles institution. The
★ menu, posted over the counter where orders are taken, also includes steamed clams, fried shrimp, grilled chicken, frankfurters, and ice cream. Drop by Friday for lobster bisque. The counter staff shouts your name when your order is ready. Sit in the dining room under watch of the colorful mural of Skaneateles, at an outdoor picnic table, or take it to go. ⊠*8 Jordan St.* ☎*315/685–3288* ⌕*Reservations not accepted* ⊟*MC, V.*

$$$ ✕**Rosalie's Cucina.** A Tuscan-style eatery, Rosalie's is upscale but relaxed.
ITALIAN On a weekend night in the downstairs dining room you can forget
★ meaningful conversation unless you read lips. (The smaller upstairs room is quieter and more romantic.) The buzz is about the food, served in generous portions. The Italian fare includes appetizers such as carpaccio—ultra-thin slices of raw beef served with capers and Parmigiano-Reggiano cheese—and main dishes like chicken scaloppine with lemon butter, pancetta, and artichoke hearts. Don't skip dessert—the Banana Budino is unbelievable: layers of creamy banana pudding, real bananas, house-made cinnamon-sugar puff pastry, almond cookies, and caramel

sauce. ⊠ *841 W. Genesee St.* ☎ *315/685–2200* ⚲ *Reservations not accepted* ⊟ *AE, D, DC, MC, V* ⊘ *No lunch.*

$$ ✕ **Sherwood Inn Dining Room & Tavern.** The original 1807 tavern, rus-
AMERICAN tic compared with the elegant dining room, is perhaps the best place around to experience Old Skaneateles—meaning pre-1980, when the village was more of a cozy bedroom community for Syracuse than a vacation destination. Menu favorites include traditional Yankee pot roast and crab cakes with scallop mousse. Seasonal offerings might be seafood bouillabaisse or chicken-and-biscuits. An enclosed porch lined with windows is open in warm weather. ⊠ *26 W. Genesee St.* ☎ *315/685–3405* ⊟ *AE, MC, V.*

WHERE TO STAY

$$ ⌂ **1899 Lady of the Lake.** Fresh flowers, lovely antiques, and touches of Portuguese lace set the mood at this Queen Anne–style beauty. Its key selling point is the location, across the street from Skaneateles Lake and Clift Park. You can easily walk to shopping, a boat ride, and dinner. The excellent breakfasts include German pancakes. **Pros:** great location; plenty of charm. **Cons:** small rooms. ⊠ *2 W. Lake St.* ☎ *315/685–7997 or 888/685–7997* ⊕ *www.ladyofthelake.net* ⇆ *3 rooms* ⚲ *In-room: no phone, DVD, Internet, Wi-Fi. In-hotel: bicycles, Internet terminal, Wi-Fi, some pets allowed, no kids under 8, no-smoking rooms* ⊟ *AE, D, MC, V* ⊚ *BP.*

$$ ⌂ **Arbor House Inn.** Furniture dating from the 1700s and other antiques outfit this 1852 brick inn. Most rooms have a gas or electric fireplace, and several have a whirlpool tub. The dominant feature of each of the individually decorated guest rooms tends to be the bed—a tall four-poster or a bird's-eye maple sleigh bed, perhaps. Floors are hardwood, with bedside throw rugs. The inn is a block from Skaneateles Lake and the restaurant and shopping district. **Pros:** central village location; attractive decor. **Cons:** not on lake; no Wi-Fi. ⊠ *41 Fennell St.* ☎ *315/685–8966 or 888/234–4558* ⊕ *www.arborhouseinn.com* ⇆ *8 rooms, 3 suites* ⚲ *In-room: kitchen (some), Internet (some). In-hotel: no-smoking rooms* ⊟ *AE, D, MC, V* ⊚ *BP.*

$$–$$$ ⌂ **Mirbeau Inn & Spa.** Understated elegance is the rule at this château-like property. Mirbeau is French for "reflected beauty" and appropriately, the complex wraps around a water garden with lovely lilies and an arched wooden walkway. The 10,000-square-foot Roman-style spa has the region's most extensive treatment menu. Rooms have fireplaces, French-country furnishings, down comforters, and soaking tubs. On Saturday night the elegant Giverny restaurant, which serves contemporary takes on seafood and game, hosts live jazz. Four- and five-course tasting menus are available. **Pros:** A-to-Z pampering; good restaurant; quiet grounds. **Cons:** pricey spa treatments; expensive restaurant. ⊠ *851 W. Genesee St.* ☎ *315/685–5006 or 877/647–2328* ⊕ *www. mirbeau.com* ⇆ *34 rooms* ⚲ *In-room: refrigerator, DVD, Internet, Wi-Fi. In-hotel: restaurant, bar, gym, spa, bar, Internet terminal, Wi-Fi, no-smoking rooms* ⊟ *AE, D, MC, V* ⊚ *BP.*

$$–$$$ ⌂ **Sherwood Inn.** This blue-shingle inn is across the street from Clift Park
★ and Skaneateles Lake. You may book a boat ride, complete with captain, on the inn's 1946 wooden Chris-Craft. Guest rooms in the traditional,

tasteful main building are individually decorated with antiques, many carved-wood four-poster beds, and crisp white moldings. Suites have fireplaces and either steam showers or Jacuzzi baths. Drinks are served from the original 1807 tavern, which connects to a refined dining room. **Pros:** near the lake; recommended restaurant. **Cons:** rooms above tavern can be noisy. ⊠*26 W. Genesee St.* ☎*315/685–3405 or 800/374–3796* ⊕*www.thesherwoodinn.com* ⌑*9 rooms, 16 suites* ⌂*In-room: Wi-Fi. In-hotel: restaurant, room service (some), bar, laundry service, Internet terminal, Wi-Fi, no-smoking rooms* ⊟*AE, D, MC, V* ⓞ*CP.*

SYRACUSE

255 mi northwest of New York City, 135 mi west of Albany.

At the southern tip of Onondaga Lake, Syracuse is considered the geographic center of the state. The Syracuse area is the ancestral home of the Iroquois Confederacy's Onondaga tribe, who lived in the surrounding hills. In the 1600s, Europeans began settling the area, which was found to be rich in salt. The Erie Canal floated Syracuse salt to the world. Salt production peaked during the Civil War, and Salt City, as Syracuse was called, diversified by producing steel, automobiles, and china, among other goods.

Syracuse University and the State University of New York's Upstate Medical University are the top employers today in terms of numbers of jobs. Parts of downtown have been reinvented as a cultural and nightlife destination. The Everson Museum, which has outdoor sculptures and a large piazza, anchors one corner of downtown; Armory, Clinton, and Hanover squares anchor other sections of downtown, which hosts ethnic festivals, outdoor winter ice-skating, and an hours-long St. Patrick's parade, among other events.

Syracusans are fond of saying their city offers the best of city living without the traffic hassles. Thanks to quick-flow bypasses, it's possible to drive from one corner of Syracuse to another in minutes. But a good map and a game plan are essential; this is a loosely knit city, with attractions scattered throughout neighborhood nooks casual travelers might overlook.

GETTING HERE AND AROUND

Interstates 690, 481, and 81 merge at Syracuse, which lies 5 mi south of the New York State Thruway (Interstate 90). The city is a hub for Amtrak and several bus lines. Trains and buses arrive and depart from the Regional Transportation Centre, at 131 Alliance Bank Parkway (near the Carousel Center Mall). Syracuse's airport is 7 mi northeast of downtown. The city has public buses, but a car is by far the best way to get around.

Airport Information Syracuse Hancock International Airport (⊠*1000 Col. Eileen Collins Blvd., Syracuse* ☎*315/454–4330* ⊕*www.syrairport.org*).

VISITOR INFORMATION
Syracuse Convention & Visitors Bureau (✉ *572 S. Salina St., Syracuse* ☎ *315/ 470–1910 or 800/234–4497* ⊕ *www.visitsyracuse.org*).

WHAT TO SEE

Armory Square. The former factory-warehouse district of redbrick buildings is now a vibrant area with shops, restaurants, and loads of nightlife. The district is named after the 1874 armory, now home to the Museum of Science and Technology, near its southern perimeter. ✉ *On sections of Jefferson, Harrison, W. Fayette, and Clinton Sts.* ⊕ *www. armorysq.org.*

★ **Erie Canal Museum and Syracuse Heritage Area Visitor Center.** Orient yourself to Syracuse and the region by watching the introductory film in the museum theater. Then make your way to a replica canal boat in a circa-1850 building where real canal boats were weighed when the Erie was a major player in U.S. commerce. A re-created general store, an 1800s canal office, and a postal area are interspersed with exhibits about Syracuse musician Libba Cotten and others who shaped the region. ✉ *318 Erie Blvd. E* ☎ *315/471–0593* ⊕ *www.eriecanalmuseum.org* ✉ *Donations accepted* ⊙ *Mon.–Sat. 10–5, Sun. 10–3.*

NEED A BREAK? The smell of its bread baking is so good that **Columbus Baking Co.** (✉ *502 Pearl St.* ☎ *315/422–2913*) could charge admission. On a side street in Syracuse's Little Italy section, the bakery has just one product and makes it 10 paces from where customers buy it.

Everson Museum of Art. Jackson Pollock and Andrew Wyeth works are part of the collection of more than 8,000 objects at the Everson, which was designed by architect I. M. Pei. Kids have their own gallery. ✉ *401 Harrison St.* ☎ *315/474–6064* ⊕ *www.everson.org* ✉ *$5 donation* ⊙ *Tues.–Fri. and Sun. noon–5, Sat. 10–5.*

☾ **Museum of Science and Technology.** Walk through replicas of the human heart and brain; crawl, jump, and slide through the five-floor Science Playhouse; and learn about cave formations exploring the Discovery Cave. The MOST, as it's called, is a hands-on science museum built to entertain and educate. It occupies a former armory and includes an IMAX theater. ✉ *500 S. Franklin St.* ☎ *315/425–9068* ⊕ *www.most. org* ✉ *$5, IMAX $9* ⊙ *Wed.–Sun. 10–5.*

☾ **Open Hand Theater/International Mask & Puppet Museum.** A multicultural approach helps children enjoy the fine arts through masks and puppets, ranging from English marionettes to Indonesian shadow puppets. Performances are given at 11 AM on some Saturdays from October to April. The theater also has a storytelling series. Browse masks, puppets, and traditional wooden toys in the gift shop. ✉ *518 Prospect Ave.* ☎ *315/476–0466* ⊕ *www.openhandtheater.org* ✉ *Free* ⊙ *Museum by appointment Fri. 10–4 year-round, and 1st 2 Sat. of month Oct.–Apr. 10–12:30.*

Rosamond Gifford Zoo at Burnet Park. Part of the half-mile loop at this zoo is a treetop boardwalk that allows you to traipse above fields of reindeer and other hoofed animals. You can touch the Asian elephants, which have been bred here for decades. Sand cats, ocelots, meerkats, penguins, red pandas, and Amur tigers reside here, too, along with hundreds of other animals. A reptile house and a free-flight aviary are among the indoor exhibits. ⊠*1 Conservation Pl.* ☎*315/435–8511* ⊕*www. rosamondgiffordzoo.org* ☜*$6.50* ☉*Daily 10–4:30.*

3

Syracuse University. The school, founded in 1870 as a private coeducational institution, enrolls more than 19,000 students in its undergraduate and graduate programs. Two centuries of building styles can be seen on the compact campus, which is crossed by city streets and includes a traditional collegiate quadrangle. A number of lectures and music performances are open to the public, as is the **SUArt Galleries** (☎*315/443– 4097* ⊕*suart.syr.edu* ☜*Free* ☉*Tues., Wed., and Fri.–Sun. 11–4:30, Thurs. 11–8*), in the Shaffer Art Building. Get campus maps online or at the **Schine Student Center,** at 303 University Place. ⊠*University Ave. at University Pl.* ☎*315/443–1870* ⊕*www.syr.edu.*

**OFF THE
BEATEN
PATH**

Sterling Renaissance Festival. Enter Warwickshire, a 1585 English village spread across a wooded hillside, and spend the day as an Elizabethan. Costumed improvisational troupes beckon you to join them for a rollicking round at the dunking pond, courtly dancing, discourse at the village "well," or cheering at the jousting field, where men astride strong steeds play medieval games. Artisan booths feature Elizabethan-style caps and clothing, handmade musical instruments, and jewelry. The festival, about an hour north of the city, is held for seven summer weekends starting in early July. ⊠*15385 Farden Rd., Sterling* ☎*315/947–5783 or 800/879–4446* ⊕*www.sterlingfestival.com.*

SHOPPING

Stores in the five-block area known as **Armory Square** (⊠*On sections of Jefferson, Harrison, W. Fayette, and Clinton Sts.* ⊕*www.armorysq.org*) feature clothing, jewelry, crafts, antiques, and other wares. Crunchy, caramel-coated popcorn in a paper box is the signature walk-around food in downtown Syracuse. **Syracuse's Original Carmelcorn Shoppe** (⊠*116 W. Jefferson St.* ☎*315/475–2390*) has been popping on this block in the Armory Square district since 1930.

Syracuse's top tourist attraction is its 1.6-million-square-foot **Carousel Center Mall** (⊠*9090 Carousel Center Dr.* ☎*315/466–7000*). And it's getting even bigger. A project is underway to nearly double the size of the mall, part of a new 75-million-square foot "green" retail complex called Destiny USA.

NIGHTLIFE AND THE ARTS

Since the 1980s, **Armory Square** (⊠*On sections of Jefferson, Harrison, W. Fayette, and Clinton Sts.*), once a weary warehouse district, has evolved into a vibrant nightlife area. The dining and dancing destination encompasses five blocks of redbrick buildings softened by dark-green awnings. On Wednesday evenings from mid-May through August, **Party in the Plaza** (⊠ *Clinton St. at Genesee St.* ☎*315/234–4797*) transforms the James M. Hanley Federal Plaza into a free outdoor party. Bands play from 5 to 8 PM and vendors sell food and drink.

★ The ornate 1928 **Landmark Theatre** (⊠*362 S. Salina St.* ☎*315/475–7980* ⊕*www.landmarktheatre.org*) hosts touring stage shows, dance performances, concerts, stand-up comics, and classic films. Ani DiFranco, Jerry Seinfeld, and the Moscow Ballet are among the past performers and shows at this 3,000-seat venue. **Syracuse Stage** (⊠*820 E. Genesee St.* ☎*315/443–3275* ⊕*www.syracusestage.org*), a professional regional theater, hosts at least seven productions at its 499-seat theater each year. Productions include musicals, dramas, and children's programs. The **Syracuse Symphony** (⊠*411 Montgomery St.* ☎*315/424–8200* ⊕*www. syracusesymphony.org*), with 80 professional musicians, makes its home in the Mulroy Civic Center in downtown Syracuse, but sometimes performs in other venues.

FESTIVALS AND FAIRS

Balloon Fest. About two dozen hot-air balloons participate in this annual three-day event ($5 per day) held the second weekend in June. Live bands, balloon rides, and food and crafts vendors are part of the fun. ⊠*Jamesville Beach Park, Apulia Rd. north of Rte. 20 E, Jamesville* ☎*315/435–5252 Apr.–Sept., 315/451–7275 Oct.–Mar.* ⊕*www. syracuseballoonfest.com.*

Great New York State Fair. Nearly a million people visit the nearly two-week-long fair each year, making it one of the most popular events in upstate New York. The 375-acre fairground hosts world-class musical entertainment, carnival rides and games, international equestrian competitions, 4-H animal shows, butter-sculpting contests, and assorted vendors. Free daily entertainment includes concerts, circus acts, and more. ⊠*581 State Fair Blvd.* ☎*315/487–7711* ⊕*www.nysfair.org* ⌨*$10 ($6 in advance)* ◷*12 days leading up to Labor Day.*

WHERE TO EAT

If variety is what you seek, head to Armory Square, which has more than 40 restaurants in a six-block radius.

$ ✕**Clam Bar.** More clams are sold here than anywhere else in the region,
SEAFOOD according to the Clam Bar, which also serves lobster, haddock, steaks, and chicken, plus daily specials. Clams come raw, steamed, in marinara sauce, and with garlic, butter, and wine. A full bar rounds out this comfortable, family-owned North Syracuse spot, which opened in 1959 in an old farmhouse. ⊠*3914 Brewerton Rd., North Syracuse* ☎*315/458–1662* ▤*AE, D, MC, V.*

$ ✕**Coleman's.** Crawl through the little front door built for the "wee peo-
IRISH ple" and you'll understand why this restaurant is the center of Tipperary Hill, Syracuse's Irish neighborhood. (Don't worry: there's also a regular-size entrance.) Green beer flows freely every March 17, and corned beef

and cabbage and open-faced Reubens lead the menu year-round. Also available: shepherd's pie, seafood, and burgers. The cozy wood-paneled, two-story pub has several fireplaces. There's a full bar and Irish bands play Thursday through Sunday. Patio dining is a summer option. ⊠*100 Tompkins St.* ☎*315/476–1933* ⊟*AE, D, DC, MC, V.*

$ ✕**Dinosaur Bar-B-Que.** What started as a darling of the biker crowd has
AMERICAN evolved into a regional hot spot for pork sandwiches, barbecued ribs, and, on most nights, live blues. Chicken, beef, and pork are prepared barbecue, Cajun, and even Cuban style. Try a side of salt potatoes for some local flavor. On Friday and Saturday, waits can run as long as 90 minutes; the full-service bar, with 17 beers on tap, helps pass the time. In July and August, you can eat at one of the sidewalk picnic tables. ⊠*246 W. Willow St.* ☎*315/476–4937* ⚖*Reservations not accepted* ⊟*AE, D, DC, MC, V.*

$$ ✕**Pascale Wine Bar & Restaurant.** Many of the contemporary dishes here,
AMERICAN including the mixed grills, are prepared in the wood-fired oven. Combos
★ might include antelope (the antelope Wellington is a signature dish), quail, duck, or venison, and come with black-currant or huckleberry sauce. The menu, tuned to the weather, changes seasonally. Breads and desserts come from Pascale Bakehouse, a nearby sister operation. A 12-page wine list includes hundreds of wines from France, California, Australia, and South America; many are available by the glass. Local artists created most of the stained-glass panels, paintings, and sculptures you see here. ⊠*204 W. Fayette St.* ☎*315/471–3040* ⊟*AE, DC, MC, V* ⊘*No lunch.*

$ ✕**Pastabilities.** A funky, urban feel infuses this downtown Syracuse
CONTINENTAL spot—a former union hall—that attracts a business crowd by day and couples at night. Lunch is cafeteria style, while dinner is full service. There's always fresh pasta with sauces like the ever-popular spicy hot tomato oil. Dinners might include homemade Boursin-cheese ravioli in a tomato-mushroom-cream sauce with pine nuts. The restaurant bakes its own bread daily. In warm weather you can sit outside at a sidewalk table or in the back courtyard. ⊠*311 S. Franklin St.* ☎*315/474–1153* ⊟*AE, D, DC, MC, V* ⊘*No lunch weekends.*

WHERE TO STAY

$–$$ ⊡**Bed & Breakfast Wellington.** This 1914 Tudor-style home is a product of the Arts and Crafts movement and regionally acclaimed architect Ward Wellington Ward. The house, on a tree-lined street, has hardwood floors, two Mercer-tile fireplaces, and Oriental rugs throughout. One guest room has two queen-size beds and two rooms share a screened-in porch. **Pros:** friendly hosts; all beds are queen or king. **Cons:** fills up quickly; "expanded Continental" breakfast weekdays. ⊠*707 Danforth St.* ☎*315/474–3641 or 800/724–5006* ⊕*www.bbwellington. com* ➯*4 rooms, 1 suite* ⚒*In-room: kitchen (some), DVD, Internet, Wi-Fi. In-hotel: Internet terminal, Wi-Fi, parking (free), no-smoking rooms* ⊟*AE, D, DC, MC, V* ⍾*CP weekdays, BP weekends.*

$$–$$$ ⊡**Genesee Grande Hotel.** About five blocks from Syracuse University, this
★ hotel has rooms with elegant, streamlined furnishings, hypoallergenic

bedding, and granite bathrooms (some with whirlpool baths). The restaurant offers fine contemporary fare with many Italian-inspired selections; the bistro offers more casual fare. The 50-seat theater is used for both business and entertainment purposes. The hotel lounge has a grand piano. **Pros:** attentive staff; nicely decorated; well-maintained rooms. **Cons:** ho-hum views; facilities are in two buildings without interior connection. ⊠*1060 E. Genesee St.* ☎*315/476–4212 or 800/365–4663* ⊕*www.geneseegrande.com* ⇨*160 rooms, 49 suites* ⌂*In-room: safe (some), kitchen (some), Internet, Wi-Fi. In-hotel: restaurant, bar, room service, gym, laundry service, Internet terminal, parking (free), no-smoking rooms* ⊟*AE, D, DC, MC, V.*

$$–$$$ 🔲**Jefferson Clinton Hotel.** This Armory Square landmark is Syracuse's oldest hotel. Most rooms and suites have kitchens, and all have flat-screen TVs and leather desk chairs. Decor is traditional, with wall-to-wall carpeting, walnut veneer furnishings, and crisp white bedding. The pillow-top mattresses were custom-designed for the hotel. **Pros:** central location; upper floors have great city views. **Cons:** fee for parking; some awkward room layouts. ⊠*416 S. Clinton St.* ☎*315/425–0500* ⊕*www. jeffersonclintonhotel.com* ⇨*28 rooms, 40 suites* ⌂*In-room: refrigerator (some), kitchen (some), DVD, Internet, Wi-Fi. In-hotel: gym, Internet terminal, Wi-Fi, laundry service, parking (free), no-smoking rooms* ⊟*AE, MC, V* ❍❘*BP.*

$$–$$$ 🔲**Renaissance Syracuse Hotel.** Staying at this upscale 20-story hotel puts you within a mile of most downtown sights and within a few blocks of Syracuse University. Interiors show contemporary flair, with some pops of bright colors and interesting textures (like velvet pillows). Rooms also have flat-screen TVs, ergonomic work chairs, and speaker phones. There are full meals in bi-level Redfield's, while light fare is served in the Library Lounge. **Pros:** central location; updated rooms; shuttle service. **Cons:** next to highway; neighborhood not walkable. ⊠*701 E. Genesee St.* ☎*315/479–7000 or 877/843–6279* ⊕*www.renaissancesyracuse. com* ⇨*276 rooms, 3 suites* ⌂*In-room: safe, refrigerator (some), Internet, Wi-Fi. In-hotel: 2 restaurants, room service, bars, gym, laundry facilities, Internet terminal, parking (free), some pets allowed, no-smoking rooms* ⊟*AE, D, DC, MC, V.*

The Adirondacks and Thousand Islands

WORD OF MOUTH

"Having just traveled through some state parks in Pennsylvania and Ohio, I have to say the Adirondack Park just blows them all away . . ."

—annikany

By Jennifer Edwards

"Upstate New York may be America's best-kept secret," wrote George Meegan, an Englishman who made a seven-year, 19,000-mi trek (ending in 1983) through the Americas, in his account *The Longest Walk.*

The "secret" world of the Adirondacks and Thousand Islands region of New York—referred to as the North Country—includes everything from refined civility to absolute wilderness. You might cross paths with the rich and famous, or you might cross paths with deer, bear, loons, and beavers. It just depends on how and where you choose to spend your time in the region.

Much of the region is part of 6-million-acre Adirondack Park, the largest park in the continental United States. In fact, it's bigger than Grand Canyon, Yellowstone, Everglades, and Glacier national parks put together. Girding the blue-green, pristine mountain wilderness are lakes and rivers, principally Lake George and Lake Champlain to the east, the St. Lawrence River to the north, and Lake Ontario to the west.

The secret character of the region came about through disregard. The rugged land, inhospitable soil, and often unmerciful winter conditions sent early American settlers elsewhere for good farmland. Only the east, from Saratoga Springs, just outside the region's southern rim, to Lake Champlain, saw any significant settlement early on.

The extended disinterest proved, in the long run, a boon for wilderness lovers. By the 1800s the idea that there was value in the wilderness itself began to gain popular support. Fans as disparate as Ralph Waldo Emerson and Teddy Roosevelt discovered the Adirondack wilds and returned praising their virtues.

After the publication in 1869 of William H. H. Murray's classic *Adventures in the Wilderness,* extolling the freshness and purity of the Adirondack air, the area became recognized as a place for recuperation. A couple of decades later, wealthy families discovered the Adirondacks, giving rise to the building of rustic "great camps." These remote lodges were built of native wood and stone and had a rough-hewn look to them, but they were otherwise spacious and luxurious. One of the great camps, Camp Sagamore, was built in 1897 in the village of Racquette Lake. Now open for tours, it's a good example of what it means to rough it upper-crust style.

Though forgotten for much of the 20th century, the 1980 Winter Olympics in Lake Placid sparked renewed interest in the Adirondacks, Lake Placid in particular. The largest city in the region, however, is Watertown (population 27,000), which is in the Thousand Islands area but not on the water. The 1959 opening of the St. Lawrence Seaway, connecting the Great Lakes and the Atlantic Ocean, prompted modest growth in the smaller cities, as did the opening of Interstate 87 in the 1960s. There are no big cities here, but cities aren't the draw in the Adirondacks—escape is.

ADIRONDACKS TOP REASONS TO GO

Mountains aflame. Visitors travel from all over the world to see fall set foliage-covered Adirondack slopes and peaks alight.

Creature features. Within the 6 million acres of park (and even more wilderness), rare wildlife—like loons, beavers, bear, and moose—roam freely.

Winter wonderland. The region hosts every winter sport imaginable, from snowmobiling, skiing, and

snowshoeing to ice fishing and dog sledding.

Peak spots. Bag gorgeous views from atop of some of the region's most famous mountains, including from 4,867-foot Whiteface Mountain.

Adirondack-style shopping. Chances to snap up the quilts, knotty-pine furniture, and iconic Adirondack chairs abound in the region.

4

In fact, it's the sparseness of civilization that visitors seem to enjoy most about the region. Hiking trails and a plethora of lakes and rivers throughout the region offer plenty of opportunities to explore. In fall, when the leaves change color, the great expanses of forested land make for one of nature's most dramatic spectacles.

ORIENTATION AND PLANNING

GETTING ORIENTED

The region is bordered by the Mohawk River valley to the south, Lake Ontario and the St. Lawrence River valley to the west and north, and Lake Champlain to the east.

While there are no major urban areas in the Adirondacks, there are several towns·of note. In the northern Adirondacks, Lake Placid is unquestionably the hub of activity. To its south is the famed High Peaks area—the 46 highest peaks in the Adirondacks, most of them surpassing 4,000 feet. At 5,344 feet, Mt. Marcy is the highest point in New York. On it, at 4,320 feet above sea level, is Lake Tear of the Clouds, which is considered the source of the Hudson River. Also in the northern region is Lake Saranac, which, like Lake Placid, offers numerous dining, lodging, recreation, and shopping opportunities; Lake Saranac also has an airport with flights to/from Albany and Boston.

At the southeastern tip of the Adirondack State Park, near the border with Vermont, is Lake George, another travel hub and an entry point into the Champlain Valley. The valley is located at the easternmost edge of the park and—as its name implies—along the edge of the lake, which forms the physical border between the two states. There are several towns of interest in the valley, including Ticonderoga, which played a key role in the French and Indian War, and Bolton's Landing, a resort town.

PLANNING

WHEN TO GO

The region is very much defined by the seasons. Tourism shifts into high gear from June through August, before slowing down in September and October, and slowing considerably thereafter. Active skiing centers, such as Lake Placid and North Creek, have visitors through the winter, and snowmobilers, cross-country skiers, and ice fishermen in the North Country enjoy the cold winter months. With sizable winter populations—from both out-of-town tourists as well as New Yorkers who have second homes here for winter sports fun—cities such as Watertown, Glens Falls, and Plattsburgh remain reasonably active during the off-seasons. Generally speaking, the North Country slows down from November through April. Black-fly season can start as early as late April, and lasts until early July.

GETTING HERE AND AROUND

⇨ *Travel Smart New York State at the end of the book for contact information for airlines, buses, and trains.*

AIR TRAVEL

As serene and wild as the Adirondacks and Thousand Islands are, they still are located near some major urban hubs with airports and easy-to-travel roadways. The main commercial airports are located in Albany, to the southeast; in Syracuse, to the southwest; and in Montreal, over the northern border in Canada. Adirondack Regional Airport in Saranac Lake has flights to and from Boston on Cape Air; there's an airport for charter flights in Lake Placid; and a municipal airport in Ticonderoga. There's also an airport in Burlington, Vermont, to the east of the park across Lake Champlain. At Watertown International Airport, Cape Air flies inexpensively between Watertown and Albany.

Airport Information Adirondack Regional Airport (⊠ *North of Rte. 186, Lake Clear* ☎ *518/891-4600* ⊕ *www.saranaclake.com/airport/index.html).*

CAR TRAVEL

The North Country has two interstate highways: Interstate 81 and Interstate 87, both running north–south. The former cuts through the region's western edge, while the latter runs near its eastern edge. There are no major east–west highways, although the Interstate 90 tollway (the New York State Thruway) traverses the state not far from the region's southern rim and connects Syracuse and Albany to the arteries that lead northward. From Syracuse, travelers going to Thousand Islands can catch Interstate 81, and follow it north.

To get to the Adirondacks Park from Syracuse, drive east to Utica, then catch Route 8/12 north to access roads going east or northeast: Routes 365, 8, or 28. Those traveling to the park from Albany can hop on Interstate 87 (not a toll at this point) which goes north through the park. From Montreal to the park, head south on Autoroute Métropolitaine 15 and be sure to bring your U.S. passport in order to cross the border. To get from the Thousand Islands into Adirondack Park, take Route 3 east out of Watertown.

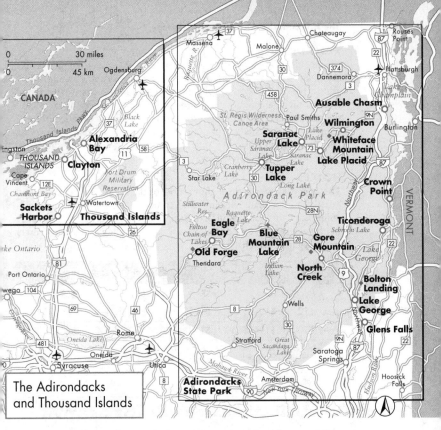

The Adirondacks
and Thousand Islands

Because the North Country gets considerable snowfall in winter, you should prep your car in cold-weather months. Distances between settlements with lodging and services can be substantial; stretches of 30 mi or more are common, especially in the central and far-north Adirondacks, so keep an eye on the gas gauge.

Some rules of thumb for when the temperature dips below freezing: keep your gas tank full (the tank can freeze if it's nearly empty); shut down all accessories before turning the car off (batteries only operate at 50% capacity when temperatures are at 0°F) and put some winter-mix windshield fluid in your wiper reservoir. You can find these mixes at gas stations throughout the region. You should be fine with all-weather tires.

TRAIN TRAVEL

Amtrak's Adirondacks line travels up from Albany–Rensselaer to Saratoga Springs and then to the eastern edge of the park, stopping at Whitehall (near Bolton Landing), Ticonderoga, Port Henry, Westport, and Port Kent (near Ausable Chasm). Amtrak's Empire line connects the northern part of western New York and Syracuse with the Adirondacks line in Albany. Bus service via Greyhound and Trailways is available into park destinations such as Lake George, Lake Placid, and Saranac Lake as well as Watertown in the Thousand Islands region.

RESTAURANTS

Haute cuisine is essentially nonexistent except for in a few places like the Lake Placid area and Lake George in the Adirondacks, and Alexandria Bay and Clayton in the Thousand Islands–Seaway area. Food is generally simple, good, and mostly American (especially steak and seafood). Meals at traditional lodges tend to be for guests, although many establishments accept nonguests for dinner. Indeed, some of the best food in the Adirondacks is served in resort and inn restaurants. There are a few fine breweries.

HOTELS

The operative words throughout most of the region are "simple" and "rustic" rather than "elegant" and "refined." Room prices and availability vary with the season. Expect to pay more in July and August, the fall foliage season, and during the December holidays. The ski centers stay busy into March.

WHAT IT COSTS					
	¢	$	$$	$$$	$$$$
RESTAURANTS	under $10	$10–$17	$18–$24	$25–$35	over $35
HOTELS	under $100	$101–$150	$151–$200	$201–$300	over $300

Restaurant prices are for a main course at dinner (or at the most expensive meal served). Hotel prices are for two people in a standard double room in high season, excluding tax.

THE THOUSAND ISLANDS AND THE SEAWAY

The name Thousand Islands is less than accurate; there might be nearly twice that number, depending on who's counting and what you consider an island. There is also much more to the region than the island-studded area of the St. Lawrence River called the Thousand Islands, usually defined as bordered by the Adirondacks to the east, the St. Lawrence River to the north, and Lake Ontario to the west.

Most of the region is flat or rolling farmland. The St. Lawrence River defines a coastline running for more than 100 mi southwest from Massena to Cape Vincent, where the river meets Lake Ontario. The St. Lawrence is the throat of a waterway that leads through the Great Lakes and which, with the completion of its lock system in 1959, formed the longest navigable inland passage—more than 2,300 mi—in the world.

The region's largest city, Watertown, is more than 30 mi south of the Thousand Islands and is not on any water itself. Alexandria Bay and Clayton are the focal points for summer visitors to the Thousand Islands. They're the ports from which most of the island's homeowners make their way to secluded summer homes. Both make good walking towns because they're away from highway traffic and fairly compact.

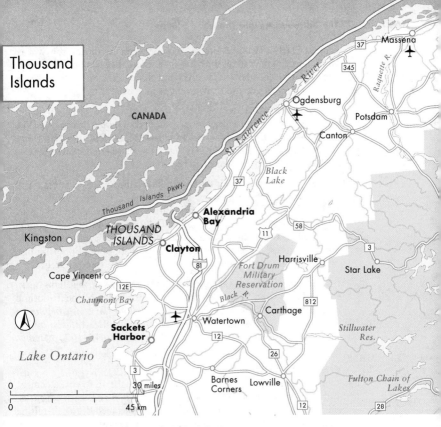

Thousand Islands

GETTING HERE AND AROUND

The main roads of the Thousand Islands area are Interstate 81, which runs north from Syracuse through Watertown, and the Seaway Trail, a combination of Routes 37, 12, and 12E that follows the St. Lawrence River to the Lake Ontario shore. These two main roadways intersect at the Thousand Islands International Bridge, leading into Canada. An inland road that parallels the Seaway Trail for much of the way is U.S. 11, which runs from northern Lake Champlain through the cities of Malone, Potsdam, and Canton to Watertown.

VISITOR INFORMATION

St. Lawrence County Chamber of Commerce (✉ *101 Main St., Canton* ☎ *315/ 386–4000 or 877/228–7810* ⊕ *www.northcountryguide.com*). **1000 Islands International Tourism Council** (☎ *800/847–5263* ⊕ *www.visit1000islands.com*).

SACKETS HARBOR

25 mi west of Watertown.

This Lake Ontario village was settled in 1800, and many of the buildings here are from the early 19th century. The visitor center has a walking-tour brochure you can follow through the historic district.

Sackets Harbor was the site of two engagements during the War of 1812, and you may stroll the battlefield where they took place. In summer the harbor bustles with boaters and charter cruises. In winter hardy cross-country skiers and snowmobilers take over.

VISITOR INFORMATION

For information on the village, stop by the **Sackets Harbor Heritage Area Visitors Center** (⊠ *301 W. Main St.* ☎ *315/646–2321* ⊕ *www.sacketsharborny. com* ⊗ *Late May–Columbus Day, daily 10–5*), where displays focus on the harbor's role in the War of 1812.

Seaway Trail National Scenic Byway. Trekking the Seaway Trail is a trip you'll remember for a lifetime. The 500-plus-mi trail has views of the St. Lawrence Seaway, Lake Ontario, the Niagara River, and Lake Erie. It spans New York and Pennsylvania. The road wends through tranquil farmland, beautiful shore, and dozens of small towns and their restaurants, lodgings, museums, art galleries, and shopping opportunities. There are lighthouses and many historical buildings and churches.

If your time is limited, take the portion of the byway that links Sackets Harbor on the Seaway to Massena, at the edge of the Thousand Islands region. ⊠ *From Sackets Harbor, follow the coast, beginning on Rte. 12E. Stay on this road, which becomes Rte. 12. The byway ends just outside Croil Island State Park* ☎ *315/646–1000* ⊕ *www. seawaytrail.com.*

WHAT TO SEE

🅒 **Robbins' Farm and Old McDonald's Farm.** Walk right up to cows, camels, and more than 200 other animals. Old McDonald's has been educating children about farm life since 1986. The complex includes a calf-raising facility as part of a 1,200-acre working farm. There's also a miniature-golf course, pony rides, and a hayride. ⊠ *14471 Rte. 145* ☎ *315/583– 5737* ⊕ *www.oldmcdonaldhasafarm.com* ⌨ *General admission $7, dairy tour $2, pony ride $2* ⊗ *Early June–Labor Day, daily 10–6; rest of Sept. and May–early June, Sun.–Thurs. 10–4, Fri. and Sat. 10–5; Oct., Sun.–Thurs. 10–5, Fri. and Sat. 10–6.*

Sackets Harbor Battlefield State Historic Site. During the War of 1812, two battles were fought here between the British and Americans. The harbor served as headquarters for divisions of the U.S. Army and Navy. Today the site includes a nicely restored commandant's house, which dates from 1850. In summer, guides reenact camp life; an audio tour and stories are available through your cell phone through mid-October. ⊠ *505 W. Washington St.* ☎ *315/646–3634* ⊕ *nysparks.state.ny.us* ⌨ *$3* ⊗ *Call for hrs.*

Seaway Trail Discovery Center. The Seaway Trail is a 454-mi federally recognized scenic byway along the shores of Lakes Erie and Ontario and the St. Lawrence River. Nine rooms in the Discovery Center present interactive exhibits that explain life along the water. Displays include agriculture, history, culture, lighthouses, architecture, and recreation. ⊠ *Ray St. and W. Main St.* ☎ *315/646–1000* ⊕ *www.seawaytrail. com/05_discoverycenter.asp* ⌨ *$4* ⊗ *May–Oct., daily 10–5; Nov.– Apr., call for hrs.*

WHERE TO EAT AND STAY

$$ ✕**The Boathouse Restaurant and Bar.** This casual restaurant right on the
SEAFOOD banks of Lake Ontario serves a robust menu with fun-loving entrée
names like That Fire Thang, (a spicy hamburger concoction featuring
salsa, jalapeños, and chipotle mayo). Other dishes include Alaskan crab
legs, steamed Canadian mussels, wraps, pasta, and the fish of the day.
There's a wine list and a martini list. Wi-Fi is available throughout the
restaurant. ⊠*214 W. Main St.* ☎*315/646–2092* ▤*MC, V* ▤*Closed
in winter.*

$$ ✕**Tin Pan Galley.** The upstairs dining room, called 110 West Main, begins
AMERICAN service at 5:30 PM daily; breakfast and lunch are served downstairs;
★ and all three meals are served outside, weather permitting. Salads and
sandwiches are popular—try the grilled portobello mushroom sandwich. Alfresco dining is in a New Orleans–style flower garden with
wrought-iron gates and a stone archway. Wine tastings are offered on
some days of the week. ⊠*110 W. Main St.* ☎*315/646–3812* ⊕*www.
tinpangalley.com* ▤*AE, D, MC, V* ⊘ *Closed Mon.*

$ 🏠**Candlelight Bed and Breakfast.** Built in 1832, this Georgian redbrick
home is next door to the Sackets Harbor Battlefield State Historic Site
and a three-minute walk from restaurants, shops, and the Seaway
Trail. Rooms have period antiques, four-poster beds, and quilts; two
have water views, the third looks out onto the village. **Pros:** clean and
relaxing; discounts are sometimes offered if you pay with cash. **Cons:**
you must cancel within 10 days of stay; no in-room TVs. ⊠*501 W.
Washington St.* ☎*315/646–1518 or 800/306–5595* ⊕*www.imcnet.net/
candlelight* ⮡*3 rooms* ⌕*In-room: no phone. In-hotel: no kids under
12, restaurant, Wi-Fi* ▤*MC, V* ▧|*BP.*

¢ 🏠**Ontario Place Hotel.** Some rooms have views of the harbor at this hotel
with a range of accommodations. In addition to standard rooms there
are larger minisuites, with roll-away beds, that can sleep up to five people. Minisuites have refrigerators, microwaves, and in-room hot tubs.
Pros: within walking distance of historical attractions; some pets are
allowed with fee. **Cons:** rooms are on the small side; no in-room TVs.
⊠*103 General Smith Dr.* ☎*315/646–8000 or 800/564–1812* ⊕ *www.
ontarioplacehotel.com* ⮡*38 rooms, 4 suites* ⌕*In-room: refrigerator,
Wi-Fi. In-hotel: no-smoking rooms* ▤*AE, D, DC, MC, V.*

CLAYTON

20 mi north of Sackets Harbor.

Clayton, which occupies a promontory jutting into the St. Lawrence
River, quietly maintains its riverine heritage. Settled in 1822, it was
once a major shipbuilding port and steamship stop. Later in the 19th
century, vacationers came here to fish and boat—two activities that
still draw people to the area. Otherwise, museums are the main attractions here.

WHAT TO SEE

☯ **Antique Boat Museum.** Boats and river memorabilia depict life on the St.
★ Lawrence River. The collection of 205 craft includes an 8-foot canoe
and a 65-foot yacht. Landlubbers may appreciate an exhibit that
shows the Thousand Islands as a vacation destination; in its heyday,
15 trains arrived daily from New York City and Boston. ✉ *750 Mary
St.* ☎ *315/686–4104* ⊕ *www.abm.org* ☞ *$12* ☉ *Early May–mid-Oct.,
daily 9–5.*

Tibbetts Point Lighthouse. One of the oldest lighthouses on the Great Lakes
looks out over the outlet of Lake Ontario. The Coast Guard left in 1981,
and the building is now used as a youth hostel. Off-season reservations
at the hostel must be made by e-mail at TibbettsPoint@hiusa.org. The
lighthouse is 12 mi west of Clayton. ✉ *33435 Rte. 6, Cape Vincent*
☎ *315/654–2700 for lighthouse, 315/654–3450 for hostel* ⊕ *www.
capevincent.org/lighthouse* ☞ *Free; small fee to stay in hostel* ☉ *Late
May–mid-June, Fri.–Mon. 10–7; mid-June–early Sept., daily 10–7.*

WHERE TO EAT

$ ✕ **Clipper Inn.** Enjoy upscale fare in a casual, comfortable space with
AMERICAN cloth-covered tables in this chef-owned restaurant. The menu at this
★ local favorite emphasizes seafood: shrimp scampi, sautéed or broiled
scallops, king crab legs. Filet Oscar is butterflied filet mignon dressed
with crabmeat, asparagus, and béarnaise sauce; veal Oscar is similar.
The menu also includes chicken Parmesan and other chicken dishes.
✉ *126 State St.* ☎ *315/686–3842* ⊕ *www.clipperinn.com* ☰ *AE, D,
DC, MC, V* ☉ *Closed Nov.–Mar. No lunch.*

$ ✕ **Foxy's.** Gaze out at the St. Lawrence River as you tuck into the Ital-
ITALIAN ian-American fare at this waterfront restaurant between Clayton and
Alexandria Bay. Families like the casual atmosphere, and the kids like
the game room. Dishes include veal preparations, lasagna, eggplant
Parmesan, sautéed chicken livers, chicken Parmesan, scampi, fried scallops with citrus sauce, and New York strip steak. Weekend reservations are strongly suggested. ✉ *18187 Reed Point Rd., Fisher's Landing*
☎ *315/686–3781* ☰ *D, MC, V* ☉ *Closed mid-Sept.–mid-Apr.*

$$ ✕ **Thousand Islands Inn.** The late-1800s inn, in downtown Clayton, is said
AMERICAN to be the first place to have served Thousand Island salad dressing. You
★ can guess what the house dressing is today. The restaurant is known for
its game dishes—broiled quail on a bed of wild rice or sautéed venison
medallions in demi-glace, for example. But the menu is extensive and
includes pasta, fish, pork, lamb, steak, chicken, and veal dishes. Try
one of its signature dishes—Beef Continental, which comes with two
cooked-to-order steaks. One is topped with a savory blue-cheese-and-
herb mix, the other with a red-wine demi-glace. ✉ *335 Riverside Dr.*
☎ *315/686–3030* ⊕ *www.1000-islands.com/inn/menus.htm* ☰ *D, MC,
V* ☉ *Closed mid-Sept.–mid-May.*

WHERE TO STAY

¢ ⊞ **Bertrand's Motel.** You'll be right in the middle of the village at this
1930s budget motel close to the shore. Exterior corridors provide access
to the rooms, which are simple and have wood-paneled walls. **Pros:**
friendly staff. **Cons:** few extras. ✉ *229 James St.* ☎ *315/686–3641 or*

800/472–0683 ⊕*www.1000islands.com/bertrand* ⤙*28 rooms, 4 efficiencies* ⌖*In-room: refrigerator (some). In-hotel: no-smoking rooms* ⊟*AE, D, MC, V.*

$ 🖼 **McKinley House.** The Queen Anne Victorian, built in 1890, is a block from the St. Lawrence River and has a turret and a curved porch. Guest rooms are tasteful, with four-poster or brass queen beds, hardwood floors, large windows, and sitting areas. **Pros:** beautiful, formal home. **Cons:** cash and checks only. ⊠*505 Hugunin St.* ☎*315/686–3405* ⤙*3 rooms* ⌖*In-room: no phone, no TV. In-hotel: restaurant, no-smoking rooms* ⊟*No credit cards* ⏿*BP.*

ALEXANDRIA BAY   4

12 mi northeast of Clayton.

★ The vacation center and heart of the Thousand Islands area, Alexandria Bay sits at the edge of the St. Lawrence River. In the late 1800s the village was a popular vacation spot and steamboat stop, attracting wealthy visitors who built homes on the islands. Today Alexandria Bay caters to visitors who want a quick look at the islands, and restaurants and motels abound. The centerpiece is Boldt Castle, on Heart Island, across from the village. Wellesley Island is home to a couple of state parks and to a cottage community called Thousand Islands Park.

WHAT TO SEE

☺ **Aqua Zoo.** This collection of more than 100 aquariums of varying sizes provides a look at creatures from lakes, oceans, and rivers around the world. There's also a petting area for kids. ⊠*43681 Rte. 12, ¾ mi south of Rte. 81* ☎*315/482–5771* ⊕*www.aquazoo.com* ▦*$7.50* ⊙*Memorial Day–Labor Day, daily 10–7.*

☺ **Boldt Castle.** George C. Boldt, proprietor of the Waldorf-Astoria Hotel
Fodor$Choice in New York, began building this 120-room Rhineland-style castle on
★ Heart Island for his wife, Louise, in 1900. Four years later, when she died suddenly, he ceased work on the castle. The building remained deserted for 73 years, abused by vandals and weather. Since 1977, millions of dollars have been poured into restoration work. It's worth a trip to the 5-acre island to see the castle. Its fleet of wooden boats is in the Boldt Yacht House, on Wellesley Island. Uncle Sam Boat Tours runs shuttle boats between Alexandria Bay, Heart Island, and Wellesley Island. ⊠*Heart Island* ☎*315/482–9724, 315/482–2501, or 800/847–5263* ⊕*www.boldtcastle.com* ▦*Castle $6.50, yacht house $3* ⊙*Yacht house mid-May–late Sept., daily 10–6:30; call for castle hrs.*

Singer Castle. Guides lead 45-minute tours, up and down many stairs, through this lovely turn-of-the-20th-century castle on Dark Island. The castle, originally known as the Towers, was built as a summer home for Frederick G. Bourne, president of the Singer sewing-machine company. Famed American architect Ernest Flagg modeled the four-story, 28-room structure on a Scottish castle, giving it all sorts of interesting nooks and crannies. To get here, take a boat from Alexandria Bay. Empire Boat Lines and Uncle Sam Boat Tours include Singer Castle

in their sightseeing cruises. ⊠*Dark Island* ☎*877/327–5475* ⊕*www.*
singercastle.com ⊠*$12* ☉*Mid-May–mid-June and Labor Day–mid-*
Oct., weekends 10–5; mid-June–Labor Day, daily 10–5; last tour leaves
the boathouse at 4.

SPORTS AND THE OUTDOORS

Wellesley Island State Park. The 2,600-acre park encompasses a beach, a
marina, boat launches, and the largest campground in the Thousand
Islands, which offers wilderness sites, tent and trailer sites, and cabins
and cottages. A highlight of Wellesley Island State Park is the **Minna
Anthony Common Nature Center** (⊠*44927 Cross Island Rd., Fin-*
eview ☎*315/482–2479* ☉*July and Aug., Mon.–Sat. 8:30–8:30, Sun.*
8:30–4:30; Sept.–June, daily 8:30–4:30), a 600-acre wildlife sanctuary
with a museum. You may hike, cross-country ski, and snowshoe the
8 mi of trails here (equipment rentals are available). The museum has
decoys, live fish and reptiles, and mounted birds, and there's a seasonal
butterfly house. To get here by car, take the Thousand Islands International Bridge to the park entrance. ⊠*Cross Island Rd., Fineview*
☎*315/482–2722* ⊕*www.nysparks.state.ny.us* ⊠*Parking $7* ☉ *Daily*
dawn–dusk.

BICYCLING   For bicycling on paved roadways, the marked **bicycle route on Route 28**
covers some pretty mountainous terrain, but the **Seaway Trail** between
Alexandria Bay and Cape Vincent runs through generally flat or rolling farmland.

BOAT
TOURS

Uncle Sam Boat Tours (⊠*47 James St.* ☎*315/482–2611* ⊕*www.usboattours.*
com ☉*Apr.–Oct.; call for schedule*) offers tours that go through the Canadian
side of the islands, but fall foliage is also worth catching. Sightseeing cruises
take 2¼ hours, with options to stop at Boldt Castle or Singer Castle. The company also runs frequent 10-minute boat shuttles to the castles. Boats have
heated, enclosed lower decks. Dinner and lunch cruises are available; reservations for meal cruises are required. Boldt Castle shuttles are $7, and dinner
and other cruises cost up to $42.50.

ARTS AND ENTERTAINMENT

FESTIVAL   **Bill Johnston's Pirate Days.** During this 10-day festival in early to mid-
August, pirates invade the village of Alexandria Bay for two weekends,
and the mayor hands the keys to the city over to these marauders. Midweek festivities include music and other entertainment. Bill Johnston,
for whom the event is named, was an 1830s pirate who looted ships
near the city. ⊠*Throughout downtown* ☎*800/541–2110* ⊕*www.*
alexbay.org/premierevents.html.

WHERE TO EAT

$$ ✕ **Captain's Landing.** This family-oriented restaurant actually floats on
AMERICAN   the water (the foundation was once used as a dredge on the New York
State Canal System). The oak-trimmed dining room has antique buf-
fet tables. Try the prime rib (also served Cajun style), seafood pasta,
porterhouse steak, or shrimp scampi. The menu also includes plenty of
chicken and pasta dishes. The restaurant is part of Captain Thompson's

Resort. A deck has open-air dining. ⊠*49 James St.* ☎*315/482–7777* ⊕*www.1000islands.com/landing* ▤*AE, D, MC, V* ⊘*Closed mid-Oct.–early May.*

$ ✕**Cavallario's Steak and Seafood.** Cavallario's is one of those places that
ITALIAN   quickly becomes a family tradition. Part steak house, part seafood eatery, the place also has a rich and lusty Italian streak. Try the bruschetta, escargot, or the hot peppers (a regional favorite) to warm you up for more-robust fare like the veal, manicotti, duckling, or the combination seafood in wine sauce. ⊠*24 Church St.* ☎*315/482–9867* ▤*MC, V.*

¢   ✕**Dockside Pub.** Despite billing itself as the village's "best-kept secret,"
AMERICAN   this sports bar and restaurant near the shore always seems to be hopping. The daily menu includes pizzas, burgers, appetizers, and dinner specials where the chef gets creative with what's in the kitchen. Cheese sauces are common. There's fish on Friday and prime rib on Saturday. ⊠*17 Market St.* ☎*315/482–9849* ▤*MC, V.*

$$$ ✕**Jacques Cartier Dining Room.** A pianist or harpist adds to the romantic
FRENCH   tone of this elegant restaurant where you have views of Boldt Castle and
★   the St. Lawrence River through floor-to-ceiling windows. The kitchen turns out fine American and French fare, all presented with flair. Broiled sea bass, New York–cut prime rib, and veal and lobster dishes are worth trying, as are the flaming desserts. The wine list is long, varied, and features several choices from New York State. ⊠*Riveredge Resort Hotel, 17 Holland St.* ☎*315/482–9917* ▤*AE, D, DC, MC, V* ⊘*No lunch.*

ADIRONDACK STATE PARK

Adirondack State Park was created by the state in 1892, and two years later a large chunk of the land was designated "forever wild," prohibiting future development. The official park boundaries encompass 6 million acres, almost three times the land area of Yellowstone National Park. There are 1,000 mi of rivers, 30,000 mi of brooks and streams, more than 3,000 lakes and ponds, and 1.3 million acres of forest. The numbers impress, but they're just an introduction to the Adirondacks.

Understanding the Adirondacks is a matter of sensory perception rather than number crunching. It's a place that not only has to be seen but also has to be heard and smelled and, in winters that are often harsh, felt as well. From spring through fall, every lake view or mountain vista or walk in the woods comes with the fragrance of hemlock and spruce and musty soil and the sounds of songbirds, woodpeckers, loons, or any of the 220 species of other birds in the region.

However, this isn't a complete wilderness area; about half the land within park boundaries is privately owned. The checkerboard of public and private lands gives the Adirondacks a different character from most national parks. Unlike in many state or national parks, motels, lodges, and restaurants are found throughout, as are private canoe rentals, seaplane services, and guide services. At the same time, most campgrounds, trails, and waterways are maintained on public land by the state, through the Department of Environmental Conservation.

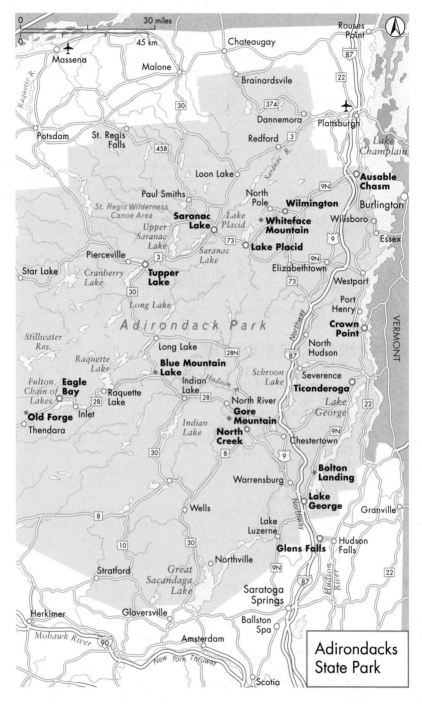

Adirondacks
State Park

Although most people associate the Adirondacks with high mountains, the southern and central landscape is primarily one of lakes, rivers, and hills. The notable exception is Blue Mountain, which stands high above everything that surrounds it. Its summit lookout tower affords a 360-degree view that includes the chain of lakes stretching west, but the price of this view is a fairly steep scramble of about a mile.

For the most part, the tranquillity of the southern and central Adirondacks turns to dormancy in winter. However, because the terrain here is gentler than in the High Peaks region to the north—and nearer the population centers of the south—snowmobiling and cross-country-skiing enthusiasts are drawn to the area. Snowmobilers tend to congregate in Schroon Lake, Speculator, and Old Forge, which is also the center of tourist activity in the southern and central area. Blue Mountain Lake, home of the Adirondack Museum, is the area's cultural center.

GETTING HERE AND AROUND

The two main roads through the southern and central Adirondacks are Routes 28 and 30. Route 28 forms an east–west arc from Warrensburg, a few miles from Lake George, through Old Forge (and continuing toward Utica). Route 30 reaches north from Amsterdam in the Mohawk River valley, passing through Tupper Lake, Saranac Inn, and Paul Smiths on its way into Canada. The two routes run together for about 11 mi between Indian Lake and Blue Mountain Lake, the approximate geographical center of the Adirondacks. Route 28N makes a northerly swing from Route 28 at North Creek before veering west and joining Route 30 at Long Lake, 11 mi north of Blue Mountain Lake. Route 8, which enters the region in the southwest corner, joins Route 30 in Speculator and is the major road in the southwestern part of Adirondack Park.

VISITOR INFORMATION

Adirondack North Country Association (⊠ *28 St. Bernard St, Saranac Lake* ☎ *518/891–6200* ⊕ *www.adirondack.org*). **Adirondack Regional Tourism Council** (✐ *Box 2149, Plattsburgh 12901* ☎ *518/846–8016 or 800/487–6867* ⊕ *www.adk.com*).

SPORTS AND THE OUTDOORS IN THE REGION
BICYCLING

For mountain biking, consider one of the Adirondacks' downhill and cross-country ski centers. The Gore Mountain Ski Center, in North Creek; the Garnet Hill Ski Lodge and Cross-Country Ski Center, in North River; the Whiteface Mountain Ski Center, in Wilmington; and the Cross Country Center at the Verizon Sports Complex at Mt. Van Hoevenberg, near Lake Placid, all have mountain-biking trails in the warm-weather months.

RESOURCES   **Bike Adirondacks** (✐ *c/o Holmes & Associates, Box 295, Saranac Lake 12983* ☎ *No phone* ⊕ *www.bikeadirondacks.org*) has loads of information about mountain-bike trails, as well as details about paved routes, multiuse paths, and bike shops, with links to various related organizations and services. The **Lake Champlain Bikeways** (☎ *802/652–2453* ⊕ *www.champlainbikeways.org*) has detailed directions and terrain descriptions as well as suggested themed rides; brochures are available. **Seaway Trail, Inc.** (⊠ *W. Main St., Sackets Harbor 13685* 🕾 *315/646–1000 or 800/732–9298* ⊕ *www.seawaytrail.com*) is dedicated to making the Seaway Trail region accessible to tourists and outdoors enthusiasts, and that includes bikers. Route maps for the Warren County Bikeway are available from the **Warren County Department of Parks and Recreation** (⊠ *Fish Hatchery Rd., Warrensburg* 🕾 *518/623–2877* ⊕ *www. warrencountydpw.com/Parks_Rec07*).

CANOEING

The vast network of rivers and lakes in the Adirondacks makes canoeing one of the best ways to experience the outdoors here. Trips of 100 mi or more are possible, as are short day trips geared for beginners.

St. Regis Wilderness Canoe Area. Motorboats aren't allowed in this pristine wilderness, which includes part of Upper Saranac Lake and stretches northwest. One of the best areas for canoeing in the Northeast, it encompasses nearly 60 ponds and lakes and more than 100 mi of navigable waters connected by portages. Primitive campsites (first-come, first-served) are scattered around the various ponds. One route, called the Seven Carries, takes you about 9 mi from Little Clear Pond to Upper St. Regis Lake. It makes a good day trip, but it's not a loop, so you need to arrange for a way to get back to Saranac Lake. The 11-mi Nine Carries route is more challenging and has tougher portages. To get to Little Clear Pond and other access points from Saranac Lake, take Route 86 north to Route 186 and turn left (west). Local outfitters and the Saranac Lake Area Chamber of Commerce (🕾 *518/891–1990 or 800/347–1992* ⊕ *saranaclake.com*) can provide more information about paddling in the area.

To the southwest, between Old Forge and Raquette Lake, is the 16-mi **Fulton Chain of Lakes,** also popular with canoeists. The Lower Fulton Chain begins with Old Forge Pond to the south and ends at Seventh Lake to the north. A 1-mi portage links this eight-lake cluster (from Eighth Lake) to Raquette Lake, from which you may paddle north. The Fulton Chain of Lakes Association (⊕ *www.fultonchainoflakesassociation.org*) has a great diagram of the lakes and a chart that shows where boat launches, beaches, islands, and picnic areas are.

RESOURCES The Web site of the **Adirondack Regional Tourism Council** (⟑ *Box 2149, Plattsburgh 12901* 🕾 *518/846–8016 or 800/487–6867* ⊕ *www.adk. com*) has a handy interactive map detailing canoe and kayak routes in the area. The council also provides a free "Adirondack Waterways Guide" with route descriptions and maps. **Franklin County Tourism** (⊠ *10 Elm St., Malone 12953* 🕾 *518/483–9470 or 800/709–4895* ⊕ *www. adirondacklakes.com*) offers canoe maps that cover the St. Regis area.

OUTFITTERS AND EXPEDITIONS Canoe rentals are available at most lakes in the Adirondacks, both on a daily and an extended basis. For extended trips, hiring a guide service is strongly recommended.

The **Adirondack Foothills Guide Service** (⟑ *Box 345, Saranac Lake 12983* 🕾 *518/359–8194* ⊕ *www.adkfoothills.com*) runs canoe day trips and overnight camping excursions and can outfit you, whether or not you need a guide. In addition to being able to outfit canoe and camping trips, **Adirondack Lakes and Trails** (⊠ *541 Lake Flower Ave., Saranac Lake* ☎*800/491–0414* ⊕*www.adirondackoutfitters.com*) offers lessons and guided excursions. **Raquette River Outfitters** (⊠*1754 Rte. 30, Tupper Lake 12986* ☎*518/359–3228* ⊕*www.raquetteriveroutfitters. com*), a great source for information about canoeing and kayaking in the area, can help you put together a paddling trip. The shuttle service brings your boat to the launch and has your car waiting for you at the end of the route. The store rents and sells canoes, kayaks, and camping equipment. You may also buy fly-fishing gear here. **St. Regis Canoe Outfitters** (⊠*73 Dorsey St., Saranac Lake* ☎*518/891–1838 or 888/775–2925* ⊕*www.stregiscanoeoutfitters.com*) has day trips as well as longer excursions into the St. Regis Wilderness Canoe Area, guiding services, and kayak and canoe rentals and instruction. Some canoe trips include mountain hikes. You may also buy camping and other gear here. From April to October, St. Regis runs a **Floodwood branch** (⊠*Floodwood Rd., Lake Clear* ☎*518/891–8040*) at the Long Pond portage. **Tickner's Canoe Rentals** (⊠*Rte. 28, Old Forge 14320* ☎*315/369–6286* ⊕*www. ticknerscanoe.com*) has canoe and kayak rentals and organizes paddles, short and long, on Moose River and in the Fulton Chain of Lakes. Floats include the kayak or canoe, a life vest, and shuttle service. One package includes return transportation on the Adirondack Scenic Railroad.

FISHING

Fishing is a year-round sport in the North Country. The St. Lawrence River offers some of the best bass fishing in the country. Muskellunges ("muskies" for short) are a member of the pike family and are a common catch between Ogdensburg and Cape Vincent. Ice-fishing tournaments give Thousand Islanders a little sport on weekends in January and February.

Many lakes, ponds, and streams in the Adirondacks are stocked with trout and salmon. For walleye, the Raquette River and Lake Champlain are the best bets. The Ausable River, near Lake Placid, is known for its fly-fishing. Hiring a guide is highly recommended, especially if you're interested in a backcountry fishing trip.

RESOURCES   The **Adirondack Regional Tourism Council** (☎*518/846–8016 or 800/487–6867* ⊕*www.adk.com*) lists fishing guides and charters on its Web site; the council also offers a free fishing guide. The **1000 Islands International Tourism Council** (☎*800/847–5263* ⊕*www.visit1000islands.com*) offers a free fishing-and-hunting booklet that lists fishing guides and charters and state boat-launch sites and describes the types of fish found in the Thousand Islands.

Fishing licenses and regulations may be obtained at town clerk offices, fishing-gear retailers, or by phone from the state. For fish and wildlife information, sporting conditions, licenses, and a list of marinas, contact the **New York State Department of Environmental Conservation** (☎*866/933–2257 fishing licenses, 518/897–1200 general information* ⊕*www.dec.state.ny.us*).

HIKING

Hiking is the simplest and one of the best ways to experience the outdoors in New York's North Country. Most trails are well maintained and marked by the New York State Department of Environmental Conservation, and many trailheads are along the major routes through the Adirondack area—including Route 28N between North Creek and Long Lake and Route 73 between Lake Placid and Keene.

The most popular—and congested—area for hiking is the High Peaks region, accessible from the Lake Placid area in the north, Keene in the east, and Newcomb in the south. Much ado is made of the so-called Adirondack "46ers"—the people who have ascended the 46 highest peaks in the region. Although the High Peaks area tends to draw the most attention, this is where you find the most rugged hiking. Many less strenuous climbs and hikes offer rewarding views and backwoods experiences, whether for half-day hikes, full-day outings, or multiday backpacking trips. The areas around Schroon Lake, for example, have good hiking with minimal climbing.

The Adirondack Loj, off Route 73 about 7 mi south of Lake Placid, is at the main trailhead to Mt. Marcy, Algonquin, and the rest of the High Peaks core. The lodge is run by the nonprofit Adirondack Mountain Club (aka the ADK), which is a good source for hiking and backcountry information. It publishes a set of regional Adirondack trail guides with topographic maps and trailhead directions. You may buy the guides through the ADK Web site or at its Lake George and High Peaks information centers.

RESOURCES   The **Adirondack Regional Tourism Council** (⌂ *Box 2149, Plattsburgh 12901* ☎ *518/846–8016 or 800/487–6867* ⊕ *www.adk.com*) features an interactive map with some North Country hikes on its Web site. You may also obtain a copy of the free "Great Walks & Day Hikes" brochure from the council.

Run by the Adirondack Mountain Club (ADK), **Adirondack Mountain Club Information Center** (✉ *814 Goggins Rd., Lake George* ☎ *518/668–4447 or 800/395–8080* ⊕ *www.adk.org Information Center* ✉ *Adirondack Loj Rd., off Rte. 73, Lake Placid* ☎ *518/523–3441*) is a nonprofit group that aims to protect forest, parkland, and other wilderness areas while supporting responsible recreational use. Information about hiking and other recreational activities in Adirondack Park is available here. The center is closed on Sunday.

TRAILS: **Baxter Mountain.** A mile-long trek leads you to the 2,440-foot peak of
EASY   Baxter Mountain, which rises over Keene Valley and affords a view of Mt. Marcy, the highest peak in New York State. The trailhead begins off Route 9 in Spruce Hill. The hike is about an hour coming and an hour going.

Cascade Lake Trail: Although the trail is a somewhat lengthy 4.6-mi round-trip hike (about 2½ hours), the going is easy and the views of the waterfall near the end are more than enough payoff. There are also swimming and fishing opportunities. To get to the trailhead, head north

THE 46ERS

In an immense park known for its Olympic-grade mountains, some peaks still manage to stick out. Over the years, hikers have compiled a list of the 46 highest peaks in the park. Although mountain climbers once believed all 46 were higher than 4,000 feet, we know now that the four shortest are not.

They all make for a good climb, though. And if you're ambitious and hardy enough to climb all of them, your feat will get you inducted into Adirondack Forty-Sixers Inc. The 46ers club (⊕ *www.adk46r.org*) promotes conservation and works with the state on projects within the park.

on Big Moose Road at Eagle Bay and drive for about an hour. Look for the parking area to your right.

Severance Hill Trail. A short trail, Severance Hill winds uphill, leading to views of Schroon Lake and vast tracts of untamed land beyond. The trailhead is located on Route 9, just north of Schroon Lake.

MODERATE **Azure Mountain.** This 2-mi (round-trip) hike leads to fabulous views atop Azure Mountain, plus two bonuses: a restored fire tower and, most days, a volunteer guide. To get to the trailhead, take Route 458 to Blue Mountain Road, then putter about 7 mi down the road.

Bald Mountain Trail. One of the more frequented trails, this moderately difficult trail measures about 2 mi round-trip and rewards hikers with magnificent views of the wilderness and the Fulton Chain of Lakes. To get to the trailhead, located in the Old Forge area, travel about 5 mi past the tourist information center on Route 28. Turn left on Rondaxe Avenue and look for the parking lot.

Blue Mountain Trail. At 3,759 feet above sea level, Blue Mountain towers over the waters of Blue Mountain Lake, and this well-maintained, 2.2-mi (one way) trail leads to the summit. At the top, you're greeted by spectacular views of the surrounding lakes and mountains. The trailhead is on Route 30/28N, 1.3 mi north of the hamlet of Blue Mountain Lake. Look for a parking area not far past the Adirondack Museum, also on Route 30/28, in Blue Mountain Lake.

Cathedral Rocks and Bear Run. This 1.6-mi (one way) trail leads to small waterfalls and some of the more interesting rock formations in the park—your reward for the sometimes-steep gradients you'll climb on the way. The trailhead is off Route 73 a couple of miles south of Keene Valley.

DIFFICULT **East Trail to Rocky Peak Ridge and Giant Mountain.** This 16-mi round-trip trail ends at the Giant Mountain summit, passing spectacular views at Blueberry Cobbles, Bald Peak, and Rocky Peak Ridge. When you get to the Giant Mountain summit, you'll have reached an elevation of 4,600 feet, and you'll also have scaled one of the highest of the 46 peaks in the park.

Lower Wolf Jaw Mountain Trail. Climbing another of the highest mountains in the park—Lower Wolf Jaw Mountain, at close to 4,200 feet—is a 13.5-mi, six- to seven-hour endeavor. Here are some of the most beautiful views in the park. The trailhead is located at the parking area opposite the Giant Mountain trailhead on Route 73.

Van Hoevenberg Trail to Mt. Marcy. If you're an ambitious hiker, it would be a shame to leave the park without reaching the top of Mt. Marcy, at 5,344 feet the highest point in all of New York State. Although there are many approaches to the top, we find that the trail from Adirondack Loj, off Rte. 73 in Lake Placid, is one of the simplest to follow. It's 14-mi, round-trip.

Whiteface Mountain Trail. This steep 10.4-mi round-trip climb leads up the slopes of one of the most prominent and well-known peaks in the park, Whiteface Mountain, which looms over Lake Placid and is one of the highest peaks in the park. By the time you get up the steep trail, you'll have reached 4,867 feet. Follow Whiteface Veterans Memorial Highway from its intersection with Route 86 about half a mile and look for a Department of Environmental Conservation sign on your left.

> ### OUTDOOR GUIDES
>
> The Adirondacks have a rich guiding tradition that dates back to the early 1800s. Whether you're going fishing, hiking, canoeing, or white-water rafting, a guide can make your trip more enjoyable. Guides, which are licensed by the state, know the best routes and are well versed in the proper safety precautions, and they also can make light work of the cumbersome preparations and logistics necessary for any outing. You may obtain a list of licensed guides from the **New York State Outdoor Guides Association** (⊠ *1936 Saranac Ave., Lake Placid* ☎ *866/469–7642* ⊕ *www.nysoga. com*).

DID YOU KNOW?

The DEC posts important advisories about the many trails located throughout the Adirondacks. For important information, such as whether you're required to wear snowshoes or if a bridge has washed away, check ⊕ *www. dec.ny.gov/outdoor/7865.html.*

OUTFITTERS AND EXPEDITIONS **High Peaks Information Center** (⊡ *Box 867, Adirondack Loj Rd., off Rte. 73, Lake Placid 12946* ☎ *518/523–3441* ⊕ *www.adk.org*), 5 mi south of Lake Placid, is run by the nonprofit Adirondack Mountain Club. It sells camping and hiking gear as well as regional guides and has information about hiking and other recreational activities in the area.

RAFTING

The real white-water daredevils like to put their kayaks and canoes into the river in spring, after the runoff from the snowmelt has swollen the waters. The most popular runs for adventurous rafters are along the Indian River from Indian Lake and then on to the Hudson River leading to North Creek. The Hudson River Gorge offers 17 mi of class III and IV white water. Also, Moose River has 14 mi of class V rapids. If you want tamer waters, consider summer family rafting and tubing on the Sacandaga River.

OUTFITTERS **Adirondack River Outfitters** (⊠ *Rte. 9N S, Old Forge* ☎ *800/525–7238*
AND ⊕ *www.aroadventures.com*) offers one-day rafting trips on the Hud-
EXPEDITIONS son, Black, and Moose rivers and tubing and family rafting on the
Sacandaga River. Trips include shuttle, equipment, guides, snacks, and
drinks. From April through October, the well-known **Hudson River Rafting Company** (⊠ *1 Main St., North Creek 12853* ☎ *518/251–3215 or
800/888–7238* ⊕ *www.hudsonriverrafting.com*) runs rafting trips for
experts as well as beginners. Trips may include camping behind its
Hudson River base.

⇨ *Sports and the Outdoors listings under each town for specific
venues.*

SOUTHERN ADIRONDACKS

OLD FORGE AND EAGLE BAY

51 mi northeast of Utica.

Located in the southwest corner of Adirondack Park, the village of Old
Forge sits at the west end of the Fulton Chain of Lakes. In years past
it was a hub for wealthy travelers who arrived by train and then continued by boat to their Adirondack hotels and summer homes. Today
it's touristy, with a water park and souvenir stores, but short side trips
take you away from the fray.

WHAT TO SEE

Adirondack Scenic Railroad. In July and August, the 12:30 train features
nature stories and a lecture by resident scholar Bernie Davis. Davis
regales passengers with stories about the Adirondacks and nearby areas.
Or, from late May to late October, you may take a scenic 20-mi train
ride south to Otter Lake. Either trip is $16. Trains leave from the sta-
tion in Thendara, 2 mi southwest of Old Forge. ⊠ *Rte. 28, Thendara*
☎ *877/508–6728* ⊕ *www.adirondackrr.com* ⊡ *$16 and up* ⊙ *Early
May–late Oct.; call or check Web site for schedule.*

Arts Center/Old Forge. The arts center sponsors exhibits, performances,
artists' receptions, and special events focusing on Adirondack traditions and artists. Classes and workshops for children and adults teach
everything from watercolor and basket weaving to poetry. The center
also organizes hikes. ⊠ *3260 Rte. 28, Old Forge* ☎ *315/369–6411*
⊕ *www.artscenteroldforge.org* ⊡ *Admission varies* ⊙ *Mon.–Sat. 10–4,
Sun. noon–4.*

☾ **Calypso's Cove Family Fun Center.** Located right next to Enchanted Forest,
this amusement complex offers go-karts, bumper boats, miniature golf,
and an arcade. A Pizza Hut is on-site. Attractions cost a ticket or more
each, and each ticket is $5. ⊠ *3183 Rte. 28, Old Forge* ☎ *315/369–6145*
⊕ *www.watersafari.com* ⊡ *$25.95* ⊙ *Late June–early Sept., daily; call
for hrs, which vary by attraction.*

ADIRONDACKS FESTIVALS AND EVENTS

WINTER

Lake George Winter Carnival.
Cold-weather activities, such as polar-bear swims, ice sculpting and fishing, snowmobile and dog-pull races, and snowmobile drags are scheduled for weekends from late January through early February. The carnival also includes a chili cook-off and fireworks. ☒ *Throughout downtown Lake George* ☎ *518/240–0809* ⊕ *www.lakegeorgewintercarnival. com.*

Saranac Lake Winter Carnival.
The annual festival, held for 10 days starting in early February, is the oldest winter carnival in the country. It includes a lighted ice palace, fireworks, and a costume parade. Inner-tube and ski races, hockey tournaments, and snowshoe-softball games are among the sporting events. The whole town gets into the action, so there are concerts, dinners, and dances at Hotel Saranac; breakfasts at the Masonic temple; and shows at the Pendragon Theatre. ☒ *Throughout downtown Saranac Lake* ☎ *518/891–1990 or 800/347–1992* ⊕ *www.saranaclake. com/carny.shtml.*

SPRING

The Adirondack Living Show.
During the first blush of spring, the annual show rolls out everything residents (and admiring visitors) need to deck their domiciles in true Adirondack Fashion . . . despite the fact that the show is technically hosted just outside park borders. $9 for admission. ☒ *Adirondack Sports Complex, 326 Sherman Ave., Queensbury 12804* ☎ *518/371–6363* ⊕ *www.adirondackliving.com.*

Hudson River White Water Derby.
In early May, this two-day event draws canoeing, kayaking, and camping enthusiasts to the North Creek area for slalom and downriver races. ☒ *Downtown North Creek, North Creek* ☎ *518/251–2612* ⊕ *www.goremtnregion.org.*

SUMMER

Americade Motorcycle Tour & Rally. Up to 50,000 motorcycle enthusiasts flock to the Lake George area for this multiday event held in early June. Activities include an exposition with hundreds of vendors and a huge motorcycle parade. ☒ *Throughout Lake George* ☎ *518/798–7888* ⊕ *www.tourexpo. com.*

No-Octane Regatta. Only boats without a motor—sailboats, sloops, rowboats, canoes, and guide boats—may participate in this race, sponsored by the Adirondack Museum. The event, held over a weekend in mid-June, includes a grand parade of wooden boats on Little Wolf Lake, a toy-boat regatta, and boatbuilding workshops among other activities. ☒ *On Little Wolf Lake, Tupper Lake* ☎ *518/352–7311* ⊕ *www. adkmuseum.org.*

Lake Placid Horse Shows. Hunter and jumper competitions are part of the back-to-back Lake Placid and I Love New York horse shows, which start at the end of June and run to early July. Participants include members of the U.S. equestrian team. ☒ *Lake Placid Horse Show Association, 5514 Cascade Rd., Lake Placid 12946* ☎ *518/523–9625* ⊕ *www. lakeplacidhorseshow.com.*

French Festival. The largest festival in the North Country celebrates Cape Vincent's French heritage over a weekend in early July. The fun includes a parade; French music, dress, bread and pastry; fireworks; band performances; and children's programs. ✉ *Downtown Cape Vincent* ☎ *315/654–2481* ⊕ *www.capevincent.org/frenchfestival.asp.*

Fodor$Choice ★ ⏱ **Woodsmen Field Days.** Skills and crafts related to the lumber industry are demonstrated during this colorful two-day event held in early July at Tupper Lake Municipal Park. Draft horses pull logs, chain-saw artists sculpt, and modern-day lumberjacks demonstrate chopping and ax throwing. ⌂ *Tupper Lake Woodsmen's Association, Box 759, Tupper Lake 12986* ☎ *518/359–9444* ⊕ *www.tupperlakeinfo.com.*

Duck, Decoy and Wildlife Art Show. Artists, carvers, painters, and taxidermists come from all over the country and Canada to show their work at this three-day event in mid-July, set in Clayton. ✉ *Recreation Park Arena, 615 East Line Rd., Clayton* ☎ *315/686–5794* ⊕ *www.timuseum.org.*

Adirondack Festival of American Music, This July-long event features well-known performers and musicians such as the Gregg Smith Singers, who travel the world singing classical chorale music. ✉ *Various locations around Saranac Lake* ☎ *518/891–1057.*

FALL

The annual **Adirondack Canoe Classic** is a three-day, 90-mi canoe race held in early September. The 250 boats participating make their way from Old Forge through Blue Mountain Lake to the village of Saranac Lake, crossing several portages. ☎ *518/891–2744* ⊕ *www.*

macscanoe.com/90-Miler/90-miler_Index.htm.

Adirondack Hot Air Balloon Festival. More than 100 hot-air balloons puff their stuff as they ascend in this annual four-day event held around the third weekend in September. There are usually two launches on Saturday and Sunday (one at sunrise and the other in the early evening), weather permitting. Smaller launches are held on Thursday and Friday. ✉ *Floyd Bennett Memorial Airport, 443 Queensbury Ave., Queensbury (off Rte. 354 [Quaker Rd.] 3 mi northeast of downtown Glens Falls)* ☎ *518/761–6366 Warren County Tourism* ⊕ *www.adirondackballoonfest.org.*

Lake George Jazz Weekend. Jazz groups from all over the state converge at the Shepard Park bandstand for an end-of-summer bash, usually in mid-September, after Labor Day. ✉ *Shephard Park, Lake George* ☎ *518/668–2616* ⊕ *www.lakegeorgearts.org.*

Whiteface Mountain Scottish Highland Festival. Held on a Saturday in early September, the festival features piping, drumming, Highland dancing, Celtic harps, Celtic fiddles, spinning and weaving, a Scottish heavy athletics competition, clan tents, and Scottish imports and food. ✉ *Whiteface Mountain Ski Center, Rte. 86, Wilmington* ☎ *518/946–2223.*

WESTERN ADIRONDACKS SCENIC DRIVE

Black River Trail Scenic Byway. The 111-mi trail traces the western extremity of the Adirondacks and leads from Rome, New York in the south nearly to Canada in the north. This is a breathtaking area of the park, especially when the leaves are changing. Along the way are fun stops at dairies, picnic areas, museums, and maple-syrup producers. Beware the winter, though, as the trail leads through the Tug Hill Plateau before ending at Ogdensburg. The plateau gets foot upon foot of snow in the winter. –>Tip: Bring along a map of the area, as there are many side roads, leading to a sometimes-confusing trek. ⊠ 46 heading north from Rome, which turns into Rte. 12, then catch Rte. 812 north from Lowville. Follow it to Harrisville, where you will catch Rte. 11 north, which turns back into Rte. 812. ⊕ www.adirondack.org/byways/bywayblackriver.php.

☾ **Enchanted Forest/Water Safari.** Highlights at this water park include a tidal-wave pool and a multiperson tube ride called the Amazon. The Black River waterslide and the Bombay Blaster chutes have you gliding through darkness. The complex includes traditional amusement rides and themed areas such as Story Book Lane for the younger set. Circus shows are offered twice daily. ⊠ 3183 Rte. 28, Old Forge ☎ 315/369-6145 ⊕ www.watersafari.com ☜ $25.95 ☾ Mid-June–Labor Day, daily; call for hrs.

★ **Old Forge Lake Cruise.** You can explore the first four lakes of the Fulton Chain on a narrated sightseeing cruise aboard one of two 125-passenger boats. The 22-mi cruises usually take two hours; kids' cruises are 15 mi and take about 90 minutes. Dinner excursions are also available. From June to mid-September you may tag along on the 35-foot *President Harrison* as it delivers mail to lakefront camps and cottages. The mail boat service dates from 1902 and was spurred by Benjamin Harrison, whose family summered on Second Lake. The mailboat can take only 10 passengers, so reservations for this three-hour cruise are a good idea. ⊠ Main St. Dock, Rte. 28, Old Forge ☎ 315/369-6473 ⊕ www.oldforgecruises.com ☜ Sightseeing and mailboat cruises $16–$20 ☾ Late Aug–mid-Oct; call or check Web site for schedule.

WHERE TO EAT

$$

AMERICAN

✕ **Old Mill Restaurant.** This popular restaurant and bar is housed in a converted mill, complete with a huge waterwheel. It's a place seasonal residents come back to, and that's probably because the restaurant does Adirondack fare—hearty, warming food in large portions—very, very well. The beef and barley stew or the cheddar cheese soup are consistent favorites. And while you may have a wait since reservations aren't accepted, the fare and comfortable surroundings will make up for it. ⊠ 2888 Rte. 28, Old Forge ☎ 315/369-3662 ⌘ Reservations not accepted ▤ MC, V ☾ Closed Nov.–late Dec. and mid-Mar.–Apr. No lunch.

WHERE TO STAY

$$ ⊡**Adirondack Lodge Old Forge.** Formerly the Best Western Sunset Inn, the property still has a heated indoor pool with an adjacent outdoor deck, but the building itself is under renovation. Still, rooms are spacious and furnished in the Adirondack style, with knotty-wood paneling and hunter-green and wine-red quilts. **Pros:** simple, clean, and comfortable. **Cons:** not much selection at breakfast. ⊠*2752 Rte. 28, Old Forge* ☎*315/369–6836* ⊕*www.adirondacklodgeoldforge.com* ⊭*52 rooms* ⍚*In-room: refrigerator, Wi-Fi. In-hotel: tennis court, pool, laundry facilities, some pets allowed, no smoking rooms* ☰*AE, D, DC, MC, V* ⭗*CP.*

$$ ⊡**Big Moose Inn and Restaurant.** The large 1903 Adirondack inn on Big Moose Lake has a central fireplace, a cozy lounge, a front porch with rockers, a floating gazebo with checkerboards, and canoes. Accommodations, located in the three-story lodge, are simple and have brass beds. Most rooms have a lake view, and one has a fireplace and a whirlpool tub, but some rooms and common areas feel a little like granny's parlor. A restaurant serves American fare in an attractive space with lake views; and a deck with umbrella-shaded tables offers lakeside dining. **Pros:** complimentary canoe and kayak use; the restaurant offers both fine and casual menus. **Cons:** some furnishings are becoming dated; no elevator. ⊠*1510 Big Moose Rd., Eagle Bay* ☎*315/357–2042* ⊕*www. bigmooseinn.com* ⭹*16 rooms, 4 with shared bath* ⍚*In-room: no a/c (some), no phone, no TV (some), Wi-Fi. In-hotel: restaurant, no-smoking rooms* ☰*AE, MC, V* ⭗*Closed Apr.* ⭗*CP.*

¢ ⊡**19th Green Motel.** Tree-lined grounds surround this motel next to the Thendara Golf Club, and snowmobiling trails are accessible from the property. Accommodations are roomy and have either one or two queen-size beds. **Pros:** near a water park and a golf club. **Cons:** no frills. ⊠*2761 Rte. 28, Old Forge* ☎*315/369–3575* ⊕*www.19thgreenmotel. com* ⭹*13 rooms* ⍚ *In-room: refrigerator. In-hotel: pool, no-smoking rooms* ☰*AE, D, DC, MC, V.*

$ ⊡**Van Auken's Inne.** Built in 1891 as a boardinghouse for lumberjacks, this historic country inn is easily identified by its two-story porch with rockers. Guest rooms, all on the second floor, have antiques and quilts; bed configurations vary from a double to two queens or a king. In the restaurant you can order a wide range of seafood or regional recipes like vodka riggies (rigatoni) or greens—a mix of sautéed escarole, cherry peppers, mozzarella, and bacon. The tavern also serves food, but you might want to try the "Fresh Seafood on the Porch" event, which features grilled seafood and live music. **Pros:** live music on the porch some nights. **Cons:** some residents say the restaurant isn't as good as it was a few years ago. ⊠*108 Forge St., Thendara* ☎*315/369–3033* ⊕*www.vanaukensinne.com* ⭹*12 rooms* ⍚*In-room: no a/c. In-hotel: restaurant, bar, no-smoking rooms* ☰*MC, V* ⭗*CP.*

$ ⊡**Water's Edge Inn & Conference Center.** The rustic-style, three-story lodge ⭗ with modern amenities sits at the edge of a lake in the Fulton Chain. Rooms have balconies, some overlooking the lake, and attractive traditional furnishings. Common areas include a library with cushy chairs, a stone fireplace, and water views conducive to lingering. **Pros:** across the street from the Enchanted Forest/Water Safari and Calypso's Cove water and amusement parks. **Cons:** noisy in some areas. ⊠ *Rte. 28, Old Forge* ⌂ *Box 1141 Old Forge 13420* ☎ *315/369–2484* ⊕ *www. watersedgeinn.com* ↪ *61 rooms, 8 suites* ↻ *In-room: Wi-Fi, refrigerator (some). In-hotel: pool, restaurant, bar, no-smoking rooms, gym* ▭ *AE, MC, V* ⦿ *CP.*

BLUE MOUNTAIN LAKE

32 mi west of Blue Mountain Lake, 31 mi south of Tupper Lake.

At the edge of Blue Mountain Lake, this hamlet is home to only a few hundred people. Outdoors lovers come to the area, the geographic heart of Adirondack Park, for the boating, fishing (largemouth bass, lake trout, brook trout, and whitefish), and the excellent hiking trails. Two major attractions, the Adirondack Museum and the Adirondack Lakes Center for the Arts, have made Blue Mountain Lake a regional cultural hub.

VISITOR INFORMATION

Blue Mountain Lake Association (⌂ *Box 245, Blue Mountain Lake 12812* ☎ *518/352–7659*).

WHAT TO SEE

Fodor'sChoice **Adirondack Museum.** More than 100,000 Adirondack artifacts are in
★ the collection of this acclaimed museum that explores the history and culture of the region. The 32-acre complex, on Blue Mountain Lake, encompasses 23 indoor and outdoor exhibit areas that examine nearly every feature of Adirondack life, including resort life, wood crafts, logging and mining, guide boats, and environmental issues. A library, snack bar, and shop are on-site. ⊠ *Rte. 30* ☎ *518/352–7311* ⊕ *www. adkmuseum.org* 🎫 *$16* 🕑 *Late May–mid-Oct., daily 10–5. Closed some days in Sept.*

Great Camp Sagamore. Sagamore Lodge and the 26 adjoining buildings that make up Great Camp Sagamore were built in the late 1800s by William West Durant, a prominent Adirondack figure. Designed in a Swiss-chalet style, the lodge was built with native spruce, cedar, and granite, and its rustic style set a precedent among the well-heeled set with retreats in the area. Bought and expanded by the Vanderbilt family in the early 1900s, Sagamore is now owned and run by a nonprofit organization that sponsors meetings, seminars, and classes, and rents rooms by the night or week. Classes and activities include canoeing, rustic furniture making, mosaic twig decoration, and mountain music. Tours (reservations required) take you to a blacksmith shop, furniture shop, icehouse, and livestock buildings, as well as to the main lodge. The camp is about 30 mi southwest of Blue Mountain Lake. ⊠ *Box 40, Rte. 28, Raquette Lake 13436* ☎ *315/354–5311* ⊕ *greatcampsagamore. org* 🎫 *Tours $12* 🕑 *Tours late May–late June, weekends at 1:30; late June–early Sept., daily at 10 and 1:30; early Sept.–late Oct., daily at 1:30.*

SPORTS AND THE OUTDOORS

BOAT TOURS

Raquette Lake Navigation Company. Cruise the waters of Raquette Lake aboard the *W. W. Durant,* a 60-foot double-deck ship that offers lunch, Sunday champagne brunch, dinner, foliage, and moonlight cruises ($7–$60), among other trips. The dining room is enclosed and heated, and there's a bar. Reservations are required for meal cruises. ✉ *Rte. 28, Raquette Lake* ☏ *315/354–5532* ⊕ *www.raquettelakenavigation.com* ⊗ *Call or visit Web site for schedule.*

THE ARTS

The **Adirondack Lakes Center for the Arts** (✉ *Rte. 28* ☏ *518/352–7715* ⊕ *www.adk-arts.org*) presents a wide variety of programs, from classical concerts to coffeehouse entertainment, films, plays, exhibits, and workshops. Galleries display regional and national artwork. Center hours change by the season.

WHERE TO STAY

$$$ ⌚ **The Hedges.** This camp, dating from 1880, is where you check in if you want to check out for a while. Forget phones, computers, and TVs—the emphasis here is on the great outdoors, and the rustic accommodations reflect that. Early-morning views from this property are of mist-covered Blue Mountain Lake and surrounding Adirondack Mountains. You might take a kayak or canoe out on the lake, hit some balls on the tennis court, try to hook a fish, or snuggle up with a book in a cozy nook. Kids will love the Ping-Pong tables, pool table, and beach access. **Pros:** breakfast and dinner are included in the price. **Cons:** no bar or pool; no pets allowed. ✉ *Hedges Rd.* ☏ *518/352–7352* ⊕ *www. thehedges.com* ⊜ *18 rooms, 13 cabins* △ *In-room: kitchen (some), no phone, no TV. In-hotel: restaurant, tennis court* ▭ *No credit cards* ⊗ *Closed late Oct.–late May* ⎗ *MAP*

¢ 🏠 **Sandy Point Motel.** The small lakefront motel has standard rooms and efficiencies with private screened-in porches and balconies with water views. Some units have kitchenettes. You can rent canoes, rowboats, and paddleboats on the property. **Pros:** near museums and restaurants. **Cons:** no breakfast included. ✉ *865 Deerland Rd. (Rte. 30), Long Lake* ☏ *518/624–3871* ⊕ *www.sandypointmotel.com* ⊜ *11 rooms* △ *In-room: kitchen (some), no a/c, no phone, Wi-Fi. In-hotel: no-smoking rooms* ▭ *AE, D, MC, V* ⊗ *Closed Nov.–Apr.*

¢ 🏠 **Shamrock Motel and Cottages.** Located right on the banks of Long Lake, the cottages, efficiencies, and motel rooms (renovated in 2007) at Shamrock are trim and tidy, though not overly luxurious. All are located a skip away from the sand and near recreation opportunities. Open year-round. **Pros:** restful, calm setting with private beach. **Cons:** reservations are not available online, no breakfast plan. ✉ *Box 205,*

Long Lake ☎518/624–3861 ⊕*www.shamrockmotellonglake.com*
↪*15 rooms, 4 suites, 2 cottages* ⬙*In-room: Wi-Fi, kitchen (some), no
a/c. In-hotel: Internet terminal, some pets allowed, no-smoking rooms*
▭*AE, D, MC, V.*

NORTH CREEK AND GORE MOUNTAIN

*29 mi southeast of Blue Mountain Lake, 21 mi northwest of Lake
George.*

Nestled between the mountains and the Hudson River gorge, the village
of North Creek makes a good base for a variety of outdoor activities.
Just southwest of the village is Gore Mountain—with a 2,150-foot
vertical drop, it's the second-largest ski area in the state (Whiteface is
the largest). Cross-country skiing and white-water rafting are options,
too *(⇨Sports and the Outdoors section).*

VISITOR INFORMATION
Gore Mountain Region Chamber of Commerce (⊠*228 Main St., North Creek*
☎*518/251–2612 or 800/880–4673* ⊕*www.goremtnregion.org*).

WHAT TO SEE
♻ **Garnet Mine Tours.** The mine, started in 1878, is one of the largest garnet
mines in the world. Guided tours, which include a walk through an
open-pit mine, leave from the Gore Mountain Mineral Shop; you follow
the guide in your car to the actual mines, at the base of Gore Mountain.
⊠*Burton Mine Rd., west off Rte. 28, North River* ☎*518/251–2706
*⊕*www.garnetminetours.com* ⊠*$10* ⊗*June–Labor Day, daily 9:30–5;
after Labor Day–mid-Oct., Mon.–Sat. 9:30–5, Sun. 11–5.*

Upper Hudson River Railroad. This scenic railroad offers unparalleled
views of the Hudson River. The two-hour, 17-mi round-trip excursion runs along a section of the old Adirondack Branch of the D&H
Railroad. ⊠*3 Railroad Pl., North Creek* ☎*518/251–5334* ⊕*www.
upperhudsonriverrr.com* ⊠ *$18* ⊗*Late May–Oct.; call for schedule.*

SPORTS AND THE OUTDOORS
GOLF
Whiteface Club & Resort. The par-72, 6,490-yard course here opened in
1898. *Golf Digest* gave it 3½ stars in 2004 and cited the well-kept fairways. Greens fees are $40 in high season. ⊠ *Whiteface Inn Rd., Lake
Placid* ☎*518/523–2551* ⊕*www.whitefaceclubresort.com.*

RAFTING
North Creek is the white-water hub of the Adirondacks and site of the
annual **White Water Derby** (☎*518/251–2613* ⊕*www./whitewaterderby.
com*).

WINTER SPORTS
SKIING **Garnet Hill Ski Lodge and Cross-Country Ski Center.** Receiving more than
★ 120 inches of snow a year, the center often has skiing into spring. It has
55 km (34 mi) of groomed cross-country-skiing trails, with 2 km (1 mi)
lighted for night schussing. Lessons, rental equipment, and a ski shop are
available; trail passes are $17. The on-property inn has lodge-and-ski

packages. In summer, mountain biking becomes the focus ($5 trail pass). It's about 5 mi northwest of North Creek. ⊠*13th Lake Rd., North River* ☎*518/251–2444 or 800/497–4207* ⊕*www.garnet-hill.com.*

Gore Mountain Ski Center. Operated by the Olympic Regional Development Authority, this state-owned center has a 2,100-foot vertical drop, 68 alpine trails, 12 snowshoeing/cross-country-skiing trails, and 95% snowmaking coverage. You find some of the longest runs in the East here; the longest stretches 2.9 mi. Intermediate trails account for 60% of the terrain; novices have 10% and advanced skiers have 30%. A ski pass is $51–$71. From August to mid-October you can ride the Northwoods Gondola Skyride ($13) up the mountain, or hit the fairly challenging terrain on a mountain bike ($14 trail passes). ⊠*Peaceful Valley Rd., North Creek* ☎*518/251–2411 or 800/342–1234* ⊕*www. goremountain.com.*

SHOPPING

Antler light fixtures and lamps are a specialty at the **Rustic Homestead Streamside Gallery** (⊠*Rte. 28N, North Creek* ☎*518/251–4038* ⊕*www. rustichomestead.com*), which also sells rustic birch rockers, cedar beds, bark-framed mirrors, and intricate desks and chests.

WHERE TO EAT AND STAY

¢ ✕**Café Sarah.** This café-bakery has light fare like soups, hot and cold
AMERICAN sandwiches, and baked goods. Bag lunches are available, too, for skiers, hikers, or anyone who just likes to brown bag it. Outdoor seating is available. ⊠*260 Main St., North Creek* ☎*518/251–5959* ▤ *MC, V* ⊘*Closed Tues. and Wed.*

¢ ▨**Black Mountain Ski Lodge.** This budget family motel is in a quiet area 5 mi from the Gore Mountain Ski Center. Its dark-wood exterior and the guest rooms' knotty-wood-paneled walls give it a rustic chalet look. Rooms are basic but spacious. There's a restaurant on-site that serves American-style fare like burgers and wraps, and an Adirondack-style pub. **Pros:** very reasonable room and dining prices. **Cons:** no frills like shampoo and scented soap. ⊠*2999 Rte. 8, North Creek* ☎*518/251–2800* ↪*23 rooms, 2 efficiencies* ᝪ *In-room: refrigerator (some). In-hotel: restaurant, bar, pool, some pets allowed, no-smoking rooms* ▤*AE, D, MC, V.*

$ ▨**Garnet Hill Lodge.** Overlooking mountains and a pristine lake 5 mi
⟳ from Gore Mountain Ski Center, this Adirondack inn was built in the tradition of the great camps. Accommodations are housed in four buildings, including the Log House, which has hewn beams and posts, a wide front porch, and mountain and lake views. Rooms combine paneled walls with contemporary, rustic-style furnishings; some rooms have balconies. The 600-acre complex includes a cross-country-skiing and mountain-biking center. The lodge also has canoes, rowboats, sailboats, and paddleboats and hosts ski programs for kids. The Saturday buffet dinner is a highlight at the restaurant. **Pros:** family and pet friendly. **Cons:** there's a fee for additional people in room. ⊠*13th Lake Rd., North River* ☎*518/251–2444 or 800/497–4207* ▤*518/251–3089* ⊕*www.garnet-hill.com* ↪*30 rooms, 27 with bath; 1 suite* ᝪ *In-room:*

no a/c (some), no TV. In-hotel: no-smoking rooms, restaurant, Wi-Fi, tennis courts, bar, bicycles, some pets allowed ☐MC, V ⦶MAP.

LAKE GEORGE AND THE CHAMPLAIN VALLEY

Long and narrow, Lake George stretches 32 mi south to north. Because the local American Indians considered its waters sacred, Lake George was originally named Lac du Saint Sacrement by the French, who had explored the region in the mid-17th century. A spit of land separates Lake George from Lake Champlain, which is 107 mi long and the sixth-largest lake in North America. The Champlain Valley is largely a farming region that stretches from the north end of Lake George to the border with Canada, west to the Adirondacks, and east into Vermont.

AREA BIKE TRAILS

The centerpiece of **Lake Champlain Bikeways** (✉ *1 Steele St. No. 103, Burlington, VT* ☎ *802/652–2453* ⦶ *www.champlainbikeways.org*), a network of bike routes and loops totaling more than 1,000 mi, is the 363-mi **Champlain Bikeway**, which circles Lake Champlain and runs north along the Richelieu River into Québec. The 10-mi **Warren County Bikeway** (*Adirondack/Glens Falls Transportation Council,* ✉ *383 Broadway, Fort Edward* ☎ *518/746–2199* ⦶ *www.co.warren.ny.us/transport/bike.php)* meanders through wooded areas and over a few hills, with glimpses of the mountains, between Lake George Village and Glens Falls.

GLENS FALLS

20 mi northeast of Saratoga Springs.

The road to Lake George begins in Glens Falls, about 10 mi south and east of Adirondack Park's formal boundary, 194 mi north of New York City and 48 mi north of Albany. With a population of more than 15,000 in the city and about 25,000 more in surrounding communities (Queensbury and Hudson Falls), Glens Falls is the only close-to-urban area in this part of the state. One good reason to visit is the Hyde Collection of art, which was started by a prominent Glens Falls family.

WHAT TO SEE
Chapman Historical Museum. A visit to the painstakingly restored home of the DeLong family—who lived here from 1860 to 1910—gives you a glimpse of life in the 19th-century Adirondacks. Guided tours of the house are available Tuesday through Friday and Sunday 1–4 and Saturday 10–4. Changing exhibits showcase regional history, and an extensive photo collection displays the work of Seneca Ray Stoddard (1843–1917). ✉ *348 Glen St.12801* ☎ *518/793–2826* ⦶ *www. chapmanmuseum.org* ☐*Free* ☉*Tues.–Sat. 10–4, Sun. noon–4.*

Fodor$Choice **Hyde Collection.** One of the finest art museums in the northeastern United
★ States, the Hyde Collection encompasses some 2,800 pieces including paintings and works on paper by artists such as Josef Albers, Sandro Botticelli, Georges Braque, Alexander Calder, Paul Cézanne, William

Merritt Chase, Leonardo da Vinci, Edgar Degas, Thomas Eakins, El Greco, Childe Hassam, Winslow Homer, Wassily Kandinsky, Pablo Picasso, Rembrandt, and Pierre-Auguste Renoir. Antiques, fine period furniture, and decorative arts are also displayed, as are temporary exhibits. Guided tours ($6) are offered between 1 and 4. ⊠*161 Warren St.* ☎*518/792–1761* ⊕*www.hydecollection.org* 🖆*Free* ⊗*Tues.– Sat. 10–5, Sun. noon–5.*

WHERE TO EAT AND STAY

$$
CONTINENTAL

✕**Bistro Tallulah** This contemporary, upscale bistro is a new edition to a newly revitalized downtown. Tallulah serves New Orleans–inspired cuisine, "small plates"—smaller portions of a main dish—and a large variety of wine including Chilean and Australian reds and Italian and New Zealand whites. Reservations are recommended. ⊠*26 Ridge St.12801* ☎*518/793–5789* ▤*MC, V* ⊗*Closed Sun.*

$
AMERICAN

✕**Davidson Brothers Restaurant and Brewery.** In the heart of downtown, this English-style brewpub serves standard pub fare and manages to project that neighborhood-meeting-place feel that Brits love. Dishes include fish-and-chips, stout-and-cheddar soup, assorted wraps and salads, blue-cheese-topped steaks, and buffalo burgers. Try the sampler for the gamut of microbrews Davidson Brothers produces. ⊠*184 Glen St.* ☎*518/743–9026* ▤*AE, D, MC, V* ⊗*Closed Sun. Jan.– Mother's Day.*

$$

🖬**Queensbury Hotel.** Ivy tendrils scale the facade of this five-story redbrick hotel built in the 1920s. A large fireplace graces the lobby, where cushy chairs invite lingering. Rooms are traditional, with lace-fringed windows, soft colors, and dark-wood furniture. The indoor pool, under a massive skylight, is a nice size. The hotel is across from the city park in downtown Glens Falls. **Pros:** lots to do on-site, including swimming and dining; near the town of Lake George. **Cons:** decor is a bit dated. ⊠*88 Ridge St.* ☎*518/792–1121 or 800/554–4526* ⊕*www.queensburyhotel. com* ⇋*114 rooms, 11 suites* ♿*In-room: refrigerator (some), Internet. In-hotel: no-smoking rooms, restaurant, pool, gym, bar, laundry service* ▤*AE, D, DC, MC, V* ⭐*CP*

LAKE GEORGE

10 mi north of Glen Falls.

The village of Lake George, in the Adirondack foothills, sits at the southern end of the lake of the same name. It's a family-focused tourist area, chockablock with motels, eateries, small outlet malls, and assorted amusements, including theme parks, miniature golf, and a wax museum. In summer, traffic through the village can crawl along U.S. 9.

Lake George also has historical significance. The area, because of its location on the lake, was inhabited before the European settlers arrived and later figured prominently in the French and Indian War. It also saw clashes during the Revolutionary War.

VISITOR INFORMATION

Lake George Regional Chamber of Commerce (⊠ *2176 U.S. 9, Lake George* ☎ *518/668–5755 or 800/705–0059* ⊕ *www.lakegeorgechamber.com*).

WHAT TO SEE

Fort William Henry Museum. The "fort" here is actually a reconstruction of the 1755 original, which was built by the British, used in the French and Indian War, and written about in James Fenimore Cooper's *The Last of the Mohicans*. The complex encompasses barracks, dungeons, and an example of an Iroquois longhouse, as well as artifacts recovered from the original fort site, which is nearby. Tours, led by guides dressed in 18th-century military garb, start on the hour; demonstrations include the firing of muskets and cannons. Ghost tours of the museum and Lake George are also available on Friday and Saturday nights ($14.95). ⊠ *Canada St.* ☎ *518/668–5471* ⊕ *www.fwhmuseum.com* ⊠ *$14 museum* ⊗ *May–late Oct., daily 9–6.*

☾ **House of Frankenstein Wax Museum.** More than 50 interactive exhibits of monsters and mayhem are on display here, including such favorites as Dracula and the Wolfman. Kindergartners and younger children may get quite a fright here. ⊠ *213 Canada St.12845* ☎ *518/668–3377* ⊕ *www.frankensteinwaxmuseum.com* ⊠ *$9* ⊗ *Daily Apr.–early Nov.; call for hrs as they vary by day and month.*

THEME PARKS **Great Escape & Splashwater Kingdom Fun Park.** Six roller coasters are
☾ among the 125-plus rides at this theme park. The water-park area (open Memorial Day through Labor Day) includes labyrinthine slides, a 25,000-square-foot wave pool, and a raft ride with waterfalls and water bombs. Shows include a high-dive act. ⊠ *1172 U.S. 912845* ☎ *518/792–3500* ⊕ *www.sixflags.com/greatescape* ⊠ *$35.99* ⊗ *Mid-May–early Sept.,daily 11–6.*

☾ **Water Slide World.** The 12-acre park has more than 35 slides, a wave pool, water and sand volleyball, and kiddie pools. Food is available, as are lockers, picnic areas, showers, and life jackets. To get here, take Exit 21 off Interstate 87. ⊠ *U.S. 9 and Rte. 9L* ☎ *518/668–4407* ⊕ *www. adirondack.net/tour/waterslideworld/* ⊠ *$24* ⊗ *Mid-June–Labor Day, daily 9:30–6.*

SPORTS AND THE OUTDOORS

SWIMMING

Lake George Beach. The popular swimming beach, also known as Million Dollar Beach, has a bathhouse, lifeguards, lockers, picnic facilities, and volleyball nets. ⊠ *Beach Rd., east of U.S. 9* ☎ *518/668–3352* ⊠ *Parking $7* ⊗ *Memorial Day–Labor Day, daily 9–6:30.*

BOAT TOURS

Lake George Steamboat Co. (⊠ *57 Beach Rd.* ☎ *518/668–5777 or 800/ 553–2628* ⊕ *www.lakegeorgesteamboat.com*) offers cruises on its three boats: the *Minne-Ha-Ha*, a steam paddle wheeler; the 1907 *Mohican*; and the 190-foot *Lac du Saint Sacrement*. Cruises, offered daily May through October, include sightseeing excursions ($11.50–$24.50) as well as brunch, lunch, and dinner cruises ($18.50–$41.50). Special themed and holiday cruises are also scheduled throughout the year.

WHERE TO EAT

$ ✕**Barnsider Smokehouse.** Smoked ribs are the specialty at this peren-
BARBECUE nial local favorite, and if you like them you might consider buying the bottled barbecue sauce. The wedge-cut fries are thick and satisfying, and the hearty breakfasts include all-you-can-eat buttermilk pancakes. In warm weather you may eat on the small deck. There's also a full bar. *2112 Rte. 9* ☎*518/668–5268* ▤*AE, D, DC, MC, V* ⊘*Closed Nov.–Apr.*

$$ ✕**East Cove Restaurant.** Cloth-covered tables add a touch of formality to
AMERICAN this cozy log-cabin space. The brunch is a local favorite and includes upscale touches like seafood Newburg and beef tips. The overall fare is American: prime rib (blackened, if you wish), surf and turf, chicken parmigiana, and fettuccine Alfredo. There's a nice wine list and full bar—try a Bloody Mary for a classic, tangy treat. ⊠*3873 State Rte. 9L* ☎*518/668–5265* ▤*AE, D, MC, V* ⊘ *Closed Mon. and Tues. Nov.– Apr. No lunch Mon.–Sat.*

$$ ✕**Log Jam.** Like the East Cove restaurant, Log Jam looks like a refined
STEAK log cabin, with three stone fireplaces and attractive wood furniture. Despite its down-home feel, the place serves upscale dishes like prime rib, roast duck, and steak au poivre, which comes with sautéed mush-rooms and shallots in mustard sauce. Fish dishes include surf-and-turf combos as well as more-complicated preparations. There's also a salad bar. ⊠*1484 U.S. 9, No. 1* ☎*518/798–1155* ▤*AE, D, DC, MC, V.*

¢ ✕**Pizza Jerks.** If you like New York City–style pizza, this is the place
PIZZA for you. This eatery has pizza on par with anything there, served up
☺ in a fun, casual atmosphere. Veggie lovers will enjoy the Tree Hugger
★ (pesto, spinach, garlic, and more), while carnivores will go for the Car-cass, loaded with every type of meat available in the restaurant. ⊠*59 Iroquois St.* ☎*518/668–4411* ▤*MC, V.*

WHERE TO STAY

$ ▦**Best Western of Lake George.** The two-story, lodge-style chain motel offsets traditional furnishings with Adirondack flair. Some rooms have sloping wood ceilings, and some suites have fireplaces, but rooms here as a rule are not fancy. The true appeal is that Lake George beaches are 1 mi away and the property has an outdoor swimming pool with a view of the mountains. **Pros:** the breakfast is usually good. **Cons:** don't expect frills. ⊠*Rte. 9N off I–87 Exit 21* ☎*518/668–5701* ⊕*www. bestwesternlakegeorge.com* ➴*79 rooms, 8 suites* ♿ *In-room: kitchen (some), refrigerator (some), Internet. In-hotel: some pets allowed, no-smoking rooms, pools, laundry service* ▤*AE, D, DC, MC, V* ❑*CP.*

$$ ▦**Colonel Williams Motor Inn.** The yellow clock tower rising above this
☺ tidy family-oriented motel clearly identifies the 10-acre property. Rooms are uncluttered, with traditional wood furniture and either one or two queen beds or two doubles. Some rooms have decks. The grounds include two playgrounds, one of which has a kiddie-size fire engine, pirate ship, and train. **Pros:** very quiet and family-friendly. **Cons:** no visitors or infants allowed; more rules than other lodgings. ⊠*U.S. 9*

1 mi north of I–87 Exit 20, Box 268, 12845 ☎ 800/334–5727 🌐 www.colonelwilliamsresort.com ⇨ 30 rooms, 15 suites ⇨ In-room: kitchen (some), refrigerator. In-hotel: no-smoking rooms, pools, gym, laundry facilities ▭ AE, D, MC, V ⊙ Closed mid-Sept.–May 🍽 CP.

$$ **Fort William Henry Resort Hotel.** The hotel property encompasses a conference center and 18 acres overlooking the southern end of Lake George. Rooms have been refurbished but retain a traditional look. Their configurations range from studios with sleeper sofas to huge suites with fireplaces; some have lake or mountain views. The large outdoor pool looks onto the lake. **Pros:** very clean. **Cons:** if you smoke, you have to do it outside and away from the building. ✉ *48 Canada St.* ☎ *518/668–3081 or 800/221–9211* 🌐 *www.fortwilliamhenry.com* ⇨ *99 rooms, 97 suites* 👍 *In-room: refrigerator (some), Internet. In-hotel: some pets allowed, no-smoking rooms, 3 restaurants, pools, gym, bicycles, laundry facilities, laundry service* ▭ *AE, D, DC, MC, V.*

$$ CONTINENTAL **The Georgian.** The sprawling, family-owned resort has a private beach and a marina. Rooms have views of the lake, the pool, or the courtyard; some have private balconies or patios. Suites have sitting areas with sleeper sofas. Traditional dark-wood furniture is used throughout. The main dining room ($$–$$$) serves mostly Continental fare: steak au poivre, lobster ravioli, roast rack of lamb, scampi, and chateaubriand. From mid-May through October, the Terrace Room hosts dinner theater. **Pros:** situated right in the center of Lake George. **Cons:** accommodations are getting a little shabby. ✉ *384 Canada St.12845* ☎ *518/668–5401 or 800/525–3436* 🌐 *www.georgianresort.com* ⇨ *150 rooms, 14 suites* 👍 *In-room: refrigerator (some), Wi-Fi. In-hotel: no-smoking rooms, room service, 2 restaurants, pool, bar, laundry service* ▭ *AE, D, DC, MC, V.*

$ **Hampton Inn & Suites.** Like many others in its chain, this Hampton Inn offers clean, modern and spacious rooms and breakfast until 10 AM. You can enjoy it with a free newspaper. **Pros:** located close to Lake George attractions; kids will love the indoor pool and hot tub. **Cons:** some say the breakfast isn't the best. ✉ *2133 Rte. 9* ☎ *518/668–4100* 🌐 *www.lakegeorgehamptoninn.com* ⇨ *93 rooms* 👍 *In-room: refrigerator. In-hotel: pool, laundry service, bar, Internet* ▭ *AE, D, DC, MC, V* 🍽 *BP.*

$ **Holiday Inn Turf.** The two-story hotel is set back 200 feet from the road, on a hill. Rooms, graced with wood furniture and soft earth-tone colors, are attractive and spacious. High-speed Internet access is available. Kids will love the kiddie pool, game room with oversize chessboard, indoor pool, and miniature golf course. Adults might dig the shuffleboard setup and basketball courts. **Pros:** lots of stuff for the kids to do; beautiful view of Lake George. **Cons:** some of the rooms have small bathrooms. ✉ *2223 Canada St.* ☎ *518/668–5781* 🌐 *www.ichotelsgroup.com* ⇨ *104 rooms, 1 suite* 👍 *In-room: safe, refrigerator, Internet. In-hotel: restaurant, room service, pools, gym, bar, laundry facilities, laundry service, no-smoking rooms* ▭ *AE, D, DC, MC, V.*

$$ **Still Bay.** The 5-acre property has an expansive patio that overlooks 300 feet of lakefront. Motel-style rooms are paneled in wood and have large windows. A private boathouse provides dock space. **Pros:** the

breakfasts are wonderful. **Cons:** bathrooms are small. ⊠*Lake Shore Dr./Rte. 9N* 🕭*Box 569, 12845* ☎*518/668–2584 or 800/521–7511* ⊕*www.stillbay.com* 🛏*19 rooms, 3 suites* ⚲In-room: *kitchen (some).* In-hotel: *restaurant* ⊟*MC, V* ⊘*Closed mid-Oct.–late May* ❛⦿*BP.*

BOLTON LANDING

10 mi north of Lake George.

A community of about 2,000 year-round residents, **Bolton Landing,** 8 mi north of the village of Lake George, hugs the western shore of Lake George, which is dotted with small coves and islands. In the 1800s it became fashionable for the well-heeled to summer in Bolton Landing. Thanks to the waterfront mansions that sprang up here, the area became known as Millionaires Row. Bolton Landing is perhaps best known as the home of the luxurious Sagamore Resort, which occupies its own island. Although the village is quieter and less touristy than the village of Lake George, you can still expect a good deal of summer traffic here.

WHAT TO SEE

Marcella Sembrich Opera Museum. Polish soprano Marcella Sembrich (1858–1935), who sang with New York's Metropolitan Opera, used the building housing this museum as a vocal-instruction studio. The studio was part of her summer estate. You can walk along Lake George here and take in the beautiful vista. The museum, on the National Register of Historic Places, includes opera costumes, paintings, and assorted memorabilia. ⊠*4800 Lake Shore Dr.* ☎*518/644–9839* ⊕*www. operamuseum.com* 🔁*Free (donations appreciated)* ⊘*Mid-June–mid-Sept., daily 10–12:30 and 2–5.*

WHERE TO EAT

$ ✕**Cate's Italian Garden.** Excellent gourmet pizza, seafood specialties,
ECLECTIC pasta dishes, a full wine list, and homemade desserts make it hard to
★ decide what to order at this pleasant spot. Dine alfresco in the warmth, and by lantern light in the chill. ⊠*4952 Main St.* ☎*518/644–2041* ⊟*AE, D, MC, V* ⊘*Closed Mar.*

$$ ✕**Villa Napoli Restaurant.** The restaurant, on the grounds of Melody
ITALIAN Manor, specializes in Tuscan dining. Candles and a marble fireplace adorn the quaint wood-paneled dining room, and Pavarotti sings or Vivaldi plays in the background. The chef-owner uses fresh herbs and vegetables from her garden. Try the gnocchi, a regional specialty. ⊠*Melody Manor, 4610 Lake Shore Dr.* ☎*518/644–9750* ⊟*AE, MC, V* ⊘*Closed mid-Oct.–mid-May and weekdays mid-May–late June and early Sept.–mid-Oct.*

WHERE TO STAY

$$ 🛏**The Boathouse Bed and Breakfast.** The grand 1917 stone-and-wood boathouse is on Millionaires Row and directly on Lake George. Most of the individually appointed rooms have hardwood floors and a king-size bed. Some rooms have private porches or balconies. One suite is decked out in Adirondack style, with a stone fireplace and cedar-post furniture;

the other is more refined, with a four-poster bed and boudoir-style upholstered chairs. The two carriage-house suites have gas fireplaces and two-person jet tubs. Breakfast is served in the great room, a lovely space with a timbered ceiling and several large windows. **Pros:** right on the placid waters of Lake George; great deals during the off-season; some rooms have hot tubs. **Cons:** children younger than 15 not allowed as guests. ⊠*44 Sagamore Rd.* ☎*518/644–2554* ⊕*www.boathousebb. com* ↩*4 rooms, 3 suites* ⌂*In-room: kitchen (some). In-hotel: no-smoking rooms, no kids under 15* ⊟*AE, MC, V* ⦿*BP.*

$ **Melody Manor.** The 9-acre property encompasses 300 feet of frontage on Lake George, where there's a beach and a dock. Accommodations are in motel-style buildings. The corner rooms are extra spacious. Some rooms have lake views and balconies or patios. The on-site Villa Napoli restaurant is a local favorite. **Pros:** right on the beach **Cons:** no in-room coffeemakers and coffee may run out at breakfast. ⊠*4610 Lake Shore Dr.* ☎*518/644–9750* ⊕*www.melodymanor.com* ↩*40 rooms* ⌂*In-room: Wi-Fi. In-hotel: no-smoking rooms, refrigerator (some), restaurant, tennis court, pool, bar* ⊟*AE, DC, MC, V* ⦿*Closed late Oct.–Apr.* ⦿*CP*

$$$ **Sagamore Resort.** Occupying a 72-acre island on Lake George, the
Fodor's Choice   Sagamore is an escape to a bygone era. Accommodations in the 1883
★   colonial-revival main house have views of the lake or gardens. The decor, including marble bathrooms and handsome wood furniture, is elegant but not formal, while accommodations in the newer lodge buildings are country-chic. Lodge rooms have garden views; suites have gas fireplaces and a terrace with a lake view. The separate condo units (starting at about $600 a night in season) have two bedrooms, two bathrooms, a kitchen, a living room, a dining area, and two lake-view terraces; leather couches, Adirondack-style furniture, and wood-burning fireplaces contribute to the lodge feel here. Notable facilities here include the spa and the sailing school. **Pros:** so much to do, you won't have to leave the resort. **Cons:** breakfast only included in some packages. ⊠*110 Sagamore Rd.* ☎*518/644–9400 or 800/358–3585* ⊕*www.thesagamore. com* ↩*172 rooms, 178 suites* ⌂*In-room: kitchen (some), Internet, room service. In-hotel: no-smoking rooms, 2 restaurants, golf course, tennis courts, pool, spa, children's programs (ages 3–12)* ⊟*AE, D, DC, MC, V.*

$ **Sugar Hill Manor.** Housed in a beautiful old Victorian home and set among rambling, 3-acre grounds, this relaxing B&B is comfortable and filled with antiques. It's run by Todd and Karen Hennessy, and Karen makes delicious sit-down breakfast in the morning and refreshments in the afternoon. The owners have chosen not to set up Internet access, and to keep the phones and TV downstairs in the main area. "This is where you go to get away," Karen says. **Pros:** relaxing; individualized attention; no smoking allowed on the property. **Cons:** minimum stay may be required; no Wi-Fi. ⊠*225 Sugar Hill Rd., Crown Point* ⦿*Box 143 12928* ☎*518/597–9545* ⊕*www.sugarhillmanor.com* ↩*4 rooms* ⌂*In-room: no a/c, no phone, no TV. In-hotel: restaurant, no-smoking rooms* ⊟*No credit cards* ⦿*BP.*

TICONDEROGA

28 mi northeast of Bolton Landing

Ticonderoga is an Iroquois term meaning "land of many waters," and Ticonderoga, 30 mi northeast of Bolton's Landing, lives up to its name. It's between Lakes George and Champlain, and the LaChute River runs through town. The French started building a fort in this strategic location in the mid-18th century. Today Fort Ticonderoga is a key attraction in the area.

WHAT TO SEE

Fort Ticonderoga. The fort, built alongside Lake Champlain by the French (in 1755–58), was originally named Fort Carillon. It was captured by the British in 1759 and renamed Fort Ticonderoga. The colonists took over in 1775, but only until 1777, when the British managed to place cannons atop **Mt. Defiance,** which overlooks the fort. You may drive up to the summit of Mt. Defiance and take in the views of the fort, the valley, and Lake Champlain. The fort presents living-history demonstrations, including cannon drills, musket firings, and fife-and-drum performances in July and August. Permanent exhibits include weapons and Revolutionary War artifacts. Thirty-minute guided tours with costumed interpreters are available. The grounds also encompass several gardens (open daily 10–4 from June to Columbus Day). ⊠ *Rte. 74* ☎ *518/585–2821* ⊕ *www.fort-ticonderoga.org* 🎫 *$15* ☉ *Early May–late Oct., daily 9–5.*

Hancock House. The Ticonderoga Historical Society resides in this grand Georgian mansion, a replica of the John Hancock home in Boston. The original, built in the mid-1700s, was destroyed in the 19th century. The replica, intended to serve as a museum, was commissioned by Horace Moses, who had built up the Strathmore Paper Company. Works by local artists are shown here, and you may tour the period rooms. ⊠ *6 Moses Circle* ☎ *518/585–7868* ⊕ *www.thehancockhouse.org* 🎫 *Free* ☉ *Wed.–Sat. 10–4.*

WHERE TO EAT

$$$ ✕ **Carillon Restaurant.** The spotlight at this casual restaurant is on steak
STEAK and seafood. Sautéed scallops, shrimp, and crabmeat are served with vodka sauce and penne; filet mignon, charbroiled, is dressed with peppered cabernet butter. If you'd rather have fowl, consider roast duckling with honey-raspberry sauce. Reservations aren't necessary, but are appreciated by restaurant staff. ⊠ *872 Rte. 9N* ☎ *518/585–7657* 🖃 *AE, D, DC, MC, V* ☉ *Closed Wed. No lunch.*

CROWN POINT

8 mi north of Ticonderoga.

The entire area near Crown Point was once known as Ironville, though that name now belongs to a small hamlet nearby. Crown Point is a quiet town, but the rich bed of iron ore discovered here in the early 1800s once made this an industrial center. The U.S. Navy was particularly eager to use Crown Point's iron ore for its new class of ironclad ships, such as the *Monitor*. Today the main attraction is the Crown Point State Historic Site, a few miles north of the village. The Crown Point Bridge takes you into Vermont.

WHAT TO SEE

Crown Point State Historic Site. Since the earliest European explorations of North America, long and narrow Lake Champlain has been considered an important strategic waterway. Both the French and English built forts along its shores. This site includes the ruins of the 1734 French fort, Fort Saint Frederic, and the 1759 British complex, Fort Crown Point. Exhibits at the visitor center give you historical context. ⊠*739 Bridge Rd., 3 mi north of Crown Point* ☎*518/597–3666* ⊕*www.nysparks. state.ny.us* ⊠*Parking $5 (weekends), visitor center $3, grounds free* ⊙ *Visitor center May–Oct., Wed.–Mon. 9–5.*

Penfield Homestead Museum. Dedicated to preserving the legacy of innovative industrialist Allen Penfield, this museum has exhibits explaining his work using electricity in the process of iron-ore separation. This was the first industrial application of electricity. The museum, 3 mi southwest of Crown Point, also houses many Civil War artifacts and equipment on its 550-acre site. ⊠*703 Creek Rd.* ☎*518/597–3804* ⊕*www.penfieldmuseum.org* ⊠*$4* ⊙ *Early June–Oct., Thurs.–Sun. 11–4, and by appointment.*

AUSABLE CHASM

50 mi north of Crown Point.

Thanks, to the impressive carving abilities of the Ausable River, which cut through deep layers of sandstone, Ausable Chasm has a trio of treasures: high cliffs (nearly 200 feet in places), waterfalls, and rapids.

VISITOR INFORMATION

Plattsburgh–North Country–Lake Champlain Regional Visitors Center (⊠*7061 U.S. 9, Plattsburgh* ☎*518/563-1000* ⊕*www.northcountrychamber.com*).

WHAT TO SEE

★ **Ausable Chasm.** The 1½-mi-long chasm opened to the public in 1870, becoming the country's first natural tourist attraction. The geological spectacle continues to be popular and is often overrun with visitors in summer.

A deck allows you to view formations such as Elephant Head with its trunk of rock. The trail around the rim provides soaring views, and stone walkways and stairways descend into the chasm. Sightseeing can be combined with a kayak, raft, or inner-tube ride on the Ausable River. Two-hour lantern tours ($20 per person) start at dusk. The flickering lights transform the 500-million-year-old mass of time-sculpted stone formations. Reservations are required. ⊠*U.S. 9* ☎*866/782-4276* ⊕*www.ausablechasm.com* ⊠*Walking trails $16* ⊙ *Mid-May–mid-June, daily 9:30–4; mid-June–early Sept., daily 9:30–5; early Sept. –late Oct., daily 9:30–4; some extended hrs.*

CHAMPLAIN VALLEY SCENIC DRIVES

Prospect Mountain Veterans Memorial Highway. The 5-mi corkscrew road takes you most of the way up 2,035-foot Prospect Mountain. From the parking lot it's just 100 feet to the summit, which you may reach via a shuttle. The views can stretch to 100 mi and take in up to five states, along with Lake George and the High Peaks region. You may also hike all the way up from the village. ⊠ *West off U.S. 9, 5 mi from Lake George* ☎ *518/668–5198* 🏷 *$6* ⊗ *May–late Oct., daily 9–5.*

Brant Lake. For a fun, colorful, and relatively short drive in the Lake George area, hop on Interstate 87 heading north from Lake George and take the Route 8 exit toward Brant Lake. Follow the densely wooded drive along the shore of Brantley Lake, ending in Hague, at the tip of the Tongue Mountain Range. The drive should be close to an hour, but may be longer if you linger. ⊠ *Rte. 8, at the southeastern tip of the park.*

LAKE PLACID AND THE NORTHERN ADIRONDACKS

LAKE PLACID

137 mi north of Albany.

The village of Lake Placid isn't on Lake Placid; it's on the shore of Mirror Lake, one of the most beautiful of the Adirondack lakes. The village's namesake lake lies just north of the village. Because both the 1932 and 1980 Winter Olympics were held here, Lake Placid is one of the best-known destinations in the Adirondacks. But it has been popular since the beginning of the 20th century, when the rich and famous first discovered the area and came here to participate in winter sports. A tight cluster of hotels, restaurants, and shops lines Main Street, where traffic often backs up, especially in summer.

VISITOR INFORMATION

Lake Placid/Essex County Convention & Visitors Bureau (⊠ *49 Parkside Dr., Suite 2, Lake Placid* ☎ *518/523–2445 or 800/447–5224* ⊕ *www.lakeplacid. com*).

WHAT TO SEE

Cornell Sugar Maple Research–Uihlein Field Station. The field station, part of a Cornell University extension program, encompasses more than 200 forested acres, a greenhouse, and orchards. An exhibit here explains how maple syrup is made. You may buy some syrup to take home with you. Tours are available by appointment and are recommended during the production season, February through April. The station is also sometimes open on weekends in March and April. ⊠ *157 Bear Cub La.* ☎ *518/523–9337* ⊕ *maple.dnr.cornell.edu* 🏷 *Free* ⊗ *Weekdays 8–4; and by appointment.*

John Brown Farm State Historic Site. Abolitionist John Brown lived for a short time on this 244-acre farm. In October 1859, Brown and his followers attempted to spark a slave revolt by taking over the federal arsenal at Harper's Ferry, West Virginia. His two sons and several of his followers were killed, and Brown was tried and executed. His body was brought back and buried here. A cross-country ski trail, a nature trail, and a picnic area are on the grounds, which are open all year. ⊠ *2 John Brown Rd., off Rte. 73* ☎ *518/523–3900* ⊕ *www.nysparks.state.ny.us* ⊠ *$2* ⊙ *House May–Oct., Wed.–Mon. 10–5. Grounds year-round.*

> **SCENIC DRIVES FOR NORTH ADIRONDACKS**
>
> Route 28N between North Creek and Long Lake and Route 73 between Lake Placid and Keene offer some of the best mountain views. For river scenery, Routes 86 and 9N from Lake Placid to Keeseville follow the Ausable River and its West Branch much of the way.

Fodor'sChoice
★
☾

Olympic Center. The center was built for the 1932 Olympics and renovated and expanded for the 1980 Games. During the latter, the arena here was the site of the U.S. ice-hockey team's win over the seemingly unbeatable Soviets, which led the men to a U.S. gold medal. The victory came to be known as the "Miracle on Ice." The center also houses other ice rinks, a museum, and convention space. Winter Olympics enthusiasts can purchase bobsled and luge rides with a professional on the competition track for $60 to $75. Tours of the center are available at 10, 11:30, and 1, Tuesday through Saturday for $8.50. A stop by the **1932 & 1980 Lake Placid Winter Olympic Museum** (⊠ *$5* ⊙ *Daily 10–5*) is a fitting way to begin your tour of Lake Placid. Displays here, including sports outfits and gear, explain the history and legacy of the Olympic Games at Lake Placid. A 50-minute audiocassette tour of the center is an option. The center hosts hockey and figure-skating tournaments and ice shows as well as other special events. ⊠ *218 Main St.* ☎ *518/523–1655 Ext. 226* ⊕ *www.orda.org* ⊙ *Daily 10–5.*

SPORTS AND THE OUTDOORS
BOAT TOUR
Lake Placid Marina. One-hour narrated cruises on Lake Placid take in many of the great camps lining the shore. Cruises leave from the Lake Placid Marina, and are offered two to four times daily. ⊠ *Mirror Lake Dr., off Rte. 86* ☎ *518/523–9704* ⊠ *$7.50* ⊙ *Mid-May–mid-Oct.; call for times.*

GOLF
Lake Placid Resort. Play at either of the two highly rated 18-hole courses: the par-71, 7,006-yard Links Course, designed in 1909 by Scottish architect Seymour Dunn; or the par-70, 6,156-yard Mountain Course, which was laid out by Alex Findlay in 1910 and remodeled by Alister MacKenzie in 1931. Greens fees, including cart, are $62–$75 on the Links Course and $30–$35 on the Mountain Course. You get stunning mountain views from both. ⊠ *1 Olympic Dr.* ☎ *518/523–4460* ⊕ *www.lakeplacidcp.com.*

WINTER SPORTS

You may see Olympic-caliber athletes in a variety of sports training in and around Lake Placid, which was the site of the 1980 Winter Olympics. National and international competitions in bobsledding and luge are held at Mt. Van Hoevenberg, alpine racing and freestyle competition at Whiteface Mountain, and speed skating at the Sheffield Speed Skating Oval in the center of Lake Placid. Hockey and figure-skating competitions are held in the ice arena next door to the Olympic oval. But you don't have to spend all your time on the sidelines.

You might strap on some skates and take a spin on the speed-skating oval or the indoor ice arena; shoot down an old ski slide in a toboggan; or hurtle down a bobsled run. Go downhill skiing at Whiteface, the largest alpine resort in the North Country, or cover a few miles on cross-country skis at Mt. Van Hoevenberg. Head to the southeastern part of Adirondack Park for the Gore Mountain Ski Center, a Whiteface sibling with a 2,100-foot vertical drop, and the Garnet Hill Cross-Country Ski Center.

During the 1980 Olympics, the Verizon Sports Complex was the site of the luge, bobsled, cross-country skiing, and biathlon events. And this is the perfect place to try some of these sports yourself. In winter you might whoosh down the ½-mi bobsled run at 50 mph–60 mph— a professional driver and brakeman accompany you—or steer a modified luge along a serpentine track. From mid-June to early November, the bobsled ride is offered on wheels. ■TIP➜**If you're prone to motion sickness, consider taking some Dramamine first or avoiding the bobsled. The ride is not only fast, but is bumpy and sways a lot.** ⊠ *Olympic Center, 2634 Main St.* ☎*518/523–4436* ⊕*www.orda.org* ⊠*Bobsled ride $75, luge $60* ☉ *Winter only. Call or check Web for times.*

ICE HOCKEY AND ICE-SKATING National Hockey League training camps are held at the **Olympic Center** (⊠*2634 Main St.* ☎*518/523–1655* ⊕*www.orda.org*) during the preseason, and the women's U.S. national hockey team makes its home here. You might catch ice-hockey tournaments or college games at the arena. From late November to mid-March, you may skate ($7) on the outdoor **Sheffield Speed Skating Oval,** where Eric Heiden won his five Olympic golds during the 1980 games, or at the indoor **1932 Olympic Rink.** From late June to late August, the indoor **Lussi Rink** is open to the public.

★ **Lake Placid Toboggan Chute.** An old 30-foot-tall ski slide right in town has been converted into a hair-raising toboggan run that spits you out onto and across iced-over Mirror Lake. The chute usually opens after Christmas but might be open as early as November and as late as February, so call to check conditions. ⊠*Parkside Dr. next to post office* ☎*518/523–2591* ⊠*$5* ☉ *Call for hrs.*

MacKenzie-Intervale Ski Jumping Complex. The towers of the 70- and 90-meter ski jumps here are stark and exposed and seem out of place, but the view from the top of the taller tower is dramatic. A glass-encased elevator takes you 26 stories to the top, where you get a bird's-eye view of the lay of the land and the High Peaks around Lake Placid. You also get a stomach-gripping view of what the jumpers see while preparing to take flight. During most of the year you may also opt to ride a chairlift up to the elevator. In summer, freestyle skiers practice twirls and somersaults into the pool at **Kodak Sports Park.** ⊠*Rte. 73 2 mi southeast of village center* ☎*518/523–2202* ⊕*www.orda.org* ⊠*$5–$10* ☉*Elevator: late Oct.– mid-Dec., Thurs.–Sun. 9–4; chairlift and elevator mid-Dec.–mid-Mar., Wed.–Sun. 9–4.*

The **Olympic Sports Complex** has 31 mi of groomed cross-country-skiing trails. Full-day trail passes are $18; lessons and rentals are available. You may also rent snowshoes here. From late June to early October, mountain bikers take over the trails (it's $10 for mountain biking). ⊠*Off Rte. 73, 7 mi south of Lake Placid, at Mt. Van Hoevenberg* ☎*518/523–4436 or 518/523–2811.*

SHOPPING

The village is full of shops, many of them with "Adirondack" in their name. The **Adirondack Store** (⊠*2024 Saranac Ave.* ☎*518/523–2646* ⊕*www.theadirondackstore.com*) sells antler chandeliers, bark frames, hand-painted Arts and Crafts–style lanterns, and pine-scented soaps, among with many other items sure to remind you of your visit.

NIGHTLIFE AND THE ARTS

NIGHTLIFE

The classy **Cottage** (⊠*5 Mirror Lake Dr.* ☎*518/523–9845*), part of the Mirror Lake Inn Resort, serves cocktails late into the night. It overlooks the lake and has a large deck. Sandwiches, salads, and other light bites are on the menu. Upstairs at the **Lake Placid Pub & Brewery** (⊠*14 Mirror Lake Dr.* ☎*518/523–3813*) is a smoke-free zone where you can shoot some pool or have lunch or dinner. Downstairs there's an Irish pub with darts and billiards, and in summer you can sit outside on the deck and bask in the lake views. The beer selection includes the dark-red Ubu Ale, the signature brew here.

THE ARTS

The **Lake Placid Center for the Arts** (⊠*91 Saranac Ave.* ☎*518/523–2512* ⊕*www.lakeplacidarts.org*), the largest arts center in the region, shows classic films and hosts theater, dance, and music performances. Gallery space is used to show works by local artists and changing exhibits.

WHERE TO EAT

$$ ✕**Dancing Bears.** This lively first-floor restaurant and bar at High Peaks
AMERICAN   Resort has been a hit with locals and out-of-town visitors ever since
★   it opened in fall 2008. The menu has classics like big hamburgers and homemade pizza as well as steak. It's also great for breakfast. ⊠*2384 Saranac Ave., High Peaks Resort, Main St. and Mirror Lake* ☎*518/523–4411* ▭*AE, D, MC, V.*

$$ ✕**Great Adirondack Steak & Seafood Company.** The extensive menu at
STEAK   this casual downtown eatery and microbrewery combines American
★   and Continental fare. For a starter you might sample the escargots and mushrooms in puff pastry and cream sauce or bite into the nicely laden bruschetta. If you want a spicy-sweet start to your meal, try the Mardis

Gras shrimp (spicy shrimp baked in jalapeño corn bread and drizzled with honey). Steak selections include a filet mignon (6- or 10-ounce options), sirloin sandwich, and New York strip steak au poivre. There are also seafood items, like the Seashore Pasta, packed with mussels, artichoke hearts, clams, portobella mushrooms, and sun-dried and grape tomatoes. The staff will know just which microbrew should go with your meal, and if you or your kids want to try a homemade brew but without the alcohol, order a root beer, made on the premises with pure mountain water and cane sugar. (If you're really curious how the brewing process works, request a tour of the small brewing facilities.) For a sweet finish, share a slice of the New York cheesecake drizzled with strawberries. ⊠*2442 Main St.* ☎*518/523–1629* ⌒*Reservations not accepted* ⊟*AE, D, DC, MC, V.*

$ ✕**Lake Placid Pub and Brewery.** This downtown eatery might be casual,
AMERICAN but it serves sophisticated appetizers like gazpacho and some very fine craft beers—if you leave without trying the Ubu Ale, you haven't been here. There's also comforting pub food like quesadillas and steak sandwiches. ⊠*813 Mirror Lake Dr.* ☎*518/523–3813* ⊟ *MC, V.*

$$$ ✕**The View Restaurant.** Nestled inside the Mirror Lake Inn, the View
CONTINENTAL warms you instantly with its mahogany paneling and views of Mir-
★ ror Lake and the mountains and a seasonal menu that leans contemporary and sounds elegant. For example, you might dine on venison loin encrusted with pepper and coffee and served with foie gras and a black-currant reduction. ⊠*Mirror Lake Inn, 77 Mirror Lake Dr.* ☎*518/523–2544* ⊟*AE, D, DC, MC, V* ☙*No lunch.*

WHERE TO STAY

$ 🏨**Art Devlin's Olympic Motor Inn.** The family-owned hotel, named for the famous ski jumper, sits on 2 acres three blocks from the Olympic Center. Every year, the owners renovate a new bit of the property. All but two rooms have been renovated since 2000, and many are now larger, have bigger flat-screen televisions and refrigerators and feature granite countertops and wood ceilings. **Pros:** very reasonable prices by Lake Placid standards; fresh, clean updated rooms. **Cons:** breakfast is minimal and includes mostly pastries and coffee. ⊠*350 Main St.* ☎*518/523–3700* ⊕*www.artdevlins.com* ↩*41 rooms* ⌂*In-room: refrigerator. In-hotel: some pets allowed, no-smoking rooms, pool* ⊟*AE, D, MC, V* ⊙*CP.*

$$ 🏨**Crowne Plaza Resort & Golf Club.** From its hilltop perch, the four-story hotel takes in the resort's 1,000-plus acres and lovely mountain and lake views. The property encompasses two highly regarded 18-hole golf courses and the well-known Veranda restaurant. It also has a private beach on Lake Placid. Guest-room furnishings are traditional and attractive, with two double beds. Some rooms have jetted tubs and fireplaces. Also on the grounds are chalets and lakeside condominiums. **Pros:** dog friendly; specials can bring down the price of a room dramatically. **Cons:** extras (a glass of wine, a cup of coffee, etc.) are pricey. ⊠*101 Olympic Dr.* ☎*518/523–2556 or 877/570–5891* ⊕ *www.lakeplacidcp.com* ↩*194 rooms, 12 suites* ⌂*In-room: refrigerator, Wi-Fi. In-hotel: Wi-Fi, room service, 4 restaurants, golf courses,*

tennis courts, pool, gym, bar, laundry facilities, laundry service, some pets allowed, no-smoking rooms ⊟*AE, D, DC, MC, V.*

$$ 🏨 **Golden Arrow Lakeside Resort.** The former Best Western Golden Arrow
CONTEMPORARY is under new management, and sits right in the heart of Lake Placid,
🕑 on Main Street. Beautiful views of Mirror Lake are available from the
★ lobby and some rooms, which have balconies. But what really sets
the property apart is the owners' decision to go as green as possible.
Expect recycled and ecofriendly gifts to greet you on arrival (perhaps a
pine-tree seed in a terra-cotta pot filled with earth, for example). Have
a seat at Charlie's, the resort restaurant, for a view of the green roof.
The roof, finished in summer 2008, is an insulating blanket of plants
grown on a flat section of the property's roof. Some of the herbs grown
there might go into dishes served at Charlie's. Kids' programs are avail-
able. **Pros:** large, clean and spacious rooms; easy access to Mirror Lake.
Cons: it's nice to have a fireplace in your room, but the smell from oth-
ers' fires lingers. ⊠*2559 Main St.* ☎*518/523–3353 or 800/582–5540*
⊕*www.golden-arrow.com* ⤵*147 rooms, 19 suites* 🛇*In-room: safe
(some), kitchen (some), refrigerator, Wi-Fi. In-hotel: room service, res-
taurant, Wi-Fi, pools, gym, bar, laundry facilities, some pets allowed,
no-smoking rooms* ⊟*AE, D, DC, MC, V.*

$ 🏨 **High Peaks Resort.** The 7-acre waterfront property that once was the
Hilton has now become the newly renovated High Peaks. The prop-
erty has accommodations in two buildings, one on Main Street in the
center of town and another on the water. The entire property has been
redone, so everything is new, including the lobby, the rooms, and three
new restaurants—the casual Dancing Bears *(see Where to Eat)*; the fine-
dining venue Reflections; and PRs, a warm, elegant bar with a double
fireplace. The breakfast plan, which includes a morning nosh at the
Dancing Bears, costs extra. Rooms throughout the updated property
are attractive, with tasteful wooden furniture and furnishings. Rooms
in waterfront buildings have either a balcony or a patio for views of the
lake. Complimentary rowboats and paddleboats are offered to guests
for use at the resort's access to Mirror Lake. **Pros:** right off Main Street
and near just about everything in Lake Placid. **Cons:** babysitting ser-
vices are no longer available, though referrals are. ⊠*1 Mirror Lake
Dr.* ☎*518/523–4411 or 800/755–5598* ⊕*www.lphilton.com* ⤵*133
rooms* 🛇*In-room: kitchen (some), Wi-Fi. In-hotel: Wi-Fi, room service,
3 restaurants, bar, pools, gym, bar, laundry service, no-smoking rooms*
⊟*AE, D, DC, MC, V* ⦿*BP.*

$$$ 🏨 **Interlaken Inn & Restaurant.** A lovely Victorian houses this classy get-
CONTEMPORARY away with individually appointed rooms and an excellent restaurant.
★ Some rooms look out onto the Adirondacks and some overlook the
Interlaken's lush gardens. Interior schemes offset old-fashioned fabrics. Rooms are handsome, with four-poster and sleigh beds, down
comforters, and Frette linens and towels. A few rooms have private
balconies, and third-floor rooms have sloping ceilings. The smallest,
least expensive rooms are simple but still attractive. **Pros:** near just
about everything in Lake Placid. **Cons:** housekeeping tips are automati-
cally added to your bill; no breakfast of any type is included with the
room, though it is served for a fee in the restaurant. ⊠*39 Interlaken*

*Ave. ☎518/523–3180 or 800/428–4369 ⊕www.theinterlakeninn.com
⇨7 rooms, 2 suites, 1 carriage house ⚙In-room: no phone, no TV
(some). In-hotel: some pets allowed, no-smoking rooms, restaurant,
bar ▤AE, D, DC, MC, V.*

$$$$ 🏨 **Lake Placid Lodge.** Accommodations at this posh lakefront retreat, a
Fodor's Choice member of the Relais & Châteaux group, have stone fireplaces, feath-
★ erbeds, twig-and-bark furniture—including many one-of-a-kind pieces
created by local artisans—and views of either the woods or Lake Placid.
Some rooms have balconies. Lodge suites include a sitting room, often
with a fireplace of its own; an extra-spacious bathroom with a large
soaking tub; and either a private balcony or patio. A stay is pricey, but
includes breakfast, afternoon tea, dinner, turndown service, and all
activities on the property. Most of the cabins are one-room units with
sitting areas and huge windows. The restaurant is a draw on its own and
prepares new American fare. **Pros:** nearly everything is included in the
price. **Cons:** some of the cabin views are limited. ⊠ *Whiteface Inn Rd.,
off Rte. 86 ☎518/523–2700 or 877/523–2700 ⊕www.lakeplacidlodge.
com ⇨13 rooms, 17 cabins ⚙ In-room: refrigerator (some), Internet,
no a/c (some), no TV. In-hotel: some pets allowed, restaurant, room
service, bicycles, bar, laundry service, Internet terminal, no kids under
14 ▤AE, MC, V ☺ ⦿MAP.*

$$$$ 🏨 **Mirror Lake Inn Resort & Spa.** The complex is on the small, pristine lake
☺ that is its namesake, and many get a view of the lake either in their rooms
Fodor's Choice or at the resort's afternoon tea. Most guest rooms here are elegant, with
★ traditional furnishings and large doses of neutral colors. Four-poster
beds, fireplaces, private balconies, and couches are available in some
rooms. Fodorites say that sitting in the big, cozy chairs next to the fire
is heaven, but the resort offers a slew of organized activities, too—sunset
cruises, kayak and fishing trips, guided hikes, snowshoe outings, cross-
country-skiing lessons, yoga classes—and there's a full-service spa on
the property. The Averil Conwell Dining Room earns high marks for
its food. **Pros:** every room has a view of the lake and/or Adirondacks.
Cons: the beach, a draw for children, can get a little noisy sometimes.
⊠*5 Mirror Lake Dr. ☎518/523–2544 ⊕www.mirrorlakeinn.com
⇨128 rooms, 11 suites ⚙In-room: Wi-Fi, refrigerator. In-hotel: room
service, restaurant, tennis court, pools, gym, bar, children's programs
(ages 3–12), no-smoking rooms ▤AE, D, DC, MC, V.*

$ 🏨 **Mountain View Inn.** Rooms at this family-owned and -operated motor
inn, neighbor to the Olympic Center, have balconies and views of the
lake and the mountains. A three-bedroom cottage on the lake is available, too. Guests have beach privileges at a nearby club. **Pros:** very well
kept. **Cons:** because it's downtown, street and pedestrian traffic can
intrude. ⊠*2548 Main St. ☎518/523–2439 or 800/499–2668 ⊕www.
lakeplacidlodging.com ⇨18 rooms, 1 cottage ⚙In-room: refrigerator,
Wi-Fi. In-hotel: no-smoking rooms, Wi-Fi ▤AE, MC, V ☺Closed Apr.
and weekdays in Nov.–late Dec.*

CAMPING 🏨 **Adirondack Loj.** The lodge, 5 mi south of Lake Placid, was built in
$ 1927 on the shore of Heart Lake. It's run by the nonprofit Adirondack
Mountain Club, which also runs the High Peaks Information Center
here. The lodge has private rooms, family bunk rooms that sleep four

to six, and a coed sleeping area with 18 beds . The main room has a stone fireplace, and the dining room serves homemade breads and soups. You may also order trail lunches here. There's a small beach on the property, and trailheads are steps away. The lodge has canoes and kayaks, and snowshoe and cross-country-ski rentals are available at the information center. Also on the grounds are two cabins, three canvas cabins, 36 campsites, and 36 lean-tos. A Modified American Plan for dining is available to lodge guests staying for three or five nights. **Pros:** very close to all kinds of outdoor adventures. **Cons:** many lodgings are multiple-occupancy. ⊠*Adirondack Loj Rd., Box 867, off Rte. 73* ☎*518/523–3441* ⊕*www.adk.org* ⏎*4 rooms, coed sleeping area with 18 beds, 4 family bunk rooms; all with shared baths* ᐧ*In-room: no a/c, no phone, no TV. In-hotel: restaurant, no-smoking rooms* ⊟*AE, D, MC, V* ⏐⊙⏐ *BP/MAP.*

WILMINGTON

8 mi northeast of Lake Placid, 20 mi southwest of Ausable Chasm.

Wilmington is home to Whiteface Mountain ski area, where the alpine events of the 1980 Winter Olympics were held.

VISITOR INFORMATION
Whiteface Mountain Regional Visitors Bureau (⌂ *Box 277, Wilmington 12997* ☎*518/946–2255 or 888/944–8332* ⊕ *www.whitefaceregion.com*).

WHAT TO SEE

Adirondack History Center Museum. An old school building houses a museum, where the rather eclectic collection includes a bobsled from the 1932 Winter Olympics, antique dolls, artifacts from Fort Crown Point, and, out back, a 58-foot fire tower. The property also includes gardens. ⊠*Rte. 9N and Hand Ave., Elizabethtown* ☎*518/873–6466* ⊕*www. adkhistorycenter.org* ⊠*$5* ⊙*Late May–Columbus Day, Mon.–Sat. 9–5, Sun. 1–5.*

High Falls Gorge. A spectacular 700-foot waterfall and ancient granite cliffs are highlights of the self-guided tour of this gorge. It was created as the Ausable River cut through the granite base of Whiteface Mountain. In winter, you can rent snowshoes, skis, or snowboards. Nearby are a shop, restaurant, and picnic areas. There are only two seasons to visit here: summer and winter. ⊠*Rte. 86 at Wilmington Notch* ☎*518/946–2278* ⊕*www.highfallsgorge.com* ⊠*$13.50* ⊙*May, June, Sept., and Oct., daily 9–5; July and Aug., daily 9–5:30; late Nov.–mid-Dec., Fri.–Tues. 10–4; mid-Dec.–Mar., daily 10–4.*

Whiteface Mountain. Though only the fifth-highest in the region, Whiteface Mountain is one of the best-known mountains in the Adirondacks. **Veterans Memorial Highway** twists and climbs 8 mi to the top of the mountain. Close to the peak is a parking lot; from here you can ride an elevator or hike the rest of the way up. Scenic gondola rides are available in the summer. ⊠*12997 Veterans Memorial Hwy.* ☎*518/946–2223 Ext. 214* ⊕*www.whiteface.com* ⊠*$9 per car and driver, $4 each additional passenger. $17 per person for gondola rides* ⊙*Access to the* *drive is available late May–early July, daily 9–4; early July–early Sept., daily 8:30–5; rest of Sept., daily 9–4; call for Oct. times. Gondola rides to the top of the mountain are available daily 10–4 mid-June–Sept. 1 and on weekends Sept. 5–Oct. 9.*

THEME PARK **Santa's Workshop.** This simple theme park (2 mi northwest of Wilmington) with rides and live reindeer is ideal for small children. Santa and his helpers talk with children, and elves practice their crafts in shops around the park. On Sunday evenings in late December, visitors can take in the brightly lighted Village of Lights. ⊠ *12946 Whiteface Mountain Memorial Hwy., North Pole (near Wilmington)* ☎ *800/806–0215* ⊕ *www.northpoleny.com* ⊠ *$17.95 general admission, $9.95 Village of Lights* ⊙ *Late June–early Sept., daily 9:30–4; early Sept.–mid-Oct. and mid-Nov.–late Dec., weekends 10–3:30.*

SPORTS AND THE OUTDOORS

SKIING

Whiteface Mountain Ski Center. Owned by the state of New York and operated by the Lake Placid Olympic Regional Development Authority, this is one of the biggest ski centers in the East. It has 10 lifts, 75 trails, 95% snowmaking, and a vertical drop of 3,430 feet—the largest such drop in the East. Experts have 44% of the trails, intermediates 36%, and beginners 20%. The views from the top are unmatched (nearly 100 mi in good visibility). Facilities include a snowboard park, rentals, a school, children's programs, and restaurants. Day passes are $89. The ski season usually runs late November to early April. Mountain bikes take over the slopes from mid-June to early October. Trail passes are $10. Rentals and gondola passes are also available. Even if you don't plan to bike, you can ride the Cloudsplitter Gondola ($17) to the top of Little Whiteface (3,676 feet), where there's an observation deck and a picnic area. ⊠ *Rte. 86* ☎ *518/946–2223, 518/946–7171 for snow conditions* ⊕ *www.whiteface.com.*

WHERE TO EAT AND STAY

$$ ╳ **Hungry Trout Motor Inn Restaurant.** This restaurant near Whiteface
AMERICAN Mountain Ski Center earns high marks for its American fare, served
Fodor'sChoice in an attractive dining space with cloth-covered tables, candles, and a
★ wall of windows. A section of the menu is devoted to the restaurant's namesake, trout. The delectable fish may be panfried or served in more-complex ways but it's not all about the fish here. Options include Long Island duck and New York strip steak. The cozy pub serves hamburgers and sandwiches. ⊠ *5239 Rte. 86* ☎ *518/946–2217 or 800/766–9137* ⊕ *www.hungrytrout.com* ☐ *AE, D, MC, V* ⊙ *Closed Apr. and Nov.*

$ ▦ **Ledge Rock at Whiteface Mountain.** The upscale two-story motel is on a big piece of land across the road from Whiteface Mountain. Rooms are spacious, with seating areas or kitchenettes and either two double beds or one or two queen-size beds. The decor is cheery, with jolts of bright color here and there. Some rooms have mountain views. Common areas include a great room with a fireplace, a large-screen TV, a pool table, and assorted board games. In fall and winter, complimentary cookies and hot beverages are served here. During fishing season, guide services are offered. **Pros:** spectacular views, even among hotels with spectacular views. **Cons:** beds are kind of hard. ⊠*5078 Rte. 86, at Placid Rd.* ☎*518/946–2302 or 800/336–4754* ⊕*www.ledgerockatwhiteface.com* ⇋*18 rooms* ♿ *In-room: kitchen (some), refrigerator. In-hotel: some pets allowed, no-smoking rooms, pool* ☰*AE, D, DC, MC, V* ⏏*CP.*

$ ⚏**Whiteface Chalet.** Serene woods surround this Swiss chalet–style inn facing Whiteface Mountain. Rooms have two double beds—some also have one or two daybeds. Wood paneling is used in the guest rooms as well as in the common areas, which include a living room and a recreation room. Rates include breakfast and dinner. **Pros:** cute Adirondack décor. **Cons:** not within walking distance of shops, restaurants. ⊠*Springfield Rd./Rte. 12* ☎*518/946–2207 or 800/932–0859* ⊕*www. whitefacechalet.com* ⇋*13 rooms, 3 suites* ♿*In-room: no a/c (some). In-hotel: restaurant, tennis courts, pool, bar* ☰*AE, D, DC, MC, V* ⏏*CP.*

$ ⚏**Willkommen Hof B&B.** The two-story European-style *Gasthof* (guest-
GERMAN   house), built in 1920 at the foot of Whiteface Mountain, has a large porch and a deck. Fireplaces, skylights, and whirlpool tubs are among the extras in some rooms. The three-room suite includes a sitting room with a TV and a bedroom with bunk beds. The dining room is centered on a German *Kachelofen* (tile stove) and features a traditional German *Stammtisch* (corner booth for regulars) and an English-style bristle dartboard. Breakfast for overnight guests includes apple pancakes and blintzes. **Pros:** pet friendly; some rooms have hot tubs. **Cons:** dinner reservations require a six-guest minimum. ⊠*Rte. 86* ☎*518/946–7669 or 800/541–9119* ⊕*www.willkommenhof.com* ⇋*8 rooms, 6 with bath; 1 suite* ♿*In-hotel: some pets allowed, restaurant, Wi-Fi, no-smoking rooms* ☰*MC, V* ⏏*BP.*

SARANAC LAKE

10 mi west of Lake Placid.

The village of Saranac Lake sits on small Flower Lake; the three lakes that go by the name Saranac—Lower Saranac, Middle Saranac, and Upper Saranac—are to the west. Although its population of about 4,800 is significantly more than Lake Placid's 2,800, Saranac Lake is much less touristy than its neighbor to the east. Settled in the early 1800s, it remained a remote community through the 19th century before becoming a center for guiding the occasional intrepid hunter and angler in the Adirondacks. Today the village remains a good base for those who want to pursue the many outdoor recreational opportunities in the area.

DID YOU KNOW?

In the late 1800s Dr. Edward Livingston Trudeau—having discovered the positive, healthful effects of a prolonged Adirondack vacation himself—established a tuberculosis treatment center in Saranac Lake. As the Trudeau Sanitarium became famous, the village suddenly boomed, becoming home to several hotels and a score of what came to be known as "cure cottages," many of which remain in existence. The sanatorium eventually developed into the Trudeau Institute, a biomedical research center.

WHAT TO SEE

Adirondack Park Agency Visitors Interpretive Center at Paul Smiths. The center has natural-history exhibits and hosts lectures and classes on wildlife and other nature-related and outdoorsy subjects. Nature trails here double as cross-country-skiing and snowshoeing trails in winter. From June through Labor Day you may observe butterflies in the Butterfly House, a greenhouse-like structure. The center is in Paul Smiths, 12 mi north of Saranac Lake. ⊠*Rte. 30, Paul Smiths* ☎*518/327–3000* ⊕*www.adkvic.org* 🖃*Free* ⊙*Center: summer, daily 9–5; winter, Tues.– Sat. 9–5. Grounds: daily dawn–dusk.*

Robert Louis Stevenson Memorial Cottage and Museum. In 1887 the author of *Dr. Jekyll and Mr. Hyde* and *Treasure Island* spent a year in Saranac Lake being treated for tuberculosis. Today the quaint farmhouse where he lived contains his original furniture as well as a collection of Stevenson memorabilia, including early photographs, personal letters, and his velvet smoking jacket. ⊠*11 Stevenson La.* ☎*518/891–1462* ⊕*www. adirondacks.com/robertlstevenson.html* 🖃*$5* ⊙*July–mid-Sept., Tues.– Sun. 9:30–noon and 1–4:30, and by appointment.*

Six Nations Indian Museum. American Indian art, crafts, and artifacts are on display at this small museum dedicated to preserving the culture of the Iroquois Confederacy—the Mohawks, Oneida, Onondaga, Cayuga, Seneca, and Tuscarora. It was started in 1954 by Mohawk Ray Fadden and his family, who still run the place. Baskets, canoes, paintings, beadwork, and other items are hung on the walls and from the ceilings. The museum is 14 mi northeast of Saranac Lake. ⊠*Franklin County Rte. 30, Onchiota* ☎*518/891–2299* 🖃 *$2* ⊙*July–Labor Day, Tues.–Sun. 10–6, and by appointment.*

★ **White Pine Camp.** President Calvin Coolidge used this great camp on Lake Osgood as his "summer White House" in 1926. Although built in 1907 and expanded in 1911 by William Massarene and Addison Mizner, the camp is noted for blending rustic architecture with a rather modern sensibility. If you're not staying at one of the guest cabins here, you may see the camp only as part of a guided tour. The tours (1½ to 2 hours) take in the bowling alley, tennis house, dining and great rooms, boathouse, and guest cabins. A Japanese teahouse on a small island is accessed by an arched stone bridge. The camp is 12 mi northwest of Saranac Lake. ⊠*White Pine Rd., off Rte. 86, Paul Smiths* ☎*518/327– 3030* ⊕*www.whitepinecamp.com* 🖃*$9* ⊙*Tours July–Labor Day, Sat. at 10 and 1:30.*

SPORTS AND THE OUTDOORS
GOLF

★ **Saranac Inn Golf & Country Club.** Seymour Dunn, the Scottish architect and professional golfer, designed this course at the turn of the 20th century. *Golf Digest* magazine gives the par-72, 6,631-yard championship course 4½ stars. Greens fees are $65, including a cart. The complex includes a restaurant as well as a 10-room motel ($) with rooms overlooking the first tee. ⊠*125 Rte. 46* ☎*518/891–1402* ⊕*www. saranacinn.com.*

Thendara Golf Club. The 6,435-yard, par-72 course here was designed by Donald Ross and has a challenging back 9 holes. It rated four stars from *Golf Digest* magazine in 2004. Greens fees are $35, excluding carts. ⊠*Rte. 28, Thendara, just west of Old Forge* ☎*315/369–3136* ⊕*www.thendaragolfclub.com.*

THE ARTS

The **Pendragon Theatre** (⊠*15 Brandy Brook Ave.12983* ☎*518/891–1854* ⊕*www.pendragontheatre.org*), a year-round professional company, performs classical and new works. Special events include mystery dinner-theater shows.

SHOPPING

With everything from camouflage jackets and bathing suits to ice-hockey skates and fishing lures, the **Blue Line Sport Shop** (⊠*82 Main St.* ☎*518/891–4680*) can outfit you for most outdoor activities

The Ray Brook Frog (⊠*Rte. 86, Ray Brook* ☎*518/891–3333*), between Saranac Lake and Lake Placid, sells twig furniture and cushy leather chairs as well as smaller items, including lamps and lanterns, baskets, and rustic frames and mirrors. The Union Depot, an old train station, is the home of the **Whistle Stop** (⊠*42 Depot St.* ☎*518/891–4759*), a showcase for wares made by local artisans and craftspeople. It's open from late May through Columbus Day.

WHERE TO EAT

$$$ ╳**A. P. Smith Restaurant.** Wooden chandeliers hang over candlelit tables,
AMERICAN and classical music usually plays in the background at this Hotel Saranac restaurant where hospitality and culinary-arts students from nearby Paul Smith's College train. The food is American: try beer-braised beef short ribs, broiled trout fillet with maple-pecan butter, chicken and dumplings, all of which are served on china specially made for Hotel Saranac. ⊠*101 Main St.* ☎*518/891–2200* ⊟*AE, D, DC, MC, V.*

$$ ╳**Belvedere Restaurant.** Locals come into this casual, family-style res-
ITALIAN taurant for hearty portions of pasta, veal Parmesan, strip steaks, and a surf-and-turf combo of steak and lobster tails. There's a lounge and pool table. ⊠*102 Bloomingdale Ave.* ☎*518/891–9873* ⊟*No credit cards* ☉ *Closed Mon. No lunch weekends.*

WHERE TO STAY

$ ▦**Best Western Mountain Lake Inn.** At this two-story chain property, interior corridors connect the rooms, which are big and bright and include desks. The heated indoor pool is a plus, as is an outdoor deck overlooking a placid pond The on-site restaurant, McKenzie's Grille, is open almost every day. **Pros:** clean. **Cons:** street noise can intrude. ⊠*487 Lake Flower Ave.* ☎*518/891–1970* ⊕*www.bestwestern.com* ⤶*69 rooms* ⚐ *In-room: Wi-Fi, refrigerator. In-hotel: restaurant, bar, pool, Wi-Fi, laundry facilities, some pets allowed, no-smoking rooms* ⊟*AE, D, DC, MC, V.*

$$$$ ▦**The Point.** Originally the home of William Avery Rockefeller, this ultra-exclusive retreat evokes the spirit of the great Adirondack camps. The secluded property occupies a forested peninsula on Upper Saranac Lake. Rooms, housed in four buildings, blend rustic furniture with

TAKE A TOUR

AIR TOURS
Adirondack Flying Service (⊠ *Rte. 73, Lake Placid* ☎*518/523–2473* ⊕*flyanywhere.com*) offers 20-minute flights over either the High Peaks region or Lake Placid and the White-face area. Flights are $40 per person, with a minimum of two passengers.

ARCHITECTURAL TOURS
Adirondack Architectural Heri-tage (⊠ *Civic Center, 1790 Main St., Suite 37, Keeseville* ☎*518/834–9328* ⊕*www.aarch.org*), a nonprofit historic-preservation organization, runs tours of Saranac Lake, Bolton Landing, Big Moose Lake, Wilmington and the Whiteface Veterans Memo-rial Highway, Camp Santanoni, White Pine Camp, and other camps. Tours cost between $30 and $55 for non-members, and some include lunch.

HORSEBACK TOURS
The horse-loving owner of **Adiron-dack Saddle Tours** (⊠ *4 Uncas Rd., Eagle Bay* ☎*877/795–7488* ⊕ *www.adkhorse.com*), a 25-year native, offers several foliage and wilderness tours through the Adiron-dacks, some of which end in Old Forge, one of the more popular tour-ist destinations in the Adirondacks. Other destinations for the tours, which take between an hour to 5½ hours, include Cascade Falls, High Peaks, and Moss Lake. Cost is $30–$125. Tours go year-round, weather permitting.

TRAIN TOURS
Adirondack Scenic Railroad (⊠ *Union Station, Utica* ☎*315/724–0700*) tours are offered by Amtrak for summer travelers and those taking in the lush fall foliage of the southwestern portion of the Adiron-dacks. The service runs from Utica, to the south of the park, through Old Forge, Thendara, and several other small communities and into Saranac Lake and Lake Placid. Running July through October, it's $36 round-trip.

4

handsome antiques and rich fabrics. Each guest room has a stone fire-place and lake views; some have pine-lined cathedral ceilings or private decks or patios. You may play billiards or darts at the intimate pub, which shares the Eagle's Nest building with three guest rooms. Over-looking the lake is the capacious Boathouse ($2,600 a night; offered from mid-April through October only), a favorite of honeymooners. Your day starts with Continental breakfast in your room or a hot meal in the dining room. Guests gather for lunch, afternoon tea, and din-ner, and menus are set, but you may opt to have a lunch to go or eat in your room. Dinner is rather formal, with jacket and tie upgraded to black tie Wednesday and Saturday evenings. The deposit alone is $500, without which you don't get directions. But that's the point of exclusivity, isn't it? **Pros:** all-inclusive. **Cons:** no one under 18 can stay here. ✑ *Box 1327, Saranac Lake 12983* ☎*518/891–5674 or 800/255–3530* ⊕*www.thepointresort.com* ⤷*11 rooms* ♦ *In-room: refrigerator (some), no phone, no a/c. In-hotel: restaurant, bar, no kids under 18* ☰*AE, MC, V* ⊘*Closed mid-Mar.–mid-Apr.* ⦿*AI.*

$ 🏨 **Sara-Placid Motor Inn.** These owner-run lodgings include a variety of accommodations, from standard motel rooms to suites with decks and lakefront cottages with fireplaces. Motel rooms are on the large side and have wood furniture and big windows. One suite has a whirlpool tub. A small park next door has tennis and basketball courts and a nearby restaurant serves breakfast and lunch. **Pros:** peaceful, bright, and clean. **Cons:** not within walking distance of most area attractions. ✉ *445 Lake Flower Ave.* ☎ *518/891–2729 or 800/794–2729* ⊕ *www. sara-placid.com* ⮑ *13 rooms, 3 suites, 3 cottages* ⚭ *In-room: refrigerator, kitchen (some), no a/c (some). In-hotel: laundry service* ☰ *AE, D, DC, MC, V.*

$$$

Fodor's Choice

★

📷 **White Pine Camp.** The camp, built in 1907, has hosted many prominent guests. It was known as the "summer White House" after President Calvin Coolidge vacationed here in 1926. The location, amid majestic pines on 35 acres on Lake Osgood, is a big draw. The property encompasses several cabins, most of them 100 feet away from the water. All have kitchens or kitchenettes and fireplaces or woodstoves and are fully furnished. Only six cabins are open all year. From late June through Labor Day, the minimum stay is a week; a two-night minimum is usually required the rest of the year. Because the property is of historic and architectural interest, small tours sometimes come through the camp, including the guest cabins. The camp is 12 mi northwest of Saranac Lake. **Pros:** historic and serene; use of canoes, kayaks, and rowboats is complimentary. **Cons:** remote from restaurants and shops. ✉ *White Pine Rd., off Rte. 86, Paul Smiths* ☎ *518/327–3030* ⊕ *www.whitepinecamp.com* ⮑ *13 cabins* ⚭ *In-room: no a/c, no phone, no TV, kitchens (some). In-hotel: no-smoking rooms* ☰ *MC, V.*

TUPPER LAKE

21 mi southwest of Saranac Lake.

Once a logging and transportation center, Tupper Lake is today a quiet spot with about 3,800 residents. The village sits on Raquette Pond (the lake named Tupper is just west of it), with smaller bodies of water dotting the area. If you follow Main Street west to where it intersects with the old railroad tracks, you'll come to the part of town known as the Junction. Here you can see well-preserved buildings from Tupper Lake's early days, including the late-19th-century Grand Union Hotel on Depot Street. The Goff-Nelson Memorial Library on Lake Street houses a large collection of photographs and accounts of Tupper Lake's beginnings.

WHAT TO SEE

Historic Beth Joseph Synagogue. Jewish peddlers in the Adirondacks built this synagogue in 1905. Listed on the National Register of Historic Places, the synagogue has been restored and contains art exhibits. It also hosts concerts and other activities. ✉ *Mill and Lake Sts.* ☎ *518/359–7229* 🎟 *Free* ☾ *July and Aug., Tues.–Fri. 1–3.*

WHERE TO EAT AND STAY

$

AMERICAN

✕ **Pine Grove Restaurant.** The restaurant's country-rustic decor is accented by plenty of ponderosa pine, and wildlife art adorns the walls. The menu includes sandwiches, burgers, steaks, and chops, which you may order at a table or at the bar. ⊠ *166 Main St.* ☎ *518/359–3669* ⊟ *AE, D, MC, V* ⊘ *Closed Tues. No lunch.*

¢ 🏨 **Shaheen's Motel.** Most rooms at this two-story motel have knotty-
♻ wood paneling and forest views; some have two queen beds and a pull-out couch. The location is convenient to canoeing, hiking, and other outdoor activities. **Pros:** near area restaurants and businesses. **Cons:** miniature-golf course closed in winter. ⊠ *314 Park St.* ☎ *518/359– 3384 or 800/474-2445* ⊕ *www.shaheensmotel.com* ⟿ *31 rooms* ♿ *In-room: refrigerator, Wi-Fi, no a/c (some). In-hotel: pool, no-smoking rooms* ⊟ *AE, D, DC, MC, V* ⏶ *CP.*

$ 🏨 **Tupper Lake Motel.** The single-level motel, a good budget option, has comfortable rooms overlooking the pool, which has a slide. You have a choice of either one or two double or queen-size beds. A supermarket and restaurants are within walking distance. **Pros:** close to dining and shopping options. **Cons:** rooms are small. ⊠ *255 Park St.* ☎ *518/359– 3381 or 800/944-3585* ⊕ *www.tupperlakemotel.com* ⟿ *18 rooms* ♿ *In-room: refrigerator, Internet. In-hotel: bicycles, no-smoking rooms* ⊟ *AE, D, MC, V* ⏶ *CP.*

Albany and Central New York

WORD OF MOUTH

"I have been to Saratoga a couple of times and always found it interesting for an afternoon. Lots of Victorian architecture, fun places to eat, and plenty of shopping. Walking around the park and taking the waters at the various springs is very interesting."

—Ackislander

By Jennifer
Edwards

Two of New York's most striking areas—the capital region and the Leatherstocking region—share a common history but have somehow managed to become flip sides of the same state coin. Although both played important roles in early American history, the capital region has become a booming governmental, business, and economic capital, while the Leatherstocking region and Mohawk Valley have matured into peaceful, pastoral, and more thinly populated destinations still basking in an industrial legacy.

It was in this geographically diverse swath of land that now known as the capital region, bordered by the Adirondack and Catskill mountains, that Iroquois Indians traded furs and Dutch settlers carved out what eventually would become some of the oldest cities in the country. This is also where the British forces were defeated in a defining moment of the American Revolution. In 1797, Albany was chosen as the state capital.

Rich in timber and iron ore from the nearby Adirondack Mountains, the region later became a leader in the Industrial Revolution as the rise of factories and steel mills altered its agricultural landscape. Prosperity continued into the 19th century, when the landmark 363-mi Erie Canal across upstate New York was built, linking the Atlantic Ocean with the Great Lakes and opening up new trade and transportation routes.

The capital region is striking, bordered as it is by deep-green mountains and the shining blue of the Hudson. Leatherstocking Country is no slouch, either. Part of New York's agricultural and dairy heartland, it epitomizes the pastoral lifestyle. As you move deep into the region, distances between towns grow and signs of industry dwindle. Rivers, streams, and brooks glisten between forests of hardwood and pine, and fields of corn and alfalfa form a shimmering patchwork.

Cooperstown, first made famous by James Fenimore Cooper's *Leatherstocking Tales,* a two-volume collection of novels, is the highlight of this region. The town sits beside Otsego Lake in the middle of Otsego County, which is wedged between U.S. 20 on the north and Interstate 88 on the south. The area is riddled with creeks, streams, and small lakes.

Along the region's northern edge is the historic Mohawk Valley, winding through the Adirondack foothills and of great tactical importance during the Revolutionary War. The valley is also rich in American Indian history, inhabited as it was by the Six Nations of the Iroquois Confederacy—the Oneida, Mohawk, Onondaga, Cayuga, Seneca, and Tuscarora tribes. In the early and mid-1800s, the Erie Canal brought prosperity and settlers to this fertile heartland.

TOP REASONS TO GO

Sports mecca. The area has not one but four halls of fame, including the National Baseball Hall of Fame, the National Distance Running Hall of Fame, the National Soccer Hall of Fame, and the International Boxing Hall of Fame.

Memorable meals. The entire region is filled with fine dining options, especially the dozens of restaurants that rely on ingredients almost entirely from central New York.

Eye-popping views. Central New York is rich in ways to get a closer look its many rivers, mountains, and forests, including train rides, boat trips, and myriad outdoor activities. The region, one of the first settled by Europeans, is home to some of the oldest and best-preserved churches, mansions, and inns in the country.

Nature's bounty. Pick fresh apples from the tree, visit a grove of sugar maples and sample their syrup, or try a dairy's freshest cheese at the region's many family-owned farms and orchards.

ORIENTATION AND PLANNING

GETTING ORIENTED

The triangular Leatherstocking region, which includes Montgomery, Schoharie, Otsego, southern Herkimer, Chenango, Broome, Madison, and Oneida counties, is sandwiched between Albany to the east, Syracuse to the west, the Adirondacks to the north, and the Catskill Mountains to the south. The Mohawk, Susquehanna, Chenango, and other, less-important rivers cut through the region, as do several highways. U.S. 20, the longest continuous highway in the country, originated in these parts as the Great Western Turnpike. It runs west–east through the heart of the region. Fewer than 15 mi to the north, Interstate 90 parallels U.S. 20. Defining the region's southern edge is Interstate 88. The north–south Interstate 81 skirts the region on the west, connecting Syracuse (part of the Finger Lakes region) and Binghamton; Route 12 links Binghamton and Utica. Several other north–south routes link Interstate 90 and Interstate 88, including (from east to west) Routes 10, 28, and 8.

The capital region consists of Albany and three smaller cities: Troy, Schenectady, and Saratoga Springs. All are accessible via Interstate 87, which runs north–south the length of the state, and Interstate 90, which runs east to west. Across the Hudson River and a few miles northeast of Albany is Troy. Schenectady, which hugs the Mohawk River, is a few miles northwest of the capital. Traveling north on Interstate 87 gets you to Saratoga Springs.

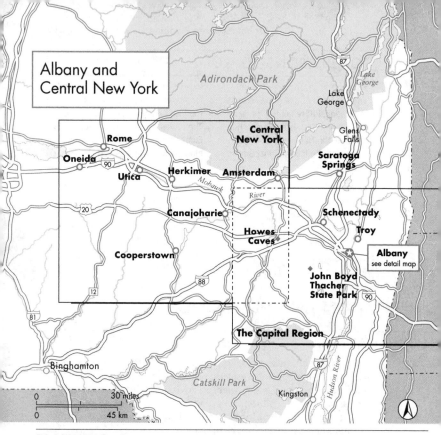

PLANNING

WHEN TO GO

After a long, snowy Northeast winter there's nothing quite like the spring here. The remaining patches of snow are quickly overtaken by early spring flowers, namely the tulip, which is the focus of a weekend-long celebration every Mother's Day. Summer temperatures are mostly moderate, with the exception of a few 90°F days. With the warm weather comes the festival season, when many regional parks stage outdoor concerts and plays. The festivals last through the fall harvest season, when the weather cools and the trees burst with colorful foliage. Late July and August are high points in Saratoga Springs, when the horse-racing season—with its attendant cultural and social activities—is in full swing.

Although the Leatherstocking region draws visitors throughout the year, the most popular time to visit is summer, when antiques hunters are out in full force, seeking treasures in the hundreds of shops scattered throughout Schoharie, Madison, and Broome counties, and baseball enthusiasts converge on Cooperstown, the home of America's favorite pastime. With its apple harvests and spectacular displays of colorful foliage, fall is also a good time to visit. In winter the region sees 100-plus inches of snow. From mid-March to early May the combination of melting snow and spring showers creates what's known as mud season.

GETTING HERE AND AROUND

Central New York is serviced by Albany International Airport, which is just east of the region as defined in this chapter, and Syracuse Hancock International Airport, just west of the region. Greyhound and Adirondack Trailways link the region with New York City and much of the rest of the state. Shortline and Otsego Express also serve the region. Many scenic, well-maintained roads crisscross and border the region. The interstates—Interstate 90 (the New York State Thruway), Interstate 81, and Interstate 88—are the fastest way to get around central New York. The thruway parallels the Mohawk River, which flows west to east across the region. Route 5, which also parallels the Mohawk River, is an alternative. Route 20 is a more southerly east–west option.

RESTAURANTS

From price to cuisine, eating out in the Leatherstocking region largely exemplifies middle-American dining. The region's best-known entrée is purely American and can be found on many restaurant menus on Friday: the fish fry, a breaded piece of haddock served with french fries and coleslaw. That said, new immigrant groups in the region continue to diversify the cuisines available here. And, although casual dining is the rule rather than the exception, the region does have several fine-dining places that hold up against the best restaurants in the state. Cooperstown, for one, has a cluster of excellent restaurants, and Utica is known for its Italian eateries.

HOTELS

With few exceptions, accommodations in the region fall within the inexpensive-to-moderate range. The cities usually have higher-end business-oriented properties (which tend to offer more amenities) as well as mid-range and budget chain properties; independent motels are found throughout the region. Bed-and-breakfasts and small inn properties are usually outside the big cities. Cooperstown is filled with this kind of lodging, but you should book six weeks in advance if you plan to visit in summer or early fall. Ask about minimum stays when booking; many B&Bs and inns require two-night stays on weekends, especially in July and August.

WHAT IT COSTS					
	¢	$	$$	$$$	$$$$
RESTAURANTS	under $8	$8–$14	$15–$21	$22–$30	over $30
HOTELS	under $100	$100–$149	$150–$199	$200–$250	over $250

Restaurant prices are for a main course at dinner (or at the most expensive meal served). Hotel prices are for two people in a standard double room in high season.

COOPERSTOWN AND OTSEGO COUNTY

On the shores of Otsego Lake—James Fenimore Cooper's beloved Glimmerglass—Cooperstown provides the backdrop for a number of museums and attractions. Fans of the great American pastime make pilgrimages to the National Baseball Hall of Fame. Other notable sites are the Farmers' Museum, the Fenimore Art Museum, and, north of the lake, a one-of-a-kind Petrified Creatures Museum. This is also the home of the Glimmerglass Opera, which presents classics in English each summer. Nearby attractions such as Howe Caverns and the Old Stone Fort Museum Complex in Schoharie are easy detours from here.

COOPERSTOWN

215 mi northwest of New York City, 72 mi west of Albany.

The village was founded in 1786 by William Cooper on the southern shore of Otsego Lake, also known as Lake Glimmerglass. William was the father of novelist James Fenimore Cooper (1789–1851), who set some of his epics in this region. By the late 19th century, word about the village and its beautiful lake spread, as New York's wealthy began building vacation homes upstate. The community is full of civic structures and residences from this period—many of them stately, most of them well preserved. Indeed, many of Cooperstown's accommodations are run by highly dedicated innkeepers in refurbished historic mansions hundreds of years old, and are a big draw for visitors. All told, a third of a million people visit the village annually.

> **SPORTS TRIPS**
>
> You could plan an entire itinerary through central New York that focuses on sports-related halls of fame. The region is home to four such attractions: the National Soccer Hall of Fame in Oneonta, the National Distance Running Hall of Fame in Utica, the International Boxing Hall of Fame in Canastota (southwest of Oneida), and the National Baseball Hall of Fame and Museum in Cooperstown.

When thinking of Cooperstown, you can't help but think of the national pastime. Home to the National Baseball Hall of Fame and Museum as well as a beautiful baseball diamond, the village draws fans of the game who feel they need to make the pilgrimage at least once in their lives. Both sites, as well as several shops and restaurants, are along a four-block stretch of Main Street, roughly between Chestnut and Fair streets.

GETTING HERE AND AROUND

Although several bus companies offer service to Cooperstown, you'll need a car if you really want to explore the area. You can also visit Cooperstown from Milford via a scenic train ride. From late May to mid-October, the **Leatherstocking Railway Historical Society** (⊠ *Rte. 7, Cooperstown Junction* ☎ *607/432–2429* ⊕ *www.lrhs.com*) offers rides from Milford (in the upper Susquehanna River valley) to Cooperstown on the Cooperstown & Charlotte Valley Railroad.

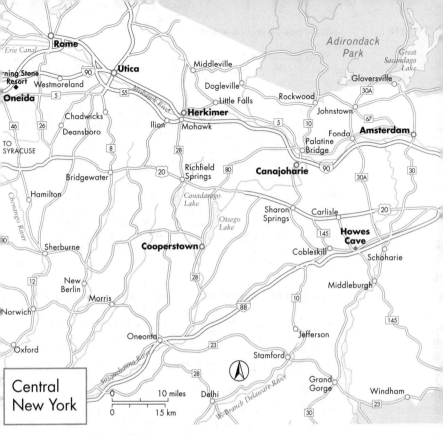

Central New York

VISITOR INFORMATION

Cooperstown Chamber of Commerce (✉ *31 Chestnut St., Cooperstown* ☎ *607/ 547-9983* ⊕ *www.cooperstownchamber.org*).

WHAT TO SEE

Brewery Ommegang. The affinity with *all* things Belgian, not just the beer, is palpable at this brewery, an elegant, white, wooden structure with an unusual round wing that has slitlike windows and would probably be called Romanesque if it were built of stone. Brews include Hennepin Farmhouse Ale, Ommegang Abbey Ale, and Rare Vos Ale, all of which are rich and excellent. Tours and tastings are possible throughout the year. In warmer months the staff makes waffles according to a traditional recipe. The brewery also hosts several seasonal events. ✉ *656 Rte. 33* ☎ *800/544-1809* 🖃 *www.ommegang.com* 🎫 *Tours $4* ☻ *Memorial Day–Labor Day, daily 11–6; rest of year, noon–5.*

Fenimore Art Museum. Native, folk, fine, and decorative American art is displayed in a brick neoclassical mansion that dates from the 1930s. Paintings of landscapes and everyday scenes enlighten you on what this country was like in the 19th century. Sculptor John H.I. Browere's (1792–1834) bronze busts were made from life masks, so they truly depict such luminaries as Thomas Jefferson and Dolley and James Madison. Furniture, portraits, other artifacts shed light on James Fenimore

Cooper and his family. Traveling exhibits are eclectic: one that explored the history of high-heeled shoes was held concurrently with another that had paintings of America's Western frontier. Photography and modern works by contemporary artists have been showcased, and so have Norman Rockwell illustrations. There's also an ever-changing roster of lectures, specialty tours, and book signings. The café, open during museum hours, serves tasty salads, soups, and other light fare. ⊠*Lake Rd. off Rte. 80* ☎*607/547–1400 or 888/547–1450* ⊕*www. fenimoreartmuseum.org* ⊠*$11* ⊙*June–Sept., daily 10–5; Apr., May, and Oct.–Dec., Tues.–Sun. 10–4.*

Glimmerglass State Park. Enjoy average summer temperatures of 72°F in the deep woods of this state park on Otsego Lake 8 mi north of the village of Cooperstown. In warm months you can swim, hike, and fish. There's a concession stand as well as 80 campsites. In winter you can snowshoe, snow-tube, cross-country ski, and ice fish. ⊠*1527 County Hwy.* ☎*607/547–8662* ⊕*nysparks.state.ny.us* ⊠*$6 per vehicle* ⊙*Daily 8* AM*–dusk.*

☺ **Heroes of Baseball Wax Museum.** It's great to read about and trade cards of your favorite players, but this museum puts you face-to-face with them. Thirty-odd baseball legends are immortalized in wax, and will perhaps interest kids more than adults. When your interest in all that wax starts to wane, you can slug it out in the virtual-reality batting cage, buy a team pennant or jersey in the gift shop, or grab lunch in the café. ⊠*99 Main St.* ☎*607/547–1273* ⊕*www.baseballwaxmuseum. com* ⊠*$8* ⊙*May–Oct., daily 9* AM*–10* PM.

Hyde Hall. Its legacy is as remarkable as its architecture: from the time it was built in 1819 until it was sold to New York State in 1964, Hyde Hall remained in the same family. Money from estates here, in Europe, and in the Caribbean enabled George Clarke (1768–1835), a prominent figure in colonial New York, to finance what is, according to many historians, the largest residence built in this country before the Civil War. Ongoing restoration projects—and the chance to question artisans about their work—add texture to a tour of the 50-room mansion. The property adjoins Glimmerglass State Park on the north end of Otsego Lake. ⊠*Mill Rd.* ☎*607/547–5098* ⊕*www.hydehall.org* ⊠*Tours $7.50–$10* ⊙*Mid-Apr.–Oct., Tues.–Thurs. 10–4.*

☺ **National Baseball Hall of Fame and Museum.** The ball that Babe Ruth hit
Fodor'sChoice for his 500th home run and Shoeless Joe Jackson's shoes are among
★ the memorabilia that help to make this shrine to America's favorite pastime so beloved. Plaques bearing the pictures and biographies of major-league notables line the walls in the actual hall of fame. The museum also has multimedia displays, exhibits geared to children, and a research library with photos, documents, and videos. New hall members are inducted during a ceremony held on the grounds of Clark's Sports Center. The event, which may be scheduled for any weekend between June and August, is free. ⊠*25 Main St.* ☎*607/547–7200 or 888/425–5633* ⊕*www.baseballhalloffame.org* ⊠*$16.50* ⊙*Labor Day–Memorial Day, daily 9–9; rest of yr daily 9–5.*

National Soccer Hall of Fame. This interactive, hands- (and feet-) on museum displays soccer-related memorabilia, equipment, trophies, and photographs. In the Kicks Zone section, you can show off your kicking, heading, and dribbling skills and test your knowledge of the sport. The collection includes the world's oldest soccer ball. ⊠ *18 Stadium Circle, Oneonta* ☎ *607/432–3351* ⊕ *www.soccerhall.org* 🖅 *$12.50* ⊙ *Apr. –June, daily 10–5; July–Labor Day, daily 9–6; Labor Day–Mar., Wed. –Sun. 10–5.*

SPORTS AND THE OUTDOORS

BASEBALL One glance at the brick entrance of **Doubleday Field** (⊠ *Main St.* ☎ *607/547–7200 or 888/425–5633* ⊕ *www.friendsofdoubleday.org*), just south of the Baseball Hall of Fame, will have you whistling "Take Me Out to the Ballgame" for the rest of the day. Local leagues play at this diamond, which opened around 1939 and can seat about 9,000 people in its bleachers. It's also used for the Baseball Hall of Fame Game held each summer, exhibition games, and other area events.

BOATING From May through October, **C. P.'s Charter Service** (☎ *315/858–3922* ⊕ *www.cooperstownfishing.com*) offers 90-minute boat tours of Otsego Lake for as many as 12 people. Vessels can pick you up from many places along the shore, and trips include free soft drinks. Rates vary. C. P.'s also conducts excursions to fish for bass, carp, perch, salmon, trout, and other game fish. Prices are $235 for four-hour trips for two people and $350 for full-day trips.

GOLF The par-72, 6,416-yard **Leatherstocking Golf Course** (⊠ *60 Lake St.* ☎ *607/547–9931 or 800/348–6222* ⊕ *www.otesaga.com*), designed by Devereux Emmet in 1909 and part of the Otesaga Resort, has a championship green that runs along Otsego Lake's southwestern shore. There's an on-site pro shop as well as a practice facility down the road. Greens fees are $90–$100. You can arrange individual lessons or take part in two- or four-day weekday or weekend training sessions (fees include hotel accommodations) through the Leatherstocking Golf School.

THE ARTS

★ National and international groups perform at the **Cooperstown Chamber Music Festival** (⊠ *Lake Rd. off Rte. 80* ☎ *607/547–1450* ⊕ *www. cooperstownmusicfest.org*), held at the Farmers' Museum throughout August. Area opera devotees staged a performance of *La Bohème* at the local high school in 1975. Twelve summers later the company they went on to form was successful enough to merit its own space. In 1987 the **Glimmerglass Opera** (⊠ *7300 Rte. 80* ☎ *607/547–2225* ⊕ *www. glimmerglass.org*) held its first production in the 900-seat **Alice Busch Opera Theater**. The company presents four operas during its July– August season. Picnics on the grounds are a good way to spend time before a performance. Tickets are $28–$92 weekdays and $56–$100 weekends.

WHERE TO EAT

$$$ ✕**Hoffman Lane Bistro.** This sunny bistro is in an alley a bit more than
AMERICAN a block from the Baseball Hall of Fame. You can eat lunch or dinner on the patio in summer or in the brightly painted dining rooms in

winter (ask for a seat near the fireplace). The dinner menu includes a wide range of dishes, including sautéed mussels served in curry sauce and seared duck breast. Locals love the live music, which takes place most weekends, and the wine list. ⊠*2 Hoffman La.* ☎*607/547–7055* 🖃*AE, MC, V.*

$$$
ECLECTIC
✕**James Fenimore Cooper Room.** Part of the Tunnicliff Inn, this sparkling restaurant overlooks Pioneer Park. The food and service are impeccable. Dishes range from regional American fare to Continental classics and contemporary preparations, including a grilled 12-ounce strip steak atop sautéed portobello and shiitake mushrooms and a pool of mustard cream sauce. Downstairs is the Pit, a historic pub where many a baseball player and fan has raised a glass and downed a burger. ⊠*34–36 Pioneer St.* ☎*607/547–9611* 🖃*AE, D, MC, V* ☻*No lunch, no dinner weekdays.*

$
AMERICAN
✕**T. J.'s Place.** The family-style restaurant's massive dining room is filled with baseball memorabilia. The menu includes everything from omelets to burgers to Italian dishes. A bar, plasma-screen TV, and gift shop provide additional distractions. ⊠*124 Main St.* ☎*607/547–4040* ⊕*www. tjsplace-thestablesinn.com* 🖃*AE, MC, V* ☻*No dinner.*

WHERE TO STAY

$
🏠**1805 Phinney House Bed & Breakfast.** This impeccable Federal-style home is just off Main Street and adjacent to Doubleday Field. The B&B recently switched hands, and the new owners cook wonderfully out-of-the-ordinary breakfasts. The decor is clean and cozy with a definite colonial feel. **Pros:** view of Doubleday Field, tasty breakfasts. **Cons:** children under eight not allowed. ⊠*14 Elm St.* ☎*607/547–2483* ⊕*www.1805phinneyhouse.com* �’*5 rooms* △*In-room: Wi-Fi. In-hotel: no kids under 8, no-smoking rooms* 🖃*AE, D, MC, V* ⋈*BP.*

$$
🏠**Barnwell Inn.** The owners of this 1850 mansion are opera lovers, and the inn tends to book up with other opera buffs during the local company's summer season. The house, on a tree-lined, flower-filled yard created from three city lots, includes rooms painted in salmon pink, malachite green, burgundy, and pale yellow. Each guest room is unique, and a coach-house apartment—a good value—has a bedroom, a living area, and a kitchenette. Breakfast includes fresh berry pies and fruit crisps as well as such standard fare as quiche. Note that a dog also resides here. **Pros:** central location; great for music lovers. **Cons:** not great for small kids. ⊠*48 Susquehanna Ave.* ☎*607/547–1850* ⊕*www. barnwellinn.com* �’*2 rooms, 2 suites, 1 apartment* △ *In-room: kitchen (some). In-hotel: Wi-Fi, no kids under 2* 🖃*MC, V* ⋈*BP.*

$$
🏠**Bay Side Inn & Marina.** Otsego Lake is the focal point at this well-run motel, which has its own beach with docks, paddleboats, canoes, and gazebos—there's even a waterside swing set. The central building has large guest rooms, a sweeping porch, a lounge, and a room with pinball machines. There are also 11 freestanding cottages, the largest of which can accommodate 10 people, but these are much more expensive than the guest rooms. **Pros:** soothing sound of the water; lovely location; nice views. **Cons:** closed in winter; no breakfast. ⊠*7090 Rte. 80* ☎*607/547–5856* ⊕ *www.baysidecooperstown.com* �’*29 rooms, 11 cottages* △*In-hotel: refrigerator, Wi-Fi. In-hotel: gym, no-smoking rooms* 🖃*AE, D, MC, V* ☻*Closed Nov.–Apr.*

$ ⊞ **Bryn Brooke Manor.** Atop a hill off Lake Street, this old mansion has lake and mountain vistas and provides a country-manor-house experience. The resident dog and cats pay you visits in the spacious public rooms, which have wood details, paneling, and floors. In the dining room the windows open so wide that you feel like you're on a porch. Guest rooms are done in dusty pastels, whites, and florals. **Pros:** excellent breakfast; friendly vibe. **Cons:** steps to climb, not for small kids. ⊠6 *Westridge Rd.* ☎607/544–1885 ⊕*www.brynbrookemanor.com* ⌁4 *rooms* ⌂ *In-room: Internet. In-hotel: pool, no-smoking rooms* ⊟*MC, V* ⎮◎⎮*BP.*

$$ ⊞ **Diastole Bed & Breakfast.** The breathtaking views from the huge porch of this hilltop B&B take in Lake Otsego's western shore. Even the name of the property—which means a rhythmic, recurrent expansion—evokes the sound of the waves. Inside, Shaker pieces are scattered throughout. The largest guest room, outfitted with Early American furnishings, is impeccable. The property encompasses miles of private hiking trails, and you can arrange for horseback riding with a nearby outfitter. **Pros:** serene view of the lake; lovely furnishings. **Cons:** closed during winter months. ⊠276 *Van Yahres Rd.* ☎607/547–2665 ⊕*www.diastolebb. com* ⌁5 *rooms* ⌂*In-room: Wi-Fi. In-hotel: restaurant, no kids under 6, no-smoking rooms* ⊟*No credit cards* ⎮◎⎮*BP.*

$$$ ⊞ **Inn at Cooperstown.** Rocking chairs are set all along the front porch, which runs the width of this inviting Second Empire building with its dormer windows. Guest rooms are uncluttered, making them seem even roomier than they are. Crisp clean walls, king- and queen-size beds, and wall-to-wall carpeting lend modernity. Pastel quilts in traditional patterns and period reproductions are nods to this inn's history and its place on the National Register of Historic Places. **Pros:** creative package deals; central location. **Cons:** steps to climb. ⊠16 *Chestnut St.* ☎607/547–5756 ⊕*www.innatcooperstown.com* ⌁17 *rooms, 1 suite* ⌂*In-room: refrigerator (some), Wi-Fi. In-hotel: no-smoking rooms* ⊟*AE, MC, V* ⎮◎⎮*BP.*

$$ ⊞ **Landmark Inn.** An expansive front lawn rolls from Chestnut Street to the sheltered entry of this truly grand 1856 Italianate mansion. Common areas are large and sunny. Gleaming wood floors and attractive furnishings are found throughout. Beds and chairs are so plump you can't resist flopping onto them as soon as you enter your room. Many rooms have special showers or tubs; one has an 11-head shower. Full breakfasts are served in a formal dining room. **Pros:** great breakfasts; good for families. **Cons:** wireless Internet isn't always dependable. ⊠64 *Chestnut St.* ☎607/547–7225 ⊕*www.landmarkinncooperstown.com* ⌁9 *rooms* ⌂*In-room: refrigerator, Wi-Fi. In-hotel: no-smoking rooms* ⊟*AE, D, MC, V* ⎮◎⎮*BP.*

$$$$ ⊞ **Otesaga Resort Hotel.** There's something almost collegiate about the **Fodor's**Choice stately Otesaga—maybe it's all the brick, or perhaps it's the cupola or ★ the neoclassical entryway. The same studied grace runs throughout the interior. But it would be hard to hit the books here, thanks to such distractions as the Leatherstocking Golf Course and fishing or canoeing on Otsego Lake. In the luxurious **dining room,** massive windows look out onto the grounds. The four-course dinner is quite formal, with

jackets required for men. The ever-changing menu lists contemporary dishes such as boneless chicken glazed in honey and lavender and sautéed sea bass. **Pros:** pretty building; afternoon tea. **Cons:** two-night minimum stay; too stuffy for some. ⊠*60 Lake St.* ☎*607/547–9931 or 800/348–6222* ⊕*www.otesaga.com* ☞*156 rooms* ⌂*In-room: safe, Wi-Fi. In-hotel: restaurant, bar, golf course, tennis courts, pool* ⊟*AE, D, DC, MC, V* ☉*Closed mid-Nov.–mid-Apr.* ⫶⊙*IMAP.*

ONEIDA, ROME, AND UTICA

The Oneida, Rome, and Utica area, a frontier in the 1750s, has played a pivotal role in the development of the state as well as of the country. It became a gateway to the West, especially after the Erie Canal opened in 1825, in what is called the Mohawk Valley. South of the valley are soft hills, lush forests, and farmed fields. North of the canal are the Adirondack foothills, and to the west are the glistening waters of Oneida Lake. The area is home to such notable industries as Revere Copper Products, Oneida Ltd., and Harden Furniture. The Oneida Indian Nation, which runs the Turning Stone Resort & Casino as well as several other businesses, is a major employer here.

VISITOR INFORMATION

Mohawk Valley Chamber of Commerce (⊠ *200 Genesee St., Utica* ☎ *315/724–3151* ⊕ *www.mvchamber.org*).

ONEIDA

67 mi northwest of Cooperstown; 32 mi east of Syracuse.

This small city off Route 5 and the thruway was settled in 1834. It's home to the Mansion House estate, where the former Oneida Community, a utopian religious sect, lived in the mid-19th century. The group produced assorted goods, including silverware, and in the 1880s, abandoning its communal way of life, it morphed into Oneida Community Ltd. This joint-stock company eventually became Oneida Ltd.

The enticements of the small town are dwarfed by the sprawling Turning Stone Resort & Casino, 4 mi away in Verona. The casino, run by the Oneida Nation, offers round-the-clock gambling, three hotels, a full-service salon and spa and several restaurants.

There are other amusements nearby, however. A few miles north, on the eastern end of Oneida Lake, Sylvan Beach offers warm-weather amusements.

VISITOR INFORMATION

Oneida County Convention & Visitors Bureau (✉ *Box 551, Utica 13503* ☎ *315/724–7221 or 800/426–3132* ⊕ *www.oneidacountycvb.com*).

WHAT TO SEE

Cottage Lawn. The 1849 Gothic Revival cottage, headquarters of the Madison County Historical Society, was designed by noted architect Alexander Jackson Davis. The group runs tours of the cottage, which contains seven rooms decked in period furnishings. Glassware from Canastota Glass and portraits of City of Oneida founder Sands Higinbotham and prominent abolitionist Garrett Smith are among the displays here. The building, which once belonged to Higinbotham's son Niles, includes a research library. Out back is the Hops Barn, where exhibits explain that the region was once the center of hops production for England. The annual summer Hops Festival celebrates this heritage. ⊠ *435 Main St.* ☎ *315/363–4136 or 315/361–9735* ⊕ *www. mchs1900.org* 🖃 *$5* ⊙ *Weekdays 9–4.*

International Boxing Hall of Fame. In 1982, residents of Canastota and boxing enthusiasts wanted to honor two hometown boxers, late 1950s welterweight and middleweight champion Carmen Basilio and his nephew Billy Backus, the 1970 winner of the world welterweight title. Their efforts resulted in the 1989 opening of boxing's first hall of fame and museum, where you may see memorabilia from such notable boxers as Muhammad Ali, Joe Louis, and Billy Graham. The hall of fame is 6 mi southwest of Oneida. ⊠ *1 Hall of Fame Dr., Canastota* ☎ *315/697–7095* ⊕ *www.ibhof.com* 🖃 *$9.50* ⊙ *Weekdays 9–5, weekends 10–4.*

Mansion House. The three-story brick house and its 34 acres were the home of the 19th-century utopian Oneida Community, founded in 1848 by John Humphrey Noyes. The sect believed that the second coming of Christ had already occurred and that a new Eden could be achieved on Earth. Followers considered themselves sinless and believed in the sharing of property and spouses. The group, which supported itself by making silk thread, animal traps, canned foods, and silverware, eventually led to the formation of tableware manufacturer Oneida Ltd. The mansion, a 93,000-square-foot National Historic Landmark with beautiful mansard roofs, was constructed in stages between 1861 and 1914 and contains 35 apartments (some occupied by descendants of the original community members), a large hall, a dining room, and a museum. Guided tours are the only way to see the interior. ⊠ *170 Kenwood Ave.* ☎ *315/363–0745* ⊕ *www.oneidacommunity.org* 🖃 *$5* ⊙ *Mar.–Dec., Wed.–Sat. 10 and 2, Sun. 2; Jan. and Feb., Sat. 10 and 2, Sun. 2.*

Shako:wi Cultural Center. The center, in a log building on the grounds of the Oneida Indian Nation, has exhibits highlighting baskets, beadwork, dolls, and wampum. You may also learn about the role of the Oneida Nation during the American Revolution, when it sided with the rebels rather than with the British. ⊠ *Oneida Indian Nation, Rte. 46, off I-90 Exit 33, Verona* ☎ *315/829–8801* ⊕ *www.oneidaindiannation. com* 🖃 *Free* ⊙ *Daily 9–5.*

⟳ **Sylvan Beach Amusement Park.** The amusement park, on the eastern shore of Oneida Lake, is loaded with old-fashioned fun. Attractions include an old-time carousel, bumper cars and boats, roller coaster, food vendors, and arcades. ⊠ *112 Bridge St., Sylvan Beach* ☎ *315/762–5212* ⊕ *www.sylvanbeach.org/amusementpark* 🖃 *Free* ⊙ *Apr.–May, weekends; June–early Sept., daily. Call for hrs.*

SPORTS AND THE OUTDOORS

GOLF   The **Turning Stone Resort & Casino** (⊠ *5218 Patrick Rd., Verona* ☎ *800/*
Fodor'sChoice   *771–7711* ⊕ *www.turning-stone.com*) has three championship golf
★   courses. *Golf Digest* chose the Rick Smith course at the **Shenendoah
Golf Club** as one of the best-conditioned courses in the United States.
The 7,129-yard course was designed with nature in mind, with efforts
made to preserve delicate wetlands. Robert Trent Jones Jr. designed
the challenging 7,105-yard course at the **Kaluhyat Golf Club,** a mix
of open links-style stretches and tight tree-lined fairways. The course
takes advantage of the rolling landscape, so you have to place shots to
remain in play; attempt the shortcut and the tall native grasses surely
will make you pay with a penalty stroke.

The newest of the resort's golf offerings is the 7,314-yard Tom Fazio
course at the off-property **Atunyote Golf Club,** designed for the long-
ball hitter. But this course, too, has a variety of challenges in its stretches
of open space and gentle slopes. The course includes several lakes, the
largest of which runs along three fairways. Greens fees run $90–$175
for resort guests and $125–$200 for nonguests. The resort also has
two 9-hole courses.

WHERE TO STAY

$ ☷ **Charlotte's Creekside Inn.** The colonial-style house, on 3 wooded acres
along the Sconondoa Creek, was built in 1813 by State Assemblyman
Sydney Breese, uncle of inventor Samuel Morse. The property includes a
multilevel deck and manicured gardens. Guest rooms, painted in bright
greens and other cheery colors, embrace the flair of the Caribbean. The
first floor houses the restaurant, which has four intimate dining rooms.
The food is mostly Italian, but you also find fresh seafood dishes. **Pros:**
not too expensive; tasty restaurant. **Cons:** Continental breakfast only.
⊠ *3960 Sconondoa Rd.* ☎ *315/363–3377* ⊕ *www.charlottescreekside.
com* ➫ *3 rooms, 2 suites* ⚹ *In-hotel: restaurant, bar, no-smoking rooms*
⊟ *AE, D, DC, MC, V* ⚹⦿⚹ *CP.*

$$$$ ☷ **Turning Stone Resort & Casino.** You have three lodging options at this
lavish resort: the all-suites **Lodge at Turning Stone,** the 19-story **Tower
at Turning Stone,** and the modern **Hotel at Turning Stone.** Rooms in the
hotel have contemporary furnishings and dramatically lighted marble
bathrooms; some suites have whirlpool tubs and patios. In the tower,
the third floor is devoted to a health club and a 65-foot-long indoor
lap pool; a rooftop terrace crowns the building. The more intimate and
luxurious lodge has chic suites with balconies with lovely views. The
resort's broad (and rich) dining options include steak, regional Italian,
Brazilian, and American. ⊠ *5218 Patrick Rd., Verona* ☎ *800/771–7711*
⊕ *www.turning-stone.com* ➫ *255 rooms, 30 suites in hotel; 98 suites in
lodge; 266 rooms, 21 suites in tower* ⚹ *In-room: safe (some), refrigerator
(some), Internet. In-hotel: 6 restaurants, room service, golf courses, pool,
gym, spa, laundry service, no-smoking rooms* ⊟ *AE, D, DC, MC, V.*

ROME

16 mi northeast of Oneida.

The Mohawk River courses through Rome, about 10 mi north of Interstate 90, and the route linking the Atlantic Ocean with the Great Lakes cuts through the area. The Oneida were the first to live in this area, and in the 1600s British and French fur traders came to barter for black-beaver pelts. In the 1750s the British built Fort Stanwix, which the Americans took over just before the Revolutionary War. And it was here, in 1817, that the first portion of the Erie Canal was dug. Today about 35,000 people live in Rome, where the former Griffiss Air Force Base has been converted into a high-tech community. The city is home to a number of historic sites that attract tens of thousands of visitors each year.

VISITOR INFORMATION

Rome Area Chamber of Commerce (⊠ *139 W. Dominick St., Rome* ☎ *315/337–1700* ⊕ *www.romechamber.com*).

WHAT TO SEE

Erie Canal Village. Digging of the Erie Canal started in 1817 on this site, now home to a re-created 19th-century canal settlement. You can visit a tavern, a blacksmith shop, a one-room schoolhouse, and settlers' houses from different eras of the 1800s. The complex also includes a cheese museum (in a former cheese factory), a carriage museum with horse-drawn vehicles, and a canal museum with displays about the construction of, and life along, the canal. A mule-drawn packet boat gives rides on the canal, or you can take a ride on a steam train. ⊠ *5789 New London Rd.* ☎ *315/337–3999 or 888/374–3226* ⊕ *www.eriecanalvillage. net* 🎟 *Village and museums $10, packet boat $6* ☉ *Late May–Labor Day, Wed.–Sat. 10–5, Sun. noon–5; rest of Sept., Sat. 10–5, Sun. noon–5.*

Fort Stanwix National Monument. In 1758, during the French and Indian Wars, the British built a fort here to protect the strategic Oneida Carrying Place—a 1-mi-long area between the Mohawk River and Oneida Lake where boats had to be carried. It was part of the route from the Atlantic Ocean to the Great Lakes. A path here allows you to walk part of the Oneida Carrying Place. The British eventually abandoned the fort, which the American rebels took over at the start of the Revolutionary War. The fort came under attack by British forces, Tories, and their Indian allies for three weeks in August 1777, but the rebels were able to fend off the siege. The structure you see today is a reconstruction of that fort, which suffered a major fire and destructive floods after the Revolution. ⊠ *112 E. Park St.* ☎ *315/338–7730* ⊕ *www.nps.gov/fost* 🎟 *Free* ☉ *Daily 9–5.*

Oriskany Battlefield State Historic Site. The August 6, 1777, battle fought here is said to have been one of the bloodiest conflicts of the American Revolution, and is viewed as key to later rebel victories. It involved Brigadier General Nicholas Herkimer and the 800 men and 60 Oneida warriors he had assembled to march to the aid of the rebels at Fort

Stanwix, which British forces had attacked. As Herkimer's group marched toward the fort, it was ambushed in a ravine by British forces, Tories, and their Seneca and Mohawk allies. The losses, heavy on both sides, caused the British side to retreat. ⊠*7801 Rte. 69, Oriskany* ☎*315/768–7224* ⊕*nysparks.state.ny.us* ⊠*Free* ☉*Mid-May–mid-Oct., Wed.–Sat. 9–5, Sun. 1–5.*

WHERE TO EAT AND STAY

$$
CONTINENTAL

✕**Michelina's.** The restaurant is part of the Beeches, an estate with a lovely manor house. The place serves top-quality Continental fare that's full of flavor and attractively presented. Rack of pork, rarely encountered on menus in these parts, is marinated and slow roasted so that it melts in your mouth. Salmon steaks are broiled and dressed with the restaurant's tasty dill sauce. The dining room, with a large fireplace and hand-painted ceiling panels, exudes 1920s style. The chandelier, crafted by Raulli Ironworks of Rome, is original. ⊠*7900 Turin Rd.* ☎*315/336–1700* ☐*AE, D, DC, MC, V* ☉*Closed Mon.*

$
ITALIAN
Fodor'sChoice
★

✕**Savoy.** At this Italian restaurant you can enjoy an intimate meal or just sip cocktails at the bar and listen to live piano music. The walls are covered with photographs of celebrities who have visited since the place opened in 1908. The menu offers pasta and seafood dishes as well as traditional preparations like manicotti and chicken cacciatore. The fried meatballs (greasy and rich as they are) are a popular appetizer. The cocktails are imaginative and generally well mixed. Try the Savoy Manhattan for a smooth, refreshing twist on an upstate favorite. The bar, separate from the dining room, has intimate seating. ⊠*255 E. Dominick St.* ☎*315/339–3166* ☐*AE, D, MC, V* ☉*No lunch weekends.*

¢
Fodor'sChoice
★

▦**The Beeches Inn and Conference Center.** This inn, part of the 52-acre Beeches estate, is the best place to stay in town. Rooms, dressed in French-country style with floral patterns, have a king bed or one or two queen-size beds; bathrooms have marble trim. The suite has a sitting area and a whirlpool tub. The restaurants alone are worth the trip. **Pros:** beautiful grounds; lovely architecture. **Cons:** no breakfast option. ⊠*7900 Turin Rd.* ☎*315/336–1776 or 800/765–7251* ⊕*www.thebeeches.com* ↪*63 rooms, 7 suites* ♿*In-room: Internet, Wi-Fi. In-hotel: 3 restaurants, pool, some pets allowed, no-smoking rooms* ☐*AE, D, DC, MC, V.*

UTICA

15 mi southeast of Rome.

Utica, near the exact geographic center of New York State, has been a magnet for immigrants since Erie Canal days. Thousands of Irish workers came here to dig the big ditch in the early 1800s; after the city was incorporated in 1832 there was a wave of German immigrants. Poles and Italians, attracted by the railroad, construction, brickyard, and mill jobs, poured into Utica in the late 1800s.

Although its industrial presence is no longer what it once was, the city continues to attract—and retain—immigrants. Some of the many Italian bakeries and restaurants for which Utica is known have been in business in the same neighborhoods for three generations. The inflow of immigrants since the 1990s has been mostly from Asia, Africa, Russia, and other parts of Eastern Europe. Indeed, 10% of the population of 60,000 is from Bosnia, and the daily newspaper once printed a weekly column in Serbo-Croatian.

GETTING HERE AND AROUND

Greyhound and Adirondack Trailways link the region with New York City and much of the rest of the state. Shortline buses, which stop in Binghamton and Utica, link central New York with New York City, the Catskills, the Finger Lakes, and western New York. To get around, however, you need a car.

WHAT TO SEE

Children's Museum of History, Natural History, Science and Technology. A brick building in the historic Main Street district houses four floors of hands-on exhibits for all ages. There's a Dinorama, with dinosaur models and fossils, and a Weather Room, with Doppler radar. Kiddies can walk into a replica Iroquois longhouse, don firefighting gear, and pretend to fly a 17-foot-long airplane. Outside you can explore the inside of an old Adirondack locomotive, dining car, and caboose parked alongside the building. ✉ *311 Main St.* ☎ *315/724–6129* ⊕ *www.museum4kids. net* ✉ *$9* ⊙ *Museum Mon., Tues., Thurs., and Fri., 9:45–3:30; Sat. 10–3:45.*

Fodor's Choice ★ **Munson-Williams-Proctor Arts Institute.** The institute is made up of a museum, an art school, and a performing-arts center. Its **Museum of Art** occupies two distinctly different buildings. The 1850 Italianate mansion, called Fountain Elms, has rooms of Victorian-era furnishings. The main gallery spaces are in the 1960 Philip Johnson structure, a rather austere building clad in polished granite. The holdings include 18th-, 19th-, and 20th-century American paintings, sculptures, and photographs; 19th- and 20th-century European paintings; Asian prints; and pre-Columbian artifacts. A highlight here is the collection of Hudson River School paintings, which include the four-part "Voyage of Life" series by Thomas Cole as well as works by Asher B. Durand and Frederic Church. ✉ *310 Genesee St.* ☎ *315/797–0000* ✉ *Free* ⊙ *Tues.–Sat. 10–5, Sun. 1–5.*

Saranac Brewery Tour Center. Learn how the **F. X. Matt Brewing Co.** creates its Saranac-brand traditional lager, pale ale, pilsner, Adirondack amber, and old-fashioned root beer. The same family has operated the seven-story brick brew house for more than a century. Inhaling the yeasty aroma of fermenting hops and malt, you can see several steps of the brewing process. Tours are on the hour and end with a beer or root-beer sampling. Call in advance for reservations. ✉ *830 Varick St., off Court St.* ☎ *315/732–0022 or 800/765–6288* ⊕ *www.saranac.com* ✉ *$3* ⊙ *June–Aug., Mon.–Sat. 1–4, Sun. 1–3; Sept.–May, Fri.–Sat. 1–3.*

Union Station. The massive limestone-and-granite building has 47-foot-high vaulted ceilings, marble pillars, a terrazzo floor, original steam-heated wooden benches, and a vintage barbershop that still gives haircuts. Train tours operated by Adirondack Scenic Railroad leave from the 1914 Italian Renaissance–style station for day trips into the Adirondack wilderness. ⊠*321 Main St.* ☎*No phone (station), 315/724–0700 (train rides)* ⊕*www.adirondackrr.com (train rides).*

TAKE A TRAIN TOUR

You can take a seasonal scenic train ride from Utica into the mountains. From Memorial Day weekend through Columbus Day, a 1950s-era locomotive chugs and whistles from Utica's historic Union Station on day trips into the Adirondack Wilderness via the **Adirondack Scenic Railroad** (⊠*Union Station, 321 Main St.* ☎*315/724–0700* ⊕*www.adirondackrr.com*).

↻ **Utica Zoo.** Siberian tigers, Alaskan grizzly bears, and California sea lions are some of the 200 animals that reside in this city park with views of the Mohawk Valley. A petting zoo and live animal shows are options in summer. ⊠*99 Steele Hill Rd.* ☎*315/738–0472* ⊕*www.uticazoo. org* ⊠*Apr.–Oct. $4.50, Nov.–Mar. free* ☉*Daily 10–5.*

SPORTS AND THE OUTDOORS

The **National Distance Running Hall of Fame** (⊠*114 Genesee St.* ☎*315/724–4525* ⊕*www.distancerunning.com*) holds its annual induction ceremony the night before the Boilermaker road race.

SHOPPING

A food lover's delight awaits at Bleecker and Albany streets 1 mi from downtown. Here, in the remnants of an old Italian neighborhood, Uticans wait patiently in line for freshly made pastries, bread, and tomato pie (pizza-like squares that are eaten at room temperature). **Caffe Caruso** (⊠*707 Bleecker St.* ☎*315/735–9712*) has glass cases packed with fresh cookies, a giant copper espresso machine, and white wrought-iron chairs and glass-topped tables. Crisp-and-creamy cannoli are $1 each, and chocolate *pasticciotti* (small custard-filled pies) are 80¢ at the **Florentine Pastry Shop** (⊠*667 Bleecker St.* ☎*315/724–8032*), open since 1918. Enjoy your treat with a cup of coffee in an adjoining storefront room decorated with maps and photos of Italy. In business since 1908, **Rintrona's Bakery** (⊠*744 Bleecker St.* ☎*315/732–2337*) sells bread, meatballs, fried dough, pizza shells, and tomato pie.

THE ARTS

At the 2,945-seat **Stanley Center for the Arts** (⊠*259 Genesee St.* ☎*315/724–4000* ⊕*www.cnyarts.com*) you can see touring Broadway shows and enjoy performances by the **Mohawk Valley Ballet** and the **Utica Symphony Orchestra.** The Mexican-baroque center was built as a movie house in 1928. It has an ornate marquee and terra-cotta and mosaic tile accents on its exterior; inside, walls are adorned with gold-leaf lions and angels, and the ceiling is scattered with stars.

WHERE TO EAT

$$

ITALIAN

Fodor's Choice

★

✕**Delmonico's** Utica's Italian community has gathered for years at Delmonico's, which bills itself as a steak house but really dishes up some of the region's most authentic Italian food. For an appetizer, try some Utica greens—sturdy greens cooked with olive oil, hot and sweet peppers, ham, and cheese. Rachel Ray did, and loved them so much she devoted a show to them. If you're not too full from the huge portions, sample the chicken Sinatra, which is simmered with hot peppers, mozzarella, and mushrooms. A waitress in pinstripes and a fedora will bring your food and offer you a selection from a long and tasty wine list. ⊠*147 N. Genesee St.* ☎*315/732–2300* ⊟*AE, D, DC, MC, V* ⊗*No lunch weekdays.*

$$
ITALIAN
✕**Dominique's Chesterfield Restaurant.** This family restaurant, a favorite for two decades, occupies a brick storefront with tin ceilings and Tiffany lamps. The kitchen serves traditional Italian dishes as well as local specialties such as chicken "riggies" (bite-size chunks of chicken breast tossed with pasta, hot and sweet peppers, cheese, and onions). Sip a selection from the nice wine and cognac list. ⊠*1713 Bleecker St.* ☎*315/732–9356* ⊟*AE, MC, V.*

$
MIDDLE EASTERN
✕**The Phoenician.** Traditional Middle Eastern cuisine is the specialty of this small restaurant just outside Utica. Stuffed grape leaves, tabbouleh, and hummus with pita bread are among the appetizers. Kebabs of marinated and grilled lamb, pork, beef, and chicken are the most popular entrée. Also on the menu are *kafta* (skewered meatballs of finely ground beef and lamb), *kibbi* (raw, ground spiced lamb), stuffed cabbage, and several vegetarian dishes. A small patio offers outdoor dining. ⊠*623 French Rd., New Hartford* ☎*315/733–2709* ⊟*AE, D, MC, V.*

WHERE TO STAY

$
Fodor'sChoice
★
🏨**Hotel Utica.** Judy Garland once sang from the mezzanine to fans in the lobby, and Mae West, Rita Hayworth, and Jimmy Durante all spent the night at this 14-story Renaissance revival–style hotel in the downtown business district. The two-story lobby of the grand 1912 building has a coffered ceiling, faux-marble pillars, large crystal chandeliers, a piano, and lovebirds that serenade you from their antique cage. Guest rooms, spacious and attractive, have swagged window treatments and traditional furnishings; many have Mohawk Valley views. **Pros:** beautiful building; great location in historic district. **Cons:** no restaurant. ⊠*102 Lafayette St.* ☎*315/724–7829 or 877/906–1912* ⊕*www.hotelutica.com* ⇆*98 rooms, 14 suites* ♿*In-room: refrigerator (some), Wi-Fi. In-hotel: bar, laundry service, no-smoking rooms* ⊟*AE, D, DC, MC, V* ¡◎¡*BP.*

$$
🏨**Rosemont Inn Bed & Breakfast.** A cupola crowns this handsome three-story brick Italianate villa built in 1866. The B&B has two large porches, a parlor with a marble fireplace, and bathrooms with claw-foot tubs. One guest room is on the first floor; the others are on the second floor. Most rooms have a queen bed, and all have rose-print bed coverings and down comforters. The Wine and Roses room, where walls are the color of claret, has a queen and a double bed. **Pros:** in city's historic district; near area attractions. **Cons:** noise from one of the city's main drags. ⊠*1423 Genesee St.* ☎*866/353–4907* ⊕*www.rosemontinnbb.com* ⇆*7 rooms* ♿ *In-room: Wi-Fi. In-hotel: no-smoking rooms* ⊟*MC, V* ¡◎¡*BP.*

5

THE MOHAWK VALLEY

The Mohawk Valley, the ancestral home of the Mohawk Indians, is so peaceful and scenic that it catches you by surprise. This is big-sky country, Northeast style: miles of rolling woodlands, farms, and pastures sliced through by the Mohawk River, a shimmering ribbon with mostly undeveloped banks. In the valley's small cities and tiny villages hidden treasures await, from Herkimer "diamonds" to Winslow Homer masterpieces.

VISITOR INFORMATION
Montgomery County Chamber of Commerce (⌂ *Box 836, Fonda 12068* ☎ *518/ 853–1800 or 800/743–7337* ⊕ *www.montgomerycountyny.com*).

HERKIMER

13 mi east of Utica.

The village, on the north bank of the Mohawk River, takes its name from a Revolutionary War general whose home, now a state historic site, was several miles east, near Little Falls. The first road through Herkimer was built in 1794; the Erie Canal came in 1825, followed by the railroad in 1833 and the thruway in 1954. The arrival of these harbingers of historic, economic, and cultural transformation is analogous to the history of Herkimer. After settlement, this village transitioned from an agricultural base to producing bicycles, shoes, furniture, matches, coat hangers, carriages, and lumber. Later, as the 20th century approached, the local economy became more reliant on the service industry, and jobs shifted to the health-care and education fields. Boosting tourism are Herkimer's "diamonds," which you may discover at one of the local mines.

VISITOR INFORMATION
Herkimer County Chamber of Commerce (⊠ *28 W. Main St., Mohawk* ☎ *315/866–7820 or 877/984–4636* ⊕ *www.herkimercountychamber.com*).

WHAT TO SEE

♻ **Ace of Diamonds Mine.** Bring your own sledgehammers and pry bars or rent them from the gift shop, stake a "claim," and begin your search for quarry. No matter where you prospect, you're not likely to be disappointed. Many open pits are an easy walk to the right or left of the visitor center, where you can see beads, stones, an extensive book section, and other rock-related items. You might venture up the steep hillside in hope of finding a pocket containing hundreds of "diamonds"—really quartz crystals with diamondlike facets. The views of the wooded valley and the Mohawk River are a find in themselves. ⊠*Rte. 28, Middleville* ☎*315/891–3855* ⊕*www.herkimerdiamonds.com* ⊘ *$7* ⊘*Apr.–Oct., daily 9–5.*

Erie Canal Cruises. Canal-history tours aboard the *Lil' Diamond*, a 36-passenger motorboat, take you from the docks at the Gems Along the Mohawk retail complex through Lock 18 and back. The tour takes about two hours, and the season runs from May to early October. ⊠*800 Mohawk St.* ☎*315/717–0350* ⊕*www.eriecanalcruises.com* ⌂*$18.*

Herkimer Diamond Mines. Try your luck at prospecting: hammer open the right rocks and you'll find double-terminated quartz crystals, aka Herkimer diamonds. Two open pits are easy to reach. The first is adjacent to the gift shop. Upstairs you can watch an explanatory video or stroll through multiple scientific displays, including exhibits about dinosaurs and fluorescent minerals. The mines are just south of Middleville. ⊠*Rte. 28 between Rtes. 5 and 29* ☎*315/891–7355 or 800/562–0897* ⊕*www.herkimerdiamond.com* ▣*$10* ☉*Apr.–Nov., daily 9–5.*

Herkimer Home State Historic Site. You can stroll the gardens, attend a multimedia show, and tour the restored Georgian-style mansion that was home to Revolutionary War general Nicholas Herkimer. Costumed historical interpreters inform you about the history, crafts, and lifestyle of the 18th century. Picnicking is encouraged. ⊠*Rte. 5S, ½ mi off Thruway Exit 29A, Little Falls* ☎*315/823–0398* ⊕*nysparks.state.ny.us* ▣*$4* ☉*May–Oct., Tues.–Sat. 10–5, Sun. 11–5.*

Suiter Mansion. The 1884 Victorian mansion is one of four buildings, all within short walking distances of one another, that make up the **Historic Four Corners.** Upstairs at the 1834 **Herkimer County Jail** (▣*$2*) is a large dollhouse assemblage. The **Reformed Church** (1835) and the **Herkimer County Court House** (1873), as well as the jail, may be visited by appointment. Adjacent to the Suiter Mansion, which you can tour, is the Eckler House, a simple Italianate house occupied by the Herkimer County Historical Society. Its holdings include gravestone files, photographs, maps, and a manuscript collection. ⊠*Herkimer County Historical Society, 400 N. Main St.* ☎*315/866–6413* ⊕*www.rootsweb.com/~nyhchs* ▣*Free* ☉*Sept.–June, weekdays 10–4; July and Aug., weekdays 10–4, Sat. 10–3.*

WHERE TO EAT AND STAY

$$
AMERICAN
★
✕**Beardslee Castle.** Thanks to the meticulous owners, you'd never know that this 1860 castle, now a fine American restaurant, had survived fires and years of abandonment. The place is said to be inhabited by ghosts, and that's not hard to imagine. Stone archways separate the five cozy dining rooms, where white cloths cover the tables. The food doesn't detract from the haunting ambience. Many entrées come grilled, such as pork loin with compote or honey-glazed duck with fig relish. Meat-free dishes like terrine of grilled vegetables also appear on the menu. For a really spooky treat, have a drink in the dungeon, located in the castle's basement. The restaurant is 6 mi east of the center of Little Falls. ⊠*Rte. 5, Little Falls* ☎*315/823–3000 or 800/487–5861* ▤*AE, D, MC, V* ☉*Closed Sun.–Wed. No lunch.*

¢
▦**Herkimer Motel.** The more popular choice in town, the Herkimer Motel gets lots of compliments on cleanliness and service. Inexpensive though it is, it offers an outdoor pool and fitness room, and is conveniently located for further excursions into the area. **Pros:** near area restaurants and shops. **Cons:** can be noisy. ⊠*Exit 30 from the Thruway (I–90)* ☎*877/656–6835* ⊕*www.herkimermotel.com* ⚗*In-room: Wi-Fi. In-hotel: restaurant, pool* ▤*AE, D, DC, MC, V* ⊠*CP.*

5

CANAJOHARIE

29 mi southeast of Herkimer.

Canajoharie is on Route 5S, on the south bank of the Mohawk River. Founded in 1730, the village is now home to a large Beech-Nut food-processing plant. The wealth of its industrial past is evident in the Canajoharie Library and Art Gallery, which has a collection of fine art donated by the late Beech-Nut factory owner, Bartlett Arkell.

WHAT TO SEE

★ **Arkell Museum at Canajoharie.** The collection of paintings, largely by American artists, includes works by such well-known painters as Winslow Homer, Gilbert Stuart, Edward Hopper, John Singer Sargent, Mary Cassatt, Childe Hassam, Charles Burchfield, and Thomas Eakins. Twenty-one Homer paintings are lent out regularly to museums around the world. ✉ *2 Erie Blvd.* ☎ *518/673–2314* ⊕ *www.clag.org* ✆ *Free* ⊙ *Mon.–Thurs. 10–7, Fri. 10–5, weekends 12:30–5.*

WHERE TO EAT

¢ ✕ **Village Restaurant.** Locals craving a Spanish omelet, baked ziti, and
AMERICAN other comfort food head for this downtown diner just off Interstate 90. Everything is made from scratch, and seasonal decorations brighten the decor. ✉ *59 Church St.* ☎ *518/673–2596* ▭ *No credit cards.*

AMSTERDAM

22 mi east of Canojoharie; 27 mi northeast of Howes Cave.

In its heyday, this Erie Canal town bustled with mills and factories churning out manufactured goods, from carpets and curtains to carriage springs. Amsterdam was once the nation's biggest producer of brooms, crafting 7 million a year from corn grown in the Mohawk Valley. Today visitors stop in the former Rug City (population 21,000) on their way to many historic sites, both American Indian and colonial. The city has one of the oldest upstate Hispanic communities and is the home of musicians Alex Torres and the Latin Kings.

WHAT TO SEE

Schoharie Crossing State Historic Site. Five miles west of Amsterdam is the only site with structures dating from all three stages of the Erie Canal's evolution, including the Schoharie Aqueduct. The earliest parts date from 1817. Exhibits in the visitor center show how the canal developed and include dress-up and coloring activities for children. The site has a small-boat launch and hiking, cross-country skiing, and bike trails. ✉ *129 Schoharie St., Fort Hunter* ☎ *518/829–7516* ⊕ *nysparks.state. ny.us* ✆ *Free* ⊙ *Grounds daily dawn–dusk; visitor center May–Oct., Wed.–Mon. 10–5 and Sun. 1–5.*

WHERE TO EAT

¢ ✕ **Happi Daze Charcoal Pit.** In the 1950s it was a teen hangout, with car-
AMERICAN hops zipping trays of burgers, fries, and colas to Chevys and Fords lined up in the parking lot. The Pit, 4 mi north of Amsterdam, is still a cool place, with tunes by Elvis and the Beatles playing from loudspeakers and

THE ERIE CANAL

Central New York was the birthplace of the Erie Canal, which was key to the development of the state and, indeed, the country. The first portion of the cross-state canal was dug in Rome in the early 1800s, and the project drew thousands of laborers to central New York, many of them immigrants. The waterway opened in 1825 and, compared with road travel, was a much more affordable way to transport goods and resources. It fueled industrial development along its 363 mi, increased trade, and prompted a major westward migration. The boom in water traffic made New York City the busiest port in the country, and the canal was expanded.

You can experience the canal in different ways throughout the region. The place where the digging of the canal started is part of the Erie Canal Village, a re-created 19th-century settlement. The Schoharie Crossing State Historic Site, 5 mi west of Amsterdam, has structures dating from all stages of the canal's development. In addition, you may take a cruise or boat on the canal, bike or walk alongside it, and dine at a canal-side restaurant.

babes in hot pants and go-go boots pictured on the big neon sign. Try the famous foot-long hot dogs or chill out with ice cream that's made on-site. You can eat in your car or relax at pine-shaded picnic tables. ⊠ *4479 Rte. 30* ☎ *518/843–8265* ⚠ *Reservations not accepted* ▭ *No credit cards* ⊘ *Closed Oct.–Mar.*

$$ ✕ **Raindancer Steak Parlour.** Everyone knows this big, busy restaurant
AMERICAN 3 mi north of Amsterdam—including Hillary Clinton, who lunched here
Fodor'sChoice during her 1999 Senate campaign. Dining is casual, in cozy booths or
★ at tables in wood-paneled nooks. Specialties include beef-and-seafood combo plates, such as salmon and filet mignon or Alaskan king crab and prime rib. Help yourself at the soup-and-salad bar. ⊠ *4582 Rte. 30* ☎ *518/842–2606* ▭ *AE, D, DC, MC, V.*

SCHOHARIE COUNTY

This picturesque region is the bridge between the capital region and Cooperstown. It also serves as a buffer between the Catskills and the Adirondacks. Soft hills and rich farmland dominate Schoharie County. The lone college town here is Cobleskill, home to a state-university campus. State and town roads throughout display numerous Revolutionary War battle markers.

HOWES CAVE

27 mi southwest of Amsterdam; 38 mi east of Cooperstown.

Howes Cave is such a small community that you could easily miss it as you motor down Route 7. But looks can be deceiving. The small town attracts thousands of visitors each year because of its underground caves. The chiseled walls of the caverns, located more than a hundred feet below the surface, even hold an underground lake.

VISITOR INFORMATION
Howe Caverns Visitor Center (⊠ *255 Discovery Dr., Howes Cave* ☎ *518/296–8900* ⊕ *www.howecaverns.com*).

WHAT TO SEE

Caverns Creek Grist Mill. At this restored 1816 mill you can take a self-guided tour and watch the 12-foot-round waterwheel power the 1,400-pound millstone. ⊠ *Caverns Rd. north of Rte. 7* ☎ *518/296–8448* ⊕ *www.cavernscreekgristmill.com* ☒ *$4* ⊙ *June–early Sept., daily 11–7; early Sept.–Oct. and May, weekends 11–7.*

☾ **Howe Caverns.** An elevator takes you down 156 feet to reach these caverns. The 80-minute guided tours lead you along paved walkways and include a ¼-mi boat ride on an underground lake. The temperature down under hovers just above 50°F all year, so dress appropriately. On Friday and Saturday evenings visitors (13 and older) can opt for a lantern-lighted tour; call ahead for a reservation. The grounds include a restaurant and a motel. ⊠ *255 Discovery Dr., off Exit 22 off I–88* ☎ *518/296–8900* ⊕ *www.howecaverns.com* ☒ *$18–$27* ⊙ *Apr.–Oct., daily 9–6; Nov.–Mar., daily 9–5.*

Iroquois Indian Museum. Displays of ancient and modern artworks, archaeological relics, and ever-changing cultural exhibits and events celebrate one of the mightiest American Indian confederacies of the Northeast. The museum, which sits on 45 park acres in a building designed to recall a longhouse, includes an area devoted to exhibits for children. ⊠ *Caverns Rd. north of Rte. 7* ☎ *518/296–8949* ⊕ *www.iroquoismuseum.org* ☒ *$8* ⊙ *July and Aug., Mon.–Sat. 10–5, Sun. noon–5; Apr.–June and Sept.–Dec., Tues.–Sat. 10–5, Sun. noon–5.*

Old Stone Fort Museum Complex. The site contains several 18th- and 19th-century buildings, including the 1772 church that served as a fort during its early years. A log stockade was erected in 1777, and the building came under attack by the British three years later. During the Civil War it was used as an armory. Converted to a museum in 1889, the interior serves as a museum within a museum, with hundreds of artifacts exhibited in cases that have changed little in the past century. ⊠ *145 Fort Rd., off Rte. 30, Schoharie* ☎ *518/295–7192* ⊕ *www.schohariehistory.net* ☒ *$5* ⊙ *May, June, Sept., and Oct., Tues.–Sat. 10–5, Sun. noon–5; July and Aug., Mon.–Sat. 10–5, Sun. noon–5.*

Secret Caverns. The cave was discovered in 1928 on a farm just outside Cobleskill. An hour-long guided tour takes you 85 feet down, via winding stairs, and features fossils, stalagmites and stalactites, natural domes, and a 100-foot-high waterfall. The cavern temperature is usually 50°F, so dress accordingly. ⊠ *Secret Caverns Rd., off Rte. 7* ☎ *518/296–8558* ⊕ *www.secretcaverns.com* ☒ *$16* ⊙ *May and Sept., daily 10–4:30; Apr. and Oct., daily 10–4; June–Aug., daily 9–6.*

WHERE TO EAT AND STAY

$$
STEAK
Fodor'sChoice
★

✕**Bull's Head Inn.** In the center of this college town, the Bull's Head Inn—in operation since 1802—is considered the grande dame of steak houses in these parts. The space is rustic and intimate, with picks, whips, yolks, and long rifles mounted on the walls. Below the restaurant

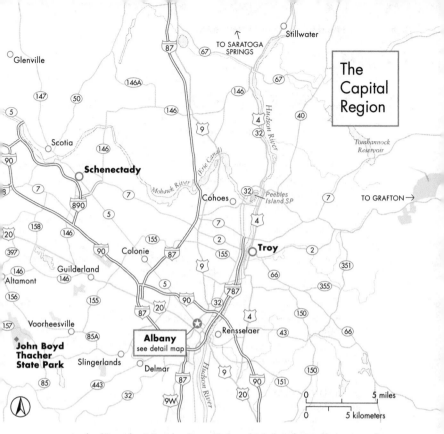

is the Timothy Murphy Brew Pub, which briefly made its own beer. ✉ *2 Park Pl., Cobleskill* ☎ *518/234–3591* ▤ *AE, MC, V* ⊗ *Closed Mon. No lunch Sat.*

$ 🏨 **Gables Bed & Breakfast.** Two graceful Victorian homes form this peaceful bed-and-breakfast. Most rooms have queen-size beds, and all are decorated in a period style of florals, lace, and wicker. Wireless Internet access is a bonus. **Pros:** period charm; beautiful views. **Cons:** modest breakfasts. ✉ *436 W. Main St., Cobleskill* ☎ *518/234–4467* ⊕ *www. nyinn.com* ➡ *4 rooms, 1 suite, 1 studio* ⚷ *In-room: kitchen (some), Internet. In-hotel: no-smoking rooms* ▤ *MC, V* ⦿ *CP.*

¢ 🏨 **Howe Caverns Motel.** Rooms at this single-level motel, on the grounds of Howe Caverns, have mountain and valley views. Choose between a queen, a king, or two double beds; family suites have four doubles. Interiors are basic, but some rooms have whirlpool tubs. The restaurant is open from July through Labor Day. **Pros:** quiet surroundings, budget-friendly rates. **Cons:** no breakfast. ✉ *255 Discovery Dr.* ☎ *518/296–8950* ⊕ *www.howecaverns.com* ➡ *21 rooms* ⚷ *In-room: refrigerator (some), Internet. In-hotel: restaurant, pool, no-smoking rooms* ▤ *AE, D, MC, V* ⦿ *CP.*

ALBANY

Since 1797 Albany has served as the capital of the state. You could say that the city, thanks to its role in state politics and to its location—about 150 mi north of New York City and roughly the same distance from Montréal—is in the thick of things. The state is the largest employer in the city (population 100,000), which helps to keep the economy fairly stable.

The heart of the state government is Empire State Plaza, where tens of thousands of people work. The city's most prominent architectural features are the towers that dominate the plaza's marble expanses. The imposing state capitol, on the north end of the plaza, looks across the mall to the classical New York State Museum. Other fine architectural specimens are easily found, like the Romanesque City Hall. In addition to the many public buildings here are historic residences, good restaurants, and interesting shops. To the west is Washington Park, which was designed by Frederick Law Olmsted and Calvert Vaux and is the site of many annual festivals and events. To the east of the plaza is the Corning Preserve, a lively waterfront park.

As the city grew more prosperous in the late 1800s, wealthy residents built homes in Mansion Hill, today a historic district south of the plaza. Although the district's historic structures suffered neglect for decades, recent years have seen a spate of renovation, fueled in part by federal grants. Adding prestige to the neighborhood is the governor's residence on Eagle Street.

GETTING HERE AND AROUND
Albany is a compact city that is easily negotiated on foot or by car. The downtown business area revolves around the state government and, thus, Empire State Plaza. The area is bounded by State, Jay, Swan, and Lark streets. Because of its nightlife, boutiques, and colorful characters, the stretch of Lark Street between Madison Avenue and State Street is often compared to New York City's Greenwich Village.

The capital region is served by Albany International Airport (ALB), as well as buses and trains. A loop of highways creates Albany's boundaries and makes traveling around the city quick and easy. Route 5, known as Central Avenue, cuts through the city from Interstate 787 to Interstate 87, but traffic lights and shopping draws can slow travel on this road. Downtown has ample parking in public lots, garages, and metered spaces.

VISITOR INFORMATION
Albany Convention and Visitors Bureau (⊠ *25 Quackenbush Sq., Albany* 🖾 *518/ 434–1217 or 800/258–3582* ⊕ *www.albany.org*).

TAKE A TOUR

Albany Aqua Ducks. From April through October, you can tour the city in a land-and-water vehicle. The 75-minute tour starts on dry ground, cruising the streets of Albany to historic sites. The U.S. Coast Guard–certified vessel then plunges into the Hudson River to give you another perspective of the city skyline. Tours start at the Albany Heritage Area Visitors Center and depart in the morning and early afternoon. ☎*518/462–3825* ⊕*www. albanyaquaducks.com* 🎫*$20.*

WHAT TO SEE

⑮ **Albany Heritage Area Visitors Center.** The center's museum gallery is a good place for an orientation. Displays trace the city's history and define its neighborhoods; some include cultural artifacts. The center, downtown, has basic visitor information and often serves as a starting point for guided tours. Within the visitor center is the **Henry Hudson Planetarium** (🎫*$3*), which presents various shows and lectures. The star-sighting program, an interactive show, is held the second Saturday of each month at 1 PM. ⊠*25 Quackenbush Sq.* ☎*518/434–0405* ⊕*www.albany.org* 🎫*Free* ☉ *Weekdays 9–4, weekends 10–4.*

⑪ **Albany Institute of History and Art.** The 1791 museum, the state's oldest, has annual rotating exhibits and an impressive permanent collection that includes Hudson River School paintings and an Egyptian mummy exhibit. Silver, furniture, and contemporary-art collections cover regional history dating from the 1500s. The building, which combines a modern expansion with the original 18th-century space, is interesting architecturally. ⊠*125 Washington Ave.* ☎*518/463–4478* ⊕*www. albanyinstitute.org* 🎫*$7* ☉ *Wed.–Sat. 10–5, Sun. noon–5.*

❻ **Cathedral of the Immaculate Conception.** The country's oldest neo-Gothic cathedral, finished in 1852, has an imposing redbrick exterior with tall twin spires. Inside you find a high vaulted ceiling, stained-glass windows, and statues. ⊠*Madison Ave. and Eagle St.* ☎*518/463–4447* ⊕*www.cathedralic.com.*

⑬ **City Hall.** American architect Henry Hobson Richardson, who also developed the state's capitol, designed this 1881 Romanesque revival–style structure. A 49-bell carillon, one of about 200 in the country, was added in 1927. ⊠*24 Eagle St.* ☎*518/434–5075* ⊕*www.albanyny.org.*

⑭ **Corning Preserve.** The Hudson River Way Pedestrian Bridge leads to this expansive green space along the Hudson River. A 5.3-mi trail, which can be used for biking and hiking, snakes through the preserve. At the north end are a public boat launch and a restaurant on a barge. June through August, the 800-seat amphitheater hosts musicians. ⊠*Off Maiden La., near Broadway* ☎No phone 🎫*Free.*

❽ **Corning Tower.** An elevator whisks you up 589 feet to the 42nd-floor observation deck of this building, the tallest structure in the state outside New York City. The views on a clear day include the Berkshire, Catskill, and Adirondack mountains. To get to the deck, you first must present a photo ID at the plaza-level security desk. ⊠*Empire State Plaza, off Madison Ave. near Eagle St.* ☎*518/474–2418* 🎫*Free* ☉ *Daily 10–4.*

❶ **Five Rivers Environmental Center.** Outdoor education programs, ¼- to 2-mi hiking and skiing trails, a wildlife garden, and an exhibit center with animals are at this 400-acre preserve 10 mi southwest of downtown. You can

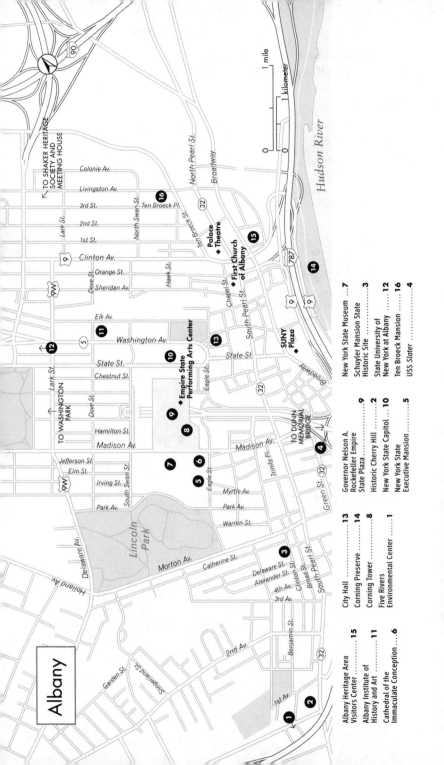

Albany

Albany Heritage Area
Visitors Center **15**
Albany Institute of
History and Art **11**
Cathedral of the
Immaculate Conception **6**

TO SHAKER HERITAGE
SOCIETY AND
MEETING HOUSE

Colonie Av.
Livingston Av.
3rd St.
2nd St.
1st St.
Clinton Av.
Orange St.
Sheridan Av.
Elk Av.
Washington Av.
State St.
Chestnut St.

Lark St.
North Swan St.
Dove St.
Hawk St.

Palace
Theatre

First Church
of Albany

Empire State
Performing Arts Center

TO WASHINGTON
PARK

Lincoln Park

Hamilton St.
Madison Av.
Jefferson St.
Elm St.
Irving St.
Park Av.

Myrtle Av.
Park Av.
Warren St.

Delaware Av.
Holland Av.

Morton Av.
Catherine St.

Delaware St.
Alexander St.
Clinton St.
Broad St.
South Pearl St.
4th Av.
3rd Av.
2nd Av.
1st Av.

Benjamin St.
Sutherland St.
Garden St.

Ten Broeck Pl.

North Pearl St.
Broadway

State St.

SUNY
Plaza

TO DUNN
MEMORIAL
BRIDGE

Madison Av.
Trinity Pl.
Green St.

Hudson River

1 mile
1 kilometer
0 / 0

City Hall **13**
Corning Preserve **14**
Corning Tower **8**
Five Rivers
Environmental Center **1**

Governor Nelson A.
Rockefeller Empire
State Plaza **9**
Historic Cherry Hill **2**
New York State Capitol ...**10**
New York State
Executive Mansion..........**5**

New York State Museum ...**7**
Schuyler Mansion State
Historic Site **3**
State University of
New York at Albany **12**
Ten Broeck Mansion **16**
USS Slater **4**

picnic on the grounds. ✉ *56 Game Farm Rd., Delmar* ☎ *518/475–0291* ⊕ *www.dec.ny.gov/education/1835.html* ✉ *Free* ⊙ *Grounds daily dawn–dusk; visitor center Mon.–Sat. 9–4:30, Sun. 1–4:30.*

⑨ Governor Nelson A. Rockefeller Empire State Plaza.
Fodor'sChoice
★ The ¼-mi-long, 98-acre concourse includes modern art and sculpture, the New York State Museum, the State Library, the elliptical performing-arts center, and the New York State Vietnam Memorial. At the center of the plaza is a rectangular reflecting pool. The capitol crowns the plaza's north end. On weekdays in July and August you can take a free hour-long tour, which examines the plaza's history, architecture, monuments, and artworks. Tours start at 11 and 1 at the concourse-level visitor center. ✉ *Bordered by Madison Ave. and State, Eagle, and Swan Sts.* ☎ *518/474–2418* ⊕ *www.ogs.state.ny.us* ✉ *Free* ⊙ *July and Aug., tours weekdays 11 and 1.*

② Historic Cherry Hill. The 1787 Georgian house was the home of Philip Van Rensselaer, one of the region's original Dutch settlers. Guided tours focus on Catherine Putnam, Rensselaer's niece, who lived in the house during the Civil War and World Wars I and II. The collection of family memorabilia encompasses more than 20,000 objects, including furniture, artworks, kitchen items, and pottery pieces; 3,000 photographs; and extensive documents and records. To visit the house you must take the tour, which lasts about an hour and starts on the hour. Note that Cherry Hill is closed currently for restoration. ✉ *523½ S. Pearl St.* ☎ *518/434–4791* ⊕ *www.historiccherryhill.org.*

⑩ New York State Capitol.
Fodor'sChoice
★ It took more than 30 years to complete this grand building (1867–99), which incorporates elaborate carvings, interesting architectural elements, and eclectic styles. The 45-minute guided tour highlights the ornate Great Western Staircase (aka the Million Dollar Staircase)—which took 13 years and 600 stone carvers to complete—and, right over it, a 3,000-square-foot skylight that had been covered from World War II until 2002. Amid the carved faces adorning the staircase pillars are several famous visages. You can visit the legislative chambers and, when open, the governor's ceremonial offices. Tours begin at the visitor center on the concourse level of Empire State Plaza. ✉ *Washington Ave. and State St.* ☎ *518/474–2418* ⊕ *www.ogs.state.ny.us* ✉ *Free* ⊙ *Tours weekdays 10, noon, 2, and 3; weekends 11, 1, and 3.*

SUMMERTIME SHOWS

Summer is the season for music and entertainment, from weekend-long jazz festivals to dance performances. Many events—such as the Live at Five concert series at the Corning Preserve, in Albany—are free. Both the New York City Ballet and the Philadelphia Orchestra hold summer residencies at the Saratoga Performing Arts Center, a cultural gem that hosts pop, rock, and jazz concerts as well. Opera and chamber-music festivals are held at the Spa Little Theatre, part of Saratoga Spa State Park. Parks in Schenectady and nearby Scotia also host outdoor concerts.

5

5 **New York State Executive Mansion.** Wraparound porches, a balconied gable, and turrets provide evidence of the 1856 building's progression of architectural phases, from Italianate to Second Empire and finally Queen Anne. The mansion has served as the official residence of New York's governors since 1875. To see the interior, you must take one of the guided tours, which last about an hour; because visiting times are so limited, reserve at least two weeks in advance. ⊠ *138 Eagle St.* ☎ *518/473–7521* ⊕ *www.ogs.state.ny.us* ☒ *Free* ⊙ *Tours Sept.–June, Thurs. noon, 1, and 2.*

7 **New York State Museum.** The museum explores the state's history, geog-
★ raphy, nature, and art; exhibits include a re-created Iroquois village, a display about New York birds, and a working 1916 carousel (with horses from the 1890s). A display about the September 11 terrorist attacks documents, through photographs and artifacts, rescue efforts at the World Trade Center. In February the museum hosts the regional flower show, "New York in Bloom." ⊠ *Empire State Plaza, Cultural Education Center, Madison Ave.* ☎ *518/474–5877* ⊕ *www.nysm.nysed. gov* ☒ *$2 suggested donation* ⊙ *Daily 9:30–5.*

8 **Schuyler Mansion State Historic Site.** Philip Schuyler, a Revolutionary War general, was the original owner of this 1763 Georgian mansion. George Washington and Benjamin Franklin were among the notable figures who visited the house. Tours of the national historic landmark (the only way to see the interior) feature original family furnishings, arti-facts, and paintings. ⊠ *32 Catherine St.* ☎ *518/434–0834* ⊕ *nysparks. state.ny.us* ☒ *$4* ⊙ *Mid-Apr.–Oct., Wed.–Sat. 11–5; Nov.–mid-Apr., by appointment.*

12 **State University of New York at Albany.** About 18,000 students are enrolled at this state university, established in 1844. The quaint downtown cam-pus, built in 1909, was modeled after the University of Virginia. The 1971 **uptown campus** is dominated by stark, massive arches. A large reflecting pool lies at the center of a quadrangle formed by four high-rise dorms and classrooms. The free **University Art Museum** (⊠ *1400 Washington Ave.* ☎ *518/442–4035*) has three galleries with frequently rotating contemporary-art exhibits. The museum's permanent collec-tion includes works by Richard Diebenkorn, Donald Judd, Ellsworth Kelly, and Robert Rauschenberg. ⊠ *Downtown campus, 135 Western Ave.* ☎ *518/442–5200* ☒ *Uptown campus, 1400 Washington Ave.* ☎ *518/442–3300* ⊕ *www.albany.edu.*

16 **Ten Broeck Mansion.** Family portraits and period furnishings fill this 1798 Greek Revival home built for General Abraham Ten Broeck, a former Albany mayor. The tour takes you through the house and well-kept gardens. ⊠ *9 Ten Broeck Pl.* ☎ *518/436–9826* ☒ *$4* ⊙ *Tours May– Dec., Thurs. and Fri. 10–5, weekends 1–4.*

4 **USS *Slater*.** This warship is the last of 565 destroyers used through-out World War II and the Cold War. Tours show the ship's restored armaments, crew and officers' quarters, radio room, and pilot house. ⊠ *Quay and Broadway* ☎ *518/431–1943* ⊕ *www.ussslater.org* ☒ *$7* ⊙ *Apr.–Nov., Wed.–Sun. 10–4.*

OFF THE BEATEN PATH

Shaker Heritage Society and Meeting House. Through exhibits and tours, the preservation group details the history of the Shaker movement. The site was home to the first Shaker settlement in the United States; it started in 1776 with about a dozen members and grew to about 350 members at its peak, in the mid-1900s. The 1848 meetinghouse, a clapboard structure with a tin roof, was the third meetinghouse built here. Guided tours ($3; Saturday 11:30 and 1:30) are available June through October. ⊠ *875 Watervliet Shaker Rd., Colonie* ☎ *51/456–7890* ⊕ *www.shakerheritage.org* ⊡ *Free* ☉ *Feb.–Oct., Tues.–Sat. 9:30–4; Nov. and Dec., Mon.–Sat. 10–4.*

NIGHTLIFE AND THE ARTS

NIGHTLIFE

The Roaring Twenties theme at **Big House Brewing** (⊠ *90 N. Pearl St.* ☎ *518/445–2739)* makes this former warehouse a three-story party palace. The microbrewery has a good number of beers on tap. The first floor has a game room. Live entertainment on weekends makes conversation difficult, but upstairs levels are more sedate. In good weather you can dine outside. The high-energy **Jillian's** (⊠ *59 N. Pearl St.* ☎ *518/432–1997*) is a three-story club inside a downtown entertainment complex. You can watch sports on large televisions, play interactive video games, or shoot pool at one of the 12 tables. Take a turn on the dance floor in the Groove Shack, the restaurant's nightclub; or grab a burger, sandwich, or slice of pizza. At **Sneaky Pete's** (⊠ *711 Central Ave.* ☎ *518/489–0000*), the largest dance club in Albany, DJs start spinning at 10 PM Wednesday through Saturday.

THE ARTS

★ The **Capital Repertory Theatre** (⊠ *111 N. Pearl St.* ☎ *518/445–7469* ⊕ *www.capitalrep.org*) is an intimate space for musicals, comedies, and dramas. Though balanced on a platform that reaches six stories underground, the futuristic **Empire State Performing Arts Center** (⊠ *Empire State Plaza, near Eagle St.* ☎ *518/473–1845* ⊕ *www.theegg.org*), known as the Egg, appears to float above the plaza like a UFO. Shows here include acts by big-name artists, touring pop and folk musicians, comedy routines, and modern dance performances. The spectacular **Palace Theatre** (⊠ *19 Clinton Ave.* ☎ *518/465–3334* ⊕ *palacealbany.com*), a restored movie-and-vaudeville house, hosts pop concerts and touring Broadway shows. It's the home of the **Albany Symphony Orchestra.** National music acts, the circus, and wrestling all make stops at the 16,000-seat **Times Union Center** (⊠ *51 S. Pearl St.* ☎ *518/487–2000* ⊕ *www.pepsiarena.com*).

FESTIVALS AND FAIRS

Pipe bands, highland dance performances, and traditional contests are the highlights of the annual **Capital District Scottish Games** (⊠ *Altamont Fair Grounds, Rte. 146, Altamont* ☎ *518/438–4297 or 518/785–0507* ⊕ *www.scotgames.com*), held on the Saturday and Sunday of Labor Day weekend. During the daylong, early September street festival **Larkfest** (⊠ *Lark St. between Madison and Washington Aves.* ☎ *518/434–3861* ⊕ *www.larkstreet.org*), more than 100 crafts and food booths line the streets. A separate area for kids has games and rides. Local

5

bands perform, in addition to area dancers and magicians. Hundreds of thousands of tulips are at their peak during the **Tulip Festival** (⊠ *Washington Park, between State St., Madison Ave., Lake Ave., and Willett St.* ☎*518/434–2032* ⊕*www.albanyevents.org*), a three-day weekend festival in mid-May celebrating Albany's Dutch heritage. Traditions include scrubbing the streets and crowning a Tulip Queen. On Saturday and Sunday, Washington Park has music, concerts, and food vendors.

WHERE TO EAT

$$$ ╳**Café Capriccio.** A favorite of local politicos, this intimate, wood-paneled eatery serves northern Italian and Mediterranean food. The breads and pastas are made on-site, and you can't miss with the risotto of the day. ⊠*49 Grand St.* ☎*518/465–0439* ▤*AE, D, MC, V* ⊗*No lunch*.

ITALIAN

$$$ ╳**Jack's Oyster House.** For great seafood, this Albany establishment with tiled floors, white tablecloths, dark wood, and polite service is the place to go. Two menus are offered at dinner: one has dishes from 1913, the year Jack's opened, and the other lists more-contemporary preparations. Oysters, steak, and prime rib are regular features. Signature dishes from the 1913 menu include calves' liver sautéed with bacon, and Jack's Seafood Grille, which contains scallops, shrimp, and salmon. ⊠*42 State St.* ☎*518/465–8854* ▤*AE, D, DC, MC, V.*

CONTINENTAL

$$ ╳**Lombardo's.** Young professionals, important legislators, and out-of-towners flock here to eat northern and southern Italian fare in a dining room where casual clothes mix easily with jackets and ties. Lombardo's is known for veal, pasta, and seafood dishes, and has some of the best waiters in the region. The lengthy menu manages to be a mix of sophistication and comfort food. The shrimp wrapped in savory prosciutto and silky mozzarella and baked in tomatoes is a winner. ⊠*121 Madison Ave.* ☎*518/462–9180* ▤*MC, V* ⊗*Closed Sun. No lunch Sat.*

ITALIAN

$$$$ ╳**McGuire's.** Whether you're looking for drinks or an interesting meal, this always-crowded spot is the place to see and be seen in Albany. The innovative chef has put together a menu that ranges from Kobe steaks to Peking duck breast to tandoori pork tenderloin. Appetizers include yellowfin tuna and fig salad. ⊠*353 State St.* ☎*518/463–2100* ▤*AE, D, MC, V* ⊗*No lunch.*

ECLECTIC

¢ ╳**Miss Albany Diner.** The Albany landmark looks just as it did before World War II. The menu has a selection of stick-to-your ribs favorites, such as fried eggs, pancakes, and one-third-pound hamburgers. Daily blue-plate specials might include turkey and pot roast. The owners pay homage to Rhode Island—where diners originated—with quahog (clam) chowder and chocolate and coffee egg creams. ⊠*893 Broadway* ☎*518/465–9148* ▤*No credit cards* ⊗*No dinner.*

AMERICAN

$$$ ╳**Yono's.** This intimate restaurant draws mostly business executives who come to savor curry and coconut-milk dishes. The menu, a blend of Indonesian and Continental fare, includes winners such as pistachio-crusted chicken breast in Madeira sauce and rack of lamb. If you want an experience to savor and linger over, order the Rijstaffel, a five-course Indonesian-style meal that includes appetizer, soup, salad, entrées, and condiments. For dessert consider the Kentucky bourbon nut pie. The

ECLECTIC
Fodor'sChoice
★

wine list, covering more than 700 bottles, has been lauded by *Wine Spectator.* ⊠*25 Chapel St.* ☎*518/436–7747* ▭*AE, D, DC, MC, V* ☉*Closed Sun. No lunch.*

WHERE TO STAY

$ 🏨**Desmond Hotel & Conference Center.** Brick courtyards, hand-painted wooden signs, Early American furniture, and staff in 18th-century attire give this large hotel the air of a colonial village with modern conveniences. Some rooms have king-size canopy beds; all have large bathrooms with phones. The complex includes a casual all-day eatery (many patrons favor the cheese blintzes for breakfast); a fine dinner-only restaurant; and a lounge with cushy upholstery seats. **Pros:** comfortable beds; close to airport. **Cons:** breakfast not included. ⊠*660 Albany Shaker Rd., Colonie* ☎*518/869–8100* ⊕*www.desmondhotels.com* ⬥*323 rooms, 18 suites* ♿*In-room: refrigerator (some), Internet. In-hotel: 2 restaurants, pools, gym, no-smoking rooms* ▭*AE, D, DC, MC, V.*

$ 🏨**Mansion Hill Inn.** The inn in the heart of downtown was built in 1861 around a central courtyard. Guest rooms are large and uncluttered, with reproduction antiques and tasteful watercolor prints. Another draw is the dozen-table storefront restaurant, which serves imaginative new American cuisine. Entrées include grilled duck breast and sesame-crusted salmon fillet with sweet soy sauce. **Pros:** central location; period charm; great restaurant. **Cons:** rooms need an update. ⊠*115 Philip St.* ☎*518/465–2038 or 888/299–0455* ⊕*www.mansionhill.com* ⬥*8 rooms* ♿ *In-room: safe (some), refrigerator (some), Internet, Wi-Fi. In-hotel: restaurant, laundry facilities, laundry service, no-smoking rooms* ▭*AE, D, DC, MC, V* ⦿*BP.*

$ 🏨**Morgan State House.** Inside the **Morgan State House,** a late-19th-century town house on Washington Park, rich cherry wainscoting complements high ceilings, hand-glazed walls, and fireplaces. Although the house is in the center of town, the views are of either the park or the inn's well-tended flower beds. Each room is different—yours might have a fireplace, a claw-foot tub, exposed brick walls, a skylight, or a reading area—but the overall look is refined. Studios are available three doors away at the **Washington Park State House,** a sibling property with an elevator. Breakfast is served in the town house. **Pros:** gorgeous building; plenty of charm; YMCA pass included in rate. **Cons:** steps to climb. ⊠*393 State St.* ☎*518/427–6063 or 888/427–6063* ⊕*www.statehouse. com* ⬥*4 rooms, 1 suite, 9 studios* ♿*In-room: kitchen (some), Wi-Fi. In-hotel: laundry service, no kids under 16, no-smoking rooms* ▭*AE, D, DC, MC, V* ⦿*BP.*

Fodor'sChoice ★

$ 🏨**State Street Mansion.** The intimate, neoclassical town home is near the state capitol, museums and other attractions, and restaurants. Rooms have either one king bed, one or two queens, or one or two doubles; some have working fireplaces. Guest-room furnishings include large flat-screen televisions. Breakfast is served in a parlorlike space with a fireplace and a European feel. **Pros:** lots of charm; looks great after recent renovation. **Cons:** breakfast is a bit meager. ⊠*281 State St.* ☎*518/462–6780* ⊕*www.statestreetmansion.com* ⬥*12 rooms*

⌂ *In-room: refrigerator (some), Wi-Fi. In-hotel: laundry service* ⊟*AE, MC, V* ⧀ *CP.*

NORTH OF THE CAPITAL

Since the late 1980s, the spa-resort city of Saratoga Springs has served as a somewhat distant suburb for the tri-city area of Albany, Schenectady, and Troy, and many of its residents make the 25-mi commute south to go to work. Beyond Saratoga Springs are several American Revolution sites. The Revolution's Battle of Saratoga, actually fought in nearby Stillwater, halted the British invasion from Canada and turned the war in the rebels' favor, thus securing the area a place in U.S. history books.

SARATOGA SPRINGS

25 mi north of Albany.

Mineral-water springs first brought American Indians and, later, American settlers to this area just south of the Adirondack foothills. Gideon Putnam opened the first inn and commercial bathhouse here in 1791, to cater to early health seekers eager to drink from and bathe in the supposedly restorative waters. By the 1870s, Victorian society had turned Saratoga Springs into one of the country's principal vacation resorts, and the city became known as the "Queen of Spas."

In 1909, after the commercial exploitation of the mineral springs diminished their flow and even dried up some wells, New York State developed the Spa State Reservation (now called Saratoga Spa State Park) to protect against excessive pumping. Today you may sample the naturally carbonated waters of more than a dozen active springs, which were created by complex geological conditions centuries ago. A "tasting tour" brochure (available from the Saratoga Visitor Center) guides you to the springs in the Congress Park and High Rock Park areas, which are downtown, and in Saratoga Spa State Park, at the south end of the city. The springs differ, offering water rich in iron or sulfur or with minute quantities of radon gas. Geysers, or spouters, spray water out of a couple of springs.

By the 1890s the city had become a horse-racing hot spot, with the Travers Stakes a highlight of the racing season. These days, Thoroughbred racing has surpassed the springs as a draw, and the Travers, first run in 1864, remains a high point.

GETTING HERE AND AROUND
Most Saratoga sites are within walking or cycling distance of downtown, and the city has a trolley that runs along Broadway from Skidmore College to the Saratoga Performing Arts Center. Rides are $1.

VISITOR INFORMATION
Saratoga Visitor Center (⊠ *297 Broadway, Saratoga Springs* ☎ *518/587–3241* ⊕ *www.saratoga.org).*

WHAT TO SEE

Children's Museum of Saratoga. At this museum with hands-on exhibits geared for kids three to nine years old, youngsters may slide down a fire pole to a pretend fire truck or imagine they're slinging hash in a model diner. ⊠*69 Caroline St.* ☎*518/584–5540* ⊕*www.childrensmuseumat saratoga.org* ⊠*$6* ⊙*July–Labor Day, Mon.–Sat. 9:30–4:30; rest of yr, Tues.–Sat. 9:30–4:30, Sun. noon–4:30.*

Congress Park. Italian gardens, ponds, fountains, and statuary punctuate wide lawns at this park in the heart of the city. Fifty cents buys you a ride on a **carousel** with 28 horses that were carved and painted about a century ago. Crowds gather outside the Italianate Canfield Casino, a former gambling hall within the park, to watch the tuxedo set enter one of the August balls. The 1870s building also houses the **Historical Society Museum of Saratoga Springs** (☎*518/584–6920* ⊠*$5*), where exhibits of Victorian furnishings, paintings, original gambling paraphernalia, and historic documents bring the city's history alive. From Memorial Day weekend through Labor Day, the museum is open Monday through Saturday 10–4 and Sunday 1–4; the rest of the year it's closed Monday and Tuesday. ⊠*Broadway between Circular and Spring Sts.* ⊠*Free.*

Crystal Spa. The spa taps into water from the **Rosemary Spring,** on property it shares with the Grand Union Motel. The original motel owner built a gazebo and then drilled water underneath (in 1964) to honor his wife, who had just delivered their 12th child. The family-run, cash-only business offers everything from an aromatherapy sauna for $15 to a package of several treatments for $175. ⊠*120 S. Broadway* ☎*518/584–2556* ⊕*www.thecrystalspa.com* ⊙*Sept.–June, Fri.–Tues. 8:30–4:30; July, Thurs.–Tues. 8:30–4:30; Aug., daily 8:30–5:30.*

National Museum of Racing and Hall of Fame. Exhibits, including memorabilia from famed horse Seabiscuit, relate the story of Thoroughbred racing in the United States. In the Hall of Fame, video clips of races bring to life the horses and jockeys enshrined here. For an additional fee you may take a tour of the training track. ⊠*191 Union Ave.* ☎*518/584–0400* ⊕*www.racingmuseum.org* ⊠*$7* ⊙*Mon.–Sat. 10–4:30, Sun. noon–4:30.*

Saratoga Automobile Museum. America's love affair with the car is celebrated in this museum in a former bottling plant in Saratoga Spa State Park. Included are three galleries and an orientation theater. Changing exhibits display classic and racing cars. ⊠*110 Ave. of the Pines* ☎*518/587–1935* ⊕ *www.saratogaautomuseum.com* ⊠ *$8* ⊙*May–early Nov., daily 10–5; early Nov.–Apr., Tues.–Sun. 10–5.*

Saratoga Harness Racing Museum and Hall of Fame. The museum, on the grounds of Saratoga Raceway, displays antique horseshoes, high-wheeled sulkies (the two-wheeled vehicles used for harness racing), and horse-related artwork. ⊠*352 Jefferson St.* ☎*518/587–4210* ⊕*www.saratogaraceway.com* ✑*Free* ⊙*July and Aug., Tues.–Sat. 10–4; Sept.–June, Thurs.–Sat. 10–4.*

Saratoga National Historical Park/Battlefield. The Battle of Saratoga, fought 12 mi southeast of Saratoga Springs at this site in 1777, is recognized as the turning point in the American Revolution. The visitor center at the Route 32 entrance provides historic information and an orientation to the park, which encompasses the battlefield and two sites in the nearby villages of Schuylerville and Victory. Ten stops along a 9½-mi tour road through the battlefield explain the battle and its significance. Reenactments and other living-history programs are scheduled throughout the summer. The road is popular with bicyclists in warm-weather months and, when closed to traffic in winter, with cross-country skiers. The **John Neilson House,** the only structure standing on the battlefield that was here in the time of the Battle of Saratoga, might have served as headquarters for Benedict Arnold.

The 155-foot **Saratoga Monument** (⊠*53 Burgoyne St., Victory*) commemorates the British surrender on October 17, 1777. The obelisk was built between 1877 and 1883, and has three niches commemorating generals Philip Schuyler and Horatio Gates, and Colonel Daniel Morgan. The fourth niche, where a statue of Benedict Arnold would have gone, has been left empty deliberately and cannot be entered. The monument is open from late May to Labor Day, Wednesday through Friday 9:30–4:30. The **General Philip Schuyler House** (⊠*1072 U.S. 4, Schuylerville*) was the general's country home before its destruction by the British in 1777. Schuyler and his soldiers rebuilt it in 29 days. The house includes some original furnishings. It's open from late May through Labor Day, Wednesday through Friday 9:30–4:30; tours are given every half hour. ⊠*Visitor center, 648 Rte. 32, Stillwater* ☎*518/664–9821 Ext. 224* ⊕*www.nps.gov/sara* ✑*Free* ⊙*Visitor center daily 9–5; tour road Apr.–mid-Nov., daily dawn–dusk.*

Saratoga Spa State Park. Developed for the study and therapeutic use of the mineral springs here, this 2,200-acre park is now listed on the National Historic Register of Historic Places. It is home to the Gideon Putnam Resort & Spa, the Saratoga Performing Arts Center, the Lincoln and Roosevelt baths, the Spa Little Theatre, and eight active springs. Recreational facilities include walking trails, 36 holes of golf, two pools, clay and asphalt tennis courts, picnic facilities, an ice-skating rink, and 12 mi of cross-country skiing trails. ⊠*S. Broadway and Rte. 50* ☎*518/584–2535* ⊕*nysparks.state.ny.us* ✑*Parking $6* ⊙*Memorial Day–Columbus Day daily 8 AM–dusk; limited access in winter.*

Yaddo. Artists, writers, and musicians from all over the United States come to this highly regarded artists' colony to work. The estate was built in 1899 by philanthropist Spencer Trask as a gift to his wife, Katrina. Although you can't visit the house, you can tour the grounds, which include a formal rose garden with fountains and an informal rock garden. ⊠ *Union Ave.* ☎*518/584–0746* ⊕*www.yaddo.org* ✉*Grounds free, tours $5* ☉*Daily dawn–dusk.*

SPORTS AND THE OUTDOORS

GOLF At the **Saratoga National Golf Club** (⊠*458 Union Ave.* ☎*518/583–4653* ⊕*golfsaratoga.com*), the 2½-story Victorian-style clubhouse and mile-long access road edged with ponds and stone walls gives the impression of an exclusive private club. But the 18-hole course, built on 400 acres of hills and wetlands in the style of the 1920s and '30s, is open to anyone willing to pay greens fees that range from $120 to $185. **Saratoga Spa Golf** (⊠*Saratoga Spa State Park, 60 Roosevelt Dr.* ☎*518/584–2008* ⊕*www.saratogaspagolf.com*), a public 18-hole course in Saratoga Spa State Park, has a championship layout. Weekend greens fees of $25 make it a good value.

HORSE RACING Top jockeys compete for six weeks (starting in late July) each year at the **Saratoga Race Course** (⊠*262 Union Ave.* ☎*518/584–6200* ⊕*www. nyra.com*), the nation's oldest Thoroughbred track. Breakfast at the track has become a tradition, with a buffet meal served 7–9:30, while the horses go through their morning workouts. You also can bring your own breakfast and sit in the stands for the free show. Afterward, get a behind-the-scenes look at the track with a free tram tour of the backstretch. The action at the **Saratoga Raceway** (⊠*Nelson Ave.* ☎*518/584–2110* ⊕*www.saratogaraceway.com*) is in the form of harness racing, and it's free and offered year-round.

WATER SPORTS You may fish, rent boats from one of several marinas, learn to water-ski, or just watch weekend sailboat races on the 8½-mi-long, 1½-mi-wide **Saratoga Lake. Brown's Beach** (⊠*712 Rte. 9P* ☎*518/587–8280*), the only public beach on Saratoga Lake, is open June through Labor Day ($6). It's about 7 mi east of downtown Saratoga Springs.

SHOPPING

Chain stores have been encroaching on the small clothing boutiques and gift shops that make wandering down Broadway and its side streets so interesting, but the majority of storefronts are still unique to the city.

Out-of-print books, first editions, and antique prints are the specialties at **Lyrical Ballad Bookstore** (⊠*7–9 Phila St.* ☎*518/584–8779*). The three covered pavilions at the **Saratoga Farmer's Market** (⊠*High Rock Park, High Rock Ave., off Lake Ave.* ☎*No phone*) are a social gathering spot on Wednesday 3–6 and Saturday 9–1, from early May to mid-December. There's a good variety of produce, poultry, and meats from area farms, baked goods, and jams from local berries. Although **Soave Faire** (⊠*449 Broadway* ☎*518/587–8448*) specializes in framing and art and office supplies, it's also the place to buy any type of hat you might want to wear to the track or a picnic on the polo grounds.

NIGHTLIFE AND THE ARTS

NIGHTLIFE Recognized as the country's oldest folk-music venue, **Caffè Lena** (⊠*47 Phila St.* ☎*518/583–0022* ⊕*www.caffelena.com*) opened in 1960 and hosted Bob Dylan and Arlo Guthrie early in their careers. The tradition continues at this upstairs coffeehouse, thanks to staff members as well as volunteers who together work the shows, a mix of well-known musicians and newcomers.

Live jazz comes to the 40-seat **9 Maple Ave** (⊠ *9 Maple Ave.* ☎ *518/583–2582* ⊕ *www.9maplavenue.com*) every Friday and Saturday evening. The centerpiece of the hand-built mahogany bar is a porcelain tap head thrown by potter Regis Brodie. The club claims to offer the largest selection of single-malt Scotches in New York State.

THE ARTS **Saratoga County Arts Council.** Changing exhibits in this 2,000-square-foot art gallery and theater-performance space showcase works by local as well as nationally known artists. At the theater here the **Saratoga Film Forum** shows mostly art-house movies (tickets $6) Thursday and Friday nights in fall, winter, and spring. ⊠ *320 Broadway* ☎ *518/584–4132* ⊕ *www.saratoga-arts.org* ☜ *Free* ☉ *Weekdays 9–5, Sat. 11–5.* The **Saratoga Performing Arts Center** (*SPAC* ⊠ *Saratoga Spa State Park, 108 Ave. of the Pines, between U.S. 9 and Rte. 50* ☎ *518/587–3330* ⊕ *www.spac. org*) is the summer home of the New York City Ballet and the Philadelphia Orchestra. The open-air venue, with both assigned amphitheater seats and lawn seating, also hosts concerts by big-name pop acts.

FESTIVALS Some of the hottest jazz musicians stop at the **Freihofer's Jazz Festival**
Fodor'sChoice (⊠ *Saratoga Performing Arts Center, 108 Ave. of the Pines, between*
★ *U.S. 9 and Rte. 50* ☎ *518/587–3330* ⊕ *www.spac.org*) in June for two days of music to kick off summer. Free pre-opera talks provide some background on the operas performed at the **Lake George Opera Festival** (⊠ *Spa Little Theatre, 19 Roosevelt Dr., off Ave. of the Pines* ☎ *518/587–3330* ⊕ *www.lakegeorgeopera.org*), which runs for two weeks at the start of summer. The **Saratoga Chamber Music Festival** (⊠ *Spa Little Theatre, 19 Roosevelt Dr., off Ave. of the Pines* ☎ *518/587–3330* ⊕ *www.spac.org*), a celebration of music written for ensemble groups, is offered for several days through the Saratoga Performing Arts Center but presented at the more intimate Spa Little Theatre, next door.

WHERE TO EAT

$$$$ ✗ **Chez Sophie Bistro.** The second generation of owners has updated the
FRENCH classic French food served at this gleaming 1950s diner. This is no casual eatery: inside are two dining rooms with cloth-covered tables and an abundance of artwork. The food on the ever-changing menu is just as refined, such as the pumpkin soup or the roasted half rack of New Zealand lamb in wine sauce. A $35 three-course "pink plate special" dinner includes soup or salad, entrée, and cheese or dessert. The restaurant is 4½ mi south of Saratoga Springs. ⊠ *2853 U.S. 9, Malta* ☎ *518/583–3538* ⊟ *AE, DC, MC, V.*

¢ ✗ **Esperanto.** The menu of this tiny basement eatery offers a smattering
ECLECTIC of inexpensive dishes from Thailand, Mexico, England, Italy, and the
★ Middle East. There's counter service only and just a few tables. Top a quick chimichanga with fresh fixings from the salsa bar. ⊠ *6½ Caroline St.* ☎ *518/587–4236* ⊟ *AE, D, DC, MC, V.*

$$ ✗ **Hattie's.** Since 1938 this casual restaurant has been serving such South-
SOUTHERN ern favorites as fried chicken, ribs, pork chops, and jambalaya—a warm

welcome to those born south of the Mason-Dixon. Meals include home-made biscuits and corn bread and a choice of sides, including macaroni and cheese and sweet potatoes. In nice weather you can eat on the courtyard patio. Inside, tables—in checkered cloths—crowd together; overhead fans and a banging screen door keep the air circulating. The place does not take reservations in July and August; you just show up and wait. ⊠ *45 Phila St.* 🕾 *518/584–4790* ⊟ *AE, MC, V* ⊗ *Closed Tues. No lunch.*

$
BARBECUE

✕**PJ's Saratoga Style Bar-B-Q.** You can smell the smoke pit for miles before you pass this '50s-style drive-in. Seating at this seasonal local favorite just south of Spa State Park on U.S. 9 is either under a roof shared with the kitchen and order counter or at outdoor picnic tables; a small section has table service. Chicken, ribs, and beef brisket are the specialties, but you can come just to have ice cream, listen to the DJ spinning oldies, and gaze at the classic cars that congregate in the lot on Saturday night. ⊠ *1 Kaydeross Ave. W at S. Broadway* 🕾 *518/583–2445* ⊟ *AE, MC, V* ⊗ *Closed mid-Sept.–Easter.*

$$$$
ECLECTIC

✕**Prime at Saratoga National.** With high ceilings, draped tables, and mahogany-stained paneling, this restaurant in the Saratoga National Golf Club's Victorian-style clubhouse exudes quiet elegance. The food lives up to the decor. The menu might include Russian caviar, Australian rack of lamb, or seared ahi tuna. A lounge with a granite-and-wood bar and an outdoor terrace are more-casual dining options. ⊠ *458 Union Ave.* 🕾 *518/583–4653* ⊟ *AE, MC, V* ⊗ *Closed Mon. and Tues.*

$
CAFÉS

✕**Ravenous.** Savory and dessert crepes are the focus at this small eatery furnished with plain wooden tables and chairs. Side orders of Belgian-style frites (fries) come in paper cones sized for an individual or a table of diners, and may include several kinds of dipping sauce. The Mamma Mia crepe wraps up Italian sausage with sweet and spicy peppers—a ubiquitous ingredient in upstate. ⊠ *21 Phila St.* 🕾 *518/581–0560* ⚐ *Reservations not accepted* ⊟ *MC* ⊗ *Closed Mon. and Tues. mid-Oct.–early Apr. No dinner Sun.*

$$
AMERICAN

✕**Springwater Bistro.** The chef, who relies largely on local ingredients, changes the menu daily to reflect what's available from area farms. Coconut rice may be paired with Atlantic salmon, for instance, or mahi-mahi may be served with pesto gnocchi. The bar area, which occupies a restored Victorian, serves tapas, and the kitchen prepares picnic baskets in summer. Works by local artists adorn the converted Victorian residence. ⊠ *139 Union Ave.* 🕾 *518/584–6440* ⊟ *AE, D, DC, MC, V* ⊗ *Closed Tues. and Wed. No lunch.*

$$
ASIAN
Fodor's Choice
★

✕**Sushi Thai Garden.** A hostess dressed in a kimono is likely to greet you at this bright and airy restaurant with pale wood furnishings. A sushi bar serves a large selection of sushi and sashimi combinations; entrées include teriyaki, tempura, and *kutsu* dishes as well as Thai curries and noodles. Try the *ika yaki* (grilled squid in teriyaki sauce) or the fried soft-shell crab for a truly delicious indulgence. ⊠ *44–46 Phila St.* 🕾 *518/580–0900* ⊟ *AE, D, MC, V.*

$$
ITALIAN

✕**Wheat Fields.** You can see fettuccine, lasagna, and other pastas squeezing out of the pasta machine in the front window of this main-street restaurant. Traditional Italian dishes share menu space with more creative fare. Smoked salmon, caviar, and scallions adorn angel-hair pasta in Alfredo sauce; the same sauce dresses breaded breast of chicken filled with asparagus mousse and served with tomato-tinted pasta. For a truly regional experience, try the handmade gnocchi—pasta made of potatoes and called "hats" in some parts. There are 24 wines by the glass. ☒*440 Broadway* ☎*518/587–0588* ▤ *AE, D, MC, V.*

$ ✕**Wine Bar.** A sealed cigar room makes this one of the few restaurants
AMERICAN in New York where you can still smoke. The lamb chops and the ahi tuna are two of the more popular items on the mostly American menu; small plates, with smaller prices, also are available. More than 40 wines are offered by the glass, but the bar pours other libations, too. Live musicians play on the weekends. ☒*417 Broadway* ☎*518/584–8777* ▤*AE, D, DC, MC, V* ◷*No lunch.*

WHERE TO STAY

$$$$ ⊡**Adelphi Hotel.** The impressive lobby of one of the city's original late-19th-century hotels has slightly worn divans, elaborately stenciled walls and ceilings, and trompe-l'oeil details. The grand staircase leads to three floors of guest rooms and common spaces, including a second-story piazza overlooking Broadway. Bedroom styles—from Victorian and French country to Adirondacks and Arts and Crafts—are diverse. The bar, which spills off the lobby and into a courtyard, is a favorite evening gathering spot for drinks and desserts. **Pros:** relaxing atmosphere; grand public areas. **Cons:** some furnishings need refurbishing. ☒*365 Broadway* ☎*518/587–4688* ⊕*www.adelphihotel.com* ☽*21 rooms, 18 suites* ♿*In-room: no phone. In-hotel: restaurant, pool* ▤*MC, V* ◷*Closed Nov.–Apr.* ⏅*CP.*

$$$ ⊡**Batcheller Mansion Inn.** The ornate architectural details of this High Victorian Gothic stunner include dormer windows crowned with clamshell arches and a mansard roof of alternating bands of red and gray slate. The common spaces include porches, a living room, and a dining room that seats 20. Two long plush-velvet couches invite lingering in the library. Congress Park is across the street. **Pros:** centrally located; period charm. **Cons:** not for those with small children. ☒*20 Circular St.* ☎*518/584–7012 or 800/616–7012* ⊕*www.batchellermansioninn. com* ☽*4 rooms, 5 suites* ♿*In-room: refrigerator, Wi-Fi. In-hotel: no kids under 14, no-smoking rooms* ▤*AE, MC, V.*

$$$$ ⊡**Gideon Putnam Resort & Spa.** This lovely Georgian revival–style brick hotel sits amid the 2,200 acres of Saratoga Spa State Park. Tall windows look out onto front and rear gardens, and the interior is decorated in a gracious, traditional style. The Sunday brunch buffet of hot and cold entrées is a favorite among locals and visitors alike. **Pros:** spacious rooms; secluded setting. **Cons:** some rooms smell stuffy; breakfast not included. ☒*24 Gideon Putnam Rd.* ☎*866/890–1171* ⊕*www. gideonputnam.com* ☽*120 rooms, 18 suites* ♿*In-room: Internet. In-hotel: restaurant, bar, tennis courts, pool, gym, spa, bicycles, laundry service, no-smoking rooms* ▤*AE, D, DC, MC, V.*

$$$$ ⊡**Inn at Saratoga.** At this 1848 inn, Victorian-inspired rooms with dark-wood furniture and tailored swags include such modern conveniences as high-speed Internet access. The four suites, in the Brunelle Cottage in the back, have heated floors. Your room key grants access to the fitness facilities at the YMCA. **Pros:** delicious breakfast buffet; modern

conveniences. **Cons:** pricey during racing season. ✉*231 Broadway* ☎*518/583–1890* ⊕*www.theinnatsaratoga.com* ⇝*36 rooms, 6 suites* ♿*In-room: Internet. In-hotel: restaurant, no-smoking rooms* ▤*AE, D, DC, MC, V* ¶◎*BP.*

$$$$ ▨**The Mansion Inn.** Paper-bag inventor George West had this 23-room villa built in 1866 across from one of his mills, 7 mi west of Saratoga Springs. Today it serves as a luxurious B&B where special services may include being picked up at the train station by the inn's Bentley or having cocktails delivered to your room on a silver tray. Intricate moldings, mirrors, and mantels grace rooms with 14-foot ceilings and Victorian furnishings. Some rooms have four-poster beds; all have down comforters. In warm weather you may opt to have breakfast on the long porch overlooking the mansion's gardens and ponds. **Pros:** beautiful furnishings; lovely grounds; heated pool. **Cons:** outside Saratoga Springs. ✉*801 Rte. 29, Rock City Falls* ☎*888/996–9977* ⊕*www.themansionsaratoga.com* ⇝*7 rooms, 2 suites, 1 cottage* ♿*In-room: Internet. In-hotel: some pets allowed, no kids under 14, no-smoking rooms* ▤*AE, D, MC, V* ¶◎*BP.*

$$$$
Fodor's Choice
★
▨**Saratoga Arms.** The Smith family greets you at this gorgeous Second Empire hotel in the heart of downtown. Rooms have country-cottage or Victorian furnishings; some have fireplaces or claw-foot tubs. Printed fabrics outfit beds and windows, and every room has a CD player. Shower stalls contain a tile with a quote about local history, characters, or landmarks painted on it. The wraparound porch is roomy and has antique wicker chairs. **Pros:** in the heart of town; walking distance to sights. **Cons:** pricey rates really climb during racing season. ✉*495–497 Broadway* ☎*518/584–1775* ⊕*www.saratoga-lodging.com* ⇝*31 rooms* ♿*In-room: Wi-Fi. In-hotel: no kids under 12, no-smoking rooms* ▤*AE, D, DC, MC, V* ¶◎*BP.*

$$$$ ▨**Union Gables Bed & Breakfast.** A sweeping front porch graces this turreted and gabled Queen Anne Victorian inn, one in a row of equally impressive homes. Benches built into the wood paneling flank the foyer sitting area, and the dining room, dressed in purple, is a Victorian fantasy. A piano figures prominently in the living room. None of the guest rooms are cramped, and those on the second floor are particularly large. Pastels are coupled with busy florals in some rooms, and in others deep greens and blues set off paisleys or plaids. Hardwood floors gleam throughout. **Pros:** quiet location; stately building. **Cons:** breakfast isn't stellar. ✉*55 Union Ave.* ☎*518/584–1558 or 800/398–1558* ⊕*www.uniongables.com* ⇝*11 rooms, 1 suite* ♿*In-room: refrigerator. In-hotel: tennis court, gym, bicycles, no-smoking rooms* ▤*AE, D, DC, MC, V* ¶◎*CP.*

$$$$ ▨**Westchester House.** Antique and reproduction furnishings fill lace-curtained rooms in this 1885 Victorian painted lady. The property, with gardens, is on a leafy residential street within walking distance of downtown and the racetrack. A formal dining room is the setting for the full cold breakfast, which includes baked goods and meat and cheese platters. The parlor houses a library and baby grand piano. **Pros:** within walking distance of many attractions; lovely decor. **Cons:** children only by special arrangement. ✉*102 Lincoln Ave.* ☎*518/587–7613* ⊕*www.*

westchesterhousebandb.com ⤳7 *rooms* ⌂ *In-room: no a/c (some).*
In-hotel: Wi-Fi, no-smoking rooms ▤*AE, D, DC, MC, V* ⊙*Closed*
Jan. and Feb. ⦿*BP.*

WEST AND EAST OF THE CAPITAL

Within 10 mi of Albany are the smaller cities of Troy and Schenectady. Although each has its own distinct character and attractions, the cities are tightly knit by common threads of industry and immigration that spin back to the 1600s. Troy, home of Rensselaer Polytechnic Institute, and Schenectady, home to a General Electric Co. site, have been vital centers of science and technology for more than a century. A visit today could include marveling at a 1930s refrigerator in the Schenectady Museum or strolling down Troy's antique-lamp-lined River Street. Parks, farms, and forest trails are never far away.

SCHENECTADY

8 mi northwest of Albany.

Founded by Dutch traders in 1661, Schenectady is one of the oldest cities in the country. Both General Electric Co. and the now-defunct American Locomotive Co. had their headquarters here in the early 1900s, and Schenectady was dubbed "the city that lights and hauls the world." At night, a giant GE emblem still glows over downtown from atop a factory. Today, with a population of nearly 62,000, the city is an interesting blend of arts, architecture, and culture. Proctor's Theatre, an old vaudeville theater, hosted the upstate premiere of Schenectady native John Sayles's 2004 movie, *Silver City*. In the city's quiet, tree-lined Stockade District—a historic district away from the downtown area—18th- and 19th-century homes and churches nestle along the Mohawk River. European immigrants, especially Italians and Poles, have left an indelible imprint on the city's churches, restaurants, and markets; festivals celebrating Italian, Greek, Polish, and Jewish food and culture, held from June through September, attract thousands. The Gazette Holiday Parade —the largest nighttime parade in the Northeast—winds through downtown the day after Thanksgiving, cheered by excited children and parents bundled in overcoats.

GETTING HERE AND AROUND

Visitors to the capital region should find it quite easy to navigate. The New York State Thruway connects downstate to upstate via its branches: Interstate 90 east and Interstate 87 north and south. Troy is located just north of Albany off Interstate 87, while Schenectady can be reached just west of Albany via Interstate 90. Amtrak also makes the region accessible, as the train stops in Schenectady, Albany, and Rensselaer to the east. Albany International Airport is a major air-travel hub that offers rental cars and bus service.

VISITOR INFORMATION
Schenectady Chamber of Commerce (✉ *306 State St., Schenectady* ☎ *518/372–5656 or 800/962-8007* ⊕ *www.schenectadychamber.org*).

WHAT TO SEE

☼ **Empire State Aerosciences Museum.** Cruise through aviation history via dioramas, models, photos, and interactive displays at the **Schenectady County Airport,** near the spot where Charles Lindbergh landed in 1928. Take a ride in the simulated-flight reality vehicle, or get an up-close look at dozens of restored aircraft, which are parked all around the 27-acre site and include an F-14A Tomcat. In September, a museum-sponsored air show roars over the city. ✉ *250 Rudy Chase Dr., off Rte. 50, Glenville* ☎ *518/377–2191* ⊕ *www.esam.org* 💲 *$8* ☉ *Wed.–Sat. 10–4, Sun. noon–4.*

Historic Stockade District. Examples of Federal, Dutch, Gothic, Victorian, and Greek Revival architecture are found among the homes and churches here, which date from 1690 to 1930. The Stockade is one of the oldest continuously occupied neighborhoods in the nation. (George Washington slept here.) In warm weather you see people running and relaxing in tiny Riverside Park, along the Mohawk River. Residents open their homes to the public for guided tours during **Walkabout Weekend,** held in September. At the **Stockade Villagers Art Show,** also in September, painters set up easels and tents to display their works. ✉ *Between Erie Blvd. and Union St. along Mohawk River* ☎ *518/374–0263 or 518/372–5656* ⊕ *www.historicstockade.com.*

Schenectady County Historical Society & Museum. A stenciled floor and a huge 1930s dollhouse are among the highlights of this museum, which fills the 1896 Georgian-style **Dora Jackson House** with its 18th-century furniture, paintings, costumes, toys, and household and military items. The **Grems-Doolittle Library** has Revolutionary War records, newspapers from the 1800s, and the papers of Charles Steinmetz, an inventor who developed alternate-current motors. ✉ *32 Washington Ave.* ☎ *518/374–0263* ⊕ *www.schist.org* 💲 *Museum $3, library $5* ☉ *Weekdays 9–5, Sat. 10–2.*

☼ **Schenectady Museum & Suits-Bueche Planetarium.** Early televisions and kitchen appliances are part of a vast General Electric archive that traces the city's scientific and cultural history. Interactive children's displays explore science and technology. ✉ *15 Nott Terrace Heights* ☎ *518/382–7890* ⊕ *www.schenectadymuseum.org* 💲 *Museum $6.50, museum and planetarium $9.25* ☉ *Tues.–Fri. 10–5, weekends noon–5.*

Union College. The 100-acre campus of this liberal-arts college founded in 1795 was the first in America to be designed by an architect. The grounds include **Jackson's Garden,** an oasis of perennials and herbs near a bubbling brook. At the campus center is the 1875 **Nott Memorial** (☉ *Daily 10–6*), a 16-sided structure with a colorful slate mosaic dome. The unusual building, a National Historic Landmark, is illuminated in the evening. The **Mandeville Gallery** (☎ *518/388–6004*), on the Nott Memorial's second floor, shows history-, science-, and art-related exhibits. ✉ *807 Union St.* ☎ *518/388–6000* ⊕ *www.union.edu* 💲 *Free.*

SHOPPING

A dozen or so shops line a pedestrians-only section of Jay Street. On Thursday in summer you can browse to the sounds of the free lunchtime concerts that take place in front of City Hall. In addition to the shops listed below, pop into the Open Door Bookstore, Two Spruce Pottery gallery, and Bibliomania, a store of rare and used books.

Civitello's (⊠42 N. Jay St. 🕾518/381–6165), a bakery and small café with booths and tables, has been selling cannoli, spumoni, and Italian cookies since 1911. The **New York Folklore Society** (⊠133 Jay St. 🕾518/346–7008) sells one-of-a-kind items made by New York folk artists: carved birds and walking sticks, quilts, hand-knitted children's sweaters, American Indian jewelry, baskets, and Ukrainian *pysanky* (decorated eggs). A line forms every afternoon at **Perreca's Bakery** (⊠33 N. Jay St. 🕾518/372–1875), in business since 1914 and the cornerstone of the city's Little Italy project. It's a Schenectady tradition to wait for a loaf of Perreca's bread, still warm from the oven. Round or rectangular, large or small, the crusty bread is the city's best-known food item. Actor Jack Nicholson developed a craving for Perreca's when he was in Albany filming the 1987 movie *Ironweed* and has friends pick up a loaf when they're in the area.

NIGHTLIFE AND THE ARTS

NIGHTLIFE One of the best clubs for jazz and blues in the capital region is the **Van Dyck** (⊠237 Union St., off Erie Blvd. 🕾518/381–1111), at the entrance to the Stockade District. Sip a martini at the first-floor antique bar before heading upstairs to the intimate, attic-like performance space.

THE ARTS Local, national, and internationally known musicians perform as part
★ of the **Central Park Concert Series** (⊠*Ashmore Ave. and Iroquois Way* 🕾518/292–0368). The outdoor concerts start at 7 PM on Sunday in July and August. **Proctor's Theatre** (⊠432 State St. 🕾518/346–6204 ⊕*www.proctors.org*), a 1926 vaudeville theater with chandeliers, balconies, and 2,700 seats, is one of the crown jewels of the capital region. Year-round schedules include Broadway shows performed by national touring companies; concerts; dance performances; and second-run movies. A recent expansion added the GE Theatre, with a huge screen. **Freedom Park** (⊠*Schonowee Ave. near Rte. 5, Scotia* 🕾*No phone* ⊕*www. freedomparkscotia.org*) comes alive from June through August with free outdoor concerts of jazz, blues, rock, and polka. Shows start at 7 PM on Wednesday.

WHERE TO EAT

$$ ✕**Cornell's.** Locals love this place and have savored its Italian specialties
ITALIAN since 1943. Start with the clams in wine, butter, oil, and garlic, or a hot
Fodor'sChoice antipasto. For a main course, consider the braciola, a longtime favorite;
★ the tender rolls of beef are filled with sausage and baked in meat sauce. The restaurant is part of Schenectady's emerging Little Italy community on North Jay Street. ⊠39 N. Jay St. 🕾518/370–3825 ▭ AE, MC, V ⊘*Closed Mon.*

$ ✕**Peter Pause.** Shirt-and-tie wearers mix with jeans-and-sneakers types
ITALIAN at this tiny Italian diner across the street from Union College. The best

seats are at the counter, where you can watch the soup simmer and smell the tomato sauce. Melt-in-your-mouth eggplant parmigiana sandwiches are the specialty. Daily pasta dishes might include spaghetti, ravioli, or linguine with red or white clam sauce. On a cold day, warm up with a bowl of *stracciatelli* (a soup made with eggs, semolina, and cheese). ⊠*535 Nott St.* ☎*518/382–9278* ▭*No credit cards* ⊗ *Closed weekends. No dinner.*

WHERE TO STAY

$$ ▦**Glen Sanders Mansion.** A former fur trapper's trading post–turned–Dutch mansion provides a swish backdrop for a room and a meal on the Mohawk River. Standard rooms have two queen beds; junior suites have a king-size sleigh bed, a desk, and a seating area. The decor throughout is a harmonious blend of patterned fabrics and wallpapers in elegant palettes. Candlelit tables set with fine china and table linens fill the pre-colonial dining room, which has two decorative fireplaces and hand-hewn beams. A cavelike, stone-walled pub downstairs offers lighter fare. **Pros:** fresh flowers; luxe accommodations; excellent Sunday brunch. **Cons:** tough cancellation policy. ⊠*1 Glen Ave., off Rte. 5/Mohawk Ave., Scotia* ☎*518/688–2138* ⊕*www.glensandersmansion. com* ⇆*10 rooms, 10 suites* ⌂*In-room: safe (some), refrigerator (some), Wi-Fi. In-hotel: restaurant, bar, no-smoking rooms* ▭*AE, D, DC, MC, V* ▮⊚▮*CP.*

$$ ▦**The Parker Inn.** This hotel dramatically transformed the Parker Building, a narrow structure that was the city's tallest building when it was erected in 1906. An antique cage-style elevator takes you to contemporary rooms with dark-wood furniture and floral-fabric accents. Maroon velvet curtains and vintage movie posters in the lounge downstairs are a nod to the inn's neighbor, Proctor's Theatre; before and after shows, a chic crowd gathers for drinks, dinner, and snacks. **Pros:** close to everything; period charm. **Cons:** older hotel. ⊠*434 State St.* ☎*518/688–1001* ⊕*parkerinn.com* ⇆*23 rooms, 6 suites* ⌂*In-room: Wi-Fi. In-hotel: bar, laundry facilities, no-smoking rooms* ▭*AE, D, MC, V* ▮⊚▮*CP.*

$ ▦**The Stockade Inn.** Before its latest incarnation, this three-story Federal-style building in the heart of the Stockade served as a bank and an exclusive men's club. The Victorian-style rooms, all on the top floor, have plush carpeting and reproduction antique poster beds; six have gas fireplaces. The first two floors hold a swanky restaurant, which has upholstered armchairs, high ceilings, and chandeliers; a billiards room; and meeting rooms. **Pros:** pretty rooms; use of facilities at the YMCA. **Cons:** Continental breakfast is limited. ⊠*1 N. Church St.* ☎*518/346–3400* ⊕*www.stockadeinn.com* ⇆*7 rooms, 2 suites* ⌂*In-room: Internet. In-hotel: restaurant, bar, no-smoking rooms* ▭*AE, D, MC, V* ▮⊚▮*CP.*

TROY

4 mi north of Albany.

At the juncture of the Hudson River and the Erie Canal and just a few miles north of Albany, Troy was an important commercial city in the early 1800s. Although the development of the railroads curtailed its commercial dominance, Troy became one of the largest industrial cities on the East Coast. Uncle Sam—actually Sam Wilson, a meat packer who acquired the moniker during the War of 1812—hailed from Troy and is buried in the Oakwood Cemetery. In the 20th century the city became known as the home of Cluett-Peabody, maker of Arrow shirts. Today Troy has a host of cultural venues as well as several excellent restaurants. It's also rich in architecture, with Federal-style farmhouses, 19th-century Georgian-style buildings and brownstones, and 20th-century bungalow-style homes. It's also home to Rensselaer Polytechnic Institute and Russell Sage College.

GETTING HERE AND AROUND

Capital District Transportation Authority (☎*518/482–8822* ⊕*www.cdta. org*) provides a way to get around the capital area by bus.

VISITOR INFORMATION

Rensselaer County Regional Chamber of Commerce (⊠*255 River St., Troy* ☎*518/274–7020* ⊕*www.renscochamber.com*).

WHAT TO SEE

Arts Center of the Capital Region. Two gallery spaces display contemporary and folk pieces by local and regional artists. One- and two-day classes are offered in art, photography, writing, culinary arts, and crafts. ⊠*265 River St.* ☎*518/273–0552* ⊕*www.artscenteronline.org* ⊠*Free* ☾*Mon.–Thurs. 9–7, Fri. and Sat. 9–5, Sun. noon–4.*

↻ **Children's Museum for Science and Technology.** Kids can learn about Mohican life or bees and pollination through the interactive exhibits here, which cover science, history, and art. ⊠*250 Jordan Rd.* ☎*518/235–2120* ⊕*www.cmost.com* ⊠*$5* ☾*Thurs. –Sun. 10–5.*

Grafton Lakes State Park. The Durham Reservoir, 20 mi of trails, and a series of ponds make this park a favorite place for such warm-weather activities as picnicking, swimming, fishing, hiking, and biking. In winter, cross-country skiers, snowshoers, and snowmobilers hit the trails, and ice-skaters take to the frozen water. The park is off Route 2 east of Troy. ⊠*61 N. Long Pond Rd., Grafton* ☎*518/279–1155* ⊕*nysparks. state.ny.us* ⊠*Free* ☾*Daily dawn–dusk.*

Rensselaer County Historical Society. The 19th-century **Carr Building** contains the historical society's offices as well as a research library that, through old photos, maps, diaries, and letters, documents Troy's development from the 1800s through the following century. Next door is the **Hart-Cluett House,** an 1827 Federal town house with a white marble exterior and period furnishings; tours are available by reservation. ⊠*57 2nd St.* ☎*518/272–7232* ⊕*www.rchsonline.org* ⊠*$5* ☾*Museum and library Tues.–Sat. noon–5.*

Troy RiverSpark Visitor Center. The staff offers an orientation to the area, including tips on local events. Exhibits cover the city's river history. ⊠*251 River St.* ☎*518/270–8667* ⊕*www.troyvisitorcenter.org* 🎫*Free* ☉*May–Sept., Tues.–Fri. 10–6, weekends 10–5; Oct.–Apr., Tues.–Sat. 11–5.*

THE ARTS

The **New York State Theatre Institute** (*NYSTI* ⊠*37 1st St.* ☎*518/2747–3200* ⊕*www.nysti.org*), a family-oriented professional theater company, presents plays and musicals from September to May. Local and touring bands play the popular **Revolution Hall** (⊠*425 River St.* ☎*518/273–2337* ⊕*revolutionhall.com*). The converted 18th-century warehouse hosts jazz, blues, and folk acts. The beaux arts **Troy Savings Bank Music Hall** (⊠*State and 2nd Sts.* ☎*518/273–0038* ⊕*www. troymusichall.org*), considered one of the few acoustically perfect concert halls in the world, attracts top international and U.S. musicians. A full lineup of classical, pop, and jazz concerts is held throughout the year, and the Albany Symphony plays a seven-concert season here from October through May.

WHERE TO EAT

$ ✕**Brown's Brewing Company.** The brewpub occupies a circa-1850 riverside warehouse. In warm weather, locals linger on the outdoor deck overlooking the Hudson; inside, exposed-brick walls set off local memorabilia, antiques, and old photos. A slew of beers is concocted on-site, including the smooth oatmeal stout, which won a gold medal at the World Beer Cup. The pub menu has been expanded and offers classics like burgers as well as sophisticated seafood dishes. ⊠*417–419 River St.* ☎*518/273–2337* ▤*AE, MC, V.*

AMERICAN
Fodor's Choice
★

$$$ ✕**Daisy Baker's.** Plank floors, small wood tables, old organ pipes, and a high ceiling flanked by rich wood walls are reminders of this dining room's former religious uses: at various times, the 1892 brownstone has been a fundamentalist church, a Christian Science reading room, and a YWCA. The menu changes frequently and might include pancetta-wrapped veal rib chop with smashed red potatoes; grilled swordfish with cucumber strips, or roasted free-range chicken with sautéed mushrooms and onions in cherry-wine sauce. After 10 PM, a young crowd fills the long bar, and local bands play until the wee hours. ⊠*33 2nd St.* ☎*518/266–9200* ▤*AE, D, MC, V* ☉*Closed Sun.*

ECLECTIC

$$ ✕**Lo Porto's.** Veal Scorsese, one of the more popular entrées at this northern Italian restaurant, is named for Martin Scorsese, who dined here regularly while directing *The Age of Innocence*. The dish pairs wafer-thin pieces of veal with mushrooms, artichoke hearts, prosciutto, and capers, all covered with cooked tomatoes. Fresh seafood and pasta dishes are also good choices. ⊠*85 4th St.* ☎*518/273–8546* ▤*AE, D, DC, MC, V* ☉*Closed Sun. and Mon. No lunch Sat.*

ITALIAN

$$$ ✕**River Street Café.** On your way upstairs to the dining room, you pass the chef working in an exposed kitchen. The comfortable brick-and-mahogany room overlooks the Troy marina on the Hudson River. The eclectic menu changes frequently to reflect the seasonal ingredients available and incorporates Asian, American, Mediterranean,

AMERICAN
★

and other flavors. The menu changes often, but some recent offerings included flat-iron steak and duck with a sauce of port, balsamic vinegar, and blackberries. A caveat: the service can be slow. ⊠*429 River St.* ☎*518/273–2740* ⊟*MC, V* ⊙*Closed Sun. and Mon. No lunch.*

WHERE TO STAY

$ 🏠**Franklin Square Plaza Inn and Suites.** The cheerful brick inn a block from the Hudson River is a good alternative to chain hotels. Standard rooms tend to be a bit run-of-the-mill and have either two double beds or a king. Suites, double the size of the standard rooms, have king-size beds, an adjoining sitting room, a refrigerator, and a whirlpool tub. **Pros:** nicely renovated; walking distance to eateries. **Cons:** breakfast is limited. ⊠*1 4th St.* ☎*518/274–8800 or 866/708–2233* ⊕*www. franklinsquareinn.com* ⊲*58 rooms, 4 suites* ⊘*In-room: refrigerator (some), Wi-Fi (some). In-hotel: no-smoking rooms* ⊟*AE, D, DC, MC, V* ⦿*CP.*

¢ 🏠**Olde Judge Mansion.** This sunny bed-and-breakfast offers family-style
Fodor'sChoice hospitality, lovely furnishings, a common parlor, and card games on
★ the weekends. The rooms are housed in a late-19th-century home, and attended to by the owner. **Pros:** made-to-order breakfast; friendly vibe. **Cons:** neighborhood is loud at times. ⊠*3300 6th Ave.* ☎*518/274– 5698* ⊕ *www.oldejudgemansion.com* ⊲*5 rooms* ⊘*In-room: Internet. In-hotel: Internet terminal* ⊟*AE, D, MC, V* ⦿*BP.*

JOHN BOYD THACHER STATE PARK

★ *15 mi southwest of Albany.*

The park sits along the **Helderberg Escarpment,** one of the most fossil-rich formations in the world and the most dramatic natural feature of the regional landscape. From the escarpment ledge you can take in panoramic views of the Hudson-Mohawk Valley, with the Adirondack foothills and the western mountain ranges of Massachusetts and Vermont off in the distance. The park is the ending point for the Long Path, a 349-mi hiking trail that starts in Fort Lee, New Jersey, and crosses public and private land. Within the park you can hike the **Indian Ladder Trail,** which runs along the Helderberg cliff. The trail, open from May to mid-November, is furnished with interpretive signs, and guided hikes are available. Another 12 mi of trails are open all year. In warm weather the trails are used for hiking, biking, and nature walks; cross-country skiing (on groomed and ungroomed trails) and snowshoeing are available in winter. Facilities include an Olympic-size pool ($2 in season) and picnicking sites. ⊠*Rte. 157 off Rte. 85, Voorheesville* ☎*518/872–1237* ⊕*nysparks.state.ny.us* ⊠*Parking $6 (late May–Labor Day)* ⊙*Daily 8* AM*–dusk.*

The Catskills

WORD OF MOUTH

"Visited the town of Woodstock and enjoyed all it had to offer. I have never seen so many 'hippies' in my life! (Hey, but I could live there! LOL.) Bought several things in this town as it proved to be the best shopping of our trip. Everything from clothes to antiques to artwork. Went back to this city another day and hiked Overlook Mountain— an excellent 5-mi r/t hike. At the top of the mountain there was a fire tower. When you went to the top of the tower, you really did feel as if you were on the top of the world."

—Paul

Updated by
Gary Catt

Verdant forests, undulating mountains, swiftly moving streams and rivers, meandering creeks, waterfalls, and abundance of wildlife lure visitors to the Catskills, particularly the northern Catskills. But there is also a deep sense of mystery and spiritual vibrancy that has drawn travelers through the centuries. Henry Hudson felt the pull of these looming, mist-shrouded mountains in 1609, as did the Dutch and English colonists who populated and farmed the fertile land in the small, upland valleys between the stony round-topped peaks.

Rising between the Hudson River to the east and the upper Delaware and Susquehanna rivers to the south and west, the Catskills—called *Onteora,* or "land in the sky," by the Algonquians and "these fairy mountains" by writer Washington Irving—are among the most visited, written-about, and painted mountain ranges in the country.

In the mid-19th century a group of artists led by Thomas Cole and Frederick Church—the rock stars of their day—followed old American Indian trails into the deep clefts between the mountains and emerged with a series of cathedral-like, supernatural paintings that spoke to the popular imagination and drew thousands of New York City urbanites to the mountains. An entire rugged-tourism industry sprouted, and more artists, writers, and early environmentalists flocked to the area, followed in the 1900s by ethnic and religious groups fleeing the heat and oppression of the city. Syrians, Armenians, Viennese, Ukrainians, Germans, Italians, Russians, Irish, and others came to the Catskills, leaving indelible stamps that still pervade the region today. The first resort, the Catskill Mountain House, was built in the 1820s near Haines Falls.

Despite the many developments here, environmental visionaries have strived to protect the Catskill's pristine landscape. Since 1904, 700,000 acres have been incorporated into the Catskill Park and Forest Preserve, with approximately 250,000 acres designated "forever wild."

The Catskills today are a destination for travelers from around the globe. Championship golf courses dot the area; world-class trout streams flow through the region (which incidentally spawned the sport of fly-fishing). More than 200 mi of marked hiking trails wind through the hills and valleys here, and both skiers and hikers aim for the high-peaks region. Hunting and fishing also are significant draws.

TOP REASONS TO GO

Bethel Woods Center for the Arts. Both a cultural hub and a museum, the center explores the cultural transformation of the 1960s at the site of the Woodstock Music and Arts Fair.

Breathtaking views. Drive the highways and byways of the Catskills during any season where winding roads cross picturesque streams and rise up and down through the hills and valleys of an undulating terrain. Be surprised by roosting eagles, soaring vultures, and roadside wildlife going about their business naturally.

Fish on. When they talk fish in the Catskills, the name is trout. The Roscoe Junction Pool, where the Willowemoc River runs into the Beaverkill Creek, is where the serious fly-fishers go.

Go for a float. Bring your floatation device, boat, tube, kayak, whatever—and don't forget your fishing pole, and head to the Upper Delaware River, which borders New York and Pennsylvania.

Thomas Cole National Historic Site. Along with the Hudson River Art trail, this restored home allows visitors to see the views that inspired America's first great landscape painters. Walk in the footsteps of Cole, Frederic Church, Asher B. Durand, Jasper Cropsey, Sanford Gifford, and other pioneering American artists.

ORIENTATION AND PLANNING

GETTING ORIENTED

The Catskills region is a two- to three-hour drive north of New York City, spilling over Ulster, Greene, Schoharie, Sullivan, Orange, and Delaware counties. This crooked arm of the Appalachians holds dense forests; mountains almost 4,200 feet tall; twisting rivers; rock-walled gorges; and lush, wide valleys. Small towns and one-store crossroad hamlets abound. Much of the terrain is protected land within the 700,000-acre Catskill Forest Preserve.

Most travelers first glimpse the Catskills from Interstate 87 (the New York State Thruway), which links New York City and Albany. About 10 mi west of Interstate 87 the mountains rise abruptly from the valley floor in a ragged blue wall some 20 mi long. In the northern Catskills, the Hudson River towns of Kingston and Catskill (New York State Thruway Exits 19 and 21) are jumping-off points for Routes 23, 23A, and 28, all of which climb the mountainous wall and snake through Greene and upper Ulster counties. From the west, Routes 23, 28, and 30 are the principal access routes running through the mountains of Delaware County, which separate the watersheds of the Hudson and Delaware rivers. Sullivan County and the Upper Delaware River region can most easily be accessed via Route 17—also Interstate 86—which runs from the Thruway westward through the Catskills.

PLANNING

WHEN TO GO

Spring in the Catskills brings the reemergence of dormant fauna, mating, and foraging for food as buds burst into flower on the branches. In summer, the mountains fill with travelers roaming dense forests, splashing in cool rivers and watering holes, and attending countless festivals. Autumn foliage burns golden amber, rich red, brilliant orange, and occasionally pink. In winter, bare, silvery branches stretch to the sky, laden with mounds of snow and icicles. The only time to avoid visiting is during mud season—usually mid-March to mid-May—when the melting snow and rainfall turn the region into a gooey mess, and many businesses close.

GETTING HERE AND AROUND

⇨ *Travel Smart New York State in the back of the book for airport, airline, and car rental contact information.*

AIR TRAVEL

The closest airports to the Catskills are Greater Binghamton Airport, Stewart International Airport, and Albany International Airport. The Albany airport puts you within an hour's drive of the northern Catskills. Continental Airlines affiliate CommutAir connects Albany airport to the Finger Lakes region, Long Island, and western New York; the carrier also flies to Westchester County Airport, in the lower Hudson Valley. US Airways Express links Albany to New York City, Long Island, and western New York. Flights into Binghamton and Stewart come from outside New York State.

BUS TRAVEL

You can get to the Catskills by bus, but you should note that public transportation within the region is limited. Shortline buses link the Catskills with New York City, Long Island, the Hudson Valley, the Finger Lakes region, and central and western New York. Stops include Bethel, Liberty, Monticello, Roscoe, and Swan Lake; depending on your destination, you may have to wait at the Monticello terminal for your connecting bus.

Adirondack Trailways travels between the northern Catskills and New York City, the Hudson Valley, the Capital–Saratoga Region, and central New York; connecting service gets you to and from the other regions of the state. Buses stop in Arkville, Delhi, Fleischmanns, Haines Falls, Highmount, Hunter, Mount Tremper, Phoenicia, Prattsville, Shandaken, Tannersville, Windham, and Woodstock. During ski season, the Hunter-, Windham-, and Belleayre-bound buses are packed with twentysomethings from New York City heading for the slopes. Special packages include lift tickets.

Bus Lines Adirondack Trailways (☎ *800/858-8555* ⊕ *www.trailways.com*). **Shortline Coach USA** (☎ *800/631-8405* ⊕ *www.shortlinebus.com*).

CAR TRAVEL

The best way to get around and explore the Catskills is by car. You can enter the northeast Catskills via Exits 19 and 21 off the New York

State Thruway (Interstate 87). Route 17/Interstate 86 (aka the Quickway) provides access to the southern and western Catskills. Weekenders heading north take to these highways on Friday evenings, when you can expect congestion and slower travel. The same is true heading south on Sunday, especially in the late afternoon and early evening.

The scenery is breathtaking on many of the region's roads. These include Route 23A, which, heading northwest toward Hunter, climbs steeply, passing Kaaterskill Falls; Route 10, which snakes its way across Delaware County past working farms and 19th-century homesteads; and Route 97, which runs parallel to the Delaware River.

Deer are plentiful throughout the region, so be on the lookout—especially at night. Also, be aware that cellular service in the region is spotty. In winter, snow and ice make for tough going, especially in the northern Catskills; having four-wheel drive is extremely helpful in negotiating the hilly (and often snowy and icy) terrain. In summer, slow-moving farm vehicles and animals along the roadside may impede travel; also be on the lookout for bikers and pedestrians on the road.

■**TIP→** Note that the New York State Thruway is composed of both Interstates 90 and 87. The Thruway is the same as Interstate 87 running north to Albany, but from there the Thruway switches to Interstate 90, running west across the state. The Thruway is a toll road, so bring along change if you don't have an E-ZPass.

TRAIN TRAVEL
The closest Amtrak stops to the Catskills is in the Hudson Valley and in the Capital–Saratoga Region. These Rhinecliff, Hudson, and Albany stops all put you near the northeastern Catskills.

■**TIP→** Once you get to the Catskills, you can enjoy train travel through the mountains of Catskill Park, as an attraction via Catskill Mountain Railroad or Delaware & Ulster Railroad (⇨ *Take a Tour by Train box later in the chapter for details*).

RESTAURANTS
Although Catskills cuisine used to be a misnomer, regional restaurants are changing their reputations, largely thanks to the nearby Culinary Institute of America in the Hudson Valley's Hyde Park. After graduation, many CIA students settle in the area and work in Catskills restaurants—or open their own. Combined with a movement to use fresh, local produce and farm products, the result is a plethora of superb dining choices. Most of the best restaurants are in the towns that draw New York City money—Windham, Woodstock, and Hunter—but smaller, more remote towns and villages also contain pleasant surprises. Dining in the region remains a casual experience, and few people dress for dinner.

HOTELS
A full range of accommodations are available in the Catskills, and well-appointed and well-tended hotels pepper the region. Winter is usually considered high season for most lodging choices near the Belleayre, Windham, and Hunter ski centers. In the northern Catskills it's not

unusual for properties to charge high-season rates in both summer and winter. Prices tend to be much lower during the week, regardless of the season.

WHAT IT COSTS					
	¢	$	$$	$$$	$$$$
RESTAURANTS	under $8	$8–$14	$15–$21	$22–$30	over $30
HOTELS	under $100	$100–$149	$150–$199	$200–$250	over $250

Restaurant prices are for a main course at dinner (or at the most expensive meal served). Hotel prices are for two people in a standard double room in high season, excluding tax.

VISITOR INFORMATION

Catskill Association for Tourism Services (✉ Box 449, Catskill 12414 ☎ No phone ⊕ www.visitthecatskills.com).

CATSKILL PARK

Designated a state treasure in 1904, Catskill Park spans Ulster, Green, Delaware, and Sullivan counties. It encompasses 700,000 acres of public and private land, and some of the wildest country south of Maine, with bears, coyotes, rattlesnakes, and other creatures. About 60% of the land is privately owned; the nearly 300,000 acres of state land within the park is called the Catskill Forest Preserve. The park has 200 mi of marked trails, campgrounds, ponds, lakes, and mountains; 98 peaks rise above 3,000 feet. At 4,190 feet, Slide Mountain is the highest of the Catskill peaks.

In summer, hikers, climbers, kayakers and canoeists, bicyclists, and tubers join Bruderhof community members, Buddhists, and Orthodox and Hasidic Jews on the streets of mountain villages; in winter most of these groups are gone, displaced by an influx of skiers from the New York City area, as well as a considerable number of snowmobilers and hardy ice climbers. The visitors mix well with the dreamers, visionaries, artists, writers, poets, and musicians who still come to the mountains seeking a corner to call their own, and a community with which to share their talents.

WOODSTOCK

105 mi north of New York City, 195 mi east of Syracuse, 53 mi south of Albany.

An arts colony and a haven for eccentricity, Woodstock is the almost mythical wellspring of alternative American culture and home to many of the now deified promulgators of the seemingly endless phenomenon of the 1960s. In having its name usurped for a seminal music festival in 1969 (actually held in Bethel, in the southwestern region of the Catskills), Woodstock has inadvertently been called upon to define an entire generation—or at least the amber-tinted soul of its lost youth.

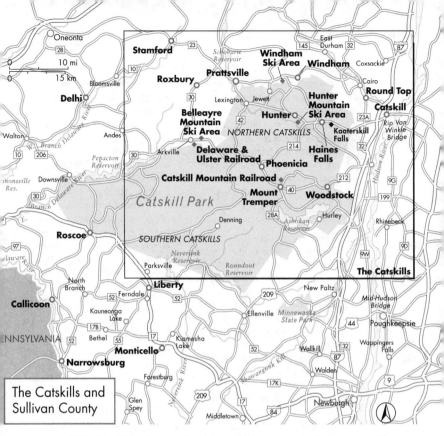

The Catskills and Sullivan County

Woodstock's main street hugs the small town green, where angst-ridden teenagers, musicians, political protesters, and the occasional pet parade convene. Although eclectic shops and art galleries help maintain the town's status as a countercultural magnet, the current scene is rather mellow. These days you're more likely to spot Land Rovers than VW buses in town, where aging hippies and baby boomers, families, and celebrities share sidewalks with out-of-towners. To enjoy Woodstock's charm, don't overlook the details—the gently gurgling brooks, the odd homegrown bench, the twinkling lights that come on at dusk—and consider visiting in winter or spring, when crowds thin out and traffic eases.

VISITOR INFORMATION

Woodstock Chamber of Commerce & Arts (⊠ *21 Tinker St., Woodstock* ☎ *845/ 679–8025* ⊕ *woodstockchamber.com).*

WHAT TO SEE

Byrdcliffe. Ralph Radcliffe Whitehead, a wealthy Englishman under the sway of William Morris and John Ruskin, decided to create a utopian arts colony. His friend and conspirator Bolton Brown, an artist, suggested Woodstock; after a visit in 1902, Whitehead agreed. Here is the result: 300 acres dotted with 35 buildings, the only intact Arts and Crafts colony remaining on U.S. soil. Although Whitehead was

Hudson River School

The Hudson River School—the name given to a group of New York landscape painters that flourished from about 1850 until the 1870s—was the nation's first brotherhood of artists. Thomas Cole is regarded as the school's father; others prominent in the movement included Frederic Edwin Church, Asher B. Durand, Jasper Cropsey, and Sanford Gifford.

You can see the Catskill views that provided inspiration for these artists by following the Hudson River School Art Trail. The driving tour features seven stops. The first (and main) site is the former home of Thomas Cole, who settled in 1825 in the town of Catskill, a ferry stop on the Hudson River. The mountain vistas that captured Cole's attention are still visible from the wraparound porch of his home, Cedar Grove, now part of the **Thomas Cole National Historic Site** (⊠ *218 Spring St., Catskill 12414* ☎ *518/943–7465* ⊕ *www.thomascole. org* ⊠ *Free*). Meticulously restored by a consortium of government and private interests, Cedar Grove's main house and separate studio are open daily from the first Saturday in May through the last Sunday in October. Guided tours are offered from 10 to 4 on Thursday, Friday, Saturday, and Sunday. Maps for the art trail can be picked up at the historic site.

Another stop on the trail is Olana (⊠ *5720 State Rte. 9G, Hudson 12543*

☎ *518/828–0135* ⊕ *www.Olana.org* ⊠ *House tours $9, call for reservations*), the home of Frederic Edwin Church, a Cole student. A gifted draftsman and a colorist, Church traveled widely and collected materials throughout New York and New England, particularly Vermont. From Olana, Church set a pattern of travel, hiking, and sketching from spring through autumn, spending winters in New York painting and socializing. A mansion in its own style, Olana rises from the hillside on the eastern shore of the Hudson overlooking the Catskill village landing. The grounds are open 8 AM–sunset throughout the year. During peak periods, there's a $5 charge per vehicle. House tours are offered Wednesday through Sunday and holiday Mondays. Grounds maps for walking and hiking are available at the visitor center.

Other stops on the Hudson River School Art Trail bring you to the breathtaking vistas that provided so much inspiration—Kaaterskill Falls, Kaaterskill Creek, and the site of the Catskill Mountain House, a premier resort of the 1800s made famous by Washington Irving and visited often by Cole because of its vistas. Most sites are within 15 mi of Catskill.

To see paintings by Hudson River School artists, visit the **Munson–Williams–Proctor Arts Institute in Utica** (⇨ *Chapter 5*).

considered dictatorial, his early efforts laid the groundwork for Woodstock's transformation into a colony of the arts. John Dewey, Thomas Mann, naturalist John Burroughs, and Isadora Duncan all fell under Byrdcliffe's spell. Artists, writers, composers, and dance and theater companies still call it home when they participate in its residency programs. Pamphlets in the mailbox outside the barn outline a self-guided walking tour. ⊠ *Upper Byrdcliffe Rd., off Glasco Tpke.* ☎ *845/679–2079* ⊕ *www.woodstockguild.org* ⊠ *Free.*

Center for Photography at Woodstock. If you come here, you're entering hallowed ground: what was once the Espresso Café—where Bob Dylan, Janis Joplin, and others entertained countercultural dreamers—remains indelibly imprinted on the town. Now a gallery space for photography, the center aims to provoke serious consideration of the medium, offering a dynamic series of exhibits, lectures, and workshops. ⊠ *59 Tinker St.* ☎ *845/ 679–9957* ⊕ *www.cpw.org* 🖃 *Free* ⊗ *Wed.–Sun. noon–5.*

Karma Triyana Dharmachakra. A giant golden Buddha resides in the colorful shrine room of this Tibetan Buddhist monastery, where you can meditate or wander the grounds. Tours are given weekends at 1:30; stroll around to discover a fishpond, guesthouse, and solitary-retreat cabins. Because this is a religious center, you aren't allowed in the shrine room wearing shoes, hats, or revealing garments. Introductory instruction in *shinay* (mind-calming) meditation is also available; call for the schedule or to make an appointment. The monastery is about 3 mi north of the village center. ⊠ *335 Meads Mountain Rd.* ☎ *845/679–5906 Ext. 10* ⊕ *www.kagyu.org* 🖃 *Free* ⊗ *Daily 6–6.*

Woodstock Artists Cemetery. Dead artists of all kinds reside here: poets, musicians, writers, painters, sculptors, dancers, and bon vivants. Many of the stones, in keeping with the wishes of their buried subjects, tell artfully rendered stories. Look for the grassy knoll behind the Evergreen Cemetery to commune with the spirits of Woodstock. ⊠ *On hill behind parking lot of Colony Cafe, which is at 22 Rock City Rd.* ☎ *No phone* 🖃 *Free.*

SPORTS AND THE OUTDOORS

HIKING Looming over Woodstock, **Overlook Mountain** (⊠ *Off Meads Mountain Rd.* ☎ *845/256–3000* ⊕ *www.catskillcenter.org*) has inspired generations of landscape artists, as well as several rock musicians. The 3,140-foot peak offers one of the best views in the Catskills, on clear days taking in five neighboring states. On the way up the 2½-mi dirt road—an almost constant ascent—you'll see the ruins of the Overlook Mountain House, a once-grand hotel; an old fire tower is at the top. To get here from the Woodstock village green, turn onto Rock City Road. Proceed to the four-way stop, after which the road becomes Meads Mountain Road. Continue for another 2½ mi. The Overlook trailhead and parking are on the right, across the road from Karma Triyana Dharmachakra.

Stretching over 47,500 acres, the **Slide Mountain Wilderness** is the largest and most popular wilderness area in the Catskills. The area includes

Slide Mountain (⊠ *Off Rte. 47, 10 mi south of Big Indian* ☎607/652–7365, 607/652–5076, or 607/652–5063 ⊕*www.dec.ny.gov*)—which, at 4,190 feet, is the range's highest peak—and encompasses several forest preserves. Its 35 mi of hiking trails take you over lofty peaks with spectacular views. The most straightforward way up Slide Mountain is via the Woodland Valley–Denning and Burroughs Range trails, accessed from the Slide Mountain trailhead parking area on Route 47, west of Woodstock. You'll trek 2.7 mi and climb 1,780 feet to the summit, where a plaque commemorates naturalist and poet John Burroughs.

SHOPPING

At **Golden Notebook** (⊠*29 Tinker St.* ☎845/679–8000), a venerable Woodstock institution since 1978, the friendly staff helps you navigate the eclectic mix of local lore, children's books, fiction, and other titles. Wander through the labyrinth and you'll find the Golden Bough, an adjacent gift shop. At **Loominus** (⊠*3257 Rte. 212, Bearsville* ☎845/679–6500), scarves, shawls, jackets, hats, and pillows fashioned from piles of lush chenille fill the front of the store. Behind the counter women work sewing machines, trying to keep pace with orders from Barneys and Bergdorf. Incense tickles your nose as you enter **Mirabai** (⊠*23 Mill Hill Rd.* ☎845/679–2100), a decidedly spiritual bookstore. Crystals give way to books, tapes, and other objects to help the flow of your chi. Two former Condé Nast graphic designers revamped Woodstock's old post office into the **Woodstock Wool Company** (⊠*105 Tinker St.* ☎845/679–0400), a 3,000-square-foot tribute to wool. A boisterous young crowd attends monthly karaoke-knitting sessions at the sleek contemporary space—this is not your grandmother's knitting store.

NIGHTLIFE AND THE ARTS

NIGHTLIFE Local and national performers play at the **Colony Cafe** (⊠*22 Rock City Rd.* ☎845/679–5342 ⊕*www.colonycafe.com*); after the first time, they always come back. A fireplace at one end and a stage at the other anchor the large space. Doors open at 7 nightly except Wednesday, when the place is closed; admission varies. Choose from beer, wine, espresso, and desserts. WDST, Woodstock's independent radio station, books top-notch acts that demonstrably enjoy performing at the open-to-the-elements **Woodstock Playhouse** (⊠*Rtes. 212 and 375* ☎845/679–4101 ⊕*www.woodstockplayhouse.org*). You can expect to interact with the performers—if you're not pulled onto the stage, the performers may work their way through the crowd to you. Seating is stadium style, but you'll be hard-pressed to remain in your seat.

ART GALLERIES **Woodstock Artists Assn. Gallery & Museum.** With three spaces capable of running concurrent exhibitions, this gallery exercises its commitment to showing—and collecting—area artists' works in all mediums. One space has monthly group exhibits; another features solo shows of contemporary artists; and the Phoebe and Belmont Towbin Wing is devoted to art from the permanent collection. ⊠*28 Tinker St.* ☎845/679–2940 ▨*Free* ⊙*Thurs.–Mon. noon–5.*

Woodstock Guild. A nonprofit arts organization with more than 600 members, the guild has been serving artists in the mid-Hudson Valley since

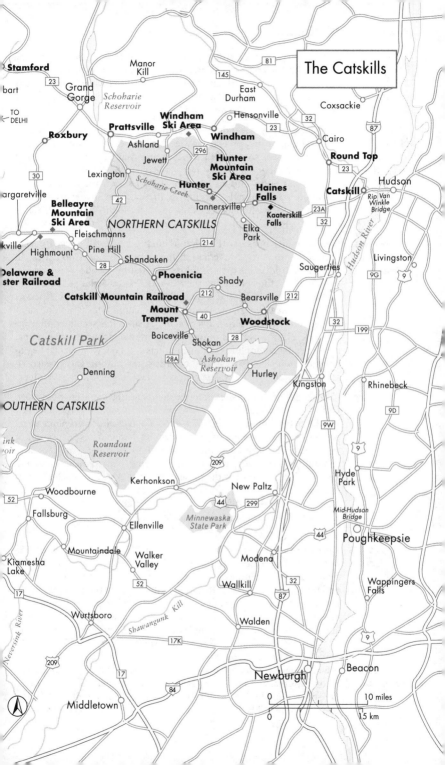

The Catskills

Stamford
Manor Kill
81
bart
23
Grand Gorge
Schoharie Reservoir
145
East Durham
Coxsackie
I-87
TO DELHI
Hensonville
32
Roxbury
Prattsville
Windham Ski Area
23
Windham
Cairo
Round Top
Ashland
296
Coxsackie
23
Jewett
Hunter Mountain Ski Area
Hudson
Lexington
Schoharie Creek
Hunter
Haines Falls
Catskill
30
42
Tannersville
23A
Rip Van Winkle Bridge
argaretville
Belleayre Mountain Ski Area
NORTHERN CATSKILLS
Kaaterskill Falls
32
Fleischmanns
Elka Park
Livingston
kville
Highmount
Pine Hill
214
Saugerties
9G
9
28
Shandaken
Delaware & ster Railroad
Phoenicia
Shady
212
Bearsville
212
Catskill Mountain Railroad
Mount Tremper
40
Woodstock
32
199
Catskill Park
Boiceville
Shokan
28
28A
Ashokan Reservoir
Hurley
Kingston
Rhinebeck
Denning
9D
SOUTHERN CATSKILLS
ink oir
Roundout Reservoir
9W
9
Hyde Park
209
Woodbourne
Kerhonkson
New Paltz
52
44
299
Mid-Hudson Bridge
Fallsburg
Ellenville
Minnewaska State Park
44
Poughkeepsie
Mountaindale
Walker Valley
Modena
Kiamesha Lake
52
Wallkill
32
Wappingers Falls
17
87
Wurtsboro
Shawangunk Kill
Walden
9
209
17K
17
Newburgh
Beacon
84
Middletown

0   10 miles
0   15 km

1939. Steward of the Byrdcliffe Arts Colony, the guild also oversees the **Fleur de Lis Gallery,** which showcases the works of 90-plus artisans, and hosts performing, visual, and literary artists at its **Kleinert/James Arts Center.** ⊠*34 Tinker St.* ☎*845/679–2079* ⊕*www.woodstockguild.org* ✑*Free* ☉*Call for open days and hrs.*

OFF THE BEATEN PATH

Elena Zang Gallery. Meander through the terraced sculpture garden, past the babbling brook, several inspired birdhouses, and other delightful art objects to the studio of Elena Zang and Alan Hoffman, creators of minimalist functional pottery. Down the hill is the gallery space, where blond-wood floors and an infusion of light set off the contemporary art on the walls. Mary Frank, Judy Pfaff, and Joan Snyder are some of the contemporary luminaries exhibiting here. ⊠*3671 Rte. 212, Shady* ☎*845/679–5432* ⊕*www.elenazang.com* ✑*Free* ☉*Daily 11–5.*

FESTIVALS AND EVENTS

Fodor's Choice ★

Hervey White broke with Ralph Whitehead to form his egalitarian enclave for the arts, Maverick, in the woods outside Woodstock. In order to subsidize his dream, White staged a music and dramatic festival in 1915, thus beginning the **Maverick Concert Series** (⊠*1 mi from junction of Rte. 375 and Maverick Rd.* ☎*845/679–8217* ⊕*www. maverickconcerts.org*), the country's oldest continuously running summer chamber-music series. Every summer since has seen a confluence of world-class musicians drawn by superlative acoustics in a chapel renowned by audiophiles. An open-admission policy reflects its beginnings as a collaborative colony of artists; the faithful gather early to secure good seats. The season runs from late June to early September.

Cinephiles flock to Woodstock for five autumnal days in September, when Hollywood converges with the fiercely independent at the well-regarded **Woodstock Film Festival** (☎*845/679–4265* ⊕*www.woodstockfilmfestival. com*). Celebrity-led seminars, film screenings, and raucous parties—most in Woodstock—will keep you buzzing until morning. Poet laureates and Pulitzer Prize winners inspire the aspiring, read to the faithful, and hold workshops praising the muse during the **Woodstock Poetry Festival** (✉*Box 450, 12498* ☎*No phone*), held the last weekend in August. Venues include the Colony Cafe, the Maverick Concert Hall, and the Center for Photography at Woodstock.

WHERE TO EAT

$–$$$
AMERICAN

✕**Bear Cafe.** Rock stars and actors find their way to this streamside restaurant 3 mi west of Woodstock, where a horseshoe bar adjoins two dining areas (one outdoors). Sit on the west side of the restaurant for an unfettered view of the Saw Kill stream; the patio is about as close to the water as you can get without falling in. The kitchen prepares American fare, such as its signature filet mignon dressed with port-garlic sauce and Stilton. The wine list includes 200 bottles, and prices range from $25 to $1,500. ⊠*295A Tinker St., Bearsville* ☎*845/679–5555* ▭*MC, V* ☉*Closed Tues. No lunch.*

$$–$$$
MEDITERRANEAN

✕**Blue Mountain Bistro.** A barn with rough-hewn beams and siding from a corncrib makes for a cozy yet elegant atmosphere. The zinc tapas bar serves duck liver pâté, Moroccan carrot salad, and other goodies. Local wisdom holds that you can't get a bad meal here. Try mushroom

The Borscht Belt

Liberty and Monticello are jumping-off points for the legendary Catskills resorts. The cool, dry atmosphere of the region and its proximity to New York City historically attracted sufferers of tuberculosis and other lung ailments. Later, Russian and Eastern European Jews flocked here to escape the heat and disease of New York City's immigrant ghettos. Over time, this network of vacation spots came to be known as the Borscht Belt, and served as boot camp for innumerable entertainers who later gained national prominence. (The Catskills churned out comedians Milton Berle, Freddie Roman, and Danny Kaye, to name a few.) Not many of the old-time resorts are still standing, although a few remain as popular golf destinations. The influence of the resorts era has faded from the landscape, but the Yiddish sayings uttered by the local high-school kids are remnants of this period of Catskills history.

panzerotti (a pizzalike tart), jumbo scallops with wild-mushroom risotto, or *moules* Marseillaise, and see if you agree. Herb gardens border the outdoor patio. ⊠*1633 Glasco Tpke.* ☎*845/679–8519* ⚑*Reservations essential* ▤*AE, D, DC, MC, V* ☾*Closed Sun. and Mon.*

$$–$$$
MIDDLE EASTERN ✕**Joshua's.** At one of the oldest eateries on Woodstock's main street, the unassuming interior gives no hint of the wonders coming out of the kitchen. The inventive Middle Eastern menu includes zucchini flat cakes and tangy Cosmic Curry Chicken served over brown-rice pilaf. Joshua's smorgasbord brings together hummus, baba ghanoush, tabbouleh, dolmas, and salad. ⊠*51 Tinker St.* ☎*845/679–5533* ▤*AE, MC, V* ☾*Closed Wed. in Jan.–Mar.*

¢–$$
CHINESE ✕**The Little Bear.** The wall of windows overlooking the Saw Kill inspires thoughts of feng shui as you ponder the extensive menu. Try chicken (or tofu) with honey walnuts or the vegetable–shark fin soup for two. Hunan shredded pork with black-bean sauce is one way to indulge carnivorous tendencies. The chef keeps it healthy by refusing to yield to the seduction of MSG, and the alert staff keeps things moving. ⊠*295B Tinker St., Bearsville* ☎*845/679–8899* ▤*AE, MC, V.*

¢–$
MEXICAN ✕**Taco Juan's.** The laid-back storefront eatery began as a humble stand behind the infamous Espresso Café. You can help yourself to utensils and sort your dirty dishes when you're finished, and a rogues' gallery of Woodstock characters lines one wall. Nothing beats the enormous wet-tofu burrito; a scoop of Jane's homemade ice cream is the perfect chaser. Park benches outside provide front-row seats for watching bongo players on the village green. ⊠*31 Tinker St.* ☎*845/679–9673* ⚑*Reservations not accepted* ▤*No credit cards.*

WHERE TO STAY

$$–$$$ 🛏 **Enchanted Manor.** This B&B eschews the farm aesthetic for the suburban. Seemingly endless decks lead to a heated pool, hot tub, and pond—all framed by 8 acres of forest. To enter the 1965 white-columned brick house you first must remove your shoes. A fireplace warms the large living room, where plush upholstery invites you to unwind. Cozy bedrooms and friendly hosts lend a comfortable vibe. The suite has its own living room and fireplace, and some rooms have hot tubs. **Pros:** smoke-free property (indoor and outdoor); full spa services. **Cons:** must drive to most activities. ⊠*23 Rowe Rd.* ☎*845/679–9012* ⊕*www.enchantedmanorinn.com* ⟿*2 rooms, 1 suite, 1 cabin (no bath in cabin)* ⌂*In-room: no phone. In-hotel: pool, gym, laundry facilities, no kids, no-smoking rooms* ⊟*AE, MC, V* �rm*BP.*

$ ▦**Twin Gables.** This Victorian B&B in the center of Woodstock has served lodgers since the 1940s; shops, restaurants, and live-music venues are within strolling distance. Patterned wallpaper provides a backdrop for period furnishings and local artists' works. Be aware that several bedrooms share hall bathrooms. **Pros:** homey atmosphere; within walking distance of many activities and diversions. **Cons:** some shared baths; limited off-street parking. ⊠*73 Tinker St.* ☎*845/679–9479* ⊕*www.twingableswoodstockny.com* ⟿*9 rooms, 3 with bath* ⌂*In-room: no phone, no TV. In-hotel: no-smoking rooms* ⊟*AE, D, MC, V* �rm*CP.*

$$–$$$ ▦**The Wild Rose Inn.** Beyond a white picket fence and a pleasant amble from central Woodstock is this rose-themed 1898 Victorian. Most rooms are draped in damask and organza swags and bedding. A dramatic, antique walnut-burl bed takes center stage in the Honeysuckle Rose Suite, which has a private entrance. The Sweetheart Room is the smallest of the accommodations, but the others are large; all have hot tubs. Complimentary brandy, truffles, and fruit add to the sweetness, and the Continental breakfast is substantial. **Pros:** heated saltwater pool; serene atmosphere. **Cons:** two-night minimum stay May-November; three-night minimum stay during holidays. ⊠*66 Rock City Rd.,* ☎*845/679–8783* ⊕*www.thewildroseinn.com* ⟿*2 rooms, 3 suites* ⌂ *In-room: no phone. In-hotel: no-smoking rooms* ⊟*MC, V* ⌑*CP.*

$$–$$$ ▦**Woodstock Country Inn.** Hidden in a meadow of wildflowers several hundred yards from the quiet main road 2 mi west of Woodstock center, this bed-and-breakfast offers peaceful seclusion. The house includes paintings by Woodstock artist Jo Cantine, who originally lived here. Guest rooms keep frills to a minimum, instead offering simple luxuries such as 300-thread-count sateen sheets, mountain views, a porch or deck, and a private entrance. Breakfast is lavish and consists of organic fare. **Pros:** lots of nearby activities; elegant setting. **Cons:** 2 mi from town; kids under 12 not welcome. ⊠*Cooper Lake Rd.* ☎*845/679–9380* ⊕*www.woodstockcountryinn.com* ⟿*3 rooms, 1 suite* ⌂*In-room: no phone, kitchen (some), no TV (some). In-hotel: pool, no kids under 12, no-smoking rooms* ⊟*MC, V* ⌑*BP.*

¢–$$ ▦**Woodstock Inn on the Millstream.** Tall pines stand sentinel at this motel-style lodging, creating a private haven a short walk from the center of Woodstock. After splashing in the swimming hole you can relax on the landscaped lawn. In the rooms, more like B&B accommodations than motel units, hanging flower planters adorn front porches, and quilts cover beds. The Continental breakfast spread is bountiful. **Pros:** short walk from town; free Wi-Fi. **Cons:** some rooms are on the small side; no pets. ⊠*48 Tannery Brook Rd.* ☎*845/679–8211 or 800/420–4707* ⊕*www.woodstock-inn-ny.com* ⟿*11 rooms, 5 studios* ⌂*In-room: no phone, kitchen (some), Internet.* ⊟*AE, MC, V* ⌑*BP.*

TAKE A TOUR BY TRAIN

The **Catskill Mountain Railroad** (✉ *Rte. 28, Mount Pleasant* ☎ *845/688–7400* ⊕ *www.catskillmtrailroad.com* ✉ *$14*) runs train tours through the northern Catskills following the famed Esopus Creek. Board the 1920s-style train and watch from the gondola car for bald eagles, great blue herons, hawks, deer, and other wildlife during the 1½-hour round-trip. During summer months, the railroad shuttles tubers back to their cars after they've floated down the Esopus Creek. At Phoenicia Station be sure to take in the Empire State Railway Museum to learn more about the region's history. On weekends and holidays from late May through October, trains depart three times daily for the 12-mi tour which passes through Phoenicia and Boiceville.

From late May through October, the **Delaware & Ulster Rail Road** (✉ *43510 Rte. 28, Arkville* ☎ *845/586–3877 or 800/225–4132* ⊕ *www.durr.org* ✉ *$7–$15*) train travels along the Catskill Scenic Trail and the East Branch of the Delaware River, providing farm, field, and mountain views. It leaves Arkville for Roxbury (1 hour and 45 minutes round-trip), home of railroad magnate Jay Gould, who created the original railway in this area. On weekends you can opt for the shorter ride to Halcottsville, which takes about an hour there and back. Special excursions include a train ride to Highmount, where you transfer to a shuttle bound for the lift ride at Belleayre Mountain (a three-hour outing), and a ride pulled by Thomas the Tank Engine. From mid-September through October, leaf peepers pack the trains.

MOUNT TREMPER

10 mi west of Woodstock.

A Woodstock neighbor and home to the acclaimed Zen Mountain Monastery, Mount Tremper has attracted its share of artists and weekenders seeking a less-expensive address. The village sits along Esopus Creek, which lures anglers and is a popular spot for tubing.

WHAT TO SEE

Emerson Country Store. This darkened 60-foot grain silo now houses an enormous **kaleidoscope.** From the silo, wander through the cobblestone courtyard of this retail complex, where upscale boutiques sell clothing, furniture, and antiques. ✉ *146 Mount Pleasant Rd.* ☎ *845/688–5800* ⊕ *www.emersonplace.com* ✉ *Kaleidoscope $7* ☉ *Mid-Sept.–May, Wed.–Mon. 10–5; June–mid-Sept., daily 10–6.*

Zen Mountain Monastery. This monastery resides in a four-story bluestone–and–white oak church on 230 acres bordered by the Beaverkill and Esopus rivers. The building, constructed by Norwegian craftsmen at the turn of the 20th century, includes a 150-person meditation hall, a dining hall, and resident and guest quarters. The only way to visit is to partake in introductory Zen instruction—offered Wednesday evenings and as weekend retreats—or in the Sunday session of services, *zazen* (or sitting) meditation, and lunch. ✉ *S. Plank Rd. off Rte. 212*

☎ *845/688–2228* ⊕ *www.mro.org* ✉ *Wed. free; Sun. $5 donation* ☾ *Wed. 7:30* PM*–9* PM*, Sun. 8:45* AM*–noon.*

SPORTS AND THE OUTDOORS

CANOEING AND KAYAKING The owner of **Cold Brook Canoes** (✉ *4181 Rte. 28, Boiceville* ☎ *845/657–2189*), Ernie Gardner, began selling canoes out of his garage in 1970. Since then his selection has expanded, and the garage now overflows with canoes, kayaks, flotation devices, wet bags, and anything else you might need on the water. Ernie, who's always friendly, can also point you to the best paddling spots.

FISHING An especially productive area of Esopus Creek is just south of Boiceville (3 mi south of Mount Tremper), near the Ashokan Reservoir, where anglers cast for smallmouth bass and walleye in addition to wild rainbow trout, brown trout, and brook trout. **Ed's Fly Fishing & Guide Services** (✉ *69 Ridge Rd., Shokan* ☎ *845/657–6393*) can teach you to fly-fish for trout in Esopus Creek or the Delaware or Neversink rivers for $150 a day. Because Ed doesn't take out more than three people at a time, personal attention is pretty much guaranteed. Book several weeks in advance—especially in spring and fall—and be sure to secure a New York State fishing permit.

SHOPPING

Soapbox-derby entries mingle with sculpture at **Fabulous Furniture** (✉ *Rte. 28, Boiceville* ☎ *845/657–6317*). Around back, owner Steve Heller does unimaginable things to rotting or dead wood and old Cadillacs and other cars. Inside are the amazing results: custom-made tables with tree-trunk bases, lamps, menorahs, and mirrors.

WHERE TO EAT

$$ × **Catskill Rose.** Architectural glass blocks flank a magenta door, hinting AMERICAN at the funky art-deco motif inside. Herb gardens line the restaurant's perimeter, with brightly painted window boxes above. If you want to eat alfresco, head for the periwinkle tables and chairs on the brick courtyard. The menu, which changes with the seasons and is mostly new American, might include smoked duck with tamarind-raspberry sauce or poached salmon flavored with lemon and basil. ✉ *5355 Rte. 212* ☎ *845/688–7100* ▤ *D, DC, MC, V* ☾ *Closed Mon.–Wed. No lunch.*

WHERE TO STAY

$$$$ ▦ **The Emerson Inn & Spa.** You're pampered from the minute you pull up ★ to this 1870s Victorian building. Before you know it, your car is parked, your luggage is delivered to your room, and you're accepting a flute of champagne. Persian, Victorian, West Indies colonial, African, and Asian decorative schemes are manifested in tailored leopard-print curtains, Asian and African artifacts, fringed lamp shades, and embroidered pillows. Bedrooms have cordless phones and Frette linens. One suite has a sauna; the duplex has two bathrooms and an indoor hammock; and others feature in-room hot tubs. Fine china and crystal adorn tables in the restaurant ($$–$$$$), where Continental fare meets contemporary flair. Roast rack of lamb, for instance, is paired with Parmesan soufflé. At the serene spa, which is open to the public, you can indulge in everything from algae wraps to shiatsu. **Pros:** great for weddings;

top-rated spa. **Cons:** pricey; no pre-teens allowed. ⊠*5340 Rte. 28* ☎*845/688–7900 or 877/688–2828* ⊕*www.emersonplace.com* ➪*20 rooms, 4 suites* ⅃*In-room: no TV (some), Internet. In-hotel: restaurant, gym, spa, bicycles, no kids under 13, no-smoking rooms* ⊟*AE, D, DC, MC, V* ⍥*BP.*

$$$–$$$$ ⊞**Kate's Lazy Meadow Motel.** The exterior of this single-story 1950s motel reveals little of what's inside the meticulously appointed suites, owned by Kate Pierson of the B-52s and kept clean by Lady Estrogen, the drag-queen maid. The funky decor includes vintage pieces—Eames furniture, Russel Wright kitchenware—as well as custom wallpaper and handcrafted bathroom tiles and shower curtains. Most of the suites have a mint '50s kitchen and a sitting area with a gas fireplace; some suites have sleeping lofts and private decks. Lush gardens designed by Dean Riddle (a nationally known garden writer and green thumb) surround the red motel. A bonfire pit overlooks Esopus Creek, where you can fish for trout or—thanks to the motel's wireless Internet access—check your e-mail on your laptop. **Pros:** *very* different property; wide variety of accommodations. **Cons:** no personal checks. ⊠*5191 Rte. 28* ☎*845/688–7200* ⊕*www.lazymeadow.com* ➪*7 suites* ⅃*In-room: kitchen (some), refrigerator, Internet. In-hotel: Wi-Fi, no kids under 15, no-smoking rooms* ⊟*AE, D, DC, MC, V.*

¢–$$ ⊞**La Duchesse Anne.** As you pull into the gravel driveway and climb the steps of this 1850s Victorian, visions of Grandma's house dance in your head. Crushed velvet and floral paper cover the walls, and period antiques grace dark rooms. Diners come from miles around to savor such French dishes as *cotriade bretonne* (fish stew), rack of lamb, and Black Angus steak with peppercorn-cognac cream sauce, served in formal surroundings with a glowing fireplace. **Pros:** great dining; very Victorian; reasonable rates. **Cons:** far from activities; no in-room telephones. ⊠*1564 Wittenberg Rd.* ☎*845/688–5260* ⊕*www. laduchesseanne.com* ➪*8 rooms* ⅃*In-room: no phone. In-hotel: restaurant* ⊟*AE, D, MC, V.*

$$–$$$ ⊞**Onteora Mountain House.** The spectacular Catskills vistas at this
★ B&B—the former summer home of mayonnaise magnate Richard Hellman—will leave you breathless. A massive stone fireplace presides over the great room, a magnificent space with a soaring ceiling. Oriental rugs, scattered across wide-plank honey-color floors, cushion your every step, and Asian antiques and American pieces enjoy an elegant coexistence. Some rooms have fireplaces and hot tubs, and one has a window seat with dazzling valley views. Play billiards in the cavernous game room, or sweat it out in the sauna. Weekends in May through August usually book up a year in advance. **Pros:** great views; perfect for romantic getaways. **Cons:** remote location; does not accept reservations more than three months in advance. ⊠*96 Piney Point Rd., Boiceville* ☎*845/657–6233* ⊕*www.onteora.com* ➪*4 rooms, 1 suite* ⅃ *In-room: no a/c, no phone, no TV. In-hotel: no kids under 12, no-smoking rooms* ⊟*D, MC, V* ⍥*BP.*

6

CAMPING   ⚠Kenneth L. Wilson Campground. At this campground, part of the Catskill
  ¢   Forest Preserve camping system, tall pine trees surround sites, which are
near a lake with a sand beach. The lake contains chain pickerel, yellow
perch, bullheads, white sucker, shiners, and sunfish. Fishing licenses
are available at the campground, as are rowboat, canoe, paddleboat,
and kayak rentals. The grounds—originally several farms—lie in the
valley of Little Beaver Kill, a tributary of Esopus Creek. Each site has a
picnic table and grill. Self-contained RVs are welcome. **Pros:** great fishing; ample opportunities for outdoor fun. **Cons:** you'll be roughing it;
reservations are a must. ⚲ *Grills, flush toilets, dump station, showers,
picnic tables, public telephone, swimming (lake)* ✉*859 Wittenberg
Rd.* ☎*845/679–7020, 800/456–2267 reservations* ⊕*www.dec.ny.gov*
🛏*76 tent sites* ⚲*Reservations essential* ▤*MC, V* ⊘*Closed Columbus Day–Apr.*

PHOENICIA

8 mi north of Mount Tremper.

Phoenicia has been undergoing a transformation since the 1990s, when
hipsters discovered the tiny hamlet. The number of creative individuals
who have settled here, establishing funky boutiques and fine restaurants, is growing. Many out-of-towners come to Phoenicia to go tubing
down Esopus Creek, and the Hunter and Belleayre ski resorts are an
easy trip from here through the High Peaks area.

SPORTS AND THE OUTDOORS

HIKING   Two trails lead you to the summit of **Tremper Mountain** (☎*607/652–
7365, 607/652–5076, or 607/652–5063* ⊕*www.catskillcenter.org*),
where an early-20th-century fire tower stands. The red-blazed Phoenicia Trail, the much shorter but steeper of the two, begins off Route 40
about 1 mi southeast of Phoenicia and climbs the western side of the
mountain for 2¾ mi to the summit (at 2,740 feet). The 4.2-mi Willow
Trail starts just west of the post office in the village of Willow, on Route
212 about 5 mi southeast of Phoenicia.

TUBING   **F-S Tube and Raft Rentals** (✉*4 Church St.* ☎*845/688–7633*), a tubing
outfitter, offers a 4-mi run down Esopus Creek. A lower 3-mi course
encounters milder rapids and is more appropriate for families. (Children must be at least nine years old to go tubing.) The season runs
from Memorial Day to the third week in September; $10 covers tube
rental and transport.

The red barn that stands guard as you enter Phoenicia houses the **Town
Tinker** (✉*10 Bridge St.* ☎*845/688–5553* ⊕*www.towntinker.com*),
which has everything you need to spend a day riding the rapids or drift-
ing on the currents of the Esopus. From mid-May through September
you can rent tubes for beginner and advanced routes on Esopus Creek
between Shandaken and Mount Pleasant. Don't feel like hiking back?
Get out at a designated spot for a ride to Phoenicia on the Catskill
Mountain Railroad. Tube and transport are $15. Children must be
older than 12, and only strong swimmers should consider this.

SHOPPING

Garden gnomes occupy the front window of **Morne Imports** (✉ *52 Main St.* ☎ *845/688–7738*), and camping and hunting gear hangs precariously above their heads. The general store sells everything you'll need to tackle nature, from fishing rods and hand-tied flies to hunting knives. Home goods are artfully displayed at **The Tender Land** (✉ *45 Main St.* ☎ *845/688–2001*), a sophisticated country housewares shop. After browsing here, head down the street to Tender Land Home, a complementary contemporary store filled with small—aka easily transportable—delights. Chic pottery and luscious pillows, window treatments, and rugs will make you want to move in.

NIGHTLIFE AND THE ARTS

ART GALLERY   A blue-sequined sign lures you inside **Upstate Art** (✉ *60 Main St.* ☎ *845/688–9881* ✐ *Free* ☉ *Call for hrs or to make an appointment*). Upstairs, six brightly lighted rooms exhibit contemporary regional artists. Nita Friedman has been running the gallery since the late 1990s, and her lively openings draw local artists out of their homes in the surrounding wooded hills.

THEATER   The **Shandaken Theatrical Society** (✉ *Church St.* ☎ *845/688–2279*) produces a show each season: a spring musical, a summer melodrama, a fall comedy or drama, and a winter holiday event. Past performances include *Cabaret, Harvey,* and *The Sound of Music.*

WHERE TO EAT AND STAY

¢–$ ✕ **Sweet Sue's.** French doors open into a bright, airy space filled with
AMERICAN   white wooden booths, marble-top café tables, and a stainless-steel counter where trays of fresh muffins keep cool. Folksy renditions of the house specialties decorate one wall; a blackboard announcing specials resides on another. Robert De Niro haunts this place, as do other area glitterati. You'll see why when you tuck into the Blue Monkey, a stack of blueberry-banana buttermilk pancakes. Pumpkin-crusted tofu over polenta and sautéed kale topped with roasted red-pepper sauce are served alongside hot meat loaf sandwiches and other comfort food. Efficient, friendly service caters to your needs. Take a note from the locals—who come armed with newspapers and books—and stay a while. Reservations are essential on weekends. ✉ *33 Main St.* ☎ *845/688–7852* ▤ *No credit cards* ☉ *Closed Tues. and Wed.*

CAMPING   ⚠ **Woodland Valley State Park Campground.** The woodsy sites here, with
¢   trails leading to Wittenberg and Cornell mountains, are favorites with hikers. Some sites are next to Woodland Valley Stream, which teems with fish. Fishing licenses are available, and self-contained RVs are welcome. **Pros:** nice amenities; wooded sites. **Cons:** reservations are a must; seasonal operation. ☖ *Flush toilets, dump station, showers, picnic tables, public telephone* ✉ *1319 Woodland Valley Rd.* ☎ *845/688– 7647* ⚲ *72 tent sites* ⚑ *Reservations essential* ▤ *MC, V* ☉ *Closed mid-Oct.–mid-May.*

6

BELLEAYRE MOUNTAIN SKI AREA

Highmount is 12 mi northwest of Phoenicia.

Some of the villages and hamlets close to Belleayre have been experiencing resurgence, spurred by an influx of city folk escaping the rat race. In Margaretville, 9 mi east of Belleayre, boutiques and upscale restaurants are beginning to take root. A couple of miles before Margaretville is Arkville (blink, and you'll miss it), home to the Erpf Cultural Center and Delaware & Ulster Railroad. With half a dozen restaurants and places to stay, Pine Hill—a stone's throw from the Highmount-based ski resort—bustles by comparison. In Fleischmanns, 3 mi east of Belleayre, locals sit on their porches and Orthodox Jewish families stroll down the sleepy Main Street. Shandaken, at the junction of Routes 42 and 28, sits beside Esopus Creek.

SPORTS AND THE OUTDOORS

Catskill Center for Conservation and Development. The center helps villages and hamlets in the region get grants for beautification and other economic stimulation programs. Its gallery in the **Erpf Cultural Center** hosts rotating exhibits of regional artists' works, with a focus on nature-inspired pieces. You can take part in twice-monthly public events, including hikes, canoe trips, bird-watching, and lectures. ✉*43355 Rte. 28, Arkville* ☎*845/586–2611* ⊕*www.catskillcenter.org* ☜*Free* ☉ *Weekdays 9–5, Sat. 10–2.*

SKI AREA   The **Belleayre Mountain Ski Center** (✉*Belleayre Mountain Rd. off Rte. 28, Highmount* ☎*845/254–5600 or 800/942–6904* ⊕*www.belleayre. com*), in the Catskill Forest Preserve, has one section for expert skiers and another for intermediates and novices. Of the 38 trails that vein the peak's 171 acres of skiable terrain, 22% are for beginners and 58% are for intermediate skiers; the vertical drop is 1,404 feet. The resort, owned by the New York State Department of Environmental Conservation, has 96% snowmaking capability, eight lifts, and more than 5 mi of cross-country trails. Families appreciate the laid-back atmosphere, while serious skiers seek out the great snow, grooming, and single- and double-black-diamond trails. Skiing and snowboarding instruction and rentals are available. Full-day peak-season lift tickets are $42. A shuttle transports skiers to and from nearby villages. From late April through October, the upper, lower, and cross-country areas offer biking tracks for beginners to experts; lifts aren't equipped for bikes, so you have to ride in both directions. From Memorial Day through Labor Day you may also swim, boat, and fish at Pine Hill Lake ($6 per car), where pedal boats, rowboats, and kayaks are for rent. A lift ($8 per person) takes you to the summit, from which you can hike or ride the lift back down. Belleayre hosts crafts, music, and other festivals, too.

SHOPPING

Vintage housewares sit alongside Nigella Lawson's kitchen line at **Home Goods of Margaretville** (✉*The Commons, Main St., Margaretville* ☎*845/586–4177*), an emporium with everything for anyone who cooks or entertains. Le Creuset cast-iron pots, neat dish towels, and cookbooks fill the large, bright store.

NIGHTLIFE AND THE ARTS

Lyle Lovett, the Neville Brothers, Herbie Hancock, and the Alvin Ailey American Dance Theater are among the performers who have appeared at the annual **Belleayre Music Festival** (✉ *Belleayre Mountain Ski Center, off Rte. 28, Highmount* ☎ *845/254–5600 or 800/942–6904* ⊕ *www. belleayre.com*), held Saturday nights in July and August. Friday nights in August bring the Jazz Club, when the audience dances up a storm under the stars.

WHERE TO EAT

¢ ✕ **The Cheese Barrel.** Locals come to this upscale deli-grocery for break-
AMERICAN fast and lunch, or to pick up specialty ingredients. You can eat a sandwich or sip an organic-coffee drink at one of the café tables in the simple dining area. While waiting, study shelves of vinegars, olives, old-fashioned candy, and Italian lemonade. ✉ *Main St., Margaretville* ☎ *845/586–4666* ⊟ *MC, V* ⊘ *No dinner.*

¢–$ ✕ **El Rey Mexican Restaurant.** Traditional Mexican celebration banners in
MEXICAN bright red, green, yellow, and pink hang from the ceiling of this convivial spot, where locals flock for good, inexpensive food. The menu leans toward Tex-Mex fare: fajitas, enchiladas, burritos, and tostadas. The salsa, infused with cilantro, is available to go, and diners inevitably grab a quart to take home. ✉ *297 Main St., Pine Hill* ☎ *845/254–6027* ⊟ *MC, V* ⊘ *Closed Tues.*

$$–$$$ ✕ **Loretta Charles' Natural Wood Grill.** Most dishes at this new American
AMERICAN restaurant overlooking Esopus Creek involve seafood. The dining room is rustic, with a wood-burning fireplace and picture windows overlooking the water. The blackboard menu, which changes weekly, might include Thai-style grilled shrimp with chilies and garlic, served with basmati rice. The food is all grilled over hickory and cherrywood, and entrées come with at least four vegetables. A piano player entertains at an upright in the dining room Friday and Saturday nights. ✉ *7159 Rte. 28, Shandaken* ☎ *845/688–2550* ⊟ *AE, D, MC, V* ⊘ *Closed Mon.– Wed. No lunch.*

$–$$ ✕ **Pine Hill Arms Hotel.** This 1882 country inn has two dining rooms—the
CONTINENTAL Catskill Mountain Room, with rustic barn-wood siding, and the Greenhouse Room—and a bar. Among the draws: charcoal-broiled steaks, blackened red snapper, a wide range of desserts, and a hearty country-style breakfast. The après-ski crowd packs the place on winter weekends, when live bands play. ✉ *Main St., Pine Hill* ☎ *845/254–4012 or 800/932–2446* ⊟ *AE, D, MC, V* ⊘ *Closed Mon. and Tues. No lunch Wed.–Fri. and Sun.*

$–$$ ✕ **Pine Hill Indian Restaurant.** Framed Indian textiles and embroidered
INDIAN curtains set the stage for tasty tandoori chicken, chicken korma, *biriani* (a layered dish of spicy meat and rice), and other Indian specialties. On weekend nights you can sample a chunk of the menu during an all-you-can-eat buffet; $12.95 lets you choose from a dozen entrées (many vegetarian) and includes dessert and coffee. You can bring your own beer or wine to accompany the meal, or enjoy a refreshing *lassi* (a cold yogurt drink). ✉ *143 Main St., Pine Hill* ☎ *845/254–6666* ⊟ *AE, D, MC, V* ⊘ *Closed Tues. and Wed.*

WHERE TO STAY

¢–$ 🖭 **Highlands Inn.** Fragrant lavender blooms near the entrance to this 1904 late Victorian. Original inlaid parquet floors and chestnut trim run through the 3,000 square feet of common space, which includes a sunroom, a library with an upright piano, two dining rooms, and a lounge with a 73-inch TV, a gas fireplace, leather couches, and a pool table. Guest rooms are outfitted in florals, toiles, or country quilts. Some have twin beds; all have private sinks. Third-floor rooms are nestled under the eaves. **Pros:** romantic rooms; kids under 12 stay free. **Cons:** no pets; no room phones/Internet. ⊠ *923 Main St., Fleischmanns* ☎ *845/254–5650* ⊕ *www.thehighlandsinn.com* ⤳ *7 rooms, 3 with bath* ⟁ *In-room: no a/c, no phone, no TV. In-hotel: Wi-Fi, no-smoking rooms* ⊟ *MC, V* ℺ *BP.*

¢–$ 🖭 **Margaretville Mountain Inn.** This 1886 Queen Anne Victorian occupies 6 acres atop Margaretville Mountain, on the site of what was the region's first cauliflower farm. Bluestone steps lead to the 80-foot porch, where you can sit on wicker love seats and chairs while taking in sweeping views of the Catskill Mountains. Lace curtains veil the windows, and vintage photographs line the stairs leading to antiques-filled rooms. One room has a dramatic canopied brass bed. Breakfast is served on Royal Dalton china in a formal dining room. A hot tub occupies the old milk house. **Pros:** reasonable rates; good starting point for regional tours. **Cons:** extra fee for children; $5-per-night service fee. ⊠ *1478 Margaretville Mountain Rd., Margaretville* ☎ *845/586–3933* ⊕ *www.margaretvilleinn.com* ⤳ *6 rooms* ⟁ *In-room: no a/c, no phone, no TV (some). In-hotel: some pets allowed, no-smoking rooms* ⊟ *AE, MC, V* ℺ *BP.*

¢–$ 🖭 **River Run Bed & Breakfast Inn.** Garden gnomes greet you on the front porch of this Queen Anne Victorian. The smell of freshly baked muffins permeates the 1887 house, which has antiques, original stained glass, and a pictorial history of the innkeeper's family. The suite—decorated with '50s furnishings and retro floral prints—has two bedrooms, two bathrooms, a private entrance, and a kitchen. You can fly-fish for brown trout at the edge of the 1-acre yard, where the Bushkill Stream flows by old stone retaining walls, or wander through a stone labyrinth. A full vegetarian breakfast is served, and there is a refrigerator in the common area. **Pros:** pets welcome (except during winter); free Wi-Fi. **Cons:** no phones in rooms. ⊠ *882 Main St., Fleischmanns* ☎ *845/254–4884* ⊕ *www.catskill.net/riverrun* ⤳ *8 rooms, 4 with bath; 1 suite* ⟁ *In-room: no a/c, no phone, no TV (some), kitchen (some), Wi-Fi. In-hotel: Wi-Fi, some pets allowed, no-smoking rooms* ⊟ *MC, V* ℺ *BP.*

HUNTER

12 mi northeast of Phoenicia.

Nestled in the shadow of Hunter Mountain, the second-highest mountain in the Catskills, the village of Hunter is all about the slopes. On winter weekends thousands of skiers flock to the area, the oldest of the Catskill ski resorts. Although it was once dominated by twenty-something rowdies from the New York metropolitan area—and still provides, along with nearby Tannersville (5 mi east), a raucous nightlife scene—Hunter is becoming more family oriented. In other seasons, fairs and special events (including a well-known Oktoberfest) are held here. The village's permanent arts scene, mostly the work of the not-for-profit Catskill Mountain Foundation (CMF), includes a gallery, movie theater, bookstore, and performing-arts center.

OFF THE BEATEN PATH Verdigris copper onion domes perch atop cedar-shingled structures at the Ukrainian cultural complex surrounding **St. John the Baptist Ukrainian Catholic Church** (⊠ *Rte. 23A, 5 mi west of Hunter* ☎ *No phone*), built without using a single nail in the 1960s by Ukrainian expatriates who settled in the surrounding mountains.

SPORTS AND THE OUTDOORS

☾ The year-round **Bear Creek Landing Family Sport Complex** (⊠ *Rte. 214 south of Rte. 23A* ☎ *518/263–3839*) has 18 holes of miniature golf, a driving range, go-karts, a trout pond, an arcade room, ice-skating, snowmobiling, and a restaurant that specializes in barbecue. On some weekends you get live music with your smoked meat.

Hunter Mountain Skyride. A lift takes you over 1 mi to the 3,200-foot summit of Hunter Mountain, where you can look out at the Catskill, Berkshire, and Green mountain ranges. The autumn foliage here is gorgeous. ⊠ *Rte. 23A* ☎ *518/263–4223 or 800/486–8376* ⊕ *www. huntermtn.com* 🎫 *$6* ◷ *Early July–Aug., Wed. noon–4 and weekends 10–5; Sept.–early Oct., weekends 10–5.*

Mountain Top Arboretum. The 11 acres of this preserve and garden are part of a 21-acre experiment that was begun in the late 1970s to see which temperate trees could grow at 2,500 feet above sea level. Wooded paths weave past lush ferns, oaks, beech, rhododendron, and mountain laurel. A circular path leads to a large, open meadow filled with finches, warblers, orioles, thrushes, sapsuckers, bluebirds, turkeys, and hummingbirds. In spring you may see ducks and geese at the pond, where great blue herons have moved in. ⊠ *Rte. 23C and Maude Adams Rd., Tannersville* ☎ *518/589–3903* ⊕ *www.mtarbor.org* 🎫 *Free* ◷ *Apr.– Nov., daily dawn–dusk.*

FISHING The **Hunter Mountain Expeditions** (⊠ *Rte. 23A* ☎ *518/263–4223, 518/263–4666, or 800/486–8376* ⊕ *www.huntermtn.com*) offers fly-fishing instruction, guide services, and equipment rentals from April through November. Once enrolled, you can expect to spend the day on Schoharie or Esopus creek, casting for rainbow, brown, or brook trout or bass. You must have a valid New York State fishing license.

HIKING **Devil's Path** (⊠ *Off Rte. 214* ☎ *607/652–7365, 607/652–5076, or 607/652–5063* ⊕ *www.dec.ny.gov*), in the Westkill Mountain Wilderness area of the Catskills, winds through the Stony Clove mountain pass and around natural rock formations. Follow the red trail markers for the scenic 7-mi hike to the summit of Westkill Mountain (3,880 feet). The trailhead is at the north end of the parking lot at the Devil's Tombstone Campground, at Diamond Notch Lake. To get here from Hunter proper, take Route 23A east to Route 214 and head south for 4 mi.

CATSKILLS SPORTS AND OUTDOORS

■TIP➜ Deer ticks—the carriers of Lyme disease—are prevalent in the Catskills; wear bug repellant, cover skin with light-color clothing, and check for ticks after outdoor excursions and activities.

BIKING

Cyclists will find a mix of endurance-testing hills and flat straightaways. Throughout the region you can find marked bike trails, wide country roads, and no-vehicles-allowed rail trails. Bike-rental locations and tourism offices can provide information about specific routes.

In its online biking guide, the **Sullivan County Visitor's Association** (⊠ *100 North St., Monticello* ☎ *800/882–2287* ⊕ *www.scva. net*) outlines 14 suggested rides. The **Delaware County Chamber of Commerce** (⊠ *114 Main St., Delhi* ☎ *607/746–2281* ⊕ *www. delawarecounty.org*) has information about the 19-mi Catskill Scenic Trail—an old railway path—and lists five bike routes on its Web site.

For challenging mountain biking, head for the ski resorts in the off-season, when they turn their trails over to two-wheeled enthusiasts. (The Ski Plattekill resort is one of the top mountain-biking spots in North America.)

CANOEING AND KAYAKING

The Class II–III Esopus Creek, which parallels Route 28 in and around Phoenicia, is a popular spot for canoeing and kayaking. Regulated by the **New York State Department of Environmental Conservation** (☎ *845/256–3161 Esopus water-release information* ⊕ *www.dec. ny.gov*), releases from the nearby Schoharie Reservoir help maintain

optimal conditions for recreational use of the creek waters—and create some awesome rapids. Contact the DEC for water-release schedules and additional information. If you're looking for a something tamer, try the Delaware River; public-access spots are scattered between Long Eddy and Port Jervis.

FISHING

Fly-fishing is said to have gotten its start in the Catskills—more specifically, at Roscoe's Junction Pool, where the Willowemoc River runs into the Beaverkill. Serious anglers make it a point, at least once in their lives, to fish the fabled waters around Roscoe, which is often called Trout Town, U.S.A. The state stocks brown trout to supplement the wild trout you can catch here. The Delaware River, another option, is less heavily fished. Esopus Creek, which runs along part of Route 28 in and around Phoenicia, is one of the most productive wild-trout streams in the Northeast. Although the number of fish—mostly wild rainbow and brown trout, but also brook trout—in the Esopus is impressive, most fish are less than 12 inches in length.

For fishing regulations, license fees, seasons, and other specific information, contact the regional headquarters of the **New York State Department of Environmental Conservation** (☎ *866/933–2257 fishing licenses, 845/256–3000 general information* ⊕ *www.dec.ny.gov*) before heading off to the water.

GOLF

Several courses in the southern Catskills (Sullivan County) are highly rated and offer good value; standouts include the Grossinger Country

Club's Big G and Little G courses and the Concord Resort & Golf Club's Monster course. (The course at the Villa Roma resort is another good option.) For the best golf in the southern Catskills, however, detour to the Nevele Grand Resort & Country's Club's 27 holes, designed by Robert Trent Jones and Tom Fazio. The resort is in Ellenville, at the eastern edge of the Catskills. In the northern Catskills you can play at the Windham Country Club, a course which earns high marks and was updated in 2008. Throughout the Catskills, the mountainous scenery provides a beautiful backdrop. Much of the terrain is rather curvy, with big elevation changes—but you'll also find gentler 9-hole courses.

HIKING

The **Catskill 3500 Club** (⊕ *www.catskill-3500-club.org*), an organization of intrepid souls dedicated to hiking all 35 Catskills peaks with summits of 3,500 feet or more, outlines high-peaks hikes in its quarterly *Catskill Canister* ($10 annual subscription). The **Catskill Center for Conservation and Development** (✉ *43355 Rte. 28, Arkville* ☎ *845/586–2611* ⊕ *www.catskillcenter.org*), in Arkville, occasionally runs guided hikes in the northern Catskills. Alternatively, you can join the **Rip Van Winkle Hikers** (☎ *845/246–8616* ⊕ *www.newyorkheritage.com/rvw*) on one of their beginner, intermediate, or advanced group hikes; nearly every weekend the hikers congregate in Saugerties (a few miles east of the northern Catskills), at the parking lot on the corner of Market and Main streets, and then carpool to their destination. In the southern Catskills, the **Catskill Hiking Shack** (✉ *169*

Sullivan St., Wurtsboro ☎ *845/888–4453* ⊕ *www.catskillhikes.com*) in Wurtsboro, about a 20-minute drive southeast of Monticello, carries hiking and camping gear and will point you to the area's best hiking spots.

Hiking in the Catskills can be amazing, but the rocky terrain and abundance of wildlife, including raccoons, skunks, porcupines, and bears, mean that extra care should be taken. For safety information, contact the **New York State Department of Environmental Conservation** (☎ *845/256–3000* ⊕ *www.dec.ny.gov*).

SKIING

With several ski resorts and hundreds of trails, the Catskill Mountains draw hordes of skiers. The northern Catskills, home to the region's main ski resorts—Hunter, Belleayre, and Windham, as well as the smaller and quieter Plattekill—see most of the action. Many skiers come for the weekend from the metro New York area, satisfied with vertical drops of 1,100 to 1,600 feet. The drive's not bad either: about 2½ to 3 hours from New York City. Buses also serve the ski areas. Facilities offer lessons and trails for all levels of experience. Snowboarding and snow tubing in terrain parks are popular, too, in part thanks to the superlative snowmaking abilities of the area resorts. Winters here are usually long and cold, allowing for the season to stretch to six months.

6

SKI AREAS   The sprawling **Hunter Mountain ski area** (⊠*Rte. 23A* ☎*518/263–4223 or 800/486–8376* ⊕*www.huntermtn.com*) has 53 trails on 240 acres, where you may ski, snowboard, snow tube, and snowshoe. In the Catskill Forest Preserve, Hunter has full snowmaking capability—a definite boon when natural conditions are less than optimal. The 3,200-foot peak offers a 1,600-foot vertical drop; 11 lifts move you up the slope. Fifteen of the trails are set aside for beginners, 8 are designed for double-black-diamond skiers, and about 16 are for intermediates. Full-day lift tickets are $52. Rentals and instruction are available. From May to early October, mountain bikers take over. The single-track trails run through dense forest and cross streams, and a lift transports bikers to the summit. Fly-fishing instruction and guidance also are available. Throughout summer and fall, music and ethnic festivals are held here.

At the **Mountain Trails Cross Country Ski Center** (⊠*Rt. 23A between Hunter and Tannersville* ☎*518/589–5361* ⊕*www.mtntrails.com*), you can cross-country ski 21 mi of groomed, wooded trails at the beginner, intermediate, or expert level, secure in the knowledge that the National Ski Patrol is on the beat. The lodge has a snack bar and rents snowshoes, cross-country skis, and sleds.

SHOPPING

The **Catskill Mountain Foundation Bookstore** (⊠*Hunter Village Sq., 7950 Main St./Rte. 23A* ☎*518/263–4448*) has the largest selection of regional books in the northern Catskills. It also has an extensive general-interest collection and gift items crafted by regional artists and artisans. You can pick up regional organic produce year-round at the **Catskill Mountain Foundation Farm Market** (⊠*7950 Main St./Rte. 23A* ☎*518/263–4908 Ext. 204*), where Francine Sherer, former owner of the Soho Charcuterie and Restaurant, presides. The staggering array of prepared foods, artisanal cheeses, and smokehouse products makes for good picnic fare.

NIGHTLIFE AND THE ARTS

THE ARTS   Part of Hunter Village Square, the **Catskill Mountain Foundation Gallery** (⊠*7950 Main St./Rte. 23A* ☎*518/263–4291*) is a bright, well-lighted space showcasing high-quality crafts and fine arts by artists with ties to the region. Exhibits change every six to eight weeks and run the gamut from contemporary to outsider to native arts. The **Catskill Mountain Foundation Cinema** (⊠*7971 Main St./Rte. 23A* ☎*518/263–4702* ⊕*www. catskillmtn.org*) shows first-runs, indie films, and foreign movies on its two screens and has a small café in a restored single-story building. As part of the Mountain Culture Festival, the Best of Mountain Film screens movies dealing with environmental issues, mountain sports, and other topics related to mountain life. Housed in a red barn behind Hunter Village Square, the **Catskill Mountain Foundation Performing Arts Center** (⊠*7967 Main St./Rte. 23A* ☎*518/263–4908 or 518/263–5157* ⊕*www.catskillmtn.org*) hosts an active program of music, dance, theater, and family events.

Every Saturday night from July 4 through Labor Day weekend you can hear classical music at the **Grazhda Music and Art Center of Greene County** (⊠*78 Ukraine Rd./Rte. 23A, Jewett* ☎*518/263–4619* ⊕*www.*

grazhdamusicandart.org ✉ *$15*). During the first two weeks in August, Ukrainian arts-and-crafts workshops are offered. At the **Pleshakov Piano Museum** (⊠ *Rte. 23A* ☎ *518/263–3333* ⊕ *www.catskillmtn.org*), acclaimed pianists Vladimir Pleshakov and Elena Winther provide call-ahead tours of an extraordinary collection of antique pianos ranging from an 1826 Tischner which was built for Russian royalty and a 1789 Longman and Broderip which may have been played by Mozart.

FESTIVALS
AND FAIRS
Celtic Festival. Caber tossing, Irish step dancing, and a march of bag-pipers down Hunter Mountain are just some of what you can expect during this celebration of all things Celtic, held the second weekend in August. ⊠ *Rte. 23A* ☎ *518/263–4223 or 800/486–8376* ⊕ *www.huntermtn.com.*

Oktoberfest. The Hunter Mountain ski resort stands in for the Alps during the first two weekends of October, when the harvest is celebrated with German and Austrian music, food, and dance. Watch men imitate courting rituals of the wood grouse during traditional dances; after a couple of beers, you may be tempted to try it yourself. Kids get free pumpkins. ⊠ *Rte. 23A* ☎ *518/263–4223 or 800/486–8376* ⊕ *www.huntermtn.com.*

WHERE TO EAT

$–$$
FRENCH
✕ **Last Chance Cheese and Antiques Café.** Most of the antiques are gone, but what remains is tasty, especially the fondue. Peruse the gourmet shop, in business since 1971. You can hang out on the front porch, choose from a selection of 320 beers—yep, 320—and dig into a hearty "knishwich" of potato knish, coleslaw, melted cheddar, pastrami, and turkey. A quick browse through the emporium yields artisanal cheeses, imported sop-pressata (a type of Italian salami), and baskets of old-fashioned candy. ⊠ *602 Main St./Rte. 23A, Tannersville* ☎ *518/589–6424* ⊟ *AE, D, MC, V* ⊘ *Closed Mon.–Thurs. in early Sept.–early Dec.*

¢–$
AMERICAN
✕ **Maggie's Krooked Café.** At this laid-back eatery with homemade muffins piled on the counter you can have breakfast all day—well, at least until closing time, at 4 or 5 PM. Mountain bikers and skiers fill the place in the morning to partake of challah French toast, steak and eggs, and freshly squeezed juices. Later in the day, sandwiches and salads are an option. Thumbtacks hold artwork on the white wood-plank walls, and aqua benches are filled with boisterous families. ⊠ *3066 Main St./Rte. 23A, Tannersville* ☎ *518/589–6101* ⊟ *No credit cards* ⊘ *No dinner.*

WHERE TO STAY

If you want to stay right on the slopes, consider booking a condo rental through the Hunter Mountain resort (☎ *518/263–4223, 800/486–8376, or 866/486–8376*). Its modern condo cluster, called Liftside, is at the base of Hunter Mountain.

¢–$$
🏨 **Eggery Inn.** Part of a working farm in 1898, this Dutch Colonial farmhouse took on a new life in the 1930s when it became a boardinghouse for Viennese guests. Many of the antiques that fill the inn are for sale. Guest rooms are simple, with brass or wooden beds covered in crocheted, matelassé, or quilted bedspreads. Relax at the bar, which faces Hunter Mountain, or in a glider on the wraparound front porch—or

wander the 12½ acres. **Pros:** close to skiing; great views. **Cons:** no pets allowed; strict smoking rules. ✉288 Platte Clove Rd./Rte. 16, Tannersville ☎518/589–5363 ⊕www.eggeryinn.com ⇆15 rooms ♿In-room: Wi-Fi. In-hotel: bar, Wi-Fi, no-smoking rooms ⊟AE, MC, V ⦙◎⦙BP.

¢–$$ ★ ⌂**Fairlawn Inn.** You can see the mountains from your room at this Queen Anne Victorian, ½ mi from the Hunter resort and 2 mi from North-South Lake. Modern-day amenities join original oil paintings, stained-glass windows, antiques, paneling, parquet floors, and wood carvings to create a seamless whole. The pristine rooms have wrought-iron, four-poster, carved-wood, or brass queen beds; some bathrooms have claw-foot tubs and antique dressing tables. Victorian touches are used throughout. Owner Chuck Tomajko sets out bottled water, carbonated drinks, snack baskets, and cookie jars. **Pros:** great front porch; awesome antiques. **Cons:** might be too kitschy for some; occasionally noisy. ✉7872 Main St./Rte. 23A ☎518/263–5025 ⊕www.fairlawninn.com ⇆9 rooms ♿In-room: Internet. In-hotel: no kids under 10, no-smoking rooms ⊟AE, MC, V ⦙◎⦙BP.

$$–$$$$ ⌂**Hotel Mountain Brook.** Originally constructed in the 1940s, this hotel has been completely rebuilt and fashioned into an upscale Adirondack-style lodge. Charming cabins, cottages, and luxury suites are available—decorated and outfitted with many modern amenities. Each room includes gourmet breakfast in the dining room. Top ski attractions are minutes away, as are most summer activities in the Hunter Mountain area. Pets are welcome with advance notification. **Pros:** completely renovated in 2008; private cottages are a couples' delight. **Cons:** must drive to most activities; group events can be a distraction ✉57 Hill St., Tannersville ☎518/589–6740 ⊕www.hotelmountainbrook.com ⇆9 rooms, 8 cabin-style rooms, 2 cottages ♿ In-room: DVD, Wi-Fi. In-hotel: Wi-Fi, some pets allowed, no-smoking rooms ⊟AE, MC, V

$$–$$$ ⌂**Hunter Inn.** This modern, chalet-style hotel is ¾ mi from the Hunter ski resort. Some rooms have mountainside patios or balconies with views of the surrounding forest and Hunter Mountain. Suites have a cathedral ceiling, a loft sleeping area, and a whirlpool tub; botanical prints adorn the walls. Odd-numbered rooms face the parking lot and road, which can be busy; even-numbered rooms face the mountains. **Pros:** outdoor hot tub; nice bar. **Cons:** can be noisy; Wi-Fi in lobby only. ✉7433 Main St./Rte. 23A ☎518/263–3777 ⊕www.hunterinn.com ⇆27 rooms, 14 suites ♿In-room: no a/c (some), refrigerator (some), Internet. In-hotel: bar, gym, laundry facilities, Wi-Fi, some pets allowed, no-smoking rooms ⊟AE, D, MC, V ⦙◎⦙CP ⊘Closed weekdays late May–late Nov.

$–$$ ★ ⌂**Washington Irving Inn.** This 1890 inn, formerly a summer home for New York's high society, was named the 2007 B&B of the Year by the New York State Hospitality Association. Many original architectural details—including lustrous dark-wood paneling, stained-glass windows, built-in bookcases, and carved fireplace mantels—adorn the rooms. Guest rooms contain antiques; some have four-poster beds and in-room hot tubs, and three have private balconies. Owner Stefania Jozic oversees the details. **Pros:** afternoon tea is delightful; good central location. **Cons:** extra charge for children; not all rooms are air-conditioned.

✉6629 Rte. 23A ☎518/589–5560 ⊕www.washingtonirving.com
↩13 rooms, 2 suites ⑁In-room: Internet. In-hotel: bar, pool, no-
smoking rooms ⊟AE, MC, V ⊚|BP ⊙Closed late Apr.–early May.

CAMPING   ⌂**Devil's Tombstone Campground.** This campground, one of the oldest in
¢   the state, attracts hikers, who access the popular Devil's Path trail at the
north end of the campground parking lot. The terrain here, about 3 mi
south of the Hunter Mountain ski resort, is mountainous and rocky.
Within the campground sits the Devil's Tombstone—a large boulder
typical of the area's natural rock formations—which came down the
mountain many centuries ago either in a landslide or via glacier. Sites
are wooded, with limited facilities (no electricity, hookups, or showers). Self-contained RVs are welcome. **Pros:** great hiking; nice tent sites.
Cons: few amenities. ✉Rte. 214 ☎845/688–7160, 800/456–2267 reservations ⊕www.dec.ny.gov ↩24 tent sites ⑁Grills, flush toilets, running water, picnic tables, public telephone, play area ⌂Reservations
essential ⊟MC, V ⊙Closed early Sept.–late May.

HAINES FALLS

6 mi east of Hunter.

Haines Falls was once filled with tanneries and mills as well as mountain houses where wealthy urbanites came to play. For much of the
19th century the famous Catskill Mountain House, which stood near
North-South Lake and the stunning Kaaterskill Falls, provided a respite
to denizens of the increasingly industrialized cities to the south. Things
have slowed down quite a bit in this hamlet, but the natural world is
still the main attraction. Haines Falls also benefits from the overflow
of visitors to nearby Hunter Mountain, which draws thousands of skiers each winter.

SPORTS AND THE OUTDOORS

BIKING   The **Mountain Bike Inn** (✉Rte. 23A ☎518/589–9079 ⊕www.mountain-
bikeinn.com) runs tours for beginning and experienced mountain and
road bicyclists; the inn has seven rooms and a five-bedroom cottage.

HIKING   **Catskill Mountain House site.** A stone's throw from North-South Lake
and Kaaterskill Falls, the mountain house was built in the early 1820s
as an intimate retreat that appealed mostly to outdoorsy folks and
artists. As the area's popularity increased, the resort expanded, topping out at just over 300 rooms. The area and its grand hotels fell out
of favor in the early 20th century, as the automobile opened up more
options for travelers. In the 1960s, following years of disrepair and
neglect, the mountain house was burned down by the state. Still, many
people make the hike to the site, which is about 2,300 feet above sea
level. The site is a short hike from the North-South Lake Public Campground, which welcomes day-trippers. ✉Rte. 18, 2 mi north of Rte.
23A ☎518/589–5058 North-South Lake Public Campground ⊕www.
dec.ny.gov ⌂Mid-May–late Oct., $6.

The **Escarpment Trail,** part of the 340-mi Long Path from Albany to New
York City, offers 23 mi of rigorous Catskills hiking and beautiful valley

views. The trail follows the 1,600-foot-tall cliff known as the Great Wall of Manitou, leading you through rugged terrain and forests, over fallen trees, across creeks, and along rock outcroppings with stunning views of North-South Lake. If you want to hike just part of this rough trail, access it at the **North-South Lake Public Campground** (⊠ *Rte. 18, 2 mi north of Rte. 23A* ☎ *518/589–5058* ⊕ *www.dec.ny.gov*); the day-use fee is $6 from mid-May to late October and free the rest of the year.

Fodor's Choice
★
Kaaterskill Falls. As you watch the waters cascade 260 feet down the gray rock of this two-tiered waterfall, you'll see why this spot was so popular with Thomas Cole and other Hudson River School painters. To access the trail that leads to the bottom of the falls, park in the public lot on Route 23A, 3 mi west of Palenville. To get to the trailhead, walk about ¼ mi down (east) along the narrow shoulder of Route 23A. (This is a very busy road with hairpin turns; you may find yourself hugging rocks as cars pass you.) Signs point the way to the path, which leads you past the delicate Bastion Falls. Although largely level, the trail does have a few steep sections. Altogether the hike is less than 1 mi long and shouldn't take a full hour. You may be tempted to climb to the top of the falls, but this is really risky and can't be recommended: missteps on the slippery rocks here have resulted in many accidents—some fatal. ⊠ *Off Rte. 23A, 3 mi west of Palenville* ☎ *No phone.*

WHERE TO STAY

CAMPING
¢
⚠ **North-South Lake Campground.** In the Catskill Forest Preserve, the facility has a recreational program (July 4 through Labor Day) that keeps the kids engaged in the natural world. North–South Lake has sand beaches, and you can swim in the brisk water from late May through Labor Day, when lifeguards are on duty. If the water's too cold—the lakes are 2,000 feet above sea level—rent a boat and go fishing (with a license) for bass, perch, or catfish, or hit the surrounding trails on a mountain bike or on foot. From here it's a short hike to the site of the old Catskill Mountain House. The campground is 3 mi northeast of Haines Falls. Reservations are essential for summer weekends. Day-trippers pay $6 entry. **Pros:** lots of family activities; great hiking. **Cons:** very busy in season. ⚐ *Grills, flush toilets, dump station, showers, picnic tables, public telephone, swimming (lake)* ⊠ *Rte. 18, 2 mi north of Rte. 23A* ☎ *518/589–5058 or 800/456–2267* ⊕ *www.dec.ny.gov* ☞ *219 tent and trailer sites* ▤ *MC, V* ⊗ *Closed late Oct.–mid-May.*

▌ EN
  ROUTE
☾ **Bailiwick Ranch and Discovery Zoo** has three attractions that will entertain children: horseback rides along scenic trails, a zoological park with exotic and farm animals (including a petting zoo and feeding area), and paintball. Educational programs and special events also take place throughout the year. The ranch is open year-round (weather permitting), but the zoo is closed November through March. Members of the military receive free admission. ⊠ *118 Castle Rd., Catskill* ☎ *518/678–5665* ⊕ *www.bailiwickranch.com* ☞ *$12* ⊗ *Call ahead for hrs.*

ROUND TOP

30 mi south of Albany, off Rte. 23; 14 mi northeast of Haines Falls, about a 30-min drive.

SPORTS AND THE OUTDOORS

GOLF Narrow tree-lined fairways, water hazards, undulating greens, and dramatic elevation changes make the par-72 **Blackhead Mountain Golf Course** (*✉Crow's Nest Rd. ☎518/622–3157 or 888/382–7474 ⊕www.blackheadmountaingolf.com*) challenging for golfers. The $40 greens fee includes cart rental. A 19th-century barn with murals of dancing gnomes and Rip Van Winkle serves as clubhouse; a bar with a stone fireplace awaits inside, where you can order lunch.

WHERE TO EAT AND STAY

¢ GERMAN ★ ✕**Hartmans Kaffeehaus.** Desserts are serious business at this simple café-bakery, where a "periodic table" of sweets hangs on the wall. The Fürst Pückler torte—layers of marzipan, buttercream, sponge cake, and apricot jam—could put you into sugar shock. Strudels are delicious, and the breakfast and lunch fare is good as well. A side of warm German potato salad accompanies midday plates, such as the bratwurst platter or chicken salad studded with bits of apple, bell pepper, and celery. Choose a German beer to wash it all down. *✉1507 Hearts Content Rd. ☎518/622–3820 ▭MC, V ⊗Closed Mon., Tues., and Christmas–Easter.*

$$$$ **Blackhead Mountain Lodge and Country Club.** The German-American Maassmann family, which owns this golf-focused lodge, has presided over this section of the Blackhead Mountains since 1967. Some of the motel-style rooms open onto balconies overlooking playgrounds, tennis courts, and the mountains. The restaurant specializes in German food: bratwurst, pepper steak, potato pancakes, sauerbraten, and Rouladen (German roulade), all with served side orders of spaetzle in a large, bright dining room with beer steins displayed on mantels. **Pros:** recently renovated; great room views. **Cons:** very focused on golf; must drive to all non-golf activities. *✉Crow's Nest Rd. ☎518/622–3157 or 888/382–7474 ⊕www.blackheadmountaingolf.com ⇨24 rooms ♿In-room: no phone. In-hotel: restaurant, bars, pool, golf course, tennis courts, no-smoking rooms ▭AE, MC, V.*

$$ **Winter Clove Inn.** A weeping willow and a grove of birch trees stand on the front lawn of this early-19th-century colonial, which has an expansive front porch. Inside you find loads of hardwood and a vast collection of antiques and reproductions. The rooms, simple and tidy, all overlook the landscaped grounds. The lounge has a TV, stone fireplace, piano, and several wing chairs and sofas to relax in. Rates include all three meals, and children's programs are offered in summer. **Pros:** good country cooking; history abounds here. **Cons:** lovers may find it a busy retreat; it's a drive to off-site attractions. *✉2965 Winter Clove Rd., off Rte. 32 ☎518/622–3267 ⊕www.winterclove.com ⇨50 rooms ♿In-room: no phone. In-hotel: restaurant, pools, golf course, tennis court, children's programs (ages 3–16), no-smoking rooms ▭MC, V ¦◎¦AI.*

6

WINDHAM

16 mi west of Round Top, about 30 mins away.

Once a private club that attracted politicians and business leaders, the Windham ski resort retains a somewhat exclusive air. Professionals from the New York metropolitan area and their broods flock to the slopes, which have a family-friendly reputation. Greater Windham is a favorite destination for hikers and hunters, and lodging options range from intimate inns and converted Victorian homes to a sprawling resort and modern hotels.

OFF THE BEATEN PATH

 Zoom Flume Waterpark. The Catskills' largest water park has a dozen squeaky-clean waterslides, tube rides, mat rides, and a lagoon activity pool with a giant waterfall, oversize raindrops, and other interactive features. The Black Vortex is a three-person enclosed tube ride; the Anaconda is an enclosed body slide; and Thrill Hill is a tube ride for young children. The park is about 2 mi north of the center of East Durham, off Route 145. ⊠*91 Shady Glen Rd., East Durham* ☎*518/239–4559 or 800/888–3586* ⊕*www.zoomflume.com* ≊*$19.95* ☉*Father's Day– Labor Day, weekdays 10–6, weekends 10–7.*

SPORTS AND THE OUTDOORS

GOLF   The par-71, 18-hole course at the **Windham Country Club** (⊠*36 South St.* ☎*518/734–9910* ⊕*www.windhamcountryclub.com*), with a Catskills backdrop, is well groomed and has been a regional favorite since 1927. The 6,005-yard course, open daily from April through November, fills up on weekends. Greens fees of $55 cover your cart rental.

SKI AREA   Professionals and families come to ski and board the 1,600-foot verticals, two terrain parks, tube park, and half pipe at **Windham Mountain** (⊠*C. D. Lane Rd.* ☎*518/734–4300, 800/754–9463, 800/729–4766 ski conditions* ⊕*www.windhammountain.com*). Of the 39 downhill trails, 10 are set aside for beginners. Eight trails are for black-diamond skiers; six are double-black-diamond trails. You can arrange for valet and caddy service to greet your vehicle, take your skis, and meet you at the lift. The facility also offers perks like First Tracks Tickets, which allow you to hit the slopes an hour before the lifts open to the public ($15 additional). At the slope-side business center, wireless Internet access keeps you connected, and the Children's Learning Center keeps kids busy while their parents are carving on the mountain. There's also night skiing and tubing Friday nights until 10 PM, snowshoeing along mountain trails, and a new ice rink, which is lighted for night skating. From Memorial Day to Columbus Day, the Windham Mountain Adventure Park is in full swing; there's rock climbing, paintball, bungee trampoline, and a skateboard park. In fall, lift rides offer treetop views of the Catskills foliage. A shuttle bus operates from the town area.

NIGHTLIFE AND THE ARTS

ART GALLERY   At **Windham Fine Arts** (⊠*5380 Main St.* ☎*518/734–6850* ⊕*www. windhamfinearts.com*), a gallery in an 1855 Federal-style house, track lighting bounces off richly hued wooden floors and illuminates the work of regional and national artists. You may see contemporary, representational, and traditional works in all mediums here. The gallery is open Thursday through Monday (Friday through Monday from Labor Day to Memorial Day).

FESTIVAL Two former Metropolitan Opera performers started the **Windham Chamber Music Festival** (✉ *Main and Church Sts.* ☎ *518/734–3868, 518/734– 6378 tickets* ⊕ *www.windhammusic.com*) in 1997. The festival makes the most of the soaring acoustics at the **Windham Performing Arts Center,** which occupies an 1826 Greek Revival church. Saturday-evening concerts are scheduled throughout the year, but many take place in summer; tickets are $18.

OFF THE
BEATEN
PATH
Windham Vineyard & Winery. Sample up to 10 wines on a spacious deck overlooking the nearby mountains at the highest vineyard and winery in the Northeast. Cornerstone wines include a Riesling, chardonnay, and a variety of sweet and dessert wines. The wines are made in small batches using grapes from Windham's vineyard, a vineyard in the Finger Lakes, and a vineyard on Long Island. Tastings, sales, and tours are offered throughout the year; hours vary by season, so it's best to call ahead. To get here, take Route 23 West out of Windham, then turn right onto North Settlement Road. Drive 2.6 mi to Route 10, and turn left; the winery is 1 mi ahead on the left. ✉ *County Rte. 10* ☎ *518/734–5214* ⊕ *www.windhamvineyard.com* ⊟ *AE, DC, MC, V* ⊗ *Seasonal hrs vary.*

6

WHERE TO EAT

$–$$$
GERMAN
✕ **Chalet Fondue Restaurant.** The decor at this German-Swiss restaurant in the heart of Windham combines a slice of Germany—owner Ute Seigies imported the two ceramic stoves, oversize wine casks, and all the ironwork and woodwork from her native country—with fireplaces, candlelight, and lush ficus and palm trees. The chef, who hails from Hungary, turns out authentic Jaegerschnitzel, Wiener schnitzel, and sauerbraten. Fondue offerings include cheese, *Chinoise* (veal and filet mignon cooked in broth), and chocolate. The wine-and-beer list is extensive, and the desserts are rich. ✉ *Rte. 296* ☎ *518/734–4650* ⊟ *AE, DC, MC, V* ⊗ *Closed Tues. No lunch.*

$$–$$$
AMERICAN
✕ **Vesuvio Restaurant.** Statues stand watch over bubbling fountains in the lush gardens that surround the outdoor seating area at this regional Italian restaurant. Inside, a large bar dominates a corner of the front dining room; an arched white trellis separates the rear dining rooms. Seafood figures prominently on the menu, which is extensive. Dishes include crabmeat-stuffed artichoke hearts in Frangelico sauce, and seafood Vesuvio—a combination of lobster, clams, mussels, calamari, scallops, and shrimp, served over pasta. ✉ *40 Goshen Rd., Hensonville* ☎ *518/734–3663* ⊟ *AE, DC, MC, V* ⊗ *Closed Apr. No lunch.*

WHERE TO STAY

¢–$$
★
🏠 **Albergo Allegria.** Antiques are scattered throughout this handsome 1892 Queen Anne Victorian, which has stained-glass windows and other original features. You can warm up by the fireplace in the parlor—which is slightly formal but inviting—or help yourself to a snack in the kitchen. The house has 12 guest rooms and four suites, all with

down comforters and plush carpeting; the decor is country-chic, and flounces are kept to a minimum. The master suite—with its king-size bed and featherbed, double whirlpool tub, and gas fireplace—is billed as honeymoon central. Behind the inn is a carriage house (formerly a horse stable) with a courtyard and outdoor lounge. Its five suites have cathedral ceilings, skylights, double whirlpool tubs, gas fireplaces, and garden views. The inn also has two sister properties—the Mountain Streams Cottage, with two suites and one room, and the Farmhouse, with three apartments—in Windham. **Pros:** overstuffed comfort; noteworthy swimming hole. **Cons:** it's all about the outdoors; three-night minimum on holidays. ⊠ *43 Rte. 296* ☎ *518/734–5560 or 800/625– 2374* ⊕ *www.albergousa.com* ➳ *12 rooms, 9 suites* ⅏ *In-room: refrigerator (some), Internet. In-hotel: laundry service, Internet terminal, no-smoking rooms* ▤ *MC, V* ⎮◎⎮ *BP.*

$$ ⛱ **Christman's Windham House Resort.** The centerpiece of this 260-acre golf resort is a white Greek Revival inn that's been taking in travelers since its opening in 1805. The rooms, although updated, retain the flavor of the past, with antiques, Victorian-inspired wallpaper, and wide-plank floors; some have fireplaces. Several attractive motel-style buildings surround the inn. If you tire of golf, you can fish in Batavia Kill or wander the grounds. Meals are served in the main building, where the excellent Messina's La Griglia ($$–$$$; no lunch) has three comfortable dining rooms with a mostly white-on-white decor; the fare is northern Italian. You can savor mussels, capellini with shrimp and scallops in white-wine sauce, or roast duck in fig-and-honey sauce while eyeing the golf course's 9th hole through the large windows. **Pros:** great golf packages; central location; nice restaurant. **Cons:** a bit pricey. ⊠ *5742 Rte. 23* ☎ *518/734–4230, 888/294–4053, 518/734– 4499 restaurant* ⊕ *www.windhamhouse.com* ➳ *50 rooms* ⅏ *In-room: refrigerator (some). In-hotel: restaurant, bars, pool, golf course, tennis court, laundry facilities, no-smoking rooms* ▤ *AE, MC, V* ⊗ *Closed mid-Oct.–Christmas and late Mar.–Apr.*

¢–$$ ⛱ **Hotel Vienna.** The rooms at this tidy hotel have exposed ceiling beams, solid cherrywood furniture, lace curtains, cheery bed and window coverings, and sliding doors that lead to a private, tiled balcony. Some rooms have in-room hot tubs. Enjoy breakfast in front of a wood-burning stove and, in the afternoon, unwind with homemade cookies and hot chocolate. The glass-enclosed pool opens onto a sundeck and provides 360-degree views of the countryside. **Pros:** central location; good package deals. **Cons:** must drive to most activities; no pets. ⊠ *107 Rte. 296* ☎ *518/734–5300* ⊕ *www.thehotelvienna.com* ➳ *29 rooms* ⅏ *In-room: Internet. In-hotel: pool, gym, Internet terminal, no-smoking rooms* ▤ *D, MC, V* ⎮◎⎮ *CP.*

$$–$$$ ⛱ **Winwood Mountain Inn.** This family-oriented property sits on 12 acres in the mountains and offers a variety of accommodations. The condos, which account for the bulk of the units, are roomy and have either private patios or balconies. Suites have one or two bedrooms. All accommodations are outfitted in a comfortable American decor with cherrywood furniture. **Pros:** in ski country; kids under 13 stay free. **Cons:** self-contained resort. ⊠ *Rte. 23* ☎ *518/734–3000 or*

800/754–9463 ⊕*www.windhammountain.com/lodging/winwood-inn*
🛏*5 rooms, 15 suites, 30 condos* 🕭*In-room: kitchen (some), refrigerator (some), Internet. In-hotel: restaurant, bar, tennis court, pool, gym,
laundry facilities, Internet terminal, some pets allowed, no-smoking
rooms* ▤*AE, D, MC, V.*

PRATTSVILLE

10 mi west of Windham.

Thick hemlock forests, abundant wildlife, and cool mountain water
lured the Mohawk and Dutch, English, and German settlers to this
area. In the early 1800s, Zadock Pratt, a tanner in nearby Jewett, saw
an opportunity and seized it, using the tannin from the trees to establish a tannery that yielded $500,000 in profits by 1825. To celebrate
his success, Pratt built 100 Federal-style buildings in the area, forming
Prattsville; 80 of them still stand. Not content to rest on his laurels, Pratt
went on to become a banker, and, eventually, a U.S. congressman. These
days, second-home owners, out-of-towners, and locals enjoy the slow-
paced life here. Main Street is lined with Arts and Crafts bungalows,
Victorian houses, and Gothic Revival and Greek Revival buildings.

WHAT TO SEE

Pratt's Rocks. A steep, serpentine, half-mile climb leads to a series of
carvings chiseled into a prominent sandstone outcropping. With only
slight sarcasm, the whitewashed carvings are noted as the "Rushmore
of the East." According to local lore, Zadock Pratt commissioned sculptor Andrew W. Pearse to create the cameo-like carvings in exchange
for room and board. Images of Pratt's son George, a colonel who was
killed in the Civil War, and Pratt's favorite horse are visible from the
mountainside as you hike. ⊠*Main St./Rte. 23, 1 mi east of Prattsville
center* ☎*518/299–3125* 🎫*Free.*

Zadock Pratt Museum. Antiques and memorabilia depicting life in the
1850s fill the former Greek Revival summer home of Prattsville's namesake. A tireless entrepreneur, Zadock Pratt—who outlived five wives—
made his initial money in tanning but went on to develop a variety of
industries, including several mills, factories, a general store, and a printing plant. The museum includes a cultural and educational center with
changing exhibits related to the history of the Catskills. ⊠*Main St./Rte.
23* ☎*518/299–3395* ⊕*www.prattmuseum.com* 🎫*Free* ☉*Memorial
Day–Columbus Day, Thurs.–Sun. 1–4:30.*

WHERE TO EAT

¢–$ ╳**Hitching Post.** Low lighting and lots of bare wood give this family-
AMERICAN   friendly restaurant about 5 mi northwest of Prattsville a roadhouse-like
aura. The building dates from the turn of the 20th century and has a
storied history; during Prohibition one enterprising owner set the attic
on fire when his still blew up. The menu is loaded with well-prepared
American favorites such as burgers and fries, steak-and-potato dinners,
shareable appetizer baskets, and scrumptious homemade desserts—save
room for co-owner Jennifer's apple crisp. Simple, reasonably priced

rooms upstairs and a sizable cottage out back are available for rent. You might have company if you choose to stay here; guests have reported benign ghostly visitors. ⊠ *37690 Rte. 23, Grand Gorge* ☎ *607/588–7078* ⊟ *MC, V.*

ROXBURY

12 mi west of Prattsville.

The headwaters of the Delaware River flow through bucolic Roxbury, meandering past tree-lined streets and the stone walls of 11-acre Kirkside Park.

The area was once known for its dairy farms, the number of which dwindled significantly in the second half of the 20th century. After naturalist John Burroughs (1837–1921) wrote lovingly about his home here and the surrounding mountains, the area captured the interest of city dwellers. In the 19th century Roxbury was shaped by financier Jay Gould and his family, whose fortune was made in railroads and the Western Union Telegraph Co. Ensuing Gould generations used their money philanthropically, building churches and community centers that still stand today.

WHAT TO SEE

Jay Gould Memorial Reformed Church. When two of Roxbury's churches were destroyed—one in a windstorm, the other by fire—Jay Gould offered to foot the bill to rebuild. The result was this church, built in 1893 at the edge of Kirkside Park under the direction of Henry Hardenburgh, architect of New York City's Dakota apartment building. Constructed of St. Lawrence limestone, the church has had only minor restoration work over the years. It has two stained-glass windows by Tiffany and two others by the Maitland Armstrong Co. ⊠ *53738 Main St.* ☎ *607/326–7101* ✉ *Free* ☉ *Early June–Labor Day, Sun. 10–11; rest of yr., Sun. 10:30–11:30.*

John Burroughs Memorial State Historic Site. Acres of fields, a small stone gravesite, and mountain views on the outskirts of Roxbury are the perfect memorial to John Burroughs, an early environmentalist whose books changed the way many Americans looked at the natural world. En route to the memorial you'll pass Woodchuck Lodge, a rustic summer home with quarter moons carved into closed shutters that Burroughs built in 1908 for his retirement years. You can stand on the front porch where Burroughs slept, and take in the vistas that inspired him. ⊠ *Burroughs Memorial Rd., west of Rte. 30* ☎ *607/326–7908* ⊕ *nysparks.state.ny.us* ✉ *Free* ☉ *Daily dawn–dusk.*

OFF THE BEATEN PATH

Brovetto Dairy and Cheese House. Cheese maker Ronald Brovetto, his wife Corinne, and son Russell have been making quality farmstead cheeses on their farm for over eight years. They make Harpersfield cheese, an aged, semihard, washed-rind, Tilsit-style cheese, cave-aged on the property, as well as flavored cheeses. All are made from milk from the resident herd of Holstein cows. The farm is about 8 mi north of Stamford, about a 40-minute drive from Roxbury. ⊠*1677 County Rte. 29, Jefferson* ☎*607/278–6622* ⊙*Daily 11–4.*

SPORTS AND THE OUTDOORS

GOLF The par-36, 3,127-yard golf course called **Shephard Hills** (⊠*Golf Course Rd.* ☎*607/326–7121* ⊕*www.shephardhills.com*) was built in 1918 as part of the estate of Helen Gould Shephard. The 1911 stone clubhouse, originally a summer guesthouse, recalls the turn of the 20th century (you can grab a quick bite in the casual dining room). Greens fees, including cart rental, are $32. It's open April through October.

MOUNTAIN BIKING From late April to early November, mountain bikers take over **Ski Plattekill** (⊠*1 Plattekill Mountain Rd., east of Rte. 30* ☎*607/326–3500 or 800/633–3275* ⊕*www.plattekill.com*). With 70 trails covering 60-plus mi, a vertical drop of 1,100 feet, and two lifts, the park is considered one of the top mountain-biking venues in North America. Races for all ages and skills levels take place monthly, during which hundreds of aficionados pitch tents in the lower parking lot. An all-day trail-and-lift pass is $25. Instruction and rentals are available.

SKI AREA The family-oriented **Ski Plattekill** (⊠*1 Plattekill Mountain Rd., east of Rte. 30* ☎*607/326–3500 or 800/633–3275* ⊕*www.plattekill.com*) sits on 75 acres with 40 mi of cross-country trails, 20 mi of downhill trails, a 1,100-foot vertical drop, and a snow-tubing area. It averages 165 inches of snowfall a year, and has 85% snowmaking capability. Of its 35 trails, 20% are for novices; 40% are for intermediates; 20% are deemed difficult; and another 20% are for experts only. Expert skiers and snowboarders soar down the longest continuous vertical in the Catskills, while those in the learning stages can cruise for a couple of miles. Full-day passes are $37. The family-run lodge includes a cafeteria, ski shop, nursery, bar and lounge, and rental shop.

NIGHTLIFE AND THE ARTS

ART GALLERIES The Roxbury Arts Group transformed a 1911 classical-revival building that had housed the YMCA into the **Walt Meade Gallery and Hilt Kelly Hall** (⊠*5025 Vega Mountain Rd.* ☎*607/326–7908* ⊕*www. roxburyartsgroup.org*), which hosts year-round dance and theater performances, concerts, and children's programs. On Sunday of Columbus Day weekend, hundreds of North American fiddlers converge for a series of concerts, jam sessions, and dance. The Todd Mountain Theatre Project premieres new plays by New York playwrights for three weeks in August, and the gallery showcases works by local artists.

WHERE TO STAY

$$$$ **The Roxbury.** There is *so* much going on here. Behind the chartreuse
Fodor'sChoice doors are 14 rooms and four suites that propel guests into the kitschy
★ days of '60s and '70s sitcoms and cartoons. "Fred's Lair" has everything a Flintstone would need, furry lamp shades and all. Other themed rooms cover "The Jetsons," "The Partridge Family," and others. The intimate spa features a sauna, hot tub, massage area, and a shower tiled with soothing, smooth river stones. Owner Gregory Henderson is an obliging and energetic concierge, making sure that everything is just right. **Pros:** a real getaway location, sense of fun pervades the property.

Cons: there isn't much near the property; some may find the decor a bit overdone. ✉*2258 Rte. 41* ☎*607/326–7200* ⊕*www.theroxburymotel. com* ⟿*14 rooms, 4 suites* ♿*In-room: kitchen (some), DVD, Internet. In-hotel: laundry facilities, Internet terminal* ⊟*AE, D, DC, MC, V.*

STAMFORD

14 mi northwest of Roxbury, 13 mi northwest of Prattsville.

Long before trappers and farmers settled in Stamford in 1790, American Indians spent time traveling the trail between the Schoharie Valley and the Catskills. With the advent of the Delaware & Ulster Railroad in 1872 came tourists, and the farms ceded way to boardinghouses, hotels, and inns, earning the village the moniker Queen of the Catskills. The village's heavy reliance on tourism suffered a blow after World War II, when the automobile became the preferred method of travel. Although many of the old boardinghouses still line the main streets, most have seen better days. Today this sleepy village of 3,000 has big plans that include extensive renovation at the park atop Mt. Utsayantha, which it hopes will help it become a prime tourist destination once again.

WHAT TO SEE

☾ **Blenheim–Gilboa Power Project Visitors Center.** Housed in a 1905 barn, the visitor center sits above the Blenheim-Gilboa pumped-storage project, which generates power by recycling water between two reservoirs. Hands-on exhibits explain the science of energy production; an enclosed porch overlooking the lower reservoir has exhibits of local fauna. Picnic tables are scattered between the historic outbuildings. Hiking trails lead to Mine Kill State Park. ✉*Rte. 30, North Blenheim* ☎*518/827–6121 or 800/724–0309* ⊕*www.nypa.gov* ✉*Free* ☾*Daily 10–5.*

Greenbriar Farm. A single-story board-and-batten farm building constructed with logs from the property contains a sap house and cider mill. You can buy tangy apple cider, cider doughnuts, homemade pies, and maple syrup. If you bring your own apples, the Powell-Wagner family will happily custom press them for you. You can tour the premises by calling ahead. ✉*146 Berg Rd., South Gilboa* ☎*607/652–7898* ✉*Free* ☾*Early Sept.–Thanksgiving, weekends 11–5.*

Lansing Manor. John Lansing, who served in the New York State Assembly (1780–88) and as mayor of Albany (1786–90), built this Federal-style manor in 1819 for his daughter Frances and son-in-law, the Honorable Jacob Sutherland, so that they could collect rent from his tenant farmers. After the Sutherlands sold the manor, it passed to the Rosseter, Spring, and Mattice families before the New York Power Authority bought it in 1972. The manor, a window onto the 19th century, is filled with period antiques, some of which belonged to the resident families. In the ladies' reception area you can see where a young member of the Rosseter clan and his friend scratched their names into the window with a diamond. Tours take place each half hour. ✉*Rte. 30, North Blenheim* ☎*518/827–6384* ⊕*www.nypa.gov* ✉*Free* ☾*May–Oct., Wed.–Mon. 10–5.*

Mt. Utsayantha. Ever since a carriage road and observation tower were created in 1882, intrepid souls have ventured to the 3,365-foot summit to take in the sweeping vistas of Delaware and Schoharie counties and the Berkshire, Green, Adirondack, and Catskill mountains. (It's a bone-rattling drive up a steep gravel road). A 1926 wooden observation tower is under renovation at this writing, as are the steel fire tower and hiking trails. According to local lore, the mountain takes its name from an American Indian princess who drowned herself in a lake after her father killed her white lover and their child; the princess is supposedly buried on the mountain. ✉*Tower Mountain Rd.* ☎*607/652–6671* ⊕*www.utsayantha.com* ✆*Free.*

SPORTS AND THE OUTDOORS

Mine Kill State Park. You may picnic, hike, swim, or walk the nature trails at this park 18 mi northeast of Stamford. The facilities include an Olympic-size pool as well as pools for divers and waders ($2 daily; open Memorial Day–Labor Day); basketball and volleyball courts; and soccer and softball fields. Because the park is adjacent to the Blenheim-Gilboa power project, you can fish from the shores of the reservoir, which is stocked with bass, trout, and walleye. A hike to Mine Kill Falls Overlook yields a glimpse of a series of small waterfalls. In winter, cross-country skiers, snowshoers, and snowmobilers hit the trails. The park doesn't have trash cans, so you must pack up and take out whatever you bring in. ✉*Rte. 30, North Blenheim* ☎*518/827–6111* ⊕*nysparks. state.ny.us* ✆*May–Oct., parking $6* ☉*Daily 7:30–dusk.*

NIGHTLIFE AND THE ARTS

The **Frank W. Cyr Center** (✉*159 W. Main St.* ☎*607/652–1200*) inhabits the former Rexmere Hotel, which was built in 1898 by local hotel magnate Dr. Stephen E. Churchill. Surrounding the center is the 100-acre Churchill Park, which Churchill created complete with man-made lakes, tree clusters, meadows, and idyllic summer homes. Local arts organizations utilize the center. The Friends of Music present classical-music concerts using a Steinway grand piano flanked by Corinthian columns, and the Mt. Utsayantha Arts League hangs regional artists' works in the gallery space. (Otsego-Northern Catskills BOCES and various administrative offices occupy other parts of the building.) On the back porch are rocking chairs from which you can survey the park's lakes and groves.

Timothy Touhey runs **The Gallery** (✉*128 Main St.* ☎*607/652–4030* ⊕*www.touhey.com*) in an old tin-ceilinged department store, where he showcases his sculptures and vibrant paintings. The congenial Touhey may let you peek into his studio, or he might play a tune for you on the upright piano. A second space, at the back of the building, displays regional artists' works.

WHERE TO EAT

¢ ✗**Greenbriar Farm Sweets, Treats and Eats.** The outgoing Powell-Wagner
AMERICAN family runs this ice-cream parlor and casual eatery in addition to its sap house and cider mill (in nearby South Gilboa). You can reap the benefits of both with a visit here. Jars of homemade pickles, salsa, and

fruit jams jostle for space with freshly baked pies and sweet breads. The Friday-night fish fry—when fresh pollack, flounder, and haddock are beer-battered and deep-fried—is becoming a local tradition. ⊠*75 Main St.* ☎*607/652–9164* ▤*No credit cards* ⊘*Closed Dec.–Apr.*

¢ ✕**T. P's Café Restaurant.** At the counter of this luncheonette, locals fill
AMERICAN the stools by the griddle at breakfast and lunch. The bright, cheerful dining room, with pale yellow walls and a tin ceiling, has five tables overlooking Veterans Memorial Park. The amiable staff will let you sit as long as you like. ⊠*7 Railroad Ave.* ☎*607/652–4752* ▤*No credit cards* ⊘*Closed Mon.*

DELHI

19 mi southwest of Stamford.

Pastures and soft hills surround this village of barely 3,000 residents. The government seat of Delaware County, Delhi has some notable Federal architecture, mostly along Main Street. The brick 1878 county clerk's building anchors the western edge of the village square, with its Victorian gazebo and Civil War monument. Farming is still the main industry here. Each Wednesday from Memorial Day through October, area farmers bring their wares to market on the square. The State University of New York at Delhi is the other industry in town. The courses offered here reflect the region's cultural shift; the school was once known for its agricultural program, but today's students are more interested in the culinary arts and golf-management programs.

WHAT TO SEE

Delaware County Historical Association Museum. The centerpiece of this museum property is the 1797 Federal-style farm of Gideon Frisbee, an original settler of Delhi. The complex includes six other historic buildings as well as an extensive genealogical library. One exhibit gallery holds a permanent collection of 19th-century farm implements; the other rotates displays of local historical interest. Special events re-create the daily life of the period. A nature trail leads to a covered bridge; when in bloom, more than 80 lilac bushes perfume the grounds. ⊠*46549 Rte. 10, 2½ mi north of Delhi center* ☎*607/746–3849* ⊕*www.dcha-ny. org* ▤*$4* ⊘*Memorial Day–mid-Oct., Tues.–Sun. 11–4; mid-Oct.– Memorial Day, weekdays 10–4.*

▌OFF THE
BEATEN
PATH
Hanford Mills Museum. An 1846 red barn overlooking a millpond was purchased in 1860 by David Josiah Hanford, who developed it into a working sawmill and gristmill. By 1898 the mill was supplying East Meredith with electricity, and it remained in operation until 1967, when it became a museum. The still-functional mill, powered by a waterwheel, is open for daily tours. The grounds include nature trails, a gallery space, and a picnic area. You can try your hand at ice harvesting during the annual Winter Ice Harvest, when period tools are used to cut ice from the frozen pond. The ice is then loaded onto a bobsled and stored until July 4, when it's used to make ice cream. ⊠*Rtes. 10 and 12, East Meredith* ☎*607/278–5744 or 800/295–4992* ⊕*www. hanfordmills.org* ▤*$6* ⊘*May–Oct., daily 10–5.*

SHOPPING

At **Good Cheap Food** (⊠ *53 Main St.* ☎ *607/746–6562*), a combination health-food shop and children's store, you can pick up everything you need for a lavish picnic as well as an outfit for your tyke. The front window holds wooden cases filled with fresh, organic, local produce; handcrafted earrings are for sale behind the counter. Built in 1820 by Colonel Robert Parker, **Parker House** (⊠ *74 Main St.* ☎ *607/746–3141 or 888/263–5573*) now serves as an upscale gift emporium. The mix includes Wedgwood pieces, handwoven scarves, Vera Bradley handbags, and children's items.

Hobart International Bookport. If you're interested in international authors or want to discover them, the Hobart International Bookport is the place to go. Italian, French, German, Spanish, and Dutch are spoken in this multicultural bookstore. ⊠ *615 Main St., Hobart, 10 mi west of Delhi* ☎ *607/538–3010* ⊕ *www.hobartbookport.com* ☉ *June–Sept., daily 10–5; Oct.–May, weekends 10–5.*

OFF THE BEATEN PATH

WHERE TO EAT

$–$$$
ECLECTIC
Fodor's Choice
★

✕ **Quarter Moon Café.** At this decidedly upscale spot at the edge of the village, cobalt-blue vases sit on blond-wood tables, sharply contrasting the deep-russet walls and tin-ceilinged bar area. Large photographs of Cuban scenes are hung between book racks, where a handpicked collection of art books await your browsing—that is, if you can pull yourself away from the seared tofu with pumpkin-seed mole, curry-crusted calamari, or truffle-and-soy risotto. Wednesday is sushi night. Reservations are essential on weekends and for sushi night. ⊠ *53 Main St.* ☎ *607/746–8886* ▤ *AE, MC, V* ☉ *Closed Tues. and early Jan.–mid-Feb.*

6

SOUTHERN CATSKILLS AND SULLIVAN COUNTY

There's a whiff of history around every bend of the two-lane byways that wend through this region. Clear lakes pool between steep, green slopes. Along the great Delaware River, eagles ride the thermals, ruling the skies. Trout and other game fish teem in some of the most famous angling waters in the world. In the aging shadow of the once-great Catskill resort industry, this region has attracted new investment and has become a country home for hundreds of artists, writers, and artisans freed from the tether of city living. The influx has spawned hundreds of shops and studios full of the unexpected, from offbeat rugs to handcrafted chairs and significant pottery.

Some 15 championship golf courses are strewn throughout the region. There's a racino (a racetrack with gaming) in Monticello. On the site of the famed Woodstock Music Festival, the Bethel Woods Center for the Arts has become a not-to-be-missed cultural centerpiece. Fast-food restaurants and a few big-box stores (large retail chain stores) are evidence of the county's development, but off the interstate and around the bend the trendy and the homey await discovery.

ROSCOE

120 mi northwest of New York City.

Known as Trout Town, U.S.A., Roscoe is the site of the protected Beaverkill and Willowemoc creeks, some of the most famous angling waters in the Northeast. Fly-fishing enthusiasts make pilgrimages to this Sullivan County community on the western edge of the Catskills to fish for rainbow, brook, and brown trout. And if that's not enough, the fabled waters of Junction Pool are where American dry-fly fishing is said to have gotten its start. You would think that the people of this village had gills—it's all fishing, all the time.

VISITOR INFORMATION

Roscoe Chamber of Commerce (⬆ *Box 443, Roscoe 12776* ☎ *607/498–6055* ⊕ *www.roscoeny.com*).

WHAT TO SEE

Catskill Fly Fishing Center and Museum. The nonprofit center, 4 mi east of Roscoe, is devoted to the preservation of the sport of fly-fishing and of the delicate ecological environment that makes the sport possible. The center maintains a vast collection of fishing accoutrements, antique flies, and fishing-related artwork. It also conducts outreach and educational programs throughout the year, with twice-yearly cane rod–making classes and an October celebration of the latest legends to be named to the Fly Fishing Hall of Fame. ⊠ *1031 Old Rte. 17, Livingston Manor* ☎ *845/439–4810* ⊕ *www.cffcm.net* 🏷 *$3* ☉ *Apr.–Oct., daily 10–4; Nov.–Mar., Tues.–Fri. 10–1, Sat. 10–4.*

New York State Catskill Fish Hatchery. Along the famed Willomeoc Creek—the birthplace of American fly-fishing—a half million brown trout are raised each year to stock the state's waterways. Visitors are welcomed year-round for guided tours; experts from the state Department of Environmental Conservation are glad to answer questions and explain all things fishy. Call for specific hours. ⊠ *402 Fish Hatchery Rd., Livingston Manor* ☎ *845/439–4810* ⊕ *www.cffcm.net* 🏷 *Free* ☉ *Weekdays 10–4, Sat. 10–4.*

Roscoe O&W (Ontario & Western) Railway Museum. Operated by the Ontario & Western Railway Historical Society on the site of the old Roscoe train station, the museum features an O&W refurbished caboose, the original trout weather vane and train signal, the Cooks Falls and Roscoe watchman's shanties, and the Beaverkill Trout Car. The museum displays O&W artifacts and memorabilia, and other exhibits showing the impact of the railroad on the community before the trains stopped running in 1957. ⊠ *7 Railroad Ave.* ☎ *607/498–4346 or 607/498–5289* ⊕ *www.nyow.org* 🏷 *Free* ☉ *Memorial Day–Columbus Day, weekends 11–3.*

SPORTS AND THE OUTDOORS

FISHING

Fodor'sChoice

★

The pioneers of trout fishing took to Sullivan County's waterways in the 1800s and, with a flick of the wrist and knot on a fly, a tradition was born. Roscoe's **Junction Pool**, where the Beaverkill and Willowemoc creeks meet, is hallowed ground for anglers who wade into these waters—the supposed birthplace of dry-fly fishing. From the April 1 opening of trout season, folks are after the approximately 2.27 million catchable-size trout the state stocks each year.

At **Beaverkill Angler** (⊠*Stewart Ave.* ☎*607/498–5194* ⊕*www.beaver killangler.com*), the official Orvis dealer in Trout Town, U.S.A., offers wade and float guide services and instruction. You also get the option to "test before buying" with a rental, and the fisherman-cashier can fill you in on the water temperature and fishing prospects before you climb into your waders. **Catskill Flies** (⊠*Stewart Ave.* ☎*607/498–6146* ⊕*www.catskillflies.com*) has everything a fly-fisherman could ask for, from Columbia sportswear and hiking boots to waders and casting lessons. And you can arrange for a licensed guide to accompany you for a day of fishing. A member of fly-fishing royalty, Joan Wulff breaks down the secret of the perfect cast into simple mechanics at the **Wulff School of Fly Fishing** (⊠*7 Main St., Livingston Manor* ☎*845/439–4060 or 800/328–3638* ⊕*www.royalwulff.com*), the school she runs on the banks of the fabled Beaverkill.

WHERE TO EAT

$–$$$

PIZZA

✕**Raimondo's Ristorante & Pizzeria.** The best pizza in town is at Raimondo's, on the main drag. The building has aged, and the decor isn't anything to write home about—but the tables are clean, and the service fast. ⊠*Stewart Ave.* ☎*607/498–4702* ▤*AE, MC, V.*

$–$$$

AMERICAN

✕**Roscoe Diner.** This quintessential upstate diner has been owned by the same family since 1969. The menu has a bit of everything: omelets for breakfast, soups and sandwiches for lunch, and hearty steaks, seafood, and chicken dishes for dinner. The restaurant holds a fond place in the hearts of regular Route 17 travelers who have stopped in for a slice of pie or a belly-bustin' breakfast—always comforted by the fact that not much has changed since their last visit. ⊠*Old Rte. 17* ☎*607/498–4405* ▤*AE, D, DC, MC, V.*

WHERE TO STAY

¢–$

🖭**Baxter House Bed & Breakfast.** If you don't want to spend a minute out of the water during your fishing vacation, the Baxter House is where you'll want to park your canoe. Breakfast comes with the latest information about water temperatures, and a guide downstairs will tell you how the fish are running. Available equipment rentals and fly-fishing lessons complete the fisherman's dream. **Pros:** all about fishing. **Cons:** if you don't fish, this probably isn't the place for you. ⊠*2012 Old Rte. 17* ☎*607/290–4022 or 607/348–7497* ⊕*www.baxterhouse.net* 🛏*6 rooms, 4 with bath* ⚅*In-room: no phone, kitchen. In-hotel: no-smoking rooms* ▤*AE, MC, V* ⊚*CP.*

$$$

Fodor'sChoice

★

🖭**Beaverkill Valley Inn.** Tucked away in the southwest corner of the Catskill Forest Preserve, this family-friendly lodge has the amenities of a small resort. The 1895 inn, which sits on a great lawn, houses guest rooms outfitted with brass and iron beds and muted country prints and quilts. A fireplace warms the game room—which is of the board, rather than video, variety. The grounds include a large barn building that contains a gym, a playroom, an indoor pool, a basketball court, and an all-you-can-eat ice-cream parlor (you serve yourself); access to these facilities costs an additional $100 per room or family. A stretch of the famous Beaverkill runs right through the property, which also has an herb garden and a pond. **Pros:** fishing heaven; great rec center. **Cons:** somewhat isolated; not all rooms have private baths. ⊠ *Off Beaverkill Rd., Lew Beach* ☎ *845/439–4844* ⊕ *www.beaverkillvalleyinn. com* ➪ *20 rooms, 15 with bath* ☖ *In-room: no phone, no TV. In-hotel: pool, tennis courts, no-smoking rooms* ⊟ *AE, MC, V* ⟊ *BP.*

¢–$ 🏠 **Reynolds House & Motel.** A 1902 Victorian house with a wraparound porch holds six of the rooms at this B&B and motel. The B&B has a proud history, including a visit from John D. Rockefeller, for whom the largest, most attractive room is named. Two of the rooms in the house have queen-size beds; the Rockefeller Room has a king-size bed, and the others have doubles. Motel rooms, each with a couple of double beds, are spacious and bright. Common areas include a reading room and a lounge. Shops and eateries are within walking distance. **Pros:** main house has historic feel; on Roscoe's main drag. **Cons:** some rooms are on the small side; extra charge for kids over five. ⊠ *Old Rte. 17* ☎ *607/498–4422* ⊕ *www.reynoldshouseinn.com* ➪ *18 rooms* ☖ *In-room: kitchen (some). In-hotel: no kids under 10 (in main house), no-smoking rooms* ⊟ *MC, V.*

¢ 🏠 **Roscoe Motel.** Popular with families on a budget, this small motel just off Route 17 has simple rooms within spitting distance of some of the world's best fishing holes. Some rooms have views of the Beaverkill River, and you can easily walk from the motel to local eateries and shops. **Pros:** great starting point for touring the region; within walking distance of town. **Cons:** can be noisy in high season. ⊠ *Old Rte. 17* ☎ *607/498–5220* ⊕ *www.roscoemotel.com* ➪ *18 rooms* ☖ *In-room: refrigerator (some). In-hotel: pool* ⊟ *AE, MC, V* ⟊ *CP.*

CAMPING ⚠ **Beaverkill Campground.** This campground, part of the Catskill Forest
¢ Preserve camping system, is adjacent to the famed Beaverkill Creek, where you can fish for brown and brook trout. There's also an 1865 covered bridge on the property. Berrybrook Road is off Beaverkill Road, which you can reach via Route 206 west of Route 17/Interstate 86. **Pros:** fishing paradise; great hiking. **Cons:** if you don't fish or hike, you'll be bored; way off the beaten path. ☖ *Grills, flush toilets, dump station, drinking water, showers, picnic tables, public telephone* ➪ *108 tent and trailer sites* ⊠ *792 Berrybrook Rd., off Beaverkill Rd.* ☎ *845/439–4281, 800/456–2267 reservations* ⊕ *www.dec.ny.gov* ⊟ *MC, V* ⊘ *Closed Labor Day–mid-May.*

LIBERTY

15 mi southeast of Roscoe.

In the pine-clad foothills at the southern edge of the Catskill Mountains—and roughly in the center of Sullivan County—this quiet community is one of the Catskill gateways. The village itself doesn't have much to offer visitors; it's the surrounding area, with its hilly forests and renowned fly-fishing streams, that's the main attraction.

VISITOR INFORMATION
Liberty Chamber of Commerce (✉ *Box 147, Liberty 12754* ☎*845/292–1878* ⊕*www.libertyshops.com*).

SPORTS AND THE OUTDOORS

GOLF **Grossinger Country Club** (✉*26 Rte. 52 E* ☎*845/292–9000 or 888/448–*
★ *9686* ⊕*www.grossingergolf.net*) has two highly rated courses: the
18-hole, par-71 Big G course and the 9-hole, par-36 Little G course.
Both were originally designed by A. W. Tillinghast. Greens fees are $20
for Little G and $45–$85 (including cart rental) for its 7,004-yard sibling. Set amid beautiful scenery, walking the par-72, 6,820-yard course
at the **Swan Lake Resort** (✉*Hope Rd., Swan Lake* ☎*845/292–0323 or*
888/254–5818 ⊕*www.swanlakeresorthotel.com*) is like spending a day
in the park. Greens fees are $40–$55; cart rental is $15.

SHOPPING

A warren of 13 rooms on three floors, **Ferndale Marketplace Antiques**
(✉*52 Ferndale Rd., off Exit 101 of Rte. 17/I–86* ☎*845/295–8701*)
brims with glassware, paintings, furniture, and vintage costume jewelry.
Built in 1894, the building served as a post office and general store and
is listed on the National Register of Historic Places. Exploring its nooks
and crannies is as much fun as studying the objects for sale (feel free to
rummage around). Remnants of the old post office are still apparent.

Memories (✉*Rte. 17/I–86, Parksville* ☎*845/292–4270 or 800/222–*
8463) is an acre-size antiques emporium with rooms devoted to carousels, lamps, the Victorian age, and collectibles.

WHERE TO EAT AND STAY

$–$$$ ✕**Grape Vine.** The full menu here ranges from classic diner cuisine to
STEAK steaks and seafood. A spacious interior filled with warm woods is hid-
den by an unassuming facade. ✉*79 Sullivan Ave.* ☎*845/295–3170*
⊟*AE, D, MC, V.*

$$–$$$ ✕**Piccolo Paese.** Intimate surroundings, white tablecloths set against a
ITALIAN burgundy backdrop, and waiters clad in tuxedos make this a romantic
spot, but it's not just couples who come to dine on the fine northern
Italian fare served here. Handmade pastas are a specialty, and Caesar
salad for two is made table-side. Linguine is tossed with tuna, capers,
olives, and wine sauce; penne in spicy tomato-cream sauce gets a splash
of vodka; and shrimp are sautéed with mushrooms and prosciutto in
champagne and cream. The menu also includes chicken, steak, and veal
preparations. The list of wines is extensive. ✉*5 Rte. 52 E* ☎*845/292–*
7210 ⊟*AE, D, MC, V* ⊗*No lunch weekends.*

¢–$ ⚲**Old House on a Hill.** If you're looking to get away from it all and want
to avoid the cookie-cutter chains and megaresorts that dot the region,
consider this modest and friendly country-style B&B. The three-story
farmhouse, built in 1860, is on a hillside overlooking a meadow. Rooms
are simple and have iron beds, quilts, and pine and maple furnishings.
Pros: adorable decor; great for a quiet weekend getaway. **Cons:** must
drive to activities. ✉*295 Lt. Brender Hwy., Ferndale* ☎*845/292–3554*
⊕*www.oldhouseonahill.com* ⇌*4 rooms* ⚘*In-room: no phone, no TV.*
In-hotel: no kids under 10, no-smoking rooms ⊟*MC, V* ⍟*BP.*

MONTICELLO

11 mi south of Liberty.

Sullivan County's largest population center, the village of Monticello is also the county's government seat. It's considered a gateway to the Catskills resort region and offers large-town conveniences. Attempts by American Indian tribes to open casinos in the area have kept Monticello in the news.

SPORTS AND THE OUTDOORS

Holiday Mountain Ski and Fun Park. Batting cages, miniature golf, a mechanical bull, paintball, a rock-climbing wall, go-karts, bumper cars, and an arcade are enough to keep the whole family engaged for a day of fun in the sun. The ski slopes are in business come December; the winter wonderland stays open until the snow is gone. ⊠*99 Holiday Mountain Rd., off Exit 107 of Rte. 17/I–86* ☎*845/796–3161* ⊕*www.holidaymtn.com* ⊠*$1.50–$8, depending on activity* ☉*June– Aug., daily 10–10; Sept.–May, weekdays noon–9, Sat. 9–9, Sun. 9–5.*

GOLF Although both courses at the **Concord Golf Club** (⊠*95 Chalet Rd., Kiame-* ★ *sha Lake* ☎*845/794–4000 or 888/448–9686* ⊕*www.concordresort. com*) earn high marks, the Monster course outshines its sibling, the International course. The 7,650-yard, par-72 Monster, opened in 1963, has greens fees of $45–$95; the 6,619-yard, par-71 International is $45–$55.

HORSE RACING **Monticello Raceway.** Opened in 1958, the track has year-round harness racing, a daily-double race, and trifectas and perfectas with wagering. Inside is a Vegas-style "racino" with video lottery terminals. The all-you-can-eat buffet is first-rate. ⊠*Rte. 17B, 1 mi west of Rte. 17/I–86* ☎*845/794–4100 or 800/777–4263* ⊕*www.monticelloraceway.com* ⊠*$1.50* ☉*Daily 10* AM*–2* AM.

NIGHTLIFE AND THE ARTS

★ A mixture of professional and nonprofessional actors brings the words of famous playwrights to life at the **Forestburgh Playhouse** (⊠*39 Forest-burgh Rd., Forestburgh* ☎*845/794–1194* ⊕*www.fbplayhouse.com*). The playhouse, one of a handful of small summer theaters left in the country, has kick-started the careers of a number of Broadway stars. Shows change frequently from June through September, ranging from popular musicals to children's events.

OFF THE BEATEN PATH

Bethel Woods Center for the Arts. This is the site of the original, legendary 1969 Woodstock festival. For years that seminal event was commemorated with a small stone monument, but today the area has exploded into a true center for the performing arts, with a 15,000-seat outdoor performing-arts venue and the Museum at Bethel Woods. These facilities are set within nearly 2,000 rolling acres, about 8 mi from Monticello. Other venues at the center include a 1,000-seat outdoor Terrace Stage, the Museum Events Gallery—an indoor space for performance, lectures, and special events—and the original Woodstock concert site, which holds a permit for 30,000 concertgoers to attend major musical events. The Museum is a captivating and, to some, emotional, multimedia experience combining advanced museum technologies with film and interactive displays, text panels, and artifacts which heighten the unique experience of the three-day Woodstock festival. While music is the centerpiece, the displays dwell in detail on the cultural and political changes that made this era so significant: civil rights, the Vietnam War and political change. The site, which was purchased by Cablevision Industries mogul Gerry Allen in the mid-1990s, hosts Saturday farmers' markets (from July though late August) and themed Sunday festivals and crafts events (weekends from Labor Day through Columbus Day). ⊠*Hurd Rd., off Rte. 17B, Bethel* ☎*866/781–2922* ⊕*www. bethelwoodscenter.org* ⊡ *$13.*

WHERE TO EAT AND STAY

$$–$$$ ✕**Hana.** The Japanese eatery has several tranquil dining rooms with
JAPANESE an indoor water garden and bar. Sushi, sashimi, and tempura are the standouts. A popular spot with vegetarians, Hana is also a good choice for when you're in the mood for something a little different. ⊠*166 Bridgeville Rd.* ☎*845/794–3700* ⊟*AE, MC, V.*

$$ ⊡ **Best Western Monticello.** Popular with race fans, this chain hotel across from the Monticello Raceway gives you plenty of bang for your buck. Rooms are nondescript (think white walls, cheap art prints, and basic furnishings), but the spacious, wood-paneled lobby is inviting, as are the heated indoor pool, sauna, and hot tub. Several restaurants are within walking distance or a short drive away. **Pros:** central location; good starting point for touring area. **Cons:** racing is the key attraction; few nearby restaurants. ⊠*16 Raceway Rd.* ☎*845/796–4000* ⊕*www. bestwesternnewyork.com* ⇆*62 rooms* ⌂*In-room: refrigerator (some). In-hotel: pool, gym, laundry service, Internet terminal, no-smoking rooms* ⊟*AE, D, DC, MC, V* ⏆*CP.*

$$–$$$$ ⊡ **Inn at Lake Joseph.** Adjacent to a 250-acre lake and surrounded by
Fodor'sChoice forest, this property includes an 1860s manor house that's listed on the
★ National Register of Historic Places. Large guest rooms have working fireplaces and whirlpool tubs; several have decks. Manor-house rooms have Victorian wallpaper, Oriental rugs, four-poster beds, and antiques. Carriage-house rooms, outfitted in Adirondacks-lodge style, have private entrances and beamed cathedral ceilings. Accommodations in the Adirondacks-style cottage have cathedral ceilings and full kitchens. Breakfast is served on the manor's veranda, and the complimentary snack bar is open all day. Recreational choices here abound. **Pros:** full range of summer/winter activities; great wildlife watching. **Cons:** far from dining, shopping. ⊠*400 St. Joseph Rd., Forestburgh* ☎*845/791–9506* ⊕*www.lakejoseph.com* ⇆*11 rooms, 4 suites* ⌂*In-room: kitchen (some), refrigerator (some). In-hotel: pool, tennis courts, pool, bicycles, some pets allowed, no kids under 12 (July, Aug., and weekends Sept.–June), no-smoking rooms* ⊟*AE, MC, V* ⏆*BP.*

6

CALLICOON

22 mi west of Monticello.

This hamlet is the restaurant capital of the Delaware River valley. You can walk from fine-dining spots serving buffalo and other exotic fare to Italian eateries dishing out pasta dripping with pesto and vodka sauces, meander past antiques shops, and then head down to the banks of the Delaware. The yearly **tractor parade** (held the second Sunday in June, rain or shine) epitomizes the flavor of Callicoon: funny and fun-loving, with a reverence for its agricultural history. Pennsylvania is just on the other side of the Delaware.

VISITOR INFORMATION
Callicoon Business Association (✉ *Box 303, Callicoon12723* ☎ *845/887–4405* ⊕ *www.visitcallicoon.com).*

SPORTS AND THE OUTDOORS

GOLF   The outstanding par-71course at the **Villa Roma Country Club** (✉ *356 Villa Roma Rd.* ☎ *845/887–5097 or 800/727–8455)*, designed by David Postlethwaite, is 6,499 yards long. The rather hilly setting is lovely, especially in fall. Greens fees are $50–$65, which includes cart rental.

NIGHTLIFE AND THE ARTS

★   Independent and foreign films are on the schedule at the **Callicoon Theater** (✉ *30 Upper Main St.* ☎ *845/887–4460* ⊕ *www.callicoontheater.com)*, one of the few single-screen theaters still operating in the country. The 1948 theater has changed with the times, but retains its old-time feel. At $5.50, ticket prices are also a blast from the past.

SHOPPING

Kids will go wild in the **Little Duck House** (✉ *4893 Main St., Jeffersonsville, 8 mi west of Callicoon* ☎ *845/482–5900* ⊕ *www.littleduckhouse. com* ☉ *Wed.–Sun. 10–5)*, a specialty toy, book, and clothes shop where everything is geared for youngsters to 12 years old.

The Rustic Cottage (✉ *4938 Rte. 52., Jeffersonsville, 8 mi west of Callicoon* ☎ *845/482–4123* ⊕ *www.therusticcottage.com)* is filled with twisty-turny furniture, embroidered pillows and throws, quilts, and linens. But it's the custom furniture that takes center stage here. From sofas and club chairs to Adirondacks-style furniture and children's pieces, Michael Barber creates one-of-a-kind works for every taste using primitive techniques

WHERE TO EAT AND STAY

¢–$$ ✗**Matthew's on Main.** This place combines the comfort and fun of a
AMERICAN   small-town tavern with a broad, ever-changing menu. If you're in the
★   mood for meat, you can't go wrong with the Big Mama Burger, laden with ham, caramelized onions, and cheese on a toasted bun, and a basket of chef Matthew Lanes's hand-sliced potato chips. For a lighter meal, try a cheesy quesadilla and a cup of chunky gazpacho. Service on the deck gives you an eagle's-eye view of the hamlet. ✉ *19 Lower Main St.* ☎ *845/887–5636* ▭*MC, V* ☉ *Closed Wed. in Sept.–May.*

$$-$$$$ ✕**The 1906 Restaurant.** Ostrich, buffalo, and venison are served along-
AMERICAN   side traditional New York strip steak, pastas, and seafood dishes at this
brick-storefront restaurant. At various times the building has housed a
bank, a dry-goods store, a luncheonette, and a clothing store; the restau-
rant takes its name from the date of the building's construction, which
appears prominently on the facade. ✉*41 Lower Main St.* ☎*845/887–
1906* ▤*AE, MC, V.*

$$-$$$$ ▦**Villa Roma Resort Hotel.** Completely rebuilt following a tragic fire and
☾   flood, this cornerstone resort now hosts more families, tours, and cor-
Fodor'sChoice porate groups than ever. The casual, friendly atmosphere and extraor-
★   dinary range of activities also attracts bus-tour groups, weddings, and
family reunions. In-house luxury boutiques provide shopping opportunities, and the resort has the only in-house Starbucks in the Catskills.
Extensive pool facilities—including a waterslide and a bar—are a major
draw, as is the indoor sports complex and fitness center. Rooms have
wall-to-wall carpeting and classic furnishings; some have balconies.
Dining options are numerous, and there are organized bus trips to
nearby gaming and shopping meccas. **Pros:** family friendly; live entertainment; activities for every taste and interest. **Cons:** far from other
major attractions. ✉*356 Villa Roma Rd. 12723* ☎*845/887–4880 or
800/533–6767* ⊕*www.villaroma.com* ⬐*139 rooms, 18 suites* ☾*In-
room: refrigerator (some), Wi-Fi. In-hotel: 2 restaurants, bar, pools,
gym, golf course, tennis courts, children's programs (ages 3–19), Wi-Fi,
no-smoking rooms* ▤*AE, D, DC, MC, V* ⎮⊙⎮*BP.*

6

NARROWSBURG

13 mi south of Callicoon.

Taking its cues from the Delaware River, Narrowsburg lets life flow
by at a slow pace. On the main drag, antiques shops and art galleries
stand side by side with hardware stores and insurance agencies. The
Delaware River's deepest point is here—113 feet deep. (It's thought to
be a drowned "plunge pool" created by a glacial waterfall or a pothole
scoured out by rock movement.)

VISITOR INFORMATION
Narrowsburg Chamber of Commerce (☎*845/252–7434 or 888/252–7234*
⊕*www.narrowsburg.org*).

WHAT TO SEE
Eagle Institute. This nonprofit institute runs guided habitat tours from
January through March, when nearly 200 bald eagles return to the area
to breed. Barryville is a 20-minute drive southeast of Narrowsburg, but
you can talk with trained volunteers and watch the birds at popular
viewing sites throughout the region. The institute also hosts slide presentations and children's programs. ✉*Rte. 97, Barryville* ☎*845/557–
6162* ⊕*www.eagleinstitute.org.*

OFF THE
BEATEN
PATH

Stone Arch Bridge. Built by German and Swiss stonemasons around 1880, this bridge crossing Calicoon Creek is listed on the National Register of Historic Places. One of few hex murders on record was committed on the bridge in 1882. A curse was placed on Adam Heidt, which was said to have caused him much distress. Heidt and his son, Joseph, decided that killing a man named George Markert would break the curse, and one night, while Markert was crossing the bridge, Joesph shot Markert five times in the head, clubbed him with a heavy chair leg he used as a cane, and dumped the body over the bridge into the icy waters below. Joseph was convicted of the murder and spent several years in prison. Sightings of a ghost walking the bridge are reported to be Markert.

Fort Delaware Museum of Colonial History. The living-history site includes a replica of the 1755 stockaded fort-settlement that was the first of its kind in the Delaware River valley. Blockhouses, cabins, and gardens, along with exhibits, films, and demonstrations, give you a glimpse of the life of an 18th-century settler. ✉ *Rte. 97* ☎ *845/252–6660* 💲 *$4* 🕓 *Memorial Day–Labor Day, weekends 10–5:30.*

OFF THE
BEATEN
PATH

Roebling's Delaware Aqueduct. At Miniskink Ford along Route 97, the Upper Delaware Scenic and Recreational River is the home of the oldest suspension bridge in the country—the Delaware Aqueduct, or the Roebling Bridge. Construction started in 1847 as one of four suspension aqueducts on the Delaware Hudson Canal; it was designed by and built under the supervision of John A. Roebling, the future engineer of the Brooklyn Bridge. Each 8½-inch-diameter suspension cable carries 2,150 wires bunched into seven strands. The Tollhouse, on the Minisink Ford side of the bridge, contains self-guiding exhibits and historic photographs. The D&H Towpath Trail is a 1-mi stroll along the 1828 towpath. The bridge itself has a walking path, too.

SPORTS AND THE OUTDOORS

CANOEING
AND RAFTING

Lander's Delaware River Trips (✉ *5666 Rte. 97* ☎ *800/252–3925* ⊕ *www. landersrivertrips.com*) operates guided canoeing and rafting trips—easy floats as well as white-water thrills—from April through December. Ten riverfront sites along the Delaware River help make family-owned and -operated Lander's king of the water. Overnight camping packages are available at sites along the Delaware River.

FISHING

Encompassing 3,000 acres of mostly untouched forest, the **Eldred Preserve** (✉ *1040 Rte. 55, Eldred* ☎ *845/557–8316 or 800/557–3474* ⊕ *www.eldredpreserve.com*) has several ponds and lakes for bass, trout, and catfish fishing. Unless you fish in the catch-and-release trout pond ($12.50), you must keep and pay for the trout you catch ($2.50 to fish, $4.25 per pound of caught fish). At the preserve's popular restaurant, the kitchen will cook your trout for you. Bass fishing is catch-and-release only; two-person bass-boat rentals are $75 for a full day, and reservations are necessary. Catch-and-release catfish fishing is $15. Other activities here include sporting clays and deer and turkey hunting. There are also motel rooms (¢) in rustic buildings.

NIGHTLIFE AND THE ARTS

The **Delaware Valley Arts Alliance** (⊠*37 Main St.* ☎*845/252–7576* ⊕*www.artsalliancesite.org*) is a haven for the artists who flock to the hills and dales of Sullivan County. Housed in the historic Arlington Hotel, it boasts a gift shop and a recital hall. Monthly receptions in its two gallery spaces bring visitors face to face with the artists who created the pots and paintings for sale. Around the corner is the Tusten Theater, a restored 160-seat space with performances year-round.

WHERE TO EAT AND STAY

$–$$$ ✕**Eldred Preserve.** At the restaurant on this 3,000-acre preserve kids
AMERICAN can slip into the kitchen to watch the chef clean and prepare the trout they caught in one of the ponds and lakes. There are 12 trout dishes to choose from, including trout champignon (panfried in butter and served with sautéed mushrooms and wine sauce). The bourbon-smoked salmon appetizer, which comes with toast points and red-pepper jelly, is another specialty. The menu also includes chicken, steak, veal, lamb, and duck. You may spot deer sipping from a stream outside the window as you eat. There are also rustic cabin-style buildings with motel rooms (¢) for overnighting in the forest. ⊠*1040 Rte. 55, Eldred* ☎*845/557–8316 or 800/557–3474* ⊟*AE, D, DC, MC, V.*

$$–$$$ ⊡ **Ecce.** Ecce is Latin for "behold," and the word fits: from a seemingly
★ precarious perch on a ridge overlooking the Delaware, travelers get a true eagle's eye view of the river's majesty from every room. Sitting on the main deck imparts a feeling not unlike being suspended 300 feet over a valley. It's not unusual for resident raptors, eagles, ospreys, and hawks to float at eye level, riding thermals in search of prey far below. Trails lace the inn's 60 acres, and a hammock graces rock outcropping above the resort. Myriad outdoor activities are close by, including hiking, rafting, kayaking, and skiing. Innkeepers Alan and Kurtis have meticulously created a serene getaway that's removed, but not distant, from other Catskill attractions. **Pros:** close to activities; superb breakfast; incredible views. **Cons:** you have to drive to most attractions. ⊠*19 Silverfish Rd., Barryville* ☎*845/557–8562 or 888/557–8562* ⊕*eccebedandbreakfast. com* ⇆*5 rooms* &*In-room: refrigerator, Wi-Fi, DVD. In-hotel: Wi-Fi, no-smoking rooms* ⊟*AE, MC, V* ⦿*BP.*

6

The Hudson Valley

WORD OF MOUTH

"If you go to Hyde Park on the Hudson River, you can visit FDR's home; Eleanor Roosevelt's home, Valkill; and a Vanderbilt mansion, all quite near one another. And then have a meal at the Culinary Institute of America in the same town."

—ellenem

"We did a driving trip in the Hudson Valley this past fall and would definitely recommend Rhinebeck. It is a real town with plenty of good restaurant options and easy drives to many of the sites."

—MaggieOB

Updated
by Amanda
Theunissen
and Kate King

In 1609 explorer Henry Hudson sailed his ship, the *Half Moon*, up the great river that would later bear his name. He was seeking a shortcut from Europe to spice-rich Asia, but instead found heady treasures of a different sort—plunging rock cliffs, lush green highlands, jagged black ridges, and massive granite domes. He called it, "as pleasant a land as one can tread upon."

A vibrant tableau of American history unfolds along the Hudson's shores, culminating in the Gothic facades of the United States Military Academy at West Point, where you can walk in the footsteps of Civil War heroes and U.S. presidents. Grand, antiques-filled mansions, the legacies of prominent New York families of yore, command breathstealing Hudson River views. Many—including the Boscobel Restoration in Garrison; Kykuit, the Rockefeller estate near Tarrytown; and Montgomery Place, the Livingston mansion in Annandale-on-Hudson—open their doors and gardens for seasonal touring.

The true spirit of the valley lives in the little river towns, scattered gems where clusters of cafés, boutiques, and galleries arrange themselves along storybook main streets. You find a treasure chest of antiques shops in Nyack, Cold Spring, and newly revitalized Hudson, where more than 60 vendors jostle for ascendancy over a span of five blocks. Beacon, home to the expansive Dia:Beacon museum, lays claim to an edgy contemporary-arts scene, and the festival town of Saugerties hosts a yearly garlic celebration. Deeper inland, particularly in the sleepy hamlets nestled near Millbrook and New Paltz, country roads wend their way to apple orchards, wine trails, horse paddocks, and farm stands.

Want outdoor adventure? A dozen-plus state parks lie within the Hudson corridor. Craggy peaks, pine-scented forests, cool mountain waterways, and the sapphire ribbon of the river itself serve as superb venues for hiking, climbing, biking, kayaking, fishing, and other outdoor diversions.

It's easy to skip upriver from New York City for a day trip to the region, but scores of country inns and bed-and-breakfasts hold all the enticements for a longer, more leisurely Hudson Valley sojourn.

ORIENTATION AND PLANNING

GETTING ORIENTED

Set on both sides of the Hudson River, the region stretches from just north of New York City all the way to Columbia County's northern border, narrowing the farther north you go.

TOP REASONS TO GO

River towns. Explore New York's rich history in its charming waterfront towns and villages.

State arks. Immerse yourself in the great outdoors by exploring the Hudson Valley's magnificent nature preserves.

Leaf peeping. Witness Mother Nature's brilliance as she shows off her full fall colors.

Shopping galore. Shop till you drop at Woodbury Common Premium Outlets—and don't miss the many eclectic boutiques and antiques shops hidden in tiny towns throughout the region.

Culinary Institute of America. Treat yourself to lunch or dinner at one of the country's leading schools for chefs.

Six bridges connect the west and east banks of the river in the region: the Tappan Zee Bridge, the Bear Mountain Bridge, the Newburgh–Beacon Bridge, the Mid-Hudson Bridge, the Kingston–Rhinecliff Bridge, and the Rip Van Winkle Bridge. Interstate 84 runs east–west across the northern section of the lower valley, crossing the Newburgh–Beacon Bridge. Interstate 87, the New York Thruway, runs northward through the Bronx and lower Westchester on the east side of the Hudson River, before crossing west at the Tappan Zee Bridge and heading north toward Albany. From New Jersey, Interstate 287 merges with 87 in southern Rockland County shortly after crossing the New York state border.

The Palisades Interstate Parkway is the other major north–south road on the west side, sometimes referred to as the "left bank"; Route 17 cuts northwest across the lower valley and into the southern Catskills. U.S. 9W travels the west bank from Nyack to Catskill, through Newburgh and Kingston.

On the east side of the river, the Saw Mill River Parkway runs north of Yonkers, hooking up with Interstate 684 in the northeast corner of Westchester County. The Taconic State Parkway, which starts north of White Plains, winds its way northward the length of the Hudson Valley. U.S. 9 mostly hugs the east bank of the Hudson River, passing through many picturesque towns, including Tarrytown, Hyde Park, and Rhinebeck.

PLANNING

WHEN TO GO

Summer and fall are the peak seasons in the valley; this is when most of the biggest festivals take place. Winter can be cold and dreary, but many of the villages look quite magical with a fresh layer of snow. If winter road conditions worry you, consider traveling by train.

GETTING HERE AND AROUND

If you want to truly explore the Hudson Valley, you'll need a car. Public transportation is available, but a car is the best way to explore the region's scenic back roads and byways. The Palisades Interstate

Parkway is your best choice for a major north–south road on the west side of the Hudson River. The Taconic State Parkway, a main route on the east side of the river, is particularly scenic, with good views of the Catskills to the west. Both are easily accessible from Manhattan.

For those arriving by air, the Hudson Valley is served by Stewart International Airport and Westchester County Airport. Albany International Airport, at the north end of the Hudson Valley, is a good option for visits to Ulster, Columbia, and Dutchess counties. Of New York City's three major airports (JFK, LaGuardia, and Newark), LaGuardia is the closest to the Hudson Valley, though all three are reasonably accessible.

TRAIN TRAVEL

The Metro-North Railroad and Amtrak can take you to many of the towns on either side of the river. If you want to do more than walk around the downtown area near the train station, you may want to rent a car once there. Enterprise is a good company to go with in this situation, since staff there will pick you up (not applicable to all stations).

Train Information **Amtrak** (☎ 800/872–7245 ⊕ www.amtrak.com). **Metro-North Railroad** (☎ 212/532–4900 or 800/638–7646 ⊕ www.mta.info/mnr).

RESTAURANTS

The area is home to a slew of talented chefs, many of whom attended the Culinary Institute of America in Poughkeepsie and decided to stay close by after graduation. Excellent cuisine is available throughout the region, and at the Culinary Institute itself. Rhinebeck and Nyack brim with high-quality restaurants. Such quality often means high prices, but you can also find appealing inexpensive eateries and high-end delis. With few exceptions (which are noted in individual restaurant listings), dress is informal. Where reservations are indicated as essential, you may need to reserve a week or more ahead. In summer and fall you may need to book several months ahead.

HOTELS

The majority of places to stay in the Hudson Valley are inns, bed-and-breakfasts, and small hotels, and they range from quaint to fairly luxurious. The area does also include a smattering of full-service resorts. A few places have pools, but these are the exception rather than the rule. On weekends, two-night minimum stays are commonly required, especially at smaller inns and B&Bs. Many B&Bs book up long in advance of summer and fall, and they're often not suitable for children.

WHAT IT COSTS					
	¢	$	$$	$$$	$$$$
RESTAURANTS	under $10	$10–$17	$18–$24	$25–$35	over $35
HOTELS	under $100	$100–$150	$151–$200	$201–$300	over $300

Restaurant prices are for a main course at dinner (or at the most expensive meal served). Hotel prices are for two people in a standard double room in high season, excluding tax.

LOWER HUDSON VALLEY–WEST

The Lower Hudson Valley on the west side is composed of Rockland and Orange counties.

GETTING HERE AND AROUND

Interstate 87 (the New York Thruway) and the Palisades Interstate Parkway are the major north–south roads on the west side of the Hudson River. Interstate 84 and Route 17 are the principal east-west routes, with I–84 going from Newburgh southwest toward New Jersey, while Route 17 heads northwest from its intersection with I–87 toward the Finger Lakes and Western New York, where it becomes Interstate 86.

VISITOR INFORMATION

Orange County Chamber of Commerce (☎845/615–3860 ⊕www.orangetourism. org). **Rockland County Tourism** (☎845/708–7300 or 800/295-5723 ⊕www. rockland.org).

PIERMONT

24 mi north of New York City.

Piermont doesn't hide its gritty, blue-collar history. A century-old flywheel, which supplied power to factories in the village until 1983, is displayed as sculpture in the village's park. Art is what helped establish Piermont as a destination for visitors; many galleries surround Flywheel Park, which has a clear view of the Hudson River and the Tappan Zee Bridge. Nowadays shops and restaurants have filled the void that industry left, and the downtown thrives with day-trippers as well as residents doing errands or enjoying a night out with friends.

GETTING HERE AND AROUND

Piermont is on the west side of the Hudson River, off Route 9W, in Rockland County. From New York City, cross the George Washington Bridge, heading west towards New Jersey, then take the Palisades Interstate Parkway north to Route 9W.

WHAT TO SEE

Bird-watchers search the skies for migratory birds such as great blue herons and American avocets at the 500-acre **Piermont Marsh**, part of Hudson River National Estuarine Research Reserve, itself part of **Tallman Mountain State Park** (⊠*Rte. 9W, Sparkill* ☎*845/359–0544* ⊕*www. nysparks.com* ✉*June–Labor Day, parking $5*). The park is open daily from dawn to dusk.

NIGHTLIFE AND THE ARTS

Long a bastion of live music, the **Turning Point** (⊠*468 Piermont Ave.* ☎*845/359–1089* ⊕*www.turningpointcafe.com*) specializes in jazz, blues, and folk, and attracts big names on occasion. Seating is general admission; tickets are usually $15–$35, depending on the act.

WHERE TO EAT

$$ ✕**Freelance Café & Wine Bar.** On weekends a line forms outside for this
BISTRO less expensive sibling of Xaviars at Piermont, with which it shares an
address. Bistro-style dishes include osso buco with barley risotto, steak
frites (with fries), and pan-roasted chicken with spaetzle and morels.
The coconut shrimp is outstanding. ⊠ *506 Piermont Ave.* ☎ *845/365–
3250* ⌕ *Reservations not accepted* ☐ *AE, MC, V* ⊘ *Closed Mon.*

$ ✕**Pasta Amore.** Families, foursomes, and large groups come to this
ITALIAN northern Italian restaurant for its signature dish, Pollo Amore (chicken
with white wine and roasted peppers), as well as for its pastas, espe-
cially the penne with vodka sauce. Try to snag a table near the windows
overlooking Flywheel Park (and, farther away, the Tappan Zee Bridge).
⊠ *200 Ash St.* ☎ *845/365–1911* ☐ *AE, DC, MC, V.*

$ ✕**Relish.** Although the decor is nothing fancy (the floor is painted ply-
ECLECTIC wood), the food and the earnest, efficient service make this restau-
★ rant worth a visit. Creative fusion cuisine—soy-cured strip loin with
roasted Jerusalem artichokes, shiitake mushrooms, and kimchi puree,
for instance—and classic dishes such as braised beef short ribs draw
crowds on weekends. Sparkill is off the Palisades Parkway about 4 mi
south of Piermont. ⊠ *4 Depot Sq., Sparkill* ☎ *845/398–2747* ☐ *AE,
MC, V* ⊘ *Closed Mon. and Tues. No lunch weekends.*

$$$$ ✕**Xaviars at Piermont.** Impeccable service, elegant decor, and extraordi-
AMERICAN nary food by chef and owner Peter X. Kelly make this 40-seat restaurant
Fodor'sChoice a not-to-be-missed special-occasion place. Dinner is a relative bargain:
★ $70 gets you a four-course, prix-fixe meal with an *amuse-bouche* (bite-
size appetizer) and petits fours. The menu, which changes seasonally,
might include roasted breast of squab served with Hudson Valley foie
gras, lobster with vanilla beurre blanc and parsnip puree, and a tasting
of raw fish. The wine cellar stores more than 600 bottles. Lunch, served
Friday and Sunday, is $35 prix fixe. ⊠ *506 Piermont Ave.* ☎ *845/359–
7007* ⌕ *Reservations essential* ☐ *AE, MC, V* ⊘ *Closed Mon. and Tues.
No lunch Wed., Thurs., and Sat.*

NYACK

3 mi north of Piermont.

Although only a 35-minute car ride from Manhattan, the Hudson River
village of Nyack retains a small-town charm. Elegant mansions and
Victorian stunners mix with modest homes as well as delightful shops
and fine restaurants. For a scenic drive with glimpses of the river, take
Main Street to North Broadway and turn left to follow it north to
Hook Mountain.

The arts have long played an important role in Nyack, the birthplace
of realist painter Edward Hopper. Today Hopper's house is a commu-
nity cultural center and exhibit space. Nyack was also the longtime
home of stage actress Helen Hayes, for whom a thriving local theater
is named.

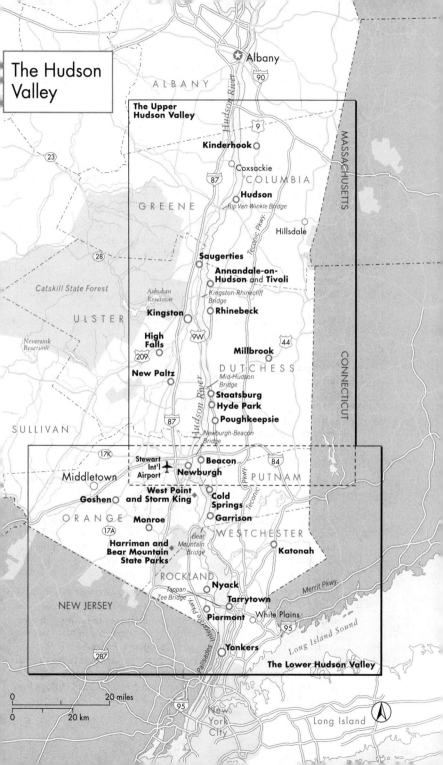

The Hudson Valley

The Upper Hudson Valley

Albany

ALBANY

Kinderhook

Coxsackie

COLUMBIA

GREENE

Hudson

Rip Van Winkle Bridge

Hillsdale

MASSACHUSETTS

Catskill State Forest

Saugerties

Annandale-on-Hudson and Tivoli

Kingston-Rhinecliff Bridge

Ashokan Reservoir

ULSTER

Kingston

Rhinebeck

Neversink Reservoir

High Falls

Millbrook

New Paltz

DUTCHESS

Mid-Hudson Bridge

Staatsburg

Hyde Park

Poughkeepsie

CONNECTICUT

Hudson River

Newburgh-Beacon Bridge

SULLIVAN

Stewart Int'l Airport

Beacon

Newburgh

PUTNAM

Middletown

West Point and Storm King

Cold Springs

Goshen

Garrison

ORANGE

Monroe

WESTCHESTER

Bear Mountain Bridge

Harriman and Bear Mountain State Parks

Katonah

ROCKLAND

Merrit Pkwy.

Nyack

Tappan Zee Bridge

Tarrytown

White Plains

Piermont

NEW JERSEY

Long Island Sound

Yonkers

The Lower Hudson Valley

New York City

Long Island

0   20 miles
0   20 km

GETTING HERE AND AROUND

From New York City, cross the George Washington Bridge, heading west towards New Jersey, then take the Palisades Interstate Parkway north to Route 9W.

WHAT TO SEE

Hopper House Art Center. The childhood home of artist Edward Hopper now serves as an arts center and exhibition space. The famed painter owned the Federal-style house, which was built in 1858 by his grandfather, until his death in 1967. A group of Nyack citizens saved the structure from ruin in 1971. Jazz concerts are held in the backyard on Thursday evenings in July. ✉*82 N. Broadway* ☎*845/358-0774* ⊕*www.hopperhouse.org* ✉*Donation suggested* ☉*Thurs.–Sun. 1–5.*

Nyack Beach State Park. The 61-acre park, known as **Hook Mountain** to locals, includes a main trail that stretches alongside the Hudson River and attracts bicyclists, dog walkers, and runners. Bird-watchers look for hawks, and area residents come with their lawn chairs and Sunday papers. Bring lunch and enjoy it at a waterfront picnic table. Parking is free daily from November through March, and on weekdays from April to mid-June and Labor Day to October. ✉*North end of N. Broadway* ☎*845/268-3020* ⊕*www.nysparks.com* ✉*Parking $6* ☉*Daily dawn–dusk.*

SHOPPING

Christopher's (✉*71 S. Broadway* ☎*845/358-9574*) brims with antique furniture and reproductions, as well as housewares and decorative items. Pet the sleeping dog on your way out. The **Franklin Antique Center** (✉*142 Main St.* ☎*845/353-0071*) houses many antiques dealers under one roof. The goods—art-deco furnishings, old cameras and typewriters, Victrolas, jadeite—are just as varied. In addition to African, Mexican, and South American furnishings and housewares, **Hacienda** (✉*70 S. Franklin St.* ☎*845/348-0300*) also has beautiful textiles.

Lord & Taylor, Macy's, and JCPenney anchor the mammoth **Palisades Center** (✉*1000 Palisades Center Dr., West Nyack* ☎*845/348-1000*), which has more than 170 stores, including Pottery Barn, Abercrombie & Fitch, and Restoration Hardware. The four-level mall, 3 mi west of Nyack, also has a skating rink, a Ferris wheel, a carousel, an IMAX theater, an AMC Loews multiplex, and many chain restaurants, including Legal Sea Foods.

NIGHTLIFE

Don't let the velvet rope outside **Luna Lounge** (✉*4 S. Franklin St.* ☎*845/358-1954*) fool you. Everyone's welcome at this comfortable, gay-friendly club that serves top-notch cocktails and has great music. The outdoor patio is a bonus for smokers. If you want to meet the locals, sidle up to the bar at **O'Donoghue's Tavern** (✉*66 Main St.* ☎*845/358-0180*), get a beer pulled from the tap, and listen to their stories. The menu stretches beyond standard pub fare and draws families (mostly for lunch and early dinner) and couples. **Olde Village Inne** (✉*97 Main St.* ☎*845/358-1160*), an Irish pub, caters to all crowds—

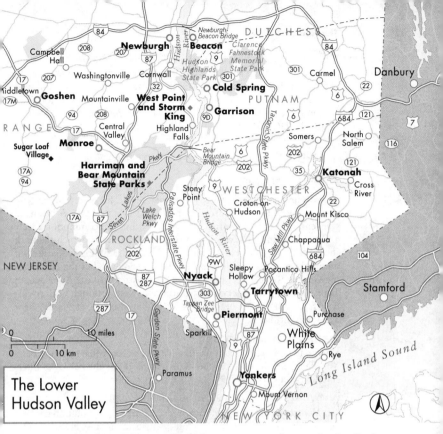

The Lower Hudson Valley

into the wee hours. Where else can you get a burger, shepherd's pie, or enchiladas until 3 AM?

WHERE TO EAT

$$
AMERICAN ✕**Hudson House of Nyack.** Save room for banana cream pie or one of the other amazing desserts at this American restaurant in the former village hall. (The wine is stored behind bars in the old jail.) Entrée favorites include shrimp and pappardelle puttanesca with anchovies, black olives, and capers, as well as Asian barbecue duck breast with whipped potato, baby bok choy, and apple-orange chutney. ⊠*134 Main St.* ☎*845/353–1355* ▤*AE, MC, V* ⊙*Closed Mon.*

$
ITALIAN ✕**Lanterna Tuscan Bistro.** The homemade pastas and the Parmesan-basket salad are your best bets at this casual Italian bistro with a good wine list. The frittatas are an excellent option for Sunday brunch. Italian-born chef Rosanno Giannini offers cooking classes and wine-tasting events. ⊠*3 S. Broadway* ☎*845/353–8361* ▤*AE, DC, MC, V.*

¢
CAFES ✕**Runcible Spoon Bakery.** Day-tripping bicyclists and locals favor this popular bakery, where you can nibble on "Hubwiches" (tasty breakfast sandwiches named after various bicycle brands), as well as scones, muffins, and pastries that will satisfy any sweet tooth. Lunch offerings include hot and cold sandwiches, and a variety of hearty soups. ⊠*37 N. Broadway* ☎*845/358–9398* ▤*AE, MC, V* ⊙*No dinner.*

$$ ✕**Wasabi.** The stylish surroundings are a match for the hip, Asian-fusion
JAPANESE cuisine served at this spot. The menu includes an innovative selection of
sushi and rolls; tasty small plates such as black cod with miso; and such
refined main courses as crispy salmon with pomegranate reduction. Res-
ervations are essential on weekends. ⊠*110 Main St.* ☎*845/358–7977*
▤*AE, D, DC, MC, V.*

HARRIMAN AND BEAR MOUNTAIN STATE PARKS

23 mi north of Nyack.

Bear Mountain, which some say resembles the profile of a reclining bear,
presides over the four-season Bear Mountain State Park. A beautiful
weekend can attract swarms of picnickers, but the commotion rarely
extends beyond the lawns and into the wooded trails, which the park
shares with adjacent Harriman State Park—a rambling wilderness of
mountain peaks, dense forests, and beach-fringed lakes that straddles
the Orange-Rockland county line. A 21-mi stretch of the Appalachian
Trail, including its first completed section, snakes through both parks,
traversing nine peaks before crossing the Hudson River via the Bear
Mountain Bridge.

GETTING HERE AND AROUND

Harriman and Bear Mountain State Parks are accessible from the New
York State Thruway (Interstate 87) via Exit 16, or the Palisades Inter-
state Parkway via Exit 19.

WHAT TO SEE

Fort Montgomery State Historic Site. Scene of a 1777 Revolutionary War
battle for the Hudson River, this fort (well, its foundation at least) is still
visible on the 14½-acre site, which is on a cliff with stunning Hudson
River views. To get to the site from New York City, take the Palisades
Parkway north to Route 9W north and proceed just over ½ mi. The
parking area is on the right.

Stony Point Battlefield State Historic Site. This is the only Revolutionary War
battleground in Rockland County. A museum with exhibits and a slide
show describes the battle, and reenactments in period costume are common.
It is also the home of the oldest lighthouse on the Hudson River. ⊠*Park
Rd., off Rte. 9W* ☎*845/786–2521* ⊕*www.palisadesparksconservancy.
org* ⊠*Weekend parking $5* ⊗*Grounds: Apr.–Oct., daily; Nov.–Mar.,
weekdays. Museum: Apr.–Oct., Wed.–Sun. Hrs vary.*

SPORTS AND THE OUTDOORS

Bear Mountain State Park. The mass of pinkish-gray granite known as
Bear Mountain looms over this enormously popular 5,067-acre park,
which hugs the Hudson River at the northern end of the Palisades Inter-
state Parkway. The park's varied terrain affords hiking, road biking, and
cross-country skiing; boat rentals and fishing are available on Hessian
Lake, and small craft can moor at a dock on the river. Of the three picnic
areas, the prettiest edges the lake. Open to the public are a swimming
pool, an ice rink, a merry-go-round, a playground, and playing fields.
The **Trailside Museums & Wildlife Center** (⊗*Daily 10–4:30*) consists

of a nature trail with outdoor exhibits and animal enclosures, as well as four museum buildings with exhibits interpreting such themes as colonial and American Indian history, geology, and wildlife. To enter the park, take the Palisades Parkway to Exit 19 and follow signs. Parking fills up quickly on nice weekends, so plan accordingly. The parking fee is charged daily from Memorial Day through Labor Day and on weekends only the rest of the year. ⊠*Rte. 9W, Bear Mountain* ☎*845/786–2701* ⊕*www.nysparks.com* ☔*Parking $6, museum and wildlife center $1, pool $2* ☉*Daily 8* AM*–dusk.*

Harriman State Park. Miles of hiking trails and biking roadways link this park with contiguous Bear Mountain State Park, with which it is considered one unit of the Palisades Interstate Park system. Nearly 10 times as large as its neighbor, the park encompasses more than 46,000 acres in the Ramapo Mountains of the Hudson Highlands. Mostly vast, pristine wilderness in which are scattered 31 lakes, ponds, and reservoirs, the park has several recreational areas, including three beaches (at Lakes Welch, Sebago, and Tiorati); two camping facilities; fishing areas; and cross-country skiing, hiking, and bridle trails. In a wooded valley the **Anthony Wayne Recreation Area** (Exit 17 off the Palisades Parkway) has picnic areas with fireplaces, playing fields, and access to hiking and skiing trails. The Silver Mine area (Exit 18 off the parkway) has lakeside picnic grounds and biking roads, as well as boat-launch sites and fishing. A visitor center, in the parkway median between Exits 16 and 17, sells trail maps and books. ⊠*Palisades Pkwy. Exits 15–18* ☎*845/786–2701* ⊕*www.nysparks.com* ☔*Parking $6 (beach parking $7)* ☉*Daily 8* AM*–dusk.*

SHOPPING

More than 220 designer outlets fill the **Woodbury Common Premium Outlets** (⊠*498 Red Apple Ct., off Rte. 32, Exit 16 off I–87, Central Valley* ☎*845/928–4000*), a sprawling shopping complex about a 20-minute drive north of Bear Mountain. Many of the top fashion retailers are here, including Giorgio Armani, Gucci, J. Crew, and DKNY. Beyond clothing, the goods range from shoes and leather goods to housewares and jewelry, with outlets for Nike, Kenneth Cole, and Williams-Sonoma. Deals can be found, but don't expect everything to be a bargain. One of the most popular destinations in the state, the center draws about 10 million visitors a year. The parking lots fill quickly and traffic can be a tangle on weekends (and certain holidays).

WHERE TO EAT

$–$$$
JAPANESE ✕**Gasho of Japan.** Housed in a 400-year-old samurai farmhouse—shipped to America from Japan and reconstructed on-site in Central Valley—this hibachi chophouse claims to deliver both "steak and theater." Skillful chefs slice, dice, flip, and grill your dinner before your eyes, while kimono-clad servers fetch appetizers and umbrella-topped specialty drinks. Proximity to Woodbury Common Premium Outlets makes this a convenient post-shopping spot. ⊠*365 Rte. 32, Central Valley* ☎*845/928–2277* ▭*AE, D, DC, MC, V.*

MONROE

15 mi west of Harriman State Park.

Although it's largely residential, Monroe blends industrial grit and old-fashioned living: it's the birthplace of Velveeta as well as home to Museum Village, a living-history museum. The town offers dining just off Exit 130 of Route 17 (morphing into Interstate 86, the Quickway), which makes it a relatively convenient place to eat near Harriman State Park and Sterling Forest.

GETTING HERE AND AROUND
Monroe is located on Route 17, in the county of Orange. From the New York State Thruway (Interstate 87), take Exit 16 toward Harriman.

WHAT TO SEE
Museum Village. Hands-on exhibits help visitors understand the United States' transition from an agricultural-based society to an industrial culture and economy. Artifacts from the 1800s are used in living-history demonstrations by interpreters dressed in period costume. They perform activities such as hammering horseshoes in the blacksmith's shop, weaving, and teaching about farm life. ⊠*1010 Rte. 17M* ☎*845/782–8247* ⊕*www.museumvillage.com* 🎫*$12* ☉ *July and Aug., daily 11–4; Apr.–June and Sept.–Nov., call ahead.*

OFF THE BEATEN PATH

Brotherhood Winery. The oldest continually operating winery in the United States, Brotherhood includes some European-style stone buildings that date from 1839. Tours and tastings are available. The winery is about 8 mi north of Monroe. ⊠*100 Brotherhood Plaza Dr., off Rte. 208 N, Washingtonville* ☎*845/496–3661* ⊕*www.brotherhoodwinery. net* 🎫*Tour and tasting $10, tasting only $5* ☉ *Apr.–Dec., Sun.–Fri. 11–5, Sat. 11–6; Jan.–Mar., weekends 11–5.*

SHOPPING
★ **Sugar Loaf Village.** The hamlet of Sugar Loaf, about 3 mi southwest of Monroe, encompasses more than 50 shops and artists' studios. Painters, sculptors, and other craftspeople ply their trade and sell their wares here, some in buildings dating from the mid-1800s. Most of the shops are open Wednesday through Sunday. ⊠*King's Hwy., off Rte. 94 south of Rte. 17/I–86* ☎*845/469–9181.*

WHERE TO EAT
$
MEXICAN
✕**Cafe Fiesta.** The come-as-you-are family-friendly eatery in Highland Mills serves authentic Mexican fare, including vegetarian and low-fat renditions. ⊠*530 Rte. 32, Highland Mills* ☎*845/928–2151* ▤*AE, D, MC, V.*

GOSHEN

12 mi west of Monroe.

With a huge park, old trees, nice restaurants, and two side-by-side hardware stores, Goshen is the kind of walkable, slow-paced village ideal for an afternoon visit. And though it remembers its past with places like the Historic Track and the Trotting Horse Museum, it is not a place that time forgot. You find a smattering of restaurants and interesting shops, as well as beautiful churches and statues to admire.

GETTING HERE AND AROUND
Goshen is located on Highway 17. From the New York State Thruway (Interstate 87), take Exit 16 toward Harriman.

WHAT TO SEE
Goshen Historic Track. The oldest harness track in the United States is also a National Historic Landmark. You can watch daily training or take a self-guided walking tour of the premises, but these days races are run only in June and July. ⊠ *44 Park Pl.* ☎ *845/294–5333* ⊕ *www. goshenhistorictrack.com* ☒ *Free* ⊙ *Daily; call for times.*

Trotting Horse Museum. Overlooking the track is this museum and hall of fame dedicated to harness racing. Exhibits include a three-dimensional racing simulator, prints, and paintings. Original track stables house some of the displays. ⊠ *240 Main St.* ☎ *845/294–6330* ☒ *Free* ⊙ *Daily 10–5.*

WHERE TO EAT AND STAY

$$

AMERICAN

✗ **Bull's Head Inn.** The kitchen of this restaurant in a restored 1786 building turns out contemporary American fare: cedar-plank salmon glazed with an orange marmalade reduction, grilled chicken and pancetta over rigatoni with sherry cream sauce, baby rack of lamb with mashed sweet potatoes. A gazebo, an herb garden, and a fountain make outdoor dining appealing. Fireplaces warm the place in winter. The restaurant is about 6 mi north of Goshen. ⊠ *120 Sarah Wells Tr., Campbell Hall* ☎ *845/496–6758* ☐ *AE, MC, V* ⊙ *Closed Mon. and Tues. No lunch.*

$–$$

⌁ **Anthony Dobbins Stagecoach Inn.** Built in 1747 as a farmhouse, this quiet Georgian B&B sits peacefully on 3 wooded acres near the foothills of the Catskills. Rooms are colonial in style, filled with family antiques and liberal doses of floral fabrics; some rooms have a fireplace. The suite is really a semidetached house with three small bedrooms, a kitchen, a living room, two bathrooms, and a back porch. **Pros:** historic and charming; easy walking distance to shops and restaurants; suite is perfect for families. **Cons:** some may find floral decor a bit much. ⊠ *268 Main St.* ☎ *845/294–5526 or 866/715–5649* ⊕ *www.dobbinsinn.com* ⇱ *4 rooms, 2 with bath; 1 suite* ⌂ *In-room: kitchen (some), Wi-Fi. In-hotel: Wi-Fi, no-smoking rooms* ☐ *AE,MC, V.*

WEST POINT AND STORM KING

West Point is 5 mi north of Bear Mountain State Park.

Though very different in purpose—one site is dedicated to military education and the other to celebrating art and nature—West Point and Storm King are among the most interesting of the lower Hudson Valley's attractions. Storm King, in Mountainville, is closed in winter, but that is high season for traveling shows at the theater at West Point's Eisenhower Hall.

WHAT TO SEE

Fodor's Choice ★ ☉ **Storm King Art Center.** More than 100 sculptures by major international artists—including David Smith, Alexander Calder, and Isamu Noguchi—are spread out on 500 acres of hills, fields, meadows, and woodlands. The relationship between art and nature is a focus for the center. For the best overview of the

WORD OF MOUTH

"If you explore west of the Hudson River, don't miss Storm King Art Center. It's a spectacular outdoor sculpture museum not far from Bear Mountain and West Point."   —NGail

grounds and collection, ride the shuttle (wheelchair-accessible), which runs every half hour. Free "Highlights of the Collection" walk-in tours are offered daily at 2. Designated picnic areas have tree-shaded tables. Whether or not you picnic, consider wearing bug repellent. Kids love to run around the grounds and the sculptures; you just need to make sure they don't touch the installations. ⊠ *Old Pleasant Hill Rd., Mountainville* ☎ *845/534–3115* ⊕ *www.stormking.org* ☜ *$10* ☉ *Apr.–Oct., Wed.–Sun. 11–5:30; early Nov.–mid-Nov., Wed.–Sun. 11–5.*

Fodor's Choice ★ **United States Military Academy at West Point.** Occupying the western shore of one of the most scenic bends in the Hudson River, the academy consists of some 16,000 acres of training grounds, playing fields, and buildings constructed of native granite in the Military Gothic style. The oldest continually garrisoned post in the U.S. Army, the citadel was founded in 1778 and opened as a military academy in 1802. Distinguished graduates include Robert E. Lee, Ulysses S. Grant, and Douglas MacArthur. The world's oldest and largest military museum, the **West Point Museum** in Olmstead Hall, showcases a vast collection of uniforms, weapons, flags, American military art, and other memorabilia. **Fort Putnam,** built in 1778 and a key component of West Point's defense during the Revolutionary War, was restored in the 1970s. Campus visits are by bus tour only (bring photo ID), but you do get a chance to step off the bus, look at a few memorials and cannons up close, and perhaps glimpse cadets in action. Civilians are also allowed on campus for sporting and cultural events, including football games, theater presentations, parades, and concerts. You can visit the museum and visitor center without taking the $11 tour. Tours aren't given during graduation week (usually late May) and on Saturdays of home football games. ⊠ *Rte. 9W, 5 mi north of Bear Mountain State Park, Highland Falls* ☎ *845/938–2638 visitor center, 845/446–4724 tours* ⊕ *www.usma.edu* ☜ *Free* ☉ *Visitor center daily 9–4:45, museum daily 10:30–4:15.*

SPORTS AND THE OUTDOORS

HIKING   Peaceful hiking trails traverse the 3,830-acre **Black Rock Forest Preserve and Consortium** (⊠ *Rte. 9W, Cornwall* ☎ *845/534–4517* ⊕ *www.blackrockforest.org*), just north of Storm King in Cornwall. In the 1800s loggers cut down the old-growth forest here to make way for farms. By the next century a restoration project was under way to bring the forest back, and the preserve remains an important educational and research site. Black Rock, the forest's highest peak, can be accessed from a number of trails. The Stillman Trail climbs through mountain laurel to the summit, which affords views of Storm King, the Schunnemunk Mountains, and the Shawangunks.

At the heart of the 1,900-acre **Storm King State Park** (⊠ *Off Rte. 9 W between Cornwall and West Point* ☎ *845/786–2701* ⊕ *nysparks.com*) is Storm King Mountain, which is veined with hiking trails, many with spectacular views. The park is undeveloped, so there are no bathrooms and parking is limited. Hikers must heed posted warnings and restrictions and stick to marked trails here, because unexploded artillery shells from the neighboring military academy might be found off trails in area B of the park, in the south.

WHERE TO EAT AND STAY

$
PIZZA
✕ **Prima Pizza.** The pizzeria is well known for its long-distance service— it'll ship a pie anywhere overnight and promise it's never frozen. But it also serves out-of-the-ordinary pizzas like lemon chicken and eggplant rollatini, as well as pastas and subs. ⊠ *252 Main St., Cornwall* ☎ *845/534–7003* ⚲ *Reservations not accepted* ▤ *AE, D, MC, V* ⊘ *Closed Mon.*

$$$–$$$$
🏨 **Cromwell Manor Inn.** After you arrive at this stately Greek Revival mansion and pass through the grand columns of the portico, any hint of formality dissolves as the innkeepers greet you with a plate of fresh-baked cookies. Combining manor-house elegance with bed-and-breakfast-style warmth, this 1820 architectural treasure is surrounded by lawns, gardens, and a patio with sunset views. Many rooms have fireplaces and four-poster beds with sheer panels or crocheted canopies; some also feature cavernous marble bathrooms. Windows provide pastoral vistas without another house in sight—except the 1764 Chimney's Cottage, which contains four of the guest rooms, all filled with period antiques. **Pros:** pastoral setting; short drive to attractions; free Wi-Fi. **Cons:** not a good place for kids. ⊠ *174 Angola Rd., Cornwall* ☎ *845/534–7136* ⊕ *www.cromwellmanor.com* ⇆ *11 rooms, 1 suite* ⚲ *In-room: no phone, no TV (some), Wi-Fi (some). In-hotel: Internet terminal, Wi-Fi, no kids under 6, no-smoking rooms* ▤ *AE, MC, V* ⧦ *BP.*

$$
🏨 **Storm King Lodge.** A vast, light-filled great room with exposed beams, comfy couches, and a massive hearth welcomes you to this white-clapboard country B&B. Rolling lawns and a peaceful feng shui garden surround the 1801 post-and-beam barn, which was converted to a guesthouse in the 1920s. The covered back porch—often a setting for breakfast or an evening drink by candlelight—looks out over the Storm King Art Center's sculpture-strewn meadows across the thruway. Upstairs guest rooms have higher ceilings and are bright; the Lavender Room has a fireplace, rocker, and wide-board floors. A separate guest cottage features two guest suites. **Pros:** convenient location near area attractions; wonderful hosts; ample breakfast. **Cons:** downstairs room is small. ⊠ *100 Pleasant Hill Rd., Mountainville* ☎ *845/534–9421* ⊕ *www.stormkinglodge.com* ⇆ *4 rooms, 1 cottage* ⚲ *In-room: no phone, no TV, Wi-Fi. In-hotel: pool, Wi-Fi, no-smoking rooms* ▤ *AE, MC, V* ⧦ *BP.*

$$$ ⬚ **Thayer Hotel.** Ethereal Hudson River views ennoble this imposing brick-and-granite hotel on the grounds of West Point. (You pass through two security checkpoints on your way to the hotel.) Sleek marble floors, iron chandeliers, and portraits of military leaders bedeck the main lobby; dark, regal furnishings and prints of river scenes adorn guest rooms. Request an odd-numbered room for river vistas or an even-numbered room for views of the academy. The restaurant lures crowds to its Sunday champagne brunch buffet ($28 prix fixe). In summer, angle for a table on the outdoor terrace. **Pros:** chance to stay at West Point; beautiful river views. **Cons:** a bit outdated, some might say musty. ⊠*674 Thayer Rd., West Point* ☎*845/446–4731 or 800/247–5047* ⊕*www. thethayerhotel.com* ☞*117 rooms, 8 suites* ⅃*In-room: Wi-Fi. In-hotel: restaurant, room service, gym, Wi-Fi, no-smoking rooms* ☰*AE, D, DC, MC, V* ❑*EP.*

NEWBURGH

15 mi north of West Point.

Toward the close of the Revolutionary War, George Washington kept his headquarters and residence here. Although the riverside city has lost much of its original architecture to urban renewal, Newburgh retains the largest historic district in the state, with elaborate Italianate mansions and fanciful Queen Anne Victorians lining Montgomery, Grand, and Liberty streets. The waterfront area has rebounded, thanks partly to the bevy of restaurants, bars, and shops that opened in the past several years at Newburgh Landing. A parade of tour boats departs from here, and piers, pathways, and alfresco tables make it a prime spot from which to enjoy valley views.

GETTING HERE AND AROUND

Newburgh lies at the intersection of the New York State Thruway (Interstate 87) and Interstate 84, on the west side of the Hudson River. The city is accessible by train from New York City. Take Metro North's Hudson Line from Grand Central Station to Beacon. From Beacon, take a cab across the bridge to Newburgh.

VISITOR INFORMATION

Newburgh Visitors Center (☎*845/565–5559* ⊕ *www.downingpark.org*).

WHAT TO SEE

Washington's Headquarters State Historic Site. From April 1782 to August 1783, General George Washington made his military headquarters and home in this Dutch fieldstone house, where he attended to the final years of Revolutionary War activity. Guided tours show how Washington, his wife, Martha, and his aides-de-camp lived and worked here as the war drew to a close. Filled with period furniture and reproductions, the house opened to the public in 1850, becoming the first official historic site in the United States. A monument to peace, the Tower of Victory, was erected here in the late 1880s. Adjacent to the house is a small museum containing artifacts collected since the mid-1880s. Lectures, live music, military and crafts demonstrations, and family programs honor Washington's birthday during a three-day extravaganza over Presidents' Day weekend. ⊠*84 Liberty St.* ☏*845/562–1195* ⊕*www.nysparks.com* ⊠*$4* ☉*Mid-Apr.– Oct., Wed.–Sat., 10–5, Sun. 1–5; Nov.–mid-Apr., by appointment.*

WHERE TO EAT AND STAY

$ ✕**Cafe Pitti.** Riverfront tables under a mandarin-orange canopy make for
ITALIAN a relaxed meal at this small eatery, perfect for lunch, dinner, or just dessert in warm weather. When the air is nippy, head inside to the slightly cramped but warm space. The chairs are rickety and the service can be slow, but all is forgiven upon the arrival of the authentic Italian fare. Try a warm panini with Brie, arugula, and truffle oil, or a thin-crusted, prosciutto-topped pizzetta from the wood-burning oven. Tiramisu and cappuccino cake pair well with a selection of dessert wines and ports. ⊠*40 Front St.* ☏*845/565–1444* ▤*AE, MC, V.*

$$ ✕**Il Cena'colo.** The flavors of Tuscany take center stage at this highly
ITALIAN regarded eatery tucked into an unlikely corner of commercial Newburgh. You'll want to toss the menu aside in favor of the exhaustive list of daily specials. Fresh buffalo mozzarella, porcini mushrooms, and sun-dried tomatoes pop up in many dishes; the osso buco is a signature dish, and the pasta with shaved black truffles has acquired nearly a cult following. For dessert, don't miss the chocolate soufflé cake. The cordial waitstaff, outfitted in ties and crisp white aprons, presides over the dining room with pressed-copper ceilings and blond-wood beams. ⊠*228 S. Plank Rd.* ☏*845/564–4494* ⟜*Reservations essential* ▤*AE, D, DC, MC, V* ☉*Closed Tues. No lunch weekends.*

$–$$ ⌂**Stockbridge Ramsdell House on Hudson.** Every bedroom in this rambling 1870 Queen Anne Victorian commands sweeping views of the Hudson River, with some windows framing scenes of Bannerman's Island and the Beacon-Newburgh Bridge. Among the spacious rooms, Beau Rivage has a high canopy bed and private enclosed porch, and Ferry Crossing has an outdoor deck with top-of-the-world vistas. The multicourse breakfast fuels a day's worth of sightseeing. Wander the block to see the 19th-century mansions, but if you stray too far west you'll come to rough-around-the-edges inner Newburgh. **Pros:** river views; walking distance to restaurants. **Cons:** few amenities; rooms could be updated. ⊠*158 Montgomery St.* ☏*845/562–9310* ⊕*www.stockbridgeramsdell. com* ⟜*5 rooms* ⌕*In-room: no phone, Wi-Fi. In-hotel: Wi-Fi, no-smoking rooms* ▤*AE, D, MC, V* ⊙*BP.*

LOWER HUDSON VALLEY—EAST

Westchester and Putnam counties and lower Dutchess County comprise the Lower Hudson Valley east side. The Metro-North commuter train line services several of the towns along the river.

VISITOR INFORMATION

Dutchess County Tourism (☏ *845/463–4000 or 800/445–3131* ⊕ *www. dutchesstourism.com*). **Putnam County Historical Society** (☏*845/265–4010* ⊕*www.pchs-fsm.org*). **Putnam County Visitors Bureau** (☏*800/470–4854* ⊕*www. visitputnam.org*). **Westchester County Office of Tourism** (☏*914/995–8500 or 800/833–9282* ⊕*www.westchestertourism.com*).

YONKERS

Just north of the Bronx border.

Settled by the Dutch in the 17th century, Yonkers takes its name from a word meaning "Djonk Herr's land." The Bronx border is to the south and Manhattan is a short drive away. The farming villages of colonial times grew into an industrial stronghold during the 19th century and home to burgeoning immigrant populations who worked in its factories. Now a modern city of shopping malls and corporate parks, Yonkers is home to almost 200,000 people. The city was made famous by author Thornton Wilder as the home of Dolly Levi, the main character in his play *The Matchmaker,* which became the hit musical *Hello, Dolly!*

Today downtown Yonkers is in the midst of an urban renaissance. Many grand 19th-century structures, including a beaux arts train station and a Victorian pier, have been rehabilitated; artists are moving into lofts; and new restaurants and businesses are being fueled by an influx of private and municipal funding. North and east of the downtown are smaller, quainter neighborhoods.

VISITOR INFORMATION
Yonkers Chamber of Commerce (☎ *914/963–0332* ⊕ *www.yonkerschamber. com*).

WHAT TO SEE
Beczak Environmental Education Center. Set along the Hudson River with views of the Palisades, Beczak is a hidden gem. Here, you'll find a sandy beach, and a tidal marsh where kids can use a spotting scope to view birds like osprey. The center offers a host of educational programs, but kids will have the most fun wading into the water and catching fish with a 30-foot net. ⊠ *35 Alexander St.* ☎ *914/377–1900* ⊕ *www. beczak.org.*

Hudson River Museum. In an 1877 Victorian Gothic mansion, the museum displays changing exhibits of 19th- and 20th-century American art and has the county's only planetarium. It specializes in combining art, history, and science in its shows. ⊠ *511 Warburton Ave.* ☎ *914/963–4550* ⊕ *www.hrm.org* 🎟 *$5* ☉ *Wed., Thurs., and weekends noon–5; Fri. noon–8.*

Philipse Manor Hall State Historic Site. Frederick Philipse I, a wealthy Dutch merchant, began building this house in the 1680s. After the Revolutionary War his great-grandson Frederick Philipse III, a loyalist to the British Crown, had to leave behind the house and a 52,000-acre estate stretching from the Bronx to Croton. The home, the oldest in Westchester County, includes some of the finest surviving examples of American rococo architecture and decor. ⊠ *29 Warburton Ave.* ☎ *914/965–4027* ⊕ *nysparks.state.ny.us* 🎟 *$5* ☉ *Tues.–Sun. 11–5.*

St. Paul's Church National Historic Site. The parish that built St. Paul's church was established in 1665. The present fieldstone-and-brick Georgian church begun in 1763 was used by British and Hessian soldiers as a military hospital during the Revolutionary War. The historic cemetery, one of the oldest in New York, contains footstones, or gravemarkers, dating back to 1704, a mass grave for Hessian soldiers, and the graves of former slaves. Guided walking tours are available. The church is in Mount Vernon, about 2 mi east of Yonkers. ⊠ *897 S. Columbus Ave., Mount Vernon* ☎ *914/667–4116* ⊕ *www.nps.gov/sapa* ⊠ *Free* ⊗ *Weekdays 9–5.*

TARRYTOWN

10 mi north of Yonkers.

On the east bank of the Hudson River, Tarrytown has a bustling downtown with a rich artistic history. In the mid-1600s this Westchester County village was settled by the Dutch, who called it Tarwe, which means "wheat." Filled with boutiques, antiques shops, art galleries, restaurants, bed-and-breakfasts, and beautiful parks, Tarrytown is a popular tourist destination whose most famous son was Washington Irving, considered the first American writer to make a living solely from his work. His classic works include *Rip Van Winkle* and *The Legend of Sleepy Hollow.* (Sleepy Hollow is the neighboring village to the north.) Irving's house, Sunnyside, is a popular attraction.

WHAT TO SEE

FodorsChoice ★ **Kykuit.** On a hill surrounded by gardens, stone terraces, and fountains sits the stunning classical-revival mansion that was home to four generations of Rockefellers, one of America's most famous families. From its regal position, Kykuit (pronounced "kie-cut"), which means "lookout" in Dutch, has breathtaking views of the Hudson River. Antiques, ceramics, and famous artworks fill the house, which was finished in 1913; sculptures by Alexander Calder, Constantin Brancusi, Louise Nevelson, and Pablo Picasso adorn the grounds, which encompass 87 acres. You must take a tour to see the estate, which is accessible only by shuttle bus from the visitor center at Philipsburg Manor. ⊠ *381 N. Broadway, Sleepy Hollow* ☎ *914/631–8200* ⊕ *www.hudsonvalley.org* ⊠ *$22–$35* ⊗ *May–early Nov., hrs vary.*

Lighthouse at Sleepy Hollow. Great views of the Hudson River and the Tappan Zee Bridge can be seen from this 65-foot-tall all-metal beacon built in 1883. ⊠ *Kingsland Point Park, Palmer Ave. (off Pierson St. west of Rte. 9), Sleepy Hollow* ☎ *914/366–5109* ⊕ *www.sleepyhollowchamber. com* ⊠ *$5* ⊗ *By appointment.*

♻ **Lyndhurst.** Noted architect Alexander Davis Jackson designed this magnificent marble mansion overlooking the Hudson River. Built in 1838, Lyndhurst is widely considered the premier Gothic Revival home in the United States. You may tour the mansion's elaborate interior and stroll the 67 landscaped acres, which include a conservatory and a rose garden. The estate also includes a turn-of-the-20th-century bowling alley and an original child's playhouse, open for children to play in today. ⊠ *635 S. Broadway* ☎ *914/631–4481* ⊕ *www.lyndhurst.org* ⊠ *$12* ⊗ *Mid-Apr.–Oct., Tues.–Sun. 10–5; Nov.–mid-Apr., weekends 10–4.*

Old Dutch Church of Sleepy Hollow. Built in 1685, this is the oldest church in New York State. It figures prominently in *The Legend of Sleepy Hollow*, by Washington Irving. Made of stone and hand-hewn lumber, the church is in a style typical of the northern Netherlands. Surrounding the Old Dutch Church is the famous **Sleepy Hollow Cemetery** (⊠ *540 N. Broadway* ☎*914/631–0081* ⊕*www.sleepyhollowcemetery.org*), which is mentioned in *The Legend of Sleepy Hollow* and was the source of some of Irving's characters' names. The cemetery is open daily 8:30– 4:30. Free tours of the church and cemetery are given Sunday at 2 from Memorial Day through October. ⊠*430 N. Broadway, Sleepy Hollow* ☎*914/631–1123* ⊕*www.sleepyhollowchamber.com* 🎫*Free* ⊗*Memorial Day–Oct., weekends 2–4, Mon., Wed., and Thurs. 1–4.*

Philipsburg Manor. On the bank of the Pocantico River sits this 18th-century farm and provisioning plant owned by Frederick Philipse III, whose Dutch family owned most of the land in the region. Guides in period costume conduct tours of the Dutch stone house filled with 17th- and 18th-century antiques. The museum focuses, however, on the lives and stories of the 23 enslaved Africans who lived here and on slavery in the colonial north. Check out the water-powered gristmill, 18th-century New World Dutch barn, slave garden, and reconstructed tenant house. ⊠*381 N. Broadway, Sleepy Hollow* ☎*914/631–8200* ⊕*www.hudsonvalley.org* 🎫*$12* ⊗*Mar., weekends 10–4; Apr.–Oct., Wed.–Mon. 10–5; Nov.–Dec., Wed.–Mon. 10–4.*

★ **Stone Barns Center for Food and Agriculture.** Founded by David Rockefeller in honor of his late wife, Peggy, Stone Barns is a groundbreaking nonprofit educational center that aims to promote sustainable, community-based agriculture. The 80-acre working farm encompasses Norman-style barn buildings, a restaurant and café, a greenhouse, and livestock, including sheep and swine. Garden tours, greenhouse workshops, and introductions to local environmentalists, winemakers, and organic farmers are among the programs. Self-guided tours are free; guided tours are $15. The dinner-only restaurant, **Blue Hill at Stone Barns,** is an outpost of Manhattan's famed Blue Hill. The Blue Hill Café serves light fare and sandwiches until 4:30. ⊠*630 Bedford Rd., Pocantico Hills* ☎*914/366–6200* ⊕*www.stonebarnscenter.org* 🎫*Free* ⊗*Wed.–Sun. 10–5.*

Sunnyside. A guide in period costume escorts you through the 1830s home of Washington Irving, whose writings include *The Legend of Sleepy Hollow* and *Rip Van Winkle*. The eclectic building, one of the nation's earliest examples of romantic architecture, includes stepped gables that recall Dutch architecture and a curved roof modeled after that of a Spanish monastery. Sunnyside was often called America's Home, because it appeared in many landscape illustrations of the period. Irving's book-lined study is a highlight. ⊠*89 W. Sunnyside La.* ☎*914/631–8200 Historic Hudson Valley* ⊕*www.hudsonvalley. org* 🎫*$12* ⊗*Mar., weekends 10–4; Apr.–Oct., Wed.–Mon. 10–5; Nov. and Dec., Wed.–Mon. 10–4.*

Fodor's Choice **Union Church of Pocantico Hills.** The nondenominational stone church
★ built in 1922 on land donated by John D. Rockefeller is loosely based
on early English Gothic buildings but deliberately devoid of sectarian
detailing. The real stars of the site, however, are the stained-glass windows by Marc Chagall and Henri Matisse, also gifts of the Rockefeller
family. ⊠ *555 Bedford Rd./Rte. 448, Pocantico Hills* ☎ *914/631–8200
Historic Hudson Valley* ⊕ *www.hudsonvalley.org* ☜ *$5* ⊘ *Apr.–Dec.,
Wed.–Fri. 11–5, Sat. 10–5, Sun. 2–5.*

Van Cortlandt Manor. At this living-history museum, costumed guides are
strategically placed throughout the estate, which includes an 18th-century
stone manor house and an 18th-century tavern. The house includes some
of its original Georgian and Federal furnishings. Spinning, weaving, and
other demonstrations are held in a tenant house adjacent to the tavern.
⊠ *S. Riverside Ave., off Rte. 9, Croton-on-Hudson* ☎ *914/631–8200
Historic Hudson Valley* ⊕ *www.hudsonvalley.org* ☜ *$12* ⊘ *Apr.–Oct.,
Wed.–Mon. 10–5; Nov. and Dec., weekends 10–4.*

SPORTS AND THE OUTDOORS
Hiking trails, fishing ponds, carriage paths, woodlands, and lush meadows make up the more than 1,000 acres of the **Rockefeller State Park
Preserve** (⊠ *Rte. 117 near Rte. 9, Sleepy Hollow* ☎ *914/631–1470*
⊕ *nysparks.state.ny.us*), 4 mi northeast of Tarrytown. The wetlands
portion is home to a number of migratory bird species, such as the
scarlet tanager and northern oriole, which breed here. Panoramic views
of the Hudson River can be seen from the former site of Rockwood
Hall, William Rockefeller's estate. The park is open daily from 7 AM to
sunset; parking is $6.

SHOPPING
Tarrytown is a walking village that prides itself on having only a few
national-chain stores. Most of its shops occupy old buildings, and the
two main drags—Main Street and Broadway—have an old-fashioned
feel. **Belkind-Bigi** (⊠ *21 Main St.* ☎ *914/524–9626*) is one of the few
shops specializing in mid-century modern furniture and accessories.
Choose from designer pieces—Mies van der Rohe's Barcelona chairs,
George Nelson's platform bench—or those with idiosyncratic pedigrees
that hold their own among such heavyweights. Antiques dealers love
the low prices and large and diverse selection at **Hank's Alley** (⊠ *15 N.
Washington St.* ☎ *914/524–9895*), set back from the street in what
was once a trolley shop. You can find 1920s mahogany dining sets and
'60s Danish modern pieces as well as vintage jewelry, beaded bags,
and clothing.

NIGHTLIFE AND THE ARTS
The 1885 **Tarrytown Music Hall** ⊠ *13 Main St.* ☎ *914/631–3390* ⊕ *www.
tarrytownmusichall.org),* a National Historic Landmark, serves as a
cultural-arts center, and is best known for its jazz concerts. Performers have included Wynton Marsalis and Tony Bennett. Theater, opera,
dance, and film fill out the offerings.

7

WHERE TO EAT

$$$$ ✕**Blue Hill at Stone Barns.** This outpost of Dan Barber's famed Blue Hill
AMERICAN restaurant (in Manhattan) occupies a barn on the grounds of Stone
Fodor'sChoice Barns Center for Food and Agriculture. The seasonal menu features
★ the center's own produce and meats as well as the bounty of other
local farms. The space is beautiful and elegant in its restraint, with high
picture windows and the barn rafters. Banquettes are dressed in brown
and set off against cream walls. Dinner is prix fixe, two to four courses.
The exceptional menu changes frequently; you might find pea-green
gazpacho, roast pork with braised bacon, or lobster-filled cannelloni.
Desserts, including a molten chocolate-and-caramel cake and passion-
fruit soufflé, are extra but worth it. ✉*630 Bedford Rd., Pocantico Hills*
☎*914/366–9600* ⊕*bluehillfarm.com* ⌕*Reservations essential* ▤*AE,
D, MC, V* ⊘*Closed Mon. and Tues. No lunch.*

$$$ ✕**Caravela.** Although small and informal, this Portuguese and Brazilian
BRAZILIAN restaurant is highly regarded. Paella brims with shrimp, clams, mussels,
chicken, and sausage; fresh cod mixes with shrimp, scallops, and clams
in fennel-and-saffron broth. Reservations are essential on Saturday.
Outdoor dining is at sidewalk tables. ✉*53 N. Broadway* ☎*914/631–
1863* ▤*AE, D, DC, MC, V.*

$$$ ✕**Equus.** A grand experience awaits at this lavishly appointed restau-
CONTINENTAL rant at the Castle on the Hudson. Choose from three dining rooms, all
of them formal: the Oak Room, with ornately carved built-ins from
France; the Tapestry Room; and the Garden Room, which has breathtaking Hudson River views. French influences make their way into the
fare, which ranges from hazelnut-crusted Hudson Valley foie gras to
pan-seared veal sweetbreads. The restaurant hosts regular wine tastings,
afternoon tea, and, on Wednesday evenings, jazz. ✉*400 Benedict Ave.*
☎*914/631–1980* ⌕*Reservations essential* ▤*AE, D, MC, V* ⊘ *Closed
Mon.–Thurs. No lunch Fri. No dinner Sun.*

$$ ✕**Horsefeathers.** A main-drag institution, the restaurant serves tradi-
AMERICAN tional pub fare, which includes its famous burgers and more than 80
microbrews from around the globe. The seemingly endless menu also
features lighter fare and 13 kinds of omelets, all served continuously
so you can have lunch at dinnertime or dinner at lunchtime. Weekend
brunch is served 11–4, however. Dine indoors in a dark, cozy, publike
environment or outdoors on the sidewalk when weather permits. ✉*94
S. Broadway* ☎*914/631–6606* ▤*AE, D, MC, V.*

$ ✕**Lefteris Gyro.** At a busy downtown corner, this family-friendly fixture
GREEK is known for using fresh ingredients and taking a light approach to tra-
ditional Greek fare. Favorites are the enormous Greek salad, which can
be shared, and platters of souvlaki, *bifteki* (Greek-style hamburger), and
gyros, served with pita, tomato, and yogurt sauce. ✉*1 N. Broadway*
☎*914/524–9687* ▤*AE, D, DC, MC, V.*

$$$ ✕**Santa Fe.** Locals flock to this casual restaurant for its fresh specialties
SOUTHWESTERN and colorful Southwestern atmosphere. Pasta de Mesilla is semolina–
and–green chili linguine with cilantro pesto; *cochinita pibil* consists of
boneless pork marinated in orange juice and achiote and slow-cooked
in banana leaves. The menu lists more than 30 premium tequilas. ✉*5
Main St.* ☎*914/332–4452* ⊕*www.santaferestaurant.com* ▤*AE, D,
DC, MC, V.*

WHERE TO STAY

$$$$ ⌂ **Castle on the Hudson.** The magnificent mansion, completed in 1910, sits amid 11 hilltop acres overlooking the Hudson River. With two impressive towers and a stone exterior, the mansion was modeled after Lismore Castle in County Waterford, Ireland. Rooms occupy the original house and a stucco wing, where you'll also fine the spa. Rooms are elegant, decorated with antiques, silk curtains, and four-poster beds. The food at the Equus restaurant is as refined as the surroundings. **Pros:** luxurious rooms; award-winning restaurant. **Cons:** difficult to reach without a car; restaurant only open weekends. ⊠*400 Benedict Ave.* ☎*914/631–1980* ⊕*www.castleonthehudson.com* ⇆*25 rooms, 6 suites* ⌂*In-room: safe, refrigerator (some), DVD (some), Wi-Fi. In-hotel: restaurant, room service, bar, tennis court, indoor pool, gym, spa, laundry service, no-smoking rooms* ▤*AE, D, DC, MC, V* ⏀*CP.*

$$ ⌂ **Tarrytown House.** Two 19th-century mansions—one Georgian, the other a stone Gothic Revival that's a National Trust site—dominate this conference-oriented property, once home to tobacco heiress Mary Duke Biddle. The grounds, high above the Hudson River, are loaded with recreational diversions and include massive specimen trees and antique garden statues. Most of the mansion rooms serve as restaurants and other public meeting places; modern wings provide the bulk of the guest rooms, each with a desk and free Wi-Fi. **Pros:** many rooms have hot tubs; lots of recreational activities. **Cons:** frenetic during conventions; not a tranquil setting. ⊠*49 E. Sunnyside La.* ☎*914/591–8200 or 800/553–8118* ⊕*www.tarrytownhouseestate.com* ⇆*207 rooms, 5 suites* ⌂ *In-room: safe, refrigerator (some), Wi-Fi. In-hotel: restaurant, tennis courts, pools, gym, laundry service, no-smoking rooms* ▤*AE, D, DC, MC, V* ⏀*BP.*

KATONAH

15 mi north of Tarrytown.

Named after an American Indian chief who sold the town its land, Katonah was a 19th-century farming center that shipped produce and milk to New York City via railroad. When New York City planned to flood parts of the old village to make way for reservoirs, some enterprising residents decided to move their homes to a newly combined commercial and residential district, Katonah's current downtown. In all, some 55 buildings were relocated in 15 years, including some gingerbread Victorian homes that make up the core of this charming village.

Katonah's downtown encompasses a shopping district populated with upscale galleries, boutiques, and restaurants, as well as a few family-owned stores that have managed to retain the feel of yesteryear. The village is also a cultural hub for northern Westchester, with the Katonah Museum of Art, Caramoor Center for Music and the Arts, and John Jay Homestead luring visitors from the tristate region.

VISITOR INFORMATION
Katonah Chamber of Commerce (☎*914/232–2668* ⊕*www.katonahchamber. org*).

WHAT TO SEE

John Jay Homestead State Historic Site. The estate of John Jay (1745–1849), the first chief justice of the United States Supreme Court, has many American classical furnishings from the period and traces Jay's life and career. The house, built in 1801, was, until the early 1950s, home to five generations of Jay's family. You can stroll the property, which includes formal gardens. ⊠ *400 Jay St.* ☎ *914/232–5651* ⊕ *www.johnjayhomestead.org* 🖃 *$7* ☉ *House Apr.–Oct., Wed.–Sat. 10–4, Sun. 11–4.*

Katonah Museum of Art. The museum's changing exhibitions span a wide range of cultures, mediums, historical periods, and social issues. It's not uncommon to see a show about banjos or puzzles followed by a more traditional art exhibit—a review of Latin American works or a retrospective of Richard Diebenkorn's prints, for example. Guided tours start at 2:30 Tuesday through Sunday. ⊠ *Rte. 22 at Jay St.* ☎ *914/232–9555* ⊕ *www.katonahmuseum.org* 🖃 *$5 (free 10–noon)* ☉ *Tues.–Sat. 10–5, Sun. noon–5.*

☾ **Muscoot Farm.** The county park, once a gentleman's farm, was named after a Lenape word meaning "by the swamp," because of its location near what is now part of the New York City watershed. A lively seasonal roster of special events is offered, including hayrides and demonstrations of blacksmithing, maple sugaring, and sheep shearing. Farm animals—sheep, chickens, pigs, goats, cows, horses—are permanent residents. ⊠ *Rte. 100 south of Rte. 35, Somers* ☎ *914/864–7282* ⊕ *www. westchestergov.com* 🖃 *Free* ☉ *Daily 10–4.*

SHOPPING

At **Boo Girls** (⊠ *151 Katonah Ave.* ☎ *914/232–8082*), which targets tweens, the leopard rug and cow-patterned dressing-room curtains compete for attention with lacy tops and lip gloss. The adjoining store, Boo Girls II, focuses on women's clothing. **Charles Department Store** (⊠ *113 Katonah Ave.* ☎ *914/232–5200*) has been selling clothing, housewares, and hardware since 1939. The salesperson-to-customer ratio is high, so expect some old-fashioned service.

NIGHTLIFE AND THE ARTS

Some of the world's finest classical and jazz performers can be heard at the **Caramoor Center for Music and the Arts** (⊠ *149 Girdle Ridge Rd.* ☎ *914/232–5035* ⊕ *www.caramoor.org*) during its summer concert season, June through August. Music is also offered year-round in the house museum, which contains an extraordinary collection of Renaissance and Asian art. Enjoy afternoon tea from May through October on Thursday and Friday.

WHERE TO EAT

$$ ✕ **Blue Dolphin.** What looks like a kitschy old diner on the outside might
ITALIAN   as well be a trattoria in Capri on the inside: photos of the island adorn the walls and the food is authentic Italian. That's why locals wait in long lines to get in. Its pastas—veal-stuffed ravioli, baked pasta with eggplant and loads of cheese—are renowned. Vegetables such as wilted broccoli rabe are also a specialty. ⊠ *175 Katonah Ave.* ☎ *914/232–4791* 🖄 *Reservations not accepted* ▭ *AE, MC, V.*

$$$ ✕**Crabtree's Kittle House.** Gardens surround this elegant colonial-style
ECLECTIC restaurant, 8 mi south of Katonah. Crabtree's is known for such cre-
ative dishes as grilled foie gras with toasted brioche, candied orange,
and Bordeaux syrup. Portobello mushrooms, served as a main course,
are roasted and given the Wellington treatment—encased in puff pastry
and served with wild mushroom sauce. ⊠*11 Kittle Rd., Chappaqua*
☎*914/666–8044* ⊕*www.kittlehouse.com* ☐*AE, D, DC, MC.*

$$ ✕**Willy Nick's.** Across the street from the Katonah train station, this is
AMERICAN the place to get a cup of joe and a freshly baked scone. Or stay for a
lunch or dinner of classic American comfort food (such as burgers and
meat loaf) and updated variations on that theme (lobster macaroni and
cheese). On weekends, families pack the place for brunch. ⊠*17 Katonah Ave.* ☎*914/232–8030* ⊕*www.willynicks.com* ☐*AE, MC, V.*

WHERE TO STAY

$$ ⊞**Holiday Inn.** This branch of the national chain has a quiet lobby with
knotty-pine paneling and a roaring fire, but on Friday and Saturday
evenings the place rocks with the sounds of a DJ in the bar, which has
a mirrored ceiling and a disco ball. Some of the guest rooms have small
sofas; executive rooms have large work areas. **Pros:** music on week-
ends; free Wi-Fi. **Cons:** can be frenzied on weekends; not a tranquil
setting. ⊠*1 Holiday Inn Dr., Mount Kisco* ☎*914/241–2600* ⊕*www.
hudsonvalleymanor.com* ⇆*122 rooms* ⏥*In-room: Wi-Fi. In-hotel: res-
taurant, room service, pool, bar, laundry service, some pets allowed,
no-smoking rooms* ☐*AE, D, DC, MC, V.*

GARRISON

35 mi north of Tarrytown.

Sleepy Garrison takes full advantage of its riverside setting with a ram-
bling waterfront park. Pleasure boats dock at the marina, and a gazebo
and willow tree–shaded benches are front-row seats to the mighty Hud-
son River; across the shore, on the west bank, loom the buildings of the
United States Military Academy at West Point. At Garrison's Landing,
as the waterfront area is known, a small clutch of art galleries, offices,
and homes surrounds the old train station, now a community theater
called the Philipstown Depot.

Beyond the Landing, restored homes and artful landscapes bespeak
the region's rich aesthetic history. Boscobel showcases architecture and
decorative arts from the early-19th-century Federalist period, whereas
Manitoga—the home, studio, and woodlands of industrial designer
Russel Wright—fast-forwards into the mid-20th century. In summer the
celebrated Hudson Valley Shakespeare Festival comes to town, gracing
Boscobel with contemporary interpretations of the hallowed plays in a
tent-theater. The Appalachian Trail passes through the region, crossing
the Hudson River at Bear Mountain and meandering through Garri-
son's many acres of protected land.

VISITOR INFORMATION
Cold Spring/Garrison Area Chamber of Commerce (☎*845/265–3200* ⊕*www. hvgateway.com/chamber.htm*).

WHAT TO SEE

Boscobel Restoration. High-style period furniture and collections of crystal, silver, and porcelain fill this restored 1808 mansion, now a museum of Federal-period decorative arts. Built by States Morris Dyckman, a descendant of one of New Amsterdam's early Dutch families, the house originally stood in Montrose, some 15 mi south. It's open by tour only, but the grounds are reason enough to visit. ✉*1601 Rte. 9D* ☎*845/265–3638* ⊕*www.boscobel.org* 🎫*Tour $15* ⊗*House Apr.– Oct., Wed.–Mon. 9:30–4:15; Nov. and Dec., Wed.–Mon. 9:30–3:15. Grounds Apr.–Dec., Wed.–Mon. 9:30–dusk.*

Constitution Marsh Audubon Center and Sanctuary. An extensive boardwalk leads you deep into the reeds and rushes of this lush, wildlife-filled tidal marshland. In winter the boardwalk is a prime lookout spot for bald eagles. Tromp through the 280-acre sanctuary's bluffs and woodlands, or visit the educational center, where a 500-gallon aquarium offers an up-close look at fish, crabs, and other resident wildlife. Note: parking is quite limited. ✉*Indian Brook Rd. off Rte. 9D* ☎*845/265–2601* ⊕*www.constitutionmarsh.org* 🎫*Donations welcome* ⊗*Center Tues.– Sun. 9–5; call ahead for center hrs in winter.*

★ **Manitoga–The Russel Wright Design Center.** Nature and art blend seamlessly throughout the home, studio, and 75-acre grounds of mid-20th-century industrial designer Russel Wright. Boulders protrude through the ground floor of **Dragon Rock,** Wright's experimental home that was named a National Historic Landmark in 2006. It is built on a rock ledge and spans 11 levels; fist-size stones serve as door handles. Four miles of paths weave through a landscape that appears natural but is actually a studied design of native trees, rocks, mosses, and wildflowers. Daily 90-minute tours take in the buildings and woodlands (wear comfortable walking shoes). ✉*584 Rte. 9D, 2½ mi north of Bear Mountain Bridge* ☎*845/424–3812* ⊕*www.russelwrightcenter.org* 🎫 *$15* ⊗*Tours May–Oct., grounds daily dawn–dusk.*

SPORTS AND THE OUTDOORS

GOLF Top-of-the-world vistas of the Hudson Highlands enhance 18 holes of championship golf at the **Garrison Golf & Country Club** (✉*2015 U.S. 9* ☎*845/424–3604* ⊕*www.garrisongolfclub.com*). The river and valley views from the driving range are positively jaw-dropping. Greens fees range from $65 weekdays to $90 on weekends. Pick up refreshments at the snack bar next to the pro shop or from the circulating beverage cart.

KAYAKING For a leisurely afternoon excursion, slip into the river from the boat launch at **Garrison's Landing,** near the Garrison train stop. Across the Hudson River loom the buildings of the United States Military Academy at West Point. Paddle upriver, past Constitution Island and Constitution Marsh, and land at Cold Spring. For quicker access to the marsh, enter the water in Cold Spring, where kayak rentals (about $60 a day) are available. Removed from the river's currents, **Constitution Marsh** is one of the most peaceful places on the Hudson to dip your paddle. Wide canals let you steer amid the marsh plants and wildlife—but take care not to lose your sense of direction in this maze of waterways. Keep in mind that because the Hudson is actually an estuary, tides affect the marsh. Avoid getting yourself grounded in the mud by leaving plenty of time to get back to the shore by low tide.

WHERE TO EAT

$$$ ✕**Valley Restaurant.** The seasonal menu of regional American fare fea-
AMERICAN tures meats, produce, and cheeses from artisanal area farms as well as from the restaurant's own kitchen garden. Ravioli are filled with Hudson Valley foie gras and scallops and served with wild-chervil-and-wine sauce; jumbo crab cakes are dressed with grainy mustard sauce and tea leaves; and organic pork gets an Asian barbecue glaze. There is also a raw bar. Sunday brunch is à la carte and includes omelets, crepes, smoked fish, and scones. Large windows frame swoon-inducing valley views. ⊠*The Garrison, 2015 Rte. 9 at Snake Hill Rd.* ☎*845/424–3604* ▤*AE, D, DC, MC, V* ⊗*Closed Mon.–Wed. No lunch Thurs.–Sat. No dinner Sun.*

COLD SPRING

5 mi north of Garrison.

7

The well-preserved 19th-century village edges one of the most dramatic bends of the Hudson River, and its true showpiece may well be the breath-stealing river-valley views. The village has a handful of sights, but the chief pleasures of Cold Spring are its mix of shops and its proximity to green spaces and hiking trails. Main Street, a few steps from the Metro-North train stop, is the commercial heart.

VISITOR INFORMATION
Cold Spring/Garrison Area Chamber of Commerce (☎*845/265–3200* ⊕*www. hvgateway.com/chamber.htm*).

WHAT TO SEE
Chapel of Our Lady. Greek Revival architecture finds expression in this 1833 chapel atop a bluff facing the Hudson River. Passing sailors have long taken pleasure in the landmark, originally built to support the spiritual lives of West Point Foundry workers. Initially a Catholic church, the nondenominational chapel now hosts ecumenical services, weddings, and other events. The chapel has no set open hours, but the facade is worth a look, and the columned porch is a great place for river gazing. ⊠*45 Market St.* ☎*845/265–5537* ⊕*www.chapelofourlady.com.*

Foundry School Museum. Local historical memorabilia and changing exhibits fill this former 19th-century schoolhouse, once attended by children of West Point Foundry workers. A permanent installation and video chronicle the history of the foundry. Paintings, drawings, photographs, and other objects and artifacts round out the museum's collection. ⊠*63 Chestnut St.* ☎*845/265–4010* ⊕*www.pchs-fsm.org* ⊠*$5* ⊗ *Wed.–Sun. 11–5*

★ **Stonecrop Gardens.** Sixty-three acres showcase the landscape design of Francis Cabot, founder of the Garden Conservancy. Display gardens span 12 of the acres, in settings ranging from rock cliffs and woodlands to placid pools and verdant lawns. Don't overlook the picture-perfect conservatory, where the winter garden includes trees and flowers native to South Africa, New Zealand, and Australia. ⊠ *81 Stonecrop La., off Rte. 301 between U.S. 9 and the Taconic State Pkwy.* ☎ *845/265–2000* ⊕ *www. stonecrop.org* ⊴ *$5* ⊙ *Weekays and 1st and 3rd Sat. of month 10–5.*

West Point Foundry Preserve. The ruins of a 19th-century iron foundry stand (barely) here amid a tangle of vines, a babbling brook, and 87 acres of preserved marshland and woodland. The original commercial hub of Cold Spring village, the West Point Foundry once buzzed with activity, as ironworkers manufactured Civil War cannons, cannon balls, and guns, as well as cast-iron facades for SoHo warehouses and even the nation's first domestically made locomotive. To get here from Main Street, turn south onto Kemble Avenue and take it to the end, proceed through the gate, turn left, and follow the path to the site. ⊠ *Off Kemble Ave., south of Main St.* ☎ *845/473–4440* ⊕ *www. scenichudson.org.*

SPORTS AND THE OUTDOORS

CROSS-COUNTRY SKIING
Nearly 10 mi of groomed trails vein the meadows, woodlands, and snowed-over lake of **Fahnestock Winter Park** (⊠ *1498 Rte. 301,Carmel* ☎ *845/225–3998* ⊕ *nysparks.state.ny.us*), part of Clarence Fahnestock Memorial State Park. Old pasture lanes weave through hemlock and hardwood groves, passing old stone walls and granite outcroppings. Come with your own gear or rent skis, boots, and poles on-site ($16 a day). Trail passes are $9. The park, open weekdays 10–4 and weekends 9–4:30, also rents skate skis and snowshoes, as well as inner tubes for use on the groomed sledding hill. Call ahead to check weather conditions, and for information about lessons and ski clinics. You can warm up with hot food and drinks in the park's lodge and café.

HIKING
A vigorous climb of about an hour leads you through an oak and hickory forest to the top of **Anthony's Nose** (⊠ *Rte. 9D immediately north of Bear Mountain Bridge*), a 900-foot mountain, for spectacular views of the Hudson Highlands and Bear Mountain across the Hudson River. The first ½ mi of the hike is part of the Appalachian Trail.

Hike past hemlock gorges and an old iron mine in **Clarence Fahnestock Memorial State Park** (⊠ *Rte. 30, ½ mi west of the Taconic State Pkwy., Carmel* ☎ *845/225–7207* ⊕ *nysparks.state.ny.us*), which encompasses some more than 14,000 acres of protected land. More than 70 mi of trails, including a segment of the Appalachian Trail, wend through the wilderness here. **Canopus Lake** has picnic spots and a beach for swimming. Another lake and four ponds dot the landscape, with excellent bass, perch, pickerel, and trout fishing. The park office has trail maps. Admission is free, but there is a fee for parking. The park is open daily from sunrise to sunset.

Hudson Highlands State Park (⊠ *Rte. 9D, ½ mi north of Main St.* ☎ *845/ 225–7207* ⊕ *nysparks.state.ny.us*), an easy walk from the Metro-North train station at Cold Spring, encompasses 5,800 acres of undeveloped land just north of town along the Hudson River. The trail to Bull Hill is the closest to the village. A moderately easy climb of about an hour through a forest offers successively grander views of Cold Spring and the river, culminating in a wide vista of the Hudson River valley at the summit. Stop for a picnic at the rocky ledge overlooking the village half-way up and watch the trains trace the shore and, in summer, sailboats, freighters, and other riverboats ply the waterway. The park is free and open daily from sunrise to sunset.

Two trails—one to a sandy beach, another to a small peak with panoramic views—traverse **Little Stony Point State Park** (⊠*Rte. 9D, ½ mi north of Main St.* ☎*845/265–7815* ⊕*www.hvgateway.com/stonypt. htm*), a short walk from the center of Cold Spring. The park is free and open daily from sunrise to sunset.

KAYAKING The relatively calm river waters close to the local shoreline make kayaking here a serene yet invigorating experience whether you're a novice or an experienced kayaker. To access **Constitution Marsh,** set out from the boat launch directly across the road from the Cold Spring train-station parking lot. Once you're in the water, paddle downriver a short distance to the railroad bridge, and pass under it to enter the marsh.

Hudson Valley Outfitters (⊠*63 Main St.* ☎*845/265–0221* ⊕*www. hudsonvalleyoutfitters.com*) runs tours for beginning to advanced kayakers that include some instruction. Half-day tours are $110; full-day tours are $120. Rentals are $60 a day. At **Outdoor Sports** (⊠*141 Main St.* ☎*845/265–2048*), kayak rentals start at $25. Bike rentals start at $15.

SHOPPING

Back-to-back antiques and specialty shops line Cold Spring's Main Street. Browse amid hanging lanterns, funky glassware, wall tiles, and garden torches at **Archipelago** (⊠*119 Main St.* ☎*845/265–3992*), an out-of-the-ordinary home-furnishings and gift shop. More than 25 dealers in antiques, vintage clothes, jewelry, art, and collectibles hawk their wares in **Bijou Galleries** (⊠*50 Main St.* ☎*845/265–4337*), a jam-packed emporium. The largest antiques center in the county, the 5,000-square-foot **Downtown Gallery** (⊠*40 Main St.* ☎*845/265–2334*) teems with furniture from Victorian through modern periods, vintage textiles and clothes, and collectible toys. You may try on a Zulu necklace, a jade pendant, or a string of Tahitian pearls at **Momminia** (⊠*113 Main St.* ☎*845/265–2260*), an avant-garde jewelry boutique.

WHERE TO EAT

$$ ✕**Brasserie Le Bouchon.** It's France-on-the-Hudson at this village hot spot
FRENCH with crimson walls, lipstick-hue banquettes, and Edith Piaf on the stereo. Although purists might claim the fare is more bistro than brasserie, the extensive menu and wine lists give you many choices. Expertly executed classics range from *croque monsieur* (egg batter–dipped ham-and-cheese sandwich) to steak au poivre with cognac-and-cream dressing. The rum-infused crème brûlée and cloud-light profiteroles have gained a following. ⊠*76 Main St.* ☎*845/265–7676* ▭*AE, MC, V* ⊙*Closed Wed.*

$$$ ✕**Cathryn's Tuscan Grill.** Swaths of sheer fabric and vibrant murals
ITALIAN   romance the interior of this rustic trattoria—a paean to northern Italian
food. Transplanted New Yorkers sip reds and whites from an extensive
wine list. Sage-browned butter laces silky calves' liver, and an espresso
demi-glace enlivens grilled hanger steak. Vegetarians choose from pasta
dishes such as whole-wheat fusilli primavera. Sunday brunch, from
noon to 3, is $20. ⊠*91 Main St.* ☎*845/265–5582* ⊟*AE, MC, V.*

$$$ ✕**Hudson House River Inn.** Watch sailboats drift by from the veranda
AMERICAN   tables at this riverfront restaurant, or dine by the window in the coun-
try-style River Room. A crust of red and blue tortillas gives crab cakes a
new twist. Notable entrées include salmon filled with sun-dried-tomato
pesto and arugula, and filet mignon wrapped in a crusty sleeve of pancetta. Sunday brunch is $26. ⊠*2 Main St.* ☎*845/265–9355* ⊟*AE,
DC, MC, V* ⊗*Closed Tues. and Wed.*

$$ ✕**Riverview.** This popular village restaurant offers great views of the
ECLECTIC   Hudson River to accompany its "modern Continental" fare. Hand-
blown sconces lend a golden glow to the dining room. The wood-oven
pizzas are praiseworthy, as are the grilled rib-eye steaks, fusilli Bolog-
nese, and fresh fish. Reservations are essential for the highly coveted
terrace tables. ⊠*45 Fair St.* ☎*845/265–4778* ⊕ *www.riverdining.
com* ⊟*No credit cards.*

WHERE TO STAY

$$–$$$ ⌂**Hudson House River Inn.** A stunning riverfront setting and a wrap-
around porch distinguish this simple three-story clapboard inn built in
1832 to house steamboat passengers. Farmhouse antiques and French-
country furnishings adorn the rooms. Be sure to request a room with a
private terrace looking out onto the Hudson River or quiet Main Street.
Pros: lovely location; historic building; near antiques shops. **Cons:**
not all rooms have views. ⊠*2 Main St.* ☎*845/265–9355* ⊕*www.
hudsonhouseinn.com* ⇆*11 rooms, 2 suites* ⌂*In-room: no TV (some).
In-hotel: restaurant, bar, no-smoking rooms* ⊟*AE, DC, MC, V.*

$$ ⌂**Pig Hill Inn.** An 1825 brick inn in the heart of the village is filled with
antiques, from Chippendale to chinoiserie. If you fall in love with that
four-poster bed or mahogany armoire, you can buy it (price tags hang
from nearly every furnishing). Most rooms have a wood-burning stove
or a fireplace; two have hot tubs. Breakfasts, served in the light-filled
Victorian conservatory or on the garden patio, are ample. Sweet aromas
also waft from the kitchen in early afternoon, when the innkeeper often
bakes cookies to serve with tea. **Pros:** close to shops and restaurants;
friendly hosts. **Cons:** some rooms have shared baths; not for kids. ⊠*73
Main St.* ☎*845/265–9247* ⊕*www.pighillinn.com* ⇆*9 rooms, 5 with
bath* ⌂*In-room: no phone (some), no TV, Wi-Fi. In-hotel: no-smoking
rooms* ⊟*AE, MC, V* ⊚*BP.*

CAMPING   △**Clarence Fahnestock Memorial State Park.** Choose from 80 campsites
¢   for an ideal jumping-off point to the park's hiking trails, beach, fishing, boating, and other outdoor activities. Only the first 50 sites are
wooded, so call to book these well in advance (reservations are essential
for these). Each simple site includes a picnic table, grill, and fire ring.
There's a convenience store at Canopus Beach. **Pros:** loop roads and
trees lend privacy; swimming, paddling, and hiking in the park; warm-

water showers. **Cons:** sometimes noisy at night. ☎*800/456–2267* ♨*Grills, flush toilets, drinking water, showers, fire pits, picnic tables, general store* ✉*Rte. 301, ½ mi west of the Taconic State Pkwy. (Cold Spring exit)* ⚑*80 tent sites, 28 RV sites* ☰*No credit cards* ☉*Closed mid-Dec.–mid-Apr.*

BEACON

8 mi north of Cold Spring.

For a touch of urban grit, arty cool, and coffeehouse grunge, head to this small river city in Dutchess County's southwestern corner. Dia:Beacon, an expansive contemporary-art museum in a former Nabisco printing plant, has put Beacon on the map. Gentrification has progressed along the eastern end of Beacon's Main Street and continues its march toward the river, bringing funky clothing boutiques, java shops, galleries, and enough antiques dealers to give neighboring Cold Spring a run for its money.

WHAT TO SEE

★ **Dia:Beacon.** Works by some of the biggest names in modern art from the 1960s to today fill this former Nabisco printing plant on the bank of the Hudson River. Highlights include Andy Warhol's *Shadows,* which includes several canvases, and works by minimalist icons Robert Ryman and Agnes Martin. Expansive spaces and luxuriant light make the nearly 300,000-square-foot building—on 34 acres with artistic landscaping—an experience in itself. If you don't know much about modern art, take the tour to gain some context. ✉*3 Beekman St.* ☎*845/440–0100* ⊕*www.diabeacon.org* ⚏*$10* ☉*Mid-Apr.–mid-Nov., Thurs.–Mon. 11–6; mid-Nov.–mid-Apr., Fri.–Mon. 11–4.*

Madam Brett Homestead. The oldest surviving home in Dutchess County, this white-clapboard dwelling housed seven generations of the Brett family from 1709 to 1954. During the Revolutionary War the homestead was used to store military supplies, and George Washington and the Marquis de Lafayette attended a Christmas party here. Original furnishings include 18th- and 19th-century pieces; hand-hewn beams, handcrafted shingles, and wide-board floors are among the architectural details. ✉*50 Van Nydeck Ave.* ☎*845/831–6533* ⚏*$5* ☉*Apr.–Dec., 2nd Sat. each month 1–4, or by appointment.*

WHERE TO EAT

$ ✕**The Piggy Bank.** Beacon's restaurant scene has yet to catch up with
BARBECUE its vibrant arts arena, but this neighborhood mainstay dishes out slow-cooked Southern barbecue favorites. It's not Memphis, but the sweet-potato fries, hickory-smoked ribs, and barbecued pulled pork over tossed greens have won over the stomachs of some locals. The restaurant occupies a circa-1880 bank building where the vault now serves as wine cellar. The dining room, with glowing copper sconces and pink-brick walls, is open and airy but visually warm. ✉*448 Main St.* ☎*845/838–0028* ☰*AE, MC, V.*

UPPER HUDSON VALLEY—WEST

The Upper Hudson Valley on the west side is essentially just Ulster County. The Catskills also are just west of the Hudson River in this area (⇨ *Chapter 6 for information on the Catskills*).

VISITOR INFORMATION
Ulster County Tourism (☎ 800/342–5826 ⊕ www.ulstertourism.info).

NEW PALTZ

18 mi north of Newburgh.

A vibrant cultural scene, a magnificent natural setting, and abundant outdoor activities are among the draws of this small college town, home to a State University of New York campus. The school lures serious students of the arts, many of whom end up living in the area after graduation. These artists, craftspeople, writers, and musicians have helped make this an energetic place with diverse shopping, dining, and arts offerings.

Founded in 1677 by Huguenots who received a patent from the colonial governor, New Paltz is one of the oldest communities in the United States. The settlers originally wanted to build on the flats, on the west side of the Wallkill River, but rethought that plan after the American Indians warned them about the river's spring floods. Building on the higher, eastern bank was an excellent decision: buildings dating from the early 1700s still stand throughout town. Several serve as bed-and-breakfasts today, so you can experience them personally.

In the distance, beyond a main street of casual eateries and quirky shops, rise the craggy cliffs of the Shawangunk Mountains. With steep faces of white quartzite conglomerate that reach more than 2,000 feet above sea level at some points, the Gunks, as they're casually known, are a premier destination for rock climbers in the northeast. Sky Top Tower, which sits atop a prominent ledge, is a landmark for miles around.

GETTING HERE AND AROUND
New Paltz is located at Exit 18 off the New York State Thruway (Interstate 87), halfway between Albany and New York City.

VISITOR INFORMATION
New Paltz Chamber of Commerce (☎ 845/255–0243 ⊕ www.newpaltzchamber. org).

WHAT TO SEE
Adair Vineyards. Tastings are offered in this small winery's centuries-old Dutch barn. The mountain views provide a pleasant backdrop for a picnic. ⊠ *52 Allhusen Rd.* ☎ *845/255–1377* ⊕ *www.adairwine.com* ⊡ *Free* ⊙ *May–Aug. and Nov.–mid-Dec., Fri.–Sun. 11–6; Sept. and Oct., daily 11–6.*

Huguenot Street. A National Historic Landmark, the street includes six stone houses that date from before 1720 and are among the oldest in the United States. Indeed, parts of the **Jean Hasbrouck, Abraham**

Hasbrouck, and Bevier-Elting houses were built in the 1680s, soon after the founding of New Paltz, in 1677. Another building, the **French church,** is a reconstruction of the 1717 structure, which was torn down in the early 19th century. The Huguenot Historical Society owns the buildings, many of which contain original furnishings and architectural details, and runs tours of them. The hour-long tour includes an orientation, one house, and the church; the longer tour, about 90 minutes, includes two additional houses. Tours begin on the hour. The tour office is in the **1705 DuBois Fort,** on Huguenot Street between Broadhead Avenue and North Front Street. During the one-day **Colonial Street Festival,** held in August, the church and the stone houses are all open; weaving, quilting, butter churning, musket firing, sheep shearing, and African-American storytelling are demonstrated. ✉ *64 Huguenot St.* ☎ *845/255–1889 or 845/255–1660* ⊕ *www.huguenotstreet.org* 💲*Short tour $7, long tour $10* ⊙ *Tours May–Oct., Thurs.–Tues. 10–4.*

Locust Lawn. Josiah Hasbrouck—a lieutenant in the American Revolution and U.S. congressman during the presidential terms of Jefferson, Madison, and Monroe—built the 1814 Federal-style mansion, which has an impressive three-story central hall. Exhibits include 18th- and 19th-century furniture and an oxcart used to carry supplies to the Continental army at Valley Forge. Nearby is **Terwilliger House** (1738), a Huguenot-era stone building with period furnishings. Tours are offered on the hour. ✉ *400 Rte. 32, Gardiner* ☎ *845/255–1660 Huguenot Historical Society* ⊕ *www.huguenotstreet.org* 💲*$7* ⊙ *June–Oct., weekends 11–4.*

Fodor's Choice **Minnewaska State Park Preserve.** The park encompasses 12,000 acres
★ in the Shawangunk Mountains. Much of the terrain is wooded and rocky, but you also come across trickling streams, gushing waterfalls, and spectacular valley views. Lake Minnewaska is its jewel; the park also includes Awosting Lake. A network of historic carriageways, now used by hikers, mountain bikers, horseback riders, and cross-country skiers, and other trails crisscross the land. Swimming is restricted to designated areas; scuba divers must be certified. Nonmotorized boating is allowed with a permit. Nature programs include walks and talks. The entrance to the **Peter's Kill Escarpment,** where you may rock climb, is 1 mi east of the main entrance. ✉ *U.S. 44/Rte. 55, 5 mi from Rte. 299* ☎ *845/255–0752* ⊕ *www.nysparks.com* 💲*Parking $6 Labor Day–Memorial Day; $7 Memorial Day–Labor Day* ⊙ *Daily 9–dusk.*

Mohonk Preserve. The 6,400-acre preserve has more than 60 mi of hiking trails and carriageways, as well as four trailheads: at the visitor center, on U.S. 44/Route 55; West Trapps, about 1.3 mi east of the visitor center; Coxing, 1 mi off Clove Road (about ¼ mi east of West Trapps); and Spring Farm, on Mountain Rest Road near the entrance to the Mohonk Mountain House. The mountain views are spectacular. A visit to the preserve, which accommodates picnickers, walkers, hikers, bikers, rock climbers, and horseback riders, gives you access to the adjacent Mohonk Mountain House grounds (with some restrictions) and the Minnewaska State Park Preserve. ✉ *Mohonk Preserve Visitor Center, 3197 U.S. 44/Rte. 55, ½ mi west of Rte. 299, Gardiner*

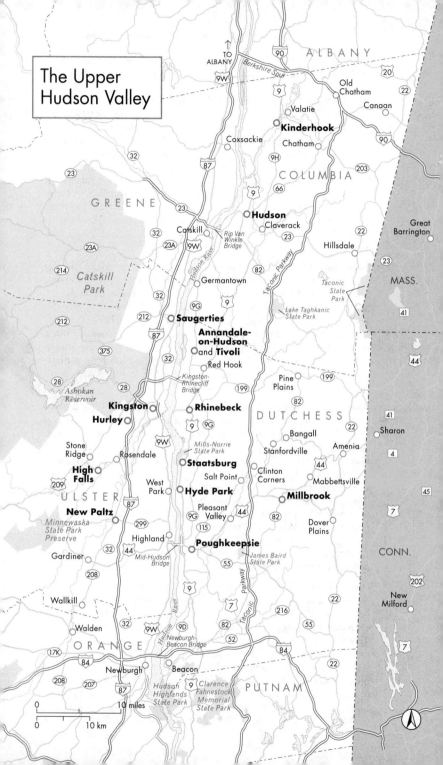

☎ *845/255–0919* ⊕ *www.mohonkpreserve.org* ⊠ *$9* ☉ *Daily sunrise–sunset. Visitor center daily 9–5.*

Shawangunk Grasslands National Wildlife Refuge. These open meadows and broken woods shelter kildeers, broad-winged and red-tailed hawks, several types of flycatchers, a few warblers, woodpeckers, eastern kingbirds, and bluebirds. In spring, listen for the evening mating rituals of American woodcocks. In fall, watch for the occasional peregrine falcon—a few breeding pairs nest in the nearby cliffs. ⊠ *Hoagerburgh Rd., 1½ mi north of Bruyn Tpke., Wallkill* ☎ *973/702–7266* ⊕ *shawangunk.fws.gov.*

State University of New York at New Paltz. The college, which long has attracted arts students, presents the community with a host of cultural offerings on its 216-acre campus. At the **Samuel Dorsky Museum of Art** (☎ *845/257–3844*), 19th- and 20th-century photographs and American and European paintings, along with a core collection of works on paper, are focal points. ⊠ *75 S. Manheim Blvd./Rte. 32S* ☎ *845/257–2121* ⊕ *www.newpaltz.edu.*

Trapeze Club at Stone Mountain Farm. From May through October, the center offers several two-hour trapeze classes each week on a 350-acre farm. All levels, from beginner to expert, are welcome; flyers may be as young as four. Classes are limited to 10 students; call to reserve a spot. ⊠ *475 River Rd. Extension* ☎ *845/658–8540* ⊕ *www.trapezeclub.org* ☉ *May–Oct.; call for class schedule.*

FESTIVALS AND FAIRS **Ulster County Fair.** Livestock, local crafts, baking and preserves competitions, pig races, and amusement rides constitute a genuine old-fashioned county fair. Held in late July/early August, it runs Tuesday through Sunday. ⊠ *Ulster County Fairgrounds, Libertyville Rd.* ☎ *845/255–1380* ⊕ *www.ulstercountyfair.com.*

Woodstock/New Paltz Art and Crafts Fair. The juried fair, held Memorial Day and Labor Day weekends, showcases potters, photographers, jewelry designers, and other artisans from across the nation. The food is better than usual fair fare, with many vegetarian and other innovative dishes. ⊠ *Ulster County Fairgrounds, Libertyville Rd.* ☎ *845/679–8087 or 845/246–3414* ⊕ *www.quailhollow.com.*

SPORTS AND THE OUTDOORS

BIKING The friendly folks at **Bicycle Depot** (⊠ *15 Main St.* ☎ *845/255–3859* ⊕ *www.bicycledepot.com*) can sell or rent you a bike, but they can also make any kind of repair, and they know *everything* about biking in the area. **Bistro Mountain Store** (⊠ *3124 U.S. 44/Rte. 55, at Rte. 299, Gardiner* ☎ *845/255–2999* ⊕ *www.bistromountainstore.com*), at the foot of the cliffs, is a little deli and ice-cream parlor that also rents bikes. It's a good place to start and end a day trip through the Gunks.

SHOPPING

Shopping in New Paltz is eclectic, largely aimed at students, creative individuals (of all ages), and outdoors enthusiasts. Nearly all the shops are on or near Main Street and within easy walking distance of one another. Farm stands are outside the village center, so you need a car to get to them.

★ Although it specializes in crafts and jewelry, **Handmade and More** (⊠6 *N. Front St.* ☎*845/255–6277*) also carries toys, clothing, and a selection of quirky cards. More than 20 varieties of apples, from Macoun and Red Delicious to Empire and Ida Red, as well as other produce, are sold at **Jenkins-Lueken Orchards** (⊠*Yankee Folly Rd. at Rte. 299* ☎*845/255–0999* ⊗*Closed mid-May–June*). You can pick pumpkins, and the apple cider, made on the premises, is fresh and good.

The **Wallkill View Farm Market** (⊠*15 Rte. 299* ☎*845/255–8050* ⊗*Closed Dec. 23–wk before Easter*) sells local produce, cheeses, baked goods, jams and preserves, maple syrup, garden supplies, fresh-pressed apple cider, and pumpkins you can pick yourself. **Water Street Market** (⊠*10 Main St.* ☎*845/255–1403*), an unassuming pedestrian mall, includes antiques stores, crafts and art galleries, cafés, clothing boutiques, and custom-furniture and other specialty shops.

NIGHTLIFE AND THE ARTS

NIGHTLIFE Thursday it's '80s Night, and Friday and Saturday it's live bands at **Cabaloosa** (⊠*58 Main St.* ☎*845/255–2400*), a gritty downstairs club on a little alley off Main. It's big with the 18-and-over college crowd. A lively sports-bar ambience, good beer, tasty food, and generous portions make **McGillicuddy's Restaurant & Tap House** (⊠*84 Main St.* ☎*845/256–9289*) a popular spot. Choose from 14 kinds of chicken wings. The "Inferno" wings are hotter than hot. ("Get the fire extinguisher," says the description in the menu—and it's not kidding.) **Oasis** (⊠*58 Main St.* ☎*845/255–2400*), upstairs from Cabaloosa, is a slightly more polished venue for jazz and other types of live music.

THE ARTS Public concerts are part of **PianoSummer at New Paltz Festival/Institute** (⊠*75 S. Manheim Blvd./Rte. 32S* ☎*845/257–3880 box office* ⊕*www.newpaltz.edu/piano*), at SUNY New Paltz; Vladimir Feltsman is the program's artistic director.

WHERE TO EAT

$ ✕**The Gilded Otter.** A gleaming copper brewery, live music, tasty pub grub
AMERICAN and more-substantial food, and views of the Gunks—what could be better after a day of rock climbing or hiking? Just don't expect much quiet on weekends. Two brews to try: New Paltz Crimson Lager and Stone House Irish Stout. Among the more unusual dishes here is pizza topped with caramelized pear, bacon, onions, Gorgonzola, fontina, mozzarella, and mesclun. ⊠*3 Main St.* ☎*845/256–1700* ▤*AE, D, MC, V.*

$ ✕**Hokkaido.** Sample sushi and other tidbits beneath handcrafted Japa-
JAPANESE nese lanterns at this informal spot. Spider rolls, hot crisp-fried soft-shell crabs in cool nori-wrapped sushi rice, are a delight. ⊠*18 Church St.* ☎*845/256–0621* ▤*AE, D, MC, V* ⊗*No lunch weekends.*

$$ ✕**La Stazione.** Dim lighting and dark mahogany trim lend romance
ITALIAN to this Italian restaurant in a converted railroad station. For starters consider sharing an antipasto platter, or try a bowl of pasta e fagioli soup. The *scaloppe di vitello alla rocco* (veal medallions with artichoke hearts, fire-roasted red peppers, and a light tomato sauce) is a savory

main course. Crowds flock to the $10.95 pasta night on Tuesday and Wednesday. ⊠*5 Main St.* ☎*845/256–9447* 🗖*AE, D, MC, V.*

$$–$$$ ✕**The Locust Tree.** A historic building houses this northern European
AMERICAN restaurant, where dishes such as crispy veal sweetbreads over wild mushroom and sweet potato fricassee, and market-fresh fish en papillote with garden vegetables display the kitchen's love for organic, local ingredients. The menu changes seasonally, and daily specials are always available. Part of the restaurant inhabits a stone Dutch Colonial with fireplaces, beamed ceilings, and hand-carved woodwork that dates from 1759. ⊠*215 Huguenot St.* ☎*845/255–7888* 🔑*Reservations essential* 🗖*AE* ☉*Closed Mon. and Tues. No lunch.*

$$ ✕**The Would.** This white-tablecloth restaurant was once a resort catering
AMERICAN to Italian families from New York City; boccie is still played here on summer evenings. The food is no throwback, however; organic produce and poultry blend with ingredients and techniques from around the world. Grilled salmon is served with a cucumber-jalapeno salsa, pan-seared chicken is complemented by shiitake mushrooms, and grilled tuna is accompanied by sweet soy and wasabi. In winter a fireplace warms the dining room. ⊠*120 North Rd., west of U.S. 9W, Highland* ☎*845/691–9883* 🔑*Reservations essential* 🗖*AE, MC, V* ☉*Closed Sun. and Mon. No lunch.*

WHERE TO STAY

$$–$$$ 🏨**Minnewaska Lodge.** Cathedral ceilings, Arts and Crafts styling, and
★ towering windows with views of white cliffs or deep forests contribute to the delight of this lodge. Works by local artists and photographers add interest. Some guest rooms have balconies. **Pros:** great mountain views; close to hiking and climbing areas. **Cons:** no restaurant; Continental breakfast is average. ⊠*3116 U.S. 44/Rte. 55, Gardiner* ☎*845/255–1110* ⊕*www.minnewaskalodge.com* ➷*25 rooms, 1 suite* ♻*In-room: refrigerator (some), DVD, Wi-Fi. In-hotel: gym, Wi-Fi, no-smoking rooms* 🗖*AE, MC, V* ⦿*CP.*

$$$$ 🏨**Mohonk Mountain House.** The rambling Victorian-era hotel—a jumble
Fodor's Choice of towers, chimneys, porches, and turrets—sits at the edge of a moun-
★ taintop lake. The resort's 2,200 acres encompass private woodland and
☾ elaborate gardens and overflow with options for recreation, including 85 mi of hiking trails. Antiques fill the guest rooms, which are luxurious and spacious. Choice accommodations in the towers have original Victorian woodwork, wood-burning fireplaces, and balconies. Your room rate includes three meals daily, plus afternoon tea and cookies. Breakfast and lunch are buffet-style; dinner is a formal affair (men may want to wear jackets). Four self-catering cottages, which sleep four to six people, are also available and include full kitchens. **Pros:** all-inclusive plan; tons of activities; great for kids. **Cons:** grounds can be packed with day-trippers; not for those looking for quiet getaway. ⊠*1000 Mountain Rest Rd.* ☎*845/255–1000 or 800/772–6646* ⊕*www.mohonk. com* ➷*265 rooms, 7 suites, 4 cottages* ♻*In-room: safe, no TV (some), Wi-Fi. In-hotel: 3 restaurants, room service, bar, golf course, tennis courts, pool, gym, spa, water sports, bicycles, children's programs (ages 2–12), laundry facilities, Internet terminal, Wi-Fi, no-smoking rooms* 🗖*AE, DC, MC, V* ☉*Cottages closed mid-Oct.–mid-May.*

$$ **Mountain Meadows Bed & Breakfast.** Linger over breakfast by the pool and hot tub, which face the Shawangunk cliffs, or in the country kitchen. Later you may want to test your badminton game in the garden or shoot some pool in the cozy rec room, which also features a fireplace. Frills and florals adorn furnishings in the guest rooms. **Pros:** short drive to New Paltz; heated pool. **Cons:** floral decor seems dated. ✉ *542 Albany Post Rd.* ☎ *845/255–6144 or 845/527–8359* 🌐 *www.mountainmeadowsbnb.com* *4 rooms* *In-room: no phone, no TV (some), Wi-Fi. In-hotel: pool, laundry facilities, Wi-Fi, no-smoking rooms* *D, MC, V* *BP.*

> **WORD OF MOUTH**
>
> "Several people have mentioned the Mohonk Mountain House, and it truly is a wonderful place. Terrific hiking, a spa, but not much of a shopping destination. The town of New Paltz has some nice little shops, it's a small college town."
>
> —KatieR

$$$$ **Rocking Horse Ranch.** Seven miles southeast of New Paltz, this all-inclusive dude ranch is loaded with activities, including a children's zoo, a waterslide, climbing walls, kayaking and water skiing, and even a video-game room with four large-screen TVs. Accommodations include rooms in the main lodge, where the lobby is hung with wagon wheels, and motel-style buildings. **Pros:** tons of activities; perfect for families with kids; all-inclusive plan. **Cons:** lobby could use updating. ✉ *Rte. 44/Rte.55 at Pancake Hollow Rd., Highland* ☎ *845/691–2927, 800/647–2624 reservations* 🌐 *www.rhranch.com* *119 rooms* *In-room: refrigerator, Wi-Fi. In-hotel: bar, tennis courts, pools, gym, spa, water sports, children's programs (ages 4–12), laundry service, Wi-Fi, no-smoking rooms* *AE, D, DC, MC, V* *FAP.*

HIGH FALLS

9 mi northwest of New Paltz.

The tiny hamlet of High Falls is a weekender's delight. Cool shops, old buildings, excellent restaurants, and cozy places to stay nestle beside the ancient locks of the Delaware and Hudson Canal. From 1828 to 1898 the canal connected Pennsylvania's coal mines to the Hudson River. "Canawlers" also shipped bluestone for New York City's sidewalks and Rosendale cement for the Brooklyn Bridge. You can see some of the locks right in town; a brochure (available at the D&H Canal Museum) outlines a walking tour. In fall, pick your own apples or taste freshly pressed cider at one of the local orchards.

GETTING HERE AND AROUND

From the New York Thruway (Interstate 87), take Exit 18 towards New Paltz. Follow Route 299 through the town of New Paltz; turn right on Route 32N, then left on Route 213W. Continue through Rosendale to High Falls.

WHAT TO SEE

A.J. Snyder Estate. The estate includes the Widow Jane Mine, cement kilns, and parts of the D&H Canal. A museum concentrates on the local cement industry and showcases antique sleighs and carriages. It's about 3 mi east of High Falls. ⊠*Rte. 213, ½ mi west of Rte. 32, Rosendale* ☎*845/658–9900* ⊕*www.centuryhouse.org* ⊠*$3* ⊙*May–Oct., weekends 1–4.*

SPORTS AND THE OUTDOORS

MOUNTAIN BIKING Owned by pro cyclist Christian Favata, **Table Rock Tours & Bicycles** (⊠*386 Main St., Rosendale* ☎*845/658–7832* ⊕*www.trtbicycles.com*) is geared toward cycling enthusiasts and beginners alike and offers the latest equipment, expert repairs, bike fittings, and tons of information about local trails and cycling events.

SHOPPING

Antiques fill the warren of rooms at the **Barking Dog** (⊠*7 2nd St., off Rte. 213* ☎*845/687–4834*), in business since 1984. You won't find the ubiquitous here, and nearly everything dates from before the 1920s. The shop specializes in country pieces, such as pine tables and cupboards, and folk art, and also offers old prints and paintings. The inventory at **Cathouse Antiques** (⊠*136 Bruceville Rd., ½ mi off Rte. 213* ☎*845/687–0457*) favors the 1940s, but pieces from the 1930s and '50s are here, too. Kitchen items and housewares in bright hues mingle with collectibles, glass and pottery pieces, and some furniture. The **Green Cottage** (⊠*1204 Rte. 213* ☎*845/687–4810*) is part florist and part gift boutique. It creates interesting bouquets and carries small gift items such as handcrafted and estate jewelry (one of the owners has a jewelry studio), ceramic vases, prettily packaged soaps, sculptural candles, children's books, and a few toys.

A bright, lovingly restored space is home to **High Falls Mercantile** (⊠*113 Main St.* ☎*845/687–4200*), which carries new and antique furniture, 1920s European paintings, and scented lotions and candles. A bevy of white platters comes in assorted shapes. At **Lounge and Linger** (⊠*8 2nd St., off Rte. 213* ☎*845/687–9463 Lounge, 845/687–7907 Linger*), sister shops that share a building off Main Street, you may indeed want to stay awhile to browse through the diverse collections. Lounge features a fun mix of home furnishings and decorative items (most new, some antique), while Linger focuses on bath-and-body lotions and potions and other self-pampering items. **Spruce** (⊠*105½ Main St.* ☎*845/687–4481*), tucked behind the Canal House, specializes in 20th-century furnishings. The rustic, wood-lined rooms are filled with Lucite lamps, mod couches, and Eva Zeisel pottery among other things.

NIGHTLIFE AND THE ARTS

★ An early-1900s firehouse was converted into the **Rosendale Theatre** (⊠*401 Main St., Rosendale* ☎*845/658–8989* ⊠*$5*) in 1949—and few changes have been made to the movie theater since. Instead of a concession counter, two ancient vending machines discharge candy.

WHERE TO EAT

$ ✕**Chefs on Fire.** In the former wine cellar of the DePuy Canal House,
ECLECTIC   this is a casual and tasty offshoot of the elegant main restaurant. Dishes
include daily quiche specials, panini, quesadillas, tamales, and pizza
(including one with a topping of broccoli rabe, black olives, and mozzarella). A new addition to the space is Amici Sushi, which is under the
watchful eye of Japanese sushi chef Makio Idesako. ✉*1315 Rte. 213*
☎*845/687–7778* ▭*AE, MC, V* ⊘*Closed Tues.*

$$$ ✕**DePuy Canal House.** The food at this 1797 stone tavern, a National
ECLECTIC   Historic Landmark, is eclectic and elaborate. Chef-owner John Novi
Fodor'sChoice   opened the place in 1969, and in 1984 was referred to as "the father
★   of new American cooking" in a *Time* magazine article. After all these
years he still manages to be creative. The menu is seasonal and often
incorporates Hudson Valley ingredients. You might find chicken-and-
fish consommé with salmon-mousse wonton or sautéed lobster with
steamed spinach, caramelized-shallot beurre blanc, and mango salsa.
The restaurant has five antiques-jammed dining rooms; you can also
dine at a balcony table overlooking the kitchen. ✉*1315 Rte. 213*
☎*845/687–7700* ⌕*Reservations essential* ▭*AE, MC, V* ⊘*Closed
Mon.–Wed. No lunch.*

$ ✕**The Egg's Nest.** Playfully cluttered and wildly painted, the Egg's Nest
AMERICAN   is fun, whether for a casual meal or a couple of drinks. "Praeseux" are
house favorites—crisp, pizzalike dishes with various toppings baked on
flour tortillas. Pasta dishes, burgers, wraps, soups, and chili also are
offered. ✉*1300 Rte. 213, at Bruceville Rd.* ☎*845/687–7255* ▭*No
credit cards.*

WHERE TO STAY

$–$$ ▦**Baker's B&B.** On frosty days you can cuddle up by one of the wood-
stoves or by the fireplace in this antiques-filled 1780 stone farmhouse
in the Rondout Valley. Breakfast, served amid spectacular farm and
mountain views in the sunroom, includes homemade granola, jams,
and jellies and home-smoked salmon or trout. **Pros:** historic building;
charming feel. **Cons:** somewhat small bathrooms; no Internet access.
✉*24 Old King's Hwy., Stone Ridge* ☎*845/687–9795 or 888/623–
5513* ⊕*www.bakersbandb.com* ➾*4 rooms, 1 suite* ⌂*In-room: no
phone, no TV (some). In-hotel: no kids under 12, no-smoking rooms*
▭*MC, V* ⊙|*BP.*

$–$$ ▦**Captain Schoonmakers B&B.** Guest rooms, each with a private balcony,
are in an 1810 carriage house at this B&B. Breakfast, including eggs
from the owners' hens, is served amid antiques in front of the fireplace
in the 1760 stone main house. The library leads to the solarium and,
just beyond, 10 acres of gardens, woods, waterfalls, and a trout stream.
Pros: serene setting; spacious rooms; excellent breakfast. **Cons:** traffic
noise. ✉*913 Rte. 213, at Mossy Brook Rd.* ☎*845/687–7946* ⊕*www.
captainschoonmakers.com* ➾*5 rooms* ⌂*In-room: no phone, no TV
(some), Wi-Fi. In-hotel: Wi-Fi, no kids under 10, no-smoking rooms*
▭*AE, D, MC, V* ⊙|*BP.*

$$ ▦**The Inn at Stone Ridge.** The 18th-century Dutch stone mansion sits on
★   150 acres (including a working apple and fruit orchard) in the village of
Stone Ridge, about 3 mi west of High Falls. Period antiques, including

an old billiard table, furnish the parlors, library, and guest rooms. Room 10 has a balcony with private access. The suites are especially spacious. Suite 3, for example, has two bedrooms, a dining table for four, and a sitting area with a TV. The inn frequently hosts weddings, often in a massive tent in back. The first floor has an intimate bar area that is open to guests only. **Pros:** spacious common areas; hot tubs in some rooms. **Cons:** no on-site restaurant. ⊠ *U.S. 209, Stone Ridge* ☎ *845/687–0736* ⊕ *www.innatstoneridge.com* ⛱ *3 rooms, 3 suites* ♨ *In-room: no TV (some), Wi-Fi. In-hotel: bar, Wi-Fi, some pets allowed, no-smoking rooms* ⊟ *AE, D, MC, V* ⦿ *BP.*

$-$$ 📷 **The Locktender Cottage.** The small, historic house sits beside a lock of the old Delaware and Hudson Canal in the center of High Falls. Across the street is the highly regarded DePuy Canal House restaurant, and quirky antiques and gift shops are a few doors away. In the rooms, pale walls dilute flowery bedspreads and curtains. The Chef's Quarters suite, under the eaves, has a kitchenette, dining area, and laundry facilities. Two additional suites are across the street in a building next to the Canal House. One has a full kitchen and a screened-in porch. **Pros:** suites are ideal for longer stays; nice location. **Cons:** no common areas; more of a self-catering room rental than a B&B. ⊠ *Rte. 213* ☎ *845/687–7700* ⊕ *www.depuycanalhouse.net* ⛱ *2 rooms, 3 suites* ♨ *In-room: no phone, kitchen (some), Wi-Fi. In-hotel: some pets allowed, no-smoking rooms* ⊟ *AE, MC, V* ⦿ *EP.*

HURLEY

7 mi northeast of High Falls.

Hurley, a National Historic Landmark, was founded by the Dutch in 1661. The area is surrounded by cornfields, which occupy the floodplain of the Esopus Creek, sitting on deep soils that accumulated during the last ice age. Hurley was burned by American Indians in 1663, during the Second Esopus War. It was rebuilt and today includes one of the largest clusters of stone houses in the United States. The 24 **Hurley Stone Houses,** as they're known collectively, date from the late 17th to early 19th century, and many are still home to descendants of the original families. On the second Saturday in July about a third of the homes are opened to the public. During Hurley's one-month stint as the state capital following the burning of Kingston by the British, the 1723 Van Deusen House (or Senate House) served as meeting space for the Colonists.

GETTING HERE AND AROUND

Hurley is located on U.S. 209, just west of the New York State Thruway (Interstate 87). From High Falls, follow Route 213 west to Main Street/U.S. 209 and turn right. Continue along U.S. 209 to Hurley.

WHAT TO SEE

Col. Jonathan Elmendorf House. The house, built between 1783 and 1790, contains the **Hurley Heritage Society Museum.** It includes a good collection of Revolutionary War materials, and has changing exhibits about local history. Walking- and driving-tour brochures are available in its front lobby. ✉*52 Main St.* ☎*845/338–1661* ⊕*www. hurleyheritagesociety.org* 🎫*Free* ⊙*May–Oct., Sat. 10–4, Sun. 1–4.*

Hurley Reformed Church. This church was built in 1853 to replace the 1801 stone church a few doors up the street. Look for the original family nameplates at the end of the pews. The parsonage is next door in the 1790 **Crispell House.** ✉*17 Main St.* ☎*No phone.*

KINGSTON

2 mi northeast of Hurley.

In 1609 Henry Hudson's ship landed at Kingston Point. Within five years a fur-trading post was established at the mouth of Rondout (from the Dutch word for a small fort) Creek. In 1658 a permanent village—Wiltwyck—was built. When the British took over in 1669, that tiny village was renamed Kingston.

It became the state's first capital in 1777. As such, Kingston became a target for the British, who set fire to every building but one (alleged to belong to a Tory sympathizer) in October of that year. Many stone houses were rebuilt, however; uptown Kingston's historic Stockade District has examples from the 17th and 18th centuries. The intersection of Crown and John streets is the only one in the United States with 18th-century stone houses occupying all four corners. The architecture throughout the city is rich and varied, and it includes representatives of Federal; Greek, Gothic, and Romanesque revival; Italianate; English Renaissance; colonial; Georgian; Second Empire; English Tudor; Dutch Colonial; and Victorian styles. The design of City Hall, which has a distinctive tower and was completed in 1875, was based on that of the Palazzo Vecchio in Florence.

Kingston thrived as a commercial port in the 19th century, especially between 1828 and 1898, when the D&H Canal was in operation and coal was shipped here from Pennsylvania for distribution elsewhere. Much of this commerce-related activity occurred in the Rondout District, just west of where the Rondout Creek joins with the Hudson River. This waterfront area, which has seen extensive gentrification since the 1980s, has a lively arts and restaurant scene. River cruises embark from the pier at the foot of Broadway (⇨*Boat Tours under Sports and the Outdoors*).

GETTING HERE AND AROUND
Kingston is located just east of the New York State Thruway (Interstate 87); take Exit 19 for State Highway 28 toward Kingston.

VISITOR INFORMATION
Kingston Heritage Area Visitor Center (☎*845/331–0080* ⊕*www.ci.kingston. ny.us*).

WHAT TO SEE
Fred J. Johnston Museum. Antiques dealer Fred J. Johnston rescued this 1812 Federal mansion from the wrecking ball in the 1930s; the Friends of Historic Kingston inherited the house in 1993 through Johnston's

will. His collection of 18th- and 19th-century Hudson Valley furniture and decorative arts is on display. ⊠*63 Main St., Stockade District* ☎*845/339–0720* ⊕*www.cr.nps.gov/nr/travel/kingston* ▦*$3* ☉*May–Oct., weekends 1–4.*

Hudson River Maritime Museum. Models, artifacts, and photographs illustrate the region's maritime history. Changing exhibits show tugboats and antique fishing and sailing craft. You may board the *Half Moon*, a replica of Henry Hudson's ship, when it's in dock. Tours to the **Rondout Lighthouse** (also known as the Kingston Lighthouse) leave from the museum's dock. ⊠*50 Rondout Landing, Rondout District* ☎*845/338–0071* ⊕*www.hrmm.org* ▦*Museum $5, lighthouse $5* ☉*May–Oct., daily 11–5.*

Old Dutch Church Heritage Museum. The church was established in 1659, and a small wooden building was erected in 1661. It was burned down in 1663, during the Second Esopus War. Today's church (the third at the site) went up in 1852 and features an 1891 window made by the Tiffany Studios. George Clinton (first governor of New York and vice president under Thomas Jefferson) and a number of Revolutionary War soldiers are buried in the graveyard. ⊠*272 Wall St., Stockade District* ☎*845/338–6759* ⊕*www.olddutchchurch.org* ▦*Free* ☉*Weekdays 10–4, tours by appointment.*

Trolley Museum of New York. The museum stands on the site of the eastern terminal of the Ulster & Delaware Railroad, which ran from Kingston through the Catskills and was affectionately known as the Up & Down Railroad. Trolley cars dating from 1907 are on display; trolley tours of historic Kingston (included in the admission fee) leave from the museum. ⊠*89 E. Strand, Rondout District* ☎*845/331–3399* ⊕*www.tmny.org* ▦*$5* ☉*Memorial Day–Columbus Day, weekends noon–5.*

Ulster County Courthouse. New York's first constitution was drafted on this site in 1777, in an earlier building. Then its first chief justice, John Jay, was sworn in on the front steps of that courthouse. He then swore in its first governor, George Clinton. Shortly thereafter, in the same year, the British burned down Kingston; the current courthouse was built in 1818. Sojourner Truth was freed in 1827, and she immediately—and successfully—sued, in this courthouse, to have her son freed from slavery in Alabama. ⊠*285 Wall St., Stockade District* ⊕*www.cr.nps.gov/nr/travel/kingston.*

MICRO-
BREWERY **Keegan Ales.** This working microbrewery offers free tours and tastings. (Stout fans should try Mother's Milk.) It also holds quarterly rock concerts, either in the brewery itself or in the parking lot, and functions as a gallery and performance space. ⊠*20 St. James St., Midtown* ☎*845/331–2739* ⊕*www.keeganales.com* ▦*Tours and tastings free* ☉*Thurs. and Fri. 3–7, Sat. noon–7.*

SHOPPING

The used and rare books at **Alternative Books** (⊠*35 N. Front St., Stockade District* ☎*845/331–5439*), including a large collection of poetry and signed first editions, reflect the artistic nature of the Mid-Hudson

Valley. **Blue-Byrd's Haberdashery & Music** (✉ *297 Wall St., Stockade District* ☎ *845/339–3174*) is a cool spot for the blues—the music, the look, the memorabilia—and for beautiful hats for guys and gals. It carries books, boxed sets, and posters of blues and jazz biggies. **Bop to Tottom** (✉ *299 Wall St., Stockade District* ☎ *845/338–8100*), a whimsical mix of gift items for children of all ages, sells fun jewelry, throw pillows, scented soaps and candles, spinning tops and jack-in-the-boxes, rice-paper lamp shades, and more. **NEXT Boutique** (✉ *17 W. Strand, Rondout District* ☎ *845/331–4537*) carries quirky handcrafted and costume jewelry and flirtatious frocks that capture the delicate allure of vintage apparel with none of the mustiness of the real thing. Michael Start, James Perse, and other casual lines are also available here. If you love to pamper your pet, don't miss **Pawprints & Whiskers** (✉ *292 Wall St., Stockade District* ☎ *845/339–5735*). Fido and Fifi will adore the souvenirs you bring home from this pet boutique. Multiple dealers of delightful antiques and other old stuff, much of it reflecting the neighborhood's nautical past, occupy **Skillypot Antiques** (✉ *41 Broadway, Rondout District* ☎ *845/338–6779*).

SPORTS AND THE OUTDOORS

BOAT TOURS **Hudson River Cruises** (☎ *800/843–7472* ⊕ *www.hudsonrivercruises. com*) offers two-hour cruises aboard the *Rip Van Winkle*. The boat leaves from Kingston's Rondout Landing, passing near the Rondout Lighthouse, and then travels south on the Hudson River to the northern edge of Hyde Park before turning around.

THE ARTS

The **Coffey Gallery** (✉ *330 Wall St., Stockade District* ☎ *845/339–6105*) shows paintings, drawings, prints, sculpture, and one-of-a-kind furniture on Tuesday from 11 to 5, or by appointment. Local artists are the focus. The **Ulster Performing Arts Center** (**UPAC** ✉ *601 Broadway, Midtown* ☎ *845/339–6088* ⊕ *www.upac.org*) resides in a beautifully restored 1927 art-deco movie palace. It's home to the 1,500-seat Broadway Theater and hosts local groups, such as the Hudson Valley Philharmonic, as well as well-known performers like Little Feat, Joan Rivers, and Randy Travis.

FESTIVALS AND FAIRS Following the 1st Ulster County Militia's reenactment of the 1777 British landing and battle at Kingston Point (held every other year in mid-October), redcoats and colonial bluecoats occupy the city for three days during the **Burning of Kingston** (☎ *845/331–7517 or 800/331–1518* ⊕ *www.firstulster.org*) event. Spectators can watch the landing and invasion. Much of the activity takes place in the Stockade District. In early May the Hudson River Maritime Museum celebrates the shad's seasonal swim up the Hudson River with the **Shad Festival.** Shad and shad-roe dinners, storytelling, crafts, jazz and blues, and boat rides are all part of the festivities. The Gourmet Society of the Culinary Institute of America prepares the food, and samplings from the menus of several waterfront restaurants are also available. ✉ *50 Rondout Landing, Rondout District* ☎ *845/338–0071* ⊕ *www.hrmm.org/museum/ festival.htm.*

WHERE TO EAT

¢ ✕**Dallas Hot Weiners.** Hot dogs are the specialty at this narrow spot
AMERICAN with a counter and a handful of tables. "One with everything" means
Fodor'sChoice a steamed dog on a steamed bun topped with slightly spicy chili sauce,
★ a dab of mustard, and a sprinkling of chopped onions. The sauce livens up fries, too; temper it with ketchup if it's too spicy for you. ✉*51 N. Front St., Stockade District* 🕾*845/338–6094* ▱*No credit cards* 🕑*Closed Sun.* ✉*490 Broadway, Midtown* 🕾*845/331–6311* ▱*No credit cards* 🕑*Closed Sun.*

$ ✕**El Danzante.** You get authentic Oaxacan food at this small and unpre-
MEXICAN tentious place. Instead of ordering the usual Americanized dishes, go for the soft tacos, tamales (especially the ones filled with rich mole poblano), or the fried squid in chipotle sauce. El Dazante carries the best selection of Mexican beers and tequilas around. ✉*720 Broadway, Midtown* 🕾*845/331–7070* ▱*AE, D, MC, V.*

$ ✕**Hickory BBQ and Smokehouse.** Savory, slow-cooked smoked meats are
ECLECTIC the draw at this casual eatery with wooden booths and a bar. The traditional Southern-style sides—collard greens, macaroni and cheese, corn bread, and flaky biscuits—are another reason to come. ✉*743 Rte. 28, 3 mi west of traffic circle* 🕾*845/338–2424* ▱*AE, D, MC, V.*

$$ ✕**Hoffman House Tavern.** You can dine by a fireplace in this late-17th-
CONTINENTAL century stone house, a National Historic Landmark. Try the aged steak or the special seafood of the day. On Saturday night, prime rib is served with Yorkshire pudding. The homemade pastas are also a treat. The dessert menu includes a different cheesecake for each day of the week. In summer, ask to sit on the patio. ✉*94 N. Front St., Stockade District* 🕾*845/338–2626* ▱*AE, D, DC, MC, V* 🕑*Closed Sun.*

UPPER HUDSON VALLEY—EAST

The fertile upper Hudson Valley, made verdant by winding rivers and copious lakes, is bordered on the east by the Berkshire Mountains. The rural landscape is graced with homes and grand manors reflecting its history; drive on U.S. 9 or Route 23 and you pass Dutch Colonial, Georgian, and Federal architecture.

Henry Hudson first stepped ashore in the area in the early 17th century. Dutch settlers, and later the English, drove the native Mohican, Lenni-Lenape, and other tribes from the area, setting up farms, mills, and taverns. A few received vast parcels of land, and many places still bear their names, Van Rensselaer and Livingston among them. With the Industrial Revolution came the train and steamboat, and visitors flocked to the region, taking the waters at natural springs in Lebanon and environs. Artists toting paintbrushes and palettes came and stayed, founding the Hudson River School.

Dairy farms and orchards still cover much of the arable land, although they are slowly finding new life as seasonal getaways. Catering to the area's growing popularity as a weekend destination are a growing number of restaurants, lodgings, and high-end stores. In the throes of resurgence, the city of Hudson lures urbanites to Warren Street, where art galleries and antiques shops jostle for space.

The counties composing this area are Dutchess and Columbia.

VISITOR INFORMATION
Columbia County Chamber of Commerce (☎ 518/828–4417 ⊕ www.columbia chamber-ny.com). **Columbia County Tourism** (☎ 518/828–3375 or 800/724–1846 ⊕ www.bestcountryroads.com). **Dutchess County Tourism** (☎ 845/463–4000 or 800/445–3131 ⊕ www.dutchesstourism.com).

POUGHKEEPSIE

25 mi north of Beacon.

Founded in 1687, this small Hudson River city has a population of about 30,000. After the British burned down Kingston in 1777, Poughkeepsie served as the state capital for several years. New York's first governor, George Clinton, lived in the city for more than two decades, and it was here that New York State ratified the Constitution in 1788. Today Poughkeepsie is the seat of Dutchess County and home to prestigious Vassar College. The downtown has seen better days, but you can see some signs of rejuvenation.

WHAT TO SEE

Locust Grove. After Samuel Morse, the inventor of the telegraph, bought this circa-1830 house, he remodeled it into a Tuscan-style villa. It still contains the possessions and keepsakes of the family that lived here after him. The Morse Gallery, inside the visitor center, has exhibits of telegraph equipment and paintings by Morse. The grounds include gardens and hiking trails. ⊠ *370 South Rd.* ☎ *845/454–4500* ⊕ *www.lgny.org* ✆ *$9* ☉ *House May–Nov., daily 10–3; grounds daily 8* AM–*dusk.*

Springside. You can walk the carriage roads and trails that vein this woodsy, 20-acre landscape. It is the only surviving example of a landscape design by A.J. Downing, the 19th-century tastemaker. Downing had designed the landscape in 1850 for the country estate of Matthew Vassar, the founder of Vassar College. A trail guide is available in the kiosk at the site. ⊠ *181 Academy St.* ☎ *845/454–2060* ✆ *Free* ☉ *Daily dawn–dusk.*

Vassar College. Begun as a women's college in 1865, Vassar has since gone coed. Today about 2,400 students attend this well-respected liberal-arts school. Vassar was the first college in the United States to have an art gallery. That gallery grew into the **Frances Lehman Loeb Art Center** (⊕ *www.fllac.vassar.edu* ☉ *Tues.–Sat. 10–5, Sun. 1–5*), housed in a 1993 Cesar Pelli building. The center's collections amount to more than 15,000 works, from Egyptian and Asian relics to 19th- and 20th-century paintings. At the free **A. Scott Warthin Geological Museum** (☉ *Weekdays 9–4*), on the ground floor of Ely Hall, you can see fossil, mineral, and rock specimens. The 1,000-acre campus, with its lakes, gardens, and 200-plus tree varieties, is a lovely place for a walk. Other Vassar highlights include the Tiffany windows in the chapel. ⊠ *124 Raymond Ave.* ☎ *845/437–7000* ⊕ *www.vassar.edu.*

SHOPPING

Absolute Auction Center. You never know what or who you'll find at an auction here: the what varies from fabulous to flea market, whereas the who ranges from well-known New York City dealers to local farmers. ⊠*45 South Ave., Pleasant Valley* ☎*845/635–3169* ⊕*www.aarauctions. com.*

SPORTS AND THE OUTDOORS

Hudson River Sloop Clearwater. Experience the Hudson River from aboard the *Clearwater,* a replica of a 19th-century Dutch sailing sloop. You'll be treated to gorgeous vistas and landmarks such as Storm King Mountain and Bannerman's Island. The three-hour sails dock at various places along the Hudson from April through mid-November. It's best to book ahead. ⊠*112 Little Market St.* ☎*845/454–7673* ⊕*www.clearwater. org* ☞*$50* ☾*Apr.–Nov., weekends; call for departure times.*

James Baird State Park. The 660 acres include hiking and cross-country-skiing trails; basketball, volleyball, and tennis courts; picnic areas; a playground; and a softball field. There's also a great golf course. A full-service restaurant overlooks the golf course. The park is off the Taconic Parkway 1 mi north of Poughkeepsie. ⊠*280 Club House Rd., Pleasant Valley* ☎*845/452–1489* ⊕*nysparks.state.ny.us* ☞*Free* ☾*Daily dawn–dusk.*

NIGHTLIFE AND THE ARTS

Fodor'sChoice The **Bardavon 1869 Opera House** (⊠*35 Market St.* ☎*845/473–5288*
★ ⊕*www.bardavon.org*), home of the Hudson Valley Philharmonic, is the state's oldest opera house. The beautifully restored auditorium has an active program of theater, music, dance, and drama. **The Chance** (⊠*6 Crannell St.* ☎*845/471–1966* ⊕*www.thechancetheatre.com*) is the premier live-music venue in the region. Bookings span all musical styles and include up-and-coming local bands as well as popular, internationally known performers. Housed in two Victorian buildings originally commissioned by the Vassar family, the **Cunneen–Hackett Cultural Center** (⊠*9 and 12 Vassar St.* ☎*845/486–4571* ⊕*www.cunneen-hackett.org*) houses nonprofit organizations, a dance studio, a workshop, an auditorium, and an art gallery.

WHERE TO EAT

$ ✕**Beech Tree Grill.** You can unwind at this popular bistro with brick
ECLECTIC walls and a bar along one wall. The menu includes Italian and Asian dishes, such as shrimp *fra diavolo* and sesame-dressed soba-noodle salad, as well as Continental comfort classics like beef Stroganoff. A few options are vegetarian, and there's a long list of beers. ⊠*1–3 Collegeview Ave.* ☎*845/471–7279* ⊕ *www.beechtreegrill.com* ▤*AE, D, MC, V* ☾*No lunch Mon.*

$$ ✕**Busy Bee Café.** Once you taste the contemporary American fare, you'll
AMERICAN know what the buzz is about—and why this place is a local favorite.
★ The menu, which changes frequently, might include white-bean-and-roasted-garlic ravioli or panko-crusted tuna on a bed of cellophane noodles. Save room for desserts such as berry-topped, warm, flourless,

chocolate cake. ⊠*138 South Ave.* ☏*845/452–6800* ▤*AE, D, MC, V* ⊗*Closed Sun. and Mon. No lunch Sat. No dinner Tues.*

$$$
FRENCH

✕**Le Pavillon.** Classical music and European paintings add to the air of refinement at this French restaurant in a 200-year-old farmhouse surrounded by well-tended grounds. The kitchen makes use of local ingredients and turns out French standards: escargots in Pernod-garlic sauce, coq au vin with leeks and mashed potatoes, and steak au poivre. When the weather's warm, you may also eat on an open-air patio. ⊠*230 Salt Point Tpke.* ☏*845/473–2525* ▤*AE, D, DC, MC, V* ⊗*Closed Sun., Mon., and 2 wks in July. No lunch.*

$
VIETNAMESE

✕**Saigon Café.** This tiny Vietnamese restaurant serves delicious noodle dishes and soups in a friendly atmosphere with prices that don't break the bank. Choices include crispy spring rolls, tender marinated steak bits, beef soup with vermicelli, lime-marinated chicken, and a few vegetarian options. Vassar College is around the corner. ⊠*6A LaGrange Ave.* ☏*845/473–1392* ▤ *D, MC, V* ⊗*No lunch Sun.*

WHERE TO STAY

$$
🏠**Inn at the Falls.** The shingle-style inn, overlooking Wappingers Creek and its falls, has a rather European feel to it. Room furnishings and styles vary, from contemporary to country and Asian-inspired to English manor; some rooms have canopy or four-poster beds. Windows are draped in yards of fabric, framing water views in some rooms. **Pros:** some rooms have hot tubs; billiards room. **Cons:** remote location; no room service. ⊠*50 Red Oaks Mill Rd.* ☏*845/462–5770* ⊕*www.innatthefalls.com* ⇥*24 rooms, 12 suites* ⚿*In-room: refrigerator (some), Wi-Fi. In-hotel: gym, spa, some pets allowed, no-smoking rooms* ▤*AE, D, DC, MC, V* ⊚*CP.*

HYDE PARK

6 mi north of Poughkeepsie.

Hyde Park dates from 1702, when an estate on this land was named for Edward Hyde, Lord Cornbury, then the provincial governor of New York. Most famous for being the boyhood home of Franklin Delano Roosevelt, it's also home to an impressive summer mansion built by one of the Vanderbilts, as well as to the East Coast campus of the renowned Culinary Institute of America.

WHAT TO SEE

Culinary Institute of America. The East Coast branch of the country's most respected cooking school is on the grounds of a former Jesuit seminary overlooking the Hudson River. Tours are available Monday to Thursday when school's in session. Five student-staffed restaurants are open to the public. The Craig Claiborne Bookstore stocks more than 1,300 cookbooks in addition to culinary equipment and specialty foods. One- and two-day workshops and lectures are offered on weekends. ⊠*1946 Campus Dr.* ☏*845/452–9600* ⊕*www.ciachef.edu* 🎫*Tour $5* ⊗*Tours Mon. at 10 and 4, Tues.–Thurs. at 4.*

Eleanor Roosevelt National Historic Site. An unpretentious cottage, **Val-Kill** was first a retreat and later the full-time residence for Eleanor Roosevelt. A biographical film, *First Lady of the World,* is shown at the site. The property encompasses 180 acres of trails and gardens. It's also the location of Val-Kill Industries, Eleanor's attempt to prevent farm workers from relocating to the city for employment; reproductions of early American furniture, pewter, and weavings were produced here. ⊠*Rte. 9G* ☎*845/229–9115* ⊕*www.nps.gov/elro* ☑*Tour $8* ☉*May.–Oct., daily 9–5; Nov.–Apr., Thurs.–Mon. 9–5.*

Fodor'sChoice **Franklin D. Roosevelt National Historic Site.** The birthplace and home of
★ the country's 32nd president, **Springwood** is just as it was when the Roosevelts lived here. It contains family furnishings and keepsakes, and Franklin and Eleanor are buried in the wonderful rose garden. At the **Franklin D. Roosevelt Library and Museum** (⊕*www.fdrlibrary. marist.edu*), photographs, letters, speeches, and memorabilia document FDR's life; a multimedia exhibit examines World War II. The first of the presidential libraries, the building was designed by Roosevelt himself. ⊠*U.S. 9* ☎*845/229–9115* ⊕*www.nps.gov/hofr* ☑*Tour $14, grounds free* ☉*Daily 9–5.*

☾ **Hyde Park Railroad Station.** Franklin D. Roosevelt used this 1914 train station, which today houses an extensive collection of railroad paraphernalia and has running displays of model trains all manned by knowledgeable enthusiasts. ⊠*34 River Rd.* ☎*845/229–2338* ⊕*www. hydeparkstation.com* ☑*Free* ☉*June 15–Sept. 15, weekends 11–5.*

Fodor'sChoice **Vanderbilt Mansion National Historic Site.** The imposing 1898 McKim,
★ Mead, and White mansion, built for Cornelius Vanderbilt's grandson Fredrick, makes a striking contrast with its Roosevelt neighbor, Springwood. A fine example of life in the Gilded Age, the house is lavishly furnished and full of paintings. It conveys the wealth and privilege of one of the state's most prominent families. The grounds offer excellent views of the Hudson River and encompass lovely Italian gardens. ⊠*U.S. 9* ☎*845/229–9115* ⊕*www.nps.gov/vama* ☑*Tour $8, grounds free* ☉*Daily 9–5.*

WHERE TO EAT

$$$ ✕**American Bounty.** Regional fare is the specialty at this student-staffed
AMERICAN restaurant at the Culinary Institute, and local and seasonal ingredients are emphasized. For instance, a salad with baked sheep-milk cheese and candied walnuts gets a dressing with Hudson Valley apple cider. The restaurant is in venerable Roth Hall, once a Jesuit seminary. ⊠*Culinary Institute of America, 1946 Campus Dr.* ☎*845/471–6608* ⚑*Reservations essential* ▤*AE, D, MC, V* ☉*Closed Sun. and Mon., 3 wks in July, 2 wks in late Dec.*

¢ ✕**Apple Pie Bakery Café.** The CIA's most casual dining option showcases
CAFES luscious desserts and breads made daily. The light lunch menu lists soups, sandwiches, pizza, and salads. The atmosphere is relaxed, and prices are reasonable. The line can get quite long around noon on weekdays, but moves fairly quickly. ⊠*Culinary Institute of America, 1946*

7

Campus Dr. ☎*845/905–4500* ⊜*Reservations not accepted* ▤*AE, D, MC, V* ⊗*Closed weekends.*

$$$ ✕**Escoffier.** The elegant Culinary Institute restaurant presents modern
FRENCH   interpretations of classic French dishes such as lobster salad, smoked
Fodor'sChoice   salmon, and sautéed beef tenderloin. Other specialties include duck-
★   liver terrine with mango chutney, seared sea scallops, and snails with
basil cream sauce. ⊠*Culinary Institute of America, 1946 Campus Dr.*
☎*845/471–6608* ⊜*Reservations essential* ▤*AE, D, MC, V* ⊗*Closed
Sun. and Mon., 3 wks in July, 2 wks in late Dec.*

$ ✕**Hyde Park Brewing Company.** American pub fare and some of the best
AMERICAN   beer in the Hudson Valley are served in this relaxed restaurant-brewery.
The menu includes sandwiches and pizzas as well as toothier fare like
steaks and pastas. The breads, desserts, and ice creams are made on the
premises. Live music three nights a week makes this a popular night-
spot, too. ⊠*4076 Albany Post Rd./U.S. 9* ☎*845/229–8277* ▤*AE,
D, DC, MC, V.*

$$ ✕**Ristorante Caterina de' Medici.** The Culinary Institute's terraced Colavita
ITALIAN   Center for Italian Food and Wine is the setting for this complex of
Italian dining areas, each with its own character. The ornately decorated main dining room has Venetian light fixtures and is the most formal; the Al Forno room has an open kitchen with a colorfully painted
wood-fired oven. Antipasti choices are plentiful, followed by first and
second courses. Panna cotta is a good dessert pick. ⊠*Culinary Institute of America, 1946 Campus Dr.* ☎*845/471–6608* ⊜*Reservations
essential* ▤*AE, D, MC, V* ⊗*Closed weekends, 3 wks in July, 2 wks
in late Dec.*

$$ ✕**St. Andrew's Café.** Contemporary fare takes on Asian influences at
AMERICAN   this casual restaurant at the Culinary Institute—chicken-and-shrimp
soup, warm spinach salad with wood-fired quail, and grilled tuna with
soba noodles, for example. The wood-fired pizza of the day is popular.
⊠*Culinary Institute of America, 1946 Campus Dr.* ☎*845/471–6608*
⊜*Reservations essential* ▤*AE, D, MC, V* ⊗*Closed weekends, 3 wks
in July, 2 wks in late Dec.*

WHERE TO STAY

$ ⌂**Roosevelt Inn of Hyde Park.** The family-owned motel, painted presiden-
tial white, has two stories and exterior corridors. Rooms have a queen
or king bed, one or two doubles, or a pair of twin beds. The smaller
rooms have knotty-pine paneling, whereas the others are more contem-
porary in style. The property is in the heart of Hyde Park, within walk-
ing distance of antiques shops, restaurants, and museums. **Pros:** within
walking distance of historic sites; free wireless. **Cons:** basic decor;
rooms can feel dated. ⊠*4360 Albany Post Rd./U.S. 9* ☎*845/229–2443*
⊕*www.rooseveltinnofhydepark.com* ⇝*24 rooms, 1 suite* ⌂*In-room:
refrigerator (some). In-hotel: some pets allowed, no-smoking rooms*
▤*AE, MC, V* ⊗*Closed Jan. and Feb.* ⎮◎⎮*CP.*

MILLBROOK

17 mi east of Hyde Park.

For many, this Dutchess County village midway between the Hudson River and Connecticut is just the right blend of town and country. Historic downtown streets lined with shops and restaurants sit amid rolling farms, country estates, and dense woodlands all laced with hiking and equestrian trails. The area, settled in the 1700s, is largely agricultural. Locals take pride in preserving this environment and go to great lengths to protect working farms, open green space, and rural practices. Where you don't see cows you're likely to see horses; meadows of them are around almost every bend outside the village, and a horsey theme threads through the village, too.

Millbrook has long attracted the rich and famous, many of whom have eschewed the Hamptons to build luxurious weekend and summer homes here. Exploring the winding back roads you can see the long, private drives that lead to their sprawling retreats. The region is also known for its wineries, with vineyards stretched along soft hills, and magnificent gardens, such as Innisfree, where views of natural features are framed for you.

WHAT TO SEE

Carey Institute of Ecosystem Studies. Devoted to teaching the public about ecology, the Carey Institute lets you explore the walking trails and roadways where you'll find fields, upland forests, and wetlands. Stroll through a fern glen and discover diverse habitats—or relax in Adirondack chairs and take in the sounds of the creek. The center also offers free lectures on ecology and birding and one-day courses about everything from Hudson Valley landscapes to rock-garden basics. ✉*2801 Sharon Tpke.* ☎*845/677–5343* ⊕*www.ecostudies.org* ☜*Free* ☾*Trails open Apr.–Oct., weekdays 8–dusk, weekends 11–dusk.*

Cascade Mountain Winery. A Hudson Valley wine pioneer, the now well-established winery produces a collection of reds and whites. A well-regarded chalet-style restaurant and a tasting room are on-site. ✉*835 Cascade Mountain Rd., Amenia* ☎*845/373–9021* ⊕*www.cascademt. com* ☜*Tour free, tasting $7* ☾*Apr.–Nov., daily 11–5.*

Clinton Vineyards and Winery. Seyval blanc is the specialty of this family-run operation housed in an 1800s converted barn. The owner, when he's around and about, conducts tours himself, displaying wit, style, and a passion for wines and winemaking. ✉*212 Schultzville Rd., Clinton Corners* ☎*845/266–5372* ⊕*www.clintonvineyards.com* ☜*Tour free, tasting $5* ☾*Fri.–Sun. noon–5.*

Millbrook Vineyards & Winery. At this 130-acre winery and vineyard you may savor a chardonnay or cabernet franc against a backdrop of spectacular views. An upstairs loft is open on weekends and offers seasonal art exhibits with regional artists and a selection of the vineyard's reds and whites. ✉*26 Wing Rd.* ☎*845/677–8383 or 800/662–9463* ⊕*www.millbrookwine.com* ☜*Tour free, tasting $7* ☾*Memorial Day– Labor Day, daily 11–6; Labor Day–Memorial Day, daily noon–5.*

☺ **Trevor Teaching Zoo.** Wallabies, chinchillas, emus, otters, parrots, snakes, and lemurs are among the more than 100 exotic and indigenous small mammals and birds that reside at this zoo on the grounds of the Millbrook School. Students, along with full-time and consulting staff, run the zoo and care for the animals as part of their curriculum at the college-preparatory school; their enthusiasm for their charges is infectious. ⊠*Millbrook School, Millbrook School Rd., about 5 mi east of Millbrook* ☎*845/677–3704* ⊕*www.millbrook.org* ⊠*$5* ☉*Daily 8:30–5.*

Wethersfield Estate and Gardens. The late owner, philanthropist Chauncey Stillman, envisioned his property as a grand Edwardian estate and fully realized his dream. The Georgian-style brick mansion surveys formal gardens (complete with resident peacocks), fountains, a sculpture garden, and a dramatic view of the Catskills. The house has an important collection of paintings assembled by the owner. The stable block houses the carriage museum and a collection of coaching memorabilia. ⊠*214 Pugsley Hill Rd., Amenia* ☎*845/373–8037* ⊠*Free* ☉*Gardens June–Sept., Wed., Fri., and Sat. noon–5; house and stables June–Sept. by appointment.*

Wing's Castle. The artist owners of this out-of-the-ordinary attraction constructed the multitowered stone castle using salvaged materials from old buildings. It's amusing to try to spot the exotic bits and pieces woven into the structure. The views take in the Catskills and the Millbrook Winery vineyard. ⊠*717 Bangall Rd. off Rte. 57* ☎*845/677–9085* ⊕ *www.wingscastle.com* ⊠*$10* ☉*Late May–early Sept., Wed.–Sun. noon–4:30; early Sept.–late Dec., weekends noon–4:30.*

SPORTS AND THE OUTDOORS

HIKING The **Stissing Mountain Fire Tower** crowns the summit (elevation 1,403 feet) of **Stissing Mountain** (⊠*Off Lake Rd., about 1½ mi off Rte. 82, Pine Plains* ☎*518/398–5247 or 518/398–5673*). The clear-day views from the 90-foot-tall structure stretch from Albany to Bear Mountain and across the Catskills. You also may see eagles, hawks, and other birds in flight from the tower, which is reached via hiking trails accessed at the mountain base. The mountain is undeveloped, with no facilities. Parking is limited to a small dirt lot across the road from a trailhead. Trail maps are available from local businesses.

HORSEBACK Millbrook is heaven for the horsey set. All manner of horse-related RIDING activity takes place here. **Cedar Crest Farm Equestrian Center** (⊠*2054 Rte. 83, Pine Plains* ☎*518/398–1034*), a 70-acre boarding and instruction facility, offers lessons in cross-country riding and stadium jumping. Adult sessions start at $53 (group lesson) and climb to $85 (private lesson with senior staff member).

SHOPPING

Antiquing is the highlight of Millbrook shopping. More than 100 dealers are represented along Franklin Avenue, the small main street, where trees shade old two-story buildings housing enticing stores. Hedges and trees shield **British Sporting Arms** (⊠*3684 U.S. 44* ☎*800/318–8693* ⊕ *www.bsaltd.com*). It's worth seeking out for its country-squire inventory: hand-carved walking sticks, flasks, bird sculptures, and all manner of shooting-related items, including antique and modern long guns. Upstairs are leather outerwear and European tweed pieces, including one local favorite—a tweedy bonnet with a large, flat bow in back. The owner of **Merritt Bookstore** (⊠*57 Front St.* ☎*845/677–5857*) promises he can access any book in print, and he means it. The store also sells offbeat greeting cards. For the best prices in town, check out the **Millbrook Antique Center** (⊠*3283 Franklin Ave.* ☎*845/677–3921*), an emporium with two floors of antiques and collectibles. A special Tiffany cabinet displays vintage Tiffany silver, objets d'art, and porcelain, all good values. With 38 dealers, the **Millbrook Antique Mall** (⊠*3301 Franklin Ave.* ☎*845/677–9311*) is the largest fine-antiques center for miles around. Almost every antiques category is represented: country furniture, botanical prints, porcelain, brass fireplace tools. The dealer collections create a series of nicely edited and presented boutique spaces.

Because **Red School House Antiques** (⊠*3300 Franklin Ave.* ☎*845/677–9786* ⊕*www.redschoolhouseantiques.com*) is the only single-dealer location in Millbrook, the collections here are more edited and focused than at other shops in town. Specialties include 18th- and 19th-century furnishings, decorative arts, and European and American oil paintings. A two-story barn in Mabbettsville, east of Millbrook via U.S. 44, has additional collections that you can view by appointment. The dealers represented at the **Village Antique Center** (⊠*3278 Franklin Ave.* ☎*845/677–5160*) are carefully chosen by the owner, and each collection is thoughtfully presented. The individual items are distinctive, with both personality and good provenance. Art-directed spiral-shape potted trees flank the double doors of the beautifully restored 1850s church that houses **Yellow Church Antiques** (⊠*U.S. 44* ☎*845/677–6779*). The fine (usually very expensive) antiques include English, American, and Continental furniture, and paintings and carpets from the 17th, 18th, and 19th centuries. The shop is open Friday through Sunday.

WHERE TO EAT

$$ ✕**Café Les Baux.** The jolly sunburst graphic on the café sign and the
FRENCH banks of colorful flowers on the front steps are très French. Warm terracotta–tone walls and vine-motif sconces continue the theme inside. The food is authentic French bistro fare, well prepared and presented. What a delight to find a really good croque monsieur and *moules* (mussels) or steak frites. Tarte tatin, baked by the chef and served with a scoop of crème fraîche, is not to be missed. ⊠*152 Church St.* ☎*845/677–8166* ⊕ *www.cafelesbaux.com* ⊟*AE, MC, V* ⊗*Closed Tues.*

$ ✕**Copperfield's.** An oval bar dominates the front room and provides
ECLECTIC plenty of space for a drink before dinner. The adjacent dining room has a casual feel with a combination of wooden booths and cloth-draped tables. The menu is long and varied, ranging from Mexican-style jalapeno chicken to French-influenced veal français. The bartender makes a great Bloody Mary to accompany the Sunday brunch. The restaurant is about 4 mi west of Millbrook. ⊠*U.S. 44, Salt Point* ☎*845/677–8188* ⊟*AE, DC, MC, V.*

$$ ✕**Millbrook Café.** With a hunter-green awning over the entrance, walls
AMERICAN covered with framed hunting prints, and wood paneling that recalls a
stable, this restaurant plays up the horse-country theme. The food is
billed as "authentic 19th-century cooking." Everything is cooked in
the wood-fired oven; the open-plan kitchen invites you to watch. The
house specialty, baked, stuffed Spanish onion, is a concoction of ched-
dar cheese and fresh vegetables that's worth trying. Entrées are served
on sizzling cast-iron platters straight from the oven. ⊠ *3290 Franklin
Ave.* ☎ *845/677–6956* ▤ *AE, MC, V* ⊘ *Closed Sun. and Mon.*

$ ✕**Millbrook Diner.** Since 1929 a diner has sat on this spot. The current
AMERICAN edition, a stainless-steel boxcar version, dates from 1952. It's a great
hangout for locals, who love how quickly that early-morning cup of
coffee is served. Order hamburgers, french fries, BLTs, and other diner
basics here. ⊠ *3266 Franklin Ave.* ☎ *845/677–5319* ▤ *MC, V.*

WHERE TO STAY

$$ ▥**Antrim House.** The 2 acres on which this Victorian-style contemporary
sits are secluded enough to appeal to wildlife, and on most mornings
various critters (deer, wild turkeys) can be seen around the grounds.
Inside, family heirlooms add plenty of charm. The largest guest room
has a queen-size bed and a deck overlooking the lawn. In winter the
glow of the constantly stoked fireplaces in the library and dining room
creates a cozy respite from the cold. The highlight of a stay may well be
the full Irish-style cooked breakfast. **Pros:** tranquil setting; tasty breakfast. **Cons:** not much within walking distance; no credit cards. ⊠ *33
Deer Pond Rd.* ☎ *845/677–6265* ⇄ *3 rooms* ⚡ *In-room: no phone, no
TV, Wi-Fi. In-hotel: no-smoking rooms* ▤ *No credit cards* ⚆ *BP.*

$ ▥**Cottonwood Motel.** The design and decor of this roadside motel are
standard issue: vending machines in one corner, lobby in the other. What
makes things interesting are the sights and sounds behind the motel.
Each room has a little patio overlooking a nature preserve. Local wildlife—deer, wild turkeys, pheasants—roam right up to your doorstep.
Towering cottonwoods frame your view. **Pros:** tranquil setting; some
rooms have hot tubs. **Cons:** remote location; drab decor. ⊠ *2639 U.S.
44* ☎ *845/677–3283* ⊕ *www.cottonwoodmotel.com* ⇄ *17 rooms, 1
suite, 1 cottage* ⚡ *In-room: refrigerator, Internet. In-hotel: some pets
allowed, no-smoking rooms* ▤ *AE, MC, V.*

$$$ ▥**Millbrook Country House.** The house, built in 1810, was remodeled
in 1838 when classical detailing was all the rage (witness the majestic
columns in the front hall). If the interior recalls 17th-century Italy, it's
because most of the furniture came from the current owner's palazzo
near Modena. Elegant marquetry tables grace the parlors (where you
may come across the owners' three cats), and lush silk draperies dress
many windows. Extensive gardens surround the house, and a sculp-
ture garden displays works by local artists. **Pros:** afternoon tea; lovely
lawn shaded by enormous maple tree. **Cons:** remote setting. ⊠ *506
Sharon Tpke.* ☎ *845/677–9570* ⊕ *www.millbrookcountryhouse.com*
⇄ *4 rooms* ⚡ *In-room: no phone, no TV, Wi-Fi. In-hotel: restaurant,
bicycles, no kids under 10, no-smoking rooms* ▤ *AE, MC* ⚆ *BP.*

$$$$ ▥**Old Drovers Inn.** Cattle herders (the "drovers" of the name) often made
a stopover at this inn, on 12 acres 15 mi southeast of Millbrook. Rooms
★

are Victorian in style; three have fireplaces. Weekend rates include full breakfast; weekday rates are considerably lower and include only Continental breakfast. In the low-ceilinged Tap Room, old favorites such as rack of lamb and turkey hash blend with more-contemporary dishes such as sesame-crusted tuna and marsala-braised Muscovy duck. **Pros:** comfortable rooms; free Wi-Fi. **Cons:** not within walking distance of sites; not for young kids. ⊠*196 E. Duncan Rd., Dover Plains* ☎*845/832–9311* ⊕*www.olddroversinn.com* ↘*7 suites* ⟡*In-room: no phone, no TV, Wi-Fi. In-hotel: restaurant, room service, bicycles, some pets allowed, no kids under 12, no-smoking rooms* ▤*AE, D, MC, V* ⊗*Closed first 2 wks in Jan.*

$$ 🏠**Porter House Bed & Breakfast.** The original chestnut woodwork and wainscoting from this 1920 stone house have been lovingly restored. Their warm patina works well with the Victorian furniture that fills the sunny parlor. Bedrooms blend rustic pieces with more-refined furnishings. The B&B is a block from the heart of Millbrook. **Pros:** some rooms have fireplaces; free Wi-Fi. **Cons:** books up in advance. ⊠*17 Washington Ave.* ☎*845/677–3057* ⊕*www.innsofmillbrook.com/ PorterHouseBandB.html* ↘*2 rooms, 3 suites* ⟡*In-room: no phone, no TV. In-hotel: no kids under 12, no-smoking rooms* ᭄*CP.*

STAATSBURG

21 mi northwest of Millbrook.

On U.S. 9 midway between Rhinebeck and Hyde Park is Staatsburg, surrounded by soft hills overlooking the Hudson River. The main attraction here is the Staatsburg State Historic Site, of which the old Mills Mansion is the centerpiece. You may hike or stroll the estate grounds, which offer stunning Hudson River views.

WHAT TO SEE

Mills-Norrie State Park. Formed from Margaret Lewis Norrie State Park and Ogden Mills and Ruth Livingston Mills Memorial State Park, the park encompasses 1,200 scenic acres along the Hudson River, about 5 mi south of Rhinebeck. The grounds include close to 9 mi of hiking, biking, and horseback-riding trails; a marina; nature center; public golf course; and the **Staatsburg State Historic Site.** Camping is an option. Eagles can sometimes be spotted from the nature center. ⊠*Old Post Rd. off U.S. 9* ☎*845/889–4646* ⊕*nysparks.state.ny.us* ᭄*Free.*

Fodor'sChoice **Staatsburg State Historic Site.** The well-known architectural firm of ★ McKim, Mead, and White was responsible for the beaux arts style of this grand 65-room mansion fronted with mammoth columns. Formerly known as Mills Mansion, the Hudson River estate was a family home of financier Ogden Mills and his wife, Ruth Livingston Mills, in the late 1800s to early 1900s. You may see the mansion's lavish interior by guided tour only. The estate, one of the most beautiful properties in the Hudson Valley, has hiking and cross-country-skiing trails, and a huge hill for sledding in winter. ⊠*Old Post Rd., off U.S. 9* ☎*845/889–8851* ⊕*www.staatsburgh.org* ᭄*House tour $5, grounds free* ⊗*Early Apr.– late Oct., Tues.–Sat. 10–5, Sun. noon–5; Jan.–Mar., weekends 11–5.*

WHERE TO EAT AND STAY

$$ ✕**Portofino Ristorante.** This out-of-the-way Italian restaurant, in an old
ITALIAN inn on the historic postal route that once connected New York City
and Albany, has a loyal following among locals and weekenders. The
menu lists 25 pasta and main dishes; nightly specials add options. Baked
artichokes with oregano, garlic, lemon, and butter are a good way
to start your meal. A popular pasta dish combines seared sea scal-
lops with sweet red-pepper cream sauce and basil. ⊠*57 Old Post Rd.*
☎*845/889–4711* ⊟*AE, D, DC, MC, V* ⊗*Closed Mon. No lunch.*

$$ ⌂**Belvedere Mansion.** The commanding neoclassical-style house sits on
a hill with distant Hudson River views. Trimmed with marble, crystal,
silk, and damask, the main-house rooms are the most elegant lodgings
on the property, which includes several other buildings. Most rooms
in what's called the Hunt Lodge, in the woods behind the main house,
are suites with fireplaces and private terraces. The more modest Carriage House building—a motel-like strip—has small rooms, some with
fireplaces. **Pros:** enchanting grounds; doting service. **Cons:** not ideal for
children. ⊠*10 Old Rte. 9* ☎*845/889–8000* ⊕*www.belvederemansion.
com* ⇆*31 rooms, 5 suites* ⌂*In-room: no phone, no TV, Wi-Fi. In-
hotel: restaurant, bar, tennis court, pool, water sports, no-smoking
rooms* ⊟*AE, DC, MC, V* ⍩*BP.*

RHINEBECK

5 mi north of Staatsburg.

At heart, Rhinebeck is a historic village with a dose of city sophistica-
tion. The influence of earlier times is present in the Victorian, Greek
Revival, colonial, and other architectural treasures scattered throughout
the village. Some two dozen, including the early Dutch-style post office,
are listed on the National Register of Historic Places. Meanwhile, up-
to-the-minute shops, restaurants, and theaters keep bringing new life to
the old churches, early educational institutions, and other repurposed
buildings they occupy.

VISITOR INFORMATION

Rhinebeck Chamber of Commerce (☎*845/876–5904* ⊕*www.rhinebeckchamber.
com*).

WHAT TO SEE

Fodor'sChoice   **Old Rhinebeck Aerodrome.** All the vintage aircraft at this museum still
★   fly; indeed, many are used during air shows, held on weekends from
♺   mid-June to mid-October (weather permitting). The collection includes
a reproduction of Charles Lindbergh's *Spirit of St. Louis* and fighter
planes from World War I. For a thrill you can don a Snoopy-style cap
and goggles and soar over the area in an open-cockpit biplane. Ride
booths open at 10 on weekends of air shows, and the rides are $65 per
person. Air shows start at 2. ⊠*44 Stone Church Rd.* ☎*845/752–3200*
⊕*www.oldrhinebeck.org* ◰*$10* ⊗*Mid-May–Oct., daily 10–5.*

Wilderstein. The grand, Queen Anne–style Victorian home with a dramatic five-story circular tower was owned by the Suckley family for

more than 140 years. The last family member to occupy the estate was Margaret "Daisy" Suckley, a distant cousin of Franklin Delano Roosevelt. The main-floor interiors and stained-glass windows were designed by Tiffany. Noted landscape architect Calvert Vaux designed the grounds, which have Hudson River views. There are weekend house tours around Christmas. ⊠*330 Morton Rd.* ☎*845/876–4818* ⊕*www. wilderstein.org* ⬛*$10* ☾*May–Oct., Thurs.–Sun. noon–4.*

SHOPPING

More than 350 artists show their crafts at **Crafts at Rhinebeck** (⊠*Dutchess County Fairgrounds, U.S. 9* ☎*845/876–4001* ⊕*www.dutchessfair. com*), a prestigious and popular juried event held in mid-June and again in October. An impressive array of handcrafted items includes jewelry, blown glass, pottery, and musical instruments. One of the best-known and -loved antiques fairs in the country, the **Rhinebeck Antiques Fair** (⊠*Dutchess County Fairgrounds, U.S. 9* ☎*845/876–4001* ⊕*www. rhinebeckantiquesfair.com*) showcases more than 200 dealers in four large exhibition halls. The fair, held three times a year (in May, July, and October), interests both casual and serious collectors.

More than 30 antiques dealers sell their wares at the **Beekman Arms Antique Market** (⊠*6387 Mill St.* ☎*845/876–3477*), which occupies a large red barn behind the Beekman Arms. The antiques mix is eclectic, with Americana, Victorian, country, and primitive pieces represented. One-of-a-kind creations by local and international artisans are artfully displayed at the exquisite **Hummingbird Jewelers** (⊠*23 E. Market St.* ☎*845/876–4585*). An exceptional collection of designer wedding bands and engagement rings is showcased. It's closed Tuesday.**Joovay** (⊠*6423 Montgomery St.* ☎*845/876–8707*) stocks fine European lingerie—teddies, slips, silk chemises, and assorted unmentionables—as well as kimono robes and vintage silk Haori jackets. **Oblong Books and Music** (⊠*Montgomery Row, 6422 Montgomery St.* ☎*845/876–0500 or 800/625–6640*), a well-stocked, all-purpose bookstore one block north of the Beekman Arms, offers a good selection of novels, books about area places and local history, and works by local writers.

"Life is chaotic, you might as well look good" is the motto of Diana Brind, owner and creative force behind the **SugarPlum Boutique** (⊠*71 E. Market St.* ☎*845/876–6729*), an accessories shop. Her eye for the delicate is evident in the array of barrettes, scarves, hats, and silver jewelry. Ever-changing window displays set the stage for the side-by-side **Winter Sun/Summer Moon** (⊠*10–14 E. Market St.* ☎*845/876–2223*). Luscious fabrics, bright colors, and rich textures give the shops the feel of a sophisticated bazaar. Comfortable, easy-to-wear, and elegant clothes, jewelry, and accessories are the signature of Winter Sun.

NIGHTLIFE AND THE ARTS

A large red barn about 3½ mi east of the village center houses the busy **Center for Performing Arts at Rhinebeck** (⊠*661 Rte. 308/E. Market St.* ☎*845/876–3080* ⊕*www.centerforperformingarts.org*). The ongoing series of Saturday children's shows is popular.

★ A cultural hub for everything about film, the small **Upstate Films Theater** (✉ *6415 Montgomery St.* ☎ *845/876–2515* ⊕ *www.upstatefilms.org*) shows documentaries, independent films, classics, and animation. Shows ($7.50) often sell out, so it's best to purchase tickets in advance.

WHERE TO EAT

¢ **✕Bread Alone.** The European-style bakery receives daily deliveries from

CAFÉS its main facility in nearby Boiceville. The loaves, shaped by hand and baked in wood-fired ovens, come in such varieties as hearty whole grain and baguettes—and can be found at many local farmers' markets throughout the Hudson Valley. The café, with six tables and a window bar, is a comfortable place for a cappuccino. ✉ *45 E. Market St.* ☎ *845/876–3108* ⊕ *www.breadalone.com* ⊟ *AE, MC, V.*

$$ **✕Calico.** There's more to this storefront patisserie than meets the eye.

CAFÉS Exquisite cakes, tarts, and baked goods fill the pastry case. The lunch

Fodor's Choice and dinner fare always includes a vegetarian option or two, such as

★ polenta layered with goat cheese, vegetables, and pesto. Bouillabaisse, brimming with shellfish in lobster broth, is a good deal. ✉ *6384 Mill St.* ☎ *845/876–2749* ⊕ *www.calicorhinebeck.com* ⊟ *AE, MC, V* ☽ *Closed Mon. and Tues. No dinner Sun.*

¢ **✕Garden Street Cafe.** The tiny café uses the freshest local ingredients,

VEGETARIAN turning them into such flavorful wraps and sandwiches as the hearty avocado supreme (avocado and melted Havarti on multigrain bread) and chili works (vegetarian black-bean chili over brown rice). Daily specials are posted on a white board decorated with funky art by a staff member. ✉ *24 Garden St.* ☎ *845/876–2005* ⊟ *AE, MC, V* ☽ *Closed Sun. No dinner.*

$$$ **✕Gigi Trattoria.** A sophisticated clientele crowds the bar, patio, and din-

ITALIAN ing rooms of this lively Italian restaurant, once the showroom of a car dealership. The food, billed as "Hudson Valley Mediterranean," includes artfully crafted salads, house-made pastas, and hearty entrées. Baby greens provide a bed for roasted butternut squash, beets, and asparagus dressed with walnuts and crumbled goat cheese. Toppings for the "skizzas" (flatbread pizzas) range from a sausage–broccoli rabe–mozzarella combo to a version with goat cheese, mozzarella, arugula, pears, and figs. ✉ *6422 Montgomery St.* ☎ *845/876–1007* ⊕ *www.gigitrattoria. com* ⌕ *Reservations not accepted* ⊟ *AE, D, MC, V* ☽ *Closed Mon.*

$$$ **✕Le Petit Bistro.** You might walk by this downtown eatery and not give it

FRENCH a second glance, but Le Petit Bistro has a spirited following. Chef Joseph Dalu is particular about ingredients, and uses local when available. Daily specials reflect his concept of "cooking with the season." The house pâté appetizer and English Dover sole are favorites on the regular menu. The dining room is warm, with worn pine floors and pale paneled walls. ✉ *8 E. Market St.* ☎ *845/876–7400* ⊕ *www.lepetitbistro. com* ⊟ *AE, D, DC, MC, V* ☽ *Closed Tues. and Wed.*

$ **✕Osaka.** You can count on a cheerful greeting when you venture into

JAPANESE this immaculate sushi bar and restaurant. The fish is super-fresh, the

★ presentation artistic, and the sake assortment excellent. In addition to sushi, the menu covers teriyaki, tempura, and udon-noodle dishes. The place isn't large and it tends to fill up on weekends, but it is worth the wait. Nearby Tivoli is home to an Osaka branch. ✉ *22 Garden*

St. 🕾845/876–7338 ⟨Reservations not accepted ⊟AE, D, MC, V ⊘Closed Tues.

$$
AMERICAN
★
✕**Terrapin.** This 1842 church contains two dining options: a casual bistro and a more-formal dining room. The bistro menu lists soups, stews, and a make-your-own-sandwich board, as well as traditional entrées. Expect a lively crowd at the bar, especially on weekends. With white-cloth-draped tables, the main dining area is quieter. The food veers from creative to comforting. A popular starter is baby-arugula salad with goat-cheese wontons. Three sauces—roasted-shallot hollandaise, mole verde, and ancho chili—accompany the salmon dish.

✉6426 Montgomery St. 🕾845/876–3330 ⊟AE, D, MC, V.

WHERE TO STAY

$$
🏨**Beekman Arms and Delamater Inn.** America's oldest operating inn, the Beekman Arms is a welcoming presence in the center of town. Beyond the massive doors are wide-plank floors, beamed ceilings, and a stone hearth. The original 1766 building has smallish though cheery and comfortable colonial-style rooms with modern baths. Contemporary motel-style rooms are available in a separate building. One block north on U.S. 9 is "the Beek's" sister, the Delamater Inn. The American Gothic masterpiece, designed by Alexander Jackson Davis, has a hidden courtyard. **Pros:** elegant rooms; plenty of charm. **Cons:** some rooms lack air-conditioning; children are not allowed in some rooms. ✉6387 Mill St. 🕾845/876–7077 ⊕www.beekmandelamaterinn.com ⌂67 rooms, 7 suites ♿In-room: refrigerator (some), Wi-Fi, no a/c (some). In-hotel: restaurant, some pets allowed, no-smoking rooms ⊟AE, D, DC, MC, V.

$$$
★
🏨**Olde Rhinebeck Inn.** On a quiet tree-lined street 3 mi from Rhinebeck center, this inn has a resident ghost who reportedly appears with some regularity in the Spirited Dove room. Jonna Paolella tends to her guests, telling them the fascinating history of this house, built by German settlers. Much of the original detail in this circa-1745 inn has been beautifully preserved. The country decor mixes rustic pieces with some finer furnishings. **Pros:** hot tubs in some rooms; fishing in bass-stocked pond. **Cons:** minimum stay on weekends; outside Rhinebeck center. ✉340 Wurtemburg Rd. 🕾845/871–1745 ⊕www.rhinebeckinn.com ⌂1 room, 3 suites, 1 cottage ♿In-room: Wi-Fi, refrigerator (some), no phone. In-hotel: restaurant, no-smoking rooms ⊟MC, V ⍩BP.

$$$
🏨**Whistlewood Farm Bed & Breakfast.** You can't help but leave the city pressures behind as you drive up the fence-lined road to this farm where horses graze. The main house is homey and rustic, with more-refined, contemporary-country guest rooms. You may sit on one of many decks

and enjoy the display of wildflowers. In winter, the fieldstone fireplace is put to use. For more privacy, stay in the Carriage House, a converted barn with two suites. Breakfast—pancakes or egg dishes—is hearty, and home-baked pie and cake are readily available. After fueling up, explore one of the trails on the grounds. **Pros:** cross-country skiing; some rooms have hot tubs. **Cons:** some rooms have baths across the hall; spotty Wi-Fi. ⊠ *52 Pells Rd.* ☎ *845/876–6838* ⊕ *www.whistlewood.com* ⟳ *4 rooms, 3 suites* ♨ *In-room: no a/c, no phone, no TV, Wi-Fi. In-hotel: some pets allowed, no-smoking rooms* ⊟ *AE* ⦿ *BP.*

ANNANDALE-ON-HUDSON AND TIVOLI

3 mi west of Red Hook.

Annandale-on-Hudson is home to the beautiful Bard College campus and its famous Fisher Center for the Performing Arts. If you travel north to the campus via River Road, which is shaded by trees and lined with old stone walls and orchards, you'll pass Poets' Walk and Montgomery Place. Tivoli, on Route 9G 2 mi north of Bard, is known for its restaurants and artistic community. It comes alive at night and is a popular spot for Bard students and professors.

WHAT TO SEE

Fodor's Choice ★ **Bard College.** A winding tree-lined road leads to this small college of liberal arts and sciences. The beautiful 540-acre campus encompasses two Hudson River estates, parklike grounds and gardens, and wooded areas. The free **Center for Curatorial Studies** (☎ *845/758–7598* ☉ *Wed.–Sun. 1–5*), on the south end of the Bard campus, is known for cutting-edge exhibits of contemporary art. Noted architect Frank Gehry designed Bard's extraordinary **Richard B. Fisher Center for the Performing Arts** (☎ *845/758–7900* ⊡ *Tours $5*). Brushed-stainless-steel panels, draped like massive ribbons over the roof and sides of the 108,000-square-foot performing-arts center, reflect the light and colors of the sky as well as the hilly surroundings. Tours are given daily at 2 most of the year. ⊠ *Annandale Rd., west of Rte. 9G, Annandale-on-Hudson* ☎ *845/758–6822* ⊕ *www.bard.edu.*

Lake Taghkanic State Park. The centerpiece of this 1,569-acre park, Lake Taghkanic has two sandy beaches, picnic areas, boat rentals, playgrounds, restrooms, and trails for hiking. You may camp here from early May through October, choosing between tent or trailer sites or rustic cabins (with bathrooms and hot and cold water). Kids enjoy climbing the water tower. Cross-country skiing, snowmobiling, ice-skating, and ice fishing are options in winter. ⊠ *1528 Rte. 82, Ancram* ☎ *518/851–3631* ⊕ *nysparks.state.ny.us* ⊡ *Parking $7 (late May–Labor Day)* ☉ *Daily sunrise–sunset.*

★ **Montgomery Place.** This 23-room mansion, once the Livingston family estate, sits on 434 acres along the Hudson River north of Rhinebeck. Built in the Federal style, the mansion was remodeled in the mid-19th century by noted American architect Andrew Jackson Davis, who applied a classical revival style. The well-maintained house is closed for restoration, but the grounds alone are worth seeing; they encompass orchards, flower gardens, and ancient trees, and offer plenty of picnic-perfect spots. ⊠*River Rd. off Rte. 9G, Annandale-on-Hudson* ☎*845/758–5461* ⊕*www.hudsonvalley.org* ☒*$5* ⊘*May–Oct., weekends 10–5.*

Poets' Walk. Spectacular views of the Hudson River and the Catskill Mountains are your reward for trekking through the fields and wooded trails (2¼ mi) at this 120-acre park. Rustic cedar benches, footbridges, and gazebos add to the park's charm and offer places to picnic and rest. ⊠*Rte. 103, ½ mi north of Kingston–Rhinecliff Bridge, Annandale-on-Hudson* ☎*845/473–4440 Ext. 270* ⊕*www.scenichudson.org* ☒*Free* ⊘*Daily 9–dusk.*

THE ARTS

A cultural hub in the area, **Bard College** (⊠*Annandale Rd., west of Rte. 9G, Annandale-on-Hudson* ☎*845/758–7900* ⊕*www.bard.edu*) hosts several outstanding performing-arts festivals. The mix of events during **Bard SummerScape,** which runs from mid-July to mid-August, might blend orchestral and choral concerts, operas, dance performances, puppetry and other theater presentations, films, and panel discussions. The annual **Bard Music Festival** is devoted to a single composer deemed worthy of a new look and is held over two consecutive weekends in August.

SPORTS AND THE OUTDOORS

A 1,720-acre nature reserve stretching for 2 mi along the east bank of the Hudson River, **Tivoli Bays** (⊠*Rte. 9G and Kidd La., about 10 mi north of Kingston–Rhinecliff Bridge, Tivoli* ☎*845/889–4745* ⊕*nerrs. noaa.gov/hudsonriver*) has several short trails that wind through and around a freshwater tidal wetland. The bays, part of the Hudson River National Estuarine Research Reserve, are used for long-term field research and education, as well as for hunting in season.

WHERE TO EAT

$ ✕**Luna 61.** Candles and Ella Fitzgerald set the stage at this artsy, funky,
VEGETARIAN vegetarian eatery. Organic ingredients are used in most of the dishes, which are served in hearty portions. The challah French toast is a morning winner; pad thai is a good dinner choice. Beer and wine, all organic, are available, too. ⊠*55 Broadway, Tivoli* ☎*845/758–0061* ▤*AE, MC, V* ⊘*Closed Mon. No lunch.*

$ ✕**Osaka.** This immaculate Japanese restaurant is popular with the
JAPANESE college crowd as well as with the locals. It offers high-quality sushi,
★ teriyaki, tempura, and noodle dishes. There's also an extensive assortment of sake. The meal always ends with a perfectly chilled orange. ⊠*74 Broadway, Tivoli* ☎*845/757–5055* ⊜*Reservations not accepted* ▤*AE, D, MC, V* ⊘*Closed Tues.*

$$$ ✕**Santa Fe.** Every year or two, owner David Weiss travels to Mexico
MEXICAN in search of new culinary inspiration—and then he changes the menu. Luckily some of the most popular dishes are mainstays, such as the grilled pork taco and the goat-cheese-and-spinach enchilada. The frozen margaritas are made from scratch. ⊠*52 Broadway, Tivoli* ☎*845/757– 4100* ▤*AE, D, MC, V* ⊘*Closed Mon. No lunch.*

SAUGERTIES

15 mi north of Kingston.

Ever since Governor Andros negotiated a deal with the Esopus tribe in 1677, Saugerties, strategically located between the Catskill Mountains and the Hudson River, has lured entrepreneurs, visionaries, and working folk. It was for centuries a no-nonsense mix of agrarian and early industry, where farmers harvested ice from the Hudson in winter, quarried bluestone and brick from surrounding hills, milled lumber, and made paper. With one of the few deepwater ports along the river, Saugerties was once a thriving riverfront town, loading its wares onto southern-bound steamboats and building racing sloops.

Today, after decades of slumber, Saugerties is thriving for completely different reasons. Mint-condition Victorian houses line its streets, and the occasional stone house evokes memories of early Palatine settlers. Civic pride blooms in flower baskets in the downtown shopping area, especially along Main and Partition streets, where antiques shops, independent bookstores, and tantalizing restaurants draw weekend crowds.

WHAT TO SEE

Kiersted House. The stone house, parts of which date from the 1720s, serves as the home of the Saugerties Historical Society and a museum. Inside you can see original architectural details, including wide-plank floors and fireplace mantels. The front lawn is the site of summertime concerts, periodic colonial reenactments, and other special events. ✉ *119 Main St.* ☎ *845/246–9529* ⊕ *www.saugertieshistoricalsociety. com* ✆ *Free* ☾ *Memorial Day–Columbus Day, weekends 1–4.*

Opus 40. The late Harvey Fite put 37 years into the making of this 6-acre outdoor sculpture, created in the rock bed of an abandoned bluestone quarry. The architectural creation is an assemblage of curving bluestone walkways, swirling terraces, and finely fitted ramps around pools, trees, and fountains. The **Quarryman's Museum** contains 19th-century tools. ✉ *50 Fite Rd.* ☎ *845/246–3400* ⊕ *www.opus40.org* ✆ *$10* ☾ *Memorial Day–Columbus Day, Fri.–Sun. noon–5.*

FESTIVALS
AND FAIRS

Esopus Creek Festival of Mask and Puppet Theater. Every August you can watch giant puppets and imaginative spectacles unfold before the Esopus Creek in Tina Chorvas Waterfront Park. You'll be dazzled once the sun goes down and local puppeteers transform the park into an otherworldly extravaganza. ✉ *E. Bridge St.* ☎ *845/246–7873* ⊕ *www. armofthesea.org.*

Hudson Valley Garlic Festival. Upward of 40,000 people make a pilgrimage to Saugerties the last weekend of September for a celebration of the "stinking rose," otherwise known as garlic. Although you find much of the usual fair fare here—crafts booths, fried-dough stands, live musical performances—one vast section of the festival is devoted to farmers, arts-and-crafts people, and food vendors all providing tributes to garlic. ✉ *Cantine Field between Washington Ave. and Market St.* ☎ *845/246–3090* ⊕ *www.hvgf.org.*

WHERE TO EAT AND STAY

$$$ ✕**Café Tamayo.** Sweep back the claret-color velvet curtains at the
AMERICAN entrance and you're transported to a turn-of-the-20th-century French
bistro. Gourmands have enthused over the new American fare—smoked
salmon–potato pancake and grilled loin of lamb, for example—since the
place opened in 1987. Chef-owner James Tamayo, a Culinary Institute
graduate, prides himself on using fresh local produce and is known for
his duck confit. ⊠*89 Partition St.* ☎*845/246–9371* ▭*DC, MC, V*
⊘*Closed Mon. and Tues. No lunch.*

$$ ✕**New World Home Cooking Co.** Colorful accents and artwork adorn
ECLECTIC this lively restaurant. A large bar and a sapphire-and-stainless-steel
open kitchen are focal points. The eclectic menu includes a sampler
with Creole-mustard shrimp, Spanish Manchego cheese, Sicilian-olive-
salad crostini, smoked Maine mussels, roasted chorizo, and pickled
vegetables. The pan-blackened string beans will have you humming
zydeco. There's Celtic music every Monday night. ⊠*1411 Rte. 212*
☎*845/246–0900* ▭*AE, MC, V* ⊘*No lunch weekdays.*

$$ ▦**Saugerties Lighthouse Bed and Breakfast.** A ½-mi hike from a small
parking lot near a Coast Guard station brings you to this romantic hide-
out, a restored lighthouse overlooking the Hudson River. Accommoda-
tions are simple and rustic—you make up your own bed at night, and
the shared bathroom has a composting toilet—but the two bedrooms
are bright and have expansive views. Be sure to climb to the lantern
house, which looks across the river at the Clermont estate. Outdoor
decks make for idyllic picnics; at low tide stairs lead to a beach. **Pros:**
unique setting; spectacular views. **Cons:** reserve a year in advance; feels
remote. ⊠*Off Mynderse St., off U.S. 9W* ☎*845/247–0656* ⊕*www.*
saugertieslighthouse.com ⟿*2 rooms with shared bath* ⚬*In-room: no*
a/c, no phone, kitchen, Wi-Fi. In-hotel: some pets allowed ▭*AE, D,*
MC, V ⊘*Closed Mon.* ▯①*BP.*

SHOPPING

★ Chocoholics beware: you could find yourself in serious trouble at
Krause's Chocolates (⊠*41 S. Partition St.* ☎*845/246–8377*), a second-
generation-run confectionery. Candy-cane-striped columns beckon
you inside, where the aroma of Karl Krause's closely guarded recipes
envelop you. Grab a basket to hold your wares; this chocolate is so
fresh it's likely to melt in your hands.

HUDSON

15 mi north of Annandale-on-Hudson andTivoli.

Rising from decades of decay and decrepitude, Hudson has, over the
past few years, finally arrived as a bona fide weekend destination for a
growing cadre of hip New Yorkers. The beautifully restored architec-
ture, the hundred-odd antiques emporiums, and the nascent reputation
of the city as an upstate offshoot of Manhattan's SoHo neighborhood
are what draw the hordes of aesthetes who descend on Hudson from
Wednesday through Sunday each week.

Warren Street, the main drag, is lined with the lion's share of the city's antiques shops, scores of quirky boutiques and art galleries, and a rising number of increasingly trendy restaurants. At its foot is Promenade Hill Park, which offers views of the river, the Catskill Mountains, and the Hudson-Athens Lighthouse.

Settled in 1783 as a whaling port, Hudson was built—from scratch—on a planned grid by a group of Quaker seafarers, artisans, and businessmen from Nantucket and New Bedford. These hardy folks felt their hometowns were sitting ducks for British warships in the uncertain days following the Revolution and wanted a safe, inland, deepwater haven. Not so long ago, into the mid-20th century, the city became famous for another industry: vice. Its red-light district, on what today is Columbia Street, was notorious. These days the old brothels have been restored by weekenders.

WHAT TO SEE

American Museum of Firefighting. The museum, a country mile from the Warren Street hub, contains 43 examples of hand-pulled engines and hose carts, including a Newsham engine built in London, imported to Manhattan in 1731, and in active service for more than 150 years. A pair of horse-drawn trucks, five steam-powered vehicles, and 15 internal-combustion engines round out the hardware, which along with other artifacts purport to tell the history of firefighting. ⊠ *117 Harry Howard Ave.12534* ☎ *518/822–1875* ⊕ *www.fasnyfiremuseum.com* ⊠ *Donations welcome* ⊙ *Daily 10–5.*

Robert Jenkins House and Museum. This Federal home, built in 1811, now houses a museum containing various articles of Hudsoniana, including historic documents, maps and books relating to whaling, military artifacts, and other archaic goodies. Tours are generally by appointment only. ⊠ *113 Warren St.* ☎ *518/828–9764* ⊠ *$3* ⊙ *July and Aug., Sun. and Mon. 1–3 or by appt.*

WHERE TO EAT

$$ ╳ **Ca' Mea.** The restaurant, clean and classic, serves northern Italian fare.
ITALIAN A mahogany ceiling and cherrywood floor in the dining room give way to a lighter, more elegant, birch-maple motif in the main dining room. Veal scaloppine with mozzarella and eggplant in a light red sauce is a crowd pleaser. Watch for the grilled octopus special. ⊠ *333 Warren St.* ☎ *518/822–0005* ⊟ *AE, MC, V* ⊙ *Closed Mon.*

$ ╳ **Mexican Radio.** Come off Warren Street into this slice of contempo-
MEXICAN rary Mexico—an outpost of Manhattan's Mexican Radio. High ceilings mean there's plenty of room for thematic art on the orange-hue walls, which are dominated by wrought-iron crucifixes and augmented by Mexican art. The cuisine is hearty, high-end Mexican; Cajun burritos filled with chorizo and shrimp and topped with jalapeno salsa, and steak and shrimp fajitas stand out. ⊠ *537 Warren St.* ☎ *518/828–7770* ⊟ *AE, MC, V.*

¢ ╳ **Muddy Cup Coffee House.** Large and comfortable, this coffeehouse is
CAFES filled with overstuffed furniture where you may lounge, read, and telecommute. More than 21 flavors of coffee compete with 10 types of

tea and a full menu of desserts. The owner is a studio musician with friends in the biz, so expect some musical surprises. ⊠*742 Warren St.* ☎*518/828–2210* ⊟*No credit cards.*

$$
ECLECTIC
✕**Red Dot Bar & Grill.** A trendy spot in the heart of the gallery district, this sleek restaurant offers a varied menu, from hamburgers and quesadillas to soft-shell crabs. The dining room has a large picture window overlooking the garden. The bar is open until 2 AM most nights. ⊠*321 Warren St.* ☎*518/828–3657* ⊟*MC, V* ☉*Closed Mon. and Tues.*

$
AMERICAN
✕**Wunderbar & Bistro.** The restaurant is a casual place to mix and mingle without putting too much of a dent in your wallet. The menu includes hearty Austrian dishes, including braised beef with potato dumplings. There are also chicken and sirloin burgers and pasta combos. ⊠*744 Warren St.* ☎*518/828–0555* ⊟*AE, MC, V* ☉*Closed Sun.*

WHERE TO STAY

$
🏠**Hudson City B&B.** This fanciful 19th-century home has a broad veranda and tower and is chock-full of period antiques. A crackling fireplace beckons in the first-floor parlor; in warmer seasons you can relax on the porch or in the garden. Bedrooms are decked out in pinks and florals; some beds are draped with swags. **Pros:** plenty of period charm; reasonable rates. **Cons:** some rooms can feel cluttered; not suitable for children. ⊠*326 Allen St.* ☎*518/822–8044* ⊕*www.hudsoncitybnb. com* ⮑*6 rooms* ��*In-room: refrigerator (some), Wi-Fi. In-hotel: some pets allowed, no-smoking rooms* ⊟*AE, MC, V* ⅋❘*BP.*

$$$
🏠**Union Street Guest House.** In an unassuming 1830 Greek Revival, this small hideaway offers two suites with private bathrooms. The rooms are spacious, high-ceilinged, and furnished with a mix of antique and mid-20th-century furniture and art. One suite has two bedrooms with queen beds; the other has one bedroom with a queen and a twin. Feather pillows and quilts abound, and wireless Internet access is available. This is not a B&B and offers no food. **Pros:** near lots of dining and shopping; pleasant rooms. **Cons:** no breakfast; not a tranquil setting. ⊠*349 Union St. 12534* ☎*518/828–0958* ⊕*www.unionstreetguesthouse.com* ⮑*8 suites* ⅋*In-room: refrigerator (some), Wi-Fi. In-hotel: some pets allowed, no-smoking rooms* ⊟*AE, D, MC, V.*

THE ARTS

The annual **Hudson ArtsWalk** (⊠*209 Warren St.* ☎*518/671–6213* ⊕*www.artscolumbia.org*), sponsored by the Columbia County Council on the Arts, takes place in October. The event, a showcase for local visual artists, attracts thousands of visitors who come to ogle a wide array of exhibits and demonstrations as well as to see concerts, dance performances, lectures, and poetry readings. Most of the action is on Warren Street.

The **Carrie Haddad Gallery** (⊠*622 Warren St.* ☎*518/828–1915* ⊕*www. carriehaddadgallery.com*) was the first art gallery to open in Hudson, in 1991, and shows a mix of established and newly discovered artists in a large two-floor complex. A cultural anchor in the city center, the **Hudson Opera House** (⊠*327 Warren St.* ☎*518/822–9003* ⊕*www. hudsonoperahouse.org*) offers a steady program of low-cost culture, including jazz, folk, blues, and classical concerts.

7

SHOPPING

Historical Materialism (✉ *601 Warren St.* ☎ *518/671–6151*), a large, airy corner store, offers antiques from all periods, with an emphasis on lighting and clean design. **Keystone on the Hudson** (✉ *746 Warren St.* ☎ *518/822–1019*) specializes in urns, fountains, cornices, and plenty of imposing statuary. The owner also offers folk art, ceramics, and furniture. **Lili and Loo** (✉ *259 Warren St.* ☎ *518/822–9492*) stocks Asian- and African-inspired pottery, furniture, and housewares. There's lots of finely crafted bamboo. **Ornamentum** (✉ *506½ Warren St.* ☎ *518/671–6770*) is a contemporary jewelry store. All the fanciful jewelry for sale is by fine artists whose work appears in museums around the world. **Rural Residence** (✉ *316 Warren St.* ☎ *518/822–1061*) carries an assortment of candles, coffee-table books, Italian and Belgian linens, and other refined trifles. **Theron Ware** (✉ *548 Warren St.* ☎ *518/828–9744*) is the archetype of Hudson antiques shops: a single storefront populated with rare and pricey treasures. It specializes in European and American antiques and artworks from the 17th through the 19th century.

KINDERHOOK

11 mi northwest of Hillsdale.

Henry Hudson disembarked from his ship, *Half Moon,* and stepped onto the fertile land we now know as Kinderhook in 1609. Shortly afterward, Dutch and Swedish settlers pushed the Lenni Lenape out, expanded their fur trade, tilled fields, established mills, made wagons, and, by the 18th century, set up taverns. Kinderhook's location at a heavily traveled crossroads made it a popular resting spot for travelers, including Benedict Arnold after he was wounded in battle.

One of Kinderhook's most notable residents was Martin Van Buren, eighth president of the United States. You can retrace the steps of early American history by walking or driving through the village, which brims with well-preserved Federal and Dutch Colonial architecture. From here it's a short hop to Chatham, where you can spend a day bouncing around the hip shopping district and checking out art galleries.

WHAT TO SEE

Shaker Museum and Library. You can learn about the daily life of the Shakers from one of the largest collections focusing on their culture. The extensive array of clothing and household textiles on exhibit is a highlight. The series of red barns also displays furniture, tools, machinery, and decorative objects from all of the major Shaker communities. ✉ *88 Shaker Museum Rd., off Rte. 13, Old Chatham* ☎ *518/794–9100* 🎫 *$8* ☯ *Late May–Oct., Wed.–Mon. 10–5.*

SPORTS AND THE OUTDOORS

If you have the need for speed, check out the **Lebanon Valley Speedway** (✉ *1746 U.S. 20, West Lebanon* ☎ *518/794–9606* ⊕ *www.lebanonvalley. com*). Gates open at 5 PM.

NIGHTLIFE AND THE ARTS

Make a detour to explore cutting-edge contemporary sculpture at **Art Omi** (⊠*59 Letter S Rd. off Rte. 22, 2 mi west of Rte. 66, Ghent* ☎*518/392–7656* ⊕*www.artomi.org*), an international center for artists where giant heads spring fully formed from the ground in **Fields Sculpture Park**; about 80 artworks are scattered around 90 acres of the park. You can bring a picnic and spend a full afternoon roaming the park. The sculpture park is free and open daily from dawn to dusk.

WHERE TO EAT

$$ ✕**Blue Plate.** The paper tablecloths and the crayons displayed in water
AMERICAN glasses reflect the relaxed nature of this eatery. From shrimp étouffée to hamburgers, everything here is just right. The kitchen makes the most of local produce and gets its cheese and lamb from the well-regarded Old Chatham Sheepherding Company. Vegetarian entrées change nightly, drawing aficionados from miles around. ⊠*1 Kinderhook St., Chatham* ☎*518/392–7711* ▤*DC, MC, V* ◷*Closed Jan. and Mon. No lunch.*

¢ ✕**Our Daily Bread.** Baskets of fresh baguettes and focaccia greet you as
KOSHER you step inside. Glass counters hold lush chocolate temptations and bags of apricot rugelach. You can pick up goodies for a picnic, or grab a table and dig into seared bok choy or grilled rainbow trout. Get here early, as the place is only open until 5:30. ⊠*54 Main St., Chatham* ☎*518/392–9852* ▤*No credit cards* ◷*Closed Mon. and Tues. No dinner.*

WHERE TO STAY

$ ⊞**Blue Spruce Inn & Suites.** You can sip your cider from Golden Harvest Farms, located directly across the street, at one of several strategically placed picnic benches scattered on the front lawn. The motel-style accommodations show signs of inspiration—some have handsome black-and-white photographs reminiscent of Ansel Adams. Suites have eat-in kitchens and living rooms with sleeper sofas. **Pros:** good for extended stays; cute coffee shop. **Cons:** drab decor; too kitschy for some. ⊠*3093 U.S. Rte. 9, Valatie* ☎*518/758–9711* ⊕*www.bluespruceinnsuites. com* ⇆*22 rooms, 6 suites* ⌂*In-hotel: kitchen (some), Wi-Fi. In-hotel: restaurant, pool, some pets allowed, no-smoking rooms* ▤*AE, DC, MC, V.*

$$ ⊞**Inn at Silver Maple Farm.** Exposed timbers, wide-plank floors, antique trunks, and custom-made cupboards evoke a Shaker spirit at this 1830 dairy farm. On the way up to the Loft Room—which recalls a romantic, shabby-chic beach cottage—you pass a shimmering hallway mural of flower sprigs, silver maples, and a rogue bunny. Ralph Lauren sheets complement the elegantly simple rooms. You could lose hours pondering the Berkshires from the expansive back deck. **Pros:** tranquil setting; lovely views. **Cons:** young children not allowed in some rooms. ⊠*1871 Rte. 295, East Chatham* ☎*518/781–3600* ⊕*www.silvermaplefarm. com* ⇆*9 rooms, 2 suites* ⌂*In-hotel: refrigerator (some), Wi-Fi. In-hotel: dining room, no-smoking rooms* ▤*AE, DC, MC, V* ⎜⎜*BP.*

$$$ ⊞ **Peter Van Schaack House.** Symmetrical topiaries flank the steps to this 1785 Georgian manor with leaded-glass windows. A major renovation in 1865 resulted in the Victorian demeanor you see today; amid all the original artwork, period architectural details, and antiques, you

could easily mistake your surroundings for a museum. In the dramatic crimson hall, stairs rise to the four guest rooms, all stocked with plush bathrobes, 360-thread-count Egyptian cotton sheets, boxes of chocolates, bottled water, and fruit baskets. **Pros:** chef prepares breakfast; plenty of period charm. **Cons:** children under 12 are not allowed; not all rooms have air-conditining. ⊠*20 Broad St.* ☎*518/758–6118* ⊕*www. vanschaackhouse.com* ⤴*4 rooms* ⌂*In-room: Wi-Fi, no TV (some), no phone, no a/c (some). In-hotel: restaurant, no kids under 12, no-smoking rooms* ⊟*AE, MC, V* ⦿|*BP.*

New York City

WORD OF MOUTH

"For us New York is always about the theater—Broadway, off-Broadway, off-off-Broadway, whatever. We've been known to see four plays in three days."

—abram

"There IS something about the Tiffany's box. Overpriced? Maybe. Iconic? Definitely . . . Even if it's something small, pulling out that blue box will definitely put a smile on her face."

—starrsville

New York, New York is a quick-change artist, famous for transforming overnight—so what's packed and popular this month may be gone by the time you arrive. It's impossible to see everything, regardless of its staying power, so instead try to soak in the sheer amount of culture, restaurants, exhibitions, and people here, and you'll be acting like a jaded New Yorker in no time.

This is a city that is made for pedestrians: Manhattan's grid makes for easy orientation, subway stations are relatively close together, and there are so many other pedestrians that you'll find strength in numbers when you choose to cross against the light (not that you heard it from us). Pick a neighborhood, any neighborhood, and simply wander around to get a feel for it. Quick visits can vary wildly based on when you visit. The Financial District is a go-go 9-to-5 zone that turns eerily quiet at night amidst the huge commercial towers and twinkling lights, while areas like the East Village operate at a sleepy crawl during the day only to come alive with shows and frenetic pub crawls when the sun goes down.

For a city so dedicated to the finer things, great swathes of it are still industry-oriented. There's a garment district in Chelsea, a diamond district in Midtown, and wholly unidentifiable exotic fruits and vegetables at markets in Chinatown. But whole areas are always in flux, reinventing themselves anew in an eye blink. There's hardly any meatpacking going on in the Meatpacking District these days compared to a decade ago, and stretches of Bleecker in the West Village have gone from ramshackle clothing shops to homes for Marc Jacobs and Ralph Lauren. In short, Manhattan always makes way for the new.

ORIENTATION AND PLANNING

GETTING ORIENTED

New York City is composed of five boroughs (Manhattan, Brooklyn, the Bronx, Queens, and Staten Island), but when you say "the city," one assumes Manhattan. The same goes for "New York"—usually a reference to the city, not state.

Manhattan is an island, 2½ mi wide, and 13 mi long. To the west is the Hudson River and then New Jersey; to the east is the East River and then Long Island, with the boroughs of Brooklyn and Queens sprawling across its western end. To the north is the Bronx (home to both the amazing zoo and the new Yankee Stadium). To the south, across the water, are Ellis and Liberty islands, and the city's fifth borough, Staten Island.

NEW YORK CITY'S TOP REASONS TO GO

Bright lights of Broadway: The Great White Way is New York's number-one attraction. The fabulously restored historic theaters—and the popular productions within them—draw crowds to the bedazzling showtime nexus at Times Square.

Magnificent museums: If Times Square didn't put you on sensory overload, New York's museums surely will. Get dizzy circling all the master canvases, bronze statues, and ancient artifacts at the Metropolitan Museum of Art (or simply, the Met); whisper your share of oohs and aahs at the Museum of Modern Art (MoMa); and romp around the towering reassembled dinosaur skeletons at the American Museum of Natural History.

Central Park: The locals' backyard playground is the lush center of the city. Come to walk, visit the zoo, ice-skate, or just relax in an oasis of green.

Fashionable finds: New York City shopping is a nonstop eye-opener, from the pristine couture houses flanking Madison Avenue and large department stores on 5th Avenue to the shops and street vendors with marked-down wares in Chinatown.

Iconic places: Thanks to TV and film, you've seen New York and its trademark buildings and bridges time and time again. Even if you don't have time to step inside, these oh-so–New York sites deserve to be at least spotted by you on your visit to the city: Rockefeller Center, the Empire State Building, Carnegie Hall, the Statue of Liberty, Grand Central Terminal, the New York Stock Exchange, and the Brooklyn Bridge.

PLANNING

GETTING HERE

If you're driving here, you'll reach the city by either a bridge or a tunnel. If you're coming from the south or west, you can come in via the Holland Tunnel (in Lower Manhattan), the Lincoln Tunnel (in Midtown), or the George Washington Bridge (on the Upper West Side/Harlem). From the north, Interstates 87 and 95 connect the Hudson Valley and Connecticut with the Bronx and Manhattan. Connecting Manhattan with Brooklyn, Queens, and Long Island are, from north to south, the Queensboro Bridge, the Queens–Midtown Tunnel, the Williamsburg Bridge, the Manhattan Bridge, the Brooklyn Bridge, and the Brooklyn–Battery Tunnel.

Three airports serve New York City: John F. Kennedy International Airport (JFK) and LaGuardia Airport (LGA) in Queens, and Newark Liberty International Airport (EWR) in Newark, New Jersey. Public buses serve all three, but slowly, so most locals opt for the train (not an option from LaGuardia), a shuttle, or a cab.

To catch a cab or other ground-transportation service, follow the GROUND TRANSPORTATION signs to baggage claim. Taxi stands are outside the baggage-claim areas, and shuttle services have designated spots along the curb. Cab fares from LaGuardia into the city are metered, but generally a ride is $25–$35 plus tip and tolls to most destinations in

Manhattan; travel time is usually 20–40 minutes. For JFK, taxis charge a flat fee to Manhattan of $45 plus tolls and tip; travel time is 35–60 minutes. Cab fare from Newark into Manhattan cost more because you're crossing state lines. It ranges from $40 to $65 plus tolls; travel time is 20 to 45 minutes.

SHUTTLES   **New York Airport Service** (☎718/875–8200 ⊕*www.nyairportservice.com*) runs buses between JFK and LaGuardia airports, as well as buses from both airports into Manhattan, stopping at Grand Central Terminal, Port Authority Bus Terminal, Bryant Park, Penn Station, and Midtown hotels between 31st and 60th streets. Fares cost between $12 and $15 one way and $21 to $27 round-trip. Buses operate from 6:15 AM to 11:10 PM from the airports and between 5 AM and 10 PM going to the airports. There is also an affiliated shuttle, Go Airlink Shuttle (⊕*www.goairlinkshuttle.com*), that goes from Newark Airport to Manhattan; the fare is $20 one way and $39 round-trip. For Go Airlink Shuttle, go to the ticket counter at baggage claim or call from a courtesy phone.

The **Newark Liberty Airport Express** (☎877/863–9275 ⊕*www.coachusa.com/ss.airport.asp*) runs its buses between Newark Airport and Manhattan, stopping at Port Authority Bus Terminal, Bryant Park, and Grand Central Terminal. Fares cost $15 each way or $25 round-trip. Buses operate daily from 4 AM to 1 AM, running every 15 minutes. Travel time is 45 minutes to an hour. Tickets must be purchased before boarding (either online or company's agent at the ground transportation center).

SuperShuttle (☎212/258–3826 ⊕*www.supershuttle.com*) vans travel to and from Manhattan to JFK, LaGuardia, and Newark. These blue vans will stop at your home, office, or hotel. You can reach a shuttle via courtesy phones near the airports' baggage-claim areas. For travel to the airport, the company recommends you make your requests at least 24 hours in advance. Fares range from $13 to $22 per person.

TRAINS AND   Taking a train is an option from JFK and Newark. Trains arrive and
SUBWAY   leave from New York's Penn Station (not to be confused with Newark's Penn Station) and they connect with AirTrain, an elevated light-rail system that winds through the airports' terminals.

If you're flying into Newark, you can travel with **New Jersey Transit** (⊕*www.njtransit.com*) by getting on the AirTrain at the airport, which will take you to the Newark Airport stop, and then boarding the train to New York Penn Station—don't get it confused with *Newark* Penn Station, which is usually the first stop. (After you get off the AirTrain, you'll need to go upstairs and purchase your train ticket from the vending machine and then go through the turnstile to head down to the train tracks. Note that you need your train ticket to get through the turnstile and to give the train conductor, so don't forget to retrieve it when it comes back out at the turnstile.) Total travel time from Newark to New York Penn Station in Manhattan is approximately 20 minutes and costs $15. AirTrain runs every three minutes from 5 AM to midnight and every 15 minutes from midnight to 5 AM. There is no cost for Newark's AirTrain, but you need your train ticket to exit.

Alternatively, if you want to save a little money and aren't in a big hurry—or if you're staying in Lower Manhattan—you can purchase a ticket ($7.75) to *Newark* Penn Station instead of *New York* Penn Station, and, from there, switch to a PATH train ($1.75), which goes to Manhattan 24 hours a day, running every 10 minutes on weekdays and every 15 to 30 minutes on weeknights and weekends. The train runs on the red line and will take you to the World Trade Center site stop in Lower Manhattan; if you want to go to the Village or Midtown instead, get off at the Journal Square stop and switch to the yellow line that makes stops at Christopher Street in the West Village, and four stops along 6th Avenue: West 9th Street, West 14th Street, West 23rd Street, and West 33rd Street.

If you're flying info JFK, you can take the AirTrain ($5) to the Jamaica or Howard Beach station stops. AirTrain JFK runs 24 hours, leaving every 4–8 minutes during peak times and every 12 minutes during low traffic times.

From Jamaica, you can take a Long Island Rail Road (⊕*www.lirr. org*) train directly into New York Penn Station (about a 20-minute ride, $7.25 or $5.25 depending on time of day), or you can access the **NYC Transit** (⊕*www.mta.info/nyct*) E/J/Z lines at the adjacent Sutphin Boulevard/Archer Avenue subway station. Consult a subway map for where each of these lines go. The subway takes a bit longer into Midtown Manhattan than the LIRR, but if you're staying on the Upper East Side, the E line may be convenient for you. From Howard Beach, AirTrain JFK links to the A subway line's Howard Beach station (if you take this option back to the airport from Manhattan, be sure to take the A train marked FAR ROCKAWAY or ROCKAWAY PARK, not LEFFERTS BOULEVARD). It's generally less than an hour on the A train from Howard Station to Midtown Manhattan. Subway fare is $2.

GETTING AROUND
In Manhattan, you can walk, take the subway, or hail a cab—or you can drive, but we advise against it. If you've driven here, you'll likely enjoy your time better if you leave your car in a garage until your stay in the city is complete. If you're flying in, there's no need to rent a car at all. Just take a cab, train, or one of the airport shuttles from the airport to your hotel *(⇨ Getting Here, above, for shuttle and train information)*.

New York City can seem daunting, but it's not as difficult to navigate as you may think. Most streets in Manhattan form a grid, with numbered streets running east and west (getting progressively higher as you go north) and numbered (and a few named, such as Madison and Park) avenues running north and south (getting progressively higher as you go west); and then there's Broadway, which runs on a diagonal from northwest to southeast until it gets to Union Square and then branches into two streets: West Broadway and Broadway, both of which head straight south. Addresses in New York are best understood when the cross streets are included (for example, 1745 Broadway, between 55th and 56th streets). We include the nearest subway stops for each of our listings, as well as noting cross streets.

When hailing a cab, don't bother to wave at cars whose rooftop lights aren't illuminated; these already have passengers inside. Taxis whose roof lights are only lighted at the edges—not the center—are off-duty, and will rarely pick you up unless your destination is on the way to the garage. Cabbies make their money in tips; for a typical ride, tack 10% to 15% onto your fare.

WHEN TO GO

New York City weather, like its people, is a study in extremes. Winter might bring bone-chilling winds and an occasional traffic-snarling snowfall, but you're just as likely to experience mild afternoons sandwiched by cool temperatures. Even in frigid February you might consider leaving your winter coat at home, opting instead for two layers, one of which you can tie around your waist when necessary.

In late spring and early summer, streets fill with parades and sidewalk concerts and Central Park yields free performances. Late August temperatures sometimes claw skyward, giving many subway stations the feel and bouquet of dingy saunas (no wonder the Hamptons are so crowded). This is why autumn brings palpable excitement, with stunning yellow-and-bronze foliage (generally at its peak in late October and early November) complementing the dawn of a new cultural season. Between October and May, museums mount major exhibitions, most Broadway shows open, and formal opera, ballet, and concert seasons begin.

VISITOR INFORMATION

Visit **NYC & Company Convention & Visitors Bureau** (✉ *810 7th Ave., between W. 52nd and W. 53rd Sts., 3rd fl., Times Square* ☎ *212/484–1222* ⊕ *www.nycvisit.com* Ⓜ *N, R, W to 49th or E, V to 7th Ave.*) for brochures, subway and bus maps, discount coupons to theaters and attractions, and multilingual information counselors. In addition to its main center near Times Square, the bureau also runs kiosks in Lower Manhattan at City Hall Park and at Federal Hall National Memorial at 26 Wall Street, in Chinatown at the triangle where Canal, Walker, and Baxter streets meet and at the Apollo Theater in Harlem at 253 West 125th Street.

The "Visitors" section of **NYC.gov,** the official New York City Web site, has particularly useful information about events around town. If the local morning news channel you've tuned in to turns out to be exasperatingly uninformative, go online to **New York 1** (⊕ *www.ny1.com*), which is frequently updated with the city's breaking stories as well as mass transit and weather information. And if our sometimes enigmatic bus or subway maps are causing you to scratch your head, pull up the site for **HopStop** (⊕ *www.hopstop.com*) for directions.

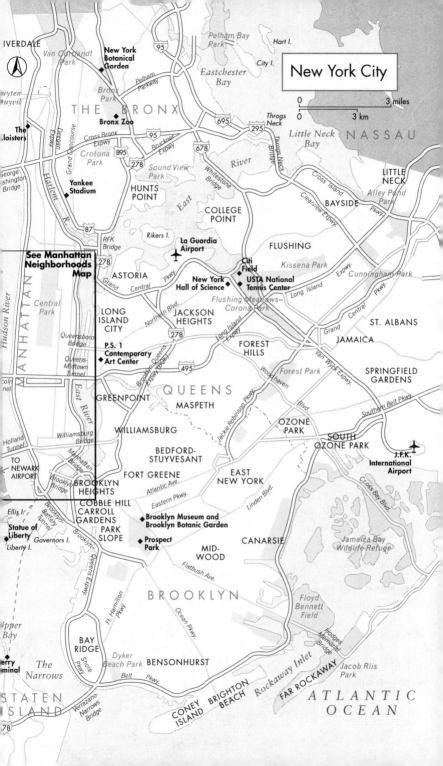

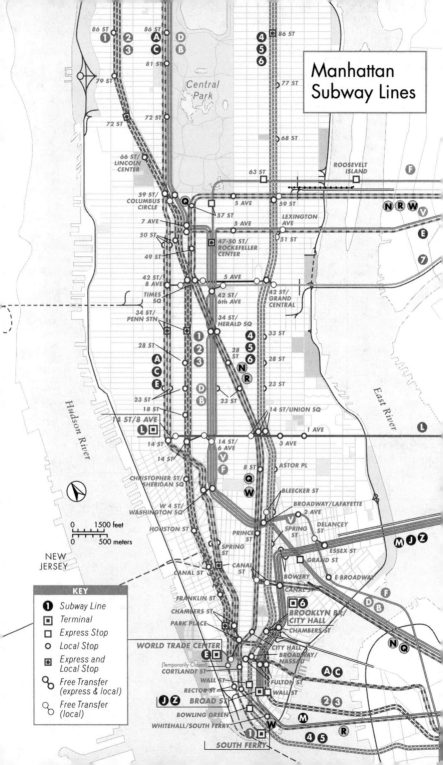

EXPLORING NEW YORK CITY

LOWER MANHATTAN

FINANCIAL DISTRICT

⇨ *Lower Manhattan map for sights in this section.*

New York was born on the southern tip of Manhattan, and a visit here provides a glimpse of the city both past and present. From the 19th-century brick facades of South Street Seaport to the skyscraper-lined canyons of Wall Street and lower Broadway, this is an area you can fully appreciate only by walking its streets.

GETTING HERE

Many subway lines service this area. The Fulton Street Broadway–Nassau station, serviced by nine different subway lines, puts you within walking distance of City Hall, South Street Seaport, and the World Trade Center site. If you're coming from New Jersey, the PATH comes into the World Trade Center station.

❷ Jutting out at the southernmost point of Manhattan, leafy **Battery Park** provides plenty of places to sit and rest, including two tiers of wood benches that line the promenade facing New York Harbor. From here, you can see Governors Island, a former Coast Guard installation now managed by the National Park Service; a hilly Staten Island in the distance; the Statue of Liberty; Ellis Island; and the old railway terminal in Liberty State Park, on the mainland in Jersey City, New Jersey. On crystal-clear days you can see all the way to Port Elizabeth's cranes, which seem to mimic Lady Liberty's stance. The park's main structure is Castle Clinton National Monument, the ticket office site and takeoff point for ferries to the Statue of Liberty and Ellis Island.

❽ **Brooklyn Bridge.** "A drive-through cathedral" is how the critic James

Fodor'sChoice Wolcott describes one of New York's noblest and most recognized

★ landmarks, which spans the East River and connects Manhattan to Brooklyn. A walk across the bridge's promenade—a boardwalk elevated above the roadway and shared by pedestrians, in-line skaters, and bicyclists—takes about 40 minutes from the heart of Brooklyn Heights to Manhattan's civic center. It's well worth traversing for the astounding views. The roadway is supported by a web of steel cables, hung from the towers and attached to block-long anchorages on either shore. Ⓜ *4, 5, 6 to Brooklyn Bridge/City Hall; J, M, Z to Chambers St. or A, C to High St.-Brooklyn Bridge.*

❹ **Federal Hall National Memorial.** It's a museum now, but this site has a most notable claim: George Washington was sworn in here as the first president of the United States in 1789, when the building was Federal Hall of the new nation. Once we lost capital rights to Philadelphia in 1790, Federal Hall reverted to New York's City Hall, then was demolished in 1812 when the present City Hall was completed. The museum within covers 400 years of New York City's history, with a focus on the life and times of what is now the city's financial district. You can spot this building easily—it was modeled on the Parthenon, and a statue of George

8

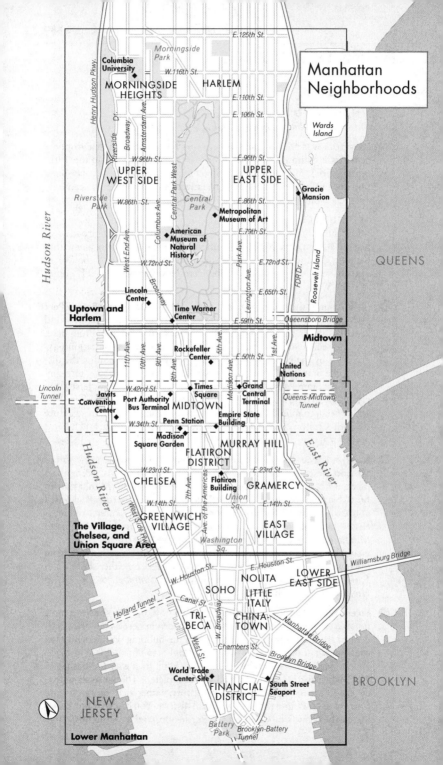

Washington is planted quite obtrusively on the steps. ✉ *26 Wall St., at Nassau St., Lower Manhattan* ☎ *212/825–6870* 🔲 *Free* 🕑 *Weekdays 9–5* Ⓜ *2, 3, 4, 5 to Wall St.; A, C to Broadway/Nassau; J, M, Z to Broad St.*

③ New York Stock Exchange (NYSE). Unfortunately you can't tour it, but it's certainly worth ogling. At the intersection of Wall and Broad streets, the exchange is hard to miss. The neoclassical building, dating to 1903, has six Corinthian columns supporting a pediment with a sculpture entitled *Integrity Protecting the Words of Man.* ✉ *Lower Manhattan* Ⓜ *2, 3, 4, 5 to Wall St.; J, M, Z to Broad St.*

> **FREE FERRY TO LADY LIBERTY**
>
> About 70,000 people ride the Staten Island Ferry every day, and you should be one of them. Without having to pay a cent, you get great views of the Statue of Liberty, Ellis Island, and the southern tip of Manhattan. You don't need to purchase a ticket; just line up and board at the Whitehall Terminal at Whitehall and South streets, near the east end of Battery Park. Once the ferry reaches Staten Island, you need to disembark and then reboard to go back. Ⓜ *1 to South Ferry; R, W to Whitehall St.; or 4, 5 to Bowling Green.*

⑦ South Street Seaport Historic District.

Fodor'sChoice ★ ☾ Had this charming cobblestone corner of the city not been declared a historic district in 1977, we have no doubt you'd be glancing indifferently at hyperdeveloped skyscrapers in this spot rather than at the city's largest concentration of early-19th-century commercial buildings. If you've been either to Boston's Quincy Market or Baltimore's Harborplace, you may feel a flash of déjà vu—the same company leased, restored, and adapted the existing buildings, preserving the commercial feel of centuries past. The result blends a quasi-authentic historical district with a homogenous shopping mall. Also here, at 12 Fulton Street, is the main lobby of the **South Street Seaport Museum** (☎ *212/748–8600* ⊕ *www.southstseaport. org* 🕑 *Apr.–Oct., Tues.–Sun. 10–6; Nov.–Mar., Fri.–Mon. 10–5*), which hosts walking tours, hands-on exhibits, and fantastic creative programs for children, all with a nautical theme. You can purchase tickets ($10) at either 12 Fulton Street or Pier 16 Visitors Center. ✉ *South Street Seaport, Lower Manhattan* ☎ *212/732–7678 events and shopping information* ⊕ *www.southstreetseaport.com* 🔲 *$5 to ships, galleries, walking tours, Maritime Crafts Center, films, and other seaport events* Ⓜ *A, C, 2, 3, 4, 5, J, M, Z to Fulton St./Broadway Nassau.*

① Statue of Liberty and Ellis Island. For millions of immigrants, the first

Fodor'sChoice ★ ☾ glimpse of America was the Statue of Liberty. You get a taste of the thrill they must have experienced as you approach Liberty Island on the ferry from Battery Park (or Liberty State Park, if you're coming from New Jersey) and witness the statue grow from a vaguely defined figure on the horizon into a towering, stately colossus. Between 1892 and 1924, approximately 12 million men, women, and children first set foot on U.S. soil at the Ellis Island federal immigration facility. The island's main building is now the Ellis Island Immigration Museum. ⇨ *"Gateway to the New World" in-focus feature in Chapter 1 for more on these two star attractions.* ☎ *212/363–3200, 212/269–5755 ferry information,*

8

CLOSE UP

A Good Walk: Financial District

Late in the evening of December 15, 1989, sculptor Arturo Di Modica left a 7,000-pound surprise gift for New York City under the Christmas tree in front of the New York Stock Exchange—his bronze Charging Bull statue. The bull quickly became the icon of Wall Street. Ask New Yorkers who don't frequent the downtown area where the statue is and they'll usually tell you it's somewhere on Wall Street near the stock exchange. But the statue actually resides in **Bowling Green**, where it was moved after police complained it was blocking traffic in its original location. Since the city never commissioned it, the bull is still officially dubbed a "temporary installation."

After you pose for snapshots with the bull, head northeast to **Wall Street**, one of the most famous thoroughfares in the world. The epicenter of Wall Street is—you guessed it—the **New York Stock Exchange**, at the intersection of Wall and Broad streets. The stock exchange traces its beginnings to a group of brokers who, in 1792, shortly after Alexander Hamilton

issued the first bonds in an attempt to raise money to cover Revolution-caused debt, were in the habit of meeting under a buttonwood tree that once grew on Wall Street. The exchange itself isn't open to visitors, but there is a related museum at the **Federal Hall National Memorial.**

Look at the facade of 23 Wall Street, just across from the exchange. The deep pockmarks and craters were created on September 16, 1920, when, at noon, a horse-drawn wagon packed with explosives detonated in front of the building, killing 33 people and injuring 400. Those responsible were never apprehended and no one ever claimed credit for what was the worst terrorist attack on American soil until the Oklahoma City bombing on April 19, 1995.

Marking Wall Street's far west end is **Trinity Church**, whose parish was founded by King William III of England in 1697. Trinity's burial ground serves as a resting place for a half dozen notables, including Alexander Hamilton.

877/523–9849 ticket reservations ⊕www.statuecruises.com ✉Free; ferry $12 round-trip ⊙Daily 9–5; extended hrs. in summer.

⑤ Trinity Church. Alexander Hamilton is buried under a white-stone pyramid in the church's graveyard, not far from a monument commemorating steamboat inventor Robert Fulton (buried in the Livingston family vault with his wife). The church (the third on this site) was designed in 1846 by Richard Upjohn. Its most notable feature is the set of enormous bronze doors designed by Richard Morris Hunt to recall Lorenzo Ghiberti's doors for the Baptistery in Florence, Italy. *Trinity Root*, a 12½-foot-high, 3-ton sculpture by Steven Tobin cast from the sycamore tree struck by debris on 9/11 behind St. Paul's Chapel was installed in front of the church on September, 11, 2005. A museum outlines the church's history; a daily tour is given at 2. ✉74 *Trinity Pl., Broadway at head of Wall St., Lower Manhattan* ☎212/602–0800 ⊕www. trinitywallstreet.org ⊙ *Weekdays 7–6, Sat. 8–4, Sun. 7–4; churchyard*

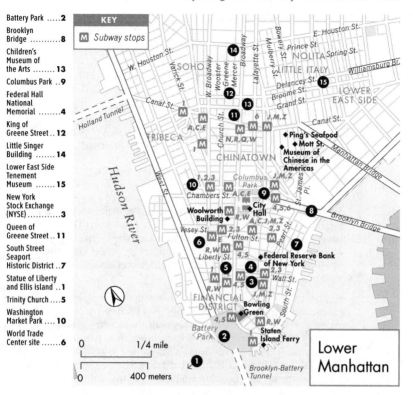

Lower
Manhattan

Nov.–Apr., daily 7–4; May–Oct., weekdays 7–5, Sat. 8–3, Sun. 7–3 Ⓜ *4, 5 to Wall St.; R, W to Rector St.*

❻ World Trade Center site. On September 11, 2001, terrorist hijackers steered two commercial jets into the World Trade Center's 110-story towers, demolishing them and five outlying buildings and killing nearly 3,000 people. Dubbed Ground Zero, the fenced-in 16-acre work site that emerged from the rubble has come to symbolize the personal and historical impact of the attack. In an attempt to grasp the reality of the destruction, to pray, or simply to witness history, visitors come to glimpse the site, clustering at the two-story see-through fence surrounding it. Temporary panels listing the names of those who died in the attacks and recounting the history of the twin towers have been mounted along the fence on the west side of Church Street and the north side of Liberty Street. ✉*Between Church and West Sts., from Vesey to Liberty, Lower Manhattan* Ⓜ*R, W to Cortland St.*

CHINATOWN AND TRIBECA
⇨*Lower Manhattan map for sights in this section.*

Tucked to the west, south of Canal Street, residential TriBeCa (Triangle Below Canal) has a quieter vibe and still owes much of its cred to Robert De Niro, whose investments in the area include the TriBeCa Grill and the nonprofit TriBeCa Film Center. Unlike the in-your-face commercial presence of nearby SoHo (for South of Houston) and NoLita (for South of Little Italy), TriBeCa keeps more to itself with self-assurance and urban grace. And while TriBeCa's money is hidden away behind grand industrial facades, you can get a taste of it at one of the posh neighborhood restaurants or when the stars turn out for the annual TriBeCa Film Festival in spring.

> **WORD OF MOUTH**
>
> You could do half day in Wall Street area. The NY stock exchange used to have a very good tour and viewing area, as did the commodities exchange, off Fulton Street. [it's] really wild to see all the trading chaos. Then I'd go by St. Paul's chapel on Broadway."
>
> —bigbomoho

Walking the photogenic streets of TriBeCa, full of cast-iron factories as well as a time-defying stretch of Federal row houses on Harrison Street, you can understand why celebrities like Robert De Niro have bought apartments here. The two-block-long Staple Street is a favorite of urban cinematographers with its connecting overhead walkway. At 60 Hudson Street is the art-deco Western Union Building—try to sneak a peek at its magnificent lobby.

Chinatown, by contrast, is a living, breathing anything-but-quiet ethnic enclave: a quarter of the city's 400,000 Chinese residents live here above storefronts crammed with souvenir shops and restaurants serving every imaginable regional Chinese cuisine, from modest dumplings to sumptuous Hong Kong feasts. What started as a 7-block area has morphed into more than 40 blocks above and below Canal Street with tea shops, restaurants, Buddhist temples, herbalists, acupuncturists, and pungent open-air markets.

GETTING HERE
Subway lines N, R, Q, W, 6, J, M and Z (Canal Street) and the B, D (Grand Street) all serve the Chinatown area. The 1 subway line stops in the heart of TriBeCa (Franklin Street).

⑨ **Columbus Park.** People-watching is the thing in this newly restored park.
Fodor'sChoice If you swing by in the morning, you'll see men and women practicing tai
★ chi; the afternoons bring intense games of mah-jongg. In the mid-19th century the park was known as Five Points—the point where Mulberry Street, Anthony (now Worth) Street, Cross (now Park) Street, Orange (now Baxter) Street, and Little Water Street (no longer in existence) intersected—and was notoriously ruled by dangerous Irish gangs. In the 1880s a neighborhood-improvement campaign brought about the park's creation with its historic pavilion. Ⓜ N, Q, R, W, 6 to Canal St.

⑩ **Washington Market Park.** This landscaped recreation space with a gazebo
Fodor'sChoice and playground—ideal for permitting the kids to blow off steam—
★ was named after the great food market that once sprawled over the
☺ area. Across the street at the elementary school are a stout red tower resembling a lighthouse and a fence with iron ship figures—reminders of the neighborhood's dockside past. There's a small greenmarket here

A Good Walk: Chinatown

For a quick taste of Chinatown, head to **Mott Street,** Chinatown's main thoroughfare. This is where the first Chinese immigrants (mostly men) settled in tenements in the late 1880s. Today the street is dense with restaurants, hair salons and barbershops, bakeries, tea parlors, and souvenir shops, most of them lying below Canal Street. If you plan it right, you can create a movable feast, starting with soup dumplings, a specialty from Shanghai, and continuing with Peking duck, a yellow custard cake, and a jasmine bubble tea, each at a different

place. Or, you can have it all come to you at **Ping's Seafood** (⊠ *22 Mott St., near Worth St.* ☎ *212/602–9988*), with dim sum for lunch.

The few blocks above Canal overflow with food markets selling vegetables and fish (some still alive and squirming). Walk carefully as the sidewalks can be slick from the ice underneath the eels, blue crabs, snapper, and shrimp that seem to look back at you as you pass by. A good place to get oriented or arrange a walking tour is the **Museum of Chinese in the Americas.**

on Wednesday and Saturday. ⊠ *Greenwich St. between Chambers and Duane Sts., TriBeCa* Ⓜ *1, 2, 3 to Chambers St.*

SOHO AND LITTLE ITALY
⇨ *Lower Manhattan map for sights in this section.*

SoHo (South of Houston) and NoLita (North of Little Italy) are both shopper's paradises, supertrendy, painfully overcrowded on the weekends, often overpriced, and undeniably glamorous. Not too long ago though, these neighborhoods were quiet warrens of artists' lofts and galleries, and the only reason to visit was to go galley hopping. Checking out the art is still a big reason to come to SoHo, but shopping has for the most part supplanted the quest for visual stimulation. In between whipping your credit card out of your wallet and feverishly searching for a café with empty seats, do take a few seconds to savor what other passersby may miss: the neighborhood's Belgian brick cobblestones and turn-of-the-20th-century lampposts.

SoHo also has the world's greatest concentration of cast-iron buildings, built in response to fires that wiped out much of lower Manhattan in the mid-18th century. Although it's hard to single out any one block, as almost all have gorgeous examples of the various cast-iron styles (Italianate, Victorian Gothic, Greek Revival), Greene Street has two standouts, the **Queen of Greene Street** and the **King of Greene Street** (⇨ *listings below)*. Even the lampposts in this neighborhood are architectural gems with their turn-of-the-20th-century bishop's-crook style, adorned with cast-iron curlicues from their bases to their curved tops; they're the perfect complement to the paving stones below.

Just east of Broadway you'll find the remains of what once was a thriving, lively community of Italian Americans: the tangle of streets that make up Little Italy. A few nostalgic blocks surrounding Mulberry Street between NoLita and ultrabusy Canal Street are all that remain of the vast community that once dominated the area. (If you want to see a modern-day Little Italy, head up to Arthur Avenue in the Bronx.) It's still a cheerful salute to all things Italian with red, green, and white street decorations on permanent display and specialty grocers and cannelloni makers dishing up delights.

GETTING HERE

SoHo is roughly bounded by Houston Street, Canal Street, 6th Avenue, and Lafayette Street. To the east, NoLita grows daily but lies pretty much between Houston, the Bowery, Kenmare, and Lafayette. There are plenty of subways that service the area; take the 6 or A, C, E to Spring Street; the R, W to Prince Street; or the B, D, F, V to Broadway-Lafayette. For Little Italy, the Canal Street stops for the N, Q, R, W, 6, J, M, and Z lines put you near Mulberry Street.

⑬ Children's Museum of the Arts. In this bi-level space a few blocks from Broadway, children ages 1 to 10 can amuse and educate themselves with various activities, including diving into a pool of colorful balls; playacting in costume; music making with real instruments; and art making, from computer art to old-fashioned painting, sculpting, and collage. ✉ *182 Lafayette St., between Grand and Broome Sts., SoHo* ☎ *212/941–9198* ⊕ *www.cmany.org* ✂ *$8* ⊙ *Wed. and Fri.–Sun. noon–5, Thurs. noon–6* Ⓜ *6 to Spring St.*

⑫ King of Greene Street. This five-story Renaissance-style 1873 building has a magnificent projecting porch of Corinthian columns and pilasters. Today the King is painted a brilliant shade of ivory. ✉ *72–76 Greene St., between Spring and Broome Sts., SoHo* Ⓜ *R, W to Prince St.*

⑭ Little Singer Building. Ernest Flagg's 1904 masterpiece reveals the final flower of the cast-iron style with a delicate facade covered with curlicues of wrought iron. The central bay windows are recessed, allowing the top floor to arch over like a proscenium. The L-shape building's second facade is around the corner on Prince Street. ✉ *561 Broadway, SoHo* Ⓜ *R, W to Prince St.*

⑪ Queen of Greene Street. The regal grace of this 1873 cast-iron beauty is exemplified by its dormers, columns, window arches, projecting central bays, and Second Empire–style roof. ✉ *28–30 Greene St., between Grand and Canal Sts., SoHo* Ⓜ *J, M, Z, N, R, Q, W, 6 to Canal St.*

THE LOWER EAST SIDE ⇨ *Lower Manhattan map for sights in this section.*

Houston Street divides the area south of 14th Street and east of 4th Avenue and the Bowery into the Lower East Side (below Houston) and the East Village (above Houston), two neighborhoods that contain some of the city's funkiest nightlife, restaurants, and shops, all backed up with loads of cultural history. Grittier than its northern counterpart, the Lower East Side has seen waves of immigration of European Jews, then Hispanics and Chinese, a legacy excellently captured in the neighborhood's soul, the Lower East Side Tenement Museum.

GETTING HERE

For the Lower East Side, it's often best to take a cab to venues, but the J, M, Z, and F subway lines do service the area, with two stops along Delancey.

⓯ Lower East Side Tenement Museum. Step back in time and into the partially restored 1863 tenement building at 97 Orchard Street, where you can squeeze through the preserved apartments of immigrants on one of three one-hour tours. This is America's first urban living-history museum dedicated to the life of immigrants—and one of the city's most underrated and overlooked. "Getting By" visits the homes of Natalie Gumpertz, a German-Jewish dressmaker (dating from 1878) and Adolph and Rosaria Baldizzi, Catholic immigrants from Sicily (1935). "Piecing it Together" visits the Levines' garment shop/apartment and the Rogarshevsky family from Eastern Europe (1918). The tour through the Confino family apartment is designed for children, who are greeted by a costumed interpreter playing Victoria Confino. Her family of Sephardic Jews came from Kastoria, Turkey, which is now part of Greece (1916). Building tours are limited to 15 people so consider buying tickets in advance. Select tours are followed by free one-hour discussions with snacks provided. Walking tours of the neighborhood are also held regularly. The visitor information center and excellent gift shop displays a video with interviews of Lower East Side residents past and present. An antiques shop at 90 Orchard Street further benefits the museum. ✉*108 Orchard St., between Delancey and Broome Sts., Lower East Side* ☏*212/431–0233* ⊕*www.tenement.org* ✉*Tenement and walking tours $15; Confino apartment tour $14* ⊙*Tenement tours leave in 40-min intervals, Tues.–Fri, 1–4:45, weekends 11–5, check Web site for full details; Confino apartment tour weekends, hourly noon–3; walking tours Apr.–Dec., weekends 1 and 3. Visitor center and gift shop Mon. 11–5:30, Tues.–Fri. 11–6, weekends 10:45–6* Ⓜ*B, D to Grand St.; F to Delancey St.; J, M, Z to Essex St.*

THE VILLAGE, CHELSEA, AND UNION SQUARE AREA

★ GREENWICH VILLAGE AND CHELSEA

⇨ *Village, Chelsea, and Union Square Area map for sights in this section.*

Home of writers, artists, bohemians, and bon vivants, the West Village is a unique section of the city where right angles and office buildings give way to twisting streets and historic homes. In the late 1940s and early 1950s, abstract expressionist painters Franz Kline, Jackson Pollock, Mark Rothko, and Willem de Kooning congregated here, as did Beat writers Jack Kerouac, Allen Ginsberg, and Lawrence Ferlinghetti. The 1960s brought folk musicians and poets, notably Bob Dylan. This primarily residential area lacks the blockbuster attractions in other parts of the city, but makes up for it with a warm local feeling and myriad small restaurants, boutiques, and coffee shops. NYU students keep the cafés full and the idealistic vibe of the neighborhood alive.

The Meatpacking District, in the far northwest section of the West Village, has cobblestone streets that are gradually giving way from swinging sides of beef to swinging clubs, trendy restaurants, and chic shops.

Overlapping the Meatpacking District to the north, stylish Chelsea has usurped SoHo as the world's contemporary-art-gallery headquarters. The west edge of the neighborhood has high-profile galleries housed in cavernous converted warehouses that are easily identified by their ultracool, glass-and-stainless-steel doors. Other former warehouses, unremarkable by day, pulsate through the night as the city's hottest nightclubs. Chelsea has also replaced the West Village as the heart of the city's gay community.

GETTING HERE

The West 4th Street subway stop—serviced by the A, C, E, B, D, F, V—puts you at the center of Greenwich Village. Farther west, the 1 train has stops on West Houston Street and Christopher Street/Sheridan Square.

The A, C, E, and 1, 2, 3, and L trains stop at 14th Street for both the Meatpacking District and Chelsea. The latter is further served by the C, E, 1, F, V lines at the 23rd Street stop and the 1 stop at 28th Street. The L train connects Union Square on 14th Street to the Meatpacking District at 8th Avenue and 14th Street.

If you're coming from New Jersey, the PATH has stops at Christopher, 9th, 14th, and 23rd streets.

❼ Chelsea Hotel. The shabby aura of the hotel is part of its bohemian allure. This 12-story Queen Anne–style neighborhood landmark (1884) became a hotel in 1905, although it has always catered to long-term tenants with a tradition of broad-mindedness and creativity. Its literary roll call of live-ins is legendary: Mark Twain, Eugene O'Neill, O. Henry, Thomas Wolfe, Tennessee Williams, Vladimir Nabokov, Mary McCarthy, Brendan Behan, Arthur Miller, Dylan Thomas, and William S. Burroughs. In 1966 Andy Warhol filmed a group of fellow artists in eight rooms; the footage was included in *The Chelsea Girls* (1967). The hotel was also seen on-screen in *I Shot Andy Warhol* (1996) and in *Sid and Nancy* (1986), a dramatization of the real-life murder of Nancy Spungen, stabbed to death here by punk rocker boyfriend Sid Vicious. Read the commemorative plaques outside, then check out the eclectic collection of art in the lobby, some donated in lieu of rent. ⊠ *222 W. 23rd St., between 7th and 8th Aves., Chelsea* ☏ *212/243–3700* ⊕ *www. hotelchelsea.com* Ⓜ *1, C, E to 23rd St.*

❺ Chelsea Market. In the former Nabisco plant, where the first Oreos were baked in 1912, nearly two dozen food wholesalers flank what is possibly the city's longest interior walkway in a single building—from 9th to 10th avenues. The market's funky industrial design—a tangle of glass and metal creates the awning, and, inside, a factory pipe has been converted into an indoor waterfall—complements the eclectic assortment of bakers, butchers, florists, and wine merchants inside. ⊠ *75 9th Ave., between W. 15th and W. 16th Sts., Chelsea* ☏ *212/243–6005* ⊕ *www.*

Fodor'sChoice
★
☺

chelseamarket.com ⊙ *Weekdays* 7 AM–9 PM, *weekends* 7 AM–8 PM Ⓜ*A, C, E, L to 14th St.*

❻ Chelsea Piers. A phenomenal example of adaptive reuse, this sports-and-entertainment complex along the Hudson River between 17th and 23rd streets (entrance on 23rd) is the size of four 80-story buildings lying flat. There's pretty much every kind of sports activity going on inside and out from golf to ice-skating, roller skating, rock climbing, swimming, kayaking, bowling, gymnastics, and basketball. Plus there's a spa, film studios, and a brewery, and it's the jumping-off point for some of the city's varied water tours and dinner cruises. ✉*Piers 59–62 on Hudson River from 17th to 23rd Sts.; entrance at 23rd St., Chelsea* ☎*212/336–6666* ⊕*www.chelseapiers.com* Ⓜ*C, E to 23rd St.*

❸ Gay Street. A curved, one-block lane lined with small row houses, Gay Street is named after Sydney Howard Gay, managing editor of the long-defunct *New York Tribune,* who lived here during the Civil War with his wife and fellow abolitionist, Lucretia Mott. In the 1930s this darling thoroughfare and nearby Christopher Street became famous nation-wide when, from No. 14, Ruth McKenney wrote her somewhat zany autobiographical stories published in *The New Yorker* and later in *My Sister Eileen,* based on what happened when she and her sister moved to Greenwich Village from Ohio. Also on Gay Street, Howdy Doody

A Good Walk: Greenwich Village

If you walk from one end of Bleecker Street to another, you'll pass through a smattering of everything Village: NYU buildings, used-record stores, Italian cafés and food shops, charming restaurants and bakeries, and funky boutiques, plus a park with a playground, tables, and benches. Because of all the shops and crowds, Bleecker Street between 6th and 7th avenues seems more of a vibrant Italian neighborhood today than does the city's eponymous Little Italy. On this extended block, you can grab an espresso and *zuppa inglese,* check out century-old butcher shops, and sample some of the city's best thin-crust pizza.

West of 7th Avenue, you can also find fashion and home-furnishings boutiques featuring antiques, eyeglasses,

shoes, and designer clothing. Also here around the northern end of Bleecker, you're sure to get lost without a map. Here, the Village turns into a picture-book town of twisting tree-lined streets, quaint houses, and tiny restaurants. Streets cross back and forth, and Greenwich Street and Greenwich Avenue bear no relation to each other. In a seemingly random way, West 4th inexplicably crosses West 10th and West 11th streets.

The area where Grove and Bedford streets intersect is among the most beautiful in the Village. These streets still feel like 19th-century New York, with simple redbrick homes from the early part of the century as well as a clapboard home and even a home built to resemble a Swiss chalet.

was designed in the basement of No. 12. ⊠*Between Christopher St. and Waverly Pl., Greenwich Village* Ⓜ*1 to Christopher St./Sheridan Sq.; A, B, C, D, E, F, V, to West 4th St.*

❹ **Patchin Place.** This little cul-de-sac off West 10th Street between Greenwich and 6th avenues has 10 diminutive 1848 row houses. Around the corner on 6th Avenue is a similar dead-end street, **Milligan Place,** with five small homes completed in 1852. The houses in both quiet enclaves were originally built for waiters who worked at 5th Avenue's high-society Brevoort Hotel, long since demolished. Later Patchin Place residents included writers Theodore Dreiser, e.e. cummings, Jane Bowles, and Djuna Barnes. Milligan Place became popular among playwrights including Eugene O'Neill. Ⓜ*A, B, C, D, E, F, V to West 4th St.*

❶ **75½ Bedford Street.** Rising real-estate rates inspired the construction of New York City's narrowest house—just 9½ feet wide—in 1873. Built on a lot that was originally a carriage entrance of the Isaacs-Hendricks House next door, this sliver of a building was home to actor John Barrymore and poet Edna St. Vincent Millay. ⊠*75½ Bedford St., between Commerce and Morton Sts., Greenwich Village* Ⓜ*A, B, C, D, E, F, V to West 4th St.*

❷ **Washington Square Park.** NYU students, street musicians, skateboarders, jugglers, chess players, and those just watching the grand opera of it all generate a maelstrom of activity in this physical and spiritual heart of the Village. The 9½-acre park had inauspicious beginnings as

FodorsChoice
★
☾

a cemetery, principally for yellow fever victims—an estimated 10,000–22,000 bodies lie below. At one time, plans to renovate the park called for the removal of the bodies; however, local resistance prevented this from happening. In the early 1800s the park was a parade ground and the site of public executions; bodies dangled from a conspicuous Hanging Elm that still stands at the northwest corner of the square. Today, playgrounds attract parents with tots in tow, dogs go leash-free inside the popular dog runs, and everyone else seems drawn toward the large central fountain.

The triumphal European-style **Washington Memorial Arch** stands at the square's north end, marking the start of 5th Avenue. In 1889 Stanford White designed a wood-and-papier-mâché arch, originally situated a half block north, to commemorate the 100th anniversary of George Washington's presidential inauguration. The arch was reproduced in Tuckahoe marble in 1892, and the statues—*Washington as General Accompanied by Fame and Valor* on the left, and *Washington as Statesman Accompanied by Wisdom and Justice* on the right—were added in 1916 and 1918, respectively. ⊠*5th Ave. between Waverly Pl. and 4th St., Greenwich Village* Ⓜ*A, B, C, D, E, F, V to West 4th St.*

THE EAST VILLAGE
⇨ *Village, Chelsea, and Union Square Area map for sights in this section.*

The East Village, best known as the birthplace of American punk and the refuge of artists, activists, and other social dissenters, is also home to a pastiche of ethnic enclaves, whose imprints are visible in the area's churches, restaurants, shops, and—of course—residents.

8

The north–south avenues east of 1st Avenue, from Houston Street to 14th Street, are all labeled with letters, not numbers, which give this area its nickname: Alphabet City. This was once a burned-out area of slums and drug haunts, but some blocks and buildings were gentrified during the height of the East Village art scene in the mid-1980s and again in the late '90s. The reasonably priced restaurants with their bohemian atmosphere on Avenues A, B, and C, and the cross streets in between, attract all kinds. A close-knit Puerto Rican community makes its home here with predominantly Latino shops and bodegas, plus a "Nuyorican" café and music venue.

North of Alphabet City, leafy Tompkins Square Park in the East Village fills up with locals year-round, partaking in picnics; drum circles; the playground; and two dog runs. The Charlie Parker Jazz Festival, honoring the former park-side resident and noted jazz saxophonist, packs the park in late August. A few blocks west of the park, St. Marks Place reigns as the longtime hub of the East Village. During the 1950s, beatniks Allen Ginsberg and Jack Kerouac lived and wrote in the area; the 1960s brought Bill Graham's Fillmore East, Andy Warhol's the Dom, the Electric Circus nightclub, and hallucinogenic drugs. The studded, pink-haired, and shaved-head punk scene followed, continuing today along with pierced rockers and teenage Goths.

GETTING HERE

To reach Alphabet City, take the L to 1st Avenue or the F or V to 2nd Avenue. Head southeast from the same stop on the F or V; or take the F to Delancey or the J, M, Z to Essex Street.

8 **Astor Place Subway Station.** At the beginning of the 20th century, almost every Interborough Rapid Transit (IRT) subway entrance resembled the ornate cast-iron replica of a beaux arts kiosk that covers the stairway leading to the uptown No. 6 train here. Inside, plaques of beaver emblems line the tiled station walls, a reference to the fur trade that contributed to John Jacob Astor's fortune. Milton Glaser, a Cooper Union graduate, designed the station's murals. ⊠ *On traffic island at E. 8th St. and 4th Ave., East Village* Ⓜ *6 to Astor Pl.*

UNION SQUARE AND ENVIRONS

⇨ *Village, Chelsea, and Union Square Area map for sights in this section.*

Union Square is the beating heart of Manhattan. The square hosts everything from concerts to protest rallies to the farmers' market, and the surrounding neighborhoods borrow its flavor while maintaining their own vibe and identity. The haste and hullabaloo of the city calm considerably as you stroll through the tree-lined neighborhoods of Murray Hill, the Flatiron District, and Gramercy Park, east of 5th Avenue between 14th and 40th streets.

Murray Hill, running roughly between 34th and 40th streets from 3rd Avenue to 5th Avenue, is partly a charming residential neighborhood, but one with some high-profile haunts, including King Kong's favorite hangout, the Empire State Building. Herald Square, home to Macy's, is just beyond the western outskirts of Murray Hill, at 34th Street and 6th Avenue.

The Flatiron District—anchored by Madison Square on the north and Union Square to the south—is one of the city's hottest neighborhoods, bustling with shoppers and lined with trendy stores, restaurants, and hotels. Here stands the photogenic Flatiron Building, Madison Square Park, the Museum of Sex, and an elegant turn-of-the-20th-century skyline.

Gramercy Park, a leafy, dignified, and mostly residential neighborhood, is named for its 1831 gated garden square ringed by historic buildings and pricey hotels. Even though you can't unpack your picnic in this exclusive residents-only park, you can bask in its historic surroundings and literary significance. Gramercy's gems are the Players Club, the National Arts Club, a street named after writer Washington Irving, and the exclusive park itself.

GETTING HERE

Both Union Square/14th Street and Herald Square/34th Street are major subway hubs, connected by the N, Q, R, and W lines. To reach the Empire State Building by subway, you can take the B, D, F, V or N, R, Q, W lines to 34th Street or the 6 to 33rd Street. The 6 also has stops at 23rd and 28th streets.

⑪ **Empire State Building.** Bittersweet though it is, this landmark is once
Fodor'sChoice again the city's tallest building. Its pencil-slim silhouette, recognizable
★ virtually worldwide, is an art-deco monument to progress, a symbol
☾ for New York City, and a star in some great romantic scenes (on- and
offscreen) Its cinematic résumé—the building has appeared in more than
200 movies—means that it remains a fixture of popular imagination and
many visitors come to relive favorite movie scenes. You might just find
yourself at the top of the building with *Sleepless in Seattle* look-alikes
or even the building's own *King Kong* impersonator.

Built in 1931 at the peak of the skyscraper craze, this 103-story limestone giant opened after a mere 13 months of construction. The framework rose at an astonishing rate of four-and-a-half stories per week,
making the Empire State Building the fastest-rising skyscraper ever built.
Many floors were left completely unfinished so tenants could have them
custom designed. ■ TIP➔ **Thanks to advance ticketing on the Internet, you
can speed your way to the observatory on the 86th floor.** If this is your
first visit, rent a headset with an audio tour from Tony, a fictional but
"authentic" native New Yorker, available in eight languages. The 86th-
floor observatory (1,050 feet high) is outdoors and spans the building's
circumference. This is the deck to go to, to truly see the city. Don't be
shy about going outside into the wind (even in winter) or you'll miss half
the experience. Bring quarters for the high-powered binoculars: on clear
days you can see up to 80 mi. If it rains, you can view the city between
the clouds and watch the rain travel sideways around the building from
the shelter of the enclosed walkway. The advantage of paying the extra
$15 to go to the indoor 102nd floor is that this observatory affords an
easy and less crowded circular walk-around from which to view the city.
It also feels more removed and quieter. Express tickets can be purchased
for front-of-the-line admission for an extra $45.

Time your visit for early or late in the day—morning is the least crowded
time, and at night the city lights are dazzling. A good strategy is to go up
just before dusk and witness nightfall. ✉*350 5th Ave., at E. 34th St.,
Murray Hill* ☎*212/736–3100 or 877/692–8439* ⊕*www.esbnyc.com*
✉*$18* ☾*Daily 8* AM*–2* AM*; last elevator up leaves at 1:15* AM Ⓜ*B, D,
F, V, N, R, Q, W, to 34th St./Herald Sq.; or 6 to 33rd St.*

Although some parents blanch when they discover both how much it
costs and how it lurches, the second-floor **NY SKYRIDE** is a favorite of
the seven- and eight-year-old set. The ride yields a movie, motion, and
sights, rolled up into New York's only aerial virtual-tour simulator.
☎*212/279–9777 or 888/759–7433* ⊕*www.skyride.com* ✉*$25.50;
$38 Combo SKYRIDE and observatory* ☾*Daily 10* AM*–10* PM.

⑩ **Flatiron Building.** When completed in 1902, the Fuller Building, as it was
originally known, caused a sensation. Architect Daniel Burnham made
ingenious use of the triangular wedge of land at 23rd Street, 5th Avenue,
and Broadway, employing a revolutionary steel frame, which allowed
for the building's 22-story, 286-foot height. Covered with a limestone
and white terra-cotta skin in the Italian Renaissance style, the building's
shape resembled a clothing iron, hence its nickname. When it became

8

apparent that the building generated strong winds, gawkers would loiter at 23rd Street hoping to catch sight of ladies' billowing skirts. Local traffic cops had to shoo away the male peepers—one purported origin of the phrase "23 skidoo." There is a small display of historic building and area photos in the lobby. ⊠*175 5th Ave., bordered by E. 22nd and E. 23rd Sts., 5th Ave., and Broadway, Flatiron District* Ⓜ*R, W to 23rd St.*

❾ **Union Square.** A park, farmers' market, meeting place, and site of rallies and demonstrations, this pocket of green space sits in the center of a bustling residential and commercial neighborhood. The name "Union" originally signified that two main roads—Broadway and 4th Avenue—crossed here, but it took on a different meaning in the late 19th and early 20th centuries, when the square became a rallying spot for labor protests; many unions, as well as fringe political parties, moved their headquarters nearby. Since 9/11, antiwar groups have led their public campaigns here. Statues in the park include George Washington, Abraham Lincoln, and the Marquis de Lafayette sculpted by Frederic Auguste Bartholdi, creator of the Statue of Liberty. Plaques in the sidewalk on the southeast and southwest sides chronicle the park's history from the 1600s to 1800s.

Union Square is at its best on Monday, Wednesday, Friday, and Saturday (8–6), when the largest of the city's **greenmarkets** brings farmers and food purveyors from the tristate area. Browse the stands of fruit and vegetables, flowers, plants, fresh-baked pies and breads, cheeses, cider, New York State wines, fish, and meat. Between Thanksgiving and Christmas, artisans sell unique gift items in candy-cane-striped booths at the square's southwest end. ⊠*E. 14th to E. 17th Sts., between Broadway and Park Ave. S, Flatiron District* Ⓜ*N, Q, R, W, 4, 5, 6 or L to Union Sq./14th St.*

MIDTOWN

Fodor'sChoice Midtown is what most people think of when they think of New York
★ City—a center of commerce, media, shopping, transportation, tourism. It's a vibrant area known both for its nose-to-the-grindstone business ethic and its shop-till-you-drop appeal. Per square foot, Midtown has more major landmarks—Carnegie Hall, Grand Central Terminal, Rockefeller Center, Times Square, and the United Nations—than any other part of the city. Plus there's 5th Avenue, probably the best-known shopping street in the world, and the renowned Museum of Modern Art.

Whirling in a chaos of flashing lights, honking horns, and shoulder-to-shoulder crowds, Times Square is the most frenetic part of New York City. Hordes of people arrive every hour by subway, bus, car, or on foot, drawn by its undeniable gravitational pull. What brings them here? There's not much to do—no great shopping, comparatively few notable restaurants, and, with the notable exception of Broadway theaters, a dearth of cultural offerings. Simply put, Times Square is a destination in itself.

GETTING HERE

New York's major transit hubs—Port Authority Bus Terminal, Penn Station, and Grand Central Terminal—are all in Midtown. From these, you can easily catch a cab or subway line to any Midtown hotel or attraction. If you're staying at a Midtown hotel, many of these sights will be within walking distance of your doorstep. To reach Rockefeller Center by subway, take the B, D, F, or V train. Times Square/Port Authority is served by the 1, 2, 3, 7, A, C, E, N, R, Q, W, and S lines. The 4, 5, 6, 7, and S take you to Grand Central, while the A, C, E, and 1, 2, 3 go to Penn Station. If you're coming from New Jersey, the PATH comes into 33rd and 7th Avenue.

⇨ *Midtown map for sights in this section.*

2 Bryant Park. An oasis amid skyscrapers, this is one of Manhattan's most popular parks. Lining the perimeter of the sunny central lawn, tall London plane trees cast welcome shade over stone terraces, formal flower beds, gravel pathways, and kiosks selling everything from sandwiches to egg creams. In the afternoon the garden tables scattered about fill with lunching office workers and people enjoying the park's free Wi-Fi (signs show you how to log on). In summer you can check out live jazz and comedy concerts and free outdoor film screenings on Monday at dusk. At the east side of the park, near a squatting bronze cast of Gertrude Stein, is the stylish Bryant Park Grill, which has a rooftop garden, and the adjacent open-air Bryant Park Café, open April 15–October 15. In February and early September giant white tents spring up here for the New York fashion shows. On the south side of the park is an old-fashioned **carousel** (🎠*$2*) where kids can ride fanciful rabbits and frogs instead of horses. *6th Ave. between W. 40th and W. 42nd Sts., Midtown West* ☎*212/768–4242* ⊕*www.bryantpark.org* ☉*Oct.–Apr., daily 7–7; May–Sept., weekdays 7 AM–8 PM, weekends 7 AM–11 PM* Ⓜ*B, D, F, V to 42nd St.; 7 to 5th Ave.*

5 GE Building. Rising up on Rockefeller Center's west side is this 70-story (850-foot-tall) art-deco testament to modern urban development. Here, Rockefeller commissioned and then destroyed a mural by Diego Rivera upon learning it featured Vladimir Lenin. He replaced it with the monumental *American Progress* by José María Sert, still on view in the lobby, flanked by additional murals by Sert and English artist Frank Brangwyn. While in the lobby, pick up a free "Rockefeller Center Visitor's Guide" at the **information desk** (☎*212/332–6868*). Sixty-five floors up, the glittering **Rainbow Room** (opened in 1934) brings the Rockefeller era to life with dancing and big-band music. The GE Building also houses **NBC Studios** (☎*212/664–7174*), whose news tapings, visible at street level, attract gawking crowds. For ticket information for NBC shows or the 70-minute studio tour, visit the NBC Experience Store at the building's southeast corner. ✉*30 Rockefeller Plaza, between 5th and 6th Aves. at 49th St., Midtown West* 🎟*NBC Studio Tour $18.50* ☞*Children under 6 not permitted* ☉*Tours depart every 30 mins Mon.–Sat. 8:30–5:30, Sun. 9:30–4:30* Ⓜ*B, D, F, V to 47th–50th Sts./Rockefeller Center.*

8

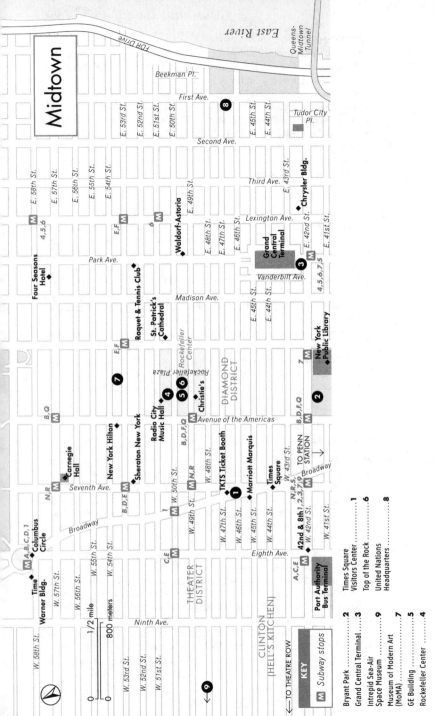

Midtown

East River

Queens-Midtown Tunnel

Tudor City Pl.

Beekman Pl.

First Ave.
Second Ave.
Third Ave.
Lexington Ave.
Vanderbilt Ave.
Madison Ave.
Park Ave.
Seventh Ave.
Broadway
Eighth Ave.
Ninth Ave.

Avenue of the Americas

E. 58th St.
E. 57th St.
E. 56th St.
E. 55th St.
E. 54th St.
E. 53rd St.
E. 52nd St.
E. 51st St.
E. 50th St.
E. 49th St.
E. 48th St.
E. 47th St.
E. 46th St.
E. 45th St.
E. 44th St.
E. 43rd St.
E. 42nd St.
E. 41st St.

W. 58th St.
W. 57th St.
W. 56th St.
W. 55th St.
W. 54th St.
W. 53rd St.
W. 52nd St.
W. 51st St.
W. 50th St.
W. 49th St.
W. 48th St.
W. 47th St.
W. 46th St.
W. 45th St.
W. 44th St.
W. 43rd St.
W. 42nd St.
W. 41st St.

FDR Drive

Four Seasons Hotel
Raquet & Tennis Club
St. Patrick's Cathedral
Waldorf-Astoria
Chrysler Bldg.
Carnegie Hall
Time Warner Bldg.
Columbus Circle
New York Hilton
Sheraton New York
Radio City Music Hall
Marriott Marquis
Times Square
Grand Central Terminal
New York Public Library
Port Authority Bus Terminal
Christie's

TKTS Ticket Booth
Rockefeller Plaza
Rockefeller Center
DIAMOND DISTRICT
THEATER DISTRICT
CLINTON (HELL'S KITCHEN)
← TO THEATRE ROW
TO PENN STATION →

A,B,C,D,1
N,R
B,Q
C,E
1
B,D,E
N,R
N,R,S
B,D,F,Q
7
B,D,F,Q
7
4,5,6,7,S
4,5,6
E,F
E,F
6
A,C,E
42nd & 8th 1,2,3,7,9

0 — 1/2 mile
0 — 800 meters

KEY

Bryant Park **2**
Grand Central Terminal **3**
Intrepid Sea-Air
Space Museum **9**
Museum of Modern Art
(MoMA) **7**
GE Building **5**
Rockefeller Center **4**
Times Square
Visitors Center **1**
Top of the Rock **6**
United Nations
Headquarters **8**

Ⓜ Subway stops

3 **Grand Central Terminal.** Grand Central is not only the world's largest (76 acres) and the nation's busiest (500,000 commuters and subway riders use it daily) railway station, but also one of the world's greatest public spaces ("justly famous," as critic Tony Hiss noted, "as a crossroads, a noble building . . . and an ingenious piece of engineering"). A massive four-year renovation completed in October 1998 restored the 1913 landmark to its original splendor—and then some. Its exquisite building is also pure eye candy for architecture buffs. Underground, more than 60 ingeniously integrated railroad tracks lead trains upstate and to Connecticut via Metro-North Commuter Rail. The subway connects here as well. *Main entrance* ⊠*E. 42nd St. at Park Ave., Midtown East* ☎*212/935–3960* ⊕*www.grandcentralterminal.com* Ⓜ*4, 5, 6, 7, S to 42nd St./Grand Central.*

9 *Intrepid* **Sea-Air Space Museum.** After reopening in November 2008 after a two-year renovation, Manhattan's floating museum had already seen more than 200,000 visitors by the end of February 2009. The renovation included rebuilding Pier 86 and refurbishing an F-14 Tomcat (the type of plane used in *Top Gun*), an A-12 Blackbird spy plane, and 14 other historic aircraft onboard the USS *Intrepid*. The 65-year-old, 900-foot aircraft carrier was used during World War II. Its most trying moment of service—the day it was attacked by kamikaze pilots—is recounted in a multimedia presentation. Docked alongside and also part of the museum is the *Growler,* a strategic-missile submarine, where children can manipulate countless knobs, buttons, and wheels, and navigate skinny hallways and winding staircases. Don't miss the museum's original Iwo Jima sculpture. ⊠*Hudson River, Pier 86, 12th Ave. and W. 46th St., Midtown* ☎*212/245–0072 or 877/957–7447* ⊕*www. intrepidmuseum.org* ⊠*$19.50* ⊙*Apr.–Sept., weekdays 10–5, weekends 10—6; Oct.–Mar., Tues.–Sun. 10–5; last admission one hour before closing* Ⓜ*A, C, E to 42nd St.; M42 bus to pier.*

7 **Museum of Modern Art (MoMA).** Novices and reluctant art enthusiasts are often awestruck by the masterpieces before them here, including Monet's *Water Lilies,* Picasso's *Les Demoiselles d'Avignon,* and van Gogh's *Starry Night.* The museum's recent $425 million face-lift by Yoshio Taniguchi increased exhibition space by nearly 50%, including space to accommodate large-scale contemporary installations. Its new building gave the museum an opportunity to shift focus from modern to contemporary art, evident in the recent creation of a media department. The museum continues to collect: most recently it obtained important works by Martin Kippenberger, David Wojnarowicz, Jasper Johns, Kara Walker, and Neo Rauch. One of the top research facilities in modern and contemporary art is held inside the museum's eight-story "Education and Research" building. In addition to the artwork, one of the main draws of MoMA is the building itself. A maze of glass walkways permits art viewing from many angles. The 110-foot atrium entrance (accessed from either 53rd or 54th Street) leads to the movie theater and the main-floor restaurant, Modern, with the Alsatian-inspired cuisine of chef Gabriel Kreuther. MoMA is a popular destination for locals and tourists, and that translates into lines that sometimes snake down the block. Weekdays tend to be less crowded. Come without bags or backpack to avoid the wait for the checkroom. Entrance after 4 on Friday is free, but come expecting to wait in line. ⊠ *11 W. 53rd St., between 5th and 6th Aves., Midtown East* ☎ *212/708–9400* ⊕ *www.moma. org* ☝ *$20; children under 16 free* ⊗ *Sat.–Mon., Wed., and Thurs. 10:30–5:30, Fri. 10:30–8* Ⓜ *E, V to 5th Ave./53rd St.; B, D, F, V to 47th–50th Sts./Rockefeller Center.*

❹ **Rockefeller Center.** If Times Square is New York's crossroads, Rockefeller
Fodor's Choice   Center is its communal gathering place, where the entire world con-
★   verges to snap pictures, skate on the ice rink, peek in on a taping of the *Today show* at NBC Studios, shop, eat, and take in the monumental art-deco structures and public sculptures from the past century. Totaling 49 shops, 28 restaurants (1.4 million square feet in all) the complex runs from 47th to 52nd streets between 5th and 7th avenues. Special events and huge pieces of art dominate the central plazas in summer, and in December an enormous twinkling tree towers above (visit ⊕ *www. rockefellercenter.com* for a schedule). ⊠ *Between 5th and 6th Aves. and W. 49th and W. 50th Sts., Midtown West* ☎ *212/332–7654 for the rink* Ⓜ *B, D, F, V to 47th–50th Sts./Rockefeller Center.*

❶ **Times Square Visitors Center.** Time Square's human and vehicular traffic can disorient even the most street-smart urbanite. Luckily, it has the city's first comprehensive visitor center, housed in the lobby of the former high-society 1925 Embassy Theater. Stop by for ATMs, MetroCards, free Internet, sightseeing and theater tickets, a video camera that shoots and e-mails instant photos, and (most important!) free restrooms. Free walking tours of Times Square start here Friday at noon. ⊠ *1560 Broadway, between W. 46th and W. 47th Sts., Midtown West* ☎ *212/768–1560* ⊕ *www.timessquarenyc.org* ⊗ *Daily 8–8* Ⓜ *1, 2, 3, 7, N, Q, R, W, S to 42nd St./Times Sq.*

❻ **Top of the Rock.** Rockefeller Center's multifloor observation deck, first
Fodor's Choice   opened in 1933, and closed in the early 1980s, reopened in 2005. Arrive
★   just before sunset to catch a view of the city that morphs before your eyes into a dazzling wash of colors, with a bird's-eye view of the tops of the Empire State Building, the Citicorp Building, and the Chrysler Building, and sweeping views northward to Central Park and south to the Statue of Liberty. Transparent elevators lift you to the 67th-floor interior viewing area, then an escalator leads to the outdoor deck on the 69th floor for sightseeing through nonreflective glass safety panels. Then, take another elevator or stairs to the 70th floor for a 360-degree outdoor panorama of New York City on a deck that is only 20 feet wide and nearly 200 feet long. Reserved-time ticketing eliminates long lines. Indoor exhibits include films of Rockefeller Center's history and a model of the building. Especially interesting is a Plexiglas screen on the floor with footage showing Rock Center construction workers dangling on beams high above the streets; the brave can even "walk" across a beam to get a sense of what it might have been like to erect this skyscraper. The local consensus is that the views from the Top of the Rock are better than those from the Empire State building, in part because the Empire State is part of the skyline here. ⊠ *Entrance on*

ARCHITECTURAL GEMS

A monument to modern times and the mighty automotive industry, the **Chrysler Building** (✉ *405 Lexington Ave., at E. 42nd St., Midtown East* Ⓜ *4, 5, 6, 7, S to 42nd St./Grand Central*), the former Chrysler headquarters, wins many a New Yorker's vote for the city's most iconic and beloved skyscraper (the world's tallest for 40 days until the Empire State Building stole the honor). Architect William Van Alen, who designed this 1930 art-deco masterpiece, incorporated car details into its form: American eagle gargoyles sprout from the 61st floor, resembling car-hood ornaments used on 1920s Chryslers; winged urns festooning the 31st floor reference the car's radiator caps. Most breathtaking is the pinnacle, whose tiered crescents and spiked windows radiate out like a magnificent steel sunburst. The inside is off-limits apart from the amazing time-capsule lobby replete with chrome "grillwork," intricately patterned wood elevator doors, marble walls and floors, and an enormous ceiling mural saluting transportation and the human endeavor.

A 1911 masterpiece of beaux arts design, the **New York Public Library** (✉ *5th Ave. between E. 40th and E. 42nd Sts., Midtown West* ☎ *212/930–0800, 212/869–8089 for exhibit information* ⊕ *www.nypl.org*

⊙ *Mon. and Thurs.–Sat. 11–6, Sun. 1–5, Tues. and Wed. 11–7:30; exhibitions until 6* Ⓜ *B, D, F, V to 42nd St.; 7 to 5th Ave.)* is one of the great research institutions in the world, with 6 million books, 12 million manuscripts, and 2.8 million pictures. But you don't have to crack a book to make it worth visiting: an hour or so at this National Historic Landmark is a peaceful (and free!) alternative to Midtown's bustle, along with some pretty incredible architecture. You can to people-watch from the block-long marble staircase at the library's grand 5th Avenue entrance, then check out the opulent interior.

The country's largest Catholic cathedral (seating approximately 2,400), **St. Patrick's Cathedral** (✉ *5th Ave. between E. 50th and E. 51st Sts., Midtown East* ☎ *212/753–2261 rectory* ⊕ *www.ny-archdiocese. org* ⊙ *Daily 8 AM–8:45 PM* Ⓜ *E, V to 5th Ave./53rd St.*) is among New York's most striking churches. As you admire the Gothic edifice, note the 330-foot spires. Among the statues in the alcoves around the nave is a modern depiction of the first American-born saint, Mother Elizabeth Ann Seton. The 5th Avenue steps are a convenient, scenic rendezvous spot. Sunday Masses can overflow with tourists; off-hours are significantly more peaceful.

50th St., between 5th and 6th Aves., Midtown West ☎ *877/692–7625 or 212/698–2000* ⊕ *www.topoftherocknyc.com* 🎟 *$17.50* ⊙ *Daily 8–midnight; last elevator at 11 PM* Ⓜ *B, D, F, V to 47th–50th Sts./ Rockefeller Center.*

❽ United Nations Headquarters. Officially an "international zone" and not part of the United States, the U.N. Headquarters is a working symbol of global cooperation. Built between 1947 and 1961, the headquarters sit on a lushly landscaped, 18-acre tract on the East River, fronted by flags of member nations. The main reason to visit is the 45-minute guided tour (given in 20 languages), which includes the **General Assembly** and major council chambers, though some rooms may be closed on any given day. The tour includes displays on war, nuclear energy, and refugees, and passes corridors overflowing with imaginatively diverse artwork. Free tickets to assemblies are sometimes available on a first-come, first-served basis before sessions begin; pick them up in the General Assembly lobby. If you just want to wander around, the grounds include a beautiful riverside promenade, a rose garden with 1,400 specimens, and sculptures donated by member nations. *Visitor entrance ⊠ 1st Ave. and E. 46th St., Midtown East ☎212/963–8687 ⊕www.un.org ✉Tour $13 ☞Children under 5 not admitted ☉Tours weekdays 9:30–4:45, weekends 10–4:30, no weekend tours Jan. and Feb.; tours in English leave General Assembly lobby every 30 mins; Delegates Dining Room, 11:30–2:30 Ⓜ4, 5, 6, 7, S to 42nd St./Grand Central.*

UPTOWN AND HARLEM

THE UPPER WEST SIDE AND MORNINGSIDE HEIGHTS

Residents of the Upper West Side will proudly tell you that they live in one of the last real neighborhoods in the city. That's arguable (as is most everything in New York City), but people actually do know their neighbors in this primarily residential section of Manhattan, and some small owner-operated businesses still flourish. On weekends, stroller-pushing parents cram the sidewalks and shoppers jam the gourmet food emporiums and eclectic stores that line Broadway and Columbus Avenue. Those who aren't shopping are likely to be found in Riverside Park, the neighborhood's communal backyard. Lively avenues, quiet tree-lined side streets and terrific restaurants and museums, all in a relatively compact area, make this the perfect neighborhood to experience life the way the locals do.

Most people think the area north of 106th Street and south of 125th Street on the west side is just part of the Upper West Side. Even many locals are unaware that it's actually Morningside Heights, and is largely dominated by Columbia University, along with the cluster of academic and religious institutions—Barnard College, St. Luke's Hospital, and the Cathedral of St. John the Divine, to name a few. Within the gates of the Columbia or Barnard campuses or inside the hushed St. John the Divine, New York City takes on a different character. This is an *uptown* student neighborhood—less hip than the Village, but friendly, fun, and intellectual.

GETTING HERE

The A, B, C, D, and 1 subway lines take you to Columbus Circle. From there, the B and C lines run along Central Park, while the 1, 2, and 3 trains run up Broadway (2 and 3 only stop at 76th and 96th, however).

⇨ *Uptown and Harlem map for sights in this section.*

❷ American Museum of Natural History. With 45 exhibition halls and more ☯ than 32 million artifacts and specimens, this is the world's largest and ★ most important museum of natural history. Three spectacular dinosaur halls use real fossils and interactive computer stations to present interpretations of how dinosaurs might have behaved. Other highlights include the popular 94-foot blue whale model in the **Hall of Ocean Life**, and the **Hayden Planetarium** which is home to the **Rose Center for Earth and Space**. Films shown on the museum's **IMAX Theater** (☎ *212/769–5034* for showtimes) are usually about nature and cost $19, including museum admission. ⊠ *Central Park W at W. 79th St., Upper West Side* ☎ *212/769–5200 for museum tickets and programs, 212/769–5100 for museum general informatio* ⊕ *www.amnh.org* ✉ *Museum $12 suggested donation; museum and planetarium show combination ticket $22. Prices vary for special exhibitions* ⊙ *Daily 10–5:45; Rose Center for Earth and Space stays open on Fri. until 8:45* PM Ⓜ *B, C to 81st St.*

WORD OF MOUTH

"The Cloisters is an amazing museum, not well-known by tourists . [it] has a priceless collection of art, furniture, jewelry, religious artifacts, all housed in a building built for the collection. Well worth the trip uptown. After your visit, walk down Ft. Washington Ave to 187th St. for dinner at Kismat, one of the BEST Indian restaurants in the city."   —travelbuff

❹ **Cathedral Church of St. John the Divine.** The largest Gothic-style cathedral in the world, even with its towers and transepts still unfinished, this divine behemoth comfortably asserts its bulk in the country's most vertical city. Episcopal in denomination, it acts as a sanctuary for all, giving special services ranging from a celebration of New York's gay and lesbian community to the annual Blessing of the Bikes, when cyclists of all faiths bring their wheels for a holy-water benediction. The cathedral hosts musical performances (⊕ *www.stjohndivine.org*) and has held funerals and memorial services for such artists as Duke Ellington, Jim Henson, George Balanchine, James Baldwin, and Alvin Ailey. Built in two long spurts starting in 1892, the cathedral remains only two-thirds complete. ⊠ *1047 Amsterdam Ave., at W. 112th St., Morningside Heights* ☎ *212/316–7540, 212/662–2133 box office, 212/932–7347 tours* ⊕ *www.stjohndivine.org* ✉ *Tours $5* ⊙ *Mon.–Sat. 7–6, Sun. 7–7; tours Tues.–Sat. at 11 and 1, Sun. at 2. A vertical tour with a climb of 124 ft to top is given on Sat. at noon and 2; reservations required, $15. Sun. services at 9, 11, and 6* Ⓜ *1 to 110th St./Cathedral Pkwy.*

❻ **The Cloisters.** Perched on a wooded hill in Fort Tryon Park, near Manhattan's northern tip, the Cloisters, which shelters the medieval collection of the Metropolitan Museum of Art, is a scenic destination on its own. Colonnaded walks connect authentic French and Spanish monastic cloisters, a French Romanesque chapel, a 12th-century chapter house, and a Romanesque apse. One room is devoted to the 15th- and 16th-century Unicorn Tapestries—a must-see masterpiece of medieval mythology. The tomb effigies are another highlight. Three gardens shelter more than 250 species of plants similar to those grown during the Middle Ages, including herbs and medicinals; the Unicorn Garden blooms with flowers and plants depicted in the tapestries. Concerts of medieval music are held here regularly (concert tickets include same-day admission to the museum) and an outdoor café decorated with 15th-century carvings

8

serves biscotti and espresso from May through October. ✉*Fort Tryon Park, Inwood* ☎*212/923–3700* ⊕*www.metmuseum.org* 🗨*$20 suggested donation* ⊙*Mar.–Oct., Tues.–Sun. 9:30–5:15; Nov.–Feb., Tues.–Sun. 9:30–4:45* Ⓜ*A to 190th St.*

❺ Columbia University. Wealthy, private, Ivy League, New York's first college has a pedigree that has always attracted students. But for a visitor, the why-go resides within its campus, bucolic and quietly energetic at once. The main entrance is at 116th Street and Broadway, site of the Columbia Graduate School of Journalism. After seeing the "J-School," follow the herringbone-pattern brick pathway of College Walk to the main quadrangle, the focal point for campus life. (When you eventually leave, exit through the quad's south gate to West 144th Street's Fraternity Row, where brownstones housing Columbia's frats display quirky signs of collegiate pride.) Dominating the quad's south side is **Butler Library** (1934), modeled after the Roman Pantheon, which holds the bulk of the university's 8 million books. Looking north, you'll see **Low Memorial Library,** its steps presided over by Daniel Chester French's statue *Alma Mater.* Low is one of the few buildings you can enter (on weekdays), either to check out the former Reading Room and marble rotunda or pick up a map or take a campus tour at the **visitor center.** North of the quad (past a cast bronze of August Rodin's *Thinker*) is the interdenominational **St. Paul's Chapel,** an exquisite little Byzantine-style dome church with salmon-color Guastavino tile vaulting inside. (This same design can be seen in Grand Central Terminal and many other buildings throughout the city.) Right across Broadway from Columbia's main gate lies the brick-and-limestone campus of women-only **Barnard College,** which also gives tours (☎*212/854–2014*). ✉*Morningside Heights* ☎*212/854–4900* ⊕*www.columbia.edu* ⊙*Weekdays 9–5. Tours begin at 1 weekdays from Room 213, Low Library* Ⓜ*1 to 116th St./Columbia University.*

❶ Lincoln Center for the Performing Arts (✉*W. 62nd to W. 66th Sts., Broadway to Amsterdam Ave., Upper West Side* ☎*212/546–2656* ⊕*www. lincolncenter.org* Ⓜ*1 to 66th St./Lincoln Center*) is the city's musical nerve center, especially when it comes to classical music. Formal and U-shape, the massive Avery Fisher Hall presents the world's great musicians, and is home to the **New York Philharmonic** (☎*212/875–5656* ⊕*newyorkphilharmonic.org*), one of the world's finest symphony orchestras. Lorin Maazel conducts, from late September to early June. Bargain-price weeknight "rush hour" performances at 6:45 PM and Saturday matinee concerts at 2 PM are occasionally offered; orchestra rehearsals at 9:45 AM are open to the public on selected weekday mornings (usually Wednesday or Thursday) for $15. The **Chamber Music Society of Lincoln Center** (☎*212/875–5788* ⊕*www. chambermusicsociety.org*) performs in Alice Tully Hall, which—while updated for the 2008–09 season—is still considered to be as acoustically perfect as a concert hall can get. In August, Lincoln Center's longest-running classical series, the **Mostly Mozart Festival** (☎*212/875–5399*), captures the crowds.

Fodor's Choice
★

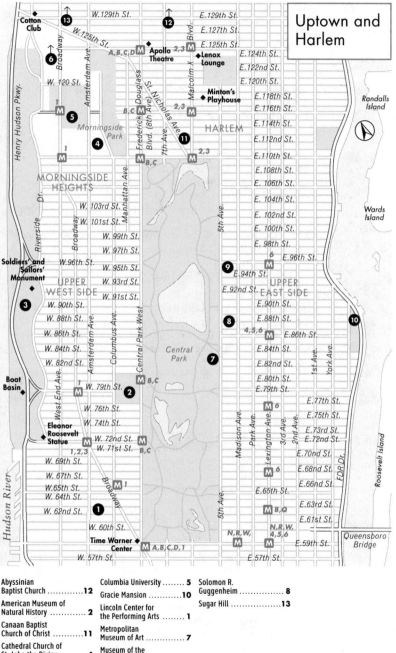

Uptown and Harlem

W.129th St.
E.129th St.
Cotton Club 13 12 E.127th St.
W.125th St. E.125th St.
A,B,C,D **Apollo Theatre** 2,3
6 Broadway **Lenox Lounge** E.124th St.
E.122nd St.
W. 120 St. E.120th St.
5 Amsterdam Ave. B,C **Minton's Playhouse** E.118th St.
E.116th St.
Morningside Park **HARLEM** E.114th St.
4 11 E.112nd St.
Frederick Douglass Blvd. (8th Ave.) 7th Ave. 2,3 E.110th St.
B,C E.108th St.
MORNINGSIDE HEIGHTS E. 106th St.
W. 103rd St. Manhattan Ave. E. 104th St.
W. 101st St. E. 102nd St.
W. 99th St. E. 100th St.
W. 97th St. E. 98th St.
Soldiers' and Sailors' Monument W.96th St. 9 E. 96th St.
W. 95th St. E.94th St.
UPPER WEST SIDE W. 93rd St. E.92nd St. **UPPER EAST SIDE**
W. 91st St.
3 W. 90th St. E.90th St.
W. 88th St. 8 E.88th St.
W. 86th St. 4,5,6 E.86th St.
W. 84th St. **Central Park** E.84th St.
W. 82nd St. 7 E.82nd St.
Boat Basin E.80th St.
W. 79th St. B,C E.79th St.
2
W. 76th St. E.77th St.
W. 74th St. 6 E.75th St.
Eleanor Roosevelt Statue W. 72nd St. E.73rd St.
W. 71st St. B,C E.72nd St.
1,2,3 Madison Ave. Park Ave. Lexington Ave. 3rd Ave. 2nd Ave. E.70nd St.
W. 69th St.
W. 67th St. 6 E.68th St.
W. 65th St. E.66nd St.
W. 64th St.
W. 62nd St. B,Q E.63rd St.
1 E.61st St.
W. 60th St. N,R,W, N,R,W, 4,5,6
Time Warner Center A,B,C,D,1 E.59th St.
W. 57th St. E.57th St.

Henry Hudson Pkwy.
Riverside Dr.
Broadway
Columbus Ave.
Central Park West
West End Ave.
Amsterdam Ave.
Broadway
Hudson River
Randalls Island
Wards Island
Roosevelt Island
FDR Dr.
1st Ave.
York Ave.
5th Ave.
Queensboro Bridge

❸ Riverside Park. Walking around concrete and skyscrapers all day, you can
easily miss the expansive waterfront park just blocks away. Riverside
Park—bordering the Hudson from 58th to 156th streets—dishes out a
dose of tranquillity. Its original sections, designed by Olmsted and Vaux
of Central Park fame and laid out between 1873 and 1888, are often
outshone by Olmsted's "other" park. But with its waterfront bike and
walking paths and lighter crowds, Riverside Park holds its own. One
of the park's loveliest attributes is a half-mile waterfront promenade, a
rare spot in Manhattan where you can walk right along the river's edge.
Reach it by heading through an underpass beneath the West Side Highway at the park's entrance at West 72nd Street and Riverside Drive (look
for the **statue of Eleanor Roosevelt**). The promenade takes you past the
79th Street Boat Basin, where you can watch a flotilla of houseboats
bobbing in the water. Above it, a ramp leads to the Rotunda, home in
summer to the Boat Basin Cafe, an open-air spot for a burger and river
views. At the end of the promenade and **up** a staircase, a community
garden explodes with flowers. Cresting a hill along Riverside Drive at
West 89th Street stands the Civil War **Soldiers' and Sailors' Monument**
(1902, designed by Paul M. Duboy), an imposing 96-foot-high circle of
white-marble columns. ⊠ *W. 58th to W. 156th Sts. between Riverside
Dr. and Hudson River, Upper West Side* Ⓜ *1, 2, 3 to 72nd St.*

THE UPPER EAST SIDE

To many New Yorkers, the Upper East Side connotes old money and
high society. Alongside Central Park, between 5th and Lexington avenues, up to about East 96th Street, the trappings of wealth are everywhere apparent: posh buildings, Madison Avenue's flagship boutiques,
and doormen in braided livery. But even more impressive, the Upper
East Side's museums, including the Metropolitan Museum of Art and
the Guggenheim stretch along "Museum Mile."

GETTING HERE

Take the Lexington Avenue 4 or 5 express train to 59th or 86th street.
The 6 local train stops at 59th, 68th, 77th, 86th, and 96th streets. If
you're coming from Midtown, another option is the F train, getting off
at 63rd; the N, R, W at 59th; or the E, V at 51st. From Port Authority
or Times Square you can take the Shuttle (S) or 7 line to Grand Central
and transfer to the Lexington Avenue line (4, 5, 6).

⇨ *Uptown and Harlem map for sights in this section.*

❿ The official mayor's residence, **Gracie Mansion** (⊠ *Carl Schurz Park, East
End Ave. opposite 88th St., Upper East Side* ☎ *212/570–4751* 🎟 *$7*
🕙 *45-min guided tours by advance reservation only; Wed. 10–2* Ⓜ *4,
5, 6 to 86th St.*) was built in 1799 by shipping merchant Archibald
Gracie and is one of New York's oldest wooden structures. Tours of
the interior—which you must schedule in advance—take you through
its history and colorful rooms furnished over centuries and packed
with American objets d'art. Nine mayors have lived here since 1942
but New York City's current mayor Michael Bloomberg isn't one of
them; he chose to stay in his own 79th Street town house, though he
uses this house for meetings and functions. ■TIP→ **If you exit the park**

at 86th Street, cross East End Avenue for a stroll through Henderson Place, a miniature historic district of 24 connected Queen Anne–style houses built in 1881 "for persons of moderate means." Note the turrets marking the corner of each block, and the symmetrical roof gables, pediments, parapets, chimneys, and dormer windows. ⊠*Carl Schurz Park spans East End Ave. to the East River, E. 84th to E. 90th Sts., Upper East Side* Ⓜ*4, 5, 6 to 86th St.*

❼ Metropolitan Museum of Art. The largest museum in the western hemisphere (spanning four blocks, it encompasses 2 million square feet), the Met is one of the city's supreme cultural institutions. Its permanent collection of nearly 3 million works of art from all over the world includes objects from the Paleolithic era to modern times—an assemblage whose quality and range make this one of the world's greatest museums. ⊠*5th Ave. at 82nd St., Upper East Side* ☎*212/535–7710* ⊕*www.metmuseum.org* 🖅*$12* ☉*Tues.–Thurs. and Sun. 9:30–5:30, Fri. and Sat. 9:30 –9* Ⓜ*4, 5, 6 to 86th St.*

❾ Museum of the City of New York. Within a colonial revival building
Ⓒ designed for the museum in the 1930s, the city's history and many
★ quirks are revealed through engaging exhibits. Permanent collections detail firefighting, theater, and New York's role as a port. Period rooms include several that John D. Rockefeller Sr. acquired when he bought a fully furnished New York mansion in the 1880s. The historic toys on view include the beloved Stettheimer Dollhouse, a miniature mansion outfitted down to postage-stamp-size artworks imitating 20th-century masters. Don't miss *Timescapes,* a 25-minute media projection that innovatively illustrates New York's physical expansion and population changes. The museum hosts New York–centric lectures, films, and walking tours. ■TIP➔ **When you're finished touring the museum cross the street and stroll through the Vanderbilt Gates to enter the Conservatory Garden, one of Central Park's hidden gems.** ⊠*1220 5th Ave., at E. 103rd St., Upper East Side* ☎*212/534–1672* ⊕*www.mcny.org* 🖅*$9 suggested donation* ☉*Tues.–Sun. 10–5* Ⓜ*6 to 103rd St.*

❽ Solomon R. Guggenheim. Frank Lloyd Wright's landmark museum building is visited as much for its famous architecture as it is for its superlative art. Opened in 1959, shortly after Wright's death, the Guggenheim is acclaimed as one of the greatest buildings of the 20th century. Inside, under a 92-foot-high glass dome, a seemingly endless ramp spirals down past changing exhibitions. The museum has strong holdings of Wassily Kandinsky, Paul Klee, Marc Chagall, Pablo Picasso, and Robert Mapplethorpe. ■TIP➔ **Gallery talks give richer understanding of the masterpieces in front of you. The museum offers tours at a terrific price: free! Eat before trekking over to 5th Avenue; restaurants on Lexington offer more varied fare than the museum's cafeteria. The museum is pay what you wish on Friday after 5:45. Lines can be long, so go early. The last tickets are handed out at 7:15.** ⊠*1071 5th Ave., between E. 88th and E. 89th Sts., Upper East Side* ☎*212/423-3500* ⊕*www.guggenheim.org* 🖅*$18* ☉*Sun.–Wed. 9–5:45, Fri. and Sat. 9–8. Closed Thurs.* Ⓜ*4, 5, 6 to 86th St.*

HARLEM

Harlem is known throughout the world as a center of culture, music, and African-American life. Today's Harlem, however, is a very different Harlem from that of a dozen years ago, when many considered it too dangerous to visit with little to offer in the way of cultural attractions, business, or residential life. Renovated and new buildings have popped up throughout the area, joining such jewels as the Apollo Theatre, architecturally splendid churches, and cultural magnets like the Studio Museum in Harlem and the Schomburg Center for Research in Black Culture. Black (and, increasingly, white) professionals and young families are restoring many of Harlem's classic brownstone and limestone buildings, bringing new life to the community.

GETTING HERE

The 2 and 3 subway lines stop on Lenox Avenue; the 1 goes along Broadway; and the A, B, C, and D trains travel along St. Nicholas and 8th avenues. The A train is among the quickest ways into Harlem.

GETTING AROUND

The city's north–south avenues take on different names in Harlem: 6th Avenue is Malcolm X Boulevard (formerly Lenox Avenue), 7th Avenue is Adam Clayton Powell Jr. Boulevard, and 8th Avenue is Frederick Douglass Boulevard; West 125th Street, the major east–west street, is called Dr. Martin Luther King Jr. Boulevard.

⇨ *Uptown and Harlem map for sights in this section.*

⑫ Abyssinian Baptist Church. This 1923 Gothic-style church holds one of Harlem's richest legacies, dating to 1808 when a group of parishioners defected from the segregated First Baptist Church of New York City and established the first African-American Baptist church in New York State. Among its legendary pastors was Adam Clayton Powell Jr., a powerful orator and civil rights leader and the first black U.S. congressman. Today, sermons by pastor Calvin Butts are fiery and the seven choirs are excellent. Because of its services' popularity, the church maintains separate lines for parishioners and tourists. Dress your best and get there early on Sunday holidays. ⊠*132 Odell Clark Pl., W. 138th St., between Adam Clayton Powell Jr. Blvd./7th Ave. and Malcolm X Blvd./Lenox Ave./6th Ave., Harlem* ☎*212/862–7474* ⊕*www.abyssinian.org* ⊗*Sun. services at 9 and 11* Ⓜ*2, 3 to 135 St.*

⑪ Canaan Baptist Church of Christ. The heavenly gospel music during Sunday-morning services makes up for this church's concrete-box-like exterior (visitors may enter once parishioners are seated). Pastor emeritus Wyatt Tee Walker worked with Dr. Martin Luther King Jr. (who delivered his famous "A Knock at Midnight" sermon here). ⊠*132 W. 116th St., between Malcolm X Blvd./Lenox Ave./6th Ave. and Adam Clayton Powell Jr. Blvd./7th Ave., Harlem* ☎*212/866–0301* ⊗*Services Sun. at 10:45* Ⓜ*2, 3 to 116th St.*

⑬ Sugar Hill. Standing on the bluff of Sugar Hill overlooking Jackie Robinson Park, outside **409 Edgecombe Avenue**, you'd never guess that here resided such influential African-Americans as NAACP founder

RELIVE THE JAZZ AGE

Many of Harlem's historic jazz venues (mostly found on 125th Street) are still active, so you can pay respect to the legends like Duke Ellington and Louis Armstrong, then listen to a legend-in-the-making. A giant digital marquee announces the **Apollo Theatre** (⊠ *253 W 125th St.*), where jazz and funk godfather James Brown debuted in 1956 and was laid out in splendor following his death in 2006. Around the corner, the **Lenox Lounge** (⊠ *288 Lenox Ave.*) buzzes with action; eat here and be transported back in time; or enjoy a swing concert or gospel brunch at the **Cotton Club** (⊠ *666 W. 125th St., off West Side Hwy.*), which continues the tradition of the celebrated original (closed in 1935). Continue the pilgrimage at the newly reopened **Minton's Playhouse** (⊠ *208 W. 118th St.*), the birthplace of bebop, where Thelonious Monk was house pianist in the 1940s.

W.E.B. Du Bois and Supreme Court Justice Thurgood Marshall, or that farther north at **555 Edgecombe,** writers Langston Hughes and Zora Neale Hurston and jazz musicians Duke Ellington, Count Basie, and others lived and played (unless you catch the Sunday afternoon jazz concerts there). Harlem's society hill from the 1920s to the 1950s is today another partly shabby–partly cleaned-up–evolving neighborhood, on its way to regentrification. Walk over to Hamilton Heights for a better-preserved taste of the Harlem Renaissance years. ■ TIP→ **If you're here after 9:30 PM, drop by the basement jazz club St. Nick's Pub (773 St. Nicholas Avenue, near 148th Street, 212/283–9728), a laid-back local fixture that's been around for ages. Bring some bills to stuff into the tip jar that circulates, grab a strong drink, and enjoy the late-night jam sessions.**

⊠ *Bounded by 145th and 155th Sts. and Edgecombe and St. Nicholas Aves., Harlem* Ⓜ *A, B, C, D to 145th St.*

CENTRAL PARK

For many residents Central Park is the greatest—and most indispensable—part of New York City. Without the park's 843 acres of meandering paths, tranquil lakes, ponds, and open meadows, New Yorkers might be a lot less sane. Every day thousands of joggers, cyclists, in-line skaters, and walkers make their daily jaunts around the park's loop, the reservoir, and various other parts of the park. Come summertime the park serves as Manhattan's Riviera, with sun worshippers crowding every available patch of grass. Throughout the year pleasure seekers of all ages come to enjoy horseback riding, softball, ice-skating or roller-skating, rock climbing, croquet, tennis, and more—or simply to escape the rumble of traffic, walk through the woods, and feel, at least for a moment, far from the urban frenzy.

No matter how close to nature New Yorkers feel when reveling in it, Central Park was in fact the first artificially landscaped park in the United States. The design was conceived in 1857 by Frederick Law

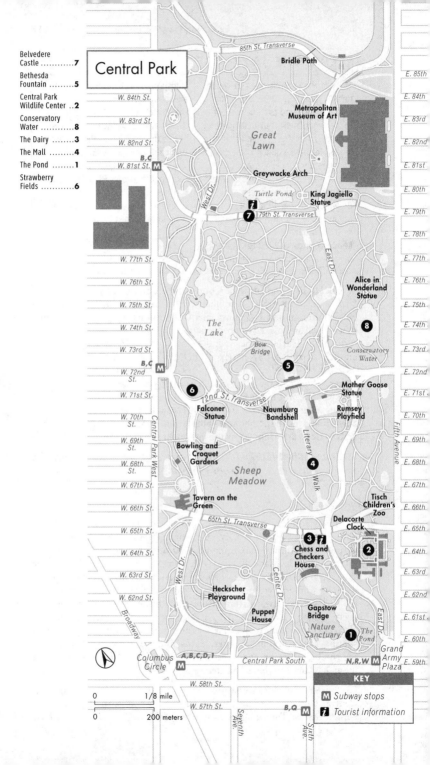

Central Park

85th St. Transverse

Bridle Path

Metropolitan
Museum of Art

Great
Lawn

Greywacke Arch

Turtle Pond

King Jagiello
Statue

79th St. Transverse

Alice in
Wonderland
Statue

The
Lake

Bow
Bridge

Conservatory
Water

Mother Goose
Statue

72nd St. Transverse

Falconer
Statue

Naumburg
Bandshell

Rumsey
Playfield

Literary Walk

Bowling and
Croquet
Gardens

Sheep
Meadow

Tavern on the
Green

65th St. Transverse

Tisch
Children's
Zoo

Delacorte
Clock

Chess and
Checkers
House

Heckscher
Playground

Puppet
House

Gapstow
Bridge

Nature
Sanctuary

The
Pond

Grand
Army
Plaza

West Dr.

East Dr.

Fifth Avenue

Central Park West

Center Dr.

West Dr.

Broadway

Columbus
Circle

Central Park South

Seventh Ave.

Sixth Ave.

W. 84th St.
W. 83rd St.
W. 82nd St.
W. 81st St. **B,C**
W. 77th St.
W. 76th St.
W. 75th St.
W. 74th St.
W. 73rd St.
W. 72nd St. **B,C**
W. 71st St.
W. 70th St.
W. 69th St.
W. 68th St.
W. 67th St.
W. 66th St.
W. 65th St.
W. 64th St.
W. 63rd St.
W. 62nd St.
W. 58th St.
W. 57th St.

E. 85th
E. 84th
E. 83rd
E. 82nd
E. 81st
E. 80th
E. 79th
E. 78th
E. 77th
E. 76th
E. 75th
E. 74th
E. 73rd
E. 72nd
E. 71st
E. 70th
E. 69th
E. 68th
E. 67th
E. 66th
E. 65th
E. 64th
E. 63rd
E. 62nd
E. 61st
E. 60th
E. 59th

A,B,C,D,1

N,R,W

B,Q

0   1/8 mile

0   200 meters

KEY

M Subway stops

i Tourist information

Olmsted and Calvert Vaux, the founders of the landscape architecture profession in the United States. The Greensward Plan, as it was called, combined pastoral, picturesque, and formal elements: open rolling meadows complement fanciful landscapes and grand, formal walkways. The southern portion of the park has many formal elements, whereas the north end is deliberately more wild.

For a recorded schedule of park events, call ☎888/697–2757. For a schedule of walking tours in Central Park, call ☎212/360–2727. Or visit the park's Web site at ⊕*www.centralparknyc.org*. Directions, park maps, and event calendars can also be obtained from volunteers at two 5th Avenue information booths, at East 60th Street and East 72nd Street.

GETTING HERE
Several entrances lead into the park. You can enter from the east, west, south, and north by paved pedestrian walkways, just off 5th Avenue, Central Park North (110th Street), Central Park West, and Central Park South. Four main roads (called Transverses) cut through the park from east to west—66th, 79th, 86th, and 96th streets. Running north-south through the park are East and West drives.

⇨ *Central Park map for sights in this section.*

❼ Belvedere Castle. Standing regally atop Vista Rock, Belvedere Castle was
☾ built in 1872 of the same gray Manhattan schist that thrusts out of the soil in dramatic outcrops throughout the park. From here you can also see the stage of the Delacorte Theater and observe the picnickers and softball players on the Great Lawn. The castle is a typically 19th-century mishmash of styles—Gothic with Romanesque, Chinese, Moorish, and Egyptian motifs. Inside, the Henry Luce Nature Observatory has nature exhibits, children's workshops, and educational programs. Free discovery kits containing binoculars, bird guides, maps, and sketching materials are available in exchange for two pieces of identification. ⊠*Midpark at 79th St. Transverse, Central Park* ☎*212/772–0210* ⊠*Free* ☾*Tues.– Sun. 10–5* Ⓜ*Subway: B, C to 81st St.*

❺ Bethesda Fountain. Few New York views are more romantic than the one
Fodor'sChoice from the top of the magnificent stone staircase that leads down to the
★ ornate, three-tier Bethesda Fountain. You might recognize it from one of the many films that have been shot here. The fountain was dedicated in 1873 to commemorate the soldiers who died at sea during the Civil War. Named for the biblical pool in Jerusalem, which was supposedly given healing powers by an angel, it features the statue *The Angel of the Waters* rising from the center. The four figures around the fountain's base symbolize Temperance, Purity, Health, and Peace. Beyond the terrace stretches the lake, filled with swans and amateur rowboat captains. ⊠*Midpark at 72nd St. Transverse, Central Park* Ⓜ*Subway: B, C to 72nd St.*

❷ Central Park Wildlife Center. Even a leisurely visit to this small but delight-
☾ ful menagerie, which has more than 130 species, will take only about an hour. The biggest specimens here are the polar bears. Clustered around

8

the central Sea Lion Pool are separate exhibits for each of Earth's major environments. The Polar Circle has a huge penguin tank and polar-bear floe; the open-air Temperate Territory is highlighted by a pit of chattering monkeys; and the Rain Forest contains the flora and fauna of the tropics. The **Tisch Children's Zoo,** on the north side of the Denesmouth Arch, has interactive, hands-on exhibits where you can pet such domestic animals as pigs, sheep, goats, and cows. Above a redbrick arcade near the zoo is the **Delacorte Clock,** a delightful glockenspiel. ⊠*Entrance at 5th Ave. and E. 64th St., Central Park* ☎*212/439–6500* ⊕*www.centralparkzoo.org* ⌑*$6* ☞*No children under 16 admitted without adult* ☉*Apr.–Oct., weekdays 10–5, weekends 10–5:30; Nov.–Mar., daily 10–4:30* Ⓜ*Subway: 6 to 68th St./Hunter College; N, R, W to 5th Ave./59th St.; F to Lexington Ave./63rd St.*

❽ Conservatory Water. The sophisticated model boats that sail this Renaissance Revival–style stone basin are raced each Saturday morning at 10, spring through fall. At the north end is one of the park's most beloved statues, José de Creeft's 1960 bronze sculpture of **Alice in Wonderland,** sitting on a giant mushroom with the Mad Hatter, March Hare, and leering Cheshire Cat in attendance. On the west side of the pond, a bronze statue of **Hans Christian Andersen,** the Ugly Duckling at his feet, is the site of storytelling hours on summer Saturdays at 11 AM. Model sailboats can be rented from a concession by the boat pond. ⊠*East side of park, from E. 73rd to E. 75th Sts., Central Park* Ⓜ*Subway: 6 to 77th St.*

❸ The Dairy. When it was built in the 19th century, the Dairy sat amid grazing cows and sold milk by the glass. Today the Dairy's painted, pointed eaves, steeple, and high-pitched slate roof harbor the **Central Park Visitor Center,** which has exhibits on the park's history, maps, a park reference library, and information about park events. ⊠*Midpark south of 65th St. Transverse, Central Park* ☎*212/794–6564* ☉*Apr.–Oct., Tues.–Sun. 10–5; Nov.–Mar., Tues.–Sun. 10–4.*

❹ The Mall. Around the turn of the 20th century, fashionable ladies and gentlemen used to gather to see and be seen on this broad, formal walkway. Today the Mall looks as grand as ever. The south end of its main path, the **Literary Walk,** is covered by the majestic canopy of the largest collection of American elms in North America and lined by statues of authors and artists such as Robert Burns, Shakespeare, and Sir Walter Scott. ⊠*Midpark between 66th and 72nd Sts., Central Park* Ⓜ*Subway: 6 to 68th St./Hunter College.*

❶ The Pond. Swans and ducks can sometimes be spotted on the calm waters of the Pond. For an unbeatable view of the city skyline, walk along the shore to **Gapstow Bridge.** From left to right you can see the brown peak-roof Sherry-Netherland Hotel; the black-and-white CBS Building; the rose-color Chippendale-style top of the Sony Building; the black-glass shaft of Trump Tower; and, in front, the green gables of the Plaza hotel. ⊠*Central Park S and 5th Ave., Central Park* Ⓜ*Subway: N, R, W to 5th Ave.*

6 Strawberry Fields. This memorial to John Lennon, who penned the classic 1967 song "Strawberry Fields Forever," is sometimes called the "international garden of peace." Its curving paths, shrubs, trees, and flower beds donated by many countries create a deliberately informal landscape reminiscent of the English parks of Lennon's homeland. ⊠ *W. Park Dr. and W. 72nd St., Central Park* Ⓜ *Subway: B, C to 72nd St.*

THE BOROUGHS: BROOKLYN, QUEENS, AND THE BRONX

Many tourists miss out on seeing these three boroughs across the East River to the east and north, and that's a shame. Within them, they contain some of the city's best museums and attractions. The Bronx, for example, contains thousands of acres of parkland and the largest metropolitan zoo in the country—not to mention the new Yankee Stadium. Meanwhile, both Brooklyn and Queens are full of diverse neighborhoods (so they're great places for tasting ethnic cuisine) and noteworthy attractions like the Brooklyn Botanic Garden and Flushing Meadows, home to the Mets. Brooklyn is the larges of the boroughs, with 2.5 million residents.

GETTING HERE

Brooklyn, Queens, and the Bronx are all served by many subway lines. To reach the Brooklyn Botanical Garden, Brooklyn Museum, and Prospect Park, take the 2 or 3 train to Eastern Parkway/Brooklyn Museum. The most direct way to the New York Botanical Garden is via **Metro-North Railroad** (⊕ *www.mta.info/mnr*) from Grand Central Terminal (Harlem Local Line, Botanical Garden stop). Round-trip tickets are $5 to $12.50, depending on time of day. A cheaper alternative is to take the D or 4 train to Bedford Park Boulevard, then walk east. ⊠ *200th St. and Kazimiroff Blvd., Bedford Park, Brooklyn* ☎ *718/817–8700* ⊕ *www.nybg.org* ▧ *Grounds only, $6, free Sat. 10–noon and all day Wed.; All-Garden Pass, $20; parking $12* ⊙ *Tues.–Sun. 10–6* Ⓜ *B, D, 4 to Bedford Park Blvd., then walk 8 blocks downhill to the Garden; Metro-North to Botanical Garden.*

⇨ *New York City map at the beginning of the chapter for sights in this section.*

BROOKLYN

Ⓒ **Brooklyn Botanic Garden.** A major attraction at this 52-acre botanic gar-
★ den, one of the finest in the country, is the beguiling Japanese Hill-and-Pond Garden—complete with a 1-acre pond and blazing red *torii* gate, which signifies (accurately) that a shrine is nearby. The Japanese cherry arbor nearby turns into a breathtaking cloud of pink every spring, and the Cherry Blossom Festival is among the park's most popular events. Also be sure to wander through the Cranford Rose Garden (5,000 bushes, 1,200 varieties); the Fragrance Garden, designed especially for the blind; and the Shakespeare Garden, featuring more than 80 plants immortalized by the Bard. Free garden tours are given every weekend at 1 PM. Entrances to the garden are on Eastern Parkway, next to the subway station; on Washington Avenue, behind the Brooklyn Museum; and on Flatbush Avenue at Empire Boulevard. ⊠ *900*

8

Washington Ave., between Crown and Carroll Sts., Prospect Heights, Brooklyn ☎*718/623–7200* ⊕*www.bbg.org* 🎟*$5; free all day Tues. and Sat. before noon. Weekend combo ticket with Brooklyn Museum $11* ⊙*Apr.–late Oct., grounds Tues.–Fri. 8–6, weekends 10–6, conservatory daily 10–5:30; late Oct.–Mar., grounds Tues.–Fri. 8–4:30, weekends 10–4:30; conservatory daily 10–4* Ⓜ*2, 3 to Eastern Pkwy.; B, Q to Prospect Park.*

★ **Brooklyn Museum.** The Brooklyn Museum has long stood in the shadow of Manhattan's Metropolitan. Though it has more than 1 million pieces in its permanent collection, from Rodin sculptures to Andean textiles and Assyrian wall reliefs, Brooklyn's is still the second-largest art museum in the United States—the Met is larger. And while the Met bustles, Brooklyn's attendance figures dwindled for many years. Pioneering museum director Arthur Lehman is out to change that. Because of a welcoming new design, more populist exhibitions, and neighborhood events, audiences have more than doubled recently.

Beyond the changing exhibitions, highlights include Egyptian art (one of the best collections of its kind in the world), African and pre-Columbian art, and Native American art. Seek out the museum's works by Georgia O'Keeffe, Winslow Homer, John Singer Sargent, George Bellows, Thomas Eakins, and Milton Avery—all stunners. Also check out the new Elizabeth A. Sackler Center for Feminist Art, which hosts traveling exhibits in addition to serving as the permanent home to Judy Chicago's installation *The Dinner Party* (1974–79). On the first Saturday of each month, the museum throws an extremely popular free evening of art, music, dancing, film screenings, and readings, starting at 6 PM. ✉*200 Eastern Pkwy., at Washington Ave., Prospect Heights, Brooklyn* ☎*718/638–5000* ⊕*www.brooklynmuseum.org* 🎟*$8 suggested donation. Weekend combo ticket with Brooklyn Botanic Garden $11* ⊙*Wed.–Fri. 10–5, weekends 11–6; 1st Sat. every month 11–11; call for program schedule* Ⓜ*2, 3 to Eastern Pkwy./Brooklyn Museum.*

Prospect Park. Brooklyn residents are passionate about this park designed in the late 1880s by Frederick Law Olmsted and Calvert Vaux. Olmsted once said that he was prouder of it than any of his other works. A good way to experience the park is to walk the entirety of its 3.3-mi circular drive and make detours off it as you wish. The drive is closed to cars at all times except weekday rush hours. Families with children should head straight for the eastern side, where most kids' attractions, such as a petting zoo and carousel (open April–October), are clustered. ✉*450 Flatbush Ave., Prospect Heights* ☎*718/399–7339* ⊕*www.prospect-parkzoo.com* 🎟*Free ($1.50 for carousel ride, $6 for zoo)* Ⓜ*2, 3 to Eastern Pkwy.; B, Q to Prospect. Park.*

QUEENS

⟳ **New York Hall of Science.** At the northwestern edge of Corona Park, the New York Hall of Science has more than 400 hands-on exhibitions that make science a playground for inquisitive minds of all ages. Climb aboard a replica of John Glenn's space capsule, throw a fastball and investigate its speed, or explore Charles and Ray Eames's classic Mathematica exhibition. ✉*111th St. at 46th Ave., Flushing* ☏*718/699–0005* ⊕*www.nyscience.org* 🎟*$11; free Fri. 2–5 and Sun. 10–11 Sept.–June* ☉*Sept.–June, Mon.–Thurs. 9:30–2, Fri. 9:30–5, weekends 10–6; July and Aug., weekdays 9:30–5, weekends 10–6* Ⓜ*7 to 111th St.; walk 3 blocks south.*

Fodor'sChoice **P.S. 1 Contemporary Art Center.** A pioneer in the "alternative-space" move-
★ ment, P.S.1 rose from the ruins of an abandoned school in 1976 as a sort of community arts center for the future. Now a partner of MoMA, P.S.1 focuses on the work of currently working experimental and innovative artists. Long-term installations include work by James Turrell and William Kentridge. The building is enormous, and every available corner is used; discover art not only in galleries but also on the rooftop spaces, in the boiler room, and even in the bathrooms. Summer Saturdays from 3 to 9 PM, outdoor dance parties attract an art-school-like crowd. ✉*22–25 Jackson Ave., at 46th Ave., Long Island City* ☏*718/784–2084* ⊕*www.ps1.org* 🎟*$5 suggested donation* ☉*Thurs.– Mon. noon–6* Ⓜ*7 to 45th Rd.–Courthouse Sq.; E, V to 23rd St.–Ely Ave.; G to 21st St.*

THE BRONX

☾ **The Bronx Zoo.** When it opened its gates in 1899, the Bronx Zoo only
Fodor'sChoice had 843 animals. But today, with 265 acres and more than 4,000 ani-
★ mals (of more than 600 species), it's the largest metropolitan zoo in the United States. Get up close and personal with exotic creatures in outdoor settings that re-create natural habitats; you're often separated from them by no more than a moat or wall of glass. ✉*Bronx River Pkwy. and Fordham Rd., Fordham* ☏*718/367–1010* ⊕*www.bronxzoo.com* 🎟*Adults $15, children $11, extra charge for some exhibits; free Wed., donation suggested; parking $12* ☉ *Apr.–Oct., weekdays 10–5, weekends 10–5:30; Nov.–Mar., daily 10–4:30; last ticket sold 30 mins before closing* Ⓜ*2, 5 to E. Tremont/West Farms, then walk 2 blocks up Boston Rd. to zoo's Wild Asia entrance; 2 to Pelham Pkwy., then walk 3 blocks west to Bronx Pkwy. entrance; Bx11 express bus to Bronx Pkwy. entrance.*

Fodor'sChoice **New York Botanical Garden.** Considered one of the leading botany centers
★ of the world, this 250-acre garden is one of the best reasons to make a trip to the Bronx. Built around the dramatic gorge of the Bronx River, the Garden offers lush indoor and outdoor gardens, acres of natural forest, as well as classes, concerts, and special exhibits. Be astounded by the captivating fragrance of the Peggy Rockefeller Rose Garden's 2,700 plants of more than 250 varieties; see intricate orchids that look like the stuff of science fiction; relax in the quiet of the forest or the calm of the Conservatory; or take a jaunt through the Everett Children's Adventure Garden, a 12-acre, indoor-outdoor museum with a boulder maze, giant animal topiaries, and a plant discovery center.

The Garden's roses bloom in June and September, but there's plenty to see year-round. The Victorian-style **Enid A. Haupt Conservatory** (🎟*$5*) houses re-creations of misty tropical rain forests and arid African and North American deserts as well as exhibitions, such as the annual

8

Holiday Train Show and the Orchid Show. The **Combination Ticket** (🖃*$13, off-peak days*) gives you access to the Conservatory, Rock Garden, Native Plant Garden, Tram Tour, Everett Children's Adventure Garden, and exhibits in the library.

SPORTS AND THE OUTDOORS

When visiting New York, you are likely going to impress yourself with just how much walking you can do every day of your trip. But if you want some other exercise or sporting adventure—or just an outdoors experience (such as the zoo and island boat tours)—New York City has plenty of options.

PARTICIPATORY SPORTS

New York City's **Parks & Recreation division** (☎*311 in New York City, 212/639–9675 or 212/NEW–YORK outside New York City ⊕www. nyc.gov/parks*) lists all of the recreational facilities and activities available through New York's Parks Department. The sports section of *Time Out New York,* sold at most newsstands, lists upcoming events, times, dates, and ticket information.

BOATING AND KAYAKING

Central Park has rowboats (plus one Venetian gondola for glides in the moonlight) on the 22-acre Central Park Lake. Rent your rowboat at **Loeb Boathouse** (⊠*Midpark near E. 74th St., Central Park ☎212/517–2233 ⊕www.centralparknyc.org*) from March through October; gondola rides are available only in summer.

In summer at the **Pier 96 Boathouse** (⊠*56th St. and the Hudson River, Midtown West ☎646/613–0740 daily status, 646/613–0375 information ⊕www.downtownboathouse.org Ⓜ1, A, C, B, D to 59th St./ Columbus Circle*) in Midtown West you can take a sturdy kayak out for a paddle for free on weekends and weekday evenings from mid-May through mid-October. Beginners learn to paddle in the calmer embayment area closest to shore until they feel ready to venture farther out into open water. More-experienced kayakers can partake in the three-hour trips conducted every weekend and on holiday mornings. Sign-ups for these popular tours end at 8 AM. Due to high demand, names are entered into a lottery to see who gets to go out each morning. No reservations are taken in advance. **Manhattan Kayak Company** (⊠*Chelsea Piers, Pier 66, W. 26th St. and the Hudson River, Chelsea ☎212/924–1788 ⊕www.manhattankayak.com Ⓜ C, E to 23rd St.*) runs trips (these are not free) and gives lessons for all levels.

BOAT TOURS Trips on the Hudson River via private yacht can be arranged by **Surfside 3 Marinemax Marina** (⊠*Chelsea Piers ☎212/336–7873*). Lunch cruises, dinner cruises, and cabaret sails can be reserved on *Bateaux New York* or *Spirit of New York,* which both leave from Pier 61 (☎*866/211–3805*).

ICE-SKATING

The city's outdoor rinks, open from roughly November through March, all have their own character. Central Park's beautifully situated **Wollman Rink** (⊠*North of 6th Ave., between 62nd and 63rd Sts., north of park entrance* ☎*212/439–6900* ⊕*www.wollmanskatingrink.com*) has skating until long after dark beneath the lights of the city. Be prepared for daytime crowds on weekends. The **Lasker Rink** (⊠*Midpark near E. 106th St., Central Park* ☎*917/492–3875* ⊕*www.laskerskatingrink.com* Ⓜ*B, C to 103rd St.*), at the north end of Central Park, is smaller and usually less crowded than Wollman.

The Pond at Bryant Park (⊠*6th Ave. between 40th and 42nd Sts., Midtown West* ☎*866/221–5157* ⊕*www.bryantpark.org* Ⓜ*B, D, F, V to 42nd St.*) offers free skating, not including the cost of skate rental (or bring your own), from late October through January, from 8 AM to 10 PM from Sunday through Thursday and from 8 AM to midnight Friday and Saturday.

★ The outdoor rink in **Rockefeller Center** (⊠*50th St. at 5th Ave., lower plaza, Midtown West* ☎*212/332–7654* ⊕*www.therinkatrockcenter.com* Ⓜ*B, D, F, V to 47th–50th Sts./Rockefeller Center; E, V to 5th Ave.–53rd St.*), open from October through early April, is much smaller in real life than it appears on TV and in movies. It's also busy, so be prepared to wait—there are no advance ticket sales. Although it's also beautiful, especially when Rock Center's enormous Christmas tree towers above it, you pay for the privilege: adult rates are $13.50–$17.50 and skate rentals are $9.

MULTISPORT

Chelsea Piers (⇨*The Village, Chelsea, and Union Square Area under Exploring New York City*) offers golf, ice-skating, roller skating, rock climbing, swimming, kayaking, bowling, gymnastics, and basketball.

TEAM SPORTS

BASEBALL

The subway will get you directly to stadiums of both New York–area major-league teams. A fun alternative, the **Yankee Clipper** (☎*800/533–3779* ⊕*www.nywaterway.com*) cruises from Manhattan's East Side and from New Jersey to Yankee Stadium on game nights. The round-trip cost is $22. The regular baseball season runs from April through September.

The **New York Mets** recently moved from Shea Stadium to the neighboring, newly constructed **Citi Field** (⊠*Roosevelt Ave. off Grand Central Pkwy., Flushing* ☎*718/507–8499* ⊕*www.mets.com* Ⓜ*7 to Willets Pt./Shea Stadium*), at the next-to-last stop on the 7 train, in Queens; the **New York Yankees** play in a stadium called the **New Yankee Stadium** (⊠*161st St. and River Ave., Bronx* ☎*718/293–6000* Ⓜ*B, D to 167th St.; 4 to 161st St.–Yankee Stadium*).

BASKETBALL

The **New York Knicks** (☎*212/465–5867* ⊕*www.nba.com/knicks*) arouse intense hometown passions, which means tickets for home games at Madison Square Garden are hard to come by. The **New Jersey Nets** (☎*201/935–3900 box office, 800/765–6387* ⊕*www.nba.com/nets*) play at the Meadowlands in the Izod Center but have plans to relocate and become the Brooklyn Nets. Tickets are generally easy to obtain.

The men's basketball season runs from late October through April.

FOOTBALL

The football season runs from September through December. The enormously popular **New York Giants** (☎*201/935–8222 for tickets* ⊕*www.giants.com*) play at Giants Stadium in the Meadowlands Sports Complex. Most seats for Giants games are sold on a season-ticket basis—and there's a long waiting list for those. However, single tickets are occasionally available at the stadium box office. The **New York Jets** (☎*516/560–8200 for tickets, 516/560–8288 for fan club* ⊕*www.newyorkjets.com*) also play at Giants Stadium. Although Jets tickets are not as scarce as those for the Giants, most are snapped up by fans before the season opener.

THE OUTDOORS

ZOOS

Want to take the kids to the zoo? In Manhattan, there's the **Central Park Wildlife Center** ⊠*Entrance at 5th Ave. and E. 64th St.* ☎*212/439–6500* ⊕*www.centralparkzoo.org* ☐*$6* ⌖*No children under 16 admitted without adult* ⊘*Apr.–Oct., weekdays 10–5, weekends 10–5:30; Nov.–Mar., daily 10–4:30* Ⓜ*Subway: 6 to 68th St./Hunter College; N, R, W to 5th Ave./59th St.; F to Lexington Ave./63rd St.),* with such creatures as polar bears, sea lions, penguins, and of course those always popular chattering monkeys. There's also a petting zoo nearby with farm animals nearby. With only 130 species, it's much, much smaller than the Bronx Zoo.

For a full-day outing at the zoo, head north to the 265-acre **Bronx Zoo** (⊠*Bronx River Pkwy. and Fordham Rd.* ☎*718/367–1010* ⊕*www.bronxzoo.com* ☐*$15, extra charge for some exhibits; free Wed., donation suggested; parking $12* ⊘*Apr.–Oct., weekdays 10–5, weekends 10–5:30; Nov.–Mar., daily 10–4:30; last ticket sold 30 mins before closing* Ⓜ*2, 5 to E. Tremont/West Farms, then walk 2 blocks up Boston Rd. to zoo's Wild Asia entrance; 2 to Pelham Pkwy., then walk 3 blocks west to Bronx Pkwy. entrance; Bx11 express bus to Bronx Pkwy.*

entrance). It has more than 4,000 animals and is the largest metropolitan zoo in the United States. Get up close and personal with exotic creatures in outdoor settings that re-create natural habitats; you're often separated from them by no more than a moat or wall of glass.

SHOPPING

New York shopping is a nonstop eye-opener, from the pristine couture houses flanking Madison Avenue to quirkier shops downtown. No matter which threshold you cross, shopping here is an event. For every bursting department store there's an echoing, minimalist boutique; for every familiar national brand there's a secret local favorite. The foremost American and international companies stake their flagships here; meanwhile, small neighborhood shops guarantee unexpected pleasures. National chains often make their New York branches something special, with unique sales environments and exclusive merchandise.

Fifth Avenue from Rockefeller Center to Central Park South pogos between landmark department stores, glossy international designer boutiques, and casual national chains. What they all have in common: massive flagship spaces.

Tomes could be written about shopping in New York City, but if you can only hit a few spots, try these for a taste of the Big Apple.

BOOKSTORE

Fodor'sChoice **The Strand.** Serious bibliophiles flock to this monstrous book emporium
★ with some 2 million volumes (the store's slogan is "18 Miles of Books"). The stock includes both new and secondhand books plus thousands of collector's items. A separate rare-book room is on the third floor at 826 Broadway (accessible through the main store). A second store is near South Street Seaport. Check out the basement, with discounted, barely touched reviewers' copies of new books, organized by author. ■ TIP→ **Don't be too goal oriented or you might end up frustrated. The beauty of the Strand is that you'll never quite leave with what you came for, and treasures will essentially find you.** ⊠*828 Broadway, at E. 12th St., Union Square* ☎*212/473–1452* ⊙*Mon.–Sat. 9:30 AM–10:30 PM, Sun. 11–10:30* Ⓜ*Union Sq./14th St.*

DEPARTMENT STORES

Fodor'sChoice **Barneys New York.** Barneys continues to provide fashion-conscious and
★ big-budget shoppers with irresistible, must-have items at its uptown flagship store. The extensive menswear selection has a handful of edgier designers, though made-to-measure is always available. The women's department showcases posh designers of all stripes, from the subdued lines of Armani and Jil Sander to the irrepressible Alaïa and Zac Posen. The shoe selection trots out Prada boots and strappy Blahniks; the cosmetics department will keep you in Kiehl's, Sue Devitt, and Frederic Malle; jewelry runs from the whimsical (Kazuko) to the classic (Ileana

Makri). Expanded versions of the less expensive **Co-op** department occupy the old Barneys' warehouse space on West 18th Street and a niche on Wooster Street. ⊠ *660 Madison Ave., between E. 60th and E. 61st Sts., Upper East Side* ☎ *212/826–8900* Ⓜ *N, R, W, 4, 5, 6 to 59th St./Lexington Ave.* ⊠ *Barneys Co-op, 236 W. 18th St., between 7th and 8th Aves., Chelsea* ☎ *212/593–7800* Ⓜ *A, C, E to 14th St.* ⊠ *116 Wooster St., between Prince and Spring Sts., SoHo* ☎ *212/965–9964* Ⓜ *R, W to Prince St.*

Bergdorf Goodman. Good taste reigns in an elegant and understated setting, but remember that elegant doesn't necessarily mean sedate. Bergdorf's carries some brilliant lines, such as John Galliano's sensational couture and Philip Treacy's dramatic hats. In the basement Level of Beauty, find a seat in the manicure–pedicure lounge (no appointments) for a bit of impromptu pampering. The home department has rooms full of magnificent linens, tableware, and gifts. Across the street is another entire store devoted to menswear: made-to-measure shirts, custom suits, designer lines by the likes of Ralph Lauren and Gucci, and scads of accessories, from hip flasks to silk scarves. The men's store is across the street at 58th street. ⊠ *754 5th Ave., between W. 57th and W. 58th Sts., Midtown* ☎ *212/753–7300* Ⓜ *N, R, W to 5th Ave./59th St.*

Bloomingdale's. Only a few stores in New York occupy an entire city block; the uptown branch of this New York institution is one of them. The main floor is a crazy, glittery maze of mirrored cosmetic counters and perfume-spraying salespeople. Once you get past this dizzying scene, you can find good buys on designer clothes, bedding, and housewares. The downtown location is smaller, and has a well-edited, higher-end selection of merchandise, so you can focus your search for that Michael Kors handbag or pricey pair of stilettos. ⊠ *1000 3rd Ave., main entrance at E. 59th St. and Lexington Ave., Midtown* ☎ *212/705– 2000* Ⓜ *N, R, W, 4, 5, 6 to 59th St./Lexington Ave.* ⊠ *504 Broadway, between Spring and Broome Sts., SoHo* ☎ *212/729–5900* Ⓜ *R, W to Prince St.*

Fodor'sChoice **Century 21.** For many New Yorkers, this downtown fixture—right
★ across the street from the former World Trade Center site—remains the mother lode of discount shopping. Four floors are crammed with everything from Gucci sunglasses and half-price cashmere sweaters to Ralph Lauren towels, though you'll have to weed through racks of less-fabulous stuff to find that gem. The best bets in the men's department are shoes and the designer briefs; the full floor of designer women's wear can yield some dazzling finds, such as a Calvin Klein leather trench coat for less than $600 or a sweeping crinoline skirt from Jean Paul Gaultier. ■ TIP→ Since lines for the communal dressing rooms can be prohibitively long, you might want to wear a bodysuit under your clothes for quick, between-the-racks try-ons. ⊠ *22 Cortlandt St., between Broadway and Church St., Lower Manhattan* ☎ *212/227–9092* Ⓜ *R, W to Cortlandt St.*

★ **Macy's.** Famous for its Thanksgiving Day Parade, Macy's is a household name. The company's headquarters store at Herald Square claims to be the largest retail store in America—so expect to lose your bearings at least once. Fashion-wise, there's a concentration on mainstream rather than on luxe. One strong suit is denim, with everything from Hilfiger and Calvin Klein to Earl Jeans and Paper Denim & Cloth. There's also a reliably good selection of American designs from Ralph Lauren, Tommy Hilfiger, and Nautica. ⊠*Herald Sq., 151 W. 34th St., between 6th and 7th Aves., Midtown/Union Sq. Area* ☎*212/695–4400* Ⓜ*B, D, F, N, Q, R, V, W to 34th St./Herald Sq.*

Saks Fifth Avenue. For concentrating on fashion- and beauty-only items, Saks sells an astonishing array of clothing. The choice of American and European designers is impressive without being esoteric—the women's selection includes Gucci, Narciso Rodriguez, and Marc Jacobs, plus devastating ball gowns galore. The footwear collections are gratifyingly broad, from Ferragamo to Juicy. In the men's department, sportswear stars such as John Varvatos counterbalance formal wear and current trends. The ground-floor beauty department stocks everything from the classic (Sisley, Lancôme) to the fun and edgy (Nars, Aussie-import Napolean Perdis). ⊠*611 5th Ave., between E. 49th and E. 50th Sts., Midtown* ☎*212/753–4000* Ⓜ*E, V to 5th Ave./53rd St.*

HAUTE DESIGN

Chanel. The Midtown flagship has often been compared to a Chanel suit—slim, elegant, and timeless. Inside wait the famed suits themselves, along with other pillars of Chanel style: chic little black dresses and evening gowns, chain-handled bags, and yards of pearls. The downtown branch concentrates more on contemporary forays, while Madison's boutique is dedicated to shoes, handbags, and other accessories. The jewelry outpost gleams with showstopper pieces based on Chanel's own jewels, as well as stars and comets sparkling with diamonds and gold worked into a quilted design. ⊠*139 Spring St., at Wooster St., SoHo* ☎*212/334–0055* Ⓜ*C, E to Spring St.* ⊠*15 E. 57th St., between 5th and Madison Aves., Midtown East* ☎*212/355–5050* Ⓜ*N, R, W to 5th Ave./59th St.* ⊠*737 Madison Ave., at E. 64th St., Upper East Side* ☎*212/535–5505* Ⓜ*6 to 68th St. /Hunter College* ⊠*Chanel Fine Jewelry, 733 Madison Ave., at E. 64th St., Upper East Side* ☎*212/535–5828* Ⓜ*6 to 68th St. /Hunter College.*

JEWELRY

Manhattan's Diamond district is centered around 47th Street just east of Sixth Avenue (Avenue of the Americas).

Cartier. Pierre Cartier allegedly won the 5th Avenue mansion location by trading two strands of perfectly matched natural pearls with Mrs. Morton Plant. The jewelry is still incredibly persuasive, from such established favorites as the interlocking rings to the more recent additions such as the handcufflike Menotte bracelets. ⊠*653 5th Ave., at E. 52nd*

8

St., Midtown East ☎212/753–0111 Ⓜ*E, V to 5th Ave./53rd St.* ✉*828 Madison Ave., at E. 69th St., Upper East Side* ☎212/472–6400 Ⓜ*6 to 68th St. /Hunter College.*

Fodor'sChoice
★   **Tiffany & Co.** The display windows can be soigné, funny, or just plain breathtaking. Alongside the $80,000 platinum-and-diamond bracelets, a lot here is affordable on a whim—and everything comes wrapped in that unmistakable Tiffany blue. ✉*727 5th Ave., at E. 57th St., Midtown East* ☎212/755–8000 Ⓜ*N, R, W to 5th Ave./59th St.*

TOYS AND GAMES

Fodor'sChoice
★   **F.A.O. Schwarz.** A New York classic that's better than ever, this children's paradise more than lives up to the hype. The ground floor is a zoo of extraordinary stuffed animals, from cuddly $20 teddies to towering, life-size elephants and giraffes (with larger-than-life prices to match). F.A.O. Schweets stocks M&Ms in every color of the rainbow; upstairs, you can dance on the giant musical floor keyboard, browse through Barbies wearing Armani and Juicy Couture, and design your own customized Hot Wheels car. ✉*767 5th Ave., at E. 58th St., Midtown East* ☎212/644–9400 Ⓜ*4, 5, 6 to E. 59th St.*

NIGHTLIFE AND THE SHOWS

New York, New York. When you're not gawking at the skyscrapers, rummaging through Chinatown treasures (or considering taking out a loan for 5th Avenue fashion finds), you just may be captivated by the Great White Way of Broadway, dazzling with its lighted signs into the wee hours of the night. In fact, you'll likely even feel safe walking down Broadway at midnight, because people are everywhere. It earned its moniker the City that Never Sleeps for good reason.

For nightlife, there's plenty to do: jazz, comedy clubs, bar hopping, dancing, attending a Ballet at the Lincoln Center, hearing a touring orchestra at Carnegie Hall, watching the Rockettes at Radio City Music Hall, and, of course, going to a Broadway show. For more nightlife options than what's listed here, see our New York City coverage on Fodors.com or pick up our acclaimed *Fodor's New York City* book.

BARS AND CLUBS

Every night of the week you'll find New Yorkers going out on the town. Nobody here waits for the weekend—in fact, many people prefer to party during the week when there's actually room to belly up to the bar. If word gets out that a hot band is playing in a bar on a Tuesday, or if a well-known DJ takes over a dance club on a Wednesday, you can be assured these places will be packed like the Saturday nights in most other towns.

The bar and clubbing scene is still largely downtown—in drab-by-day dives in the East Village and Lower East Side, classic jazz joints in the West Village, and the Meatpacking District's and Chelsea's see-and-be-seen clubs—but you don't have to go below 14th Street to have a good time. Midtown, especially around Hell's Kitchen, has developed quite the vibrant scene, too, and there are still plenty of preppy hangouts on the Upper East and Upper West sides. And across the East River, Brooklyn's Williamsburg neighborhood has become a mecca for artists, hipsters, and rock-and-rollers.

The *New York Times* has listings of cabaret shows. You may also get good tips from an in-the-know hotel concierge. Keep in mind that events change almost weekly, and venue life spans are often measured in months, not years.

Most clubs charge a cover, which can range from $5 to $25 or more, depending on the venue and the night. Be sure to take some cash, because many places don't accept credit cards. (Nothing will enrage the people behind you in line like whipping out the plastic.) Remember to dress properly, something that is easily accomplished by wearing black and leaving your beat-up sneakers at home. Smoking is prohibited in all enclosed public places in New York City, including restaurants and bars. Some bars have gardens or fully enclosed smoking rooms for those who wish to light up, but in most places you'll have to step outside.

McSorley's Old Ale House. Joseph Mitchell immortalized this spot, which claims to be one of the city's oldest, in *The New Yorker.* Opened in 1854, it didn't admit women until 1970. Fortunately, it now offers separate restrooms. The mahogany bar, gas lamps, potbelly stove, and yellowing newspaper clips are originals. Try to visit on a weekday before 7 PM so you can enjoy one of the two McSorley's ales and a cheese plate with onions in relative peace. Be warned: on weekends, this place is a zoo. ⊠ *15 E. 7th St., between 2nd and 3rd Aves., East Village* ☎ *212/473–9148* Ⓜ *6 to Astor Pl.*

8

BROADWAY

Even if you're just a legend in your own mind, there's nothing quite like making your own grand entrance at a show on the Great White Way. As you find your seat, the anticipation starts to rise; you sit, the houselights dim, and the orchestra strikes up the first notes of the overture, filling the theater with excitement. There is no other experience like it and no visit to the city—at least your first or second visit—is really complete if you haven't seen a Broadway show (or three). So secure your tickets, settle in, and prepare to be transported.

Scoring tickets is fairly easy, especially if you have some flexibility. But if timing or cost is critical, the only way to ensure you'll get the seats you want is to make your purchase in advance—and that might be months ahead for a hit show. In general, tickets for Saturday evenings and for weekend matinees are the toughest to secure.

For full-priced tickets, you can order them directly from the box office. To find out what's playing and available promotions, go online to ⊕ *www.Broadwaybox.com.* For day-of, up-to-half-off tickets, head to the TKTS booth in Times Square, at 47th and Broadway.

Also, inside the Times Square Visitors Center in Midtown is the League of American Theatres and Producers' **Broadway Ticket Center** (⌂*1560 Broadway, between W. 46th and W. 47th Sts. Midtown West* ☎*888/BROADWAY* ⊕*www. livebroadway.com* Ⓜ*1, 2, 3, 7, N, Q, R, W, S to 42nd St./Times Sq.; N, R, W to 49th St.*).

WORD OF MOUTH

"For us New York is always about the theater—Broadway, off-Broadway, off-off-Broadway, whatever. We've been known to see four plays in three days."   —abram

Ticket hours are Monday–Saturday 10–7, Sunday 11–6. You can find a selection of discount vouchers here; it also serves as a one-stop shopping place for full-price tickets for most Broadway shows.

CONCERT HALLS

Carnegie Hall (⌂*881 7th Ave., at W. 57th St., Midtown West* ☎*212/247-7800* ⊕*www.carnegiehall.org* Ⓜ*N, Q, R, W to 57th St.; B, D, E to 7th Ave.*) is, of course, one of the world's most famous concert halls. Virtually every important musician of the 20th century performed in this century-old Italian Renaissance–style building, often at the peak of his or her creative powers. Tchaikovsky conducted the opening-night concert on May 5, 1891, Leonard Bernstein had his debut here, and Vladimir Horowitz made his historic return to the concert stage here. Performances are given in the grand 2,804-seat **Isaac Stern Auditorium,** the 268-seat **Weill Recital Hall,** and the modern and stylish 644-seat **Judy and Arthur Zankel Hall** on the lower level. Although the emphasis is on classical music, Carnegie Hall also hosts jazz, pop, cabaret, and folk music concerts.

Fodor'sChoice   The titan of American opera companies, the **Metropolitan Opera** (⌂*W.*
★   *62nd to W. 66th Sts., Broadway to Amsterdam Ave., Upper West Side* ☎*212/362–6000* ⊕*www.metopera.org* Ⓜ*1 to 66th St./Lincoln Center*) brings the world's leading singers to its vast stage at **Lincoln Center** from October to April. The company's music director and principal conductor, James Levine, ensures the orchestra rivals the world's finest symphonies. Ranging from the traditional to a growing emphasis on the modern (Doctor Atomic in 2008), all performances, including those sung in English, are unobtrusively subtitled on small screens on the back of the seat in front of you. ■TIP➔ **For programs Monday–Thursday, a limited number of same-day $20 Rush orchestra-seat tickets are available for seniors (by phone or online beginning at noon); they are released two hours prior to that day's performance to the general public, at the box office only. Standing-room tickets go on sale at 10 AM on the day of the performance (buy them online, by phone, or at the Met box office); they are $20 for the orchestra level and $15 for the family circle.**

☾   **Radio City Music Hall** (⌂*1260 6th Ave., between W. 50th and W. 51st Sts. Midtown West* ☎*212/247–4777* ⊕*www.radiocity.com* Ⓜ*B, D, F to 47th-50th/Rockefeller Center*) is the famed home of the scissor-kicking Rockettes and the Radio City Christmas Spectacular, but this stunning art-deco showplace also packs its some 6,000 seats for musical events, kids entertainment like Dora the Explorer Live!, and the occasional film.

More kids programming is held at its affiliates, the Beacon Theatre and the theater at Madison Square Garden.

■TIP→ **For tickets for most events at Radio City Music Hall and Madison Square Garden, contact Ticket Master (** ☎*212/307–4100, 866/448–7849 automated service, 212/220–0500 premium tickets* ⊕*www.ticketmaster. com*)**. If you're coming at Christmastime and want to see the Rockettes in the Radio City Music Hall's Christmas Spectacular, be sure to book early and be flexible with show timing (you can see a show on Sunday morning, for example).**

TV SHOW TAPINGS

Tickets to tapings of TV shows are free, but can be very hard to come by on short notice. Most shows accept advance requests by e-mail, phone, or online—but for the most popular shows, like *The Daily Show with Jon Stewart,* the request backlog is so deep you might even have to wait a few months before they'll accept any new ones. Same-day standby tickets are often available—but be prepared to wait in line for several hours, sometimes starting at 5 or 6 AM, depending on how hot the show is, or the wattage of that day's celebrity guests.

The Daily Show with Jon Stewart. The smirking, amiable, and incisive Jon Stewart pokes fun at news headlines on this half-hour cable show. The program tapes from Monday through Thursday; you can request advance tickets by e-mailing the studio or by checking the calendar on the Web site. For standby tickets, show up well before the 5:45 PM doors-open time. Audience members must be 18 or older. ⊠*733 11th Ave., between W. 51st and W. 52nd Sts., Midtown West* ☎*212/586–2477* ⊕*www.thedailyshow.com* ✉ *requesttickets@thedailyshow.com* Ⓜ*C, E to 50th St.*

Good Morning America. Diane Sawyer, Robin Roberts, Chris Cuomo, and Sam Champion host this early-morning news and entertainment standby. *GMA* airs live, weekdays from 7 AM to 9 AM, and ticket requests (online only) should be sent four to six months in advance. ⊠*7 Times Sq., at W. 44th St. and Broadway, Midtown West* ☎*212/456–7384* ⊕*www.abcnews.go.com/GMA* Ⓜ*1, 2, 3, 7, N, Q, R, W, S to 42nd St./Times Sq.*

The Late Show with David Letterman. Letterman's famously offbeat humor and wacky top-10 lists have had fans giggling for more than two decades. Call ☎*212/247–6497* starting at 11 AM on tape days—Monday through Thursday—for standby tickets. For advance tickets (two maximum), you can submit a request online or fill out an application in person at the theater. You must be 18 or older to sit in the audience. ⊠*Ed Sullivan Theater, 1697 Broadway, between W. 53rd and W. 54th Sts., Midtown West* ☎*212/975–5853* ⊕*www.lateshow.cbs.com* Ⓜ*1, C, E to 50th St.; B, D, E to 7th Ave.*

Live! with Regis and Kelly. The sparks fly on this morning program, which books an eclectic roster of guests. Standby tickets become available weekdays at 7 AM at the **ABC Studios** (⊠*7 Lincoln Sq., corner of W.*

8

67th St. and Columbus Ave., Upper West Side). Otherwise, write for tickets (four tickets maximum) a full year in advance or fill out a form online. Children under 10 aren't allowed in the audience. ☍*Live Tickets, Ansonia Station, Box 230-777, 10023* ☎*212/456–3054* Ⓜ*1 to 66th St./Lincoln Center.*

The Martha Stewart Show. Master baker, craft maker, and champion of all "good things," Martha Stewart hosts her show with a live studio audience and various celebrity guests. The program generally tapes weekdays at both 10 AM and 2 PM. You can request tickets through the Martha Stewart Web site. Often, show producers are recruiting for groups of people (like nurses, new moms, or brides-to-be) and if you fit that category, your chances of scoring tickets increase. Occasionally, two hours prior to showtime, standby tickets are given out. Audience members must be at least 10 years old. ✉*221 W. 26th St., between 7th and 8th Ave., Chelsea* ☎*212/727–1234* ⊕*www.marthastewart. com* Ⓜ*C or 1 to 23rd St.*

The Mike Huckabee Show. A newcomer to the TV talk show scene, Mike Huckabee has a weekend show on Fox News. In his first year out of the gate he's interviewed a diverse roster of celebrities, from Jerry Springer to Steve Forbes. His show is taped on Saturday afternoons. Request tickets in advance by calling ☎*877/225–8587* or emailing ✍*hucktix@foxnews.com* (include how many tickets you need, what weekend you're coming, and your email address and phone number). ✉*Fox News studio, 1211 Sixth Ave.* Ⓜ*Rockefeller Center.*

Saturday Night Live. Influential from the start, *SNL* continues to captivate audiences. Standby tickets—only one per person—are distributed at 7 AM on the day of the show at the West 49th Street entrance to 30 Rockefeller Plaza. You may ask for a ticket for either the dress rehearsal (8 PM) or the live show (11:30 PM). Requests for advance tickets (two per applicant) must be submitted by e-mail only in August to ✍*snltickets@ nbcuni.com*; recipients are determined by lottery. You must be 16 or older to sit in the audience. ✉*NBC Studios, Saturday Night Live, 30 Rockefeller Plaza, between W. 49th and W. 50th Sts., Midtown West* ☎*212/664–3056* Ⓜ*B, D, F, V to 47th–50th Sts./Rockefeller Center.*

Today. America's first morning talk–news show airs weekdays from 7 AM to 10 AM in the glass-enclosed, ground-level NBC studio across from its original home at 30 Rockefeller Plaza. You may well be spotted on TV by friends back home while you're standing behind anchors Meredith Vieira and Matt Lauer. ✉*Rockefeller Plaza at W. 49th St., Midtown West* Ⓜ*B, D, F, V to 47th–50th Sts./Rockefeller Center.*

WHERE TO EAT

Updated by
Jay Cheshes,
Erica Duecy,
and Carolyn
Galgano

Besides satisfying a taste for the finer things in life, restaurants serve Gothamites and visitors in other crucial ways. They're a vital catalyst for exploring the city (the hunt on Museum Mile for a bite before museum-hopping), a communication device ("Let me tell you about this great little Mexican place way uptown"), and a standby of cocktail-party one-upmanship ("What? You haven't been to Per Se yet?!"). Perhaps most important, restaurants serve as extensions of New Yorkers' usually minute kitchens and nonexistent dining rooms.

So whether you decide to go for a delectable downtown *banh mi* Vietnamese hero with its surprising counterpoint of flavors and textures, or a prime porterhouse for two with creamed spinach and *pommes* Lyonnaise at a fancy uptown steak house, note that some of the dishes recommended in the following reviews may not be on the menu you receive when you sit down to eat. Many menus around town are market-driven and seasonal. Use our recommendations as guidelines and you won't be disappointed.

Also, plan to east dinner later than you ordinarily would—if you want to experience the real New York dining scene, that is. Or, alternatively, if you like to go when it's quieter and less crowded, dine earlier. Most New York restaurants are empty at around 6 PM and don't fill up until at least 7:30 or 8. Prime-time dinner reservations—between 8 and 10 o'clock—are the hardest to score.

WHAT IT COSTS AT DINNER				
¢	$	$$	$$$	$$$$
under $10	$10–$17	$18–$24	$25–$35	over $35

Price per person for a median main course or equivalent combination of smaller dishes. Note: if a restaurant offers only prix-fixe (set-price) meals, it has been given the price category that reflects the full prix-fixe price.

DOWNTOWN MANHATTAN

LOWER MANHATTAN

¢   ✕**Financier Patisserie.** On the cobblestone pedestrian street that has
CAFÉ   become the financial district's restaurant row, this quaint patisserie serves
Lower   up excellent pastries and delicious savory foods, like paninis, soup, salad,
Manhattan   and quiches. After lunch, relax with a cappuccino and a *financier,* an almond tea cake, or an elegant French pastry. In warm weather, perch at an outdoor table and watch Manhattanites buzz by. ✉*62 Stone St., between Mill La. and Hanover Sq.* ☎*212/344–5600* Ⓜ*2, 3, 4, 5 to Wall St.; J, M, Z to Broad St.* ✚ *C6* ✉ *35 Cedar St., between Pearl and William Sts.* ☎*212/952–3838* Ⓜ*E to World Trade Center; 4, 5 to Fulton St.* ✚ *C6* ✉ *3–4 World Financial Center, in Battery Park City* ☎*212/786–3220* Ⓜ*2, 3 to Wall St.; 4, 5 to Bowling Green* ⊕*www. financierpastries.com* ✍*Reservations not accepted* ▤*AE, DC, MC, V* ✪*No dinner (Stone St. location closed Sun. also).* ✚ *1:B6*

CHINATOWN AND TRIBECA

$ ✕**Bubby's.** Crowds clamoring for coffee and freshly squeezed juice line
AMERICAN   up for brunch at this TriBeCa mainstay, but the restaurant serves fine
TriBeCa   lunches and dinners as well. The dining room is homey and comfort-
☾   able with big windows; in summer, neighbors sit at tables outside with their dogs. For brunch you can order almost anything, including homemade granola, sour-cream pancakes with bananas and strawberries, and

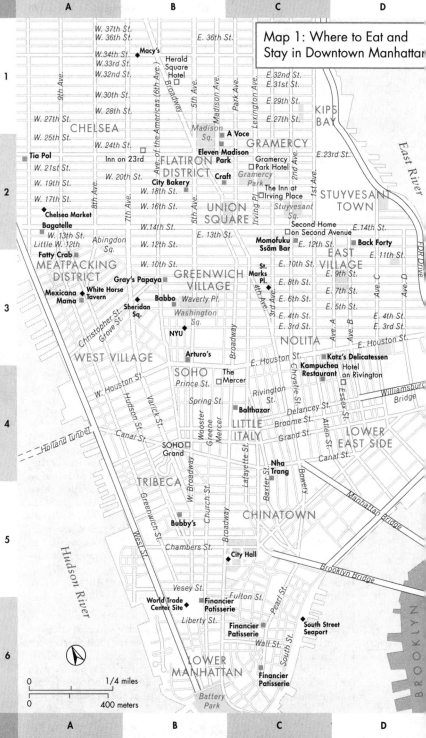

Map 1: Where to Eat and Stay in Downtown Manhattan

A   B   C   D

W. 37th St.
W. 36th St.
E. 36th St.
W. 34th St.   Macy's
Herald
Square
Hotel
W. 33rd St.
W. 32nd St.
E. 32nd St.
E. 31st St.
W. 30th St.
E. 29th St.
KIPS
BAY
W. 28th St.
E. 27th St.
W. 27th St.

CHELSEA
W. 25th St.
Madison
Sq.
A Voce
GRAMERCY
W. 24th St.
Eleven Madison
Park
E. 23rd St.
East River
Tia Pol
Inn on 23rd
FLATIRON
DISTRICT
Gramercy
Park Hotel
W. 21st St.
W. 20th St.
City Bakery
Craft
Gramercy
Park
W. 19th St.
The Inn at
Irving Place
STUYVESANT
TOWN
W. 17th St.
W. 18th St.
UNION
SQUARE
Stuyvesant
Sq.
Chelsea Market
W. 16th St.
Second Home
on Second Avenue
E. 14th St.
Bagatelle
W. 14th St.
W. 13th St.
Little W. 12th
Abingdon
Sq.
E. 13th St.
Momofuku
Ssäm Bar
E. 12th St.
Back Forty
E. 11th St.
Fatty Crab
W. 12th St.
EAST
VILLAGE
MEATPACKING
DISTRICT
W. 10th St.
GREENWICH
VILLAGE
St.
Marks
Pl.
E. 10th St.
E. 9th St.
Gray's Papaya
E. 8th St.
Mexicana
Mama
White Horse
Tavern
Babbo
Waverly Pl.
E. 7th St.
E. 6th St.
Sheridan
Sq.
Washington
Sq.
E. 5th St.
E. 4th St.
E. 3rd St.
NYU
E. 4th St.
E. 3rd St.
NOLITA
WEST VILLAGE
Arturo's
E. Houston St.
SOHO
The
Mercer
Katz's Delicatessen
W. Houston St.
Prince St.
Kampuchea
Restaurant
Hotel
on Rivington
Spring St.
Rivington
St.
Holland Tunnel
Canal St.
Balthazar
Delancey St.
LITTLE
ITALY
Broome St.
LOWER
EAST
SIDE
SOHO
Grand
Grand St.
Williamsburg
Bridge
TRIBECA
Nha
Trang
Canal St.
Manhattan
Bridge
CHINATOWN
Bubby's
Chambers St.
City Hall
Brooklyn Bridge
Hudson River
Vesey St.
World Trade
Center Site
Financier
Patisserie
Fulton St.
Liberty St.
Financier
Patisserie
South Street
Seaport
Wall St.
BROOKLYN
LOWER
MANHATTAN
Financier
Patisserie
Battery
Park

0   1/4 miles
0   400 meters

huevos rancheros with guacamole and grits. Eclectic comfort food—macaroni 'n' cheese, fried chicken—make up the lunch and dinner menus. ✉*120 Hudson St., at N. Moore St.* ☎*212/219–0666* ⊕*www. bubbys.com* ☐*D, DC, MC, V* Ⓜ*1 to Franklin St.* ✥*1:B5*

¢ ✕**Nha Trang.** You can get a great meal for under $10 at this low-atmo-
VIETNAMESE sphere Vietnamese restaurant in Chinatown. Start with crispy spring
Chinatown rolls, sweet-and-sour seafood soup, or shrimp grilled on sugarcane. For a follow-up, don't miss the thin pork chops, which are marinated in a sweet vinegary sauce and grilled until charred. Another favorite is deep-fried squid on shredded lettuce with a tangy dipping sauce. If the line is long, which it usually is, even with a second location around the corner, you may be asked to sit at a table with strangers. ✉*87 Baxter St., between Bayard and Canal Sts.* ☎*212/233–5948* ✉*148 Centre St., at Walker and White Sts.* ☎*212/941–9292* ☐*No credit cards* Ⓜ*6, J, M, N, Q, R, W, Z to Canal St.* ✥*1:C4*

SOHO AND LITTLE ITALY

$$ ✕**Balthazar.** Even with long waits and excruciating noise levels, most
BRASSERIE out-of-towners agree that it's worth making reservations to experi-
SoHo ence restaurateur Keith McNally's flagship, a painstakingly accurate reproduction of a Parisian brasserie. Like the decor, entrées re-create French classics: Gruyère-topped onion soup, steak-frites, and icy tiers of crab, oysters, and other pristine shellfish. Brunch is one of the best in town—if you can get a table. The best strategy is to go at off-hours, or on weekdays for breakfast, to miss the crush of hungry New Yorkers. ✉*80 Spring St., between Broadway and Crosby St.* ☎*212/965–1785* ⌁*Reservations essential* ☐*AE, MC, V* Ⓜ*6 to Spring St.; N, R to Prince St.; B, D, F, V to Broadway–Lafayette.* ✥*1:C4*

THE LOWER EAST SIDE

$ ✕**Kampuchea Restaurant.** Cambodian-born Ratha Chau, a former man-
CAMBODIAN ager at the upscale French restaurant Fleur de Sel, is the driving force
Lower East Side at this sophisticated Southeast Asian street-food spot. With exposed-brick walls, elevated bar-style seating, and a well-planned wine list, it's the most stylish noodle bar we've ever encountered. Start with grilled corn lathered in coconut mayo, coconut flakes, and chili powder. The unusual combination of flavors alerts your taste buds that they're in for a wild ride. Follow it up with falling-off-the-bone grilled quail with house-cured pickles or ginger-rubbed prawns. Don't miss Cambodian savory crepes filled with Berkshire pork and chives. Then move on to bountiful noodle dishes like chilled rice vermicelli with pork and Chinese sausage, topped with a thick crown of herbs and bean sprouts, or the hot filet mignon noodle soup with beef broth, peppercorn-encrusted fillet, and braised brisket. Finally, cool off with a refreshing glass of Riesling, and revel in the knowledge that you found one of New York's best hidden eats. ✉*78 Rivington St., at Allen St.* ☎*212/529–3901* ⊕*www.kampucheanyc.com* ☐*AE, D, DC, MC, V* Ⓜ*F to Delancey St.; J, M, Z to Essex St.* ✥*1:C4*

$ ✕**Katz's Delicatessen.** Everything and nothing has changed at Katz's since
DELI it first opened in 1888, when the neighborhood was dominated by
Lower East Side Jewish immigrants. The rows of Formica tables, the long self-service

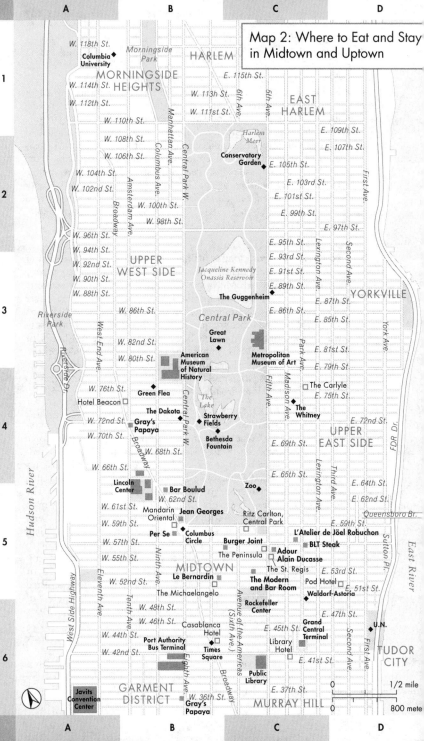

BEST BETS FOR NYC DINING

With thousands of restaurants to choose from, how will you decide where to eat? Fodor's writers and editors have selected their favorite restaurants in the Best Bets lists below. In the first column, Fodor's Choice properties represent the "best of the best" in every price category. You can also search by neighborhood for excellent eats—just peruse the following pages.

Fodor's Choice ★

Adour Alain Ducasse, Midtown

Bar Boulud, Upper West Side

Fatty Crab, Meatpacking District

L'Atelier de Joël Robuchon, Midtown

Momofuku Ssäm Bar, East Village

Tía Pol, Chelsea

Best By Price

¢

Burger Joint, Midtown

Gray's Papaya, Various locations

Nha Trang

$

Back Forty, East Village

Bubby's, TriBeCa

City Bakery, Flatiron District

Fatty Crab, Meatpacking District

Katz's Delicatessen, Lower East Side

$$

Arturo's, Greenwich Village

Balthazar, SoHo

Tía Pol, Chelsea

$$$

Craft, Flatiron District

The Modern (Bar Room)

$$$$

Adour Alain Ducasse, Midtown

Eleven Madison Park, Flatiron District

Jean Georges, Upper West Side

L'Atelier de Joël Robuchon, Midtown

Le Bernardin, Midtown

Best By Experience

BRUNCH

Balthazar, SoHo

Bubby's, TriBeCa

BUSINESS DINING

BLT Steak, Midtown

Jean Georges, Upper West Side

CELEB-SPOTTING

Balthazar, SoHo

LATE-NIGHT DINING

Balthazar, SoHo

Fatty Crab, Meatpacking District

SPECIAL OCCASION

Adour Alain Ducasse, Midtown

Jean Georges, Upper West Side

Le Bernardin, Midtown

Per Se, Upper West Side

8

counter, and such signs as "send a salami to your boy in the army" are all completely authentic. What's different are the area's demographics, but all types still flock here for succulent hand-carved corned beef and pastrami sandwiches, soul-warming soups, juicy hot dogs, and crisp half-sour pickles. ⊠ *205 E. Houston St., at Ludlow St.* ☎ *212/254–2246* ⊕ *www.katzdeli.com* ⊟ *AE, MC, V* Ⓜ *F, V to 2nd Ave.* ✛ *1:C3*

THE VILLAGE, CHELSEA, AND UNION SQUARE AREA

$$$
ITALIAN
Flatiron District

✕ **A Voce.** There's a warm glow in this 90-seat dining room, with its walnut floors and soft-green leather-top tables. Executive chef Missy Robbins shows her appreciation for simple, ingredient-driven, regionally inspired Italian dishes through her contemporary take on the Italian classics. Duck meatballs have a depth of flavor and texture that is not to be missed. Spaghetti all' Amatriciana is a piping-hot blend of spicy tomatoes, pancetta, and pecorino cheese, with truly *al dente* pasta. Red-wine-braised short ribs Piedmontese are partnered with fontina cheese potatoes. Chocolate bread pudding is not too sweet but rather complex, with roasted bananas along for the ride. In warm weather there's additional seating on the patio. ⊠ *41 Madison Ave., between 25th and 26th Sts.* ☎ *212/545–8555* ⊕ *www.avocerestaurant.com* ⊟ *AE, MC, V* Ⓜ *N, R to 23rd St.* ✛ *1:B2*

$$
PIZZA
Greenwich
Village
🔄

✕ **Arturo's.** Few guidebooks list this classic New York pizzeria, but the jam-packed room and pleasantly smoky scent foreshadow a satisfying meal. There's a full menu of Italian classics, but don't be fooled: pizza is the main event. The thin-crust beauties are cooked in a coal oven, emerging sizzling with simple toppings like pepperoni, sausage, and eggplant. Monday to Thursday, you can call ahead to reserve a table; weekends, be prepared to wait and salivate. ⊠ *106 W. Houston St., near Thompson St.* ☎ *212/677–3820* ⊟ *AE, MC, V* ◎ *No lunch* Ⓜ *1 to Houston St.; F, V to Broadway–Lafayette St.* ✛ *1:B3*

$$$
ITALIAN
Greenwich
Village

✕ **Babbo.** After one bite of the ethereal homemade pasta or tender barbecued squab, you'll understand why it's so hard to get reservations at Mario Batali's casually elegant restaurant. The complex and satisfying menu hits numerous high points, such as "mint love letters," ravioli filled with pureed peas, ricotta, and fresh mint, finished with spicy lamb sausage ragù; and rabbit with Brussels sprouts, house-made pancetta, and carrot vinaigrette. Babbo is the perfect spot for a raucous celebratory dinner with flowing wine and festive banter. But be forewarned: if anyone in your party is hard of hearing, or bothered by loud rock music, choose someplace more sedate. ⊠ *110 Waverly Pl., between MacDougal St. and 6th Ave.* ☎ *212/777–0303* ⊕ *www.babbonyc.com* ✍ *Reservations essential* ⊟ *AE, MC, V* ◎ *No lunch* Ⓜ *A, B, C, D, E, F, V to W. 4th St.* ✛ *1:B3*

$$$
FRENCH
Meatpacking
District

✕ **Bagatelle.** Situate yourself at a table in Bagatelle's elegant and spacious white dining room, sip a cocktail like La Poire Royale (pear vodka, pear brandy, pear purée, Cointreau, and champagne), and watch the Meatpacking District's beautiful people strut and coo at the bar. Executive chef Nicolas Cantrel's appealing menu of Provençal bistro classics includes some excellent appetizers: buttery elbow pasta with veal juice, ham, and Swiss cheese, and a tartine with goat cheese and tomato confit are highbrow, addictive, comfort food. There are still a few kinks to work out though. Filet mignon was nicely cooked and seasoned but accompanied by unmemorable frites, and the flavorful bouillabaisse—a Provençal fish stew with rouille and croutons—suffered from rather bland seafood. Leave room for dessert, especially "le Paris Brest"—choux pastry, praline cream, and almonds. The wine list includes many French varietals; only a few are offered by the glass. ⊠ *409 W. 13th St., between 9th Ave. and Washington St.* ☎*212/675–2400* ⊟*AE, D, MC, V* ⊘*No lunch weekdays* Ⓜ *A, C, E to 14th St.; L to 8th Ave.* ✛*1:2A*

$ | CAFÉ | Flatiron District | ☕ — ✕**City Bakery.** This self-service bakery-restaurant has the urban aesthetic to match its name. Chef-owner Maury Rubin's baked goods—giant cookies, flaky croissants, elegant tarts—are unfailingly rich. A major draw is the salad bar that's worth every penny—a large selection of impeccably fresh food, including whole sides of baked salmon, roasted vegetables, and several Asian-accented dishes. Much of the produce comes from the nearby farmers' market. In winter the bakery hosts a hot-chocolate festival; in summer it's lemonade time. Weekend brunch includes limited table-side service. ⊠*3 W. 18th St., between 5th and 6th Aves.* ☎*212/366–1414* ⊕*www.thecitybakery.com* ⌃*Reservations not accepted* ⊟*AE, MC, V* ⊘*No dinner* Ⓜ*L, N, Q, R, W, 4, 5, 6 to 14th St./Union Sq.; F, V to 14th St.* ✛*1:B2*

$$$ | NEW AMERICAN | Flatiron District — ✕**Craft.** Dining here is like a choose-your-own-adventure game in the pantry of the gods. Every delectable dish comes à la carte, including sides for your roasted guinea hen or braised monkfish. Craft is Tom Colicchio's flagship in a mini-empire of excellent restaurants around the country, including the upscale Craftbar and Craftsteak brands, as well as grab-and-go sandwich bars called 'wichcraft. Just about everything here is exceptionally prepared with little fuss, from simple yet intriguing starters (grilled French sardines) and sides (sautéed sugar-snap peas) to desserts (lemon steamed pudding with rhubarb jelly and vanilla ice cream). The serene dining room features burnished dark wood, custom tables, a curved leather wall, and a succession of dangling radiant bulbs. ⊠*43 E. 19th St., between Broadway and Park Ave.* S☎*212/780–0880* ⊕*www.craftrestaurant.com* ⌃*Reservations essential* ⊟*AE, D, MC, V* ⊘*No lunch* Ⓜ*L, N, Q, R, W, 4, 5, 6 to 14th St.-Union Sq.* ✛*1:B2*

$$$$ | NEW AMERICAN | Flatiron District — ✕**Eleven Madison Park.** Under Swiss-born chef Daniel Humm, who was lured from San Francisco's Campton Place by restaurateur Danny Meyer, this art nouveau jewel overlooking Madison Park has become one of the city's most consistently exciting places to dine. Humm announces his lofty intentions with dishes like foie gras with golden raisin brioche and African kili pepper, butter-poached Scottish langoustines with carrot-orange nage, and Jamison Farm herb-roasted lamb with tomato confit and niçoise olives. Don't forget your breakfast cake—a gift from the chef—as you walk out the door. ⊠*11 Madison Ave., at 24th St.* ☎*212/889–0905* ⊕*www.elevenmadisonpark.com* ⌃*Reservations essential* ⊟*AE, D, DC, MC, V* ⊘ *Closed Sun. No lunch Sat.* Ⓜ*N, R, W, 6 to 23rd St.* ✛*1:B2*

$ | MEATPACKING | DISTRICT | **Fodor's**Choice | ★ — ✕**Fatty Crab.** This rustic Malaysian cantina showcases the exciting cuisine of chef Zak Pelaccio, who spent years cooking at famous French restaurants before escaping to Southeast Asia, where he fell in love with the flavors of the region. Start with the addictive pickled watermelon and crispy pork salad, an improbable combination that is refreshing and decadent. The can't-miss signature dish is chili crab—cracked Dungeness crab in a pool of rich, spicy chili sauce, served with bread for dipping. It's messy for sure, but worth rolling up your sleeves for. The restaurant stays open until 4 AM Thursday through Saturday, making it a late-night hangout for chefs and others in the restaurant industry. ⊠*643 Hudson St., between Gansevoort and Horatio Sts.* ☎*212/352–3590* ⊕*www.fattycrab.com* ⌖*Reservations not accepted* ▭*AE, MC, V* Ⓜ*A, C, E to 14th St.; L to 8th Ave.* ⊹*1:A3*

¢   ✕**Gray's Papaya.** It's a stand-up, take-out dive. And, yes, limos do some-
FAST FOOD   times stop here for the legendary hot dogs. More often than not, though,
Multiple   it's neighbors or commuters who know how good the slim, traditional,
Locations   juicy, all-beef dogs are. Fresh-squeezed orange juice, a strangely tasty
☺   creamy banana drink, and the much-touted, healthful papaya juice are available along with more-standard drinks, served up 24/7. You'll find other Gray's Papaya outposts around the city, but the Greenwich Village location is our favorite. ⊠*402 6th Ave., at W. 8th St., Greenwich Village* ☎*212/260–3532* ⌖*Reservations not accepted* ▭*No credit cards* Ⓜ*A, C, E, B, D, F, V to W. 4th St.* ⊹*1:B3* ⊠*539 8th Ave., at 37th St.,Midtown West* ☎*212/904–1588* ⌖*Reservations not accepted* ▭*No credit cards* Ⓜ*A, C, E to 42nd St./Times Square or to 34th St./ Penn Station* ⊹*2:B4* ⊠*2090 Broadway, at 72nd St., Upper West Side* ☎*212/799–0243* ⌖*Reservations not accepted* ▭*No credit cards* Ⓜ*1, 2, 3 to 72nd St.* ⊹*2:B6*

$ ✕**Mexicana Mama.** This quaint and colorful—and very popular—space
MEXICAN   serves vividly flavored fare. The kitchen is serious enough to create a
Meatpacking   dozen different salsas daily, and several dishes come with your choice
District   of salsa and filling. The tomato-habanero salsa is simply unforgettable; cream tames the habaneros, but only slightly. Three chili-roasted pork tacos are also filled with piquant chihuahua cheese and black beans, and served over Mexican rice and avocado cubes. Quesadillas are made with fresh corn tortillas (for a change!), filled with that melted chihuahua cheese and your choice of chicken, barbacoa beef, chicken mole, or a daily special vegetable filling. For dessert, look no further than the eggy flan topped with caramel. ⊠*525 Hudson St., near Charles St.* ☎*212/924–4119* ▭*No credit cards* Ⓜ*1 to Christopher St./Sheridan Sq.; A, B, C, D, E, F, V to W. 4th St./Washington Sq.* ⊹*1:A3*

$$ ✕**Tia Pol.** This tiny, dark, out-of-the-way, but highly popular tapas bar
SPANISH   is usually packed, but there are good reasons for that: it's the best in
Chelsea   town. The tables and stools are small and high, but the flavors are
Fodor'sChoice   enormous. One highly original tapa that everyone was talking about
★   is a signature here: bittersweet chocolate smeared on a baguette disc and topped with salty Spanish chorizo. Rough-cut potatoes are deep-fried and served with a dollop of spicy aioli. You won't want to share them. The pork loin, piquillo pepper, and mild tetilla cheese sandwich is scrumptious, and so is the Galician octopus terrine. In fact, everything on the menu is transporting and delicious. ⊠*205 10th Ave., between 22nd and 23rd Sts.* ☎*212/675–8805* ⊕*www.tiapol.com* ⌖*Reservations essential for groups of 6–8* ▭*AE, D, MC, V* ⊘*No lunch* Ⓜ*C, E to 23rd St.* ⊹*1:A2*

THE EAST VILLAGE

$ ✕**Back Forty.** Pioneering chef Peter Hoffman, a longtime leader in pro-
AMERICAN
East Village
moting local, sustainable food, attracts a devoted crowd at this casual restaurant that feels like a neighborhood joint. Despite Hoffman's pedigree, Back Forty displays plenty of humility. Prices on the short, rustic, greenmarket menu are extremely low and the homey decor features a pastoral mural behind the bar and rusty farm tools on the walls. Begin with bar snack bacon-and-shrimp beignets washed down with a fine house cocktail like the rum–and–Concord-grape fizz. The simple family-style dinner selections include a perfect grilled trout; a moist, shareable, whole rotisserie chicken; and a wide array of seasonal sides including cauliflower gratin and roasted Brussels sprouts with dried cherries. ✉*190 Ave. B, at 12th St.* ☎*212/388–1990* ⊘*AE, MC, V* Ⓜ *L to 1st Ave.* ✛*1:D2*

$$ ✕**Momofuku Ssäm Bar.** New York foodies have been salivating over chef
ASIAN
East Village
Fodor'sChoice
★
David Chang's Asian-influenced fare since he opened his first restaurant, a Japanese noodle shop, in 2004. Momofuku Ssäm Bar, the wunderkind's much larger follow-up, is packed nightly with downtown diners cut from the same cloth as the pierced and tattooed waitstaff and cooks. The no-reservations policy means you'll likely have to wait for a chance to perch at the communal food bar and nibble on Chang's truly original small-plate cuisine. Dishes from the seasonally changing menu arrive like tapas for sharing. Although the chef works mostly with Asian flavors, his food is impossible to pigeonhole. Chang's not-to-be-missed riff on a classic Chinese pork bun helped build his cult following. ✉*207 2nd Ave., at 13th St.* ☎*212/254–3500* ⬧*Reservations not accepted* ▭*AE, MC, V* Ⓜ*L to 1st Ave.* ✛*1:C2*

MIDTOWN AND UPTOWN

MIDTOWN

$$$$ ✕**Adour Alain Ducasse.** Master chef Alain Ducasse adds to his grow-
MODERN FRENCH
Midtown East
Fodor'sChoice
★
ing empire with the upscale and elegant Adour, located in the equally sophisticated St. Regis Hotel. Celebrating couples of all ages gravitate to the Left and Right Bank rooms, while a mix of tourists, shoppers, and businessmen settle on plush burgundy chairs and banquettes in the regal but relaxed main dining room. Beautifully baked baguettes and fragrant olive and sourdough rolls are flown in from Paris. Deep pockets splurge on artfully arranged dishes, such as foie-gras ravioli with black truffles, and lobster Thermidor. Sommeliers help decipher an international wine list (displayed on interactive computer screens at the bar) with bottles that range from $35 to $19,000. ✉*2 East 55th St., near 5th Ave.* ☎*212/710–2277* ⊕*www.adour-stregis.com* ⬧*Reservations essential* ▭*AE, D, DC, MC, V* ⊘*No lunch* Ⓜ*E, V to 5th Ave./53rd St.; F to 57th St.* ✛*2:C5*

$$$ ✕**BLT Steak.** Chef Laurent Tourondel sets a new steak-house standard
STEAKHOUSE
Midtown East
in this classy space decked out in beige and suede and resin-topped black tables. The no-muss, no-fuss menu is nonetheless large, and so are the portions of supple crab cakes with celery-infused mayonnaise and luscious ruby tuna tartare with avocado, ramped up with soy-lime

8

dressing. As soon as you're settled, puffy Parmesan popovers arrive still steaming. A veal chop is crusted with rosemary and Parmesan, which imbue the veal with more flavor than veal ever has. At lunch, the quintessential BLT includes Kobe beef, foie gras, bacon, and tomato in a split ciabatta. Sides and desserts are all superior. ⊠*106 E. 57th St., between Lexington and Park Aves.* ☎*212/752–7470* ⊕*www.bltsteak. com* ⌲*Reservations essential* ☰*AE, DC, MC, V* ☾*No lunch Sat. Closed Sun.* Ⓜ *4, 5, 6, N, R, W to 59th St./Lexington Ave.* ✛*2:C5*

¢ ✕**Burger Joint.** What's a college burger bar, done up in particleboard and
BURGER rec room decor, doing hidden inside a five-star Midtown hotel? This
Midtown tongue-in-cheek lunch spot buried in the Parker Meridien does such boisterous midweek business that lines often snake through the lobby. Stepping behind the beige curtain you can find baseball-cap-wearing, grease-spattered cooks dispensing paper-wrapped cheeseburgers and crisp thin fries. The burgers—featuring no Kobe beef or foie gras—are straightforward, cheap, and delicious. ⊠*118 W. 57th St, between 6th and 7th Aves.* ☎*212/245–5000* ⊕*www.parkermeridien.com* ☰*No credit cards* Ⓜ*F, N, Q, R, W to 57th St.* ✛*2:C5*

$$$$ ✕**L'Atelier de Joël Robuchon.** The New York branch of Joël Robuchon's
FRENCH superluxurious tapas bar, inside the Four Seasons Hotel, features essen-
Midtown East tially the same food (with a more-natural-hue decor) as the Paris origi-
Fodor'sChoice nal. And that, it turns out, is a very good thing. The perfectionist chef
★ installed a longtime Japanese protégé to uphold the standards that can make a Robuchon meal a life-changing experience. Skip the regular-size appetizers and entrées. Instead, secure a seat at the pear-wood counter and cobble together your own small-plate feast. But be warned; with heady ingredients like Scottish langoustines (tempura fried), steak tartare (with hand-cut french fries) and foie gras (paired with caramelized eel), Robuchon's little bites come at a steep price. ⊠*57 E. 57th St., between Madison and Park Aves.* ☎*212/350–6658* ⊕*www.fourseasons.com/ newyorkfs/dining.html* ⌲ *Reservations essential* ☰*AE, MC, V* Ⓜ*4, 5, 6 to 59th St.* ✛*2:C5*

$$$$ ✕**Le Bernardin.** Owner Maguy LeCoze presides over the teak-panel din-
FRENCH ing room at this trendsetting French seafood restaurant, and chef-part-
Midtown West ner Eric Ripert works magic with anything that swims—preferring at times not to cook it at all. Deceptively simple dishes such as poached lobster in rich coconut-ginger soup or crispy spiced black bass in a Peking duck bouillon are typical of his style. It is widely agreed that there's no beating Le Bernardin for thrilling cuisine, seafood or other-wise, coupled with some of the finest desserts in town. ⊠*155 W. 51st St., between 6th and 7th Aves.* ☎*212/489–1515* ⊕*www.le-bernardin. com* ⌲*Reservations essential Jacket required* ☰*AE, DC, MC, V* ☾*Closed Sun. No lunch Sat.* Ⓜ*1 to 50th St.; R, W to 49th St.; B, D, F, V to 47th–50th Sts./Rockefeller Center.* ✛*2:B5*

$$$–$$$$ ✕**The Modern and Bar Room.** Both spots competing for the title of the
FRENCH country's best museum restaurant sit side by side on the ground floor
Midtown West of the New York MoMA. The Modern ($$$$), run by restaurateur Danny Meyer, is two restaurants in one. Both offer the dazzling food of Alsatian chef Gabriel Kreuther. The formal dining room has a view of the museum's sculpture garden and an ambitious, pricey, prix-fixe

menu. The far more accessible and popular Bar Room ($$$) lies just beyond a partition. Here you can find a dizzying collection of shareable plates like the refreshing Arctic char tartare and oysters with leeks and caviar. Two or three make a fine if extravagant afternoon snack—double that number for a full meal. ⊠*9 W. 53rd St., between 5th and 6th Aves.* ☎*212/333–1220* ⊕*www.themodernnyc.com* ▤*AE, D, MC, V* Ⓜ*E, V to 5th Ave./53rd St.* ⊹*2:C5*

UPPER WEST SIDE

$$ ✕**Bar Boulud.** Acclaimed French chef Daniel Boulud brings diners his

BISTRO most casual venture yet with this lively contemporary bistro. The long

Upper West Side narrow space accommodates 100 people and has a 14-seat round table

Fodor's Choice for special tastings. An additional level has three rooms for larger parties.

★ The menu emphasizes charcuterie including terrines and pâtés designed by Parisian charcutier Gilles Verot, as well as traditional French bistro dishes like steak frîtes and *poulet rôti à l'ail* (roast chicken with garlic mashed potatoes). The 500-bottle wine list is heavy on wines from Burgundy and the Rhône Valley. A pretheater three-course menu starts at $39, and weekend brunch has two hearty courses for $28. ⊠*1900 Broadway, between W. 63rd and 64th Sts.* ☎*212/595–0303* ⊕*www. barboulud.com* ▤*AE, DC, MC, V* Ⓜ*1 to 66th St./Lincoln Center; 1, A, C, B, D to 59th St./Columbus Circle* ⊹*2:B5*

$$$$ ✕**Jean Georges.** This culinary temple focuses wholly on *chef celebre*

FRENCH Jean-Georges Vongerichten's spectacular creations. Some approach the

Upper West Side limits of the taste universe, like foie gras brûlée with spiced fig jam and ice-wine verjus. Others are models of simplicity, like slow-cooked cod with warm vegetable vinaigrette. Exceedingly personalized service and a well-selected wine list contribute to an unforgettable meal. For Jean Georges on a budget, try the prix-fixe lunch in the front room, Nougatine. ⊠*1 Central Park W, at W. 59th St.* ☎*212/299–3900* ⊕ *www. jean-georges.com* ⚐*Reservations essential Jacket required* ▤*AE, DC, MC, V* ⊗*Closed Sun.* Ⓜ*A, B, C, D, 1 to 59th St./Columbus Circle.* ⊹*2:B5*

$$$$ ✕**Per Se.** Thomas Keller, who gave the world butter-poached lobster

AMERICAN and the Napa Valley's French Laundry restaurant, has given New York

Upper West Side Per Se, which serves his witty, magical creations to well-heeled diners. Come with an open mind and open wallet, and discover his inventive combinations of flavors reduced to their essences. Waiters can, and may, recite the provenance of the tiniest turnip. For reservations, call exactly two months in advance of your hoped-for dining date. ⊠*Time Warner Center, 10 Columbus Circle, 4th fl., at W. 60th St.* ☎*212/823–9335* ⊕*www.perseny.com* ⚐*Reservations essential Jacket required* ⊗*No lunch Mon.–Thurs.* ▤*AE, MC, V* Ⓜ*A, B, C, D, 1 to 59th St./ Columbus Circle.* ⊹*2:B5*

WHERE TO STAY

Updated by
Michael de
Zayas

It's the thrill of a lifetime. Finding a hotel room in New York can be a real challenge: just like in the real estate market, space is at a premium, and high prices are dictated by high demand. Rooms are smaller than you would have thought possible and noise can be a problem. So why put up with the hassle? Easy. There's nothing like staying in the city that never sleeps. To truly feel the center-of-the-universe energy that New York is famous for, you have to stay here—even if it's only for one night.

Remember the real-estate adage "location, location, location," and bear in mind that you'll pay prime prices for a prime piece of real estate. Many visitors to New York City cram themselves into hotels in the hectic Midtown area, but other neighborhoods are often just as convenient for travelers. Less touristy areas, like Gramercy, Murray Hill, and the Upper East Side, offer a far more realistic sense of New York life.

Deals do exist—if you know where and when to look. Weekdays in the financial district are pricey, but discounted rooms often become available on weekends. Also consider timing: the least expensive months to book rooms in the city are January and February. If you're flexible on dates, ask the reservationist if there's a cheaper time to stay during your preferred traveling month. That way you can attempt to avoid peak dates, like Fashion Week and the New York marathon.

Also, many chains have moved into the city, offering reasonable room rates. In addition to favorites like the Sheraton, Hilton, and Hyatt brands, there are Best Westerns, Days Inns, and Comfort Inns. But don't expect these chains to offer the same low rates you'll find outside Manhattan. Depending on the season, even budget chains may charge upward of $300 a night.

WHAT IT COSTS				
	$$$$	$$$	$$	$	¢
FOR TWO PEOPLE	over $600	$450–$599	$300–$449	$150–$299	under $150

Prices are for a standard double room, excluding 13.625% city and state taxes.

DOWNTOWN MANHATTAN

SOHO AND LITTLE ITALY

$$$ **The Mercer.** Owner Andre Balazs, known for his Chateau Marmont in Hollywood, has a knack for dating Hollywood starlets and channeling a neighborhood sensibility. Here, it's SoHo loft all the way. It's superbly situated in the heart of SoHo's shopping district, although you wouldn't know it once you're inside the lobby, a minimalist oasis created by acclaimed French designer Christian Liagre. Most guest rooms are generously sized with long entryways, high ceilings, and walk-in closets, although the lowest-priced rooms are a slightly snug 250 square feet. Dark African woods and custom-designed furniture upholstered in muted solids lend serenity with sophistication. Some bathrooms feature decadent two-person marble tubs surrounded by mirrors. Downstairs is the always happening Mercer Kitchen, and the submercer, with a separate entrance, is one of the city's hottest doors. Beware the inconsistent service, which runs the gamut from friendly to indifferent. **Pros:** great location; sophisticated design touches; celebrity sightings in lobby. **Con:**

BEST BETS FOR NYC LODGING

Fodor's offers a selective listing of quality lodging experiences in every price range, from the city's best budget motel to its most sophisticated luxury hotel. Here, we've compiled our top recommendations by price and experience. The very best properties—in other words, those that provide a particularly remarkable experience in their price range—are designated in the listings with the Fodor's Choice logo.

Fodor'sChoice★

The Carlyle, Upper East Side

Gramercy Park Hotel, Union Square Area

Hotel on Rivington, Lower East Side

Pod Hotel, Midtown

Ritz-Carlton Central Park, Midtown

The St. Regis, Midtown

Best By Price

¢

Pod Hotel, Midtown

Second Home on Second Avenue, East Village

$

Casablanca Hotel, Midtown

Hotel Beacon, Upper West Side

$$

Hotel on Rivington, Lower East Side

Inn on 23rd, Chelsea

Library Hotel, Midtown

$$$

Gramercy Park Hotel, Union Square Area

The Michelangelo, Midtown

SoHo Grand, SoHo

$$$$

The Carlyle, Upper East Side

Mandarin Oriental, Midtown

Ritz-Carlton Central Park, Midtown

The St. Regis, Midtown

Best By Experience

BEST AFTERNOON TEA

Inn at Irving Place, Union Square Area

The St. Regis, Midtown

BEST FOR HISTORY BUFFS

The Carlyle, Upper East Side

Inn at Irving Place, Union Square Area

The St. Regis, Midtown

BEST HOTEL BAR

Bemelmans Bar at The Carlyle, Upper East Side

King Cole Bar at St. Regis, Midtown

Rose Bar at Gramercy Park Hotel, Union Square Area

BEST VIEWS

The Carlyle, Upper East Side

Ritz-Carlton Central Park, Midtown

MOST ROMANTIC

Inn at Irving Place, Union Square Area

Library Hotel, Mitown

8

service inconsistent. ✉ *147 Mercer St., at Prince St., SoHo* ☎ *212/966–6060 or 888/918–6060* ⊕ *www.mercerhotel.com* ⮑ *67 rooms, 8 suites* ⌂ *In-room: safe, DVD, Wi-Fi. In-hotel: restaurant, room service, bars, Internet terminal, Wi-Fi, some pets allowed, no-smoking rooms* ▤ *AE, D, DC, MC, V* Ⓜ *R, W to Prince St.* ✛ *1:B4*

$$$ 🏨 **SoHo Grand.** The SoHo Grand defines what SoHo is today—cosmopolitan, creative, and a place where you spend a bit more cash than you intended. When it opened in 1996, it had been a century since a new hotel debuted in the neighborhood. Today, as new hotels crowd the field, the Grand's low-key sophistication stands out more clearly. The Grand Bar & Lounge is sometimes called SoHo's Living Room for its comfortable, social atmosphere. Public spaces as well as guest rooms use an industrial-chic design to mimic the architecture of the neighborhood, though this can come across as spartan to some. Comfortable contemporary rooms are mainly focused on the view out the ample windows; bathrooms are stark but have deep soaking tubs. A great seasonal pleasure is The Yard—a large outdoor space where you can have a drink or meal and then spread out on the grassy lawn—the only one of its kind in the city. The staff here is attractive and professional, but a bit older and more polished than you'll find at other fashionable hotels. **Pros:** fashionable, laid-back sophistication; great service; surprisingly discreet setting; diverse eating and drinking options. **Cons:** closer to Canal Street than prime SoHo; rooms on small side. ✉ *310 West Broadway, at Grand St., SoHo* ☎ *212/965–3000 or 800/965–3000* ⊕ *www.sohogrand.com* ⮑ *365 rooms, 2 suites* ⌂ *In-room: safe, refrigerator, Internet, Wi-Fi. In-hotel: restaurant, room service, bars, gym, laundry service, parking (paid), some pets allowed, no-smoking rooms* ▤ *AE, D, DC, MC, V* Ⓜ *6, J, M, N, Q, R, W to Canal St.* ✛ *1:B4*

DOWNTOWN

$$ 🏨 **Hotel on Rivington.** The rooms here have something completely origi-
Fodor's Choice nal and breathtaking—when you hit a button on a remote control, your
★ curtains slowly open to reveal floor-to-ceiling glass windows. Seen that trick before? Well, this is the only tall building around, and the views of the Lower East Side and Midtown are unadulterated New York. The bathrooms don't shy away from the scene either—you'll either want to shower with your glasses on, or you'll blush at being completely naked before the entire city (privacy curtains can be requested). Downstairs is quite possibly the hottest hotel bar in the city—this and the jumping restaurant are velvet-roped mayhem on weekends. (Staying here also gives you access to a small VIP bar next door.) The mezzanine bar–art library–billiard room is a hangout you can call your own. **Pros:** superhip location and vibe; huge windows with wonderful New York views; happening bar and restaurant. **Cons:** feels like a club on weekends; spotty service; small rooms and suites. ✉ *107 Rivington St., between Ludlow and Essex Sts., Lower East Side* ☎ *212/475–2600 or 800/915–1537* ⊕ *www.hotelonrivington.com* ⮑ *110 rooms* ⌂ *In-room: safe, refrigerator, Internet, Wi-Fi. In-hotel: restaurant, room service, bar, laundry service, parking (paid), some pets allowed* ▤ *AE, D, DC, MC, V* Ⓜ *F, J, M, Z to Delancey/Essex Sts.* ✛ *1:D4*

¢ 🖼**Second Home on Second Avenue.** If you like the East Village, reserve your room now, because these eight rooms are the only way to experience the neighborhood like a local. A loyal core of regular patrons, mainly Europeans, keeps it booked at least five months in advance. Far from tourists, it's easy to blend into the scene here. The punctilious owner keeps the large rooms spotless and the prices cheap. Two caveats: you have to walk up to the third or fourth floor, and the bar downstairs can be noisy, especially on weekends. The six largest rooms are themed: two are modern, plus Caribbean, Peruvian, skylight, and tribal. Guests have use of a communal kitchen. **Pros:** spacious rooms; very clean; rare East Village rooms. **Cons:** walk-up building; two rooms share a bath. ⊠ *221 2nd Ave., between 13th and 14th Sts., East Village* ☎ *212/677–3161* ⊕ *www.secondhomesecondavenue.com* ⊸ *8 rooms, 6 with bath* ⏰ *In-room: no phone, safe, Wi-Fi. In-hotel: Wi-Fi, no kids under 5* ⊟ *AE, D, DC, MC, V* Ⓜ *4, 5, 6, L, N, Q, R, W to 14th St./ Union Sq.; L to 3rd Ave.* ✛ *1:C2*

THE VILLAGE, CHELSEA, AND UNION SQUARE AREA

$$ 🖼**Inn on 23rd.** Charming and friendly innkeepers Annette and Barry Fisherman will welcome you to this five-floor, 19th-century building in the heart of Chelsea. They took care to make each guest room spacious and unique. One exotic and elegant room is outfitted in bamboo, another in the art moderne style of the 1940s. Although it's small and homey, the inn provides private baths and satellite TV in all rooms. Dorothy, the house cat, is very friendly, and has an endearing quirk: she loves to ride the elevator. A big Continental breakfast is cooked daily by famous-chefs-to-be: members of the New School college's culinary program, who use the kitchen in the mornings as a laboratory. If you're a B&B person, you've found your New York retreat. **Pros:** charming innkeepers; comfy and relaxed library; affordable for location. **Cons:** few services for businesspeople; some older amenities; beware if you have cat allergies. ⊠ *131 W. 23rd St., between 6th and 7th Aves., Chelsea* ☎ *212/463–0330* ⊕ *www.innon23rd.com* ⊸ *13 rooms, 1 suite* ⏰ *In-room: DVD (some), Internet, Wi-Fi. In-hotel: laundry service, Internet terminal, Wi-Fi, no-smoking rooms* ⊟ *AE, D, DC, MC, V* ⏺*CP* Ⓜ*F, V to 23rd St.* ✛ *1:B2*

$$$ 🖼**Gramercy Park Hotel.** The GPH is on such a different plane of cool

Fodor'sChoice in comparison to all other New York City hotels, it might as well have

★ its own hospitality category. Ian Schrager, who forged the boutique-hotel concept just over a decade ago, turned the design reins of this hotel over to famed painter and director Julian Schnabel. Embracing a spirit of High Bohemia, the property has a rock-and-roll baroque feel. You've just got to see it. Works by Cy Twombley, Andy Warhol, and Jean-Michel Basquiat aggressively decorate the lobby and the two exclusive, ground-level bars that have become key components in the city's nightlife. Only guests, however, enjoy access to the rooftop deck and its interesting lounges—no small privilege. Rooms are an assemblage of specific tastes: opulent velvets; studded leathers; moodily dark bathrooms and showers; photo prints from the famed Magnum collective. If it's your thing, you've just found your new favorite hotel, but the hipper-than-thou aspects can make some people feel out of sorts. **Pros:**

8

great discreet city location, near all but private; radical design; super-hip bars and lounges. **Cons:** if you don't like the moody design it will be hard to be comfortable here; dark bathrooms; tiny spa; inconsistent service. ✉ *2 Lexington Ave., at Gramercy Park, Gramercy Park/Union Square Area* ☎ *212/920–3300* ⊕ *www.gramercyparkhotel.com* ⇶ *140 rooms, 40 suites* ⬥ *In-room: safe, refrigerator, DVD, Internet. In-hotel: restaurant, room service, bars, gym, laundry service, parking (paid), no-smoking rooms* ☰ *AE, D, DC, MC, V* Ⓜ *6 to 23rd St.* ⊹ *1:C2*

$ ⛢ **Herald Square Hotel.** The sculpted cherubs on the facade and vintage magazine covers adorning the common areas hint at the Herald's previous incarnation as *Life* magazine's headquarters. The hotel is a great value. Rooms are basic and clean; all have TVs and phones with Wi-Fi; some were recently renovated with flat screens. Shabby-chic fixtures and white-on-white bedspreads round out the look. There's no concierge and no room service, but the staff is friendly and nearby restaurants will deliver. It's a great bargain for the convenient neighborhood. **Pros:** cheap; centrally located. **Cons:** unattractive lobby; readers report inconsistent service. ✉ *19 W. 31st St., between 5th Ave. and Broadway, Murray Hill/Union Square Area* ☎ *212/279–4017 or 800/727–1888* ⊕ *www.heraldsquarehotel.com* ⇶ *120 rooms* ⬥ *In-room: safe, Wi-Fi. In-hotel: Internet terminal, Wi-Fi, some pets allowed* ☰ *AE, D, MC, V* Ⓜ *B, D, F, N, Q, R, V, W to 34th St./Herald Sq.* ⊹ *1:B1*

$$ ⛢ **Inn at Irving Place.** Fantasies of old New York—Manhattan straight from the pages of Edith Wharton and Henry James, an era of genteel brick town houses and Tiffany lamps—spring to life at this discreet 20-room inn, the city's most romantic. There is no sign outside the 1830 town house, a hint of the somehow small-town qualities of Irving Place, a lightly trafficked street on the south side of Gramercy Park. One of the city's most famous tea salons, Lady Mendyl's, is run on the lobby level. Rooms have ornamental fireplaces, four-poster beds with embroidered linens, wood shutters, and glossy cherrywood floors. The room named after Madame Olenska (the lovelorn Wharton character) has a bay window with sitting nook—this is one of the most memorable spots in New York; reserve it for anniversaries. **Pros:** romantic; quaint; big rooms; excellent breakfast and tea service; Mario Batali's Casa Mono is downstairs; martini bar. **Cons:** dainty; rooms aren't flawless, with imperfections like older grouting. ✉ *56 Irving Pl., between E. 17th and E. 18th Sts., Gramercy Park/Union Square Area* ☎ *212/533–4600 or 800/685–1447* ⊕ *www.innatirving.com* ⇶ *5 rooms, 6 suites* ⬥ *In-room: refrigerator. In-hotel: restaurant, room service, bar, laundry service, no kids under 8* ☰ *AE, D, DC, MC, V* ⑩ *CP* Ⓜ *4, 5, 6, L, N, Q, R, W to 14th St./Union Sq.* ⊹ *1:C2*

MIDTOWN AND UPTOWN

MIDTOWN

$ ⛢ **Casablanca Hotel.** When entering the hushed Casablanca, it's hard to believe you're a stone's throw from all the Times Square hoopla. Evoking the locale of its namesake film with Humphrey Bogart, the hotel has a sultry Mediterranean feel, from mirrors and mosaics in public spaces to the room's ceiling fans, wooden blinds, and dainty little bistro tables. Huge tiled bathrooms, many with windows, feature Baronessa Cali amenities. On the second floor, classical music plays while guests linger in the spacious librarylike Rick's Café for the complimentary breakfast buffet and wine-and-cheese evenings. **Pros:** great access to the theater district; all rooms are smoke-free. **Cons:** exercise facilities at nearby New York Sports Club, not on premises; heavy tourist foot traffic. ⊠*147 W. 43rd St., Midtown West* ☏*212/869–1212* ⊕*www.casablancahotel. com* ⇌*48 rooms* ⚲*In-room: safe, DVD, Wi-Fi. In-hotel: restaurant, room service, bar, laundry, Wi-Fi, no-smoking rooms* ▤*AE, MC, V* Ⓜ*1, 2, 3, 7, N, Q, R, S, W to 42nd St./Times Sq.* ✦*2:B6*

$$ Ⓣ**Library Hotel.** Boutiquey and bookish, this handsome landmark brownstone, built in 1900, gets its inspiration from the New York Public Library. Each of its 10 floors is dedicated to one of the 10 categories of the Dewey Decimal System; modern rooms are stocked with art and books relevant to a subtopic such as erotica, astronomy, or biography—let your interests guide your room choice. Either way, many of the rooms are surprisingly big and offer good bang for the buck. The staff is very hospitable, and the whole property is old-leather-armchair comfortable, whether you're unwinding in front of the library fireplace, partaking of the complimentary wine and cheese or Continental breakfast, or relaxing in the roof garden. **Pros:** fun rooftop bar; themed book room concept is lively; stylish rooms. **Cons:** rooftop often reserved for events; more books in rooms would be nice. ⊠*299 Madison Ave., at E. 41st St., Midtown East* ☏*212/983–4500 or 877/793–7323* ⊕*www. libraryhotel.com* ⇌*60 rooms* ⚲*In-room: safe, refrigerator, DVD, Internet, Wi-Fi. In-hotel: restaurant, room service, bar, laundry service, parking (paid), no-smoking rooms* ▤*AE, DC, MC, V* ⦿*CP* Ⓜ*4, 5, 6, 7, S to 42nd St./Grand Central.* ✦*2:C6*

$$$$ Ⓣ**Mandarin Oriental.** The Mandarin brings some Asian style to a rather staid corner of New York. Its cavernous lobby sizzles with energy from the 35th floor of the Time Warner Center. Here you'll find two wonderful lounges, and the restaurant Asiate, from which to soak in the dramatic views above Columbus Circle and Central Park. On the higher floors, silk throws abound on plush beds, and the marble-ensconced bathrooms prove the Mandarin's commitment to excess. That said, contrasted with the monumental frame created by floor-to-ceiling glass, and the view it presents, regular rooms feel small. Suites are really what set this hotel apart, by creating enough stage space to make the hotel's Asian-influenced decor, and the views, really kindle. The swimming pool is one of the city's best in a hotel, with panoramic Hudson River views. The elaborate spa is impressive. **Pros:** a vibrant urban hotel; luxury all the way; fantastic pool with views; best spa in the city. **Cons:** Trump hotel blocks portion of park views; expensive; mall-like environs. ⊠*80 Columbus Circle, at 60th St., Midtown West* ☏*212/805–8800* ⊕ *www.mandarinoriental.com* ⇌*203 rooms, 46 suites* ⚲*In-room: DVD, refrigerator, Internet. In-hotel: restaurant, room service, bar, pool, gym, spa, laundry service* ▤*AE, D, DC, MC, V* Ⓜ*A, B, C, D, 1 to 59th St./Columbus Circle.* ✦*2:B5*

8

$$$ 🏨**The Michelangelo.** Italophiles will feel that they've been transported to the good life in the boot at this deluxe hotel, whose long, wide lobby lounge is clad with multihue marble and Veronese-style oil paintings. Upstairs, the decor of the relatively spacious rooms (averaging 475 square feet) varies. You can choose contemporary, neoclassic, art deco, or French country—all have marble foyers and marble bathrooms equipped with bidets and oversize 55-gallon tubs, but the different styles translate to swapped bedspreads and different colored furniture. Complimentary cappuccino, pastries, and other Italian treats are served each morning in the baroque lobby lounge. The hotel is located a few blocks from Rockefeller Center and 5th Avenue shopping. Insieme, Marco Canora's exemplary modern Italian restaurant, is on the ground floor. **Pros:** good location; fantastic restaurant; spacious rooms. **Cons:** noisy air-conditioning units; some rooms have limited views; small closets. ⊠*152 W. 51st St., at 7th Ave., Midtown* ☎*212/765–1900 or 800/237–0990* ⊕*www.michelangelohotel.com* 💬*123 rooms, 56 suites* ♿ *In-room: Internet. In-hotel: restaurant, room service, bar, gym, laundry service, Internet terminal, parking (paid), no-smoking rooms* ▭*AE, D, DC, MC, V* ⫿❚*CP* Ⓜ*B, D, E to 7th Ave.; 1 to 50th St.; B, D, F, V to 47th–50th Sts./Rockefeller Center.* ✛*2:B5*

$$$$ 🏨**The Peninsula.** And as you step through the Peninsula's beaux arts facade and head up the grand staircase overhung with a monumental chandelier that announces a taste for glitz, you know you're in for a treat. Service is world-class, and personalized: expect to be referred to by name as you make your way through the hotel. Rooms have the latest touches in luxury comfort. The views are stunning: see the northward sweep up 5th Avenue to Central Park past church steeples; or look east towards the beautiful St. Regis across the street. The high-tech amenities are excellent, from a bedside console that controls the lighting, sound, and thermostat for the room to a TV mounted over the tub for bath-time viewing (in all but standard rooms). The rooftop health club, with indoor pool, is monumental. The Salon de Ning, a rooftop bar bedecked with chinoiserie, has dazzling views of Midtown. **Pros:** brilliant service; fabulous rooms, including best room lighting of all city hotels (good angles, easy to use); unforgettable rooftop bar. **Cons:** expensive. ⊠*700 5th Ave., at 55th St., Midtown East* ☎*212/956–2888 or 800/262–9467* ⊕*newyork.peninsula.com* 💬*185 rooms, 54 suites* ♿ *In-room: safe, refrigerator, Internet, Wi-Fi. In-hotel: restaurant, room service, bars, pool, gym, spa, laundry service, parking (paid), some pets allowed, no-smoking rooms* ▭*AE, D, DC, MC, V* Ⓜ*E, V to 5th Ave.* ✛*2:C5*

¢ 🏨**Pod Hotel.** This is the hotel that made bunk beds cool again. By
offering spotless stainless-steel bunks with pull-out flat-screen TVs,
★ Pod makes tiny, tiny rooms and sharing a bath fun. If you can tolerate cramped quarters this is one of the best deals in Midtown. About half the rooms come with standard queen beds and private bath. The rooms, starting at a meager 100 square feet, borrow space-saving ideas from mass transit, with sink consoles like those in an airplane restroom, and built-in shelves tucked under the beds. But you may be willing to trade space for the convenient location and modern amenities like

in-room iPod docking stations and free Wi-Fi. The common areas are cheerful and modern, with an outdoor bar-café and a stylish roof deck. Don't expect luxe linens or fab toiletries. Do expect to book well in advance, as budget-minded hipsters and stylish spendthrifts of all ages are sure to keep this hotel hopping. **Pros:** an inexpensive and fun way to save money. **Cons:** many will hate the small rooms; shared bathrooms. ⊠*230 E. 51st St., between 2nd and 3rd Aves., Midtown East* ☎*212/355–0300 or 800/874–0074* ⊕*www.thepodhotel.com* ⟲*347 rooms, 195 with bath* ⤶*In-room: Wi-Fi* ▤*AE, DC, MC, V* Ⓜ*6 to 51st St./Lexington Ave.; E, V to Lexington–3rd Aves./53rd St.* ✛*2:D5*

$$$$ 🏨 **Ritz-Carlton New York, Central Park.** A luxurious retreat with stellar
Fodor'sChoice views of Central Park, the former St. Moritz hotel is easily one of the
★ top properties in the city. No request is too difficult for the superlative Ritz staff, one reason the hotel is a favorite of celebrities and royalty. Even the regular rooms are the size of a small New York apartment, boasting a marble bath and shower, Wi-Fi, flat-screen TVs, Frédéric Fekkai amenities, and 400-thread count linens. Chef Laurent Tourondel opened a BLT Market here in late 2007, featuring a seasonal menu that changes monthly. For getting around town in style, Bentley car service is available upon request. The club levels features six food servings a day, including a champagne-and-caviar reception overlooking the park from the second floor. **Pros:** great concierge and personalized service; stellar location and views. **Cons:** pricey; limited common areas. ⊠*50 Central Park S, at 6th Ave., Midtown* ☎*212/308–9100 or 800/241–3333* ⊕*www.ritzcarlton.com* ⟲*259 rooms, 47 suites* ⤶*In-room: safe, DVD (some), Internet, Wi-Fi. In-hotel: restaurant, room service, bar, gym, spa, laundry service, no-smoking rooms, parking (paid), some pets allowed* ▤*AE, D, DC, MC, V* Ⓜ*F, V to 57th St.* ✛*2:C5*

$$$$ 🏨 **The St. Regis.** World-class from head to toe, the St. Regis comes as
Fodor'sChoice close to flawless as any hotel in New York. Even without the hive of
★ activity in its unparalleled public spaces, this 5th Avenue beaux arts landmark would rank near the top of any best-of list. But there's more: you can dine in two dining rooms—including a new Alain Ducasse restaurant, Adour—as well as the legendary King Cole Bar, a dimly lighted institution with its famously playful Maxfield Parrish murals. Guest rooms feature the best technology in the city, including easy-to-use bedside consoles (developed by an in-house R&D team) that control lighting, audio, and climate; and huge flat-screen TVs that rise via remote control from the foot of your bed. Each floor is serviced by its own butler, a touch no other hotel here can match. Rooms have high ceilings, crystal chandeliers, silk wall coverings, Louis XVI antiques, and world-class amenities such as Tiffany silver services. If you require the best, the St. Regis delivers. **Pros:** rooms combine true luxury with helpful technology; easy-access butler service; superb in-house dining; prestigious location. **Cons:** expensive; too serious for families seeking fun. ⊠*2 E. 55th St., at 5th Ave., Midtown East* ☎*212/753–4500 or 877/787–3447* ⊕*www.stregis.com* ⟲*164 rooms, 65 suites* ⤶*In-room: safe, refrigerator, DVD, Internet. In-hotel: restaurant, room service ,bar, gym, laundry service, parking (paid), no-smoking rooms* ▤*AE, D, DC, MC, V* Ⓜ*E, V to 5th Ave.* ✛*2:C5*

UPPER EAST AND UPPER WEST SIDES

$$$$
Fodor's Choice
★

⬚ **The Carlyle, A Rosewood Hotel.** On the well-heeled corner of Madison Avenue and 75th Street, this hotel's fusion of venerable elegance and Manhattan swank is like a Chanel boutique: walk in chin high, wallet out, and ready to be impressed. As you might expect, everything about this Upper East Side landmark suggests cultivated refinement: rooms decorated with fine antique furniture, vast Central Park views, white-gloved operators working the elevators 24 hours a day. It's all overwhelmingly spiffy—it's a wonder real people feel comfortable staying here. The range of the hotel's dining and entertainment options impresses: cabaret luminaries take turns holding court at the newly refurbished Café Carlyle (and yes, Woody Allen still visits once a week). Bemelmans Bar may never lose its title as greatest old-school cocktail spot in New York. The polished, black, key slots behind the reception desk are the old guest-key deposits, though now they're a fashionable reminder of the hotel's storied history as host to presidents and celebrities. **Pros:** perhaps New York City's best Central Park views; refined service; delightful array of dining and bar options. **Cons:** removed from tourist Manhattan; stuffy vibe may be inappropriate for families. ⊠ *35 E. 76th St., between Madison and Park Aves., Upper East Side* ☎ *212/744–1600* ⊕ *www. thecarlyle.com* ↴ *122 rooms, 57 suites* ⌂ *In-room: safe, kitchen, refrigerator, DVD, Internet. In-hotel: restaurant, room service, bar, gym, spa, laundry service, parking (paid), no-smoking rooms, some pets allowed* ⊟ *AE, DC, MC, V* Ⓜ *6 to 77th St.* ✛ *2:C4*

$

⬚ **Hotel Beacon.** The Upper West Side's best buy for the price is three blocks from Central Park and Lincoln Center, and footsteps from Zabar's gourmet bazaar. All of the generously sized sea-green rooms and suites include marble bathrooms, kitchenettes with coffeemakers, pots and pans, stoves, and microwaves. Closets are huge, and some of the bathrooms have Hollywood dressing room–style mirrors. High floors have views of Central Park, the Hudson River, or the Midtown skyline; the staff here is especially friendly and helpful. The Hotel Beacon makes a nice choice to explore a different corner of New York in a safe, exciting residential neighborhood. **Pros:** kitchenettes in all rooms; heart of UWS location; affordable. **Cons:** rooms emphasize comfort over style. ⊠ *2130 Broadway, at W. 75th St., Upper West Side* ☎ *212/787–1100 or 800/572–4969* 🖷 *212/724–0839* ⊕ *www.beaconhotel.com* ↴ *120 rooms, 110 suites* ⌂ *In-room: safe, kitchen, refrigerator. In-hotel: laundry facilities, parking (paid), no-smoking rooms* ⊟ *AE, D, DC, MC, V* Ⓜ *1, 2, 3 to 72nd St.* ✛ *2:B4*

Long Island

WORD OF MOUTH

"Most of the nicer places to stay in the Hamptons are either B&Bs or Country Inns. . . . Be prepared to pay a small fortune for modest accomodations or a large fortune for nicer digs. Budget accomodations, which consist mainly of circa-1950 motels, will be merely expensive. Shopping and spas are in ample supply, but again, are geared towards the well-heeled. Obviously the beaches are a big attraction and are among the nicest on the eastern seaboard."

—ripit

Updated
by Vanessa
Geneva Ahern

At 1,377 square mi, Long Island is the largest island on the East Coast, as well as the most varied. From west to east the island shifts from overcrowded roads and suburban sprawl to verdant farmland and fruit-laden vineyards punctuated by historic seaside villages.

The island is notable for having one of the nation's finest stretches of white-sand beach, along its South Shore, as well as one of its most congested highways, the notorious Long Island Expressway. In addition to superb beaches, nature has given Long Island bountiful harbors and coves, rich soil, and a fascinating geology, whereas its inhabitants have given it a long and distinguished history, beautiful old homes, and, more recently, wonderful places to eat and stay.

Agriculture, particularly potato farming, was the basis of Long Island's early economy, and later, in the 18th and early 19th centuries, whaling brought a brief period of wealth and prominence to Sag Harbor, Greenport, and Cold Spring Harbor. After the Civil War, when well-to-do Americans discovered the pleasures of saltwater bathing and cool sea breezes, the farming and fishing communities of the Hamptons were slowly transformed into fashionable summer resorts, and the North Shore became the playground of the Vanderbilts, Whitneys, and Roosevelts. It wasn't until after World War II, when highways were constructed and Americans began owning cars as a matter of course, that vast numbers of the middle class moved out to Long Island, converting farm fields into new suburbs and shopping centers.

Today, even amid the sprawl of new homes and commercial districts, old village centers remain intact. Historic sites and museums protect many of the oldest, finest, and most magnificent homes. New farms growing wine grapes, herbs, and nursery plants have been established on old potato farms. Beyond the hubbub of development and traffic, the beaches and the waters of the sound and ocean beckon swimmers, surfers, sailors, sunbathers, and beachcombers as they always have.

ORIENTATION AND PLANNING

GETTING ORIENTED

Although two of New York City's boroughs, Brooklyn and Queens, occupy the island's western section, the *real* Long Island begins only when you leave the city behind and cross into Nassau County. East of Nassau is the more rural Suffolk County, with its North and South forks extending far into the Atlantic Ocean. The north–south distinction also applies to the North and South shores that run the length of the island.

TOP REASONS TO GO

Beaches. Whether you prefer the white sand of Fire Island, the more expansive beaches of Southampton, or the surf culture of Montauk, Long Island has beaches to accommodate every sun-and-surf worshipper.

Hampton hobnobbing. Browse the stylish boutiques and enjoy dining alfresco at trendy Hamptons restaurants. In peak season, Memorial Day to Labor Day, the town plays host to vacationing New Yorkers, international travelers, and the occasional celebrity.

Historic homes. History buffs and architecture enthusiasts can take guided tours of Teddy Roosevelt's summer home at Sagamore Hill and Walt Whitman's birthplace at Huntington Station. Drive by the Gold Coast mansions—or even stay in one (the Glen Cove Mansion is now a hotel).

Seaside villages. Don your fisherman's gear and a good appetite for fresh seafood in seaside Sag Harbor, Shelter Island, and Greenport.

Wineries. The North Fork is a wine lover's year-round paradise. Many wineries offer tours and tastings so you can see the wine-making process firsthand.

There's plenty to see on the island, but you'll spot nothing but traffic from the Long Island Expressway (U.S. 495, known to most residents as the LIE), which runs through the middle of the island from Long Island City in Queens all the way east to Riverhead in Suffolk. Summer weekends can be particularly problematic, when people head straight for either the South Shore's Fire Island or the South Fork's Hamptons and points east to Montauk. If you're more interested in the museums, stately mansions, nature preserves, and other attractions of the North and South shores, take the more leisurely roads that follow the two coastlines. On the North Shore, your best bet is Route 25A; on the South Shore, follow Route 27 (Sunrise Highway). Many north–south roads connect the shores, so cutting back and forth is easy. If your schedule is tight, stick to the LIE or the Northern State or Southern State parkways to make the best time between points of interest.

By choosing the most direct route, it's possible to drive from Manhattan to Montauk Point in less than three hours—although rush-hour and weekend traffic can cause significant delays. Once you reach Riverhead on the LIE, Long Island separates into the North and South forks. Each fork is traversed by a two-lane highway (Route 25 on the North Fork, Route 27 on the South Fork), and the surroundings become increasingly rural the farther east you go. Be prepared for travel to slow considerably once you are on the forks, especially in the height of summer; there are, however, lots of interesting farm stands and shops along the way to take your mind off the slowdown. Shelter Island, between the two forks, is a destination in itself; the only way to get here is by a short ferry ride from either Sag Harbor, on the South Fork, or Greenport, on the North Fork.

Noteworthy attractions of the North Shore, which stretches from Great Neck to Port Jefferson, include Teddy Roosevelt's summer home at

Sagamore Hill, Walt Whitman's birthplace at Huntington Station, and Gold Coast mansions. North Fork highlights include quiet villages, bountiful farm stands, and the vineyards and tasting rooms of a burgeoning wine industry. The cultured yet buzzing Hamptons, the fascinating old whaling village of Sag Harbor, and majestic Montauk Point are the essence of the South Fork.

PLANNING

WHEN TO GO

Long Island beach connoisseurs know that early autumn is the best time to visit; the water stays warm into September and sometimes even early October, and the crowds thin considerably. Of course, if you love the action, you'll want to be here in summer, when everything's open and the weather is most predictable. Book rooms a couple of months in advance for summer travel. Spring usually bursts onto Long Island in late March; suddenly everything is newly green, the gardens awaken, the shorebirds build their nests, and even the ocean loses its winter gray and starts to sparkle. Winter is good for solitary, though cold and windy, beach walks, and it's the only time of year you'll see seals and sea turtles.

BUDGETING YOUR TIME

Budget your time in a way that will allow for enough flexibility and spontaneity; the North and South forks have so much in terms of relaxation and new gastronomic, athletic, and outdoors adventures. Draw up a "must-see" or "must-do" wish list, and pack your bag. If you are planning on visiting the Hamptons during peak season, Memorial Day through Labor Day, be prepared for slow-moving traffic on Montauk Highway, the Hamptons' main throughway.

GETTING HERE AND AROUND

⇨ *Travel Smart New York State in the back of the book for airport, airline, and car rental contact information.*

Manhattan is 118 mi and two hours from the Hamptons. The most practical way to get from the New York metro area to Long Island is by car, but there are also efficient and reliable public transportation options.

AIR TRAVEL

Long Island is served by LaGuardia Airport and John F. Kennedy International Airport, both in the New York City borough of Queens, as well as by the smaller but more centrally located Long Island MacArthur Airport. American Eagle, Delta, Southwest Airlines, and US Airways fly into MacArthur. ⇨ *Air Travel in Travel Smart for more information about LaGuardia and JFK airports, as well as for airline contact information.*

Airport Information Long Island MacArthur Airport (ISP ✉ *100 Arrivals Ave., Ronkonkoma* ☎ *631/467–3210* ⊕ *www.macarthurairport.com).*

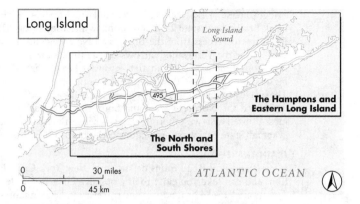

Long Island

Long Island Sound

495

The Hamptons and Eastern Long Island

The North and South Shores

0   30 miles
0   45 km

ATLANTIC OCEAN

BUS TRAVEL

Carless Manhattan residents board the Hampton Jitney bus on Friday afternoons to the North or South shore. Drinks, snacks, and newspapers are available during the two- to three-hour trip. The jitney picks up passengers along 3rd Avenue in Manhattan, and drops off at more than 20 different towns on the South and North forks, as well as making a stop in Fresh Meadows, Queens (the "Airport Connection" stop: a 30-minute cab ride from JFK Airport, and 20-minute cab ride from LaGuardia). The round-trip Hampton Jitney fare is $53. Those who want roomier, plusher seats and extra pampering can splurge for a ride on the Hampton Jitney's Ambassador Service bus for $63 round-trip.

The Hampton Luxury Liner links Manhattan with North and South Fork towns and offers connections to MacArthur Airport. Fares are $26–$38 one way. Reservations are required for all trips.

Long Island Bus, part of the Metropolitan Transportation Authority, travels throughout Nassau County and western Suffolk County, stopping at nearly 50 Long Island Rail Road stations. From late May through August, the LIRR offers special train-bus packages to Jones Beach State Park.

Contacts Hampton Jitney (☎631/283–4600 or ⊕*www.hamptonjitney.com*). **Hampton Luxury Liner** (☎631/537–5800 ⊕*www.hamptonluxuryliner.com*). **Long Island Bus** (☎516/228–4000 *weekdays 7–5* ⊕*www.mta.nyc.ny.us*).

CAR TRAVEL

Unless you plan to stay in one town or resort for the duration of your visit, a car is necessary for exploring and getting from place to place on Long Island. If you're coming from more than 200 mi away, consider flying into one of the airports and renting a car. Although train and bus service is regular, you may have to wait around for connections, depending on your destination. Taxi and car services can get you from place to place, but this is an expensive way to go if you're using them as your only mode of transportation.

The Queens Midtown Tunnel (leading to the Long Island Expressway), Queensboro Bridge (Northern Boulevard, Route 25A), and RFK

Bridge (Interstate 278) connect Long Island with Manhattan. The Throgs Neck Bridge (Interstate 295) and Bronx Whitestone Bridge (Interstate 678) provide access from the Bronx and New England. From points south, take the Verrazano Narrows Bridge (Interstate 278). Traffic in and around the metropolitan area is always heavy; the 7–9:30 morning rush and the 4–6:30 evening peak are the most harrowing times. The heavily traveled Long Island Expressway (aka the LIE or Interstate 495), and the Northern State and Southern State parkways are the most-utilized east–west thoroughfares, whereas the Meadowbrook and Wantagh state parkways are major north–south connectors.

TRAIN TRAVEL

Long Island Rail Road trains depart from New York City's Penn Station, and can take you close to any popular Long Island destination. Tickets are $15–$42 round-trip and travel can take 30 minutes to three hours depending where you're going. Passengers may have to change trains at Jamaica Center in Queens. Local taxi companies can be found at train stations and Hampton Jitney stops.

Memorial Day through Labor Day, the LIRR offers One-Day-Getaway packages to more than 25 popular Long Island destinations, with discounts and coupons. One-day packages include round-trip fare to Jones Beach ($15), Long Beach ($18), and towns in Fire Island ($24–$28), and shuttle bus, ferry ride, and beach admission.

Bicycles are allowed with a permit ($5; applications are available on the LIRR Web site). On weekdays trains are congested during the 7–9:30 morning rush and the 4–6:30 evening peak. In summer the LIRR offers Hamptons Reserve service (aka "the Cannonball"), express trains with reserved seats, air-conditioning, and bar and snack service. The LIRR also offers different themed bus tours during the summer months, including Wine Country tours and a shopping excursion at Freeport's Nautical Mile.

Information Long Island Rail Road (☎ *516/822–5477 or 631/231–5477* ⊕ *www. lirr.org)*

BEACHES

Clean white-sand beaches are Long Island's main attraction for most visitors, whether their idea of beach fun is lounging on the warm sand, watching the sun drop slowly into the water, swimming or surfing in the rolling waves, or just strolling along the shore and breathing the fresh salt air. The pounding surf and endless horizons make the South Shore unforgettable. For serious waves, head to the magnificent South Shore beaches like Jones Beach and Robert Moses, as well as Fire Island. The seashore tends to get crowded on summer weekends, but as you move out east, the crowds thin—especially all the way out in Montauk. Most Hamptons beaches are open only to residents, but lodging properties usually have beach passes for their guests. Fronting Long Island Sound, the beaches on the North Shore are tame in comparison. The shores also are rocky.

WINERIES

The white-sand beaches of the North Fork encircle a broad, central agricultural belt that, it turns out, has near-perfect conditions for ripening European grape varieties like merlot and chardonnay. Now that the quality of Long Island wines rivals that of the world's top labels, the North Fork draws serious wine lovers and sightseeing fun seekers alike. Navigating the North Fork wine trail is really about deciding how often to stop, as all but 3 of the region's 30 wineries are on Route 25, which runs east–west through the fork, or on Route 48, running north of and parallel to Route 25. Each winery has its own personality; some encourage a quiet focus on the wine, whereas at others you jostle for a place at the lively bar. Some are in old barns that retain rural charm in wide-planked wood floors, heavy beams, and old farming equipment. Summer weekends—particularly when bad weather foils beach plans—attract droves of winery-hoppers. Fall brings harvest festivals and day-trippers buying fresh vegetables at farm stands and mixed cases of wines for the holidays. Off-season, the wineries are very quiet, and you're likely to be showered with extra attention. ⇨ *For information on the North Fork Wine Trail, see Close Up box in this chapter.*

Information **Long Island Wine Council** (☎ *631/369–5887* ⊕ *www.liwines. com*).

RESTAURANTS

Every conceivable cuisine is served at restaurants, cafés, and diners across Long Island, but fresh seafood is the most notable regional specialty. It's not uncommon for chefs to prepare delectable dishes in the evening using seafood caught that same morning. A trend toward using organic foods and fresh local produce has increased the quality of restaurant meals here. If you enjoy good wine with your meal, try the Long Island chardonnays and merlots. The soil and climate on the North Fork have been compared to those in the finest wine-producing areas of France, and the wines reflect that quality. On the North and South forks, many restaurants change their schedules depending on the time of year, so it's always a good idea to call ahead in the off-season.

HOTELS

More than 340 lodging properties across Long Island—chain hotels, oceanfront condos, cottages, and bed-and-breakfasts—provide close to 15,000 rooms. Most resort-town lodgings are booked far in advance in summer, but occasional cancellations mean you can sometimes travel on a whim. In beach areas, many lodging properties offer their guests day-use beach passes, giving you access to sandy stretches reserved for residents. Some places on Fire Island and on the North and South forks institute three-night minimums during the peak season. Island real-estate agents have listings for seasonal and weekly rentals, and local chambers of commerce can point you in the right direction for a place to stay. Parking is typically free at all hotels unless otherwise noted.

WHAT IT COSTS					
	$	$$	$$$	$$$$	
RESTAURANTS	under $10	$10–$17	$18–$24	$25–$35	over $35
HOTELS	under $100	$100–$150	$151–$200	$201–$300	over $300

Restaurant prices are for a main course at dinner (or at the most expensive meal served). Hotel prices are for two people in a standard double room in high season, excluding tax.

TOURS

BOAT TOURS Atlantis Explorer Environmental Boat Tours organizes two-hour boat tours ($17) down the Peconic River, during which naturalists explain the geological history of the Peconic Estuary system and discuss local flora and fauna. There's also a shoreline walking tour. The tours, run by the Cornell Cooperative Extension Marine Program, are offered twice daily April through September.

From April through October, you may take a 2½-hour tour from Greenport around Long Island Sound aboard the *Mary E.*, a 1906 schooner, for $20–$25.

Nautical Cruise Lines offers dinner cruises (starting at $65 per person) year-round on the 100-foot *Nautical Princess*, a tri-level yacht, and the 85-foot *Nautical Belle*, an old-style paddle wheeler. Specialty cruises include magic shows, brunches, and seal watching.

Boat Tours Information **Atlantis Explorer Environmental Boat Tours** (⊠ *431 E. Main St., Riverhead* ☎ *631/208–9200* ⊕ *www.atlantismarineworld.com*). **Mary E.** (⊠ *Preston's Dock, Main St., Greenport* ☎ *631/477–8966* ⊕ *themarye.netfirms. com*). **Nautical Cruise Lines** (⊠ *395 Woodcleft Ave., Freeport* ☎ *516/623–5712* ⊕ *www.nauticalcruiselines.com*).

VISITOR INFORMATION

Long Island Convention and Visitors Bureau (⊠ *350 Vanderbilt Motor Pkwy., Suite 103, Hauppauge* ☎ *631/951–3440 or 800/441–4601* ⊕ *www.licvb.com*).

9

THE NORTH SHORE

Jagged in its coastal outline and gentle in its topography, the North Shore is lapped by Long Island Sound, which F. Scott Fitzgerald called "the most domesticated body of saltwater in the Western Hemisphere." The Gold Coast, a string of wealthy suburbs, stretches along the shore for about 18 mi from Great Neck, 22 mi east of New York City, to Huntington. The mansions here inspired the wealthy estates F. Scott Fitzgerald wrote about in his classic novel *The Great Gatsby*.

GETTING HERE

Drive east along Route 25A into Nassau County, cutting across the bases of two peninsulas that make up the towns of Great Neck and Port Washington.

PORT WASHINGTON

5 mi east of Great Neck.

Antiques and collectibles stores, gift shops, and old buildings line this town's Main Street, and tall ships bob in the water beyond the town dock at Port Washington Harbor. This area was originally settled in 1674; early residents made their living farming oysters and raising cattle until the 20th century, when the sand and gravel industry took off.

VISITOR INFORMATION
Port Washington Chamber of Commerce (⌂ *Box 121, Port Washington 11050* ☎ *516/883–6566*).

WHAT TO SEE
Sands Point Preserve. Overlooking Long Island Sound, this 216-acre preserve, once part of a Gold Coast estate, occupies the tip of the Port Washington Peninsula. The grounds include natural and landscaped areas, with forests, meadows, freshwater ponds, and shore cliffs. Also here are three castlelike mansions. The 1904 Castlegould, the visitor center, houses changing exhibits on natural history. Falaise is a Normandy-style manor house built for Harry F. Guggenheim in 1923; the home is notable for its medieval and Renaissance style and artwork. The Tudor-style Hempstead House, used for various exhibits, overlooks the harbor. Tours through Falaise and nature walks are available. ⊠ *95 Middle Neck Rd., Sands Point* ☎ *516/571–7900* ⊕ *www.sandspointpreserve. org* 🎫 *Preserve weekdays free, weekends $2; Falaise $6* ☉ *Preserve daily 9–4:30; Falaise May–Oct., Wed.–Sun. noon–3.*

OFF THE BEATEN PATH

Sea Cliff. This tiny village 4 mi north of Roslyn is filled with turn-of-the-20th-century homes, most lovingly restored to their original grandeur. Shops and restaurants in the village make it a pleasant destination for an afternoon visit. At the **Sea Cliff Village Museum,** displays of documents and photos trace the history of Sea Cliff. A scale model of a village Victorian house is also on exhibit. ⊠ *95 10th Ave., Sea Cliff* ☎ *516/671–0090* 🎫 *$1 suggested donation* ☉ *Weekends 2–5.*

SHOPPING
Among the many antiques shops in Port Washington is **Bubba Browns Treasures** (⊠ *302 Main St.* ☎ *516/767–0750*), which sells artwork, vintage Italian silks, Victorian ephemera, chandeliers, and plenty of decorative angels. The shop occupies two stores separated by a garden filled with stone angels, bronze statuary, Victorian garden furniture, and fountains.

WHERE TO EAT
$$ ✕ **Finn MacCool's.** Part restaurant, part postwork social pub, Finn's has
IRISH   the feel of an Irish tavern, with lots of wood and a noise level that rises as the evening wears on. In addition to a large selection of domestic and imported beers, the pub serves hearty homemade stews and sandwiches. ⊠ *205 Main St.* ☎ *516/944–3439* ▤ *AE, D, DC, MC, V.*

$$ ✕ **Louie's Oyster Bar and Grill.** This rustic, wood-paneled seafood restau-
SEAFOOD   rant with high ceilings, moldings, and brass railings at the wooden bar affords views of the harbor. Try the classic fish-and-chips or the salmon

fillet with a soy-ginger glaze, asparagus, and black olives. ⊠ *Main St.* ☎*516/883–4242* ▤*AE, MC, V.*

OLD WESTBURY

6 mi southeast of Port Washington.

The community of Westbury dates to 1657, when Captain John Seamann purchased 12,000 acres from the local Algonquin tribe. Later, in 1700, Quakers fleeing persecution settled in the area, naming their settlement Westbury after their hometown in England. Over time, estates replaced the farms of early settlers, and today horse trails wind across the area's soft hills.

WHAT TO SEE

★ **Old Westbury Gardens** (⊠*71 Old Westbury Rd.* ☎*516/333–0048* ⊕*www.oldwestburygardens.org* ▤*$10* ⊙*Apr.–mid-Dec., Wed.–Mon. 10–5*) is one of the few former Long Island estates still intact, and today the grounds and 1906 Gold Coast mansion built by financier-sportsman John S. Phipps are open to the public. The mansion showcases the home's original furniture and the family's art and belongings; the beautiful 160-acre property includes formal gardens, fountains, woodlands, and lakes.

OYSTER BAY

9 mi northeast of Roslyn.

The history of this quaint town on an inlet off Long Island Sound can be traced to 1615, when a Dutch explorer, impressed by the area's bountiful shellfish, named it Oyster Bay. The hamlet's distance from Long Island's more urbanized areas has helped preserve a small-town feel. Today, thousands of oyster lovers descend on the town every summer for its annual Oyster Bay Festival.

The area's most famous resident was President Teddy Roosevelt, who built his home, Sagamore Hill, here in 1885. Not all of Oyster Bay's visitors had such positive pedigrees, however. It is reported that Oyster Bay was the last port of call for Captain Kidd before he was arrested in Boston and sent back to London to be hanged in 1701. A local cook, Mary Mallon, received lots of publicity in 1906 after being dubbed Typhoid Mary for allegedly infecting dozens of people with typhoid fever. Singer Billy Joel is the town's most recent claim to fame.

WHAT TO SEE

★ **Planting Fields Arboretum State Historic Park.** The home of insurance magnate William Robertson Coe from 1910 to 1955, Planting Fields is now a public arboretum with 160 acres of gardens and plant collections and 250 acres of lawns and woodlands. Two greenhouse complexes nurture native plants. **Coe Hall,** the estate's magnificent Tudor-style manor, is filled with period furnishings and antiques, including windows from the home of Henry VIII's second wife, Anne Boleyn. Guided tours of the house are available. ⊠*Planting Fields Rd.* ☎*516/922–9210 for manor,*

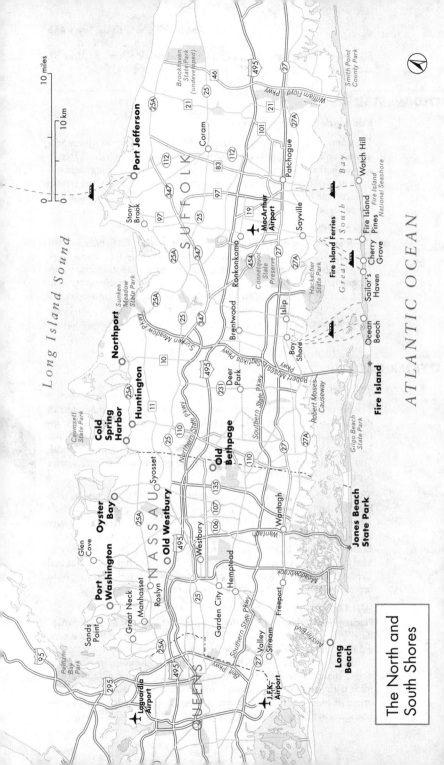

The North and South Shores

516/922–8600 for arboretum ⊕*www.plantingfields.org* 🅿*Parking $6, manor $6.50* ⊙*Daily 9–5.*

Raynham Hall Historical House Museum. Three generations of the Townsend family, renowned merchants and ship traders, lived in this colonial saltbox structure dating from the American Revolution. Sally Townsend was responsible for alerting her father to the fact that a certain Benedict Arnold was going to betray his country. Many of the original family furnishings are in the house, and there are rotating exhibits of Civil War memorabilia and holiday decorations. The house-museum reveals much about Oyster Bay from the time of the Revolution through the town's affluent Victorian period. ⊠*20 W. Main St.* ☎*516/922–6808* ⊕*www. raynhamhallmuseum.org* 🖾*$4* ⊙*Labor Day–June, Tues.–Sun. 1–5; July–Labor Day, Tues.–Sun. noon–5.*

★ **Sagamore Hill National Historic Site.** Known for a time as the "summer White House," this 23-room Victorian was President Teddy Roosevelt's cherished family retreat from 1885 until his death in 1919. In addition to the original furnishings and some personal effects, the house contains animal heads and skins from Roosevelt's many hunting expeditions. The servants' quarters offer a behind-the-scenes look at life here. ⊠*Cove Neck Rd.* ☎*516/922–4788 or 516/922–4447* ⊕*www.nps.gov/ sahi* 🖾*$5* ⊙*Grounds daily dawn–dusk. House Memorial Day–Labor Day, daily 10–4; Labor Day–Memorial Day, Wed.–Sun. 10–4.*

Theodore Roosevelt Sanctuary and Audubon Center. Down the road from Sagamore Hill, Teddy Roosevelt's family home, is this 12-acre bird sanctuary—the perfect legacy of the environmentally active president. More than 125 species of birds live here. Roosevelt is buried in a cemetery on the grounds. ⊠*134 Cove Rd.* ☎*516/922–3200* 🖾*$5* ⊙*Grounds daily 9–5; center Mon.–Thurs. 8–4:30, Fri. 8–2, weekends 1–4:30.*

WHERE TO EAT

$$ ✕**Canterbury Ales Oyster Bar and Grill.** This bistro-grill serves everything
AMERICAN from horseradish–honey mustard salmon and Japanese ahi tuna to Parmesan-and-herb-crusted chicken and wild game. To wash down your meal you have a choice of 99 beers from around the world. A children's menu is available. ⊠*46 Audrey Ave.* ☎*516/922–3614* ⊕*www. canterburyalesrestaurant.com* ⊟*AE, MC, V.*

$$$ ✕**Mill River Inn.** A fireplace, white linens, fresh flowers, and candlelight
CONTINENTAL are among the romantic touches at this quiet restaurant. Dishes are contemporary—sautéed Hudson Valley foie gras, grilled rack of lamb with poached pears and spinach, and pork chops stuffed with Swiss chard, roasted peppers, and pecorino cheese. ⊠*160 Mill River Rd.* ☎*516/922–7768* ⊟*AE, DC, MC, V* ⊙*No lunch.*

COLD SPRING HARBOR

5 mi east of Oyster Bay.

One of the North Shore's most enchanting towns, Cold Spring Harbor has always been valued for its location on the water. The Matinecock Indians are said to have called it Wawapex, meaning "place of good water." In 1653 three Englishmen from Oyster Bay bought the land around the harbor from the Matinecocks and named it Cold Spring after the area's freshwater springs. It became a U.S. Port of Entry in 1799 and during the mid-1800s was home to a fleet of nine whaling vessels and numerous cargo ships.

Time hasn't eroded any of the landscape surrounding this attractive village. As you drive east along Route 25A, the town's harbor suddenly comes into view from beyond the trees. After you take the turn that leads up the hill around Cold Spring Harbor, breathtaking trees draw the eye. At the crest of the hill, the shops and restaurants on Main Street (part of Route 25A) merit a stop. Note that parking is at a premium in the village's few and small lots.

WHAT TO SEE

Cold Spring Harbor Fish Hatchery and Aquarium. Eight outdoor tanks at this educational center hold the largest collection of native freshwater fish, turtles, and amphibians in New York State. For a fee, visitors can try their hand at trout fishing. It's 1½ mi from downtown Cold Spring Harbor. ⊠*South side of Rte. 25A at Rte. 108* ☎*516/692-6768* ⊕*www.cshfha.org* ⊠*$6* ⊙*Daily 10–5, Oct.–Labor Day until 6 weekends.*

Cold Spring Harbor Whaling Museum. One of the highlights of this museum's permanent exhibits exploring Long Island's whaling industry is a fully equipped 19th-century whaleboat. Whaling implements, paintings, scrimshaw, and ship models are also on display. ⊠*Main St./Rte. 25A* ☎*631/367–3418* ⊕*www.cshwhalingmuseum.org* ⊠*$5* ⊙*Memorial Day–Labor Day, daily 11–5; Labor Day–Memorial Day, Tues.–Sun. 11–5.*

WHERE TO EAT AND STAY

$$
CONTINENTAL
✕**105 on the Harbor.** The stately dining room in this Victorian house is a great place from which to view magnificent summer sunsets over Cold Spring Harbor. Delectable dishes include rack of lamb with mustard sauce and filet mignon with peppercorn sauce; dessert runs to fruit tarts and cheesecake. The restaurant has dock space. ⊠*105 Harbor Rd.* ☎*631/367–3166* ☐*AE, DC, MC, V* ⊙*Closed Mon.*

$$
⊡**Swan View Manor.** The Victorian house, 1½ blocks from the center of town, overlooks the harbor. When the weather's warm you may eat breakfast on the front porch, which is cozy with flowers and wicker chairs. The guest rooms are frilly, with queen- and king-size beds and floral duvets fluffed to perfection. Complimentary tea is served every afternoon in the sitting room, which is warmed by a fireplace in winter. **Pros:** complementary beverages served all day and afternoon tea. **Cons:** not walking distance to town; 14-day cancellation policy. ⊠*45 Harbor Rd.* ☎*631/367–2070* ⊕*www.swanview.com* 🛏*18 rooms, 1 suite* ⼧ *In-room: safe (some), Wi-Fi. In-hotel: no kids under 10, no-smoking rooms* ☐*AE, D, DC, MC, V* ⊙*CP Closed Jan.–Mar.*

HUNTINGTON

2 mi east of Cold Spring Harbor.

The township of greater Huntington embraces five navigable harbors, several beaches on the gentle waters of Long Island Sound, and 17 communities, including the attractive Huntington village (the township also includes Cold Spring Harbor and Northport). The township's most famous resident, the poet Walt Whitman, was born here in 1819. Later, he founded a local newspaper, the *Long Islander,* which is still published today. The late 1800s and early 1900s saw the development of this region of the North Shore's Gold Coast, which attracted estate owners William K. Vanderbilt, Marshall Field III, and Walter B. Jennings, among others.

Today, Huntington village is the heart of the township; historic buildings and excellent restaurants and shops pepper the bustling downtown. Among the stores here are a large independent bookstore, charming gift shops, trendy boutiques, and antiques stores.

WHAT TO SEE

Walt Whitman Birthplace State Historic Site & Interpretive Center. This was the boyhood home of Walt Whitman, one of America's greatest poets. A typical example of native Long Island craftsmanship of the time, the snug house, built by the poet's father circa 1819, has survived virtually intact since the Whitmans left it in 1823. Whitman portraits, letters, and manuscripts are on display. The home is off Route 110, across from Walt Whitman Mall. ⊠*246 Old Walt Whitman Rd., Huntington Station* ☎*631/427–5240* ⊕*www.waltwhitman.org* ⊠*$5* ☽ *Wed.–Fri. 1–4, weekends 11–4.*

WHERE TO EAT

$$$$
ECLECTIC
✕**Panama Hatties.** Artful cuisine is served in this upscale yet relaxed art-deco dining room. Dinner is a prix-fixe three-course affair for $65; the prix-fixe lunch is more reasonable at $21. Specialties include rare seared tuna, foie gras, pistachio-crusted rack of lamb with roasted eggplant, and New Zealand venison with wild rice, cling peaches, and macadamia nuts. ⊠*872 E. Jericho Tpke., Huntington Station* ☎*631/351–1727* ▭*AE, D, DC, MC, V.*

NORTHPORT

4 mi east of Huntington.

The Matinecock Indians were the first inhabitants of what is now one of the North Shore's oldest and most charming villages. Originally known as Cow Harbor, Northport was incorporated in 1895. Victorian houses, some built by old sea captains, fill the scenic harbor area. The downtown shopping district is east of the harbor. Northport retains a rarity on Long Island, a true main street that runs through the heart of the village and still bears the original tracks of the trolley line, now defunct, built in 1902 to relieve town horses of the chore of meeting trains.

WHAT TO SEE

★ **Suffolk County Vanderbilt Museum and Planetarium.** William K. Vanderbilt's 24-room Moroccan-style mansion, called Eagle's Nest, sits on 43
acres and houses collections that Vanderbilt acquired as he traveled
throughout the world. Summer brings various theatrical performances
to the mansion's courtyard. The adjacent planetarium is one of the
best equipped in the nation, with a 60-foot domed Sky Theater. Sky
and laser shows are held regularly. ⊠ *180 Little Neck Rd., Centerport*
☎ *631/854–5555* ⊕ *www.vanderbiltmuseum.org* ⊠ *Grounds $5, man-
sion tour $8, planetarium show $7* ⊙ *May, June, Sept., and Oct., Tues.–
Fri. noon–5, weekends 11:30–5; July and Aug., Tues.–Sat. 10–5, Sun.
noon–5; Nov.–Apr., Tues.–Fri. noon–4, Sat. noon–5, Sun. 11:30–5; call
for planetarium schedule.*

SPORTS AND THE OUTDOORS

Sunken Meadow State Park *(Governor Alfred E. Smith State Park).* A
3-mi beach edges this 1,200-acre park, which also has three 9-hole golf
courses, a driving range, playgrounds, basketball courts, softball fields,
a soccer field, and trails for biking, running, and cross-country skiing.
Facilities include showers and an aid station. Take Sunken Meadow
Parkway north and follow signs for the park. ⊠ *Off Sunken Meadow
State Pkwy.* ☎ *631/269–4333* ⊕ *nysparks.state.ny.us* ⊠ *Parking $8
(Memorial Day–Labor Day)* ⊙ *Daily sunrise–sunset.*

GOLF   The challenging 18-hole **Crab Meadow Golf Course** (⊠ *Waterside Ave.*
☎ *631/757–8800*) is hilly and windy. Most holes have panoramic views
of Long Island Sound and Connecticut's waterways. Greens fees are
$42–$45 for nonresidents; carts are available for $16.

WHERE TO EAT

$$ ✕ **Pumpernickels Restaurant.** This cozy German restaurant at the edge of
GERMAN   Northport village is known for its sauerbraten and seafood. Candles
and fresh flowers adorn the dining room, and there's often live music
on the weekends. ⊠ *640 Main St.* ☎ *631/757–7959* ⊟ *AE, D, DC,
MC, V* ⊙ *No lunch Sun.*

$$ ✕ **Ship's Inn.** Sit in a candlelit booth and savor grouper française, crab
AMERICAN   cakes, or prime rib (on Wednesday). Polished mahogany and brass
nautical details highlight the ship theme. A children's menu is available.
⊠ *78 Main St.* ☎ *631/261–3000* ⊟ *AE, D, DC, MC, V.*

PORT JEFFERSON

26 mi northeast of Northport

The Setauket Indians, the first to live here, began selling the land to settlers in the mid-1600s. By the time of the Revolutionary War the village
was home to many patriots, and during the War of 1812 the harbor was
attacked. In 1836 the local residents named the village after Thomas
Jefferson. Construction of a large dock began several years later.

Shipbuilding was Port Jefferson's major industry until the size and
weight of ships required larger shipyards in the late 1800s. A passenger ferry that crosses Long Island Sound to Bridgeport, Connecticut,

docks here. Across from the busy harbor you find a slew of restaurants, souvenir shops, antiques stores, and art galleries. Waterfront estates, charming Victorians, and old sea-captains' homes crowd its downtown. Along its cliffs lies some of the most cherished real estate on Long Island, including such posh neighborhoods as Belle Terre.

VISITOR INFORMATION

Port Jefferson Chamber of Commerce (⊠118 W. Broadway, Port Jefferson ☎631/473–1414 ⊕www.portjeffchamber.com).

WHERE TO EAT AND STAY

$$ ✕**Papa Joe's Seafood Factory.** Etched-glass windows overlook the har-
SEAFOOD bor at this spacious family-style restaurant known for its seafood. The dining room has a nautical theme; a saltwater fish tank sits by the bar. There's open-air dining on the deck. A children's menu is available. ⊠111 W. Broadway ☎631/473–5656 ☐AE, D, DC, MC, V.

¢ ✕**Tiger Lily Café.** There's a definite West Coast vibe to this café. Head to
VEGETARIAN the counter to order chicken salad, a wrap, carrot-ginger soup, or one of the satisfying home-cooked vegetarian selections, then settle into a big comfortable chair or couch in the rear (adults only here). Occasionally there's live music on weekend afternoons. The place is open only until 5 PM. ⊠156 E. Main St. ☎631/476–7080 ☐No credit cards ⊙No dinner.

$$$ 🏨**Danfords Hotel and Marina.** This inn near a marina on the harbor has spacious rooms with antiques and views of Long Island Sound. The nautical-themed rooms are techie-friendly with iPod docking stations and flat-screen televisions. Guests can enjoy the sea breeze while multitasking or relaxing on the plush sofas. Some guest rooms have fireplaces and balconies. **Pros:** granite bathtubs and glass-enclosed waterfall showers. **Cons:** $10 fee for Wi-Fi; only one building has elevator; shared balconies are not private. ⊠25 E. Broadway ☎631/928–5200 or 800/332–6367 ⊕www.danfords.com ⇔85 rooms, 7 suites ⚬ In-room: refrigerator (some), Wi-Fi. In-hotel: restaurant, room service, bar, gym, spa, laundry service, no-smoking rooms ☐AE, D, DC, MC, V.

THE SOUTH SHORE AND FIRE ISLAND

The Atlantic Ocean sends its rollers onto the white-sand beaches that fringe the South Shore. Several of these beach areas, such as Jones Beach, are actually long, narrow barrier islands that wind and tide have thrown up as a kind of sandy protection for Long Island's southern coast. The South Shore stretches from Nassau County to Suffolk County and encompasses diverse communities, from residential suburbia to hard-partying summer-resort areas.

LONG BEACH

11 mi south of Garden City.

A series of large barrier islands, which protect the mainland from ocean surges, sits off the south shore of Long Island. The city of Long Beach occupies the westernmost of these islands, in Nassau County. Thanks to the ocean breezes, the weather is moderate—on average 10F warmer in winter and 10F cooler in summer than the rest of the county.

The city, aptly named for its 5-mi-long stretch of pristine beach, was established as a warm-weather resort community in the 1870s. Teeming with restaurants, nightlife, and shops, it's still a popular vacation spot. The 2-mi-long boardwalk is a hub of activity, especially in summer, when the permanent population of 35,000 swells to 50,000. The Long Island Rail Road makes it easy to get here from New York City. The water's edge is only a third of a mile walk from the last stop on the railroad's Long Beach line.

WHAT TO SEE

Boardwalk. The 2-mi boardwalk, overlooking a beautiful stretch of Atlantic Ocean beach, is the heart of the community. It was constructed in the early 1900s with the help of elephants from Coney Island's Dreamland Park. The pachyderms pulled materials for the boardwalk's pilings along what is known today as Sunrise Highway. You can hear live music throughout summer; on weekends, vendors and entertainers attract lively crowds. ⊠*Between New York Ave. and Neptune Blvd.* ☎*516/431–3890* ☑*Free.*

OFF THE BEATEN PATH

Rock Hall Museum. Built in 1767 by Josiah Martin, a wealthy West Indian planter and British Loyalist during the Revolutionary War, this Georgian Colonial manor was acquired in 1824 by another Tory family, the Hewletts, and served as their family home. In 1948 it was given to the Town of Hempstead and is presently on the National Register of Historic Places. The home is now a museum with period furnishings and programs for all ages, and was recently added to the New York State Revolutionary War Heritage Trail. ⊠*199 Broadway, Lawrence* ☎*516/239–1157* ☑*Free* ⊙ *Wed.–Sat. 10–4, Sun. noon–4.*

SPORTS AND THE OUTDOORS

BEACHES

Fodor's Choice

★

Jones Beach State Park. Eleven miles east of Long Beach, the 6½ mi of white sand is one of the best known and most popular of Long Island's beaches. The 2,500-acre park is loaded with facilities, including two pools, bathhouses, piers, two surf-casting areas (by permit), picnic areas, concession stands, a restaurant, and four basketball courts. A 1½-mi-long boardwalk has deck games and hosts special events. Lifeguards are on duty from late May to mid-September. The **Tommy Hilfiger at Jones Beach Theater** (☎*516/221–1000* ⊕*www.jonesbeach.com*), a 14,000-seat amphitheater in Jones Beach State Park, presents such big-name musicians as Alanis Morissette, David Bowie, and Tom Petty, as well as other performers. The concert season usually runs June through August. The park can be reached from the Wantagh and Meadowbrook parkways (head south). ⊠*Ocean Pkwy., Wantagh* ☎*516/785–1600* ⊕*nysparks.state.ny.us* ☑*Parking $8 June–Aug.*

Ocean Beach Park. Sun seekers throng this beach park, which stretches for 5 mi on the barrier island's south side, to play volleyball, surf, swim, and sunbathe—all under the watchful eyes of lifeguards (on duty weekends late May to mid-June, daily mid-June to early September).

The park's indoor pool is open to the public all year. ✉*Magnolia St. between Nevada Ave. and Maple Blvd.* ☎*516/431–1810, 516/431–1021, or 516/431–5533* ⚏*Beach $6 (late May–early Sept.), pool $5* ⏱*Pool daily 9–6.*

NIGHTLIFE AND THE ARTS

During warm-weather months free concerts are held on the boardwalk on many afternoons and evenings. Bar-strewn Beech Street is the setting for a lively "bar crawl"; each place has a distinct flair and flavor. **The Inn** (✉*943 W. Beech St.* ☎*516/432–9220*) is the only live-music venue in the area that's open four nights a week (Thursday through Sunday). A mixed-age crowd enjoys the music as well as brunch, lunch, dinner, and late-night noshes. **The Saloon** (✉*1016 West Beech St.* ☎*516/432–9185*), the local neighborhood classic, has large windows opening to the sidewalk; there's always a crowd (mostly twentysomethings) spilling out onto the backyard deck. ⇨*For concerts, see the Tommy Hilfiger at Jones Beach Theater above under Beaches.*

WHERE TO EAT

$ ✕**Cabana's.** Bright colors and a tropical motif set the stage at this
SOUTHWESTERN upbeat, kid-friendly restaurant. Try a "Mexican Pizza" or the "Clams Cabana" for a local seafood fix. ✉*1032 W. Beech St.* ☎*516/889–1345* ⊟*MC, V* ⏱*No lunch.*

$$ ✕**Duke Falcon's Global Grill.** Memorabilia from around the world adorn
ECLECTIC this casual but intimate eatery. The menu is all over the globe, too, covering a range of cuisines from new American to South American. Argentine gaucho steak, grilled rib eye served with garlic-mashed potatoes and roasted peppers, is a popular choice. Sidewalk café–style dining is available in summer. ✉*36 W. Park Ave.* ☎*516/897–7000* ⊟*AE, D, DC, MC, V.*

$$$ ✕**Jimmy Hays Steak House.** Great steaks are the draw at this fun and
STEAK lively restaurant. Favorite main dishes include Black Angus rib eye, paired with sautéed spinach and a potato pancake, and Lobster Jimmy (pan-sautéed lobster with lemon, butter, and garlic). For dessert, consider chocolate mousse, peach melba, or crème brûlée. The restaurant is about a five-minute drive from Long Beach. ✉*4310 Austin Blvd., Island Park* ☎*516/432–5155* ⊟*AE, D, DC, MC, V* ⏱*No lunch.*

OLD BETHPAGE AND FARMINGDALE

34 mi northeast of Long Beach.

Golf fans know all about Old Bethpage and nearby Farmingdale. Bethpage State Park has five municipal courses, including the Black Course, host of the 2002 and 2009 U.S. Open. It's considered one of the top courses in the United States.

WHAT TO SEE

☾ **Old Bethpage Village Restoration.** A re-created pre–Civil War farm village, this living-history museum sits on 200 pastoral acres with soft hills and lovely meadows. The buildings were moved to this spot from other parts of Long Island; the 45 structures, all original, include two general stores, nine homes, a schoolhouse, a tavern, a church, and a working farm with animals. The guides, dressed in period costume, love sharing their knowledge. ⊠*1303 Round Swamp Rd., 1 mi south of LIE Exit 48, Old Bethpage* ☎*516/572–8401* ⊕*www.nassaucountyny.gov* ☜*$10* ⊙*Mar.–Dec., Wed.-Sun. 10–4.*

SPORTS AND THE OUTDOORS

Fodor'sChoice ★

GOLF

Bethpage State Park. The 1,500-acre park encompasses bridle, hiking, biking, and cross-country-skiing trails; tennis courts; and picnic areas. A polo field hosts weekly matches from mid-June to mid-October. But Bethpage is renowned for its golf complex, one of the best public golf facilities in the country. It has five 18-hole regulation golf courses, most designed by A. W. Tillinghast. The renowned par-71 **Black Course,** site of the U.S. Open in 2002 and 2009, is tough to play and tough to get on, especially on weekends. With small greens, soft slopes, and a good selection of holes, the par-71 **Green Course** is much less difficult. At the par-72 **Blue Course,** the level of difficulty drops after the challenging front 9 holes. The par-70 **Red Course** is formidable overall, but its opening hole is considered particularly tough. Although it has some steep slopes, the par-71 **Yellow Course** is probably the easiest course in the complex. Black Course greens fees are $100–$120 (nonresidents); at the other four courses, greens fees are $31–$41 (regardless of whether you're a resident) and carts are available. Blue, Green, and Yellow courses are open year-round. The Red Course is open from April 1 to December 1 and the Black Course is open from April 15 to November 15. ⊠*99 Quaker Meetinghouse Rd., off Powell Ave. east of Rte. 135, Farmingdale* ☎*516/249–0701 park, 516/249–0700 golf* ⊕*nysparks. state.ny.us* ☜*Free (park)* ⊙*Daily dawn–dusk (park).*

WHERE TO EAT

$$–$$$
CONTINENTAL

✕**56th Fighter Group.** The World War II–theme restaurant sits on a local airport runway with real planes and jeeps out back. Big-band music is piped throughout the place, enhancing the 1940s mood. You can watch planes take off and land while you dig into steaks, chops, or seafood. Signature items include beer-cheese soup, prime rib with cheddar mashed potatoes, and pot roast with chive dumplings. Sunday brunch is also popular. ⊠*7160 Republic Airport, Farmingdale* ☎*631/694–8280* ⚑*Reservations essential* ▭*AE, D, DC, MC, V.*

$$
JAPANESE

✕**Ozumo Japanese Restaurant.** At $21, the dinner box—soup; salad; steamed dumplings; fruit; California roll; and chicken, beef, salmon, or shrimp teriyaki, or another main dish—is a deal. The sushi cuts are high quality and the prices are moderate. ⊠*164 Hicksville Rd., Bethpage* ☎*516/731–8989* ▭*AE, D, MC, V*

FIRE ISLAND

24 mi southeast of Bethpage.

With the Atlantic Ocean to its south and the Great South Bay to its north, Fire Island is basically a long stretch of pristine beach. Most of the 32-mi-long barrier island belongs to the **Fire Island National Seashore.** Deer roam freely here, finding shelter in the thickets, and migrating ducks and geese seek sanctuary in the marshes; wildlife is abundant along the seashore. Vehicles aren't allowed on most of the island, which is accessible by ferry, private boat, and water taxi, although you can drive to Robert Moses State Park and Smith Point County Park, on opposite ends of the island.

One of the outer playgrounds of Long Island's majestic coastline, Fire Island is home to a string of small communities, each with its own personality. In most, boardwalks lead to a vast expanse of beach. Slightly funky Cherry Grove and the male-dominated Pines are the two gay-and-lesbian communities. Ocean Beach, the largest residential area, has restaurants, stores, and bars and attracts day-trippers and families as well as summerhouse sharers. In Ocean Bay Park, weekending twentysomethings whoop it up late into the night. Kismet, Saltaire, Fair Harbor, Seaview, and Robbins Rest, mostly inhabited by private-home owners, are more exclusive. Kismet is also known for its restaurants.

In summer the population swells to the tens of thousands. The island doesn't have many lodging places, so most of these fair-weather visitors rent houses. You can see them and Fire Island homeowners coming off the ferries, pulling behind them little red wagons filled with their belongings. Enterprising youngsters meet the boats with their own wagons, in hopes of making a few dollars by helping you to your destination. After Columbus Day, the island pretty much shuts down until Memorial Day, and only a few hundred souls live here in winter.

GETTING HERE AND AROUND

On Fire Island, only Robert Moses State Park, on the west end, and Smith Point County Park, on the opposite end, are accessible by car, so plan on taking a ferry. If you drive to the ferry, park your car in one of the lots by the boat terminals. Alternatively, consider taking the Long Island Rail Road to a South Shore village with ferry service (Sayville or Patchogue, for example).

Three passenger ferries service Fire Island. The Sayville Ferry Service shuttles from Sayville to Cherry Grove, the Pines, and Sailor's Haven. Fire Island Ferries links Bay Shore, on the mainland, with eight Fire Island communities, including Fair Harbor, Kismet, Ocean Bay Park, Ocean Beach, Saltaire, and Seaview. Davis Park Ferry runs from Patchogue to Davis Park and Watch Hill. The services offer long-term parking, (from $8 weekdays to $38 weekends) on the mainland side. Round-trips are about $16, depending on your destination.

VISITOR INFORMATION

Ferry Contacts Davis Park Ferry (☎631/475–1665 ⊕ www.davisparkferry.com). **Fire Island Ferries** (☎631/665–3600 ⊕ www.fireislandferries.com). **Sayville Ferry Service** (☎631/589–0810 ⊕ www.sayvilleferry.com).

WHAT TO SEE

Fire Island Lighthouse. The 168-foot-tall lighthouse—Long Island's tallest—marks the western tip of Fire Island. The black-and-white-striped beauty, built in 1858, replaced the original 1826 lighthouse which, at 74 feet tall, was deemed too short to be effective. Tours of the tower are offered; call for tour times and reservations. On clear days Manhattan skyscrapers are visible from the top of the lighthouse, a climb up 192 winding steps. To get to the lighthouse, park in Field 5 of **Robert Moses State Park** (park on the lot's east side) and then walk ¾ mi following the marked trail. ⊠ *Off southern end of Robert Moses Causeway* ☎ *631/661–4876* ⊕ *www.fireislandlighthouse.com* 🖾 *$6* ☉ *Apr.–June, daily 9:30–4; July–Labor Day, daily 9:30–5; Sept.–Mar., weekends noon–4.*

SPORTS AND THE OUTDOORS

Robert Moses State Park. A 5-mi stretch of ocean beach is the highlight of this 1,000-acre park. Facilities include four bathhouses, a fishing pier, a picnic area, and miniature golf; a boat basin with pump-out and bait stations is nearby. The park, one of only two parts of Fire Island accessible by car, is open year-round (Fields 2 and 5 only). Special summer events include fishing contests. To get here, take the Sagtikos Parkway south to Robert Moses Causeway and follow the latter to the end. ⊠ *Off southern end of Robert Moses Causeway* ☎ *631/669–0470* ⊕ *nysparks.state.ny.us* 🖾 *Parking $8 (late May–mid-Sept.)* ☉ *Daily dawn–dusk.*

Sunken Forest. Protected by big dunes and stunted by the wind and the salt air, the Sunken Forest actually does look like it's sunken. Some of the trees here, which include sassafras and pine, are thought to be more than 200 years old. A 1½-mi boardwalk winds through flora, marsh, and swamp, offering viewing spots and benches at various points. Twisted trees form a canopy overhead. The area is protected, so you must stick to the marked trails. (Doing so also decreases your chances of encountering poison ivy and ticks.) Guided tours are an option in summer; call for tour times. The Sunken Forest is part of **Sailors Haven** (☎ *631/597–6183 visitor center* ⊕ *www.nps.gov/fiis*), which is near the middle of Fire Island and has a beach with lifeguards, on duty from late June through Labor Day; picnic areas; a snack bar; a marina; changing rooms; and a visitor center. Sailors Haven doesn't have lodgings, however, so you can't overnight here. 🖾 *Free* ☉ *Visitor center mid-May– mid-Oct., weekdays 10–5, weekends 9:30–6.*

WHERE TO EAT

$$$ ✕ **The Hideaway.** The views at this casual waterside eatery are spec-
AMERICAN   tacular, whether you eat on the deck or inside. The food is American with contemporary touches; seafood is emphasized. Pan-seared day-boat scallops, for example, are flavored with preserved lemons and carrot-ginger juice and served with couscous. The menu also includes duck, veal chops, and filet mignon. The earlier you come, the less rambunctious the crowd. ⊠ *Houser's Hotel, Bay Walk, Ocean Beach* ☎ *631/583–8900* ⊟ *AE, MC, V* ☉ *Closed Oct.–mid-May.*

$$$ ✕ **Top of the Bay.** You can eat outside at this harborside eatery, one of the
AMERICAN   more upscale places on Fire Island. Winners include stone-crab cakes and rack of lamb. ⊠ *1 Dock Walk, Cherry Grove* ☎ *631/597–6699* ⊟ *AE, MC, V* ☉ *Closed Sept.–May and Tues.*

WHERE TO STAY

$$$ ⊞ **Fire Island Hotel & Resort.** Water views, the short walk (100 yards) to the beach, and a pool (uncommon on Fire Island) are all reasons to stay here. Rooms have either one double bed, two doubles, or a twin and a double. The suites sleep six. There's a three-night minimum on weekends, which includes a $50 voucher for the hotel restaurant. Rates are significantly less expensive on weekdays. The hotel also has a few cabins, studios, and apartments, but these are usually booked up by its time-share members. **Pros:** pool; updated bathrooms. **Cons:** no Wi-Fi; not all rooms are air-conditioned. ⊠ *25 Cayuga Walk, Ocean Bay Park* ☎ *631/583–8000* ⇆ *30 rooms, 4 suites* ⚭ *In-room: no a/c (some). In-hotel: restaurant, room service, bar, pool, laundry service, no-smoking rooms* ⊟ *AE, D, MC, V* ⊘ *Closed early Oct.–mid-May.*

$ ⊞ **The Seasons Bed & Breakfast.** This small, white, porched house is a couple of blocks away from the ocean and half a block from the bay. You're sent off to the water with beach chairs, umbrellas, and towels. Rooms have hardwood floors and either a full or queen bed or two twins. Rates include "afternoon tea"—really a small meal—pizzas, sandwiches, salads, or quiches, with options for vegetarians. On weekends, the tea takes the form of a big barbecue. Breakfast is served buffet-style in the great room. The owners also run the Bay House, which has one-, two-, or three-bedroom condo apartments. **Pros:** hearty homemade breakfasts; close to other restaurants and bars. **Cons:** two-night minimum on weekends. ⊠ *468 Dehnhoff Walk, Ocean Beach* ☎ *631/583–8295* ⊕ *www.fivacations.com* ⇆ *9 rooms with shared baths, 1 cottage, 4 3–4 bedroom houses* ⚭ *In-room: no phone. In-hotel: no kids under 12, no-smoking rooms* ⊟ *AE, MC, V* ⦿*BP Closed Jan.–Mar.*

THE NORTH FORK AND SHELTER ISLAND

9

Stretching from Riverhead in the west to Orient Point at its easternmost tip, this sedate sister of the South Fork forms the upper finger of what looks like a sideways peace sign. Not long after you take the last exit of the LIE the roads become distinctly rural. As you head east, tidy wood-frame farmhouses and fancier Victorians are followed by acres of green, once chiefly potato farms, that now hold row after row of meticulously tended grape vines.

The New England–style hamlets of the western North Fork, particularly Jamesport, Cutchogue, and Southold, are peppered with unpretentious restaurants and interesting shops that seem transported from another era. Clean, uncrowded beaches lie to the south on Great Peconic Bay and to the north on Long Island Sound.

Farther east is the fishing village of Greenport. From here you can take a short ferry ride to Shelter Island, a small, quiet island that lies between Long Island's North and South forks.

RIVERHEAD

22 mi east of Port Jefferson.

The town of Riverhead was established in 1792 at the junction of the North and South forks, with the Peconic River and Great Peconic Bay bordering the town on the south and Long Island Sound on the north. Riverhead, like most other places on the North Fork, began as a farming village. Although agriculture remains a key factor in its economy, the town's main industries today are shopping and tourism. The sprawling Tanger Outlet Stores annually draws thousands of bargain hunters and tour groups, and several major shopping centers have sprung up along Route 58.

VISITOR INFORMATION

Riverhead Chamber of Commerce (⊠ *524 E. Main St., Riverhead* ☎ *631/727–7600* ⊕ *www.riverheadchamber.com*).

WHAT TO SEE

Atlantis Marine World. Indoor exhibits, such as a natural rockscape pool and a sand-shark lagoon, offer a compelling glimpse of regional marine life. Kids love watching the frisky resident sea lions that put on outdoor shows in summer. The aquarium even has a submarine-simulator ride. ⊠ *431 E. Main St.* ☎ *631/208–9200* ⊕ *www.atlantismarineworld.com* 💲 *$13.50* ⊙ *Daily 10–5.*

Splish Splash. At this 96-acre water park you may ride an inner tube down the 1,300-foot-long Lazy River, passing waterfalls, geysers, and wave pools. Other attractions include Monsoon Lagoon, Mammoth River Ride, and Kiddie Cove. The park has three pools, a beach area, and two restaurants. ⊠ *2549 Splish Splash Dr.* ☎ *631/727–3600* ⊕ *www.splishsplashlongisland.com* 💲 *$36* ⊙ *Memorial Day–Labor Day, daily 10–6.*

WINERIES **Jamesport Vineyards.** A wood-shingled, circa-1850 barn holds a modern winery and tasting room; the feel is casual and friendly, with knowledgeable pourers willing to give extra attention. The crisp sauvignon blanc is a highly accomplished expression of a grape that's gaining ground in this region. ⊠ *Main Rd., Jamesport* ☎ *631/722–5256* ⊕ *www.jamesport-vineyards.com* 💲 *Tasting $4* ⊙ *Daily 10–6, tours by appointment.*

Martha Clara Vineyards. Once a roadside farm stand, Martha Clara now has a large, barn-style summer tasting room and patio as well as a more intimate winter tasting room. Original old barns serve as art galleries and event spaces; pet goats, live music, and antique-carriage tours pulled by resident Clydesdales add to the down-on-the-farm feel. ⊠ *6025 Sound Ave., Jamesport* ☎ *631/298–0075* ⊕ *www.marthaclaravineyards.com* 💲 *Tasting $3, tour $4* ⊙ *Weekdays and Sun. 11–5:30, Sat. 11–6.*

Palmer Vineyards. A small, old-fashioned tasting room leads out to a wooden deck and lawn—a top spot for watching the sun set over acres of vines and farm fields. Palmer wines regularly impress top critics, especially its "41/72" merlot cuveé. ⊠*Sound Ave. off Osborne Ave., Aquebogue* ☎*631/722–9463* ⊕*www.palmervineyards.com* ⊠*Tasting fees vary, tour free* ⊙*Daily 11–6.*

Paumanok Vineyards. The Massoud family tends the vines, makes the wine, and greets visitors in a tasting room that has a great view of the whole wine-making operation; ask and you might be shown the extensive catwalk system. Paumanok wines, traditionally crafted, consistently receive top marks. ⊠*1074 Main Rd., Aquebogue* ☎*631/722–8800* ⊕*www.paumanok.com* ⊠*Tasting fees vary, tour free* ⊙*Tastings daily 11–5, tours by appointment.*

SPORTS AND THE OUTDOORS

BEACHES **South Jamesport Beach.** On Peconic Bay, this 3,000-foot-long beach has shallow-water areas for children. Lifeguards are on duty weekends from mid-May through June and daily from July to early September. ⊠*Off Peconic Bay Blvd., Jamesport* ☎*631/727–5744* ⊠*Parking $35 (Memorial Day–Labor Day).*

CANOEING Renting a canoe or kayak at **Peconic Paddler** (⊠*89 Peconic Ave.*
AND ☎*631/369–9500* ⊕*www.peconicpaddler.com*) is the best way to see
KAYAKING the ecologically diverse Peconic River, which flows for 15 mi before emptying into Flanders Bay.

GOLF **Long Island National Golf Course** (⊠*1793 Northville Tpke.* ☎*631/727–*
Fodor'sChoice *4653* ⊕*www.islandsendgolf.com*), designed by Robert Trent Jones Jr.,
★ is an 18-hole, 6,838-yard course surrounded by farmland. Greens fees are $70–$99, depending on the season.

WHERE TO EAT AND STAY

$ ✕**Jamesport Country Kitchen.** The food outshines the decor at this eatery,
AMERICAN which looks like a simple, wood-shingled country store. The menu is
★ contemporary, and dishes feature local ingredients such as fresh seafood and Long Island duck. The wine list also has a local focus. It's in Jamesport, about 7 mi northeast of Riverhead. ⊠*Main Rd., Jamesport* ☎*631/722–3537* ⊟*AE, DC, MC, V.*

$$ ✕**Meetinghouse Creek Inn.** The seafood at this waterside restaurant 4 mi
CONTINENTAL east of Riverhead is a big draw, but the kitchen also turns out good steaks and pasta dishes. A patio offers open-air dining. ⊠*177 Meeting House Creek Rd., Aquebogue* ☎*631/722–4220* ⊟*AE, D, MC, V* ⊙*Closed Tues. mid-Sept.–mid-May.*

$$ ⊞**Red Barn Bed & Breakfast.** At this lovingly restored 1877 farmhouse you can relax in a hammock, sip lemonade on the porch, and stargaze through the owner's telescope. Rooms are tidy and uncluttered. Breakfast features free-range local eggs, homemade scones, and desserts such as strawberry-rhubarb cobbler. **Pros:** astronomy buffs will bond with the owner in his backyard observatory. **Cons:** no TVs in room; two-night minimum stay in peak season. ⊠*733 Herricks La., Jamesport* ☎*631/722–3695* ⊕*www.redbarnbandb.com* ⇘*3 rooms* ⌂*In-room: Wi-Fi. In-hotel: some pets allowed, no-smoking rooms* ⊟*MC, V* ⊚*BP.*

9

CUTCHOGUE

12 mi east of Riverhead.

White, steepled churches and a small collection of old-fashioned shops line Cutchogue's Main Street. Here you can stroll to an ice-cream parlor, browse a handful of art and crafts boutiques, and eat blueberry pie at the landmark Cutchogue Diner. In summer, people flock to the antiques fairs, tag sales, and concerts on the village green.

WHAT TO SEE

WINERIES **Bedell Cellars.** Merlot is the benchmark of the region, and Bedell's reputation as the area's premier maker of this wine attracts serious wine lovers. The tasting room, in a New England farm–style building, has a modern-art collection and a stainless-steel bar. ⊠ *36225 Main Rd.* ☎ *631/734–7537* ⊕ *www.bedellcellars.com* ✉ *Tastings $8–$12* ⊙ *Tastings daily 11–5, tours by appointment on weekends only.*

Castello di Borghese Vineyard & Winery. Long Island's founding vineyard has been transformed into a lively venue for festivals, opera, and art exhibits in a former barn off to the side of the tasting room. The Novella wine, a fruity pinot noir bottled young in the classic Italian style, is an annual sellout. ⊠ *Rte. 48 at Alvah's La.* ☎ *631/734–5111* ⊕ *www.castellodiborghese.com* ✉ *Tastings $9–$12; tours on Sat. only $15, includes tasting* ⊙ *May–Dec., weekdays 11–5:30, weekends 11–6; Jan.–Apr., Thurs.–Mon. 11–5.*

Osprey's Dominion Vineyards. Osprey's top wines, like the rich cabernet sauvignon, are becoming serious players. During a late-afternoon summer tasting on the patio, you might see the owners, avid flyers, buzz in for a 4 PM "visit" on an antique plane. ⊠ *44075 Main Rd., Peconic* ☎ *631/765–6188* ⊕ *www.ospreysdominion.com* ✉ *Tours $10 with tasting; single tasting $5* ⊙ *Daily 11–5.*

★ **Pindar Vineyards.** At the region's largest producer, it can be three-deep at the bar, with a fun crowd enjoying ample free tastes of approachable wines. Tours are a real education for beginners and experienced hands alike; on November weekends, a special tour shows how sparkling wine is made. ⊠ *Main Rd. between Bridge La. and Peconic La., Peconic* ☎ *631/734–6200* ⊕ *www.pindar.net* ✉ *Tasting fee $4, tour free* ⊙ *Daily 11–6.*

Pugliese Vineyards. The Pugliese family makes down-to-earth wines that are local favorites. Its sparklers really shine: the Blanc de Blanc Brut regularly ranks in national competitions, and the off-dry sparkling merlot is an unusual treat. ⊠ *Main Rd. between Cox La. and Bridge La.* ☎ *631/734–4057* ✉ *Tasting $5* ⊙ *Daily 11–5.*

Raphael. The winery is a boutique producer of high-end merlot, but the lavish Spanish mission–style winery, built with wrought iron and stone, is worth a visit on its own. ⊠ *39390 Main Rd., Peconic* ☎ *631/765–1100* ⊕ *www.raphaelwine.com* ✉ *Tastings $6–$9, tour $12* ⊙ *Daily 11–5. Closed Tues. and Wed. in winter.*

The North Fork Wine Trail

CLOSE UP

When Louisa and Alex Hargrave planted their first grapevines at their eponymous vineyard in 1973, they also planted the seeds of a new North Fork industry. Little more than a quarter century later, the area's burgeoning wine industry is attracting ever-more attention. (The Hargraves sold the winery in 1999 and the place was renamed Castello di Borghese Vineyard.)

Chardonnay and merlot together account for more than 60% of the varietals grown on Long Island; cabernet franc, cabernet sauvignon, sauvignon blanc, chenin blanc, malbec, pinot blanc, pinot gris, pinot noir, Riesling, and viognier are among the others planted here. Land devoted to

vineyards on the East End exceeds 3,000 acres.

From Aquebogue to Greenport, 20-plus wineries and vineyards—the majority on or close to Routes 25 or 48—are open to the public for tastings and, at some, tours; most host special events as well. To follow the North Fork Wine Trail, take the last LIE exit (73) and follow it to Route 25 (via Route 58), where green WINE TRAIL road signs guide you to the wineries. Before making a special trip or taking a detour to visit a winery or vineyard, call to confirm hours. At the Tasting Room (⊠ *2885 Peconic La., Peconic* ☎*631/765–6404*), open Wednesday through Monday 11–6, you may try (and buy) wines from small North Fork producers not open to the public.

SHOPPING

The local artists and craftspeople of the **Old Town Arts and Crafts Guild** (⊠*28265 Rte. 25* ☎*631/734–6382*), first established in the late 1940s, sell their artwork in this converted old house. It's open daily May through December. In summer you can buy fresh fruit at **Wickham's Fruit Farm stand** (⊠ *28700 Rte. 25* ☎*631/734–6441*); the Wickham family has been growing apples, peaches, and vegetables on Long Island for more than 300 years.

9

SOUTHOLD

6 mi east of Cutchogue.

With its wineries and beautiful farmland, the village of Southold is at the heart of the North Fork. Like its neighboring villages and hamlets, it exudes New England charm. Southold was settled in 1640, at the same time as the South Fork's Southampton, making them the oldest towns in New York State.

VISITOR INFORMATION

North Fork Chamber of Commerce (☐ *Box 1415, Southold 11971* ☎*631/765–3161*).

WHAT TO SEE

Custer Institute. Taking advantage of some of the darkest night skies on Long Island, this observatory is a prime viewing spot for astronomy buffs and star-deprived urbanites. Atop the barnlike structure is a motorized dome with a telescope you can use to track the heavenly view. ✉ *1115 Main Bayview Rd.* ☎ *631/765–2626* ⊕ *www.custerobservatory.org* ✆ *Free* ⊙ *Sat. after dusk–midnight.*

Horton Point Lighthouse and Nautical Museum. The 58-foot-tall lighthouse, operated by the Southold Historical Society, was built in 1847. Together with the adjoining lighthouse keeper's home, it resembles a church. The museum, in the keeper's residence, displays sea captains' journals, sea chests, paintings, and maps. The 8-acre park surrounding the lighthouse includes public barbecue grills. ✉ *Lighthouse Rd.* ☎ *631/765–5500* ⊕ *www.longislandlighthouses.com* ✆ *$3 suggested donation* ⊙ *Memorial Day–Columbus Day, weekends 11:30–4.*

Old Field. Christian and Rosamund Baiz's family homestead is the only place on Long Island where rows of vines run right up to sparkling Peconic Bay. The wines are made by one of the area's top winemakers. Tastings are in an old barn or picnic-style by the beach. ✉ *59600 Main Rd.* ☎ *631/765–2465* ⊕ *www.theoldfield.com* ✆ *Tastings $2–$3, tour free* ⊙ *Thurs.–Mon. 11–5.*

SPORTS AND THE OUTDOORS

CANOEING AND KAYAKING
Eagle's Neck Paddling Company (✉ *49295 Main Rd.* ☎ *631/765–3502* ⊕ *www.eaglesneck.com*) offers guided kayak tours and rents boats. **Sound View Scuba** (✉ *46770 County Rd. 48* ☎ *631/765–9515* ⊕ *www.soundviewscuba.com*) runs kayak tours in the area.

WHERE TO EAT

$$$
SEAFOOD
★
✕ **Seafood Barge.** The airy, nautically themed restaurant—one of the best on the North Fork—offers sweeping views of Peconic Bay and refined seafood and other contemporary dishes, including sushi. Local ingredients are emphasized. Try the pan-seared local fish or the grilled salmon over lobster succotash with sweet-potato sticks. ✉ *Port of Egypt Marina, 62980 Main Rd.* ☎ *631/765–3010* ▭ *AE, DC, MC, V.*

GREENPORT

6 mi east of Southold.

A fleet of commercial fishing boats still operates out of this down-to-earth, working-class village, but shops and restaurants have grown increasingly upscale due to an influx of summer visitors and second-home owners. Since the late 1600s, Greenport's saga—which includes a brisk rum-running business during Prohibition—has depended on the sea. In summer the deep waters of Long Island Sound still summon home tall ships reminiscent of the whaling boats that once docked in the safe waters of Greenport Harbor. Waterfront Mitchell Park is the perfect place to watch yachts and sailboats, or to catch an outdoor performance in the landscaped amphitheater.

WHAT TO SEE

★ **East End Seaport and Maritime Museum.** A former Long Island Rail Road passenger terminal contains exhibits about lighthouses, ships, East End shipbuilding, and yacht racing. ✉ *3rd St. at ferry dock* ☎ *631/477–2100*

⊕*www.eastendseaport.org* ⊡*$2* ☉*Late May, weekends 11–5; June–Sept., Wed.–Mon. 11–5.*

☉ **Mitchell Park Carousel.** You can still play "catch the brass ring" at this 1920s carousel, housed in a round, gleaming, glass structure, the highlight of Greenport's renovated waterfront. ⊠*Front St., near the post office* ☎*631/477–0248* ⊡*$2* ☉*June–Labor Day, weekends 11–5; rest of yr, weekends (call for hrs).*

SHOPPING

★ An old-time emporium with wide-plank floors, **Arcade Department Store** (⊠*14 Front St.* ☎*631/477–1440*) carries a little bit of everything, including boots, buttons, and North Fork necessities like lobster crackers. The owners of the antiques shop **Beall & Bell** (⊠*18 South St.* ☎*631/477–8239*) source serious treasures from the area, where many of the grand houses are passed down through the generations and have odds and ends in their attics going back centuries.

NIGHTLIFE

Late at night, the funky, eclectic **Bay & Main Restaurant** (⊠*300 Main St.* ☎*631/477–1442*) turns into a busy bar that specializes in martinis. In warm weather the older crowd gravitates to the outdoor patio, where there's live acoustic music. Saturday nights draw twentysomethings who dance to the local rock, jazz, and funk bands. The **Whiskey Wind** (⊠*30–32 Front St.* ☎ *631/477–6179*, a bar that's popular with fisherfolk and laborers, is the real Greenport. A fixture from the old days, it's still frequented mainly by local residents and their dogs, and has dartboards, a pool table, and a jukebox.

WHERE TO EAT

$$$
ECLECTIC
Fodor'sChoice
★

✕**The Frisky Oyster.** This modern restaurant is a little piece of Manhattan in Greenport. North Fork sophisticates come for the small, lively bar and contemporary fare, such as seared foie gras atop roasted pineapple and mâche, and penne with pancetta, littleneck clams, leeks, and tomatoes. ⊠*27 Front St.* ☎*631/477–4265* ⊟*AE, D, DC, MC, V* ☉*No lunch.*

OFF THE
BEATEN
PATH

Heavenly homemade lemonade—well known on the North Fork—and authentic Greek appetizers and main courses are the draws at **Hellenic Snack Bar** (⊠*5145 Main Rd., East Marion* ☎*631/477–0138* ⊟*AE, D, DC, MC, V*).

WHERE TO STAY

$$$ 🏨 **The Greenporter Hotel.** A 1950s motel a block from the waterfront has been converted into this sleek, minimalist lodging with a green interior scheme. Rooms have light-wood platform beds, graphic rugs, and metal accents. **Pros:** within short walking distance to LIRR train station and Hampton Jitney drop-off. **Cons:** restaurant closed weekdays in winter and spring. ⊠*326 Front St.* ☎*631/477–0066* ⊕*www.thegreenporter.com* ⇗*30 rooms* ⌂ *In-room: safe (some), Wi-Fi. In-hotel: restaurant, room service, bar, pool, laundry service, Wi-Fi, some pets allowed* ⊟*AE, MC, V.*

$$$$ 🖼The Harborfront Inn. Most rooms at this three-story, gray-and-white
★ inn have balconies, some with harbor views; all rooms have high-
speed Internet access, flat-screen TVs, and CD players. Interiors are
contemporary and bright, with cherrywood furniture, leather arm-
chairs, and light-color carpeting. Down comforters and Frette linens
outfit the beds. For a really big splurge, you might consider the Terrace Suite; at 800 square feet, it's double the size of the regular rooms,
and it has a 1,000-square-foot deck. **Pros:** hotel is within walking
distance of restaurants and shops. **Cons:** three-night minimum stay
on weekends in July and August. ⊠*209 Front St.* ☎*631/477–0707*
⊕*www.theharborfrontinn.com* ☞*32 rooms, 4 suites* ⌂ *In-room: safe,
refrigerator, Internet, Wi-Fi. In-hotel: bar, pool, gym, Wi-Fi, no-smoking rooms* ▤*AE, D, MC, V* ⍣*CP.*

SHELTER ISLAND

3 mi south of Greenport, via ferry.

Shelter Island lies between Long Island's North and South forks. Reach-
able only by boat (there's regular ferry service), the 11½-square-mi
island offers at least a partial escape from the summer traffic-and-crowd
snarls of the Hamptons. Quiet country lanes wind across the island's
rolling land, nearly a third of which has been set aside as a nature preserve that's a bird-watcher's delight.

Taking advantage of its hilltop elevation, Shelter Island Heights is the
island's center of activity. Its Queen Anne, Victorian, and colonial-
revival houses, stores, and inns show off embellished porches, scalloped
shingles, and carved friezes. This relaxed place becomes even mellower
in the off-season, when many restaurants and other businesses reduce
their hours or close for extended periods. If you're planning an off-
season visit, call ahead to see what's open.

GETTING HERE AND AROUND

The North Ferry and the South Ferry service Shelter Island from Long
Island's North and South forks. The North Ferry, which leaves from
Greenport, is the best way to get to the Chequit Inn and other places
in Shelter Island Heights from the North Fork. The fare is $9 one way
for a car and driver, and a same-day round-trip is $13. The South Ferry
leaves from Sag Harbor; the fare (cash only) is $7 one way for a car and
driver, and a same-day round-trip is $8. On both ferries, pedestrians and
additional car passengers pay $2 each way. North and South ferry lines
are prone to backups on summer weekends, in both directions.

VISITOR INFORMATION

Shelter Island Chamber of Commerce (⊠*47 W. Neck Rd., Shelter Island* ☎*631/*
749–0399 ⊕*www.shelterislandchamber.com*).

Ferry Contact North Ferry (☎*631/749–0139* ⊕*www.northferry.com*). **South**
Ferry (☎*631/749–1200* ⊕*www.southferry.com*).

SPORTS AND THE OUTDOORS

★ **Mashomack Nature Preserve.** Marked hiking trails of 1½ to 10 mi lace the preserve's 2,000-plus acres of beech and oak forest, meadows, tidal wetlands, beach, and freshwater ponds. A large population of ospreys nests here, along with many other bird species. The preserve is also home to harbor seals, turtles, and foxes. At the visitor center, ask for directions to the nearby gazebo, which has a water view. The Nature Conservancy, which owns the preserve, also runs tours and educational programs here. ⊠*79 S. Ferry Rd.* ☎*631/749–1001* ⊕*www.nature. org/mashomack* ⊠*$2 suggested donation* ☉*Mar.–Sept., daily 9–5; Oct.–Feb., Wed.–Mon. 9–4.*

BEACHES **Crescent Beach.** The bay beach, a long sandy strip across the street from the trendy Sunset Beach restaurant, faces northeast and is especially popular at sunset. It has picnic tables and restrooms. Island lodging properties have parking permits for guests; otherwise, contact the town clerk to get one. ⊠*Shore Rd. off W. Neck Rd.* ☎*631/749–1166* ⊠*Weekly parking $35 (Memorial Day–Labor Day).*

Wades Beach. The shallow, sandy beach, on the island's south side, has picnic tables, restrooms, and a lifeguard. Locals comb the beach's salt-marsh area for clams and crab. Island lodging properties have parking permits for guests, or contact the town clerk for one. ⊠*Heron La. off Shorewood Rd.* ☎*631/749–1166* ⊠*Weekly parking $35 (Memorial Day–Labor Day).*

FISHING Fluke, flounder, striped bass, and skate are some of what you might catch in these parts. Guides and full- and half-day captained charters are available; a half day for two anglers costs about $325. **Jack's Marine & True Value Hardware** (⊠*Bridge St. at Rte. 114* ☎*631/749–0114*) offers transient mooring and a marine-supply store, paints, toys, and summer goods. **Light Tackle Challenge** (⊠*91 W. Neck Rd.* ☎*631/749– 1906*) conducts full- and half-day sportfishing trips for striped bass and bluefish.

KAYAKING The waters around Shelter Island are perfect for kayaking. If you set out on a kayak you have the option of exploring on your own or taking a guided tour. The Mashomack Nature Preserve, rich with birdlife and other animals, is a favorite kayaking destination. A solo kayak from **Shelter Island Kayak Tours** (⊠*Rte. 114 at Duval Rd.* ☎*631/749–1990* ⊕*www.kayaksi.com*) rents for about $30 for two hours for single kayaks and $50 for double kayaks; tours are $60.

WHERE TO EAT

$$ ✕**Planet Bliss.** You can't miss this brightly painted, funky restaurant in a
ECLECTIC converted Victorian. The menu of healthful but delicious fare includes everything from rice-and-bean dishes to fruit smoothies and fine wine. Weekend brunch on the porch and patio is busy. ⊠*23 N. Ferry Rd.* ☎*631/749–0053* ⊟*AE, MC, V* ☉*Closed Mon.–Thurs. Oct.–May.*

$$ ✕**Sweet Tomato's.** The smell of Italian cooking draws you toward this
ITALIAN converted storefront outfitted with a patio and tables. High ceilings and a comfortable bar await inside. Daily specials complement the menu's

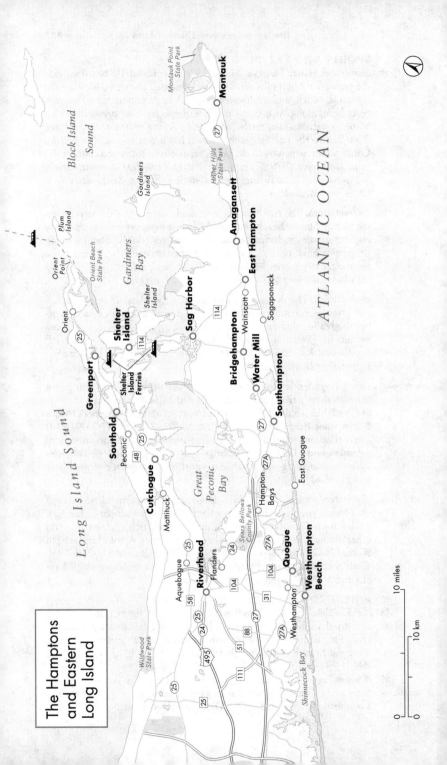

The Hamptons and Eastern Long Island

Long Island Sound

Block Island Sound

Plum Island

Orient Point

Orient Beach State Park

Orient

Greenport

Southold

Peconic

Cutchogue

Mattituck

(25)

(48)

(25)

Shelter Island Ferries

Shelter Island

(114)

Gardiners Island

Gardiners Bay

Sag Harbor

(114)

Montauk Point State Park

Montauk

(27)

Hither Hills State Park

Amagansett

East Hampton

Wainscott

Sagaponack

Bridgehampton

Water Mill

Southampton

(27)

ATLANTIC OCEAN

Great Peconic Bay

Riverhead

Aquebogue

Flanders

Sears Bellows County Park

Hampton Bays

(24)

(25)

(58)

(24)

(25)

495

(51)

(88)

(111)

(104)

(27)

(31)

(104)

(27A)

(27A)

Quogue

East Quogue

Westhampton

Westhampton Beach

(104)

Shinnecock Bay

Wildwood State Park

0 — 10 miles

0 — 10 km

pasta, seafood, and fish dishes. ⊠*15 Grand Ave., Shelter Island Heights* ☎*631/749–4114* ▤*AE, D, MC, V* ⊗*No lunch*.

$$$ ✕**Vine Street Cafe.** Husband-and-wife team Terry and Lisa Harwood create ate casual but sophisticated dishes, and their staff provides exceptional service. Diners can savor daily specials, such as bouillabaisse and crispy duck confit, and staples such as steak frites and miso-glazed salmon. The simple interior includes beige walls, exposed beams, and a wooden bar. In warm weather you may dine alfresco under tiki lights. Save room for dessert. ⊠*41 S. Ferry Rd.* ☎*631/749–3210* ⚑*Reservations essential* ▤*AE, MC, V* ⊗*Closed Tues. and Wed. in Oct.–Apr.*

ECLECTIC

WHERE TO STAY

$$$$ 🏨**Ram's Head Inn.** At this 1929 colonial-style inn, Adirondack chairs are scattered across lawns sloping down to Coecles Harbor. The secluded spot at the end of Ram Island has a small beach for swimming (bring insect repellant) or sailing. Rooms, furnished in a simple country style, are bright; they often book up months ahead of time. The restaurant is known for its outstanding seasonal fare. Jazz musicians play during Sunday brunch, served late May to late October. **Pros:** hotel pick-up at the Shelter Island Ferry House. **Cons:** located in remote section of the island and not within walking distance to stores or restaurants. ⊠*Ram Island Dr.* ☎*631/749–0811* ⊕*www.shelterislandinns.com* ⚑*13 rooms, 4 suites* ⚐*In-room: safe, DVD, kitchen, Wi-Fi. In-hotel: restaurant, room service, bar, golf, tennis court, pool, gym, laundry service, Wi-Fi, no-smoking rooms* ▤*AE, MC, V* ⊗*Closed Nov.–Mar.* ⫶◎⫶*CP.*

Fodor'sChoice
★

$$$$ 🏨**Sunset Beach.** An international crowd has flocked to this trendy hotel ever since celebrity hotelier Andre Balazs (of Los Angeles's Chateau Marmont and SoHo's Mercer) opened it in the late 1990s. Each retro-style guest room has a sundeck that looks out over the parking lot to the water. The beachfront restaurant provides the best sunset- and people-watching around. French bistro dishes, such as *moules frites* (mussels and fries) and fried calamari, are the things to get here, but choose an American finale and go for the chocolate sundae. **Pros:** luxurious bedding; bicycle rentals. **Cons:** service can be slow during peak season. ⊠*35 Shore Rd.* ☎*631/749–2001* ⊕*www.sunsetbeachli.com* ⚑*20 rooms* ⚐*In-room: DVD, kitchen (some), Wi-Fi. In hotel: restaurant, room service, bar, water sports, bicycles, some pets allowed, no-smoking rooms* ▤*AE, D, MC, V* ⊗*Closed Oct.–Apr.* ⫶◎⫶*CP.*

THE HAMPTONS AND THE SOUTH FORK

The sand-and-pine-covered finger of land that is Long Island's South Fork starts about 75 mi east of Manhattan and stretches another 50 mi east into the Atlantic Ocean. It is home to several communities dating from the 1600s, as well as a group of celebrated villages known as the Hamptons. At the eastern tip of the South Fork is Montauk, a low-key, family-friendly fishing community; just beyond the village is Montauk Point, the very end of the island. The beaches—making up one of the finest stretches of white sand in the United States—are the main draw here. Rolling farmland and vineyards are juxtaposed with historic villages, sophisticated restaurants and shops, and spectacular mansions and farms.

One could say the Hamptons mystique began in the late 1800s, when residents of Westhampton Beach and other villages out east began renting rooms to travelers who reached the area first by horse-drawn stage and later on the newly constructed Long Island Rail Road. It wasn't long before the Hamptons had become a resort area of renown, to which affluent city dwellers would escape for cool sea breezes, relaxed country living, and a hefty dose of high society. Today the villages are a curious mix of year-round communities and full-blown summer resorts, drawing vacationers, summer-home owners, and twentysomething "summer share" renters by the carload between Memorial Day and Labor Day. June is still relatively quiet, however, and in May and September you can enjoy pleasant weather while avoiding the peak-season prices and crowds.

WESTHAMPTON BEACH

78 mi east of New York City, 27 mi east of Sayville.

So many seasonal visitors have fallen in love with Westhampton that it has become one of the fastest-growing year-round communities on eastern Long Island. Excellent restaurants, chic shops, a regionally famous performing-arts center, and magnificent ocean beaches are the major draws. Along scenic Dune Road, which you can follow east to the nearby village of Hampton Bays, extravagant mansions are interspersed with simple beach houses and condominium complexes.

VISITOR INFORMATION
Greater Westhampton Chamber of Commerce (⌂ *Box 1228, Westhampton Beach 11978* ☎ *631/288–3337* ⊕ *www.whbcc.org*).

SPORTS AND THE OUTDOORS
BEACHES **Cupsogue Beach County Park.** This 296-acre barrier-beach park on Moriches Inlet has lifeguards from late May to early September, a 1-mi stretch of white-sand beach, a snack bar, restrooms and showers, and a first-aid station. Outer-beach camping and saltwater fishing are permitted away from swimming areas. ⊠ *West end of Dune Rd.* ☎ *631/852–8111 park, 631/288–7670 snack bar* ⊕ *www.co.suffolk.ny.us* 🖃 *$10 (May–Sept.)* ⊙ *Daily 8:30–4:30.*

Lashley Beach. A secret spot for locals and surfers, this is a pristine white-sand beach with parking, showers, restrooms, and lifeguards (on duty weekends 10–5 from mid-May to mid-June and daily 10–5 from mid-June through Labor Day). ⊠ *Dune Rd.* ☎ *631/288–6306* 🖃 *Seasonal nonresident permit $225.*

Rogers Beach. Parking is by village permit only at this white-sand beach. In addition to a lifeguard (on duty weekends 10–5 from mid-May to mid-June and daily 10–5 from mid-June through Labor Day), there's a pavilion with showers and restrooms. ⊠ *Beach La.* ☎ *631/288–6306* 🖃 *Seasonal nonresident permit $225.*

WHERE TO EAT AND STAY

$$$
ITALIAN
✕**Rene's Casa Basso.** Sculptures dot the front and side lawns of this upscale, traditional restaurant. To enter, you walk under the swords of two concrete 12-foot-tall fencing musketeers, after which you come upon a miniature castle complete with mythological figures. The fare, a mix of northern and southern Italian, includes well-prepared pasta, seafood, veal, and steak dishes. Try the delectable osso buco, veal Milanese, or fresh seafood-laden bouillabaisse. ✉ *59 Montauk Hwy.* ☎*631/288–1841* ▤*AE, MC, V* ⊘*Closed Mon. No lunch.*

$$$
SEAFOOD
✕**Starr Boggs.** The dining room of this sophisticated see-and-be-seen restaurant has artwork, white linens, large windows, and simple wooden chairs. The new American fare featuring prime steaks and local seafood is just as attractive. The menu changes daily, and each dish, while on the expensive side, is unforgettable. Start with Starr's clam chowder followed by laquered Half Crescent Farm duckling. Diners with heartier appetites can opt for the grilled Kobe flat-iron steak. There's open-air dining on the patio, which has a waterfall. ✉ *6 Parlato Dr.* ☎*631/288–3500* ⌕*Reservations essential* ▤*AE, MC, V* ⊘*Closed mid-Oct.–Apr. No lunch.*

$$$
▥**1880 House.** The rooms in this 1880s B&B are elegantly decorated with antiques and homemade quilts, and have cozy beds. Two rooms have an adjoining sitting room, and the third is a suite in an old carriage house. A large fireplace greets guest upon arrival. The ocean is a five-minute walk away. **Pros:** homemade sweet breads for breakfast; walking distance to town and beach. **Cons:** most guests are couples so owner expects children to be well supervised. ✉ *2 Seafield La.* ☎*631/288–1559 or 800/346–3290* ⊕*www.1880seafieldhouse.com* ⇆*3 rooms* ♨ *In-room: kitchen (some), refrigerator, Wi-Fi. In hotel: tennis court, pool, some pets allowed, no-smoking rooms* ▤*AE, MC, V* ⊚❘*BP.*

QUOGUE

9

3 mi east of Westhampton Beach.

Settled in the mid-17th century, Quogue, part of the greater Westhampton area, is one of the oldest communities on Long Island. Today, thanks to the stately Victorians nestled along its tree-lined streets and the contemporary mansions along the ocean on Dune Road, Quogue is one of the most desirable residential areas in the Hamptons. Just east is East Quogue, which was settled in 1686 and was originally known as Fourth Neck. Its acres of farmland and pine forest, beautiful bay, and ocean beaches are enlivened by Main Street shopping and the seasonal influx of visitors.

SPORTS AND THE OUTDOORS

Quogue Wildlife Refuge. At the 300-acre wildlife preserve, managed by the State Department of Environmental Conservation, you can birdwatch, hike along a self-guided trail, or visit a complex where injured animals are rehabilitated. There's also a nature center with exhibits and a library. Classes about field ecology and wildlife photography are available, and the refuge also has children's programs. It's open daily dawn to dusk. ⊠*3 Old Country Rd.* ☎*631/653–4771* ⊕*www.quoguewildliferefuge.org* ☜*Free* ☉*Daily dawn–dusk.*

WHERE TO EAT AND STAY

$$$

SEAFOOD

✕**Dockers.** People stop in at this casual, lively waterfront restaurant on their way home from the beach just across the road. Try the calamari appetizer, Black Angus aged steak, clambake platter, or lobster. The large deck overlooking the bay has good views of the sunset. There's live music Friday through Sunday, and early-bird dinner specials are available. ⊠*94 Dune Rd., East Quogue* ☎*631/653–0653* ⚘*Reservations not accepted* ▤*AE, D, DC, MC, V* ☉*Closed mid-Nov.–mid-Mar.*

$$$

FRENCH

Fodor'sChoice

★

✕**Stone Creek Inn.** At this bright and airy restaurant, the talented chef-owner relies on the freshest local produce and seafood—as well as on his considerable talent—to provide a memorable dining experience. Oven-roasted halibut, rack of lamb with Mediterranean spice, and braised Montauk lobster with baby vegetables are among the dishes on the French-leaning menu. Homemade desserts—such as ricotta mousse and lemon tart—may make you swoon. The dining spaces are elegantly spare, with polished hardwood floors, countless windows, and white-clothed tables. ⊠*405 Montauk Hwy., East Quogue* ☎*631/653–6770* ▤*AE, DC, MC, V* ☉ *Closed Jan. and Feb. No lunch.*

$$$–$$$$

🏠**Inn at Quogue.** This tranquil complex in the center of Quogue village consists of a house from the 18th century, another from the 19th century right across the road, and private cottages. Ralph Lauren designers supervised the interior scheme here, and each comfortable, antiques-filled room is different. The inn's restaurant, Q Restaurant East, has a hint of the antebellum South about it. The chef is known for such innovative dishes as apple-and-Gorgonzola salad, seared ahi tuna, and tangy lemon-lobster risotto. **Pros:** warm and inviting hotel; walking distance to town and beach. **Cons:** the bar on the property can be busy and noisy during peak season. ⊠*47–52 Quogue St.* ☎*631/653–6560* ⊕*www.innatquogue.com* ↩*67 rooms, 2 cottages* ⚲ *In-room: DVD, refrigerator, Wi-Fi. In-hotel: restaurant, room service, bar, pool, bicycles, laundry service, Wi-Fi* ▤*AE, D, MC, V.*

SOUTHAMPTON

15 mi east of Quogue.

Southampton is not only steeped in rich history but also in contemporary affluence. Pristine area beaches framed by sparkling Atlantic waters are a draw, but so are upscale shops, fine restaurants, polo matches, and antiques shows.

The village was settled in the 17th century by Puritans who had set sail from Lynn, Massachusetts, and landed at what is today known as Conscience Point. Southampton, which was formally incorporated in 1894, was named after the third earl of Southampton, Henry Wriothesly, who was sympathetic to the early British settlers and widely respected.

Southampton has several districts and buildings included on the National Register of Historic Places. The village is part of the much larger town of Southampton, which spans from parts of Eastport to the west all the way east to Sagaponack, with its potato farms and seaside estates. A drive through the "estate section" of Southampton takes you past graceful mansions surrounded by 20-foot privet hedges. Gin Lane, in particular, is worth a peek.

VISITOR INFORMATION

Southampton Chamber of Commerce (⊠ *72 Main St., Southampton* ☎ *631/283–0402* ⊕ *www.southamptonchamber. com*).

WHAT TO SEE

Fodor's Choice ★ **Parrish Art Museum.** Samuel Longstreth Parrish built this museum in 1898 as a repository for his Italian Renaissance art. Through the years the museum has also developed a strong collection of American paintings, including works by renowned

STAR POWER

The rich and famous have been drawn to the Hamptons since the 1800s, even before the Long Island Rail Road line made a day trip doable for sun seekers. The LIRR's "Hit the Sunrise Trail" campaign of the 1920s lured tourists with cheap and speedy travel to visit the emerging resort towns. In the 1970s, Truman Capote, Mick Jagger, and Andy Warhol made the area their summer retreat. Today, it is hard to find a Manhattan-based celebrity without a second home on Long Island's East End. Tourists do double-takes. Is that Paul McCartney looking for a snack in Amagansett? Billy Joel riding a Harley?

Long Island artists. Traveling exhibits have ranged from pieces by sculptor August Saint-Gaudens to photographs of the civil rights movement by Herbert Randall. The gardens are filled with reproductions of sculpture from the museum's permanent collection. There's a full calendar of lectures, workshops, concerts, and children's programs. Juried art exhibitions hang on the walls during the year. ⊠ *25 Jobs La.* ☎ *631/283–2118* ⊕ *www.parrishart.org* ✉ *$7 suggested donation* ☉ *Mon.–Sat. 11–5, Sun. 1–5.*

NEED A BREAK? Agawam Park off of Jobs Lane in Southampton is a 4-acre oasis of calm and tranquillity. Bring bread to feed the ducks, swans, and the aggressive geese that make Agawam Lake their home. Beginning in late June, music concerts are held on Wednesday nights. Swing sets accommodate both adults and big kids.

SPORTS AND THE OUTDOORS

BEACHES ★ **Cooper's Beach.** For a fee, you can stretch out on the sand of this Southampton Village beach, studying the sea in one direction and historic mansions—including Calvin Klein's massive manse (the one with the turrets)—in the other. Facilities include lifeguards (9–5 daily from Memorial Day through Labor Day), restrooms, outdoor showers, and a snack bar. ⊠ *268 Meadow La.* ☎ *631/283–0247* ⊕ *www. southamptonvillage.org* ✉ *Memorial Day–Labor Day $25 weekdays, $30 weekends.*

⚠ Pay close attention to Southampton village parking signs. Village beaches require parking permits and the police strictly enforce these rules.

SHOPPING

BAKED GOODS It's hard not to be drawn in by the smell of fresh-baked bread and pastries at **Blue Duck Bakery and Café** (⊠ *30 Hampton Rd.* ☎ *631/204–1701* ⊕ *www.blueduckbakerycafe.com*). It's the place to pick up that perfect "thank-you" dessert or breakfast indulgence. The scent of homemade fudge wafts into the street in front of the cheery **Fudge Co.** (⊠ *67 Main St.* ☎ *631/283–8108*), which is closed New Year's to mid-March. Storefront displays of colorful, scrumptious confections—including many novelty items—delight kids as well as grown-ups. **Tate's Bake Shop** (⊠ *43 N. Sea Rd.* ☎ *631/283–9830*) is famous for its yummy chocolate-chip cookies; it also sells freshly baked pies, scones, muffins, and specialty cakes.

CLOTHING AND ACCESSORIES Minimalist boutique **Intermix** (⊠ *64 Main St.* ☎ *631/283–8510*) caters to fashionistas, selling clothing from designers such as Chloé, Theory, and 7 for All Mankind. Southampton's former town hall makes an intimate outpost for the venerable **Saks Fifth Avenue** (⊠ *1 Hampton Rd.* ☎ *631/283–3500*) department store. It's all about designer stuff here: resort wear by Donna Karan, Juicy Couture, and Calvin Klein, bags by Burberry and Prada, cosmetics and skin-care products by Chanel and Kiehl's.

NIGHTLIFE

Most of the nightclubs in the Hamptons close after Labor Day weekend, but might open sporadically for fall and winter holiday weekends. If you need a little help making it past the velvet ropes, contact the **Hampton Angels** (☎ *646/963–0378* ⊕ *www.hamptonangels.com*), a concierge and event planning service that caters to visitors planning the perfect weekend.

Rub shoulders with models and fashionistas at **Nello Sumertimes** (⊠ *136 Main St.* ☎ *631/287–5500*). The hot spot serves sinfully delicious but pricey fare: Lobster bisque doesn't come cheap at $27, but you might end the night with a story to tell. Located right on the East Quogue beach, **Neptune's Beach Club** (⊠ *70 Dune Rd.* ☎ *631/653–8737* ⊕ *www.neptunebeachclub.net*) is popular with the unpretentious college crowd that prefers dancing under the stars in flip-flops rather than in stilettos. If the scene at the **Pink Elephant** (⊠ *281 County Rd., Rte. 27 and N. Main St.* ☎ *631/287–9888* ⊕ *www.pinkelephantclub.com*) gets too hot, there's a liquid nitrogen machine that creates cold air and snow. Getting beyond the velvet ropes here requires connections. Choose a bed in the man-made beach area and lounge, sip champagne, and groove to pop and hip-hop music. Thousands of local and Manhattan revelers flock to the **Whitehouse** (⊠ *239 E. Montauk Hwy.* ☎ *631/728–4121* ⊕ *www.whitehousenightclub.com*) on summer weekends to dance the night away. Different music genres keep dancers from getting in a groove rut. Satisfy midnight munchies at the sushi bar. Drinks are affordable for the area and range from $6 to $8

WHERE TO EAT

$$$
ECLECTIC

✕**75 Main.** The interior of this old clapboard building in the middle of town is light and airy. Dishes have international (mostly Asian) twists and may include duck-and-vegetable spring rolls with tamarind barbecue sauce and jicama slaw, or grilled Nova Scotia salmon served over Beluga lentils with Swiss chard and red-onion marmalade. There's a weekend brunch as well as a menu for kids. The bar gets busy after 11 PM on Friday and Saturday thanks to a DJ and a crowd that likes to dance. ⊠*75 Main St.* ☎*631/283-7575* ▱*AE, MC, V.*

$
AMERICAN

✕**Barrister's.** Simple but good American fare is the rule here, as are friendly service and a general conviviality. Try for a table at the front for an entertaining view of Main Street. There are daily specials as well as a steady menu of burgers, seafood entrées, and pasta dishes; salads rise above the usual. The bar draws locals for after-work drinks. ⊠*36 Main St.* ☎*631/283-6206* ⩔*Reservations not accepted* ▱*AE, D, DC, MC, V.*

$
ITALIAN
Fodor's Choice
★

✕**La Parmigiana.** Everyone seems to love this family-style place for its "red-sauce" Italian menu, its huge portions, and its reasonable prices. Spaghetti *celestino* (with tomato-cream sauce) and prosciutto with tomato and basil are favorites. Be prepared for a wait on summer weekends. ⊠*44–48 Hampton Rd.* ☎*631/283-8030* ▱*AE, MC, V* ⊘*Closed Mon.*

$$$
FRENCH

✕**Le Chef.** A warm, welcoming, busy little bistro, Le Chef serves mainly French food. Standouts include baby rack of lamb and noisettes of veal. Prix-fixe menus are available Thursday through Sunday before 6:45 PM. ⊠*75 Jobs La.* ☎*631/283-8581* ▱*AE, MC, V.*

$$$
SEAFOOD

✕**Lobster Inn.** This crowded, family-friendly seafood restaurant was once a marina and boat shop. It's still nautical and rustic—the perfect place to dine on Manhattan clam chowder, lobster, and mussels. Seafood lovers with extra-hearty appetites can feast on a "Splat for 1 or 2" which includes lobster, clams, shrimp, and king crabs. There's also a salad bar. ⊠*162 Inlet Rd.* ☎*631/283-1525* ⩔*Reservations not accepted* ▱*AE, D, MC, V* ⊘*Closed Columbus Day–early May.*

$$$
AMERICAN
★

✕**Red Bar Brasserie.** Candle sconces line the wonderful wraparound windows at this popular American restaurant. Fried calamari, grilled salmon with local corn, filet mignon, and Long Island duck are all good choices. Part of the space, which has bentwood chairs and white-clothed tables, is devoted to the bar. The social scene is lively here on summer nights. ⊠*210 Hampton Rd.* ☎*631/283-0704* ▱*AE, MC, V* ⊘ *Closed Mon., Tues., and Nov.–Apr. No lunch.*

WHERE TO STAY

$$$$

▦**1708 House.** It's truly a colonial, from the wide clapboards outside to the wood beams within. Antiques, Asian rugs, and rich fabrics fill this B&B in the heart of Southampton Village. Public areas include an informal card room, a more formal dining room, and an even more formal parlor. Guest quarters in the house and in the two-bedroom cottages have four-poster beds. Some rooms are elegantly rustic; others are simply elegant. All are true to the age and style of the house. **Pros:** cozy wine cellar; each room feels soundproof despite being right in the village; complimentary beach parking passes. **Cons:** two- to three-night minimums on high-season weekends. ⊠*126 Main St.* ☎*631/287–1708* ⊕*www.1708house.com* ⇨*6 rooms, 3 suites, 3 cottages* ♿*In-room: DVD (some), Wi-Fi. In-hotel: Wi-Fi, no-smoking rooms* ☰*AE, MC, V* ��❚*BP.*

$$$$ 🍴**The Atlantic.** On the outside it looks like any other raised ranch circa 1975. Inside, however, rooms are up-to-date with sleek, contemporary maple furniture, stainless-steel headboards, lamps, and other details. Plump white duvets, soft sheets, and Aveda bath goodies are among the comforts. The grounds are well manicured, and the pool seems to stretch on for an eternity. **Pros:** beach passes and beach gear available; free Continental breakfast. **Cons:** no gym; not close to beach. ⊠*1655 Rte. 39* ☎*631/283–6100* ⊕*www.hrhresorts.com* ⇨*62 rooms, 5 suites* ♿*In-room: kitchen (some), refrigerator (some), Wi-Fi (some). In-hotel: tennis court, pool, laundry service, Wi-Fi, no-smoking rooms* ☰*AE, MC, V* ⓞ❚*CP.*

$$$$ 🍴**A Butler's Manor.** Be prepared to be spoiled silly at this gorgeous bed-and-breakfast owned by Chrispher Allen, who worked as a butler before opening this with his wife. Rooms are decorated to represent the estates the owner worked in. Home-cooked hot breakfast includes a frittata with veggies from the garden and Kim's delicious banana-stuffed French toast. **Pros:** free ride to Southampton beaches; CD and iPod jack in room. **Cons:** no safes; three-night minimum on summer weekends. ⊠*244 N. Main St.* ☎*631/283–8550* ⊕*www.abutlersmanor.com* ⇨*5 rooms* ♿*In-room: DVD, refrigerator, Internet, Wi-Fi. In-hotel: no-smoking rooms, pool, Internet terminal, no kids under 12* ☰*AE, MC, V* ⊗*Closed Jan.*

$$$–$$$$ 🍴**The Inn Spot on the Bay.** Guest quarters here are in seaside villas or the main house, which dates from 1857; all rooms are beautifully decorated and have private bathrooms. You can cycle the neighborhood or cross the Ponquogue Bridge to the ocean beaches just minutes away. A covered veranda overlooks Shinnecock Bay. Seasonal and short-term accommodations are available. **Pros:** award-winning restaurant on-site. **Cons:** no Internet access or phones. ⊠*32 Lighthouse Rd., Hampton Bays* ☎*631/728–1200* ⊕*www.theinnspot.com* ⇨*4 rooms, 9 villas* ♿*In-room: no phones, refrigerators (some). In-hotel: restaurant, no-smoking rooms* ☰*AE, MC, V.*

WATER MILL

1 mi east of Southampton.

This small village, settled in the mid-17th century, is the nation's only community with a functional, working water mill and windmill. The original settlers used the mills as power sources to grind grain, saw wood, and make paper and clothing materials. Today there are several restaurants in this tiny village, and the block-long Main Street has the South Fork's only old-time penny-candy store, in existence for more than 50 years.

WHAT TO SEE

Water Mill Museum. Originally built in 1644, the oldest operating water mill on Long Island is still fully operational today. You can work the lathe and learn the arts of quilting and weaving here. ⊠*41 Old Mill Rd.* ☎*631/726–4625* ⊕*www.watermillmuseum.org* ☜*$3 suggested donation* ☾*June–Sept., Thurs.–Mon. 11–5, Sun. 1–5.*

WINERY **Duck Walk Vineyards.** A Normandy-style château sits on 56 acres of vineyards. There are daily tours (free, at noon, 2, and 4) and tastings. Special events include live music on the patio overlooking the vineyards weekends in summer and fall, as well as complimentary hot mulled wine on December weekends. ⊠*231 Montauk Hwy.* ☎*631/726–7555* ⊕*www.duckwalk.com* ☜*Free* ☾*Daily 11–6.*

WHERE TO EAT

$ ✕**Hampton Coffee Company.** If the smell of coffee roasting doesn't intoxi-
MEXICAN cate you enough, order the homemade nachos and salsa. Take your breakfast to go or eat in the bright dining area. Chicken enchiladas à la Mexicana and *huevos divorciados* (two eggs over-easy on a bed of tortillas with dollops of red and green salsa) will get your heart going. Bring home a pound of the hand-roasted, estate-grown coffee. ⊠*869 Montauk Hwy.* ☎ *631/726–2633* ⊰*Reservations not accepted* ▱ *AE, DC, MC, V.*

$$$ ✕**Mirko's.** The warm atmosphere and the talented chef-owner's use of
ECLECTIC only the freshest local ingredients have consistently won this gem of a
Fodor'sChoice restaurant rave reviews from respected foodies. The menu is a blend
★ of Mediterranean, Continental, contemporary, and American dishes. Try the pan-roasted striped bass, the herb-crusted rack of lamb, or the grilled veal chop with corn-tomato salsa. You can dine inside by the fireplace or out on the terrace. ⊠*Water Mill Sq., 670 Montauk Hwy.* ☎*631/726–4444* ⊰*Reservations essential* ▱*AE, DC, MC, V* ☾*Closed Jan.–mid-Feb. No lunch.*

9

BRIDGEHAMPTON

7 mi east of Water Mill.

The beautiful beaches are just part of the attraction at this quiet, classy Hamptons community. Elegant Bridgehampton has antiques shops, art galleries, and restaurants in which you can sip wine made from locally grown grapes. This is also horse country, and in summer Bridgehampton hosts the prestigious annual Hampton Classic Horse Show and the Mercedes-Benz Polo Challenge. South of the village of Bridgehampton, running along the ocean, is the area called Sagaponack, a traditional agricultural community dating from 1656 and known for having some of the richest soil on Long Island. Even though more grand homes are being built on this precious farmland every year, you can still buy outstanding local berries, vegetables, and flowers at the farm stands here.

WHAT TO SEE

Children's Museum of the East End. This is a perfect place to let kids run off some steam on a rainy day, or just to take a break from the beach. There's a fire engine replica, painting room, library, climbing ship, and a separate play area for toddlers. ⊠*376 Bridgehampton/Sag Harbor Tpke.* ☎*631/537–8250* ⊕*www.cmee.org* 🖃*$7* ⊙*Wed. –Sat. 9–5, Sun. 10–5.*

Madoo Conservancy. A stroll around this whimsical, plant- and sculpture-studded 2-acre preserve designed by artist Robert Dash reveals why *HomeStyle* magazine once described it as one of the 10 most beautiful gardens in America. Photographs are permitted, but not dogs, strollers, or children under six. ⊠*618 Sagg Main St., off Rte. 27, Sagaponack* ☎*631/537–8200* ⊕*www.madoo.org* 🖃*$10* ⊙*May–Sept., Wed. and Sat. 1–5.*

SPORTS AND THE OUTDOORS

Late in August, the Hampton Classic show grounds host the **Hampton Classic Horse Show** (⊠*Snake Hollow Rd.* ☎*631/537–3177* ⊕*www. hamptonclassic.com*), one of North America's most prestigious equestrian shows. Participants from around the globe compete in several events that challenge their hunter and jumper skills. Huge cash prizes are put up by Calvin Klein, David Yurman jewelers, and other deep-pocketed entities.

BEACH   **Sagg Main Beach.** This Town of Southampton beach stretches along the ocean for 1,500 feet. Lifeguards are on duty (weekends 10–5 from late May to late June and daily 10–5 from late June to early September), and facilities include showers, restrooms, a food stand, picnic tables, and volleyball. Beachgoers must have a parking permit. ⊠*Sagg Main St., Sagaponack* ☎*631/728–8585* 🖃*Parking $20 (late May–early Sept.).*

WHERE TO EAT

$$$ ✕**Pierre's Restaurant.** Take your appetite on a mini-vacation to Paris,
FRENCH   where diners eat close to one another in true Parisian style. Try the roasted free-range chicken or a scrumptious plat du jour, which might include *paella valenciana* or *Boullabaisse Marsellaise.* Desserts such as *crepe au chocolat chaudare* are too good to share so be sure to get your own. For those who really want to splurge, play chef for a day and help prepare your favorite meal for a group of your friends. ⊠*2468 Main St.* ☎*631/537–5110* ▤*AE, MC, V*

$$ ✕**World Pie.** A friendly staff and mouthwatering Italian food make this
ITALIAN   down-to-earth eatery a popular choice. Artichoke hearts, goat cheese, and basil are among the toppings used on the more than 20 varieties of pizza baked in the wood-burning oven. The fresh salads—such as the chopped romaine with tomatoes, red onions, and blue cheese—are delectable, as are such daily specials as seared lamb chops with polenta. Enjoy your pie alfresco at outdoor tables in summer. ⊠*2402 Main St.* ☎*631/537–7999* ▤*AE, MC, V.*

WHERE TO STAY

$$$$ ⚏**Bridgehampton Inn.** On Main Street and within walking distance of the village center is this stately 1795 clapboard inn, operated by the same family that owns the Loaves & Fishes food shop in Sagaponack. Beautiful antique dressers and mirrors decorate the rooms, many of which have four-poster beds. The sumptuous English breakfast, served in the dining room or on the veranda, is one of the biggest treats here. **Pros:** accepts young children; on-site cooking school. **Cons:** cancellation policy is strict, 50% deposit is nonrefundable on cancellations made less than 14 days before arrival. ✉*2266 Main St.* ☎*631/537–3660* ⊕*www.bridgehamptoninn.com* ↩*5 rooms, 1 suite* ⚭*In-room: Wi-Fi. In-hotel: restaurant, room service, bar, Wi-Fi* ▤*AE, MC, V* ⦿*BP.*

SAG HARBOR

5 mi northeast of Bridgehampton.

On the South Fork's north coast, Sag Harbor has a strong maritime flavor that largely stems from its history as a whaling port. The first white settlers arrived in the late 1600s, learned a thing or two about whaling from the resident American Indians, and started sending out whaleboats in the mid-1700s. By the time the industry hit its peak in the mid-1800s, Sag Harbor had become one of the world's busiest ports.

Sag Harbor's centuries-old Main Street, lined with boutiques, galleries, and restaurants, leads to the wharf where tall ships from around the world would arrive. Today impressive sailboats and powerboats line the marina and bay. Thanks to careful preservation, much of Sag Harbor's 18th- and 19th-century architecture remains intact, including Greek-revival houses once owned by whaling captains. Also abundant are early-colonists' homes as well as Victorian houses built for wealthy industrialists.

VISITOR INFORMATION

Sag Harbor Chamber of Commerce (✉*Box 2810, Sag Harbor 11963* ☎*631/ 725–0011* ⊕*www.sagharborchamber.com*).

SPORTS AND THE OUTDOORS

Morton National Wildlife Refuge. The 187-acre refuge, on a small peninsula that juts into Little Peconic and Noyac bays a few miles west of Sag Harbor, encompasses beaches and woody bluffs inhabited by terns, osprey, and songbirds as well as deer. Hiking trails vein the area. ✉*Noyac Rd., Noyac* ☎*631/286–0485* ⛱*Parking $4* ⊗*Daily ½ hr before sunrise–½ hr after sunset.*

BEACHES **Foster Memorial Beach.** The slightly rocky bay beach, also known as Long Beach, runs along Noyac Bay a couple of miles west of Sag Harbor and is a great spot from which to watch sunsets. In season, the beach has a snack truck, lifeguard, and restrooms. You need a nonresident daily permit, sold at the beach, for parking. ✉*Long Beach Rd.* ☎*631/728– 8585* ⛱*Parking $20 (Memorial Day–Labor Day).*

9

Havens Beach. A walk or bike ride from the village center, this long sandy stretch of bay beach has calm waters for swimming, a swing set and playing field, and public restrooms. It's necessary to obtain a parking permit at the Sag Harbor municipal hall, at 55 Main Street. ⊠ *Off Bay St. near Hempstead St.* ☎ *631/725–0222* ⊠ *Parking $10 (Memorial Day–Labor Day).*

SHOPPING

At **Christy's Art and Design** (⊠ *3 Madison St.* ☎ *631/725–7000*), housed in a Victorian, you may buy antiques as small as a vintage vase or as large as enormous fireplaces and columns. Modern tableware is also for sale here, and everything is from Europe. A working glassblowing studio, **Megna Hot Glass Studio** (⊠ *11 Bridge St.* ☎ *631/725–1131*) sells handmade doorknobs, lighting, sculptures, and art glass. You can watch the work in process here.

CLOTHING AND ACCESSORIES Indonesian crafts, penny candy, candles, and a large selection of casual women's clothes and shoes populate the eclectic but chic **Flashbacks** (⊠ *69B Main St.* ☎ *631/725–9683*). **Simpatico** (⊠ *82 Main St.* ☎ *631/725–2210*) is a brightly painted shoe boutique that carries name-brand sandals, dress shoes, boots, and sneakers for men and women. You can match your pairs with the purses and wallets on display.

GALLERY The mix of international artwork, music, and books at the **Romany Kramoris Gallery** (⊠ *41 Main St.* ☎ *631/725–2499*) makes for good browsing. Goods include Brazilian CDs and Indonesian jewelry.

NIGHTLIFE AND THE ARTS

NIGHTLIFE Locals and out-of-towners drink to the strains of lounge music at **Cigar Bar** (⊠ *2 Main St.* ☎ *631/725–2575* ⊕ *www.hamptonscigarbar.com*), a late-night hot spot and intimate space. During the day, before things get hopping, visitors can take advantage of the free Wi-Fi. For true local flavor head for the **Corner Bar** (⊠ *1 Main St.* ☎ *631/725–9760*). Open when everything else has closed for the night, it's ideal for a late-night snack—the burger is one of the best in town. Trendy locals and visitors come to **Grappa Wine Bar** (⊠ *62 Main St.* ☎ *631/725–0055* ⊕ *www.grappawinebar.com*) to enjoy a glass of Long Island wine at the stylish wraparound bar. The inventive Italian cuisine includes baby veal meatballs.

WHERE TO EAT

¢ ✕ **Bay Burger.** This gourmet-cheeseburger nirvana is popular with locals.
AMERICAN Burgers are delicious, and you'll wish they made them a bit bigger. Save room for ice cream. ⊠ *1742 Sag Harbor Tpke.* ☎ *631/899–3914* ⊠ *Reservations not accepted* ⊟ *No credit cards.*

$$ ✕ **Conca D'oro.** Large portions, down-home cooking, and reasonable
ITALIAN prices make this a good choice for families. A casual pizza parlor in front serves slices to go, whereas the Italian restaurant in back can seat the whole gang for platters of antipasto, spaghetti and meatballs, and carafes of Chianti. ⊠ *Main St. near Washington St.* ☎ *631/725–3167* ⊠ *Reservations not accepted* ⊟ *AE, MC, V.*

$$ ✕ **Dockside Bar & Grill.** On the first warm day of the season, locals
SEAFOOD flock to the umbrella-shaded patio tables of this casual spot next to

the American Legion Hall. Have a bowl of steamers and watch the boats head into the marina. Traditional seafood favorites such as seared scallops and fried oysters share the menu with paella and chicken potpie. Inside are two simple dining rooms and a small bar. ⊠*26 Bay St.* ☎*631/725–7100* ⚐*Reservations not accepted* ▤*AE, MC, V. Closed Tues. and Wed.*

$$
JAPANESE
✕**Sen.** An attractive, black-clad staff serves sushi and other Japanese dishes to the hip crowd that frequents this place. Sashimi and rolls of all varieties are available; vegetable, noodle, and fresh-fish dishes help fill out the menu, which includes an extensive sake list. You may encounter a wait, but the beeper system lets you be mobile. ⊠*23 Main St.* ☎*631/725–1774* ⚐*Reservations not accepted* ▤*AE, MC, V.*

WHERE TO STAY

$$$$
★
🏨**The American Hotel.** Victorian elegance defines this hotel dating from 1846. The three-story brick facade and white-pillared porch look out on Main Street. Guest rooms have turn-of-the-20th-century antiques and spacious bathrooms with fine Italian towels and bathrobes. The restaurant and bar inhabit four intimate antiques-filled rooms, including a front room with a piano and a bar room with a fireplace. The wine list runs 85 pages. The bar and lounge attract a sophisticated crowd. **Pros:** ideal location in the center of town so you don't need a car. **Cons:** strict cancellation policy and minimum stays may apply in high season. ⊠*45 Main St.* ☎*631/725–3535* ⊕*www.theamericanhotel.com* ⇋*8 rooms* ⚘*In-room: Wi-Fi. In-hotel: restaurant, room service, bar, laundry service, Wi-Fi, no-smoking rooms* ▤*AE, D, DC, MC, V* ⎮⎯⎮*CP.*

$$$$
🏨**Sag Harbor Inn.** The two-story hotel is across from the marina and within walking distance of Main Street. Each room is simple but spacious, with a sitting area and modern pine furniture. French doors open onto patios and balconies, which look over the water in front rooms and the pool in back rooms. The breakfast room and promenade deck have harbor views. **Pros:** centrally located in town. **Cons:** skimpy complimentary breakfast. ⊠*W. Water St.* ☎*631/725–2949* ⊕*www.sagharborinn.com* ⇋*42 rooms* ⚘*In-room: Wi-Fi. In-hotel: pool, no-smoking rooms* ▤*AE, MC, V* ⎮⎯⎮*CP.*

9

EAST HAMPTON

7 mi east of Bridgehampton, 5 mi southeast of Sag Harbor.

Graced with ancient elm trees, majestic gray-shingled homes, and historic windmills, the village of East Hampton has evolved into a busy, expensive, and sophisticated combination of thriving summer resort and year-round community of hardworking locals and transplanted urbanites. A group of Puritan farmers and fisherfolk from Connecticut and Massachusetts settled the village in 1648, and agriculture remained its main source of livelihood until the 1800s, when the area began to develop into a fashionable resort. Cooled by Atlantic Ocean breezes, East Hampton is noted today for its lovely beaches and fine food and shopping. Its considerable wealth and the sustained effort by local government and residents to maintain East Hampton's precious heritage have combined to preserve much of the village architecture and landscape as it was during the 18th century.

VISITOR INFORMATION

East Hampton Chamber of Commerce (✉ *79A Main St., East Hampton* ☎ *631/ 324–0362* ⊕ *www.easthamptonchamber.com*).

WHAT TO SEE

East Hampton Historical Society. The society operates several local historic sites and museums, all near stately Main Street. The society's headquarters are in the circa-1740 **Osborn-Jackson House,** a period museum. The 1784 **Clinton Academy** (tours scheduled upon request) was the town's first preparatory academy for young men and women. Dating from approximately 1731, **Town House** is the only remaining town government building from colonial times. It's also the oldest surviving one-room schoolhouse on Long Island. The circa-1680 **Mulford Farm,** complete with a farmhouse and barn, hosts several wonderful programs each year, including a Colonial Kids Club, A Day in 1776, and various colonial reenactments. Each year, the farm plants Rachel's Garden with heirloom flowers and vegetables. The **Marine Museum** has three floors of exhibits devoted to East Hampton maritime history, including the eerie Shipwreck Hall. Call the society or visit the Web site for a complete list of activities at all the sites. ✉ *101 Main St.* ☎ *631/324–6850* ⊕ *www.easthamptonhistory.org* ✉ *Marine Museum $4, other buildings free* ☉ *Osborn-Jackson House (society headquarters), daily 9–5; opening days and hrs vary for other sites.*

Guild Hall Museum. Changing exhibitions at this fine-arts museum and cultural center focus on regional artists. The **John Drew Theater** presents several stage productions a year and also hosts concerts, film festivals, lectures, and readings. ✉ *158 Main St.* ☎ *631/324–0806 or 631/324–4050* ⊕ *www.guildhall.org* ☉ *June–Labor Day, Mon.–Sat. 11–5, Sun. noon–5; Labor Day–May, Thurs.–Sat. 11–5, Sun. noon–5.*

"Home Sweet Home" Museum. This circa-1720 saltbox is said to be the inspiration for the famous song "Home Sweet Home" written by 19th-century poet, playwright, and actor John Howard Payne. Guided tours lead you through the collections of English ceramics, American furniture, and textiles. The museum is in a historic district, within walking distance of 19th-century windmills, including the Old Hook Mill. ✉ *14 James La.* ☎ *631/324–0713* ✉ *$4* ☉ *May–Sept., Mon.–Sat. 10–4, Sun. 2–4; Apr., Oct., and Nov., Fri. and Sat. 10–4, Sun. 2–4. Closed Dec.–Mar.*

★ **Long House Reserve.** The gallery, arboretum, sculpture gardens, and special programs at this 16-acre preserve all underscore the mission of Long House—to show that experiencing art and nature together is essential to living a whole and creative life. You can explore the grounds on your own. ✉ *133 Hands Creek Rd., off Stephen Hands Path*

☎631/329–3568 ⊕www.longhouse.org ☜$10 ☉ Late Apr.–June and Sept.–mid-Oct., Wed. and Sat. 2–5; July and Aug., Wed.–Sat. 2–5.

Pollock-Krasner House. The house where abstract expressionist Jackson Pollock painted his masterpieces is now a museum and study center. You can see the paint-splattered floor of his studio, plus exhibits on Pollock and his wife and fellow artist, Lee Krasner. Call for a schedule of art exhibits, lectures, workshops, and guided tours. ✉830 Fireplace Rd. ☎631/324–4929 ⊕www.pkhouse.org ☜$5 ☉ Guided tours $10 May–Oct. by appointment.

SPORTS AND THE OUTDOORS

KAYAKING AND SURFING You can explore the beauty of Accabonac Harbor in a stable, easy-to-paddle kayak available for rent by the hour from **Kayak at Springs General Store** (✉29 Old Stone Hwy., off Springs Fireplace Rd. ☎631/329–5065). **Main Beach Surf and Sport** (✉Montauk Hwy., 1 mi west of East Hampton, Wainscott ☎631/537–2716 ⊕www.mainbeach.com), a premier surf, skate, and snowboard shop with great clothing and equipment, rents two- and four-person kayaks for excursions on Georgica Pond and other local bodies of water.

GET IN GEAR For beach clothing and accessories, as well as biking, surfing, and skating gear and rentals, check out **Khanh's Sports** (✉60 Park Pl. ☎631/324–0703.

SHOPPING

East Hampton's Main Street and the perpendicular Newtown Lane are lined with upscale shops that are great for browsing. **BookHampton** (✉41 Main St. ☎631/324–4939) is a fully stocked bookstore with a friendly and knowledgable staff. **London Jewelers** (✉2 Main St. ☎631/329–3939) has stunning and expensive jewelry and watches. The **Polo Country Store** (✉31–33 Main St. ☎631/324–1222) sells Ralph Lauren's classic clothes and accessories. **Steph's Stuff** (✉38 Newtown La. ☎631/329–2943) has a mind-boggling and absolutely delightful assortment of toys and other whimsical goodies for kids and grown-ups.

WHERE TO EAT

$$$ ✗**East Hampton Point.** You can watch the sun go down over Three Mile Harbor through a wall of windows at this resort restaurant known for its fresh, creative, contemporary menu. The emphasis is on seafood, like 3-pound lobsters with roasted potatoes and corn salad or pan-seared halibut served with black olives, tomatoes, fennel, and baby artichokes. Outside tables have umbrellas for shade. ✉295 3 Mile Harbor Rd. ☎631/329–2800 ⚭Reservations essential ▤AE, MC, V.

SEAFOOD

$ ✗**Nichols.** This cozy, wooden-antiques-filled restaurant serves good, old-fashioned, home-style food. Try the meat loaf and mashed potatoes, roast-turkey dinner, or fresh local seafood. ✉100 Montauk Hwy. ☎631/324–3939 ▤AE, MC, V.

AMERICAN

$$$ ✗**Nick and Toni's.** The dining room at this upscale, trendy restaurant has a wood-burning brick oven in which Mediterranean and northern Italian house specialties are cooked daily. Local artist Eric Fischl designed the oven's mosaic mural. Wood-roasted chicken and fish are popular,

MEDITERRANEAN

and on Sunday you can order oven-roasted pizza. There's open-air dining on the porch. ⊠ *136 N. Main St.* ☎ *631/324–3550* ⚓ *Reservations essential* ⊟ *AE, MC, V* ☺ *No lunch Sun.*

WHERE TO STAY

$$$ ⚏ **Bassett House–a Country Inn.** Within walking distance of shops and restaurants is this Victorian inn built in 1830 as a farmhouse. Trees and gardens surround the house, and eclectic antiques fill the rooms. Beds range from twin to queen-size. Two rooms have fireplaces. **Pros:** rates include home-cooked breakfast and beach equipment. **Cons:** no phones or safes in rooms. ⊠ *128 Montauk Hwy.* ☎ *631/324–6127* ⊕ *www.bassetthouseinn.com* ⟿ *12 rooms* ⚐ *In-room: no phone, no TV (some), refrigerator, Wi-Fi. In-hotel: some pets allowed, no-smoking rooms* ⊟ *AE, MC, V* ⍾ *BP.*

$$$$ ⚏ **Mill House Inn.** Built in the 1790s as a classic Cape Cod cottage, this B&B has been turned into anything but typical. Each room has a fireplace and private bathroom, but from there they diverge stylistically, with influences ranging from Asian to nautical to floral. Beds, either queen or king, have feather mattresses and high-thread-count cotton sheets that would be hard to leave if it weren't for the savory smell of the professionally cooked brunch wafting up the stairs. **Pros:** free beach passes; bed turndown service; cookies served around the clock. **Cons:** caters to dog owners so might not be good for those with pet allergies. ⊠ *31 N. Main St.* ☎ *631/324–9766* ⊕ *www.millhouseinn.com* ⟿ *4 rooms, 6 suites* ⚐ *In-room: DVD, refrigerator (some). Wi-Fi. In-hotel: room service, some pets allowed* ⊟ *AE, DC, MC, V* ⍾ *BP.*

AMAGANSETT

3 mi east of East Hampton.

Amagansett is a small hamlet in the town of East Hampton, which takes its name from an American Indian word meaning "place of good water." From the very beginning, the town's tranquil setting was perfectly suited to fishing and offshore whaling. Downtown Main Street has retained many of its original buildings as private residences, shops, B&Bs, and good restaurants. There's also a small outlet center on the village green. The town's Main Street is a designated historic district so visitors will never find food franchises here.

WHAT TO SEE

Miss Amelia's Cottage and Roy Lester Carriage Museum. Built in 1725 and full of beautifully preserved colonial antiques—including a collection of rare Dominy furniture—the museum contains artifacts and exhibits illustrating Amagansett life from the colonial period through the 20th century. On summer weekends, pony rides are given on the museum lawn from 10 to 2, and twice during the season there are huge antiques sales full of local treasures. In a barn to the rear of the property is the Roy Lester Carriage Museum, which displays locally made horse-drawn carriages. ⊠ *Main St.* ☎ *631/267–3020* ⚏ *Museum $2, pony rides $5* ☺ *Late May–early Sept., Fri.–Sun. 10–4.*

SPORTS AND THE OUTDOORS

BEACH **Atlantic Avenue Beach.** The beach is convenient to the center of Amagansett, and there are food concessions right on the sand, making it possible to stay all day. Lifeguards are on duty daily 10–5 from Memorial Day through Labor Day. An East Hampton parking permit is required on weekends and holidays, but during the week you can pay to park without a permit. ⊠ *South end of Atlantic Ave. off Bluff Rd.* ☎ *631/324–2417* ⊞ *Parking $10 (weekdays; parking permit required weekends and holidays).*

MONTAUK ANNUAL FALL FESTIVAL

Every year around Columbus Day weekend, the Montauk Chamber of Commerce hosts its annual fall festival featuring a famous clam chowder contest. Buy a mug and sample the area chefs' best chowders and seafood. A carousel, children's activities, and farmers' market add to the festivities. Call the Montauk Chamber of Commerce for more information (☎ *631/668–2428* ⊕ *www. montaukchamber.com*).

NIGHTLIFE AND THE ARTS

Fodor's Choice ★ You can hear live rock, jazz, and blues music, including many well-known acts, nearly every summer night and most off-season weekend nights at the **Stephen Talkhouse** (⊠ *161 Main St.* ☎ *631/267–3117* ⊕ *www.stephentalkhouse.com*). Paul McCartney, Jimmy Buffett, Billy Joel, Paul Simon, and Jon Bon Jovi have played there either spontaneously or for charities. With two bars, a small stage, and a dance floor, it's usually a laid-back scene, but the place can get packed on the weekends. Cover charges start at around $25. Doors open one hour before showtime.

WHERE TO EAT

$ ✕ **Astro Pizza Felice's Ristorante.** Its facade is unassuming, but you can't go
PIZZA   wrong with any of the pizzas or house specialties at this family-owned pizzeria that has been around since 1971. ⊠ *237 Main St.* ☎ *631/267–8300* ⚑ *Reservations not accepted* ⊟ *AE, MC, V.*

$ ✕ **Lobster Roll.** Set along the no-man's-land between Amagansett and
SEAFOOD ★   Montauk, this local institution (affectionately known as "Lunch") is the proverbial shanty by the sea. Its booths and outdoor picnic tables are filled with people coming and going from the beach. They come for the fresh lobster rolls, fish-and-chips, puffers (blowfish), and mouthwatering grilled tuna and swordfish. ⊠ *1980 Montauk Hwy.* ☎ *631/267–3740* ⊟ *MC, V* ⊗ *Closed Nov.–May.*

MONTAUK

12 mi east of Amagansett.

Twelve long miles of windswept road, aptly named the Napeague Stretch, separate Montauk from the Hamptons, and as you roll into the small seaside village it becomes immediately apparent that here is a place apart in other respects as well. Surrounded by water on three sides, Montauk is known for its distinct natural beauty. The spectacular undeveloped beaches and parks attract surfers and hikers, and the waters are superb for fishing.

Continue east past the village center and you arrive at land's end, where the Montauk Lighthouse, commissioned by President George Washington in 1792 and the oldest operating lighthouse in the state, perches on a rocky bluff overlooking the wild surf and craggy coastline of Montauk Point State Park.

More than 50 hotels, inns, and guesthouses, along with top-notch restaurants and shops, are concentrated in two distinct sections of Montauk—the village center, including Old Montauk Highway, and the harbor area, which is home to the local fishing fleet as well as dozens of party, charter, and whale-watching boats.

VISITOR INFORMATION
Montauk Chamber of Commerce (⊠ *Main St., Montauk* ☎ *631/668-2428* ⊕ *www. montaukchamber.com*).

WHAT TO SEE
The **Montauk Lighthouse** (☎ *631/668-2544* ⊕ *www.montauklighthouse. com*), the oldest lighthouse still in operation in the state and a well-known Long Island landmark, is perched solidly on a bluff in Montauk Point State Park. President George Washington signed an order to build the lighthouse in 1792. Climb the 137 iron steps to the top for spectacular views of the Atlantic Ocean and, to the northeast, Block Island, or take a moment to ponder the touching memorial to local fishermen lost at sea. The museum, in the former lightkeeper's quarters, displays a wealth of photos and artifacts. ⊠ *East end of Rte. 27* ☎ *631/668-3781* ⊕ *nysparks.state.ny.us* ▧ *Parking $8* ⊙ *Park daily dawn-dusk. Lighthouse Mar.–late May and mid-Oct.–Nov., weekends 10:30–4:30; late May–early Sept., daily 10:30–5:30; early Sept.–mid-Oct., weekdays 10:30–4:30, weekends 10:30–5.*

SPORTS AND THE OUTDOORS
Hither Hills State Park. This 1,755-acre park, with rolling moors and forests of pitch pine and scrub oak, encompasses a campground, picnic areas, a playground, general store, miles of ocean beach, and hiking and bicycling trails. An unusual natural phenomenon in the park is known as the Walking Dunes, so named because strong northwest winds cause the 80-foot dunes to travel 3 or more feet per year. The ¾-mi loop through cranberry bogs, beaches, and pine forests submerged in sand is not too far for little feet to travel, and most people find the natural lore of the area fascinating. Pick up the descriptive brochure, which includes trail maps, at the park office or the chamber of commerce before you set out. ⊠ *Old Montauk Hwy.* ☎ *631/668-2554, 800/456-2267 camping reservations* ⊕ *nysparks.state.ny.us* ▧ *Parking $8 (late May–early Sept.)* ⊙ *Daily dawn-dusk.*

Montauk Point State Park. About 6 mi east of the village, the 724 acres of rocky shoreline, grassy dunes, and bayberry-covered moors surrounding Montauk's lighthouse have been so well protected that you might feel as if you're standing at an undiscovered frontier of pounding surf and pristine land. Frequently, a wild riptide (this is not a swimming beach) sets up perfect conditions for exciting surf casting. This is one of the best spots in Montauk to try your luck at catching the "big one." A fishing permit isn't necessary. Other activities include hiking (trail maps are available at the information booth), bird-watching, and beachcombing. Depending on the tide and weather, during certain weekends from early December to late April naturalists lead two- to three-hour **Guided Seal Walks** (☎631/668–5000) in Montauk Point State Park. Hikers are guided to the haul-out sites along the north beach to observe seals and winter birds, and to learn about marine geology. Tours are $5; call for tour times.

BEACHES **Gin Beach.** On Block Island Sound, this beach east of the jetty has calm water and sparkling clean sand—perfect for families with little ones. You can watch the boats go in and out of the harbor all day. There are public restrooms, a snack trailer, and outdoor showers. Lifeguards are on duty Memorial Day to early September (weekends only from May to late June and after Labor Day). A resident permit is required for parking. ✉*End of East Lake Dr., off Montauk Hwy.* ☎*631/324–2417* ☞*Free (resident pass required for parking).*

Kirk Park Beach. This sandy, clean, protected ocean beach has a picnic area across the street; public restrooms are in the parking lot. Lifeguards are on duty Memorial Day weekend through late September (weekends only from late May to June 20 and Labor Day to the end of the season). ✉*Montauk Hwy. near IGA supermarket* ☎*631/324–2417* ☞*Parking $10 (Memorial Day weekend–late Sept.)* ☉*Daily dawn–dusk.*

FISHING Excellent surf casting (at Montauk Point or along the ocean beaches) and inshore or offshore trips on party and charter boats make Montauk one of the premier fishing destinations on the East Coast. A trip to the chamber of commerce on Main Street or to the Harbor area (off West Lake Drive) yields the information you need to choose from the many fishing options. ■TIP→**For summer trips, make reservations in advance.**

Breakaway (✉*Montauk Harbor* ☎*631/668–2914*), a 42-foot Downeaster, can take up to six people inshore fishing for striped bass and fluke, or offshore for tuna and shark. Half-day fishing for up to 40 people takes place on *Lazy Bones* (✉*Montauk Harbor* ☎*631/668–5671*), a popular party boat. You might catch flounder, fluke, striped bass, or bluefish, depending on the season. Choose from deep-sea fishing or a half-day inshore haul for bass and bluefish on the *Oh Brother* (✉*Montauk Harbor* ☎*631/668–2707*), which welcomes families.

Johnny's Tackle Shop (✉*786 Main/Montauk Hwy.* ☎*631/668–2940*) is the place to go for custom-designed rods, excellent surf-casting advice, and a complete selection of fishing tackle. **tar Island Yacht Club** (✉*Star Island Rd.* ☎*631/668–5052* ⊕*www.starislandyc.com*) includes a marina, yacht club, restaurant, and the East End's largest nautical store, which is filled with bait and tackle, clothing, footwear, and supplies. Star Island hosts Montauk's famous shark tournaments in summer.

9

FISHING

Lined on one side by the Long Island Sound and on the other by the Atlantic Ocean, and nicked by numerous bays and harbors, Long Island provides countless chances for anglers to indulge their passion and fisherfolk to make their living. The waters here draw commercial-fishing vessels and sporting boats, pros, and weekend warriors. In virtually every village that snuggles up against the water, you find docks, marinas, bait-and-tackle shops, and people willing to discuss the tides, weather, and best places to fish. Depending on the season and area, you can try your rod at striped bass, fluke, bluefish, flounder, skate, and even tuna and shark offshore. There's good surf casting at Montauk Point and Jones Beach. Charter boats glide in and out of harbors at Greenport, Shelter Island, and Montauk, filled with people seeking a prize for their wall or freezer.

GOLF The 18-hole, par-72, Robert Trent Jones–designed golf course at ★ **Montauk Downs State Park** (⊠ *50 S. Fairview Ave.* 📞 *631/668–5000, 631/668–1234 reservations*) is one of the top public courses in the nation. Club and cart rentals, instruction, a driving range, a putting green, and a restaurant are available. Greens fees are $30–$36 for New York residents and $60–$72 for nonresidents. Call at least a week in advance in summer to reserve tee times. The Downs is off West Lake Drive, near the harbor.

SURFING If you want to surf in Montauk, head for **Ditch Plains** (⊠ *Ditch Plains* ★ *Rd.*). It's an insider's spot, but the locals welcome newcomers who have a modicum of surfing etiquette. You can grab a wrap sandwich or an iced coffee at Lily's Ditch Witch wagon. You need a town parking permit or temporary beach sticker to park here. Take Montauk Highway east through town, make a right on Ditch Plains Road, and follow it to the beach.

The **Air and Speed Board Shop** (⊠ *795 Main St.* 📞 *631/668–0356*) offers group and private surfing lessons. The shop also sells surfing, snowboarding, and skateboarding equipment, plus the latest in clothing and accessories. **Plaza Sports** (⊠ *716 Main St.* 📞 *631/668–9300*) sells surfing equipment as well as biking paraphernalia, surfing and swimming gear, and beach sportswear.

SHOPPING

Downtown Montauk has an eclectic mix of shops that sell books, clothing, jewelry, antiques, home furnishings, and gifts. At a similar but more limited grouping of shops in the harbor area, you can find Irish knits, pricier clothing shops, and a great toy store.

HOME Walk into **Strawberry Fields Flowers and Gifts** (⊠ *Main St.* 📞 *631/668–* FURNISHINGS *6279*) and your senses are filled with the fragrance of flowers and spice and a riot of color. Flowers, baskets, plants, unusual gifts, candles, and wrought-iron wall hangings are just the beginning. The talented owner of **Willow** (⊠ *41 The Plaza* 📞 *631/668–0772*) designs and sews beautifully crafted quilts, as well as outfits for American Girl dolls. The assortment of unusual gifts includes garden ornaments, linens, stationery, and candles.

WHERE TO EAT

$$$ ✕**Dave's Grill.** Unpretentious yet stylish, Dave's is at the Montauk fish-
SEAFOOD ing docks. Indoor seating is in a small, candlelit room or around a cozy adjoining bar; outdoor seating is on a deck next to the harbor. Come for succulent steaks, vegetarian delights, and contemporary dishes prepared with fresh local seafood. Leave room for dessert and try the famous "Chocolate Bag." This is a popular spot with locals, and there's always a wait for a table. ⊠*468 W. Lake Dr.* ☎*631/668–9190* ⚲*Reservations not accepted* ▭*MC, V* ⊙*Closed Nov.–Apr. No lunch.*

¢–$ ✕**The Dock.** Seafaring-related antiques festoon the rustic wood walls
AMERICAN and ceiling of Montauk's favorite dockside restaurant. Great nachos, burgers, fish sandwiches, specials, and a cozy, local bar scene are hallmarks here. ⊠*Montauk Harbor near the town dock* ☎*631/668–9778* ⚲*Reservations not accepted* ▭*No credit cards* ⊙*Closed Dec.–Mar.*

$$$$ ✕**Harvest on Fort Pond.** The glass-enclosed dining room of this seafood
SEAFOOD restaurant affords stunning views of sunsets on Fort Pond. There's
★ family-style service—entrées are huge and serve at least two. Try the calamari salad and the sizzling whole red snapper. You can dine outside in the herb garden in summer. ⊠*11 S. Emory St.* ☎*631/668–5574* ⚲*Reservations essential* ▭*AE, MC, V.*

$$ ✕**Inlet Cafe at Gosman's Dock.** The view from the waterside tables and
SEAFOOD sushi bar is so mesmerizing that you may forget to bite into the sushi or succulent local lobster on your plate. There are four Gosman's eating establishments on the dock; this one serves fresh seafood right off the boat. ⊠*Gosman's Dock, Montauk Harbor* ☎*631/668–2549* ⚲*Reservations not accepted* ▭*AE, MC, V* ⊙*Closed mid-Oct.–mid-May.*

¢ ✕**John's Pancake House.** Omelets and delicious pancakes are served all
AMERICAN day at this bustling Main Street restaurant, along with hearty homemade soups and chowders, thick burgers and shakes, spicy chicken-salad wraps, and fried ice cream. Come at off-hours especially on weekends, because there's always a line. Breakfast begins at 6:15. ⊠*Main St.* ☎*631/668–2383* ⚲*Reservations not accepted* ▭*No credit cards* ⊙*No dinner.*

WHERE TO STAY

$$$$ ⊞**Gurney's Inn Resort and Spa.** Long popular for its fabulous location on a bluff overlooking 1,000 feet of private ocean beach, Gurney's has become even more famous in recent years for its European-style spa and its indoor heated seawater pool. The large, luxurious rooms and suites all have ocean views. **Pros:** cozy, nostalgic, nautical theme; right on the ocean; small playground on the beach will delight kids. **Cons:** parking is packed and up a steep hill. ⊠*290 Old Montauk Hwy.* ☎*631/668–2345* ⊕*www.gurneys-inn.com* ⇴*100 rooms, 4 suites, 5 cottages* ⚫*In-room: safe, kitchen (some), refrigerator (some), Wi-Fi. In-hotel: restaurant, room service, bar, tennis courts, pool, gym, spa, beachfront, laundry service, Wi-Fi, no-smoking rooms* ▭*AE, D, DC, MC, V* ⦿*MAP.*

9

$$$$ ⚑**Montauk Manor.** The sprawling, family-friendly "American castle"
★ has views of the bay and myriad amenities. The Tudor-style Manor,
built in 1927 as a luxury resort, is now a condominium, so each unit
is decorated differently. Most units are bright and have contemporary
furnishings; some have loft bedrooms with skylights, patios, or balconies. Jitneys take you to the beaches, and beach passes are available. The
restaurant, Breakwater Café, offers New American fare accented with
Japanese dishes and flavors. **Pros:** myriad sport facilities. **Cons:** not close
to beach; hotel is very spread out and requires long walks to get around.
⊠*236 Edgemere St.* ☎*631/668–4400* ⊕*www.montaukmanor.com*
⬦*18 studios, 81 suites* ⚐ *In-room: DVD, kitchen, Wi-Fi. In-hotel:*
restaurant, room service, bar, tennis court, pool, gym, spa, laundry
service, Wi-Fi, no-smoking rooms ⊟*AE, D, DC, MC, V.*

$$$$ ⚑**Montauk Yacht Club, Resort and Marina.** The plush resort on Star Island,
in Montauk Harbor, has its own mini-replica of the Montauk Lighthouse as well as a 232-slip marina. Rooms, contemporary and bright,
have floor-to-ceiling windows and private terraces. The villas contain 23
rooms. **Pros:** free shuttle to town and beaches. **Cons:** hotel is 2 mi from
Montauk village. ⊠*32 Star Island Rd.* ☎*631/668–3100 or 888/692–*
8668 ⊕*www.montaukyachtclub.com* ⬦*107 rooms* ⚐ *In-room: safe,*
DVD, Wi-Fi. In-hotel: restaurant, room service, bar, pool, tennis courts,
gym, spa, children's programs (ages 5 and up), laundry service, Wi-Fi,
no-smoking rooms ⊟*AE, DC, MC, V* ⊙*Closed Nov.–early Apr.*

$$$ ⚑**Ocean Resort Inn.** Hanging baskets of flowers and picnic tables on
the deck invite you to relax and enjoy the surroundings at this in-town
two-story inn, a half block from the ocean. Some rooms have whirl-
pool baths and more than one bathroom; all are well maintained and
clean. **Pros:** Hampton Jitney bus stop is down the street; complimentary
beach pass. **Cons:** no DVD player; no restaurant. ⊠*95 S. Embassy*
St. ☎*631/668–2300* ⊕*www.oceanresortinn.com* ⬦*17 rooms* ⚐ *In-*
room: refrigerator (some), Wi-Fi. In-hotel: no-smoking rooms ⊟*AE,*
MC, V ⊙*Closed Nov.–Apr.*

Travel Smart
New York State

WORD OF MOUTH

"Yes, it's that time again. Time to travel, sure, but also time to obsess about what I'm going to bring and how to fit it all in my carry-on. Why carry-on? Because carry-on is the single easiest thing you can do to make your trip go smoothly. No concerns about your luggage going missing, no problems using the cheapest possible public transportation to get where you need to go, and no issues adjusting to last-minute changes in your itinerary.

—Therese

GETTING HERE & AROUND

▌ BY AIR

New York is one of the easiest states in America to reach by plane, and international fares to New York City are among the least expensive in the United States (except for Asian and Australian flights, which are cheaper to California). Just about every major international airline with U.S. service flies to New York City, via either JFK or Newark airports. Nearly a dozen other airports in New York State have direct service throughout the United States and Canada on anywhere from 3 to 12 airlines. Some sample flying times to New York City: from Chicago (2½ hours), London (7 hours), Los Angeles (6 hours), Sydney via Los Angeles (21 hours).

Air Travel Resources in New York The Office of the Attorney General of the State of New York (⊕ www.oag.state.ny.us) handles complaints about airlines and air travel.

AIRPORTS AND FLIGHTS

The major air gateways to New York City are LaGuardia Airport and JFK International Airport in Queens, and Newark Liberty International Airport in New Jersey. Regional airports with direct service on several commercial carriers to many cities are Albany International Airport, Buffalo Niagara International Airport, Greater Binghamton Airport, Greater Rochester International Airport, Long Island Islip Macarthur, Stewart International Airport in Newburgh, Syracuse Hancock International Airport, and Westchester County Airport in White Plains. If you're headed to the Adirondacks, consider flying into Montréal (Aéroports de Montréal), which is about a two-hour drive from Lake Placid. Except for some rural areas upstate, nearly every major region in New York is within a 90-minute drive of two or more airports.

AIRPORT INFORMATION

Aéroports de Montréal (YMQ ☎ 514/394–7377 ⊕ www.admtl.com). **Albany International Airport** (ALB ☎ 518/242–2200 ⊕ www.albanyairport.com). **Buffalo Niagara International Airport** (BUF ☎ 716/630–6000 ⊕ www.nfta.com/airport). **Greater Binghamton Airport** (BGM ☎ 607/763–4471 ⊕ www.binghamtonairport.com). **Greater Rochester International Airport** (ROC ☎ 585/753–7020 ⊕ www.rocairport.com). **JFK International Airport** (JFK ☎ 718/244–4444 ⊕ www.kennedyairport.com). **LaGuardia** (LGA ☎ 718/533–3400 ⊕ www.laguardiaairport. com). **Long Island Islip Macarthur** (ISP ☎ 631/467–3210 ⊕ www.macarthurairport. com). **Newark Liberty International Airport** (EWR) (☎ 888/397–4636 or 973/961–6000 ⊕ www.newarkairport.com). **Stewart International Airport** (SWF ☎ 845/564–2100 ⊕ www.stewartintlairport.com). **Syracuse Hancock International Airport** (SYR ☎ 315/454–4330 ⊕ www.syrairport.org). **Westchester County Airport** (HPN ☎ 914/995–4850 ⊕ www.westchestergov.com/airport).

AIRLINE CONTACTS

Air Canada (☎ 888/247–2262 ⊕ www. aircanada.ca). **American Airlines** (☎ 800/433–7300 ⊕ www.aa.com). **Continental Airlines** (☎ 800/523–3273 for U.S. and Mexico reservations, 800/231–0856 for international reservations ⊕ www.continental. com). **Delta Airlines** (☎ 800/221–1212 for U.S. reservations, 800/241–4141 for international reservations ⊕ www.delta.com). **jetBlue** (☎ 800/538–2583 ⊕ www.jetblue. com). **Southwest Airlines** (☎ 800/435–9792 ⊕ www.southwest.com). **United Airlines** (☎ 800/864–8331 for U.S. reservations, 800/538–2929 for international reservations ⊕ www.united.com). **Virgin Atlantic Airways** (☎ 800/862–8621, 01293/450–150 in U.K. ⊕ www.virgin-atlantic.com).

TRAVEL TIMES FROM NYC TO	BY AIR	BY BUS	BY CAR	BY TRAIN
Albany	1¼ hours	2¾–3 hours	2½–3¼ hours	3¼ hours
Buffalo	1¼ hours	7¾–9 hours	6½–8 hours	8–8½ hours
Catskills (Kingston)	no direct flight	1¾–2¼ hours	1¾–2¼ hours	2½ hours (Rhinecliff)
The Hamptons (Riverhead)	no direct flight	2¾–3¼ hours	2–3 hours	2¼ hours
Lake George/ Adirondacks	no direct flight	5–5½ hours	5–6 hours	4¾ hours (Fort Edward)
Montréal	1½ hours	7–9 hours	7 hours	10 hours
Niagara Falls	no direct flight	8–9½ hours	7 hours	9 hours
Rochester	1½ hours	6–7½ hours	5½–6½ hours	7½ hours
Syracuse	1¼ hours	4½–6¼ hours	4–5 hours	6¼ hours
Utica	no direct flight	5¼–6½ hours	4 hours	5¼ hours

BY BUS

Within most large cities it's possible to use municipal bus service to get around, especially within New York City. For traveling by bus to or from New York City, the major bus terminal is at Port Authority, one block west of Times Square and directly accessible via the subway from city airports. Adirondack, Pine Hill, and New York Trailways has service from New York City to several communities in upstate New York and parts of Canada. Greyhound Lines has extensive national service. Hampton Jitney connects New York City and Boston to eastern Long Island. Peter Pan Trailways serves New York City, Boston, Philadelphia, Baltimore, and Washington, D.C. Shortline connects New York City to upstate New York and parts of New Jersey and Pennsylvania.

Bus Information **Adirondack, Pine Hill, and New York Trailways** (☎ *800/225–6815* 🌐 *www.trailways.com*). **Greyhound Lines** (☎ *800/231–2222* 🌐 *www.greyhound.com*). **Hampton Jitney** (☎ *631/283–4600 or 800/327–0732* 🌐 *www.hamptonjitney.com*). **New Jersey Transit** (☎ *973/491–7000* 🌐 *www.njtransit.state.nj.us*). **Peter Pan Trailways** (☎ *413/781–2900 or 800/343–9999* 🌐 *www.peterpanbus.com*). **Shortline** (☎ *800/631–8405* 🌐 *www.shortlinebus.com*).

BY CAR

New York has a bit of a Jekyll-and-Hyde complex when it comes to car travel. You need a car to explore the upper reaches of the state, where driving is generally painless, but a car can be more hindrance than help in New York City, and even on parts of Long Island. Just north of the city in Westchester County can be just as frustrating owing to traffic-choked highways that seem forever plagued by construction projects, and to the complex and confusing network of interstates and parkways enveloping New York City.

Morning and evening rush-hour traffic ranges from ugly to catastrophic on the highways leading in and out of every decent-size city in New York. Also, most bridges and tunnels in and out of New York City charge significant tolls (as high as $6 each way for any of the six major bridge and tunnel crossings between New York City and New Jersey), as do those stretches of New York's interstate system that fall under the auspices of the New York Thruway (Interstate 90 from the New York–Pennsylvania border east to the New York–Massachusetts border, and Interstate 87 from Albany south to New York City). Toll booths in New York State all accept E-ZPass, an automated electronic toll pass used by many residents and frequent travelers; if you don't have the pass, be careful not to pull into one of the E-ZPass-only lanes when you approach a toll.

Despite the congested city areas, the state has quite a few scenic drives, even along certain spans of interstate (notably Interstate 87 north of Albany to the Canadian border and parts of Interstate 90 across the center of the state). The suburbs outside Manhattan are traversed by a series of narrow, twisting, and in many places beautiful parkways, mostly consisting of limited-access roads often bordered by verdant landscaping. (Note that although these parkways often make for pleasant drives, some of the twists and turns can be tricky in snow or rain.) New York also has hundreds of miles of U.S. and state highways that pass through dense forests, open farmland, and pastoral historic hamlets. When time permits, it's worth venturing off the interstate system to behold some of the delightful scenery fringing the state's country roads.

PARKING

In most of New York State parking is not a serious problem—this is true even for larger cities, with the exception of New York City, which has arguably the most expensive and hard-to-find parking of any U.S. city. The state's more touristy communities also suffer from limited or expensive visitor parking, including the Hamptons and some of the suburbs in Nassau, Westchester, and Rockland counties.

RENTAL CARS

Choosing the right car-rental strategy depends significantly on whether you intend to spend any time in New York City, which has exorbitant rental rates and myriad driving obstacles, from expensive off-street parking to heavy traffic. It's best

to tackle New York City, with its excellent public transportation, without a vehicle and rent a car only to explore the rest of the state.

Rates at New York City airports, as well as at Long Island's Macarthur airport, begin at around $70 a day and $240 a week for an economy car with air-conditioning, automatic transmission, and unlimited mileage; in Manhattan itself, rates begin at around $60 a day but increase to about $325 a week and up. These rates do not include state tax on car rentals, which is 5% in addition to the local sales tax rate. The New York City Yellow Pages list countless local car-rental agencies, some renting secondhand vehicles, in addition to the national chains.

If you're traveling during a holiday period, make sure that a confirmed reservation guarantees you a car; if in doubt, call the local branch of the car-rental agency. Remember to allow plenty of time to return your car—upward of an hour to be safe—especially at airports in the immediate vicinity of New York City.

Also, check out local car-rental companies—whose prices may be lower still, although their service and maintenance may not be as good as those of major rental agencies—and research rates on the Internet. Remember to ask about required deposits, cancellation penalties, and drop-off charges if you're planning to pick up the car in one city and leave it in another.

You can save money and avoid New York City's traffic by taking a bus or train to a suburban station near car-rental agencies, such as Hoboken (in New Jersey), North White Plains, Poughkeepsie, or even Stamford, Connecticut, which borders New York's Westchester County. In North White Plains, for example, expect prices to start at $34 per day and $180 per week. As you travel farther upstate, rates continue to decrease, meaning that if you're spending part of your time in

Car Rental Resources

Alamo	800/462–5266	www.alamo.com
Avis	800/331–1212	www.avis.com
Budget	800/527–0700	www.budget.com
Enterprise Rent-a-Car	800/261–7331	www.enterprise.com
Hertz	800/654–3131	www.hertz.com
National Car Rental	800/227–7368	www.nationalcar.com
Thrifty	800/847–4389 or 918/669–2168	www.thrifty.com

the northern or western parts of the state, it may make sense to fly or take a train or bus to Albany, Rochester, Buffalo, or elsewhere upstate and rent a car once you arrive there. Rates at these destinations usually begin at around $30 per day and $175 per week.

In New York you must be 18 to rent a car. Although rental agencies based in New York are technically required to rent to qualified drivers under 25, hefty surcharges of as much as $115 a day effectively remove this option. Surcharges in New Jersey tend to be lower.

Surcharges may apply if you're under 25 or if you take the car outside the area approved by the rental agency. You'll pay extra for child seats (about $8 a day), which are compulsory for children under five, and usually for additional drivers ($3 a day).

RULES OF THE ROAD

On city streets the speed limit is 30 mph unless otherwise posted; on rural roads, the speed limit is 55 mph unless otherwise posted. Interstate speeds range from 50 to 65 mph. Within New York City limits you may not turn right on a red light; you're permitted to do so elsewhere in the state unless signs indicate otherwise. Be alert for one-way streets and "no left turn" intersections. State law requires that front-seat passengers wear seat belts at all times. Children under 16 must wear seat belts in both the front and back seats. Always strap children under age five into approved child-safety seats. It is illegal to use a handheld cell phone while driving in New York State or New Jersey (good to know if you're renting a car from Newark). Police will immediately seize the car of any DWI (driving while intoxicated, defined as having a blood alcohol count of .08 or higher) offenders in New York. First-time offenders might face a minimum fine of $500, loss of license for six months, and one year in jail.

∎ BY TRAIN

Compared with most of the country, New York enjoys extensive rail service and utilizes it heavily, especially in and out of New York City. As a result, rail service tends to be not only convenient but on time and reliable. Amtrak routes traverse two key regions in New York: the Hudson Valley, running south–north from New York City through Albany and the Adirondacks to Montréal; and central New York, running east–west across the state from western Massachusetts through Albany, Syracuse, Rochester, and Buffalo before heading down into Erie, Pennsylvania, and on into Ohio. Both of these routes are extremely scenic, especially the Hudson River run. There are also several major Amtrak routes in the northeastern United States that cut through New York City, most of them connecting stations on the Washington, D.C.–Boston corridor. New York City's Penn Station is the hub for all of the state's Amtrak service except for the central New York runs.

Nowhere else in the country can you find more comprehensive commuter-rail service than in greater New York City. From Manhattan, Metro-North Commuter Railroad trains take passengers from Grand Central Terminal to points north of the city, both in New York State and Connecticut. For trains to Long Island and New Jersey, take the Long Island Railroad and New Jersey Transit, respectively; both operate from Penn Station. The PATH trains run between Manhattan and the New Jersey towns of Newark and Jersey City.

You can often save money by avoiding travel at peak periods (generally Friday and Sunday on Amtrak, and weekdays during rush hour on the commuter rails), when tickets are generally more expensive. Amtrak occasionally offers deals that allow a second or third accompanying passenger to travel for half price or free. Amtrak's USA rail pass allows unlimited travel within the United States and Canada during any 15-, 30-, and 45-day period ($389–$749).

Tickets can run 10% to 50% higher if you don't purchase them seven days in advance. The following are approximate one-way fares, trip times, and routes on Amtrak (times and fares vary depending on the train service and number of stops): Boston to New York City, 3½–4¼ hours, $62–$93; Washington, D.C., to New York City, 2¾–3¼ hours, $72–$103; Montréal to New York City, 10 hours, $62; Chicago to Buffalo, 12–14 hours, $72; Toronto to Buffalo, 2¼ hours, $38; Toronto to Rhinecliff (mid–Hudson Valley), 8¾ hours, $96; Philadelphia to Syracuse, 8–10 hours, $62–$89; New York City to Niagara Falls, 9 hours, $55–$78; Cleveland to Albany, 6 hours, $45.

One-way fares on the commuter lines are usually $5–$12, and the cost is highest during peak hours (morning and early-evening rush hours). Also, you pay a surcharge if you purchase your tickets on the train rather than at the station.

Information Amtrak (800/872–7245 www.amtrak.com). **Long Island Railroad** (718/217–5477 www.mta.nyc.ny.us/lirr). **Metro-North Commuter Railroad** (718/330–1234 www.mta.info/mnr). **New Jersey Transit** (973/491–7000 www.njtransit.com). **PATH** (800/234–7284 www.pathrail.com).

ESSENTIALS

▌ ACCOMMODATIONS

New York City commands the highest hotel prices in the nation, and occupancy rates can be quite high, too. In seasonal destinations, such as the Hamptons and Fire Island, it can be tough to find weekend hotel rooms in summer, so it's wise to book several weeks or months ahead; you'll also pay the steepest rates in seashore destinations in summer. These same rules apply to popular fall-foliage destinations, especially the Catskills, Finger Lakes, and Hudson Valley. When visiting towns with a large college presence (Poughkeepsie, Ithaca, Hamilton), be aware that rooms can be extremely tough to come by on weekends throughout the school year. Also take into consideration major cultural and sporting events, which can push up prices and greatly reduce availability in certain places—everything from New Year's Eve in New York City to the Baseball Hall of Fame inductions in Cooperstown.

The lodgings we list are the cream of the crop in each price category. We always list the facilities that are available, but we don't specify whether they cost extra; when pricing accommodations, always ask what's included and what costs extra. Properties are assigned price categories based on the range between their least and most expensive standard double rooms in high season (excluding holidays). You'll be charged a hotel tax, which varies between towns and counties throughout the state from approximately 11% to 14%.

Assume that hotels operate on the European Plan (EP, no meals) unless we specify that they use the Breakfast Plan (BP, with full breakfast), Continental Plan (CP, Continental breakfast), Full American Plan (FAP, all meals), Modified American Plan (MAP, breakfast and dinner), or are all-inclusive (AI, all meals and most activities).

BED-AND-BREAKFASTS

Historic B&Bs and inns are plentiful throughout New York, including a handful in New York City. In many rural or less touristy areas B&Bs offer an affordable and homey alternative to chain properties, but in tourism-dependent destinations you can expect to pay about the same or more for a historic inn as for a full-service hotel. Although many B&Bs and inns are low-key and lack TVs and other amenities, the scene has changed somewhat in cities and upscale resort areas, where many such properties now cater to business and luxury travelers by offering high-speed Internet, voice mail, whirlpool tubs, and VCRs. Many of the state's finest restaurants are also found in country inns. Quite a few inns and B&Bs serve substantial full breakfasts—the kind that may keep your appetite in check for the better part of the day.

American Country Collection is a reservation service for eastern upstate New York, from the Hudson Valley up through the eastern Adirondacks to the Canadian border. Bed and Breakfast Network of New York serves New York City.

Reservation Services American Country Collection (☎ 800/810–4948 or 518/370–4948 ⊕ www.bandbreservations.com). **Bed and Breakfast Network of New York** (☎ 800/900–8134 or 212/645–8134 ⊕ www.bedandbreakfastnetny.com). **Bed & Breakfast. com** (☎ 512/322–2710 or 800/462–2632 ⊕ www.bedandbreakfast.com) also sends out an online newsletter. **Bed & Breakfast Inns Online** (☎ 800/215–7365 ⊕ www.bbonline.com). **BnB Finder.com** (☎ 212/432–7693 or 888/547–8226 ⊕ www.bnbfinder.com).

CAMPGROUNDS

Within New York's extensive state-park system, much of it concentrated in the Adirondacks and the Catskills, campgrounds offering both primitive and developed sites abound. For state parks, you can call or book online through Reserve America to claim a campsite at any of the state's camping parks as early as nine months in advance and as late as two days before you arrive. Most park campgrounds are open from Memorial Day through Labor Day; some of them remain open throughout the year, even in winter. Some have cabin rentals, too. Based on availability, state parks also accept walk-ins without reservations, but it's best to call ahead to avoid disappointment.

New York also has hundreds of private commercial campgrounds for RV and tent camping.

Contact Campground Owners of New York (☎ 585/586–4360 ⊕ www.campcony.com). **Reserve America** (☎ 800/456–2267 ⊕ www. reserveamerica.com).

HOSTELS

HI has hostels in New York City, Buffalo, Niagara Falls, Syracuse, and Cape Vincent (in the Thousand Islands).

Information Hostelling International—USA (☎ 301/495–1240 ⊕ www.hiusa.org).

HOTELS

Chain hotels can be found at big cities throughout the state. Here are their contact numbers:

Toll-Free Numbers Best Western (☎ 800/780–7234 ⊕ www.bestwestern. com). **Choice** (☎ 877/424–6423 ⊕ www. choicehotels.com). **Comfort Inn** (☎ 800/424–6423 ⊕ www.choicehotels.com). **Days Inn** (☎ 800/325–2525 ⊕ www.daysinn.com). **Doubletree Hotels** (☎ 800/222–8733 ⊕ www.doubletree.com). **Embassy Suites** (☎ 800/362–2779 ⊕ www.embassysuites. com). **Fairfield Inn** (☎ 800/228–2800 ⊕ www. marriott.com). **Hilton** (☎ 800/445–8667 ⊕ www.hilton.com). **Holiday Inn** (☎ 800/465–4329 ⊕ www.ichotelsgroup.com). **Howard Johnson** (☎ 800/446–4656 ⊕ www.hojo.com). **Hyatt Hotels & Resorts** (☎ 800/233–1234 ⊕ www.hyatt.com). **La Quinta** (☎ 800/531–5900 ⊕ www.lq.com). **Marriott** (☎ 800/236–2427 ⊕ www.marriott.com). **Quality Inn**

(☎ 800/424–6423 ⊕ www.choicehotels. com). **Radisson** (☎ 800/333–3333 ⊕ www. radisson.com). **Ramada** (☎ 800/333–3333 ⊕ www.ramada.com or www.ramadahotels. com). **Sheraton** (☎ 800/325–3535 ⊕ www. starwood.com/sheraton). **Sleep Inn** (☎ 800/424–6423 ⊕ www.choicehotels.com). **Westin Hotels & Resorts** (☎ 800/228–3000 ⊕ www.starwood.com/westin).

▌EATING OUT

New York has developed an impressive reputation for creative, sometimes downright daring, cuisine—and not just in Manhattan. You can expect to find stellar restaurants, many of them helmed by culinary luminaries, throughout the Hamptons and much of Long Island, up and down the Hudson Valley, and in some of the more tourism-driven areas in northern and western New York, such as the Finger Lakes and parts of the Adirondacks. That said, restaurant food tends to become simpler, more traditional, and more conservative as you move away from the greater New York City area.

MEALS AND MEALTIMES

Unless otherwise noted, the restaurants listed in this guide are open daily for lunch and dinner. In New York City, it's never a problem finding a restaurant open late (sometimes all night). Elsewhere in the state, hours and days of operation will vary.

RESERVATIONS AND DRESS

Regardless of where you are, it's a good idea to make a reservation if you can. In some places, it's expected. We only mention them specifically when reservations are essential (there's no other way you'll ever get a table) or when they are not accepted. We mention dress only when men are required to wear a jacket or a jacket and tie.

▋ FAMILIES AND SPECIAL TRAVELERS

CHILDREN IN NEW YORK

New York is an enjoyable part of the country for family road trips, and it's relatively affordable once you get outside greater New York City—there are plenty of comparatively inexpensive kid-friendly hotels and family-style restaurants in the northern and western sections of the state, and these regions offer some of the top kid-oriented attractions. Favorite New York destinations for families are the Long Island shoreline (including much of Fire Island and parts of the Hamptons), Lake George, the Catskills, the Finger Lakes, the Adirondacks, and Niagara Falls. Note that some of the quieter and more rural parts of the region—although exuding history—lack child-oriented attractions. New York City is full of fun things for kids. Cultural institutions host programs introducing children to the arts; large stores put on fun promotional events; and many attractions, from skyscrapers to museums, engage the whole family.

LODGING

Many of the state's fine, antiques-filled bed-and-breakfasts and inns really aren't suitable for kids; many flat-out refuse to accommodate children. Rooms in New York City, particularly in Manhattan, are small by national standards, so ask just how large the room is into which you're adding a cot or fold-out couch. Most hotels in New York allow children under a certain age to stay in their parents' room at no extra charge, but others charge for them as extra adults; be sure to find out the cutoff age for children's discounts. Amenities for youngsters often include movies for in-room use, pools, and an occasional playground.

INFORMATION

Visit the dedicated children's section of the state tourism Web site (⊕*www.iloveny. com/kids*) for more information on traveling with children.

DISABILITIES AND ACCESSIBILITY

New York has come a long way toward making life easier for people with disabilities. On most Manhattan street corners, curb cuts allow wheelchairs to roll along unimpeded. Statewide, many restaurants, shops, and movie theaters with step-up entrances have wheelchair ramps.

LODGING

Most hotels in New York comply with the Americans with Disabilities Act. The definition of accessibility, however, seems to differ from hotel to hotel. Some properties may be accessible by ADA standards for people with mobility problems but not for people with hearing or vision impairments, for example. When you call to make reservations, specify your needs and make sure the hotel can accommodate them. Newer and chain hotels are likely to be the most accessible.

INFORMATION

The U.S. Department of Transportation Aviation Consumer Protection Division's online publication *New Horizons: Information for the Air Traveler with a Disability* offers advice for travelers with a disability, and outlines basic rights. Visit ⊕*DisabilityInfo.gov* for general information.

SENIOR-CITIZEN TRAVEL

The Metropolitan Transit Authority (MTA) offers lower fares for passengers 65 and over for New York City buses and subways. Show your Medicare card to the bus driver or station agent, and for the standard fare ($2) you will be issued a MetroCard and a return-trip ticket.

To qualify for age-related discounts, mention your senior-citizen status up front when booking hotel reservations (not when checking out) and before you're seated in restaurants (not when paying the bill). Be sure to have identification on hand. When renting a car, ask about promotional car-rental discounts, which can be cheaper than senior-citizen rates.

STUDENTS IN NEW YORK

With several prominent private universities and colleges and 64 State University of New York (SUNY) campuses throughout the state, it's no wonder that New York offers countless discounts for students. Wherever you go, especially museums, sightseeing attractions, and performances, identify yourself as a student up front and ask if a discount is available. ∎ TIP→ **Be prepared to show your student ID** for discounts.

Information STA Travel (☎ *800/781–4040 24-hr service center* ⊕ *www.sta.com*). **Travel Cuts** (☎ *212/674–2887* ⊕ *www.travelcuts. com*).

∎ HEALTH

There are relatively few health issues specific to New York. In coastal regions, swimmers and boaters should be respectful of the ocean's powerful surf. Adhere to posted riptide warnings, and to be safe stick to areas that have lifeguards. Summers can be hot and humid throughout New York, especially at lower altitudes and in the southern part of the state; wear light-color clothing in summer, drink plenty of fluids (and bring along bottled water on hikes, boat trips, and bike rides), and consider staying indoors during the hottest times of the day.

Mosquitoes, seasonal black flies, and just about every other annoying insect known to North America proliferates in New York. Exercise common precautions and wear appropriate lotions or sprays.

Lyme disease, which is spread by bites from tiny deer ticks, is not uncommon in New York, especially where there are significant deer populations (eastern Long Island, the Hudson Valley, and most rural areas). Symptoms vary; most victims show a red ring-shape rash around the deer-tick bite, somewhat resembling a bull's-eye and appearing from one to several weeks after the incident. Flulike symptoms (fever, achy joints, swelling) often follow.

One common problem is delayed diagnosis; the longer you go without treatment, the more severe the disease's effects.

When spending time in areas where ticks are a concern, wear long-sleeve clothing and pants, tuck your pants legs into your boots and/or socks, apply insect repellent generously, and check yourself carefully for signs of ticks or bites. It's a good idea to don light-color clothing, as you'll have an easier time sighting ticks, which are dark. Remember that the more common wood ticks do not carry the disease, and that deer ticks are extremely small—about the size of a pinhead.

∎ HOURS OF OPERATION

Shops and other businesses tend to keep later hours in New York City and its suburbs than in rural areas.

Banks are usually open weekdays 9–3 and sometimes Saturday morning. Post offices are generally open weekdays 8–5 and often on Saturday morning.

Most major museums and attractions are open daily or six days a week (with Monday the most likely closed day). Hours are often shorter on Saturday and especially Sunday. Some prominent museums, especially in New York City, stay open late one or two nights a week, usually Tuesday, Thursday, or Friday. New York's less populous areas have quite a few smaller museums and sights that open only a few days a week, and sometimes only by appointment in the off-season.

Shops in urban and suburban areas, particularly in malls, typically open at 9 or 10 AM daily and stay open until anywhere from 6 to 10 PM on weekdays and Saturday, and until 5 or 6 PM on Sunday.

∎ MONEY

Prices for services and travel vary tremendously throughout the state. In Manhattan, New York City suburbs, eastern Long

Island, and even parts of the Hudson Valley, it's easy to get swept up in a cyclone of $60-per-person dinners, $100 theater tickets, $20 nightclub covers, $10 cab rides, and $300 hotel rooms. Elsewhere in the state, prices for dining, hotels, and entertainment tend to be consistent with national averages. But one of the good things about New York, even in Manhattan, is that there's such a wide variety of options; you can spend in some areas and save in others.

Prices throughout this guide are given for adults. Substantially reduced fees are almost always available for children, students, and senior citizens.

CREDIT CARDS
Throughout this guide, the following abbreviations are used: **AE**, American Express; **D**, Discover; **DC**, Diners Club; **MC**, MasterCard; and **V**, Visa.

Reporting Lost Cards American Express (☎ 800/528-4800 in the U.S., 336/393-1111 collect from abroad ⊕ www.americanexpress. com). **Diners Club** (☎ 800/234-6377 in the U.S., 303/799-1504 collect from abroad ⊕ www.dinersclub.com). **Discover** (☎ 800/347-2683 in the U.S., 801/902-3100 collect from abroad ⊕ www.discovercard.com). **MasterCard** (☎ 800/627-8372 in the U.S., 636/722-7111 collect from abroad ⊕ www. mastercard.com). **Visa** (☎ 800/847-2911 in the U.S., 410/581-9994 collect from abroad ⊕ www.visa.com).

▌SAFETY

Most of New York is comparable to the rest of the country with respect to safety and crime. And although New York City is one of the safest large cities in the country today, don't be lulled into a false sense of security. New York City and the state's other urban areas still have significantly higher rates of crime than suburban and rural areas. Tourists can be relatively easy targets for pickpockets and thieves, especially in New York City. Your wisest approach in the state's urban and touristy

areas is to avoid venturing out alone at night, rely on cabs when getting around at night, and if you're driving, lock your car and never leave important items unattended. Keep jewelry out of sight on the street; better yet, leave valuables at home.

In the wake of the World Trade Center disaster, security has been greatly heightened in New York City and generally increased statewide. Expect thorough inspections of your apparel and personal belongings in airports, sports stadiums, museums, and government buildings.

In New York City, ignore panhandlers, people who offer to hail you a cab, and limousine and gypsy-cab drivers who (illegally) offer you a ride. Men should carry their wallets in their front pants pocket. When in bars or restaurants, never hang your purse or bag on the back of a chair or put it underneath the table. Avoid deserted blocks in unfamiliar neighborhoods. A brisk, purposeful pace helps deter trouble wherever you go.

New York City's subway system runs around the clock and is generally well trafficked until midnight (even later on Friday and Saturday nights); overall it is very safe. If you do take the subway at night, ride in the center car (avoid empty cars), with the conductor, and wait on the center of the platform or right in front of the station agent. Watch out for suspicious characters lurking around the inside or outside of stations, particularly at night. When waiting for a train, stand far away from the edge of the subway platform. If a fellow passenger makes you nervous while on the train, trust your instincts and change cars. When disembarking, stick with the crowd until you reach the street.

Travelers Aid International helps crime victims and stranded travelers and works closely with the police. Its office at JFK airport is staffed weekdays 10–6 and weekends 11–7.

Someone who appears to have had an accident at the exit door of a bus may flee with your wallet or purse if you attempt to give aid. The individual who approaches you with a complicated story probably hopes to get something from you. Beware of people jostling you in crowds, or someone tapping your shoulder from behind. Never play or place a bet on a sidewalk card game, shell game, or other guessing game—they're all rigged to get your cash, and they're illegal.

▌ TAXES

Municipalities throughout the state charge a variety of taxes on hotel rooms, car rentals, and parking in commercial lots or garages. These range from 4% to park in a commercial lot to 5% to rent a car; keep in mind that these taxes are in addition to any other taxes, such as local sales taxes. Some of the larger airports, such as JFK and LaGuardia, charge a departure tax of $4.50.

New York City's sales tax of 8.375% applies to almost everything you can buy at retail, including restaurant meals. Nonprepared foods (from grocery stores) and prescription drugs are tax-exempt. Sales tax rates elsewhere in the state are 7%–8.75%.

▌ TIME

New York operates on Eastern Standard Time. When it is noon in New York it is 9 AM in Los Angeles, 11 AM in Chicago, 5 PM in London, and 3 AM the following day in Sydney.

▌ TIPPING

The customary tipping rate for taxi drivers is 15%, with a minimum of $2; bellhops are usually given $2 per bag in luxury hotels, $1 per bag elsewhere. Hotel maids should be tipped $3 or $4 a night for rooms that cost up to $250 a night (before taxes), $5–$7 a night for rooms in the $250–$350 range, and $8–$10 a night when you stay in more-expensive lodgings. If the hotel charges a service fee, be sure to ask what it covers, as it may include this gratuity. A doorman who hails or helps you into a cab can be tipped $1–$2. You should also tip your hotel concierge for services rendered; the size of the tip depends on your request and the quality of the concierge's work. For an ordinary dinner reservation or tour arrangements, $3–$5 should do; if the concierge scores seats at a popular restaurant or show or performs unusual services, $10 or more is appropriate.

Waiters should be tipped 15%–20%. Many restaurants add a gratuity to the bill for parties of six or more. Ask what the percentage is if the menu or bill doesn't state it. Tip $1 per drink you order at the bar; at an upscale establishment, those $15 martinis might warrant a $2 tip, however.

▌ VISITOR INFORMATION

Contacts New York State Division of Tourism (☎ *800/225-5697 or 518/474-4116* ⊕ *www.iloveny.com*).

INDEX

Photo Credits

25, Photodisc. 27 (top), Liberty Helicopters, Inc. 27 (bottom), Ken Ross/viestiphoto.com. 29 (top), Bettmann/CORBIS. 29 (bottom), Library of Congress Prints and Photographs Division.

ABOUT OUR WRITERS

Vanessa Geneva Ahern, who updated the Long Island chapter, moved with her parents to Southampton when she was a toddler in 1971. Since earning her MFA in Writing at Columbia University in 2002, she has been published in dozens of magazines, including *SELF, Fit Pregnancy, Hudson Valley,* and *New York House.* She has traveled to Brazil, Greece, India, and Australia, but for her nothing compares to the beaches on the South shore of Long Island.

Gary Catt is executive editor for Eagle Media in Upstate New York. The winner of several awards from the Associated Press for local reporting, he has authored travel and lifestyle articles for numerous newspapers and magazines. He has lived and worked in the Catskills as a writer and newspaper editor. He often follows the footprints of history through the Catskills.

Jennifer Edwards, who updated the Adirondacks and the Albany and Central New York chapters, is the day local editor at the *Utica Observer-Dispatch.* She's won multiple Associated Press awards for her work as a journalist, and her articles have appeared in several magazines and dozens of newspapers, including the *Dallas Morning News* and the *New York Sun.* She also wrote chapters for *Fodor's Complete Guide to the National Parks of the West,* winner of a 2008 Lowell Thomas Award. Jennifer says she wasn't born in Central New York, but she got here as quickly as she could.

Freelance writer and editor **Shannon Kelly** is originally from the Rochester area, where she grew up thinking that everyone understood the wonders of Abbott's Frozen Custard and "white hots." She had a blast re-exploring her native state for the "Finger Lakes" and "Western New York" chapters, and she thanks family members and friends from Corning to Penn Yan to Buffalo for their aid and insight. Shannon has edited dozens of Fodor's guides and has contributed to *Fodor's Toronto, Fodor's New York City,* and *Fodor's San Francisco.* She lives in Toronto, Ontario.

Kate King is a Hudson Valley-based freelance writer and editor who has covered travel, film, and green issues. When she's not at her desk, she can be found hiking in the Palisades or poking around local antiques stores.

New York City-based freelance writer and editor **William Travis,** who wrote the Experience New York chapter, lives and breathes travel and music. As a former editor for Fodor's, he developed many guides, including *Fodor's New York City* and the first online post-Katrina New Orleans travel guide. He covers everything from culture, restaurants, hotels, beaches, nightlife, and music.